Microsoft® Office Access™ 2007:
The Complete Reference

About the Author

Virginia Andersen became a writer and consultant after retiring from a career in defense contracting. Since then, she has written nearly 40 books about PC–based applications, including database management, word processing, spreadsheet analysis, and VBA programming. Virginia spent nearly 15 years teaching computer science, mathematics, and systems analysis at the graduate and undergraduate levels at several Southern California universities. During her years as a programmer/systems analyst, Virginia used computers for many diverse projects, including lunar mapping for the Apollo astronauts' landing, reliability engineering, undersea surveillance, weapon system simulation, and naval communications. She has also recently published her memoirs, *Digital Recall: Computers Aren't the Only Ones with Memory*, describing many of these hands-on experiences.

Microsoft® Office Access™ 2007: The Complete Reference

Virginia Andersen

New York   Chicago   San Francisco
Lisbon   London   Madrid   Mexico City
Milan   New Delhi   San Juan
Seoul   Singapore   Sydney   Toronto

Cataloging-in-Publication Data is on file with the Library of Congress

McGraw-Hill books are available at special quantity discounts to use as premiums and sales promotions, or for use in corporate training programs. For more information, please write to the Director of Special Sales, Professional Publishing, McGraw-Hill, Two Penn Plaza, New York, NY 10121-2298. Or contact your local bookstore.

Microsoft® Office Access™ 2007: The Complete Reference

1234567890 CUS/CUS 01987

ISBN-13: Book P/N 978-0-07148991-1 and CD P/N 978-0-07-148992-8
of set 978-0-07-226350-3

ISBN-10: Book P/N 0-07-148991-6 and CD P/N 0-07-148992-4
of set 0-07-226350-4

Sponsoring Editor
Megg Morin

Editorial Supervisor
Jody McKenzie

Project Manager
Rasika Mathur

Acquisitions Coordinator
Carly Stapleton

Technical Editor
Jocelyn Fiorello

Copy Editor
Lisa Theobald

Proofreader
Linda Leggio

Indexer
Kevin Broccoli

Production Supervisor
Jean Bodeaux

Composition
International Typesetting
and Composition

Illustration
International Typesetting
and Composition

Art Director, Cover
Jeff Weeks

Cover Designer
Jeff Weeks

Contents at a Glance

Contents

Part III   **Improving the Workplace**

Acknowledgments

Revising this book for the fourth edition was once again a pleasure, due especially to working with the talented and highly professional McGraw-Hill editorial and production staff. Megg Morin, my sponsoring editor, is not only an efficient and professional member of the staff—I also consider her a good friend. Carly Stapleton, my acquisitions coordinator, was once again responsive and helpful throughout the effort. I would also like to thank Jody McKenzie, editorial supervisor, for making sure the book kept on track, and Rasika Mathur, project manager, for her guidance in moving the many chapters smoothly through the production maze.

The other editorial staff, including technical editor Jocelyn Fiorello and copy editor Lisa Theobald, were very helpful in spotting missteps in logic and style. My sincere thanks also go to Linda Leggio for proofing, to Kevin Broccoli for indexing, and to International Typesetting and Composition for the great job illustrating and laying out this large, complicated book.

Thanks go, too, to the Coronado Police Department for sharing its Access database with me and my readers, as well as to my friends and neighbors who posed good-naturedly for the badge photos you can see in one of the databases. They tell me it's a good thing I'm a writer, not a photographer.

I also owe a big debt of gratitude to my literary agents of many years, Waterside Productions, for their continuing support and encouragement.

Finally, my husband, Jack, and all the cats must get a lot of credit for being so patient with me throughout this long, involved process. The cats don't really mind because, when I am working, I have a lap.

Introduction

A successful database is efficient, quick, accurate, and easy to use. This book shows you how to create just such a database with Microsoft Office Access 2007. The clearly written explanations of the database processes present exactly what you need to create an Access object or present information. The step-by-step exercises that follow the explanations further enhance your understanding by illustrating exactly how to complete the process successfully. The many tips, notes, and cautions help guide you to faster and better database management.

Who Should Read This Book?

This book is the ideal resource for anyone currently using Microsoft Office Access 2007 or who wants to learn how to use it. In planning this book, I envisioned it in the form of a large triangle, with the base scaled from the beginning user at the left end to advanced user at the right end. This book has enough material to get even the newest user of Access started with relational database management and has enough at the other end to help advanced users wade into the depths of customizing the Access workplace and designing special user interactive tools.

The bulk of the material lies between the two extremes under the peak of the triangle, and that is of the utmost interest to the readers who fall in between. This book is extremely rich in the art of designing and creating efficient relational databases with all the appropriate queries, forms, and reports. Many different approaches are taken with respect to extracting and summarizing information in useful arrangements, including charts and graphs. After all, what good is data stored in a database if you can't get it out and turn it into useful and easy-to-interpret information?

This book is also intended for users of the other Office applications, such as Word and Excel, who need to know how to interface those programs with Access. With the boundaries between the programs rapidly vanishing, use of Access isn't limited to database managers. All the Office members can now interact with each other smoothly and with little translation.

What's in This Book?

This book is organized so you can progress at your own pace, beginning with basic database and Access principles and followed by increasingly advanced topics. The book is divided into four parts, each focusing on a specific aspect of Access database management.

Part I: Getting Started

Part I takes a quick tour of Microsoft Office Access 2007 and examines the concept of relational databases. Many tips are included to help you design an efficient database that is easy to maintain and can ensure data integrity. In Part I, the reader creates and relates tables, and then enters data into them. Several methods of validating new data are investigated and means of presenting data for editing are also addressed.

Part II: Retrieving and Presenting Information

Part II is concerned with retrieving information with filters and queries, as well as presenting that information in forms and reports. This important set of chapters includes how to create expressions to extract exactly the information you want. Five chapters are devoted to creating form and report designs (including synchronized data entry forms), creating reports that summarize grouped information, and even printing mailing labels in conjunction with Word 2007. The final chapter in this part describes how to create charts and graphs to include in forms and reports.

Part III: Improving the Workplace

Part III is a little more advanced and discusses working with and customizing the new user-interactive workplace that uses a Navigation Pane, ribbons and tabbed documents. It also shows how to create dialog boxes for the more interactive applications. Several important means of optimizing Access performance are included in this part. Part III also introduces programming techniques with chapters about using macros, as well as understanding events and when events occur.

Part IV: Exchanging Data with Others

Part IV discusses the important topic of exchanging information with other users of Access and with other applications. Importing and exporting information in many forms, including text, is an integral part of developing a complete user application. This part also covers using Access in a multiple-user environment and investigates measures to ensure information security.

In Every Chapter

Every chapter is constructed to include basic learning tools, such as the following:

- Complete explanations of all processes involved in the creation and management of effective relational databases
- Numbered, step-by-step exercises with illustrations and explanations of each step
- Many tips, notes, and cautions that add shortcuts for many of the activities and pinpoint potential pitfalls
- A summary at the end of each chapter that reviews the material covered and highlights the more important topics discussed in that chapter

Quick Reference

In addition to the chapter material, this book includes a Quick Reference section on the accompanying CD. The Quick Reference contains complete lists and descriptions of elements of Microsoft Office Access 2007 database design and maintenance. This reference serves as an immediate resource for any details in question. It is accompanied by an index that can save you time when you need a specific piece of information by presenting concise lists and tables that you can jump directly to without having to browse through the more descriptive chapter material in the book itself.

What's on the Companion CD?

Appendix B presents a thorough explanation of the contents of the CD that accompanies this book. This appendix explains how to install the Access databases on your computer and how to look up specific information in the Quick Reference.

The CD includes the following:

- The Quick Reference lookup resource
- The complete Home Tech Repair database
- A set of tables containing the data to use as the basis for creating the Home Tech Repair database
- The complete Police database
- A set of tables containing the data to use as the basis for creating the Police database
- Scanned image files required by the two databases

Conventions Used in This Book

To help make this book more useful and interesting, we included a few conventions that will attract your attention to important pieces of information. Following are descriptions of these conventions:

NOTE *Notes further define terms used in the text or point you in the direction of more information about the subject under discussion.*

TIP *Tips often provide shortcuts to the process under discussion or offer useful pieces of advice about how to make better use of Access 2007.*

CAUTION *Cautions warn you to be careful when you're about to make crucial decisions or take risky steps. Access tries hard not to put you in harm's way, but mistakes do happen now and then.*

Sidebars
Sidebars are set somewhat apart from the normal text. They include information related to the current subject that doesn't necessarily fit in the flow of information. Rather than interrupt the flow, sidebars offer tangential information set aside from regular text that you can visit later.

What's New in Microsoft Office Access 2007?

This book attempts to show you the new look and feel that comes with Microsoft Office Access 2007. Many time-saving and user-friendly features make Microsoft Office Access 2007 a complete and manageable tool for tracking, reporting, and sharing information.

Some of the new features in Microsoft Office Access 2007 apply to the new user interface; others apply to creating database objects or to customizing the workplace itself. Here are some of the more significant improvements covered in this book:

- The new user interface is a ribbon that takes the place of the menus and toolbars used in earlier versions. The ribbon provides all the actions and tasks that relate to the current activity.

- The new Navigation Pane replaces the Database window and displays lists of all the objects in the current database. The Navigation Pane lists can be customized to suit your application.

- Open database objects are now displayed as tabbed documents instead of overlapping windows. You can move from one to another by clicking the object tab.

- New security features make it easier to protect your database, improving on features in previous versions. By default, all potentially unsafe components are disabled. You then have the option of trusting the database for the current session or permanently. The new Trust Center lets you set and change security settings in one place.

- The new Layout view for forms and reports lets you make design changes in place so you can see the effects in the finished product immediately.

- You can now store more than one value in a single field. Multivalued fields actually provide the same model as the many-to-many relationship.

These are just a few of the new features that you will see when you get to work on your database with Microsoft Office Access 2007.

Got Comments?

During my years spent teaching at the University of Southern California, I discovered, to my dismay, that I often learned as much from my students as I hoped they would learn from me. With this philosophy in mind, I invite you to share with me any new tricks or clever shortcuts that you have devised. Please e-mail them to me at **vandersenz@aol.com**. In fact, I would enjoy hearing any comments, good and bad, that you might have about the book or the databases I have developed as examples. Only by tapping fresh minds can I hope to make these books better and better.

I've been delighted to hear from readers all over the world about the last three editions of *The Complete Reference*. Some readers hail from places as varied as South Africa, Scotland, and Japan. I have certainly benefited from the correspondence, and I hope I've resolved some of the readers' problems as well.

PART

Getting Started

CHAPTER 1

Quick Tour of Microsoft Office Access 2007

In this, the Information Age, we are surrounded by mountains of data. To use this data effectively, the information must be stored in such a way that it can be retrieved and interpreted with flexibility and efficiency. Microsoft Office Access 2007 is a top-notch database management system that you can use for all your information management needs—from a simple address list to a complex inventory management system. It provides tools not only for storing and retrieving data, but also for creating useful forms and reports, and sharing your database with others. All you need is a basic acquaintance with Microsoft Windows and a sense of exploration to build the database you need.

This chapter shows you how to start Microsoft Office Access 2007 and provides a tour of the Access work place. If you're an experienced user, you will be amazed at the new, visually upgraded user interface.

Starting Access and Opening a Database

You can start most software built for the Windows environment in the same way: by clicking the Start button and pointing to Programs in the Start menu. Depending on how you installed Access 2007, the name might appear as a separate item in the Programs (or All Programs, if you're using Windows XP) list or as one of the programs in the Microsoft Office menu. If you don't see Microsoft Access in the Programs list, choose Microsoft Office, and then click Microsoft Access 2007.

The Getting Started with Microsoft Office Access window, where your session begins, appears with four options (see Figure 1-1):

- Start a new database with one of the Access templates. The left pane lists available templates and samples.

- Start with a new blank database.

- Connect to Microsoft Office Online. The database templates offered online may differ each time you start Access.

- Select a recently used database from the list in the right pane (no doubt your list will be different).

Microsoft Office button   Quick Access toolbar

FIGURE 1-1 Getting Started with Microsoft Office Access window

Touring the Access Window

The Access window shows a title bar and a status bar. In addition to displaying the program name, the title bar contains the Microsoft Office button, a Quick Access toolbar, and buttons you can use to manipulate the window.

The Microsoft Office button offers a choice of nine menu items that you can use to work with a database, such as New, Open, Save, Save As, and Close. The other four menu items deal with managing the database, printing documents, sending e-mail, and publishing your database. The button also displays a list of recently used documents. Two buttons at the bottom of the display let you set specific Access options or exit Access altogether.

The buttons on the Quick Access toolbar offer shortcuts to three of the commonly used menu commands: Save, Undo, and can't Undo. You can rest the mouse pointer on a button and see its name displayed below the button in a ScreenTip. You can use the Customize button to the right of the Quick Access toolbar to add more commands to the toolbar so all the actions you need are at your fingertips. You'll find out how to customize the toolbar in Chapter 20.

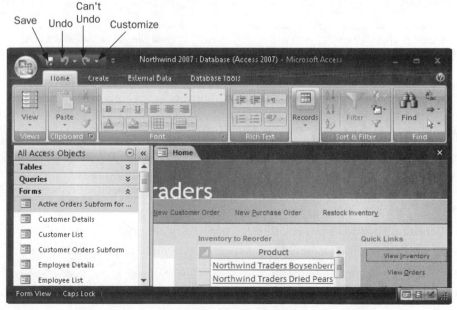

Three more buttons appear at the right end of the title bar. These buttons are common to all Windows applications.

- The *Maximize* button appears only when the window is less than maximum size and enlarges the window to fill the screen.
- The *Restore* button replaces the Maximize button when the window is maximized and returns the window to its previous reduced size.
- The *Minimize* button reduces the window to an icon on the Windows taskbar.

When the window is less than maximum size, you can move it to a new position on the desktop by dragging its title bar. You can also change its height and width by dragging either its borders or the resize handle in the lower-right corner, where you see a triangle of dots.

The status bar, located at the bottom of the Access window, provides a running commentary about the ongoing task and the Access working environment. The center of the status bar also shows boxes that indicate the presence of a filter and the status of various toggle keys on your keyboard, such as INSERT, CAPS LOCK, SCROLL LOCK, and NUM LOCK. The right end of the status bar contains buttons that can change the view of the current object. For example, you can change an open form from Form View to Design View. You'll see some of these when you start working with a database.

Opening a Database

If the database you want to open is listed in the Open Recent Database pane that appears in the Getting Started with Microsoft Office Access window, you can open it by clicking the filename. If the database you want isn't on the list, click More. The Open dialog box appears, as shown in Figure 1-2. (Your list of folders and files will be different.) The same dialog box appears if Access is already running when you click the Microsoft Office button and choose Open.

TIP *If Access is already running, you can open a recently opened file by clicking the Microsoft Office button and selecting the filename from the list.*

The Favorite Links pane at the left contains a list of places to look for the database. Select Documents to see a list of the available documents in the current folder.

The trick is to know where you stored your database. Click the arrow to the right of Folders and zero in on the folder that contains the database. Then double-click the folder name or icon to open it, and select the one you want from the list that appears in the dialog box. You can also type the name of the database in the Search box and press ENTER.

The Open dialog box contains several buttons that help you find the file you want to open. You can see the name of each button by resting the mouse pointer on the button in the command bar.

- Back and Forward move you through previously accessed folders.
- Recent pages shows a drop-down list of folders you have previously opened.
- Folders opens the Folders pane with the current list.

FIGURE 1-2   Choosing a database in the Open dialog box

The Views drop-down list offers different ways of showing the document list. As you drag the scroll button on the left margin, the display gradually changes to match.

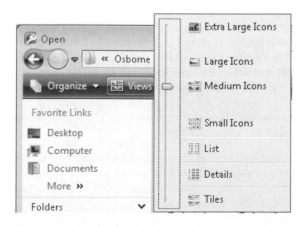

To choose a different file type to open, click the down arrow next to the Microsoft Office Access box and choose from the list of 24 types or choose All Files. The default file type for Access 2007 is Microsoft Office Access, which includes all Access databases and any other Office documents that have been linked to an Access database, such as an Excel spreadsheet or a Word document. Other Access file types are also available from the list.

Once you locate the database you want to open, double-click the name or select it and click Open.

NOTE *The Open button offers other ways to open the database, such as read-only, exclusive, or both. Another Open option is show previous versions which offers earlier versions of the selected database. More about these options appears in later chapters.*

If You Are Using Windows XP
When you click More in the Getting Started window and you are using Windows XP, you will see a unique Open dialog box with other options for finding the database you want.

The Groups pane at the left contains five buttons that you can click to open other folders or return to the Windows desktop.

- The top button, My Recent Documents, opens the Recent folder that contains the name, size, type, and date of the last modification for each recently accessed database. When you click the My Recent Documents button, the Recent folder name appears in the Look In box.

- The Desktop button displays a list of the desktop components on your computer to which you can move, including such items as My Computer, My Documents, and Network Neighborhood.

- The My Documents button (or the name of your personal default folder) shows the contents of that folder. This is the default display in the Open dialog box.

- The My Computer button displays the list of available hard disks, floppy disk drives, CD drives, and other data storage systems.

- The My Network Places button displays the network drives on your network, as well as the names of any web folders that you've set up.

The Look In box shows the name of the currently open folder and the window below displays a list of all the folders and files in that folder.

The Open dialog box also contains several buttons that help you find the file you want to open. You can see the name of each button by resting the mouse pointer on the button in the toolbar.

The Views drop-down list includes several ways to display the names of the files in the selected folder as well as graphics with file type and size. The Tools drop-down list includes options such as Delete, Rename, Map Network Drive, and Properties. To choose a different type of file to open, click the down arrow next to the Files Of Type box and choose from the list of 24 types or choose All Files.

When you find the database you want, select the name and click Open.

To start working with a database in Access 2007, let's open the Northwind Traders sample database that comes with Microsoft Office. This database is an order-processing application that demonstrates the power and usefulness of a relational database. Even though the purpose of the database seems straightforward enough—taking and filling orders from customers for the company products—a lot of data still must be manipulated. The database is introduced in this chapter and discussed further in Chapter 2.

The easiest way to install and open the Northwind Traders database is through the Getting Started window.

1. In the From Microsoft Office Online section in the left pane, double-click Sample. The Sample window displays a thumbnail for accessing the Northwind Traders database (see Figure 1-3).

NOTE *If you have already downloaded the database, you'll see two thumbnails—one to create a new copy of the database and the other to download it for the first time, as shown in Figure 1-3.*

2. Click the thumbnail to see the option. The right pane offers the option to download the database file into your default folder—for example, C:\\Documents and Settings\ Virginia Andersen\My Documents\.

3. Click the folder icon in the right pane to browse for a different destination, if necessary.

4. Enter a different database name, if desired.

5. Click Download (or Create).

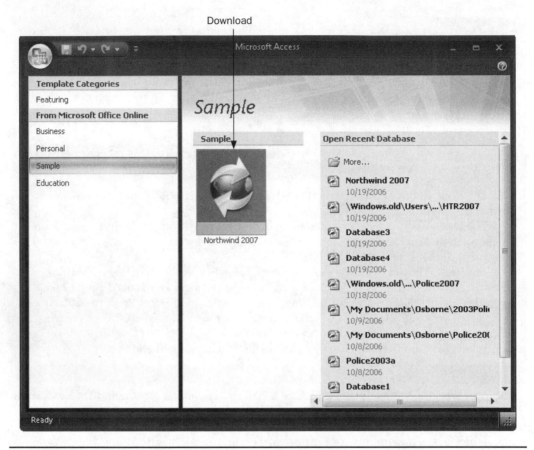

FIGURE 1-3 Choosing the Northwind sample from the Sample pane

Figure 1-4 shows the Northwind Traders database in the startup window.

New security features have been added to Access 2007. In previous versions, when you opened a database containing macros or Visual Basic for Applications (VBA) code, you were asked whether you wanted to enable them. In Access 2007, you see a Security warning message across the window between the opening ribbon and the database itself. To enable the contents, do the following:

1. Click the options button.

2. In the Microsoft Office security options dialog box (see Figure 1-5), check Enable This Content.

3. Click OK.

NOTE *More about security and how you can keep your database safe is found in Chapter 25.*

Now you are ready to sign on to the Northwind Traders database. Click Login as an employee in the Login dialog box to get started.

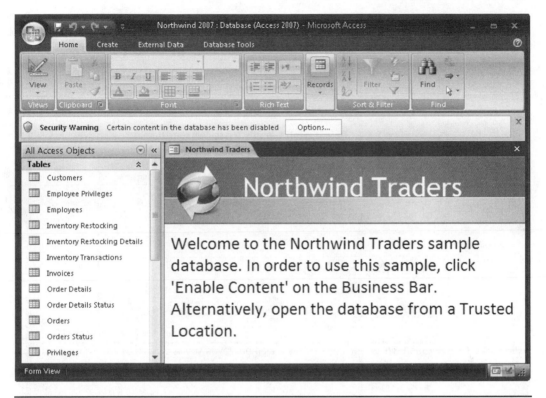

FIGURE 1-4 The Northwind Traders database in the startup window

Touring the Navigation Pane and the Object Window

The left pane in the application, labeled All Access Objects, is the new Navigation Pane that replaces the database window featured in previous versions of Access. The names of all the database objects appear in the Navigation Pane, where you can also see the complete list of objects without having to tab to other windows. You can also open any of the database objects from the Navigation Pane.

NOTE *When you change the arrangement of objects in the Navigation Pane, the header changes to Navigate to Category.*

You can resize the Navigation Pane by dragging the right border. You can also hide the Navigation Pane if you need more screen space by clicking the Shutter Bar Open/Close Button, the << or >> button in the upper-right corner. Or just press F11. To reopen the pane, click the Open button or press F11 again.

To change the display of items in the Navigation Pane, right-click the menu at the top of the pane and point to View By. The options include Details, Icon, and List. If you choose

FIGURE 1-5   The Microsoft Office Security Options dialog box gives you a chance to enable the contents in the database

Details you can view the date the object was created and when it was last modified. You can also use the menu to sort objects by name, type, date created, or date modified.

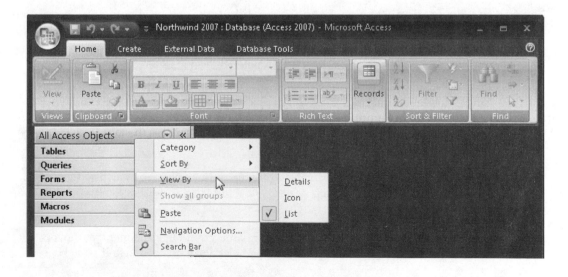

To see all the ways you can arrange and view your database objects in the Navigation Pane, click the down arrow next to All Access Objects at the top of the pane.

The upper section of the pane gives you five options for accessing objects. The lower section offers the option to filter the objects by a specific type or include all objects in the display. For now, let's leave the Navigation Pane to show all objects by type.

The Navigation Pane also replaces the common switchboard user interface by allowing you to place specific actions in a custom group in the pane (more about this in Chapter 21).

NOTE *If you have an established switchboard that you want to keep, you can turn off the Navigation Pane and use the switchboard as before.*

The Object window where you view the database objects represents what Microsoft calls the "single-document interface model." All open objects are placed in the window, each marked with a tab. In Figure 1-4, the only open object is the Northwind Traders database, as you can see. With more than one object open, you can use the tabs to switch from one object to another.

Looking at the Ribbon

While you are browsing around in the window, you might as well take a look at the new Access ribbon. The ribbon replaces the stacks of menus and toolbars you saw in earlier versions of Access.

The major advantage of this new user interface is that the ribbon makes available all the tasks related to the current activity. So rather than searching through a series of menus for the action you want, all the appropriate commands are right in front of you. For example, if you are building a report, the ribbon includes a group of report-related "contextual" commands such as Report Wizard, Labels, Report Design, and so on.

The standard ribbon appears in the Access window when you open a database. Not all the options are available to all of the database objects, and some, such as the Save command, are not available until a table or other object is opened. It also makes sense that the Paste command is dimmed until you have copied something to the clipboard.

The commands on each contextual tab are arranged in groups as designated at the bottom of each group. For example, the Clipboard group includes Cut, Copy, Paste, and AutoFormat commands. The Font group includes all the style, alignment, fore and back color settings, and gridlines.

The tabs that appear on the ribbon depend on the currently active object. For example, if you open a table, you will see a Datasheet tab on the ribbon. If you switch to table Design view, Access automatically changes the Home tab to the Design tab.

To see what a command will do, hover the mouse pointer over the command and look at the ScreenTip that appears briefly. A lot of the commands also have shortcut keys that might appear in the ScreenTip or with the command name. (See Chapter 16 for more information about showing shortcut keys.)

You can still use earlier version keyboard shortcuts to execute a command. To see what keyboard shortcut works with a command on a tab, press and release ALT. The KeyTips appear over each feature that is currently available. If you need more space, you can hide the ribbon and leave only the contextual tabs in view. To hide the ribbon, double-click the active command tab. Repeat to restore the ribbon.

Table 1-1 lists the command keys you can use to move among the commands and other items on the ribbon. Press ALT or F10 first to select the ribbon, and then press the command keys.

Checking out the Galleries and the Mini Toolbars

The ribbon contains a new control type called the *gallery*. A gallery presents the optional results of a specific command. For example, with a table open, if you click the down arrow next to the Gridlines command, you can select from the displayed arrangements—horizontal, vertical, both, or none.

A mini toolbar is a temporary display of text formatting options. After you select the text you want to format, the automatic mini toolbar appears above the text. Move the mouse pointer closer to the toolbar and you can use it to apply italic, boldface, font size, color, and other formatting options. When you select a formatting option, the selected text adopts it and you can see how it will look without actually changing it. If you move the mouse pointer away from the mini toolbar, it disappears.

Key	Action
RIGHT or LEFT ARROW	Moves to another tab on the selected ribbon
CTRL-F1	Hides or shows the ribbon
SHIFT-F10	Displays shortcut menu for selected command
F6	Moves focus between active ribbon tab, Navigation Pane, current document, and status bar toolbar
TAB or SHIFT-TAB	Moves focus back or forward to each command on the ribbon
UP, DOWN, LEFT, or RIGHT ARROW	Moves among items in the ribbon
SPACEBAR or ENTER	Activates selected command or control on the ribbon; opens the selected menu or gallery in the ribbon
ENTER	Activates a command or control in the ribbon or finishes an action and returns to the document
F1	Displays Help for the selected command or control or opens the general Help window

TABLE 1-1   Command Keys for Ribbon Commands

Using Shortcut Menus

Shortcut menus are context-sensitive menus that appear when you click the right mouse button. The commands in the menu depend on where the mouse pointer is located and what's happening when you click the button. Click anywhere outside the menu to close it. Pressing ENTER, ESC, or ALT also closes the shortcut menu. Only the most commonly used commands are included in the shortcut menu, but they might also include commands from several different ribbon tabs. Figure 1-6 shows the shortcut menu that appears when you right-click a table name in the Navigation Pane.

To choose a command from a shortcut menu, click the command or type the letter underlined in the name of the command. A right arrow next to a command, such as Import in Figure 1-6, means that a submenu is available. Rest the mouse pointer on the item to open the list of subcommands, and then click to choose one from the list. If the command shows an ellipsis (...), a dialog box opens when you click it.

NOTE *See Chapter 20 for information on how to customize the Navigation Pane, ribbons, and the Quick Access toolbar.*

Looking at a Table

To open one of the tables in the current database, first expand the list of tables in the Navigation Pane by clicking the expansion arrow next to Tables. Then double-click the table name or right-click the name and choose Open from the shortcut menu. The table appears with the data in rows and columns, much like a spreadsheet. This view of table data is called *Datasheet view.*

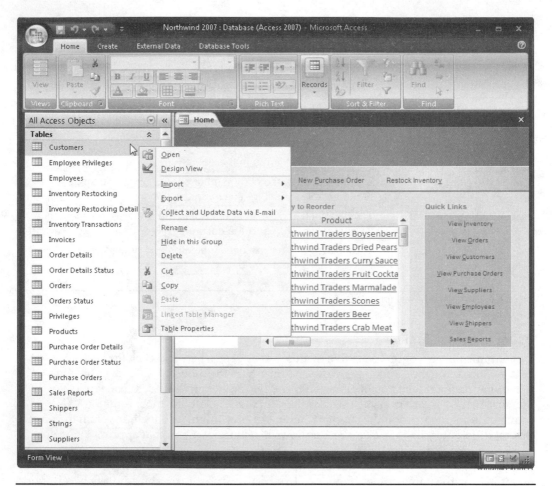

FIGURE 1-6 Shortcut menus help speed up database tasks

Figure 1-7 shows the open Northwind Orders table in Datasheet view. Each row contains a single record with information for one order. Each column contains values for one field. Each field has a unique name and contains a specific item of data, such as the customer or employee name. The column headings show the field names. When you enter data in the table, you're putting actual values in the cells at the intersections of rows with columns.

Touring the Datasheet View

You might have noticed some changes that occur in the window when you open a table. For example, the window now shows the name of the open table in a tab above the table document. The Home tab of the ribbon now shows more available commands in the contextual command groups—that is, they are no longer dimmed and are now available to activate.

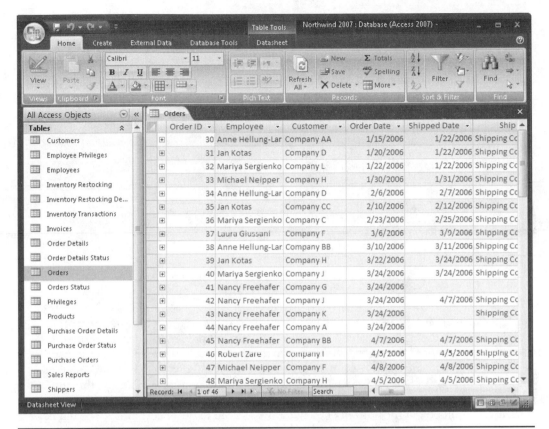

FIGURE 1-7 The Northwind Orders table in Datasheet view

The datasheet window shows scroll bars at the right side and along the bottom. To the left of the bottom (horizontal) scroll bar is a set of navigation tools you can use to move through the records in the table.

Navigating among Records and Fields

You need to be able to access your data if you want to enter new information or edit existing records. As always, you can move the cursor around the records and fields in your table in several ways, including simply clicking in the desired location if it is visible. You should try them all and settle on the one that works best for you. The methods are as follows:

- Using keystrokes such as TAB and the arrow keys
- Clicking the record navigation buttons at the bottom of the datasheet
- Dragging the vertical and horizontal scroll boxes
- Clicking Go To (the blue arrow) in the Find command group at the right end of the Home ribbon

---

NOTE *Clicking Go To in the Find command group also allows you to move to the first, last, next, previous, or an empty new record, similar to the buttons on the navigation bar.*

The Record navigation buttons at the bottom of the datasheet window provide the same options as the Go To ribbon command. You can also enter a specific record number (if you know the number of the record you want to see) in the text box between the navigation buttons and then press ENTER. This area also tells you what record the cursor is in and the total number of records in the table.

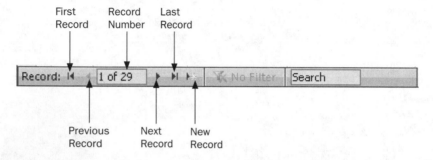

You can also find a specific record by placing the cursor in the column you want to search and enter the desired value in the Search box in the navigation bar. The cursor immediately moves to the record containing that value.

To scroll to a particular record in the table, drag the scroll box to that record. As you drag the scroll box, a helpful ScreenTip appears next to the pointer. It tells you the number of the current record and the total number of records in the table. You can also use the horizontal scroll box at the bottom of the window to drag to other columns in the datasheet.

⊞ Nancy Freehafer	Company K	3/24/2006	Shipping Company C	1
⊞ Nancy Freehafer	Company A	3/24/2006		1
⊞ Nancy Freehafer	Company BB	4/7/2006	4/7/2006 Shipping Company C	1
⊞ Robert Zare	Company I	4/5/2006	4/5/2006 Shipping Company A	1
⊞ Michael Neipper	Company F	4/8/2006	4/8/2006 Shipping Company B	1
⊞ Mariya Sergienko	Company H	4/5/2006	4/5/2006 Shipping Company B	1
⊞ Anne Hellung-Lar	Company Y	4/5/2006	4/5/2006 Shipping Company A	1
⊞ Anne Hellung-Lar	Company Z	4/5/2006	4/5/2006 Shipping Company C	1
⊞ Nancy Freehafer	Company CC	4/5/2006	4/5/2006 Shipping Company B	1
⊞ Andrew Cencini	Company F	4/3/2006	4/3/2006 Shipping Company C	1

Pressing a key or combination of keys can be a faster way to move around the datasheet once you get used to the correlation between the keys and the resulting cursor movement. Here are some examples of what happens when you press various keys and key combinations:

- UP or DOWN ARROW moves to the same field in the previous or next record.
- RIGHT ARROW or TAB moves right one field in the same record. If you're in the last field in the record, the cursor moves to the first field in the next record.

- LEFT ARROW or SHIFT-TAB moves left one field in the same record. If you're in the first field in the record, the cursor moves to the last field in the previous record.

- PGUP or PGDN moves up or down one screen of records.

- HOME or END moves to the first or last field in the same record, respectively.

- CTRL-HOME or CTRL-END moves to the first field of the first record or the last field of the last record, respectively.

TIP *You can change the behavior of the Enter and Arrow keys. For example, you can prevent the cursor from moving to another record after you fill in the last field in one record. See Chapter 16 for information about customizing your work place by setting options.*

Change the Current View

With a table open, the Datasheet view status bar shows four buttons at the right end that can change the current view of the table data: Datasheet View, PivotTable View, PivotChart View, and Design View. (See Chapter 3 for more information about the ways you can view table data.)

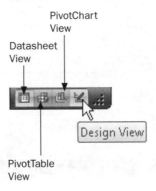

PivotChart View

Datasheet View

Design View

PivotTable View

Looking at a Subdatasheet

In a relational database, it's important that you be able to view information related to the current data on the screen. This has always been possible with forms and subforms in which the main form contains data from one record in one table, while the subform contains data from one or more records in a related table.

When viewing data in Datasheet view, the related data is contained in a *subdatasheet,* which can easily be displayed. If the records shown in Datasheet view display a plus (+) sign at the left end of the row, additional information in another table in the database is related to that record. To see this data, expand the subdatasheet by clicking the plus sign. The plus sign changes to a minus (–) sign when the subdatasheet expands. To collapse the subdatasheet, click the minus sign.

You can have as many subdatasheets expanded as you want in a single Datasheet view. Each subdatasheet corresponds to one record in the datasheet. You can expand them individually or set a table property that automatically expands all the subdatasheets when the table opens in Datasheet view. (See Chapter 4 for information about setting tables and other properties.)

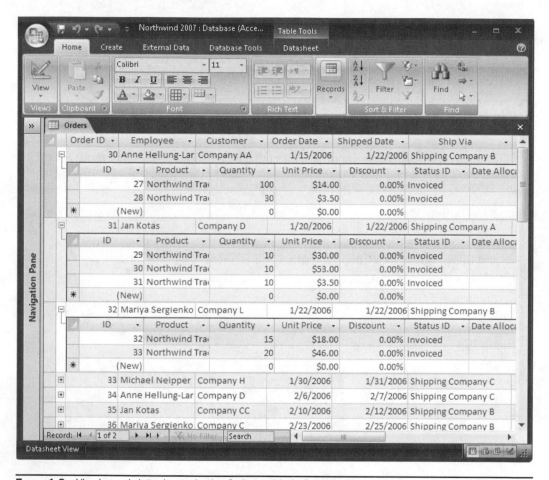

FIGURE 1-8 Viewing subdatasheets in the Orders table in Datasheet view

Figure 1-8 shows the Northwind Orders table with three subdatasheets expanded to show the products from the Order Details table, which were included in three of the orders in the Orders table. Notice the plus and minus signs indicating the current state of the subdatasheet.

NOTE *If fields haven't been specified with which to link records in the subdatasheet with records in the datasheet, when you expand the subdatasheet, you'll see all the records in the related table. See Chapter 3 for more information about relating tables and what that can do.*

Looking at Data in a Form

So far, you've viewed the Northwind Orders table data only in Datasheet view. This view is fine for reviewing the data in small tables, but the full datasheet is often too wide to fit all the fields on a single screen. A much more convenient way to see the data is in a form with only one record on the screen at once. Any related data appears automatically in a subform. Then you can usually see all the fields and move freely among them without having to use the scroll bars. Forms are dual-purpose objects: You can use a form to look up data or to enter and edit data.

Creating the Form

To create a form for a table, you don't need to open the table first. Simply select the table's name in the Navigation Pane and click the Create tab. Then click the Form command in the Forms group.

The Form command starts a special wizard that doesn't ask you for any input about how you want the form to look or what data you want it to show: it falls back on a default form layout and style. The form includes every field in the table, arranged in one or more columns with the field names to the left, so you can identify the fields. The name of the table appears in the title bar of the form and on the Object tab. Figure 1-9 shows the Northwind Orders table in Layout view.

The Orders table has a related table—Order Details—which was available as a subdata-sheet (refer to Figure 1-8). When Access creates a form with this tool, it automatically creates a subform containing data from the related table, which corresponds to the current record in the main form. Notice the automatic change in the Formatting tab of the Form Layout Tools ribbon.

NOTE *If more fields exist than can fit on a single screen, you can use the vertical scroll bar to see the rest.*

To use the form to add a new record to the Orders table, click the New (Blank) Record button in the navigation bar to display an empty form. Use the TAB key to move from field to field as you enter data. To add a new record in the subform, enter the data in the blank row at the bottom of the subform datasheet.

When you finish with the form, you can give it a name and save it as a new database object, or you can close the form without saving it. You can also choose to enter the form Design window and make changes, and then save it as a custom form. (You will learn more about form design in Chapter 10.)

Navigating in Form View

Moving through the table when it's in Form view isn't very different from moving around in Datasheet view. The navigation buttons are at the bottom of the window, which you can use to move to other records (and the Go To options are in the Find group at the right end of the Home tab). The subform also has a navigation bar referring to the records in the subform. Moving from one field to another is a little different, however. Of course, you can simply click in the field in which you want to work, but you might find using keystrokes easier. Experiment with the keystrokes to see where they take you in the form.

If the form contains a subform, pressing TAB cycles the cursor through all the fields of the main form, and then through the fields and records of the related subform. After leaving the last field of the last record in the subform, the cursor moves to the first field in the next record in the main form when you press TAB. The path is reversed when you press CTRL-TAB.

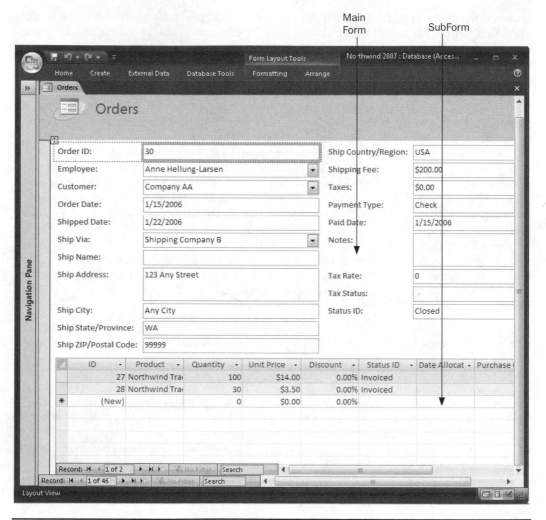

FIGURE 1-9   Creating a form for the Orders table

Looking at the Wizards

If you used earlier versions of Access, you've already met some of the *wizards*, the experts that guide you through complicated processes in a few simple steps. Wizards can help you create new databases, tables, and queries, as well as customize forms and reports with special features. A wizard presents each step as a dialog box in which you choose what you want to do and how you want the results to look. As you make choices, the wizard works in the background to create the Visual Basic code that can accomplish your goals.

Access 2007 has improved many of the old wizards and has added new ones, so you can get help with virtually anything you want to create. You can use the Control Wizards to add command buttons, lookup fields or add a subform to your existing form. See "Changing the

Access Environment" in the Quick Reference on the CD for a complete list of the wizards and builders, as well as how to reach them.

Getting Help

No matter how easy Access makes database management, you can't possibly remember how to do every task. That's where the Access Help feature comes in. You can get help with what you're doing in two ways:

- Click the question mark icon at the upper-right corner above the ribbon
- Press F1

Using the Microsoft Access Help Window

When you press F1 or click the question mark button, the Access Help window opens, showing the list of subjects you can reach through the Access Help and How-to window (see Figure 1-10). You can click a topic to see the information or you can type specific words in the Search box at the top of the screen and click Search.

FIGURE 1-10   Browse in the Access Help window for information

The Access Help window has its own toolbar with buttons that you can use to browse for help.

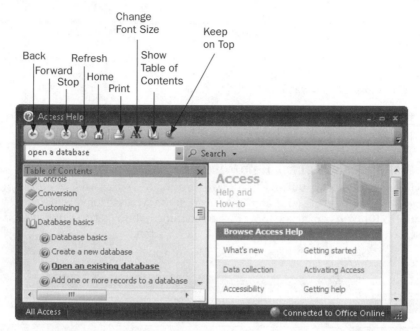

If you want to browse through the Help file table of contents, click the Table of Contents toolbar button. The Table of Contents pane displays a list of topics marked with the closed book icon. Click these to expand the topics into individual Help articles (see Figure 1-11).

If you are currently connected to the Internet, you also have access to all the up-to-date Help topics. Additional online help includes assistance, training courses, the latest product updates, clip art and media, and a research library.

Asking What's This?

Most of the Access dialog boxes include the What's This? tool that provides brief information about a specific element or choice in the box. Activating the What's This? help feature is a two-step process. First, click the question mark (?) button in the dialog box title bar. The mouse changes to an arrow accompanied by a question mark. Then, click the element you want to know more about.

To return the mouse pointer to its normal state without opening the What's This? help, feature, press ESC.

Getting Help with What You're Doing

Without opening the Help window, Access gives you many hints and clues while you're working. The status bar offers information about the current activity or the position of the cursor. Many design windows include hint boxes that tell you about aspects of the design. Other windows and dialog boxes include samples or previews of the selections made.

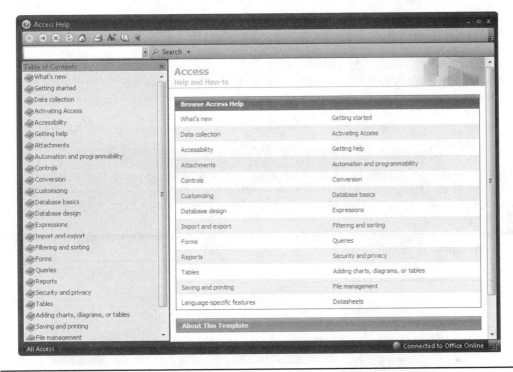

PART I

FIGURE 1-11   Open the Table of Contents pane to find more information

For example, when you're working in a table, the Design window status bar information tells you how to move around the Design view and get help. The hint box on the right describes what should appear in the Field Size Property box.

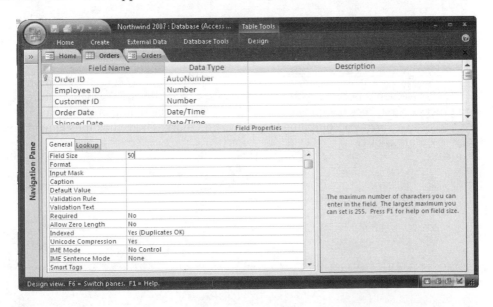

Summary

This chapter has shown you ways to start Access 2007 and get around in the Access window. You had a chance to try out the viewing options, the Navigation Pane, and the new command ribbons. Using the Access 2007 Northwind Traders sample database, you were given a tour of the Datasheet window and a glimpse of the power behind the Access design capabilities, including the many available wizards.

The final section covered the ways to get help while you're working with Access by using the Microsoft Access Help window and the Table of Contents pane.

Armed with this familiarity with the Access database management system, you can move on to the next chapter, which introduces you to the concepts behind the relational database model and examines the types of relationships you can define between tables. Chapter 2 also looks at the structure and components of a sample database, and how the data is related for efficiency.

Subsequent chapters present details about designing and creating a database, as well as populating it with tables and other Access objects.

The World of Relational Databases

We're surrounded by databases—ranging in complexity from a list of weekend gardening chores to data that resides in the archives at the Internal Revenue Service. Our ability to succeed in this Information Age is directly related to our ability to manage and track information. Managing information means storing it efficiently, and tracking means retrieving it quickly—in a form that can be instantly useful. The relational database model has been developed to meet those requirements.

What Is a Relational Database?

A *database* is an organized collection of related information used for a specific purpose, such as keeping track of ongoing work order activities or maintaining a library. A collection of data about clothing manufacturers in New York and coal production in Kentucky probably doesn't constitute a database, because the data wouldn't normally be used together for a specific purpose. If you collected information about your company's work orders, the customers who contracted for the work, and your employees who would carry out the work, however, this would constitute a database.

NOTE *The terms data and information aren't interchangeable. Bits of data are combined in a logical way to impart specific information. For example, the numbers 999090009 constitute an item of data, but they don't constitute information until modified with special characters: 999-09-0009. Then the numbers become information in the form of a Social Security Number.*

When you use a computerized database management system such as Access, the database is called *relational.* The principle behind a relational database is this: The information is divided into separate stacks of logically related data, each of which is stored in a separate table in the file. *Tables* are the fundamental objects at the heart of a relational database. They form the active basis for the information storage and retrieval system.

Once the information is arranged in separate tables, you can view, edit, add, and delete information with online forms; search for and retrieve some of or all the information with queries; and print information as customized reports.

In Access, the term *database* is more precisely used to define the collection of objects that store, track, manipulate, and retrieve data. These components include tables, queries, forms, reports, macros, and modules.

NOTE *Access 2007 no longer supports the data access page object. It makes use of the SharePoint services to send data over the Internet.*

Purpose of Relationships

Rather than storing data in one large two-dimensional table, called a *flat file,* such as you might find in a Word document or an Excel spreadsheet, Access lets you distribute data among individual tables. Topping the list of advantages of using a relational database structure is the reduction of data redundancy, which not only reduces the required disk storage space, but also speeds processing. Other important advantages gained by implementing a relational database are the following:

- **Flexibility**   If data changes, you can update the value in only one place. All queries, forms, and reports look in that place for the current values.

- **Simplicity**   The flat-file model used as the basis for a relational system dictates a simple, nonredundant method of data storage. Each table in the relational design is a single object containing data pertinent to a particular aspect of the database, such as an employee, a product, or an order.

- **Power**   Storing the data in separate related tables allows grouping, searching, and retrieving the information in almost unlimited ways.

- **Ease of management**   With smaller, less-complicated tables, the information is much easier to locate and manage.

For example, if you're tracking customer work orders, you could put all the data in a single table, creating a flat-file database. A separate record would exist for every work order under contract. Storing all the customer data with the work order information would mean repeating the same customer information. In addition, if a customer's phone number changed, every record containing that customer's information would have to be updated. Employee information in the work order table would also be repeated.

It is far more efficient to have one table for work order information and separate tables for customer and employee information. A short field containing a customer identifier could be added to the customer and work order tables to form a connection between the tables, called a *relationship.* Similarly, an employee identifier can link the work orders to the employee who is acting as the job supervisor.

Figure 2-1 shows how to implement the work order database as a relational database. The information is split into an efficient relational database containing three tables, with special fields added to provide the relationships.

In Figure 2-1, the relationship line drawn between the Customer ID field in the Customers table and the Customer ID field in the Workorders table links the two tables. This relationship enables you to look up all the work order information for one customer, as well as the customer's name and phone number for a specific work order.

Similarly, the three relationship lines from the Supervisor, Principal Worker, and Helper fields in the Workorders table to the Employees table, link the two tables in three ways. For example, you can ask Access for the name and pager number of the supervisor on a specific job. When Access creates a second relationship with a table, it actually adds another instance of the table to the Relationships layout. So you see three instances of the Employees table to accommodate the three links with different fields in the Workorders table.

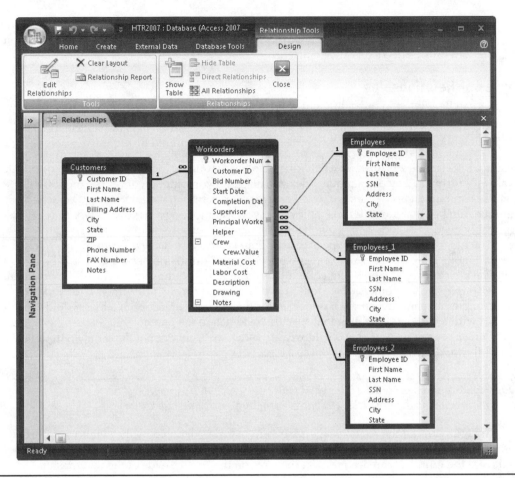

Figure 2-1   An example of a relational database

When you're building a database, one of your main tasks is to decide how to distribute the data. Four clues guide you while designing a relational database:

- The data that can be divided by user, such as by the personnel office or the production manager.

- The data redundancy. For example, in a customer-related service company, one customer might contract for several services. Storing all the customer data with the work order information would mean repeating the customer information in every work order record. This would result in many copies of the same information (if your business were successful enough to encourage repeat business).

- How many records you'll have in each category. For example, if you have 500 employees and 1500 work orders, you can see that employees and work orders belong in separate tables.

- The dimension of time. If you have information you seldom use, such as an archive of completed work orders, storing this separately—and out of the way—and bringing it out only as needed is more efficient.

Types of Relationships

Tables can be related in three different ways: one-to-many, one-to-one, and many-to-many. The type you define depends on how many records in each table are likely to have the same value.

To relate tables, one of them must include a field that contains a unique value in every record. This can be a primary key field or a field with a unique index that allows no duplicate values. A primary key or a unique index can also be a combination of two or more fields whose combined value is unique for all records. For example, the Employee ID can be a unique number that identifies an employee. If you want to use names in a key or index, you'd probably need to include both the first and last names to ensure unique values.

The most commonly used type of relationship is the *one-to-many relationship,* in which one record in one table can have one or many matching records in another table, or maybe none at all. The table on "one" side is often called the *parent* table and the other is called the *child* table. For example, the Customers table would have one record for each customer. The Workorders table might have more than one work order for the same customer. Both tables would include a field with a value representing that specific customer. In the parent table—Customers—the field must be the *primary key* or a field with an index that contains a unique value. In the child table, the field is called the *foreign key* and does not need to be unique.

Tip *You can speed processing if the child table is indexed on the foreign key. See Chapter 4 for information on defining table structures including specifying indexes.*

In Figure 2-1, all the relationships are one-to-many, as denoted by the symbols at the ends of the relationship lines. The *1* appears at the end of the line attached to the table on the "one" side and the infinity symbol appears at the table on the "many" side of the relationship. Primary key fields are indicated by the field name appearing in boldface in the field lists. As you can see in the figure, all three tables in the database have primary keys. The foreign keys are identified by the relationship line pointing to the field name in the child table field list.

The *one-to-one relationship* is sometimes used as a form of lookup, in which each record in one of the tables has a matching record in the other table. Neither table is designated as the parent. The key fields in both tables are the primary keys. One use for this type of relationship is to store additional, seldom-accessed information about an item in the first table, such as an abstract of a book or the details of a work order.

The *many-to-many relationship* isn't permitted as such in a relational database. Many records in one table have the same values in the key field as many records in the second table. To implement this in Access, you must create a third table, called a *junction table,* to place between the first two, converting the many-to-many to two one-to-many relationships. Office Access 2007 introduces a new field type, the *multivalued field,* that can replace the need for the junction table when creating a many-to-many relationship. (See Chapter 4 for information about the different data types you can use in a table.)

Figure 2-2 shows how the three types of relationships differ. Chapter 5 contains more information about defining and modifying relationships.

A one-to-one relationship links the Bid Data table to the Workorders table:

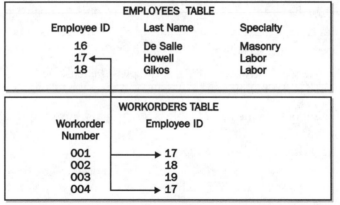

A one-to-many relationship links the Employees table to the Workorders table:

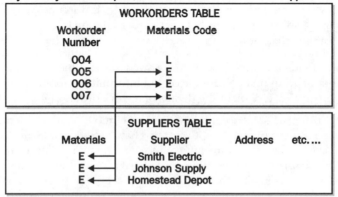

A many-to-many relationship links the Workorders table to the Suppliers table:

FIGURE 2-2 Three types of database relationships

Referential Integrity

Referential integrity is an optional system of rules that guarantees the relationships are valid and the database will remain intact as data is entered, edited, or deleted.

The basic rule of referential integrity is this: For every record in a child table (the "many" side), one and only one matching record must be in the parent table (the "one" side). For example, in the relationship between the Customers table (parent) and the Workorders table (child), every current work order must have a reference to a customer. You cannot have a work order without a customer. The referential integrity rules also prevent you from deleting a customer record if work orders are still in progress.

Here's a summary of the referential integrity rules that Access can enforce:

- You cannot enter a child record for which no parent exists (start a work order without a customer).

- You cannot delete a parent record if related child records still exist (remove a customer before the job is completed).

- You cannot change a child record so its foreign key doesn't have a match in the parent table (change the customer field in a work order record to a nonexistent customer).

- You cannot change the primary key value in a parent table as long as related records are in the child table (change a customer link before the work order is finished).

These rules help to maintain an accurate and complete database with no loose ends. Before you can set referential integrity, you must make sure you meet the following conditions:

- The matching field in the parent table is the primary key or at least has a unique value, such as an AutoNumber field.

- Related fields are the same data type.

- Both tables are in the same Access database. You can set referential integrity between linked tables, provided they are both in Access format and you open the database that contains the linked tables.

The same rules can apply to a one-to-one relationship. Enforcing the referential integrity rules in such a relationship guarantees that every record in one table has one and only one matching record in the other table.

Defining Database Objects

Before going any further, let's take a closer look at the objects that make up a database. Access is an object-oriented database management system (DBMS), which means that the entire database is composed of objects with certain characteristics or attributes called *properties* that determine their structure, appearance, and behavior. For example, table properties include a description of the table, the subject of the table, and the arrangement of records in the table, such as in alphabetic or chronological order, based on one or more fields.

In turn, each of the major Access objects is a container for other objects, which also have properties. For example, tables are made up of fields that are considered objects with properties of their own, such as name, size, format, and data type. Reports and forms contain design objects, such as data fields, titles and labels, command buttons, page numbers, and graphics. Each of these has a list of properties you can set to achieve the effect you want.

As you see in the Navigation Pane, the major database objects are tables, queries, forms, reports, macros, and modules. The *tables* are the containers for all the data in your database. As mentioned earlier, in a relational database system, the data is distributed among several related tables instead of being placed in one large table.

A *query* is a question that you ask of your database. You usually use a query to extract a specified set of records from one or more tables. For example, you might ask the database to show you a list of delicatessen customers who are vegetarians or who have a preference for exotic pasta products. Access answers your question by displaying the requested data. Because a query is a stored question instead of a stored answer, when you ask the question again, the results include the latest information. You can not only view the results, you can also use them in reports and forms.

Forms are often more convenient than a tabular datasheet for entering and editing table data, especially if a table includes more data than can fit across the screen and you have to scroll right to see the rest. A form can display a single record at a time, so all the data is visible at once, and you can arrange the fields in any way you want in a form design. You can also include data from more than one table or query as the basis for a single form. Forms are especially useful for creating a comfortable visual environment for data management. For example, you can create a form that resembles the paper form used to collect data in the work place.

When you want to print the data, you usually create a *report*. The report can be a quick and easy dump of the table data—useful for checking specific data items—or it can be a glossy presentation of the data in a custom format suitable for the stockholders or a business manager. The report can also include totals and other summaries of values in a particular field, such as gross sales and monthly profits. Adding charts and graphs to a report makes it even more visually informative.

Access provides a special type of report through the Label Wizard that you can use for printing mailing labels or envelopes. If you keep a mailing list in a database table, this type of special report can come in handy. You can also create form letters and merge them with the address list to print a personalized copy for each recipient.

The final two types of objects are macros and modules. *Macros* contain a sequence of commands that perform a certain task and are useful for defining the automatic actions that respond to button clicks or other events. Several new features have been added to macros in Office Access 2007 that make them more useful and secure. (See Chapter 19 for details.) *Modules* are programs written in Visual Basic for Applications (VBA), the programming language used by Office Access 2007. Procedures contained in the modules are the cornerstone of advanced Access applications.

Inspecting the Sample Database

The Northwind Traders sample database introduced in Chapter 1 is an order-processing application. If it weren't for the use of the Access relational-database management features, the process could be both cumbersome and time-consuming. The following sections examine the sample database in more detail.

Looking at the Data Distribution

As mentioned earlier, a relational database consists of several tables, each of which contains data focused on an aspect of the database. After distributing the data among the tables, the tables are related to one another by means of identifying the matching fields.

The Northwind data is distributed among 20 tables, as shown in the Navigation Pane in Figure 2-3. The principal tables are Products, Orders, and Customers. The other tables support the order processing by providing additional data, such as the name of the employee who took the order, the category of the product, product suppliers, order status, and shipping methods. Each of these tables is a good example of grouping data items used for the same purpose.

The Orders table contains all the order information, such as the order number; customer identifier; employee identifier; order date, date required, and date shipped; shipping method; and the complete name and address of destination. Additional fields track the payment and

FIGURE 2-3   Northwind Traders data distributed among many tables

tax information. Three other tables are related to the Orders table: Order Details, Orders Status, and Order Details Status.

The Customers table contains the customer identifier, as well as the customer's complete address and telephone numbers. It also includes a new attachment field type and a hyperlink to a web page. If this information wasn't included in a separate table, it would be repeated in every order placed by the customer.

The Products table contains the current state of the inventory of each product. The fields include the product identifier, name, supplier identifier, category, quantity per unit, unit price, units in stock and on order, the reorder level, and a field that indicates whether or not the product has been discontinued. The table also includes a new attachment field.

Inventory tracking is accomplished with three tables: Inventory Transactions, Inventory Restocking, and Inventory Restocking Details. Purchase orders are also tracked in the Northwind database with three tables: Purchase Orders, Purchase Order Details, and Purchase Order Status.

Other tables contain peripheral information for the purpose of reducing data redundancy. The Employees table contains the employee identifier, birth date and hire date, name and address, telephone numbers, the name of the employee's supervisor, and a memo field for notes. The Suppliers table includes the supplier identifier, name and address, and a point of contact. The Shippers table contains the company name and telephone numbers, as well as the shipper identifier. The Invoices table lists the order and shipping dates as well as the costs billed to the customer.

Viewing Table Relationships

Most of the tables in the Northwind database are related in some way. To see the relationship scheme, choose the Database Tools tab in the ribbon and click the Relationships command in the Show/Hide command group. The Relationships window (Figure 2-4) shows eight tables with their relationship lines.

NOTE *To simplify the view, many of the peripheral tables were hidden in this view of the Relationships window. When you choose Relationships, you may see all the tables in a tangled arrangement.*

Each of these eight tables is related to at least one other table, thereby creating a relational database. Take a look at a few of the most important relationships:

- The Orders table is the centerpiece of this display and is related to several tables: Customers, Shippers, Order Details, Invoices, and Employees. The Orders and Invoices are linked by the Order ID field. Customers and Shippers are linked to the Orders table by their ID fields. The Employees table is linked to the Orders table by the Employee ID field.

- The Products table is related to two tables: Order Details and Suppliers, all using the Product ID field.

Identifying Primary Keys and Linking Fields

As you can tell from the symbols at the end of the relationship lines, all of these relationships are one-to-many, the most common type. The parent table must be linked to the child table by its primary key. The primary key field appears with a key icon in the table field list. Notice all

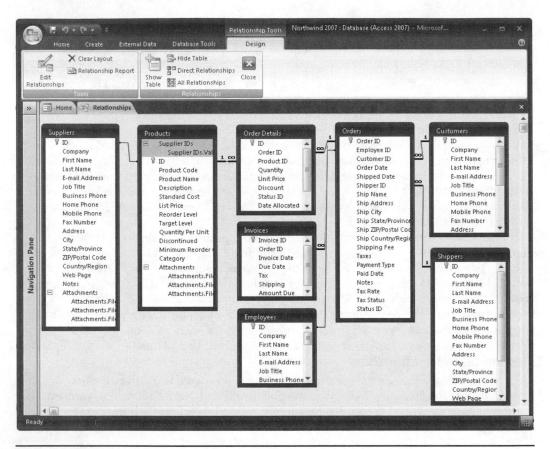

Figure 2-4   Some important relationships among the Northwind database tables

the primary keys use the ID either alone or with a table name. This practice helps to identify which field contains the primary key.

Looking at Relationship Properties

In addition to the relationship type, you can find out more about a relationship, such as whether referential integrity is enforced, the specific names of the linking fields, and the type of join implemented. The Edit Relationships dialog box opens when you right-click the middle of a relationship line and choose Edit Relationship from the shortcut menu, or when you choose Edit Relationships in the Tools command group in the Design tab. This dialog box specifies which are the linking fields in each table, the enforcement of referential integrity, and the type of relationship. Two other properties, Cascade Update Related Fields and Cascade Delete Related Records, when selected automatically make changes in related tables when you change data in the related fields or delete a record from the table on the one-side of the relationship.

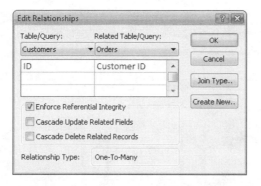

PART I

NOTE *If you click the Join Type button, a second dialog box opens in which you can choose the join property you want to use for the relationship. See Chapter 5 for more information on join types and how they affect the data displayed.*

The Payoff

In addition to the efficiency of data storage, a relational database system offers large benefits when it comes to data retrieval. Forms can be designed for entry or display of data from related tables. As you enter data in the form, it is dispersed to and updates the proper table. As you view data in a multiple-table form, the data is synchronized automatically.

A Custom Form

The Northwind sample database includes several custom forms. To view the Purchase Order Details form (shown in Figure 2-5), do the following:

1. Open the Northwind Traders database as before and log in as an employee.

2. In the Navigation Pane, click the down arrow in the header and choose Object Type in the upper Navigate to Category pane and All Access Objects in the lower Filter by Group pane.

3. Click the header arrow again to see the list of objects.

4. Click the Forms expansion arrow in the Navigation Pane to show the list of forms in the database.

5. Double-click the Purchase Order Details form name, or right-click it and choose Open from the shortcut menu.

The form is used to enter new purchase orders by supplier or to view existing orders. Each purchase order includes data from the related tables containing the purchase order details, inventory receiving data, and payment information. While this form looks complicated, you'll see in Chapter 12 that such forms are easy to construct with Access 2007.

The Supplier field has a down arrow button that controls the display of a list of Supplier IDs derived from the Suppliers table. When the supplier name is selected from the list, related information is displayed in the subform. The subform has three pages that show purchase details, inventory, and payment information.

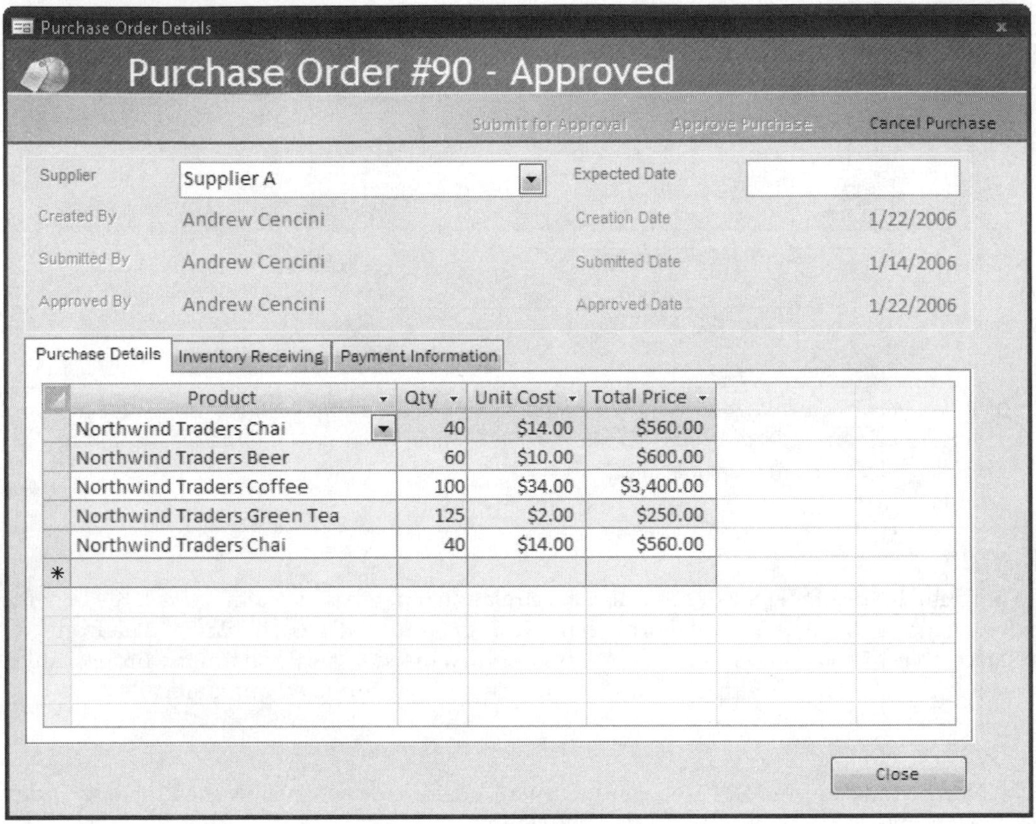

FIGURE 2-5   The Northwind Traders Purchase Order Details form

A Custom Report

To preview the Product Sales Quantity by Employee report in the Northwind database, expand the Reports list in the Navigation Pane. Then double-click the report name, or right-click it and choose Open from the shortcut menu. This is an example of a report containing information from more than one table. The report is based on a select query that gathers information from the Employees, Products, and Sales Reports tables. The sales are grouped by employee with a chart showing the volume of sales in each category for each employee. Figure 2-6 shows a preview of this report.

Summary

This chapter contains some insight into the theory of relational database systems and how they can be used for efficient information storage and retrieval. The major building blocks of an Access database—tables, queries, forms, reports, macros, and modules—were briefly

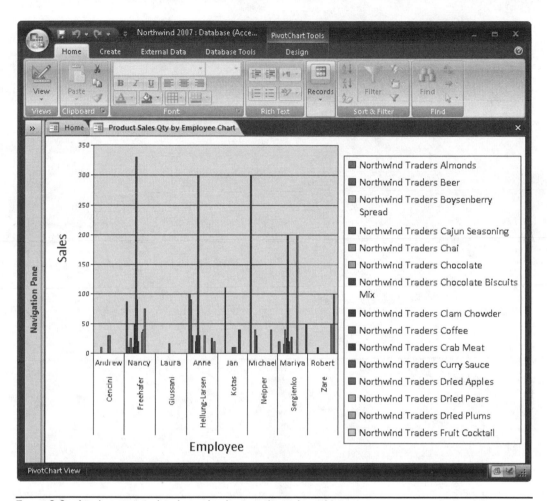

FIGURE 2-6   A sales report showing sales by quantity and employee

discussed and samples were shown. The relationships among the tables in the Northwind sample database were examined.

The next chapter discusses in-depth the process of designing a relational database and how to distribute data among tables. You will see how to create a new database from a template that you can download and how to create a blank database without a predetermined design.

Creating a Database

The information in a relational database system is distributed among related tables to optimize information storage and retrieval. Common fields relate the tables so information can be extracted and presented in useful ways. A database can be an essential tool in tracking and managing personal or business information if it's properly designed and constructed. A poorly designed database is of little or no value. The more time spent on task and data analysis, the better the results. Once the design is completed and reviewed, building the database with Access 2007 is easy, with or without a predefined database template.

Designing the Database

The design process begins with an analysis of the tasks to be required of the database. First, you must determine what the system is intended to do for the prospective users. Interview all the users and get thorough descriptions of their expectations. What's essential to remember is that the design process is also an iterative one: as the users get accustomed to a new system, they can think of more features that they can use, such as an additional data entry form, a special query, or a calculated field.

On the other hand, freezing the design at some point is critical, so you can proceed with the development. Then you can accumulate the users' later requirements and desires for the upgraded version.

It is also important to acquaint the users with the comprehensive form and report capabilities of Access 2007 by demonstrating some data entry forms and showing examples of printed reports.

The database design process can be broken down into seven steps, each with specific goals and products:

1. Determine what the users want from the database and what data is needed to provide the output.

2. Decide what tables to include in the database.

3. Identify the fields for each table.

4. Assign a unique field or combination of fields for each table that ensures no two records are the same.

5. Determine how the tables are related to one another.

6. Review design and step through procedures with users.

7. Create tables and enter data.

While numbering steps in a process implies one step is completed before the next begins, in reality, the design process is more fluid, with each step overflowing into the next. You can return to a previous step at any time in the process.

This chapter covers only the design and creation of the database itself. Chapter 4 discusses creating tables with and without a table template, Chapter 5 describes how to relate the tables, and Chapter 6 contains more information on entering and editing data in the database.

Introducing Home Tech Repair

The example we'll use is the Home Tech Repair database. Home Tech Repair is a small company specializing in maintenance and improvement of home structures. Its specialties are electrical, plumbing, structural, painting, and heating and air conditioning systems in the home. It doesn't undertake large construction or remodeling jobs.

The database's main purpose is to track work orders and print invoices. Figure 3-1 shows an example of the manual record-keeping system in use before the development of the Access database.

Determining the Goals of the Database

Step 1. Determine the Purpose of the Database   What do the users need from the database? What kind of reports do they want, and how do they want the information arranged and summarized? If adequate data collection forms already exist, use them as patterns for the database forms. Look at other databases that address similar information management situations. After the tasks are defined, you can develop a list of the required data items.

The main purpose of the Home Tech Repair database is to maintain up-to-date information about current work orders. The information must include forms for data entry and viewing of all table data, and it must relate the individual work orders to specific customers or employees.

In addition to work order tracking, the owner wants to conduct financial analyses, for example, to determine how much revenue has been generated by each employee or to review the total sales on a monthly basis. These analyses can include summary reports with charts and graphs depicting trends, as well as proportional distributions of types of jobs over a period of time. Such studies are helpful when planning for future work.

Distributing the Data

Step 2. Determine How the Information Should Be Divided among Tables   This isn't as easy as it sounds, but you can follow these guidelines:

- A table shouldn't contain duplicate information among its records. With only one copy of each data item, you need to update information in only one place.

- The information in a table should be limited to a single subject. This enables you to maintain data about each subject independently of the others.

Home Tech Repair

```
Order #_____          Date/Time_____

Customer_____

Address_____

        _____

Phone  _____          Taken by_____
```

```
Description    _____

              _____

              _____

              _____

Bid Number_____      Total Bid_____   Date_____

Supervisor_____

Work in Progress                        Date Started_____

Date Finished_____              Supervisor_____
```

Labor			Costing Data	
Hours	Rate	Cost	Parts	_____
____x ____ = ____			Sales Tax	_____
____x ____ = ____				
____x ____ = ____			Sub Total	_____
____x ____ = ____			Labor	_____
____x ____ = ____				
Total Labor:		_____	Total	_____
Cost Estimate _____ Date _____			Amount Paid _____	

FIGURE 3-1   The Home Tech Repair manual work order record

In the Home Tech Repair case, employee and customer information is repeated on several work order sheets. To reduce the redundancy, pull out both sets of information and put them in separate tables. Keeping payments in a separate table will add flexibility, especially if the work is paid for in installments, such as a deposit at the start of the contract and the remainder during the work.

If specific parts are routinely used, such as plumbing fixtures or electrical devices, the parts list should be kept in a separate table. The data in the parts table can be accessed by the form or report that brings the work order expenses together.

Other peripheral data can be included in separate small tables, such as shipping or payment methods. The Home Tech Repair company information can also be kept separately in one place, accessible to the report that prints the invoice. This table can include the company address, telephone and fax numbers, e-mail and web addresses, and any short, standard message to include in correspondence.

Step 3. Determine the Fields to Contain the Individual Facts about Each Subject   All the fields should relate directly to the subject and not include any information that can be derived from other fields. Include all the information you need, but nothing extra. Break up the information into small logical parts, such as First Name and Last Name fields, rather than a single name field. Name the fields, so that you can locate specific records and sort by individual field values. You can always combine the fields later for finding and searching, if necessary.

CAUTION   *The word* Name *is a reserved word in Access.* Name *is one of the properties of Access objects and controls, as discussed in later chapters. Using a word that has a special meaning to Access as a field name isn't a good idea because this can cause unpredictable problems.*

Access offers nine data types that cover all the types of data you're going to include in your database. For example, text, memo, date/time, currency, Yes/No, OLE Object, Hyperlink, and Attachment are some of the data types offered. You meet all these data types in later chapters. Meanwhile, try to categorize the data into specific data types.

Table 3-1 lists the fields in each of the Home Tech Repair tables and shows the data type and size, as well as a brief description of the data to be stored in the field.

Field	Data Type	Field Size	Description
Workorders Table			
Workorder Number	Number	Integer	Unique workorder number
CustomerID	Number	Integer	Unique customer ID
Bid Number	Text	5	Original bid number that contained text as well as numbers
Start Date	Date	N/A	Scheduled start date
Completion Date	Date	N/A	Expected completion date
Supervisor	Number	Integer	ID of employee in charge
Principal Worker	Number	Integer	ID of employee who is second in charge
Helper	Number	Integer	ID of helper
Material Cost	Currency	2 decimals	Cost of materials
Labor Cost	Currency	2 decimals	Cost of labor
Description	Memo	N/A	Description of work order
Drawing	Hyperlink	N/A	File of drawing, as required

TABLE 3-1   Fields and Data Types in Home Tech Repair Tables

Field	Data Type	Field Size	Description
Employees Table			
Employee ID	Number	Integer	Unique employee identification number
First Name	Text	20	Employee's first name
Last Name	Text	25	Employee's last name
SSN	Number	10	Social Security number
Specialty	Text	25	Special labor skills
Address	Number/Text	50	Employee's home address
City	Text	50	City
State	Text	2	State
ZIP	Number	9	ZIP code
Work Phone	Number	12	Office phone or pager
Pager	Number	12	Home phone
Hourly Rate	Currency	2 decimals	Salary/hourly rate
Billing Rate	Currency	2 decimals	Employee's billing rate
Comments	Memo	N/A	Additional information
Badge Picture	OLE Object	N/A	Employee picture
Customers Table			
CustomerID	Number	Integer	Unique customer ID
First Name	Text	20	Customer's first name
Last Name	Text	25	Customer's last name
Billing Address	Number/Text	50	Address to send bill
City	Text	50	City
State	Text	2	State
ZIP	Number	9	ZIP code
Phone Number	Number	12	Customer's phone number
FAX Number	Number	12	Customer's fax number
Notes	Memo	N/A	Additional customer information

TABLE 3-1   Fields and Data Types in Home Tech Repair Tables *(continued)*

NOTE *The AutoNumber data type would be better for the fields you intend to use as the primary key fields, such as Employee ID, Customer ID, Bid Number, and so on. Access creates the AutoNumber values to ensure they're unique within a table. However, if the Home Tech Repair business already had a system of identifying the employees, work orders, and so on and would like to keep them, it's easy to accommodate the users with codes with which they're familiar. You can set those field properties so that the value is always unique.*

After arranging the data in the tables, review the distribution carefully for further normalization. Remove any redundancies and make sure all the fields in each table apply directly to that subject. Do not include any fields that are derived from data in other table fields. For example, the overhead and the total work order costs are calculated fields, so they aren't included as separate fields in the Workorders table.

Specifying Key Fields and Relationships

Step 4. Be Sure Each Table Has a Key Field That Contains a Unique Value If no such field exists, let Access assign a special field to act as the primary key, so you can be sure each record in the table is unique.

Each of the three main tables of the Home Tech Repair database has a field that uniquely identifies a record: Workorder Number, Employee ID, and Customer ID. The values in these fields can be entered by the user or assigned by Access in the form of an incremental AutoNumber. If the number has no other significance, such as identifying the general location of the job, Access can provide an AutoNumber, and then you can be sure no duplicates occur.

Step 5. Determine How the Tables Will Relate to One Another Identify the common fields and the types of relationships among them.

The Workorders table has a field named Customer ID. Instead of using the customer's name to link to another table, use the Customer ID, which is the primary key in the Customers table and can be used as the linking field between the two tables. Similarly, use the Employee ID instead of the employee names in the Supervisor, Principal Worker, and Helper fields in the Workorders table. The Employee ID is the primary key field in the Employees table, which links it to three foreign keys in the Workorders table.

The relationship between the Customers and Workorders tables is one-to-many because a customer might contract for more than one job. The relationship between the Employees table and the Workorders table is also one-to-many because an employee can work on more than one job at a time and in one of three slots in a single job.

Figure 3-2 shows the Home Tech Repair tables in the Access Relationships window. The field lists have been lengthened to display all the fields. The figure also shows a fourth table, Bid Data, which you'll add later in the chapter.

Three instances of the Employees table appear in the Relationships window because the table is linked to three separate fields in the Workorders table. The table isn't really replicated, it's simply displayed in the Relationship window three times, to illustrate the three separate relationships. (Chapter 5 contains information about working in the Relationships window and defining or editing relationships.)

Completing the Database

Step 6. Thoroughly Review the Design, Complete with Sketches of Planned Reports and Prototype User Interfaces Now it's time to consult with the users for additional comments and suggestions. Step through the operations you plan to carry out with the information.

Step 7. Create the Table Structures in Accordance with the Design and Enter the Data You might want to limit the data to just enough to test the application and then complete the tables later. Create the forms, reports, and queries with this limited data. If the database is intended for inexperienced users, you can add custom categories and groups in the Navigation Pane and other

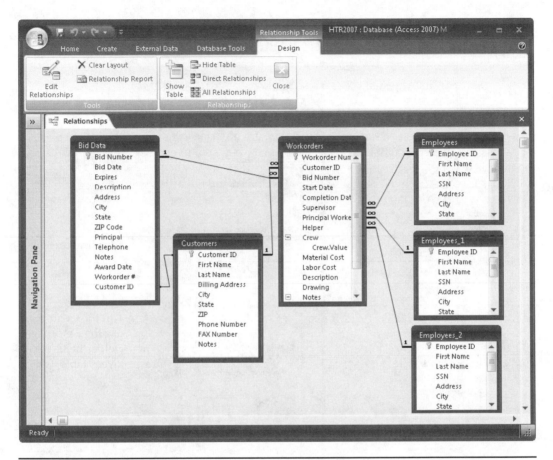

FIGURE 3-2   The Home Tech Repair tables showing their relationship

custom tools to make their jobs easier. A custom group of database objects in the Navigation Pane can be the user's main interface with the database. A custom group replaces switchboards used in previous versions of Access. You can, however, still use your switchboards in Access 2007 if your users are accustomed to them. The only problem you may find is if the Visual Basic for Application (VBA) code behind the switchboard includes a command to open a database window, which no longer exists in Access 2007.

A custom group in the new Navigation Pane displays a list of actions the user can take. Clicking an item in the list opens a data entry form or a dialog box, previews a report, or provides access to a macro or VBA module. Carefully test the entire system. Time spent refining and verifying the design at this stage can save time revising the database later, after it's been populated with data.

After the design is established, Access gives you two ways to create a new database:

1. Download a predesigned template.
2. Start from scratch with a blank database.

If you decide to start a new database using a template, you can choose among different types of commonly used database templates relating to Business, Education, and Personal categories.

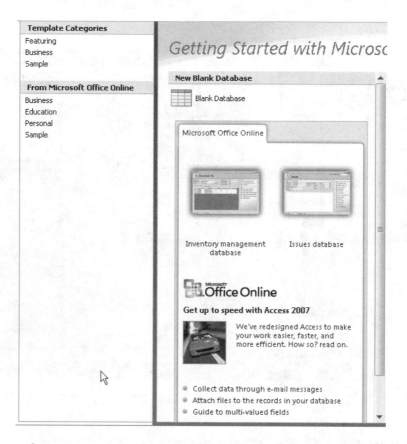

When you choose a category—for example, Business—several database templates are shown in the Business pane. The templates provide a complete version of the database, with all the relevant tables, forms, reports, and queries. They may also include data, but many do not.

When you build a new database from scratch, the Navigation Pane and object pane open with a new table listed in the Navigation Pane and the beginning of the first new table in the tabbed document window.

Creating a Database from a Template

If you need a database for a common personal, business, or educational purpose, you can get started by using a template provided by Microsoft Office Access. After you build the database from a template, you can add your own data and make modifications to the forms and reports that came with the turnkey application.

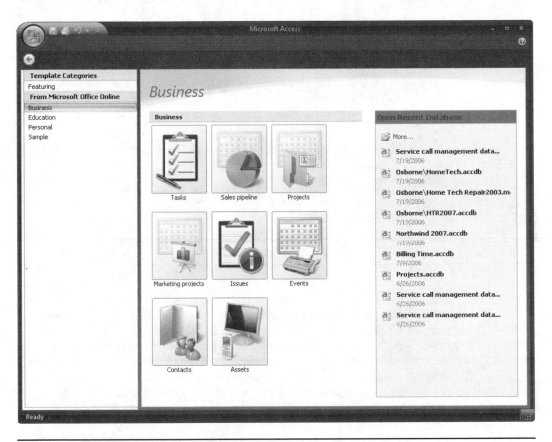

FIGURE 3-3   Database templates in the Business category

The Getting Started with Microsoft Office Access window shows a couple of templates in the center pane. If you double-click one of the thumbnails, you can see a sample form in the right pane along with instructions for downloading the template. For example, enter a name for the database and click the folder icon to change to a different destination directory.

To see more templates, double-click one of the subjects in the Template Categories group in the left pane. Figure 3-3 shows eight different templates available in the Business category. Double-click a template thumbnail again to get more information.

If none of the templates match your requirements, you can browse online for more templates, some from earlier versions of Access:

1. Click the Back button in the upper left corner to return to the Getting Started window and scroll down to the bottom of the center pane.

2. Click Templates under More on Office Online.

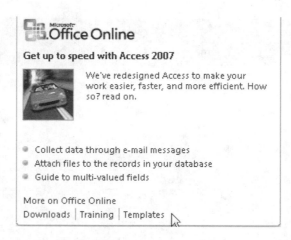

3. Scroll to the bottom of the window and enter **Databases** in the Search text box and select Access from the Program list.

4. Click Search (Figure 3-4).

For Home Tech Repair, the best template seems to be the Service Call Management database. To download the template, select the database in the search list (see Figure 3-5) and click Download Now. Microsoft Office downloads the file automatically to your default directory and opens the database.

When the database opens, the Security Warning message appears. Click the Options button and in the Microsoft Office Security dialog box, check Enable This Content. Then click OK to continue. Once the database is open, you can convert the new database to Access 2007. Then you can give it a new name and save it in your company folder. (For more about converting to other versions of Access, see Appendix A.) Let's view the database in Access 2007 (Figure 3-6) with the main form, Workorders by Customer, open in the document pane and the objects listed in the Navigation Pane.

NOTE *If you don't see tabs in the document pane after converting the database to Access 2007, you can restore the Tabbed Documents option. Click the Microsoft Office button and then click Access Options. On the left pane, choose Current Database. In the Application Options group, check Tabbed Documents and then click OK. Close and restart the database for the change take effect. More about setting work place options can be found in Chapter 16.*

You can now add more objects and delete those you don't need or change the names to fit your business. You can also add and remove fields from the tables and change report and form styles and content. You may need to change relationships if you remove a related table or field that is used as a link.

After you have tailored the database to fit your needs, you can create custom group categories in the Navigation Pane that include related activities. For example, place all the work order–related forms and reports in a group named Workorders. This group will include the following:

- Workorders by Customer form
- Workorders form

FIGURE 3-4 Searching for database templates online

- Invoice report
- Print Invoice form
- Payments form

A second custom group, named Preview Reports, will include the following reports:

- Revenue by Employer
- Sales by Month
- Finished Workorders in House
- Unfinished Workorders
- Workorder Summary

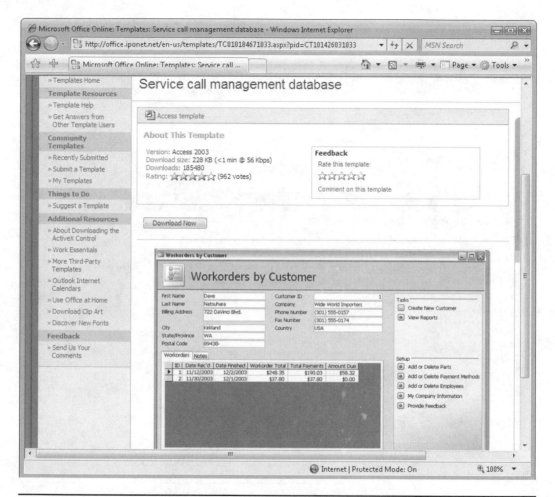

FIGURE 3-5 Downloading the Service Call Management database

A third custom group, named Other Information, will include the following forms for data viewing and entry:

- Parts
- Payment Methods
- My Company Information
- Employees

Each of these groups replaces a choice from the main switchboard that opened at startup in Access 2003.

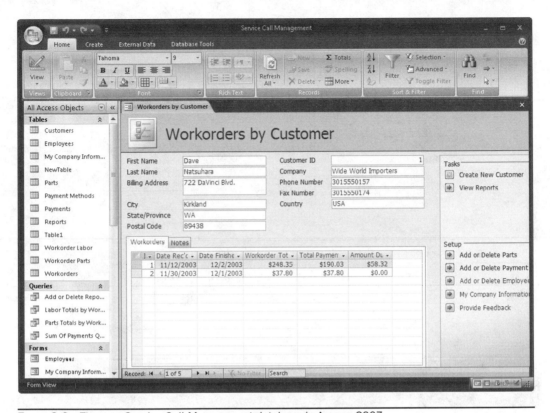

FIGURE 3-6   The new Service Call Management database in Access 2007

Running the New Application

When it opens, the Home Tech Repair application automatically displays the main form, Workorders by Customer (as shown in Figure 3-6), where you can enter new work orders or edit an existing record.

The Workorders form (Figure 3-7) contains specifics about a single work order, including the employees who work on the job, their billing rate, and the hours spent. The costs are calculated and displayed with payments credited to the work order and the remaining balance computed. To return to the previous form, close this form by right-clicking the document tab and choosing Close in the shortcut menu.

To make the template database conform to the needs of the Home Tech Repair company, you need to make many changes. Some fields are unnecessary and need to be removed; others should be renamed. Additional forms and reports that depend upon different queries, filters, or sort orders might be necessary. All these changes can be made to the Home Tech Repair database built from the Service Call Management template. (Changes to a table design are discussed in the next chapter. Queries are covered in Chapter 8, and form and report designs are discussed in Chapter 10 and later chapters.)

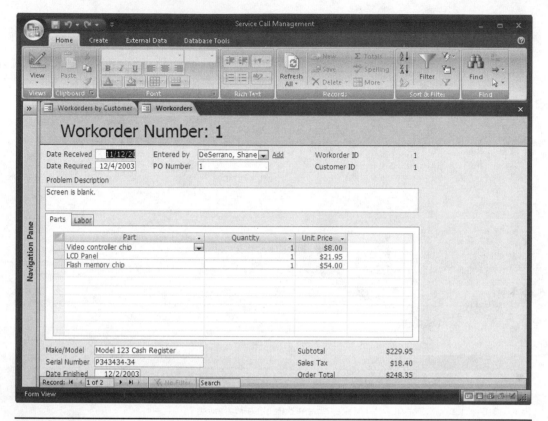

FIGURE 3-7   Reviewing the details of a Workorder

Starting with a Blank Database

To create a new blank database, do the following:

1. If the Getting Started window is not already open, click the Microsoft Office button and choose New. Then select Blank Database in the center pane.

2. The blank database pane opens, where you can enter a name for the new database and click the folder icon to browse for the folder in which you want to store it.

3. After entering a custom name for the new database and opening the folder where you want to store the database, click Create.

A new empty table is started for you in the tabbed document window and the new table name, Table1, is listed in the Navigation Pane (Figure 3-8). The Datasheet tab is active and contains all the tools you need to build the new table in Datasheet view.

Notice that the first field in the new table, ID, is the primary key field, which is an AutoNumber data type. Click in the ID field and you can see the data type in the Data Type text box in the Data Type and Formatting group on the ribbon. The Unique field property is also checked to prevent duplicate values.

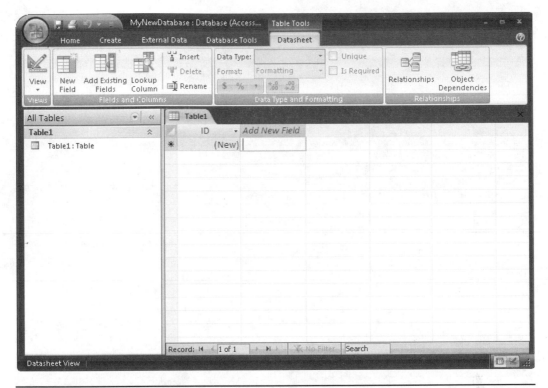

Figure 3-8 Starting with a new blank database

All you need to do now is one of the following:

- Enter data in the new table and save it with a name.
- Switch to Design view and build the table structure.

More information about creating and modifying tables is available in Chapter 4.

Summary

In this chapter, the seven-step database design process was described and put into practice in the design of the Home Tech Repair database. You saw how to distribute the data among the tables, and then how to determine the key fields and specify the relationships among the tables. After completing the design, a template was invoked to create a database similar to the one Home Tech Repair requires.

This chapter also addressed starting a new application from a blank database, rather than a prefabricated template. In the next chapter, you will learn how to create new and modify existing table structures. The many field properties that determine the appearance and behavior of the data are also discussed. You will also learn how to improve the value of the information in a database by adding validation rules, default field values, and other features.

Creating and Modifying Tables

Tables form the essential foundation of a relational database, and one of the first tasks in database development is building the tables to store the distributed data. Carefully designed table structures can make the difference between a smooth-running, error-free information system and a total disaster.

Access 2007 provides many useful tools for creating and customizing tables that help ensure accurate data entry and facilitate information selection and retrieval. This chapter covers not only how to create a new table structure, but also how to customize the design for your specific data requirements. You'll learn to create a table from a template with the Table Wizard, and you'll learn how to create a table in Datasheet view and Design view.

Creating a New Table from a Template

Access 2007 provides several built-in table templates you can use to start a new table structure. Not only are these templates appropriate for common office usage, they are compatible with the Microsoft SharePoint Services lists of the same name.

To start a new table from a template, open the database, and on the Create tab in the Tables command group, click Table Templates.

Look over the list of templates and choose one that best suits your needs. The new table is added to your database. Figure 4-1 shows a new table built from the Contacts

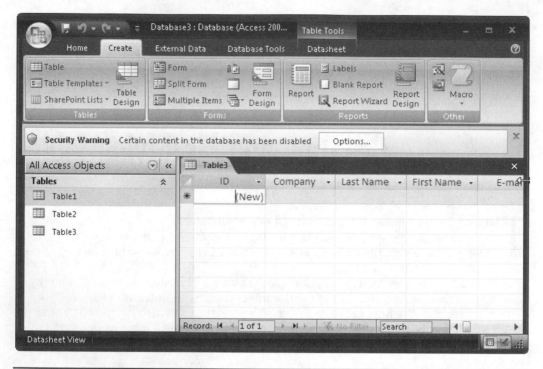

FIGURE 4-1 Creating a new table from a template

template. You can make changes in the fields and their properties, as described later in this chapter.

Creating a New Table in Datasheet View

When you start a new database, Access automatically creates a new table for you and displays it in Datasheet view. If you have already started the database and want to add a new table, you can go to the Create tab and click Table in the Tables command group. A new table opens in Datasheet view in the object pane with two fields showing:

- **ID**   The automatic primary key field.
- **(Add New Field)**   Where you begin entering data.

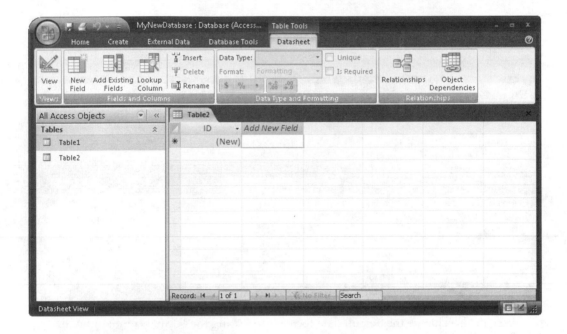

Adding Fields to the New Table

You build a new table in Datasheet view by entering the data in the cell just below the column header Add New Field. As you enter data in each new field, Access chooses the appropriate data type for the field, such as Text, Number, or Date/Time. Here are some examples:

- *John Brown* becomes a Text data type.
- *1/15/07* becomes a Date/Time data type.
- *12.99* becomes a General Number data type, with the Double field size property because of the digits to the right of the decimal point.
- *$15,000.00* becomes a Currency data type.

***

NOTE   *See the section "Creating a New Table in Design View" later in the chapter for a list and description of all the Access data types.*

***

Changing Data Types and Formats

To check on what data type Access has assigned to a field, do the following:

1. Click the Datasheet tab and select the field you want to change.
2. In the Data Type and Formatting group, click the Data Type down arrow.

3. If you want the field to use a different data type, choose the type from the list. The selected data type must be compatible with the data you have already entered in the field.

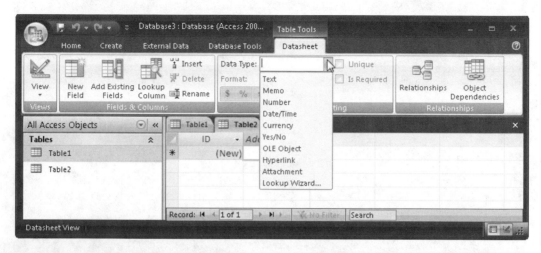

You can also change the default data format by clicking the Format command in the Data Type and Formatting group. Then choose from the list of formats that apply to the selected field's data type.

Changing Field Names

As you enter new fields, Access automatically names the fields *Field1*, *Field2*, and so on. To change this to a more meaningful name, right-click the field header and select the Rename Column from the shortcut menu. You can also use the Rename command in the Fields and Columns group of the Datasheet tab. Then enter the new name in the column header.

Field names can have up to 64 characters, including letters, numbers, and spaces. Using a mixture of uppercase and lowercase letters can help explain the field to the user, but Access doesn't differentiate between cases in field names.

NOTE *You cannot begin a field name with a space. You also can't use any of the characters to which Access attaches special meanings, such as a period, exclamation mark, and square brackets. See the Help topic, "Access 2007 reserved words and symbols" for a complete list.*

Using a Field Template

Access 2007 has included the field templates from previous versions and grouped them in the table templates. You can save time by placing these templates in your new table. To see the list of the templates you can add to your table in Datasheet view, do the following:

1. On the Datasheet tab in the Fields and Columns group, click New Field.

2. In the Field Templates pane, click the plus sign (+) next to one of the table template names to see the fields in that table.

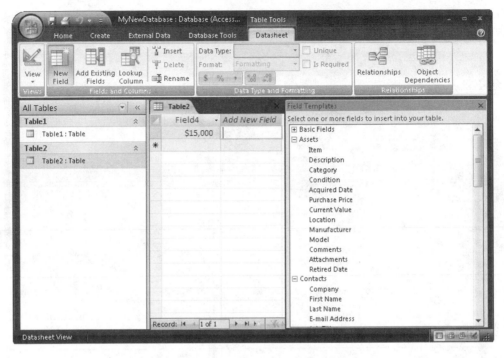

3. When you find the field you want, click and drag it through an existing row to the table. Drop the field when the insertion line appears in the column divider.

4. When finished, click the Close button in the Field Templates pane or click the New Field command again to add more.

NOTE   *You can select more than one field from the Field Templates pane and drag the group to the Datasheet view. To select contiguous fields, select the first field in the list and hold down* SHIFT *as you select the last field. If the fields are not contiguous, hold down* CTRL *as you select them individually. They will appear in the table in consecutive columns.*

Adding Fields from an Existing Table

When you build a relational database, the related tables will have fields with matching data types. If you have already built one of the tables and are working on a new table that may or may not yet be related, you can add fields from the existing table.

To do this, you need to see the list of all existing fields in all the tables in the database. In the Fields and Columns group on the Datasheet tab, click Add Existing Fields. The Field List pane opens, as shown in Figure 4-2, with the names of all the tables currently in your database. The list contains two categories of tables:

- **Fields Available in Related Tables**   Lists all the tables to which the current table is related.

- **Fields Available in Other Tables**   Lists tables not yet related to the current table.

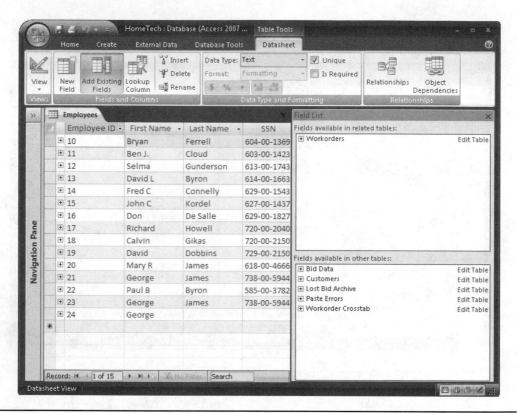

FIGURE 4-2   Selecting fields from existing tables

To see the list of fields in a table, click the plus sign (+) next to the table name. If you want to add one of the fields in the list to your new table, drag the field name to the Datasheet view and drop it when you see the insertion line. This starts the Lookup Wizard, which helps you add lookup columns to the table that contain the values from the field you chose. (There is more about lookup fields later in this chapter; see Chapter 6 for details of using the Lookup Wizard in Design view to create lookup fields.)

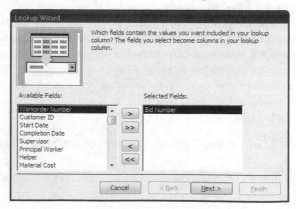

Save the New Table

When you are satisfied with the new table structure, you can name it and save it in the database. The table name can contain up to 64 characters, including spaces. You have three ways of saving the table:

- Click the Microsoft Office button and click Save.
- Right-click the table document tab and choose Save from the shortcut menu.
- Click Save on the Quick Access toolbar.

If you have not already assigned a name to the table, enter the name in the Save As dialog box and click OK.

TIP *It is a good idea to save a new object several times during development, especially if the process takes a while, so that you won't lose your work in case the worst happens.*

Creating a New Table in Design View

The easiest way to start a new table is to click the Table Design command in the Tables group on the Create tab. An empty table appears in the Design window, ready to add fields, as shown in Figure 4-3. The Design tab in the Table Tools ribbon appears.

Touring the Table Design View

The table Design view window is divided horizontally into two panes. The upper pane is the field entry area where you enter the field name, data type, and an optional description. You also specify the field to serve as the primary key for the table in the upper pane. The lower pane is devoted to specifying the individual field properties that correspond to the field selected in the upper pane, such as size, display appearance, validity rules, and so on. The list of properties depends on the type of field you're entering. To the right of the Field Properties pane is a description of the currently active area of the screen. Once you start adding fields to the design, you can jump from one pane to the other by clicking where you want to be or by pressing F6 with the cursor in an active row.

Some new commands on the Design tab of the Table Tools ribbon relate to the task of creating and modifying a table definition:

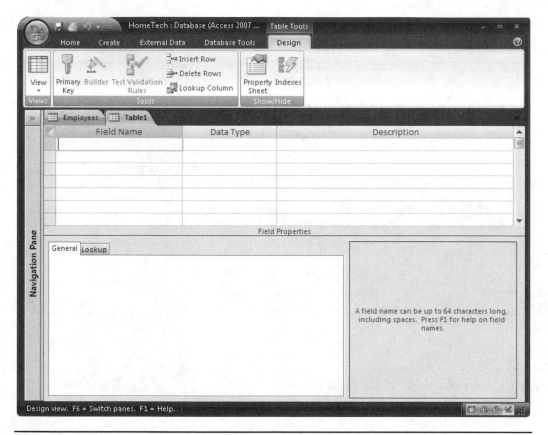

FIGURE 4-3   Starting a new table in Design view

Adding Fields

To begin adding fields to the table structure, do the following:

1. Click the first row of the field entry area and type the first field name.

2. Because the most commonly used field type is Text, Access automatically specifies a new field as a Text data type by default. To change it to another type, select the type from the Data Type drop-down list.

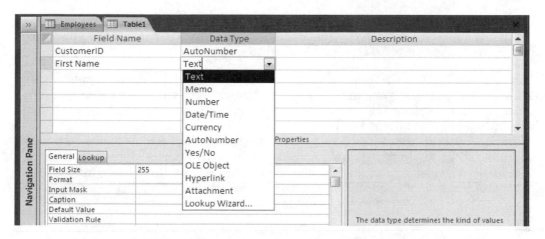

3. Enter an optional description that can provide additional information about the field. The description appears in the status bar when the field is selected in a datasheet or form.

4. Move to the Field Properties pane and set any desired properties for each new field, such as a Default Value, a custom Format, or a Validation Rule.

CAUTION *Although including spaces in field names makes them easier to read, if there's a possibility that you might want to export the table or the complete database to another database program, use a mixture of uppercase and lowercase characters instead. Access accepts spaces in field names, but other applications may not.*

TIP *Once you get used to the names of the available data types, you can simply type the first letter of the data type name and Access fills in the rest.*

Specifying Field Data Types

Several factors come into play as you decide what data types to use:

- The kind of values you plan to allow in the field and how you plan to use them.
- The availability of storage space. With some data types, the field size can be reduced for efficiency.
- The types of operations you can execute with the data. You can count the number of records containing a specific value of most data types in a field, but you can perform mathematical operations on values only in the Number and Currency fields.
- The way you want to sort or index records. You can sort or index any field data type except OLE Object and Attachment.
- The way you want to group records for a report or query. You can group on any field data type except Memo, Hyperlink, OLE Object and Attachment.

The following paragraphs briefly describe each of the 11 data types and how they're used. If you're interested in the amount of disk space each type requires, refer to the Quick Reference section "Table Fields" on the CD that accompanies this book.

Text The Text data type is the most common data type and can contain any combination of up to 255 characters and/or numbers. You would use the Text data type for storing values that contain combinations of numbers and letters, such as addresses and job descriptions. Even when you think the field will contain only numbers, but you aren't expecting to perform any calculations with the values in the field, using the Text data type is best. For example, ZIP codes might seem like numbers, but they often contain a dash, which isn't considered a number or a leading 0 that would be truncated. In addition, you won't be computing the sum or average of all ZIP codes, so using a Text type is more efficient.

TIP *If you're planning to sort records on a field that will contain only numbers, even if you won't be using the values in any calculations, you're better off using the Number data type rather than the Text data type. When Access sorts numbers in a Text field, it reads the numbers from left to right, instead of right to left. So, for example, the numbers 9, 46, and 175 in a Text field would be sorted (ascending) in the reverse of their numerical order: 175, 46, and 9 because Access reads the first digits and sorts accordingly. If the first digits are the same, it reads the second digit, and so on.*

Access gives Text fields a default size of 255 characters, but you can reduce the size to 1. If you expect the field to contain more characters than 255, you should consider using the Memo field type instead, which can contain much more data.

Memo Use a Memo field to store long, but variable-length text possibly relating to the other field data. For example, you could add comments to your employee records about their efficiency on the job or their skills when dealing with customers. You don't expect every record to include memo data, but when one does, the text can vary in size from a few words to up to 65,535 characters. Memo fields also support rich text format (rtf) editing.

NOTE *The handy spelling checker can be used to catch misspelled words in both Text and Memo fields. See Chapter 6 for more information about this useful tool.*

Number Select the Number data type when you plan to sort the values or use them in calculations, such as adding up the labor hours for a plumbing job or the hours worked by a certain employee during the fall season. If you're working with dollar sales figures, it's better to use a Currency type because you can choose from several monetary display formats. Currency values also maintain higher precision during calculations.

Date/Time The Date/Time data type is most useful when you want to sort records chronologically by the value in the field. You can also use a Date/Time field in calculations to determine elapsed time. This data type provides a variety of ways to display the data as well. Formatting Date/Time and other data types is discussed in the section "Date/Time Fields" later in this chapter.

Currency   Use the Currency data type when you want to store monetary values, such as the cost and bid price of contracted jobs. Currency fields can be used in arithmetic calculations, just like the Number fields. You have many more ways to specify the display appearance of Currency fields than Number fields, including the display of negative values. Currency values are accurate up to 15 digits to the left of the decimal point and 4 digits to the right. Using Currency instead of the Number data type prevents inaccuracies caused by rounding off the results of calculations to two decimal points.

CAUTION   Number and Currency fields are automatically assigned 0 as the default value. This can cause a problem if you plan to use the field to store lookup values. This also becomes a problem if you want to count records that contain a value in the field. Zero is considered a value and the record is then falsely included in the count. To prevent this complication, remove the setting in the Default Value property. See Chapter 6 for more information about lookup lists.

AutoNumber   When you specify an AutoNumber field, Access guarantees that each record in the table has a unique value in the field, thereby creating a field you can use as a primary key. Access generates a unique value for the field as you enter each new record. You have a choice of two types of AutoNumbers: Long Integers and Replication ID numbers. If you choose Long Integers, you have a choice of how Access generates new values: Increment or Random. The most commonly used are incremental numbers, which start with 1 and simply count the records as you add them.

Yes/No   The Yes/No field is useful when you want the equivalent of a check mark in your records. For example, suppose you want to know whether a transaction has been posted or a job has been completed. By default, a Yes/No field appears as a check box in a datasheet as well as in forms and reports. You can choose to display Yes or No, On or Off, or True or False. You can also create your own custom display for Yes/No fields.

NOTE   The Yes/No data type is also called "Boolean" because of its binary logic.

OLE Object   When you want to embed or link an object from another source in your table, you use an OLE Object type field. With this type of field, you can acquire data from such objects as an Excel spreadsheet, a Word document, graphics, sound, or other binary data.

Hyperlink   When you want the field to jump to another location, or to connect to the Internet or an intranet, store the hyperlink address in a hyperlink field. A hyperlink field can contain up to four parts, separated by the pound sign (#):

- **DisplayText**   Optional text that's displayed instead of the full hyperlink address (commonly referred to as a "friendly" link).

- **Address**   A Universal Resource Locator (URL) or a Universal Naming Convention (UNC) path.

- **SubAddress**   A page within the web address or a location within the file.

- **ScreenTip**   Text that displays when the mouse pointer rests on the hyperlink. You often see these when you rest the mouse pointer on a ribbon command.

Only the address is required unless the subaddress points to an object in the current Access database. The other parts are optional.

Attachment   An Attachment field is used to store pictures, images, files from other Office programs, and binary files. This data type is similar to attaching files to an e-mail message. An attachment field offers more flexibility than the OLE Object data type. An attachment field appears in a form or report with a paper clip icon.

When you attach a file to a field, Access creates a system table in the background and you use the Attachments dialog box to work with them. You can open and edit an attachment if the program that created it is installed on your computers.

Lookup Wizard   The Lookup Wizard creates a field limited to a list of valid values. When you select this data type, a wizard helps you create the list and attaches it to your table. You can type in the values you want to use or have the Lookup Wizard consult another table for the set of valid values. Then, as you enter table data, you can choose the value you want from a drop-down list. The field inherits the same data type as the primary key field in the lookup list, which is the value stored in the lookup field.

TIP *Field descriptions are helpful. For example, if the field name itself isn't informative enough or you want to remind yourself that the field is a link to another table, add a description. The text you enter in the Description column appears at the left end of the status bar when the field is highlighted in Datasheet view or in a form.*

Setting Field Properties

Field properties determine how the values in the field are stored and displayed. Each type of field has a particular set of properties. For example, you might want certain currency values displayed with two decimal places, a dollar sign, and a comma as the thousands separator. Or, you can specify that the currency values be rounded off to the nearest whole dollar. While you can set many field properties in Datasheet view, it is more efficient to use Design view.

To specify a property setting, first select the field in the field entry pane (the upper portion of the window) in Design view, and then click the desired property in the Field Properties pane (the lower portion). Many of the properties show a down arrow when they're selected. Clicking the arrow displays a list of property options from which you can choose. In most cases, you can also type in the setting you want. If you need more space to view the property setting, press SHIFT-F2 to open the Zoom box.

A useful field property is the Caption, which is the text that appears in the column header in Datasheet view and as the label attached to a field in a form or report. The Caption property can display a more descriptive name for the values than the field name itself.

Access attaches default properties to every field. You can accept or change the settings to customize your fields. Because Text fields are the most common and most of the field properties apply to the Text data type, let's look at their properties first. Table 4-1 describes the properties of a Text field, most of which are also available to other types of fields, although different default settings are used for different data types.

The Text, Number, and AutoNumber field types are the only types for which you can specify a field size. Access automatically sets fixed field sizes for the other types. Number and Currency fields have a property that lets you specify the number of decimal places to

Property	Effect
Field Size	Specifies the number of characters allowed in the field. Default is 255 characters, which is the maximum.
Format	Determines the display appearance, such as forcing uppercase or lowercase characters. In a Text field, a default format isn't specified.
Input Mask	Provides a template for data conforming to a pattern, such as telephone numbers or Social Security numbers, and adds literal characters to the field, if desired. Default is none.
Caption	Displays a name other than the field name in datasheets, forms, and reports. Default is none.
Default Value	Automatically enters the specified value in the field. Default is none.
Validation Rule	Specifies an expression that checks for invalid data. Default is none. (Unless the Validation Rule specifies that the field can be left blank, it can also have the same effect as setting the Required property to Yes.)
Validation Text	Displays this message if the entered data fails the validity rule. Default is none.
Required	Indicates this field cannot be left blank. Default is No.
Allow Zero Length	Differentiates between a blank field and a field containing an empty string of text (""). Helpful when a value is known not to exist (such as a fax number). Default is Yes.
Indexed	Indicates the table is indexed on this field. Default is No.
Unicode Compression	Allows string data that is now stored in Unicode format to be compressed to save storage space. Default is Yes.
IME Mode	Sets the IME mode for a field when the focus is moved to it. *IME* is a program that enters East Asian text into programs by converting keystrokes into East Asian characters. Default is No Control.
IME Sentence Mode	Sets the type of IME sentence. Default is None.
Smart Tags	Recognizes and labels the field as a particular type. Default is none.
Text Align	Specifies the default alignment of the field in a control. Default is General.

TABLE 4-1   Text Field Properties

display as well. The AutoNumber data type also has the New Values property, which determines the method of assigning a unique number to the new record.

Other properties such as Input Mask and Validation Rule include a Build button that appears as a button displaying an ellipses (...) to the right of the property text box, which you can click to get help with the property. For example, if you click the Build button next to the Validation Rule property, the Expression Builder dialog box opens, where you can get help with creating a valid expression. If you don't need help building an expression, you can simply type it into the property box. If the expression is invalid, Access lets you know.

You will learn more about validation rules in the section "Ensuring Data Validity" later in this chapter.

Choosing a Field Size

A Text field, such as a ZIP code or a job number that contains only a few characters, does not need to take up the default 255 characters. You can change the size of the field by entering a different number. Another reason to specify the field size is to prevent data entry errors by limiting the number of characters that can be entered.

Number fields are sized a little differently, specifying the name of the number layout, rather than the number of characters. The options are as follows:

- **Byte**   Stores positive integers (whole numbers) between 1 and 255. Uses 1 byte of storage.

TIP *Save space with Number field sizing. If you know the field will contain only small integers, choose the Byte field size property to save disk space. This might not sound like much, but with extremely large tables, the results are significant.*

- **Integer**   Stores larger integers and negative integers, between –32,768 and +32,768. Uses 2 bytes of storage.

- **Long Integer**   Default Number field size, which stores even larger integers between roughly –2 billion and +2 billion. Uses 4 bytes.

- **Single**   Stores single-precision floating-point numbers in IEEE format. Floating point numbers are expressed in exponential terms—for example, $.35 \times E05$. Uses 4 bytes.

- **Double**   Stores double-precision floating-point numbers in IEEE format. Uses 8 bytes.

- **Replication ID**   Stores a globally unique identifier (GUID). Replication is not supported in the new Access 2007 ACCDB file format.

- **Decimal**   Makes the Precision and Scale properties available to control number entries.

AutoNumber fields are limited to Long Integer and Replication ID field sizes.

Changing the size of a Number field only changes the way it's stored, not the appearance of the numbers. To change their appearance, you need to change the Format property.

Formatting Field Data

The Format property is used to specify the appearance of the value when displayed. This has no effect on the way the value is stored and it doesn't check for invalid entries. A format makes sure all the field values look alike, no matter how you entered the data. For example, you can force all names to be displayed in uppercase characters or all dates to include four-digit year values by using this property. Access provides predefined formats for most data types, but you can also create custom formats for all data types except OLE Object.

TIP *You can go through the Windows Control Panel to change the Country setting on the Formats tab of the Regional and Language Options dialog box to apply foreign currency and other formats to field values. For example, changing English (United States) to English (United Kingdom) changes the currency symbol from dollars ($) to pounds (£).*

When you set a field's Format property in Design view, Access applies that format to the values in Datasheet view. Any new controls on forms and reports also inherit the new formatting. Controls added to the form or report design prior to setting the custom formats are unaffected.

You can use the following custom formatting symbols with any data type:

- **!**   Enters characters from left-to-right instead of right-to-left, forcing left alignment.
- **(space)**   Enters a space as a literal character when the SPACEBAR is pressed.
- **"xyz"**   Displays the characters or symbols within the quotation marks.
- *****   Fills available space with the character that follows.
- ****   Indicates that the character that follows is to be treated as a literal character. Often used with reserved symbols and characters.
- **[color]**   Displays the field data in the color contained within the brackets: black, blue, green, cyan, red, magenta, yellow, or white.

Text and Memo Fields   Text and Memo fields use the same format settings, some of which are character placeholders that apply to individual characters and other settings affecting the entire entry. You can use the following symbols with Text and Memo field format settings:

- **@**   Indicates a character or a space is required.
- **&**   Indicates a character or a space is optional.
- **<**   Converts all characters to lowercase.
- **>**   Converts all characters to uppercase.

Custom Text and Memo format settings can have two sections, separated by a semicolon. The first section applies to fields containing text and the second applies to fields containing zero-length strings or null values.

Here are some examples of using the Text and Memo Format settings:

Format Setting	Entered As	Displays
@@@-@@-@@@@	123456789	123-45-6789
>	jimmy	JIMMY
<	JIMMY	jimmy
@@\!	Hello	Hello!
@@;"No Data"	Horse	Horse
@@;"No Data"	(blank)	No Data

Number and Currency Fields   You can format your Number and Currency data with one of Access's predefined formats or create your own using the special formatting symbols. The Format property of a Currency field is automatically set to Currency, but you can change it

Setting	Effect
General Number	Displays number as entered.
Currency	Displays number with currency symbol and thousands separator. Negative values appear in parentheses. Default is two decimal places. Default setting for Currency fields.
Euro	Displays number with Euro currency symbol and thousands separator. Negative values appear in parentheses. Default is two decimal places.
Fixed	Displays at least one digit. Default is two decimal places.
Standard	Displays thousands separator. Default is two decimal places.
Percent	Displays value multiplied by 100 with added percent sign (%). Default is two decimal places.
Scientific	Uses standard scientific notation with exponents. For example, 243 displays as 2.43E+02.

TABLE 4-2   Number, AutoNumber, and Currency Predefined Format Settings

to any of the other settings. The Format property of a Number or Currency field displays a list of the predefined formats as described in Table 4-2.

TIP *When you specify the Percent format for a number field, you must change the Field Size property from the default Long Integer to Single. Otherwise, the field displays only the integer portion of the number you enter and leaves off the fraction. For example, it you enter 1, the field displays 100.00%, but if you enter 1.25, the field still displays 100.00%.*

Date/Time Fields   Date/Time fields include seven predefined format settings, in addition to some symbols you can use to create your own custom formats. Here are the formats Access provides:

Setting	Description
General Date	(Default) Combination of Short Date and Long Time settings. If no time, only date is displayed, if no date, only time. Examples: 5/21/07 3:30:00 PM (US) 21/5/07 15:30:00 (UK)
Long Date	Uses Long Date Regional setting. Examples: Friday, May 25, 2007 (US) Friday, 25 May, 2007 (UK)
Medium Date	21-May-07
Short Date	Uses Short Date Regional setting. Examples: 5/21/07 (US) 21/5/07 (UK)
Long Time	3:30:00 PM
Medium Time	3:30
Short Time	15:30

Date and Time format settings are specified according to the setting in the Regional and Language Options dialog box in the Windows Control Panel.

NOTE *In Access, Date/Time field data is always stored with four-digit year values. However, the user could have entered only two digits to represent the year. The Short Date setting assumes any dates between 1/1/00 and 12/31/29 are in the twenty-first century, that is, between January 1, 2000, and December 31, 2029. Dates between 1/1/30 and 12/31/99 are assumed to be in the twentieth century, between January 1, 1930, and December 31, 1999.*

Using special characters to represent the hour, minute, and second in a time format and the day, week, month, and year in a date format, you can create almost any display format you choose. The letter *d*, for example, can display the day of the month as one or two digits or as the full name, depending on how many times you use the letter *d* in the string. The letter *m* can also be used to represent the month from one or two digits to the full name. The character *n* is used as the minute format symbol to avoid confusion with the month symbol, *m*.

To include literal characters other than the date and time separators with the Date/Time values, enclose them in quotation marks. Some examples of using these special formatting symbols are the following:

Setting	Displays
ddd", "mmm d", "yy	Mon, Jan 15, 07
dddd", "mmmm d", "yyyy	Monday, January 15, 2007
h:n:s AM/PM	9:15:35 AM

In addition, you can add other characters to the display format by enclosing them in quotation marks. For example, entering the value 5/25/07 in a field with the format setting

"Today is " dddd " in week number " ww "."

displays

Today is Friday in week number 21.

Notice the spaces within the quotation marks that separate the characters in the string from the date values and the period added to the end of the expression.

NOTE *If you specify a custom Date/Time format that's inconsistent with the settings in the Regional and Language Options dialog box, the custom format is ignored.*

Yes/No Fields   Access automatically displays a default check box control when you specify a Yes/No data type. Any format settings you make are ignored with this choice. To display values in any other format, first change the Display Control setting on the Lookup tab to a text box or a combo box, and then you can have some fun formatting Yes/No field values. Access provides three predefined formats for displaying Yes/No, On/Off, or True/False, but you can also create a custom format that displays other text for the two values.

To change a Yes/No field Display Control property, open the table in Design view and do the following:

1. Select the Yes/No field.
2. Click the Lookup tab in the Field Properties pane.
3. Select Text Box from the Display Control list.
4. Return to the General tab to choose the desired display format.

The Yes/No custom format contains up to three sections, separated by semicolons. The first section isn't used, but you still need to enter the semicolon before entering another section. The second and third sections specify what to display when the value is Yes and No, respectively. For example, the following format:

;"Yes, indeed!"[Green];"No, never!"[Red]

displays

Yes, indeed!

in green when the value is Yes, and

No, never!

in red when the value is No.

If you choose Combo Box as the Display Control property instead of Text Box, more properties appear on the Lookup tab, where you can set the appearance and values of the list the Combo Box will display. (More about using combo boxes and lookup lists in Chapter 6.)

Setting the Number of Decimal Places

The Field Size, Precision, Scale, Format, and Decimal Places properties of Number and Currency fields are all related.

The Field Size property determines whether the number is stored as an integer or with fractional values, and also specifies the degree of mathematical precision.

The Precision property applies only to Number fields with the Field Size set to Decimal. This property is used to limit the total number of significant digits that can be entered on both sides of the decimal point in a Number field. Leading and trailing zeros aren't counted; they're truncated. Enter a positive integer between 0 and 28 in the Precision property of the Number field. The default setting is 18.

The Scale property also applies only to Number fields with a Decimal Field Size property. Scale limits the number of significant digits that can be entered to the right of the decimal point, not counting any trailing zeros. Enter a positive integer between 0 and 28 in the Scale property. The default setting is 0.

The Format property adds display features, such as dollar or percent signs, and commas as thousands separators.

The Decimal Places property determines how many digits to display to the right of the decimal point in a Number or Currency field. The Decimal Places setting has no effect on the precision of the stored number; that's specified by the Field Size or the Precision property. If the value is stored as an integer (Byte, Integer, or Long Integer data type), a number of zeros appear to the right of the decimal point equal to the setting in the Decimal Places property.

The default Decimal Places setting for Number and Currency fields is Auto, which displays two decimal places for fields with Format property settings of Currency, Fixed, Standard, Percent, and Scientific. You can choose any number from 0 to 15. However, the Decimal Places property has no effect unless you already specified the appropriate Format property for the field.

To change the number of Decimal Places in the display, click the arrow in the Decimal Places property box and choose a number from the list or enter the desired number. If the field retains the default Long Integer property, the values are rounded to the nearest integer, no matter how many decimal places you specify for the display.

TIP *You can also set the Decimal Places property in a query, report, or form design and override the setting you specified in the table design.*

To change the number of decimal places stored in the field, change the Field Size property to one of the settings for real numbers, such as Single, Double, or Decimal, which aren't limited to integers.

Including a Caption

If someone else is going to use the database and you think the field names aren't descriptive enough, you can use the Caption property to change the column headings in the Datasheet view. A caption can contain up to 2048 characters, in any combination of letters, numbers, special characters, and spaces. Be aware, however, that the space where the caption will be displayed might be limited.

The new caption also appears in queries and replaces the text in the field labels attached to controls in report and form designs. The field names remain the same; only the labels show the new caption text.

CAUTION *If you rename the field later in Datasheet view, the Caption property is deleted. To prevent this, rename fields only in table Design view.*

Choosing a Primary Key

In a relational database system, you must be able to gather and retrieve related information from separate tables in the database. To do this, each record in one table must be unique in some way. The field or fields that contain the unique value is called the *primary key*. Access neither permits duplicate values in the primary key nor does it permit null values. A valid unique value must be in the primary key field or field combination throughout the table. In Design view, you can tell which field contains the primary key by the key icon that appears in the left margin.

When you create a new table in Datasheet view, Access automatically adds the first field and assigns it as the primary key with the AutoNumber data type.

Letting Access Set the Key

The AutoNumber field type is an Access tool that can guarantee unique records in a table. Designating an AutoNumber field as the primary key for a table is probably the simplest way to set the key. You do not need to worry about inadvertently entering duplicate values, because Access uses unique numbers to identify each record. Once the number is generated, it can't be changed or deleted. Access will also ensure that no other record contains the same value in that field.

You can choose to use incremental numbers or random numbers for records. With incremental values, Access adds 1 to the value for each record you add. When you choose random numbers for the AutoNumber field format, Access uses a random number generator to create the value. Replication ID numbers, also called globally unique identifiers (GUIDs), are not supported in the 2007 ACCBD file format.

When you finish a table design without having designated a primary key, Access asks if you want it to create one for you. If you answer Yes, Access either applies the primary key to an AutoNumber field—if one exists—or creates an AutoNumber field, which it then designates as the primary key. You can respond No and leave the table without a key for the time being.

Setting a Single-Field Key

If your table has a field that you're sure won't contain any duplicate values, you can use that field as the primary key.

- In the table Design view, click the field row you want to use as the primary key, and then on the Design tab in the Tools group, click Primary Key.

- To remove the primary key designation, repeat the step. You may be warned that you must delete a relationship using that field before removing it. (Read more about creating and deleting relationships in Chapter 5.)

NOTE   *If you choose the field as the primary key after you enter data and duplicate values occur or one of the records has a blank value in that field, Access won't set the key. However, you can run a Find Duplicates query to locate and correct any duplicate entries. Read more about queries in Chapters 8 and 9. You can also solve the problem by choosing a different field as the primary key, adding another field to the key, or adding an AutoNumber field to use as the key.*

Setting a Multiple-Field Primary Key

With Access 2007 automatically adding a primary key when the table is created, you probably will not need to create a multiple-field primary key on your own. But, just in case you need to, here is how you can do that.

If you can't guarantee that the values in a single field will be unique throughout the table, you can combine two or more fields as the primary key. For example, in a list of customer names, several may have the same last name, so that field couldn't be used as a primary key. You could combine first and last names to create unique values, or, if that still doesn't work, you could combine first, last, and middle initial or ZIP code. But, better yet, you could use an AutoNumber ID field instead.

To set a primary key that combines two or more fields, hold down CTRL while you select each field. If the fields are contiguous in the list, select the top field row and hold down SHIFT while you select the last row you want to include. After you select all the fields you want in the key, click the Primary Key command in the Tools group on the Design tab. Key icons appear in each row included in the multiple-field primary key.

TIP *The multiple-field primary key is constructed in the same order as the fields in the table structure. If a different field order is important, you can rearrange the fields in the Indexes window. More about the Indexes window in the section "Creating a Multiple-Field Index" below.*

Creating Other Indexes

Indexes help Access find and sort records faster, just as an index helps you find topics in a reference book. An index contains a pointer to the location of the data, rather than the data itself. The primary key in a table is automatically indexed; secondary indexes can be created for other fields. An index can include a single field or multiple fields. You can index any field except an OLE Object or Attachment field.

When deciding which fields to use as indexes, look at the fields for which you expect to search frequently for particular values or look for those by which you want to sort. Also, if you expect to use a field to create a relationship with another table, you might want to create an index on the field to improve performance. A field that may have many records containing the same value isn't a good candidate for an index because an index on such a field won't speed things up much.

Adding a Single-Field Index

To set a single-field index, simply change its Indexed property in the Field Properties pane to Yes and decide whether to permit duplicate values.

To view the indexes specified for a table, on the Design tab in the Show/Hide group, click the Indexes command. The Customers table includes two currently defined indexes. The primary key, Customer ID, is listed with the key icon as the first index, and a single-field index based on the customer's last name is the second. Click the first row of the index, which contains the index name, to display the Index Properties pane. Notice the primary key properties shown here; specify the index as Primary with Unique values and select No for the Ignore Nulls property to ignore null values in the field.

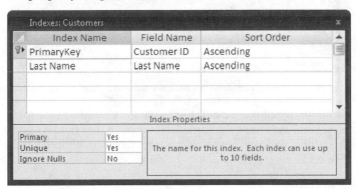

Creating a Multiple-Field Index

In many cases, you might want to search or sort records based on more than one field at once. Creating a multiple-field index enables you to do just that. When you sort records using a multiple-field index, the records are sorted initially by the first field in the index.

If Access finds duplicate values in the first field, it sorts by the next field, and so on. For example, suppose you want to see records for customers in particular areas of the city. To do this, you can create an index using both the City and ZIP fields.

To create a multiple-field index, follow these steps:

1. With the Customers table open in Design view, on the Design tab's Show/Hide group, click the Indexes command.

2. Click in the first empty row in the Indexes window.

3. Enter a name for the new index, such as **City Region**. Then press TAB to move to the Field Name column.

4. Click the down arrow and select City from the list of available fields.

5. Accept Ascending as the sort order for the City field and click the Field Name in the next row (leaving the Index Name blank, because both fields are used in the same index).

6. Choose ZIP from the Field Name list and change the sort order, if necessary.

7. If the index is intended to be the primary key, set the Primary property to Yes. (You must click the first row of the index, which contains the index name, to display the Index Properties pane.) If you want the index to contain unique values for each record, change the Unique property to Yes. Leave Ignore Nulls set as No because a primary key cannot allow null values.

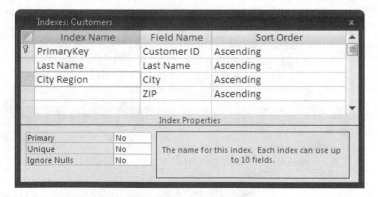

8. Close the Indexes dialog box, and then save the changes to the table.

You can specify up to 10 fields in one index with a mixture of ascending and descending orders for the fields.

Saving the Table Design

The table design does not need to be complete before you save it. In fact, a good idea is to save the design after you've worked through the tasks covered so far, and then save it again during the design process to guard against potential loss. Access requires you to save the design before you can switch to Datasheet view to enter data. To save the table design, do one of the following:

- Right-click the table tab and choose Save from the shortcut menu.
- Click the Save button on the Quick Access toolbar.
- Click the Microsoft Office button and choose Save.

The first time you save a new table, Access prompts you for a name. The table name can be up to 64 characters in any combination of letters, numbers, and spaces, but it cannot begin with a space. You can also include special characters, except for those that have a special meaning to Access, such as a period (.), an exclamation point (!), an accent grave (`), or brackets ([]). You also cannot use any control character with an ASCII value between 0 and 31.

TIP   *If you want to undo the changes you just made to the table design, close the table design and respond No when Access asks if you want to save the changes.*

Modifying the Table Design

Even though you try to include all the necessary features and properties in your table design, you'll undoubtedly find things that need changing. You might want to change Text fields to Memo fields so you can enter more information, add default values, or include validation rules. Or, you might want to add a new field or delete one that isn't needed after all. Maybe some of the field properties aren't quite what were expected or you want to change the field size or type.

You can make any of these changes to an empty table with no problems, but after you enter data, you risk losing data with some of the changes. Adding fields, increasing a field size, and rearranging the field order won't cause data loss. But if you decide to delete a field or reduce a field size in a table that already contains data, Access displays a warning that data loss could occur. Problems can also occur when changing a field type. Making a backup of the data before you make any changes to the table design is always a good idea.

TIP   *The quickest way to make a backup copy of a table is to right-click on the table name in the Navigation Pane and choose Copy from the shortcut menu. Then right-click in the Tables group header in the Navigation Pane and click Paste. Make sure the Structure and Data option is selected. Accept the default name, Copy of ..., and click OK. You can use this method to copy other database objects as well.*

Adding/Deleting Fields

A new field can be added to the bottom of the list of fields or inserted anywhere among the existing fields. To add a field to the bottom, click the first blank field and enter the field definition. To insert a field among existing fields, click the row selector (the gray button to the left of the field name) in the row below where the new one is to appear, and then do one of the following:

- On the Design tab in the Tools group, click the Insert Rows command.
- Right-click the row and choose Insert Rows from the shortcut menu.

Whichever method you choose, the new blank field row is inserted above the row that contains the cursor and all the fields below are moved down one row. The insertion point is in the new row ready to enter the field definition.

For example, you can add a new field to the Workorders table that will contain a hyperlink to a drawing used for that job, such as a schematic for installing a bay window. To add the new field, do the following:

1. Right-click on the Workorders table in the Navigation Pane, and then choose Design View from the shortcut menu.

2. Click in the first empty row in the Field Name column and enter **Drawing**.

3. Click the Data Type arrow and choose Hyperlink from the list.

4. Add a description, such as **Layouts of project**, and then click Save on the Quick Access toolbar.

TIP *Another way to add a new field that inherits the same properties as one already in your table is to copy the existing field to the clipboard and then paste it in an empty row. Of course, you must change the new field's name before you can save the table because no two fields can have the same name. Only the field definition is copied; no previously entered data is copied. You saw earlier how to drag a field from another table in the database.*

If you want to add several new rows at once, select the number of contiguous rows in the table design equal to the number of new fields you want to insert, and then use one of the previously discussed methods. The same number of new blank rows appears above the top row in the selected group. Then click one of the new rows and begin entering the field definitions.

When you delete a field from the table design, you aren't deleting only the field name, but also any data entered in the field. Before deleting a field that contains data, Access warns that you'll permanently lose the data and asks if you really want to delete the field.

To delete a field in Design view, click the row selector for the field (the gray button to the left of the field name) and do one of the following:

- Press the DEL key.
- On the Design tab in the Tools group, click Delete Rows.
- Right-click in the row and choose Delete Rows from the shortcut menu.

To delete several rows at once, select them all and delete them as a group.

NOTE *Using the DEL key works only if the row is selected. The other two methods delete the row that contains the insertion point, even if it isn't selected.*

CAUTION *You can cause a problem by deleting a field you've used in a query, form, or report. Be sure you remove any references to the field you're about to delete from the other objects before you try to delete it. Access won't let you delete a field that's a link in a relationship to another table without your deleting the relationship first.*

Changing the Field Order

To change the order of fields in both the stored table and in Datasheet view, rearrange them in Design view. To move a field to a new position in the table design, click the row selector to select the row, and then drag the row selector to move the field to its new position.

You can move several contiguous fields at once by selecting them all and then dragging them as a group. To select more than one, use one of the following methods:

- Click the top field row selector and drag through the row selectors until all are selected.

- Click the top field row selector and hold down SHIFT while you click the field row at the end of the group.

NOTE *While you can select noncontiguous field rows by holding down* CTRL *as you select the rows, you cannot drag the group to a new position.*

If you want to keep the field order in the stored table, but you would like to view them in a different order in the datasheet, you can rearrange the datasheet columns. See Chapter 6 for information about changing the appearance of a datasheet.

Changing a Field Name or Type

You saw earlier how to change the name that appears in the column heading in Datasheet view by changing the field Caption property. You can also change the actual field name in the design. Changing the field name has no effect on the data already entered into the field. However, any references to the field in other objects, such as queries, forms, and reports, or in an expression, must be changed as well, unless you have checked the Name AutoCorrect option, accessed by clicking the Microsoft Office button and clicking Access Options.

To change a field name in Design view, simply type in the new name. After changing the name, you must save the table again.

NOTE *The Name AutoCorrect feature automatically corrects most side effects that occur when you rename a field, such as changing the name of a bound control in a form or report. This is one of the options you can turn on or off by clicking the Microsoft Office button and clicking Access Options. If you have an unassociated label, a circular reference, or invalid sorting and grouping options, the errors are automatically identified and flagged in the design. When you click the flag, you will see an explanation of the error and can choose from a list of options that will correct it. See Chapter 10 for more information about creating form designs.*

Changing a field type is a little more complicated if the table already includes data. If no data is in the table, you can safely change any field data type. Some types convert easily to another type, but other conversions could result in loss of data. If data is going to be lost, Access displays a message showing the number of values that will be affected before it makes any changes. If you used the field in an expression, you might also need to change the expression. You cannot change an Attachment field to any other type.

To change a field type in Datasheet view, do the following:

1. Select the field.

2. On the Datasheet tab in the Data Type and Formatting group, click the arrow next to Data Type and select the new data type.

3. Save the table. If Access displays a warning message, respond No to cancel the changes or Yes to go ahead and make the changes. If no data is in the table, Access doesn't display any warnings.

To change the data type in Design view, do the following:

1. Select the field.

2. Select the new type from the Data Type drop-down list.

3. Save the table.

You won't encounter any difficulties converting other data types to Text. Number fields convert to Text with a General Number format, while Date/Time fields convert to Text with the General Date format. Currency fields convert accurately to Text, but without the currency symbols. You cannot change an Attachment field to another type.

Table 4-3 describes the relevant considerations when converting between data types.

CAUTION *If the field you're converting is a primary key field or a unique index and the conversion would result in duplicate values, Access deletes the entire record. Access warns you first, so you can prevent the deletion.*

TIP *If a table contains data, you cannot change any type of field to AutoNumber, even if you know that the field contains unique values. If you need an AutoNumber field, add a new field and select the AutoNumber data type. Access assigns each existing record a sequential or random number.*

Changing a Field Size

Changing the Field Size property has no effect on the data if you're increasing the size. Obviously, if you want to reduce the field size, especially for a Number field, you should make sure that no values are larger than permitted by the new field size. If the values are too large to fit the new field size, they're replaced with null values. If the new field size doesn't permit the number of decimal places currently specified, the values are rounded off.

Modifying or Deleting the Primary Key

You might find the primary key doesn't always have a unique value after all and decide to use a different field or create a primary key with two or more fields.

To change the primary key, select the row you want as the primary key and on the Design tab in the Tools group, click the Primary Key command. The key icon is removed from the old key field and appears in the new one.

From	To	Results	Comments
Text	Number, Currency, Date/Time	Converts to appropriate values	Values must fit new data type. Others are deleted. Date/Time and Currency formats follow Regional Settings.
Text	Yes/No	Converts to appropriate values	Yes, True, and On (value –1) convert to Yes. No, False, and Off (value 0) convert to No.
Number	Yes/No	Converts to appropriate values	Zero or null values convert to No and non zero values to Yes.
Memo	Text	Direct conversion	Memo data longer than field size is truncated.
Number	Text	Converts values to text	Numbers appear in General Number format.
Currency	Text	Direct conversion	No currency symbols are included.
Date/Time	Text	Direct conversion	Values appear in General Date format.
Yes/No	Text	Direct conversion	None.
AutoNumber	Text	Direct conversion	Values might be truncated depending on field size.
Currency	Number	Direct conversion	Values might be truncated depending on field size.
AutoNumber	Number	Direct conversion	Values might be truncated depending on field size.

TABLE 4-3   Converting Between Data Types

To add another field to the existing primary key, select both the old and new key fields, and then click the Primary Key command. The key icon appears in the row selector of both rows.

At times, you might want to disable the primary key temporarily—for example, if you're importing records from another table, some of which might contain values that duplicate your original table. You must remove any duplicates in the new data before restoring the primary key. This has no effect on the data stored in the field designated as the key: it simply removes the key field feature temporarily.

To remove the primary key designation, select the primary key field and click the Primary Key command. If the key is used in a relationship, you must delete the relationship before you can remove the key.

Modifying or Deleting an Index

To delete a single-field index, change the field's Indexed property to No in the Field Properties pane. This removes only the index; it has no effect on the field itself or the underlying data.

In the Indexes dialog box (on the Design tab's Show/Hide group, click the Indexes command), you can add or delete fields from a multiple-field index, change the sort order for any field in the index, or change the index properties. You can also change the field order in the index.

- To remove a field from a multiple-field index, display the Indexes dialog box, select the field row, and then press the DEL key.

- To remove the entire index, display the Indexes dialog box, select all the rows in the index, and then press the DEL key.

- To insert an additional field into the index, display the Indexes dialog box and select the field below where you want the new field to appear. Then press INSERT and enter the new field name.

- To change the field order in a multiple-field index, select and drag the field selector to the desired position in the index definition.

- To change the sort order for any of the fields in the index, choose Ascending or Descending from the Sort Order list.

After making changes to the table's indexes, be sure to save the table. Access reminds you to do so if you try to close the table or if you return to Datasheet view without saving.

Ensuring Data Validity

You've seen a few of the ways Access helps you ensure that the values entered in your database are valid. The data type you choose for the field can limit the values to, for example, date and time values. You can also limit the number of characters in a Text field and prevent duplicate values. A direct way to ensure valid data is to set some rules that the values must obey.

You can specify two kinds of data validation rules: A *field validation* rule can limit the value to a few specific values or to a range of values. The rule is checked when you try to move to another field in the same or another record. For example, a rule could limit a numeric value to a range between 1 and 100 or insist a date value fall in 2007. A *record validation* rule is handy for comparing the values in two fields in the same record. The rule is checked when you move out of a record and Access attempts to save the record. Access won't save a record with a conflict between fields. For example, a record validation rule could prevent saving a record in which the Job Cost is greater than the Bid Price. Another record validation rule could ensure that the elapsed time between dates in two separate fields doesn't exceed a specific value.

NOTE   *You can also add validation rules to controls on a form. For information, see Chapter 12.*

When either type of rule is broken, Access displays a message in a warning box that explains the violation and doesn't leave the field or record. The message you want to display is the Validation Text property in the table or field property (see the following section). If you don't enter message text there, Access creates a standard default message, such as the one shown here:

Defining Field Validation Rules

To define a field validation rule, follow these steps:

1. Select the field name in the upper pane of the Design window, and then click Validation Rule in the General tab of the Field Properties pane.

2. Type the expression you want in the Validation Rule property window. For example, if the value must not exceed 100, enter **<=100** (less than or equal to 100).

3. Then move to the Validation Text property box and enter the message you want to display when the rule is broken.

NOTE   *The Validation Rule property box includes a Build button you can click to open the Expression Builder if you need help with the expression. See Chapter 8 for information about using the Expression Builder.*

You can also type wildcards in the expression. These are the same placeholders used in search strings: *?* stands for a single character and * stands for any number of characters. When you enter an expression with a wildcard, Access converts it to an expression using the *Like* operator and adds quotation marks. For example, if you type **C*** in the property text box, it turns into Like "C*" when you move out of the property box. This expression means all values entered in the field must begin with the letter *C* or *c*. The expression is not case-sensitive.

A validation rule defined for a Date/Time field also includes special symbols when translated by Access. To enter a rule that says the date entered must be earlier than January 1, 2008, you would type **<01/01/08** and Access converts it to <#01/01/08# to make sure it isn't confused with a Number value.

Validation rules can include more than one criterion for the same field by combining them using the AND or OR operators. Table 4-4 describes some examples of validation rules, the corresponding Access expression, and an appropriate Validation Text message.

NOTE   *You will see much more about creating expressions for queries in Chapter 8.*

Figure 4-4 shows the Bid Data table structure with a validation rule added to the State field. The rule specifies that the State value must be *CA, AZ or NV* and, if the rule is violated, the message "Bid contracts only in California, Arizona or Nevada" displays in an information box.

Rule	Access Version	Typical Message
<>0	<>0	Value must not be 0, but it can be negative.
100 Or 200	100 Or 200	Value must be either 100 or 200.
C*	Like "C*"	Value must begin with C or c.
C* Or D*	Like "C*" Or Like "D*"	Value must begin with C, c, D, or d.
C??t	Like "C??t"	Value must be four characters long, begin with C or c, and end with T or t.
>=01/01/07 And <01/01/08	>=#1/1/07# And <#1/1/08#	Value must fall within the year 2007.
Not CA	Not "CA"	Field can contain any value but CA.

TABLE 4-4   Examples of Validation Rules and Text

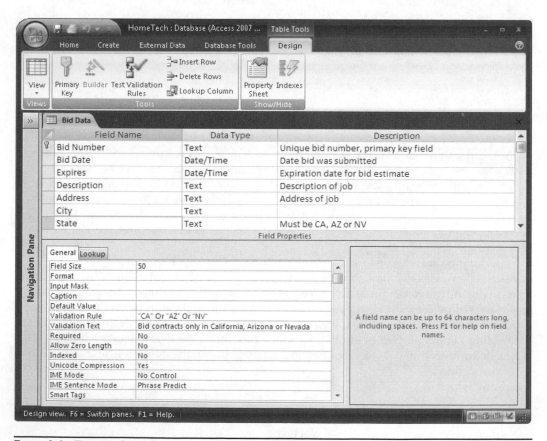

FIGURE 4-4   The new State field properties with a validation rule

If you enter a state value other than those specified, you'll see the error message when you try to move to the next record.

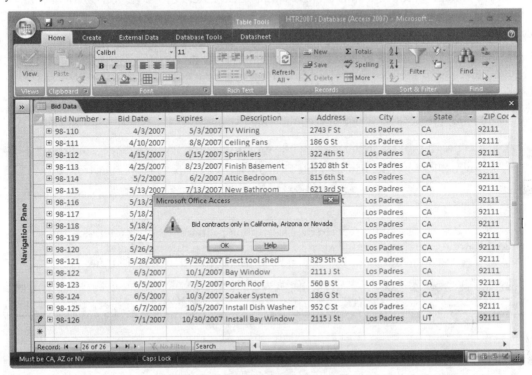

NOTE *The previous State validation rule also causes a violation if the field is left blank, because it insists on one of the three values. If you want to leave the field blank, add Null to the list of valid values. You can also create a more complex record validation rule that insists on a value only if a "no value" is in the corresponding City field to allow for customers who deal solely over the Internet instead of by mail.*

As you add validation rules to a table, you can test them against existing data to see if any of the field values violate the new rule. To do this, on the Design tab in the Tools group, click Test Validation Rules. Access warns you that the process also checks the Required and Allow Zero Length properties, could take a long time, and asks if you want to do it anyway. If Access finds no violations, it displays a message saying all the data was valid for all the rules you defined. If a violation is found, Access stops checking and displays a message indicating which rule was violated and asks if you want to continue with the rule testing.

NOTE *You may be asked to save the table design before testing the rules.*

Field validation rules are enforced whenever you enter or edit data, whether it's in the datasheet, in a form, or by means of an append or update query. These rules are also enforced on data entered by Visual Basic for Applications (VBA) code or imported from another table.

Defining a Record Validation Rule

A record validation rule is a table property rather than a field property. You can define only one record validation rule for a table, but if you want to apply more than one criterion, you can combine them in an expression using the AND or OR operator.

The record validation rule is applied whenever you enter or edit table data. When you leave a record, Access checks the new record against the rule you defined. As with field validation rules, if you define a record validation rule for a table that contains data, Access asks if you want the rule applied to the existing data when you save the table.

To add a record validation rule to a table, open the table in Design view and then open the Table Properties pane by one of the following methods:

- On the Design tab in the Show/Hide group, click the Property Sheet command.
- Right-click anywhere in the table Design view and choose Properties from the shortcut menu.
- Press ALT-ENTER.

Enter a description of the table in the Description property for later reference, the validation rule expression, and the text to display when the rule is violated. For example, the Expires date for a bid in the Bid Data table must be later than the Bid Date.

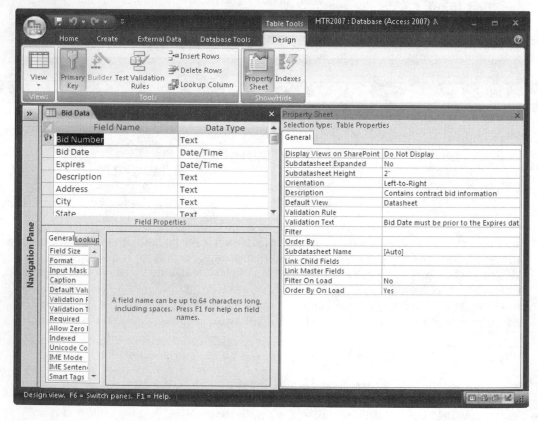

Requiring an Entry and Preventing Duplicates

One of the field properties in the Field Properties pane is Required, which is set to Yes or No. The default value is No, but you can change it to Yes if the field should never be left blank. For example, every employee record must have a Social Security number, so you would change that field's Required property to Yes.

TIP   *All field and index properties that have only Yes and No settings can be toggled back and forth by double-clicking the property box.*

The Indexed property helps prevent duplicate values. A single-field primary key field always requires unique values, but you can have only one such field in a table. You might want to prevent duplication in other fields without assigning them as the primary key. To add this restriction, change the field's Indexed property to Yes (No Duplicates). If you open the Indexes window, you'll see the new single-field index with its Unique property set to Yes.

You can prevent duplicate values in a group of fields by creating a multiple-field index on the combination of fields. Once the index is created, change the Unique property in the lower pane of the Indexes window to Yes. Then no two combinations of the values in these fields can be the same.

Handling Blank Fields

You might leave a field blank because you don't know the value or because no value exists for that field in that record. Access distinguishes between those two kinds of blank values with null values and zero-length strings.

A *null value* indicates a missing or unknown value for the field. You would leave a field blank if you don't know the value or if it isn't relevant to the current record. Access recognizes this and stores the value as a null value. Pressing ENTER without entering anything stores a null value.

A *zero-length string* is a string that contains no characters. If you know that no value exists for this field (not that you simply don't know what the value is), you enter a zero-length string by pressing the SPACEBAR or by typing a pair of double quotation marks ("") with no space in between. The marks disappear when you move to the next field, but Access stores the zero-length string.

A good demonstration of the difference between null values and zero-length strings involves the Pager field in the Customers table. If you don't know whether the customer has a pager or, if she does, you don't know the number, leave it blank. If you know the customer doesn't have a pager, enter a zero-length string.

Two special field properties control how blank fields are handled. The Required property determines whether a blank field is acceptable or whether the field must contain a value. The Allow Zero Length property, when set to Yes, permits zero-length strings. This property is available only to Text, Memo, and Hyperlink fields.

These two properties work together as follows:

- If you want to leave the field blank and don't care why it's blank, set both the Required and Allow Zero Length properties to No.

- If you never want to leave a field blank, set Required to Yes and Allow Zero Length to No. You cannot leave the field without entering a value, even if it's only "Don't know" or "None."

- If you want to tell why the field is blank, set Required to No and Allow Zero Length to Yes. Then you would leave the field blank if the information isn't known or enter quotation marks ("") to indicate the field doesn't apply to the current record (no pager exists).

- If you want to leave the field blank only if you know the field isn't relevant to a record, set both properties to Yes. Then the only way for you to leave the field blank is to enter a zero-length string, either by typing "" or pressing the SPACEBAR.

NOTE *When you allow blank fields, you can still use the Find and Replace options to locate fields with null values or zero-length strings. To find records with blank values, place the insertion point in the field and choose the Find command in the Find group on the Home tab. Type null in the Find What box to find the null values or type "" to find fields with zero-length strings. In the Match box, be sure to ask Access to match the whole field or you'll find a lot of fields with blanks between words. Also be sure to clear the Search Fields As Formatted check box and then click Find Next. See Chapter 6 for more information about locating specific records.*

Assigning a Default Value

If one of your fields usually has the same value—for example, the State field in a list of local customers—use the Default Value property to have that value automatically entered when you add a new record. You can still change it to a different value when you enter data, but using a default value can save time during data entry, especially if it's a long value such as California or Pennsylvania. A newly assigned default value doesn't affect values already entered in the table; only new entries are affected.

A default value can be assigned to any type of field except an AutoNumber, an OLE Object, or an Attachment. To assign a default value, enter the value in the Default Value property for the field. The type of value you enter depends on the data type. The value must also conform to the property settings and data type requirements. Some examples of default values are shown here:

Field	Data Type	Value
State	Text	CA
City	Text	"Los Padres" (If the value contains punctuation or spaces, it must be enclosed in quotation marks)
Hours	Number	8
Deposit	Currency	500
Entry Date	Date/Time	Date() (Automatically enters current system date)

TIP *If you assign or change a default field value after entering record data, you can change the existing values to the new value by pressing CTRL-ALT-SPACEBAR with the insertion point in the field.*

NOTE *If you want to assign a Yes/No field default value for use in a foreign country, enter an equal sign before the choice (=Yes) and the equivalent word from the local language of the computer will be displayed. For example, a Yes value would be displayed as* Oui *in French.*

NOTE *For information about importing and linking to other sources to create a new table, see Chapter 22.*

Copying an Existing Table Structure

If you already have a table with a structure similar to what you need now, you can save time by copying the structure to a new table without the data. Then change the field names and properties as necessary. To copy the table structure without opening the table, follow these steps:

1. Right-click the existing table name in the Navigation Pane and select Copy from the shortcut menu.

2. Right-click the Tables group title bar in the Navigation Pane and select Paste from the shortcut menu. The Paste Table As dialog box opens.

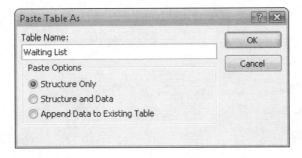

3. Enter a name for the new table, choose Structure Only, and then click OK.

The new table inherits the field properties from the original table.

If the table is open in Design view, you can use the Clipboard group commands to copy and paste the table structure. The Paste Table As dialog box opens as before.

Setting Table Properties

Two types of table properties are available in an Access database: table object properties and table definition properties. *Table object properties* include name, owner, dates of creation and last revision, and attributes, such as Hidden or Replicable. You can view these properties by one of the following methods:

- Right-click the table name in the Navigation Pane and choose Table Properties from the shortcut menu.

- Select the table name in the Navigation Pane and on the Database Tools tab in the Show/Hide group, check the Property Sheet command.

Table definition properties related to the table structure itself are available when the table is open in Design view. To open the table property sheet, do one of the following:

- Check the Property Sheet command as before.
- Right-click anywhere in the table design and choose Properties from the shortcut menu.

How to Change the Default Table Design Properties

You learned earlier that the default field size for a Text field is 50 characters. This is one of the default table design properties you can change. To modify this and other default properties, do the following:

1. Click the Microsoft Office button and click the Access Options button.
2. Select Object Designers in the left pane (see Figure 4-5).

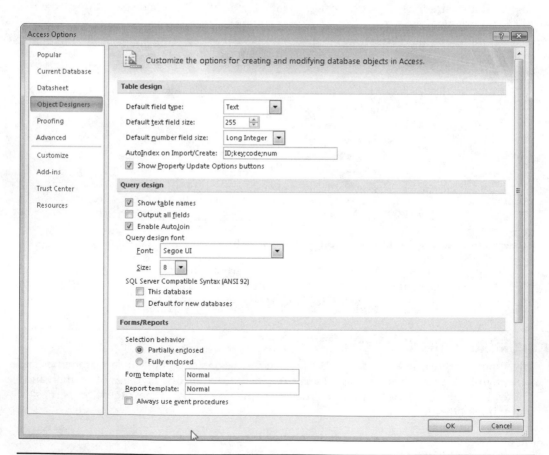

FIGURE 4-5   Setting the table design default properties

Following are the Table Design options:

- **Default Field Type (default Text)**   To change the default field type, choose from the drop-down list of field types. Notice the list doesn't include Lookup Wizard as a field type.

- **Default Text Field Size (default 255)**   To change the default Text field size, enter the desired number.

- **Default Number Field Size (default Long Integer)**   To change the Number field, choose from the drop-down list of Number field sizes.

- **AutoIndex on Import/Create**   This option gives you the opportunity to specify text often used at the beginning or ending of a field name as the basis for indexes when importing or creating tables. For example, typing **ID;Key;code;num** automatically creates indexes for all fields containing those characters either at the start or at the end of the field name. With this setting, an imported table would be indexed on fields named Customer ID, JobNum, and ZIP code.

- **Show Property Update Options Buttons**   Shows or hides the Property Update Options button that you can use to update the changed property in any controls on forms and reports that are bound to the field.

Summary

This chapter contained a great deal of information about constructing and modifying new Access tables, beginning with the built-in templates. You created a table by entering data directly into a blank table in Datasheet view and from scratch in Design view. It included choosing the best data type depending on what value you intended to store in the field and the operations with which you intended to use it. Other field properties were discussed as were primary key fields and creating indexes on one or more fields.

Modifying a table structure can be troublesome in some cases, such as changing the data type or shortening the field size. Ensuring data validity is one of the most important features Access offers. Several ways of doing this were discussed, including requiring specific fields, adding validity rules, and assigning default values.

In the next chapter, you will learn how to relate tables by linking the common field. The chapter also covers specifying the type of relationship and modifying an existing relationship. In addition, it will discuss the types of joins that control the way data is retrieved by queries.

Relating Tables

The advantages of relating tables in a database are many. For example, information retrieval routines operate much faster with matched fields, and errors are less likely to be introduced into the database during data entry. Tables related at the table level in the Relationships window are ready for use in queries, forms, reports, and data access pages. When tables are related, you can add a subform or subreport that includes corresponding information from the related table. Relating tables also helps maintain data integrity and cohesiveness.

You can define relationships between tables at any time, but the best time to do it is when the tables are new and contain little or no data. When you design the database, one of the important steps is to define the relationships between the tables and the fields that they have in common.

Defining a Relationship

To define a relationship between two tables, you specify which fields the tables have in common. In a one-to-many relationship, the field in the parent table is called the *primary key* and must be either the table's primary key or a unique index. The field in the child table is called the *foreign key*, and it does not need to have a unique value. Data retrieval is faster, however, if the child table is indexed on the foreign key.

In a one-to-one relationship, both fields are primary keys or unique indexes in their tables. A many-to-many relationship is actually two, one-to-many relationships in which a third table is created. The primary key of this third table is a combination of the common fields from the other two tables. The junction table becomes the "one" side for relationships to both the original tables. You can still create a junction table to join the two tables, but a better solution is to use a multivalued field, new with Access 2007. This new field type models the many-to-many relationship and allows you to store more than one value in a single field. (Read more about multivalued fields in Chapter 6.)

TIP *Defining table relationships at the table level keeps the relationships active and makes the database easier to use. You can link two tables temporarily in a query when you want to draw information from more than one table, but the permanent relationship is preferred. You can always break it later, if necessary.*

Using the Relationships Window

The Relationships window provides all the tools you need to define and modify relationships—add a table or query to the relationship, relate the tables and queries, specify the type of relationship, set up the referential integrity rules, and choose the join type. To open the Relationships window, on the Database Tools tab's Show/Hide group, click Relationships. If no relationships are defined in the current database, the Show Table dialog box appears in a blank Relationships window. The dialog box displays a list of all the tables and queries in the current database.

Relationships usually occur between tables, but queries can also be related. Queries can give you access to data from several tables at once without having to add all the tables referenced in the query.

NOTE *If a relationship already exists between tables in the database, Access goes directly to the Relationships window when you click the Relationships command without displaying the Show Table dialog box. To add a table to the Relationships window, go to the Design tab's Relationships group and click the Show Table command to open the Show Table dialog box.*

To add the tables or queries you want to relate from the Show Table dialog box list, do one of the following:

- In the Tables tab, double-click the table's name, or select the table and click the Add button.

- To select multiple adjacent tables, select the first table to be included, hold down SHIFT as you select the last table in the list to be included, and then click the Add button. If the table names aren't adjacent in the list, hold down CTRL while you select the names.

- Click the Queries tab to add a query to the Relationships window.

- Click the Both tab to access a combined list of tables and queries.

After you add all the tables and queries you want to work with into the Relationships window, click Close in the Show Table dialog box.

Touring the Relationships Window

The Relationships window shows the field lists of the tables you chose. The lists display the primary key field, if any, with a key icon. Use the scroll bars to see all the fields, or resize a field list box by dragging the bottom border to see more names or the right border to see complete field names. You can also drag the field list boxes around in the window for better viewing. The following Relationships window shows four tables from the Home Tech Repair database. Relationships exist only among the first three tables:

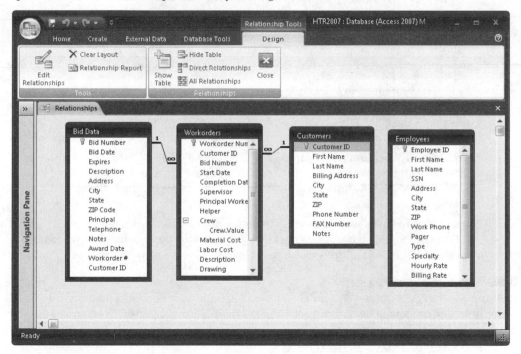

Before you join the tables, take a look at the new commands in the Relationships group on the Design tab.

Command	Description
Show Table	Opens the Show Table dialog box with lists of all tables and queries in the current database.
Hide Table	Removes the selected table from the Relationships window.
Direct Relationships	Displays the relationships for the selected table.
All Relationships	Displays all relationships in the current database.
Close	Closes the window after asking if you want to save changes to the layout.

Three shortcut menus are available in the Relationships window by right-clicking a field list box, an empty area in the Relationships window, or on the center part of a relationship line:

- **Field list shortcut menu**   Includes—in addition to Show Direct—the Table Design (or Query Design) option, which opens the Design view for the selected table or query, and the Hide Table option, which temporarily removes the table or query from the display, not the layout. Hide Table is also available from the Relationships group.

- **Relationships window shortcut menu**   Includes—in addition to Show Table and Show All—the Save Layout option, which saves the current arrangement of field list boxes in the Relationships window. It also includes Close, which closes the Relationships window.

- **Relationship line shortcut menu**   Includes Edit Relationship, which opens the Edit Relationships dialog box, and Delete, which removes the relationship you right-clicked. Edit Relationship is also available in the Tools group on the Design tab.

Drawing the Relationship Line

Relating two tables in Access couldn't be easier. You simply drag a field (usually the primary key) from one table and drop it on the corresponding field (the foreign key) in the other table. The field names do not need to be the same, but they usually need to be the same data type and contain the same kind of information. If you intend to enforce referential integrity, the fields must be the same data type. If the fields are Number fields, they must also have the same Field Size property.

One exception applies to the requirement to match data types when you relate an AutoNumber field to a Number field. An AutoNumber field with the New Values property set to Increment can be linked to a Long Integer Number field. AutoNumber values are stored as 4-byte numbers. For the foreign key to have a matching value, it must contain a number of the same size: a Long Integer.

TIP *Dragging the foreign key field from the related table to the primary key field in the primary table creates the same relationship.*

To relate the Employees table to the Workorders table by Employee ID, do the following:

1. Click the Employee ID field in the Employees field list and drag it to the Principal Worker field in the Workorders field list.

2. Drop the linking field into the child table. The Edit Relationships dialog box opens.

TIP *Notice that Access recognizes this relationship as a one-to-many, because one of the fields is a primary key and the other isn't. If both fields were primary keys, Access would recognize the relationship as one-to-one. If the fields are neither primary keys nor unique values, Access calls the relationship* Indeterminate.

3. Verify the field names that relate the tables, and then do one of the following:

- If you want to change the field at either side of the relationship, you can select a different field from the drop-down field list under the table name.

- If you want to add another relationship between the same tables that relates two different fields, move to an empty row in the grid, click the down button, and choose from the list for each table.

- If you chose the wrong foreign key, choose Cancel in the Edit Relationships dialog box and start over in the Relationships window.

- If you type the first few letters of the field name in the Edit Relationships dialog box grid, Access will fill in the rest for you.

4. To complete this relationship, click Create, and you will return to the Relationships window. Figure 5-1 shows the Relationships window with the new link drawn between the Workorders and Employees tables.

5. To complete the relationships in the window, repeat the previous procedure to draw the relationship line from the Employee ID field in the Employees field list to the Supervisor field in the Workorders field list.

Relating to Two or More Foreign Keys

If you need to create relationships from a primary table to two or more foreign keys in the same table, Access creates additional instances of the table in the Relationships window. You don't have two copies of the table in the database, only in the Relationships layout.

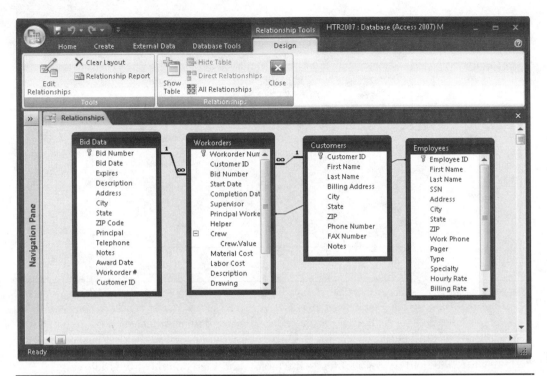

FIGURE 5-1 A new relationship line is drawn between the two tables

Figure 5-2 shows a Relationships window with three copies of the Employees table with the Employee ID primary key field relating to the Supervisor, Principal Worker, and Helper foreign keys in the Workorders table.

Note that the relationships all have referential integrity enforced, as you can see by the infinity symbol at the end of each relationship line. Referential integrity is discussed in the next section.

Enforcing Referential Integrity

As discussed in Chapter 2, *referential integrity* is a set of rules that attempts to keep a database complete and without loose ends. These rules say that no related records can exist without a parent. When you want Access to enforce the referential integrity rules on the relationship that you're defining, check Enforce Referential Integrity in the Edit Relationships dialog box. If, for some reason, the tables already violate one of the rules, such as the related fields not being of the same data type, Access displays a message explaining the violation and doesn't apply the enforcement.

NOTE *Referential integrity isn't enforced on queries included in a relationship.*

When you check the Enforce Referential Integrity option, two options become available that let you override some restrictions.

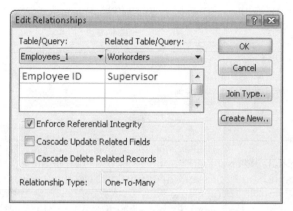

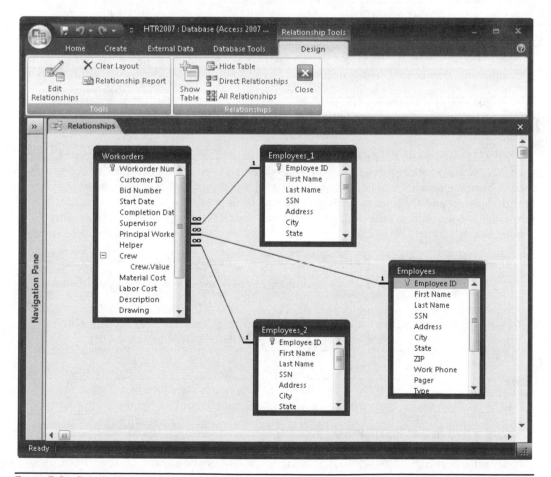

FIGURE 5-2 Relating one table to three fields in another table

With these options checked, if you delete a record from the parent table or change one of the primary key values, Access automatically makes changes to the child table to preserve the referential integrity. Without checking one of these options, Access displays a warning message if you try to delete a parent record that still has child records.

The Cascade Update Related Fields option lets you change the value in the primary key field in the parent table, and Access automatically changes the foreign key value in the child table to match. For example, if you change the Customer ID value in the Customers table, all records for that customer in any related table are automatically updated to the new value. This option preserves the relationship. Access doesn't display a message that the update operation is taking place. If the primary key in a table serves as a link to more than one table, you must set the Cascade Update Related Fields property for each of the relationships. If not, Access displays a message that referential integrity rules would be violated by the cascading operation and refuses to delete or update the record.

NOTE *Setting the Cascade Update option has no effect if the primary key is an AutoNumber field because you can't change the value of an AutoNumber field.*

The Cascade Delete Related Records option enables you to delete a parent record, and then Access automatically deletes all the related child records. When you try to delete a record from the parent table of a relationship with this option selected, Access warns you that this record and the ones in related tables will be deleted. For example, if you delete an employee record, Access automatically deletes all the records for that employee in the related tables.

CAUTION *Setting the Cascade Delete Related Records property can be dangerous. If you delete records using a Delete query, Access automatically deletes the related records without issuing a warning.*

Creating a One-to-One Relationship

At times, you might want to store information about a particular subject—such as an item of merchandise or an employee—separate from the main pieces of information. For example, you might have data about an employee, such as name, address, and Social Security number, in one table where the data is readily available, but you keep other data, such as the resume and employment history, in another table. These two tables are then related using a one-to-one relationship because only one record in each table matches one record in the other table. Both tables include a primary key field, such as the employee identification number.

To relate two tables with a one-to-one relationship, do the following:

1. On the Database Tools tab's Show/Hide group, click the Relationships command.

2. If the tables you want to relate don't appear in the Relationships window, click the Show Table command.

3. Select the tables in the Show Table dialog box and click Add; then click Close.

4. Drag the primary key field from one table and drop it on the key field on the other table. The direction you go doesn't matter; the same one-to-one relationship is created.

Specifying the Join Type

One of the most powerful Access tools is the query that extracts and brings together data from more than one source. Many queries also carry out an action with the data. For example, you might want to see how much time each employee spent working on a job for each current customer. To do so, you need information from the Workorders, Employees, and Customers tables. Once the data is extracted, the query adds up the hours for records with matching employees and customers. (See Chapter 8 for a full description of the power of queries.)

For a query to know how to associate records from the three tables, the tables must be related. When you define each relationship, you can also specify the type of join you want for the tables. The join type specifies which records to display in a query based on related tables when they don't correspond exactly. For example, do you want the parent record to appear only if corresponding child records exist, or do you want to see all parent records even if there are no related child records?

NOTE *The join type doesn't affect the relationship; it simply tells Access which records to include in the result of a query.*

To modify the relationship between the Employees and Workorders tables, and to set the join type, do the following:

1. In the Relationships window, right-click in the middle of the relationships line joining the Employees table with the Workorders table and choose Edit Relationship from the shortcut menu. The Edit Relationships dialog box opens.

2. Click the Join Type button to open the Join Properties dialog box.

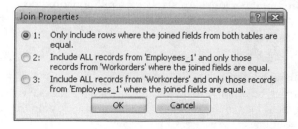

3. Select Option 2 as the type of join for this relationship, because you want to see all the employee records even if they have no related records in the Workorders table. Notice the explanatory text is specific with respect to the tables you related.

4. Click OK in the Join Properties dialog box.

5. Click OK in the Edit Relationships dialog box.

Understanding Joins

You can specify three types of joins through the Join Properties dialog box:

- Option 1 includes only records for which both parent and child have the same values in the linking fields (no orphans and no childless parents). This is called an *inner join* or an *equijoin* and it's the default join type.

- Option 2 includes all the records from the table on the left, even if no corresponding values are in the other table, and only the matching records from the table on the right. This is called a *left outer join* (all parents, including the childless, but no orphans).

- Option 3 is the opposite of Option 2 and includes all the records from the table on the right and only matching records from the left table. It is called a *right outer join* (all children, but no childless parents). If Referential Integrity is enforced, there will be no children without a parent.

NOTE *Left and right in these descriptions refer to the position of the tables in the Edit Relationships dialog box, not their position in the layout.*

If you select an outer join, an arrow at one end of the relation line points to the table whose value must match to be included in the query results. In a one-to-many relationship, the *one* side is considered the left table and the *many* side is the right table.

NOTE *You can also create a fourth type of join, a self join, which includes records from two instances of the same table. For example, you can add a self join to a query design to display the Supervisor's Name instead of the Supervisor ID when extracting records from the Employees table. The Supervisor's Name is in the Name field in the Employee record with the Supervisor ID value in the Employee ID field.*

Figure 5-3 shows the completed layout for three tables in the database that tracks bid data, work orders, customers, and employees. The relationships that include referential integrity show a 1 on the "one" side and an infinity sign on the "many" side. Relationships with no referential integrity enforced appear as lines with small dots at each end. Relationship lines with no arrows represent inner joins. An arrow on a relationship line means that the join is an outer join and the arrow points to the table whose values must match to be included in the query results. The relationship between Employees and Workorders tables is a left outer join with referential integrity enforced.

Saving the Relationships Layout

All relationships are saved when you create them. You can also save the *layout*, the arrangement of the field lists in the Relationships window. Saving the layout has no effect on the tables in the database.

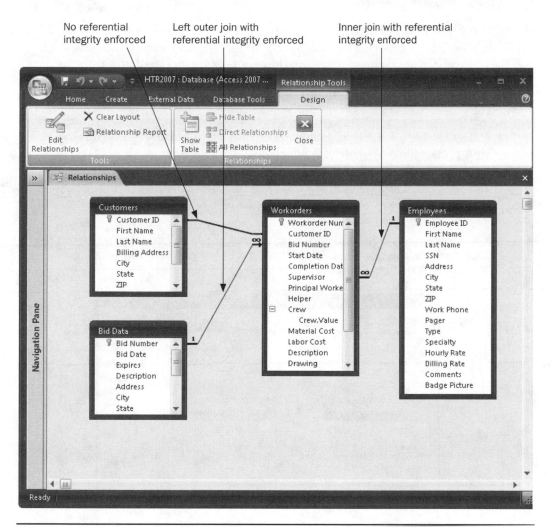

FIGURE 5-3   This layout contains four related tables

To save the layout, do one of the following:

- Right-click anywhere in the Relationships window (except on a field list) and choose Save Layout from the shortcut menu.
- Click the Save button on the Quick Access toolbar.
- Click the Microsoft Office button and choose Save.
- Press CTRL-S.

If you made changes in the layout and try to close the Relationships window without saving the layout, Access prompts you to save it. If you want to discard the changes, choose No. When you open the Relationships window again, the previously saved layout is displayed.

Using the Field List Pane

After you have added tables to your database, it is time to build their relationships. Or if you have already created some relationships but need more, you can do this using the Field List pane. For example, suppose you want to add another field to the Workorders table that will name extra helpers on the job. To do this, open the Workorders table in Datasheet view and open the field list as follows:

1. With the table open in Datasheet view, on the Datasheet tab's Fields and Columns group, click the Add Existing Fields command.

2. Find the table in the Field List pane that contains the data you want to use in the relationship—Employees, in this case. The tables are listed as available from related tables or unrelated tables. Then click the plus sign to the left of the table name to see the complete list of fields in the table.

3. Click the Employee ID field and drag it to the datasheet. Drop the field when the insertion line appears. The Lookup Wizard dialog box opens, showing the Employee ID field in the Selected Fields list.

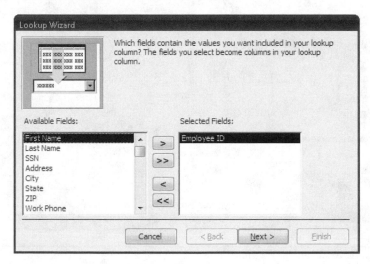

4. You will want to see the Employee's name instead of the ID, so select Last Name in the Available Fields list and click the right arrow; then click Next.

5. Skip the Sort Order options by clicking Next, and accept the Hide Key Column option and click Next.

6. Enter a new name for the lookup field, such as Crew2, and click Finish.

7. Close the Field List pane, and on the Database Tools tab's Show/Hide group, click the Relationships command. Figure 5-4 shows the new relationship between the Employees table and the Workorders table linking the Employee ID field to the new Crew field.

TIP *You can call upon the Lookup Wizard later to change the Crew field to a multivalue field where you can store more crew members. See Chapter 6 for more information.*

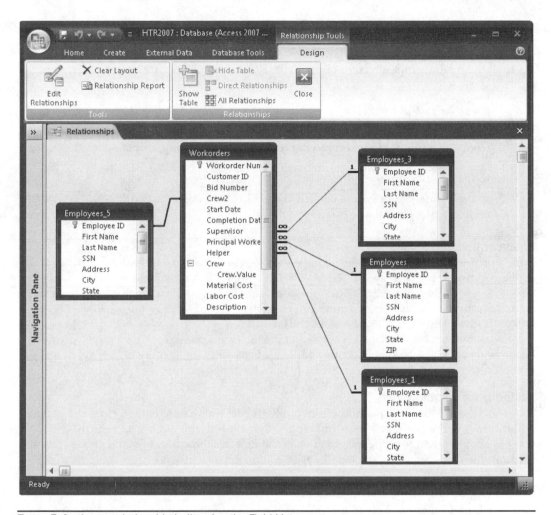

FIGURE 5-4   A new relationship built using the Field List pane

Viewing and Editing Relationships

To look at the relationships you defined for a database, open the Relationships window. If you plan on making any changes, be sure to close all open tables first.

Viewing Existing Relationships

You have a choice of viewing all the relationships you set in your database or only those involving a specific table.

Open the Relationships window as before, and on the Design tab's Relationships group, do one of the following:

- To view all the relationships in the current database, click the All Relationships command.

- To see only the relationships for the table selected in the Relationships window, click Direct Relationships.

If all the relationships already appear in the Relationships window, perform the following steps to see only one table's relationships:

1. Clear the layout by clicking the Clear Layout command in the Tools group. Click Yes to confirm the action.

2. Click the Show Table command in the Relationships group, double-click the table name in the Show Table dialog box, and then choose Close. This adds the table back to the Relationships window.

3. In the Relationships group, click the Direct Relationships command. All the tables related to the first table are added to the layout and the relationship lines are drawn.

Hiding or Deleting a Table

If the Relationships window becomes too crowded, you can hide a table temporarily or delete it entirely from the layout. To hide the table, first select the table, and on the Design tab's Relationships group, click Hide Table; or right-click the table and choose Hide Table from the shortcut menu. The next time you open the Relationships window, all the tables will reappear even if you choose to save the layout.

To delete the table from the layout, select the table and press DEL; or, on the Home tab's Records group, click the Delete command. This affects only the display of the layout and doesn't remove the relationship or the table from the database.

Restoring All Relationships

To restore the Relationships window's layout to its previous arrangement, close the window without saving the changes. When you reopen the window, the old layout returns. If you want to keep the window open, right-click in the Relationships window and choose Show All from the shortcut menu, or click the All Relationships command.

Modifying or Deleting a Relationship

Relationships aren't cast in concrete. You use the same window to edit a relationship that you used to create one.

TIP *You can even switch to table Design view from the Relationships window and modify the table structure, as you'll see in the next section. This comes in handy if you need to make sure the related fields are the same data type or if you want to create an index to speed processing.*

Editing a Relationship

To edit an existing relationship, do the following:

1. Open the Relationships window.

2. If you don't see the relationship you want to change, on the Design tab's Relationships group, choose Show Table. Then double-click the missing table, and choose Close.

3. When you see the relationship line that represents the relationship you want to change, do one of the following to open the Edit Relationships dialog box:

- Double-click the line.
- Right-click the line and choose Edit Relationship from the shortcut menu.
- Select the line and click the Edit Relationship command in the Relationships group.

4. Make the changes you want, and then click OK.

Deleting a Relationship

To delete a relationship, click the relationship line to select it and do one of the following:

- Press DEL.
- Right-click the line and choose Delete from the shortcut menu.

Access asks for confirmation before permanently deleting the relationship, no matter which method you use. Be careful not to delete a relationship used by a query.

NOTE   *Pressing* DEL *with a table selected only removes the table from the layout, while pressing* DEL *with a relationship line selected permanently removes the relationship between the tables.*

Changing a Table Design from the Relationships Window

You might need to make a change in a table design to create the relationship you want. For example, the primary key might be a Text field, while the foreign key is a Number field. This is alright unless you want to enforce referential integrity, which requires the same data type in both fields. You can open the child table design and change the field type to Text. If you already set a relationship between the tables, you must delete the relationship before you can change the table design. You might also want to add a secondary index on the foreign key in the child table to speed processing.

To switch to the table Design view from the Relationships window, right-click in the title bar of the table's field list box and choose Table Design from the shortcut menu. When you finish changing the table design, save the changes and close the window. You will then return automatically to the Relationships window.

Printing the Relationships

Documentation is always helpful, especially if you work with several databases or develop applications for others. Once you define all the relationships for the database, graphically documenting the structure is easy.

To print the table relationships diagram, do the following:

1. In the Relationships window, right-click in an empty area and choose Show All.
2. When all tables appear in the layout, click Relationship Report in the Tools group on the Design tab. Figure 5-5 shows the Print Preview of the Home Tech Repair database relationships.

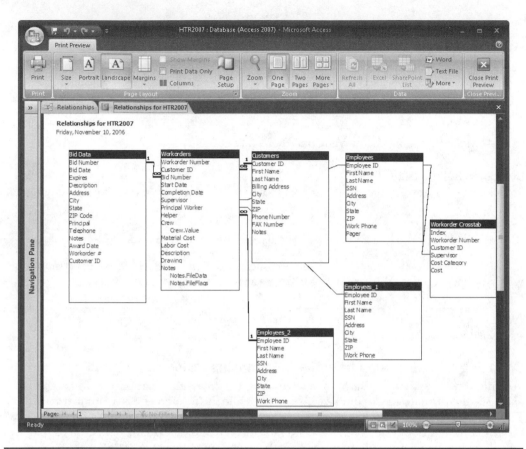

FIGURE 5-5   Print Preveiw of the database relationships diagram

You can use the relationship line symbols as a guide to the linking fields.

TIP *You might need to run Page Setup, and then reduce the left and right margins or change to Landscape orientation to print the entire diagram on one page.*

If you want more precise information about the relationships you established in the database—including the attributes such as referential integrity and the relationship type—you can use the Documenter, one of the Access analytical tools.

1. On the Database Tools tab's Analyze group, click the Database Documenter command (the top icon). The Documenter dialog box opens, showing eight tabs applying to the database objects and the database itself. If you see a message saying the Documenter isn't installed, you can have it installed now.

Relationships

EmployeesWorkorders

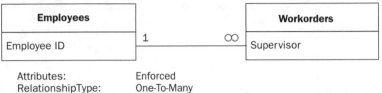

| Attributes: | Enforced |
| RelationshipType: | One-To-Many |

EmployeesWorkorder Crosstab

| Attributes: | Not Enforced |
| RelationshipType: | One-To-Many |

Bid DataWorkorders

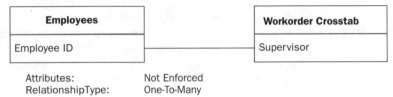

| Attributes: | Enforced, Cascade Updates |
| RelationshipType: | One-To-Many |

CustomersWorkorders

| Attributes: | Enforced, Cascade Updates |
| RelationshipType: | One-To-Many |

EmployeesWorkorders

| Attributes: | Enforced |
| RelationshipType: | One-To-Many |

Figure 5-6   Printing the database relationships

2. When the Documenter dialog box opens, click the Current Database tab, and then click the Relationships check box.

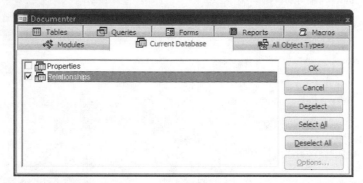

3. Click OK to print the relationships in table form. A preview of the Relationships document appears after a few moments. Figure 5-6 shows the printed first page of the documented relationships that exist in the Home Tech Repair database that we have been constructing.

Summary

In these first five chapters, you learned the importance of creating relationships among tables in a database. The tables and their relationships form the structure on which the other database objects are based. Queries can extract related information from multiple sources. Forms and reports can include data from many tables.

You saw how to create and modify tables and, in this chapter, you learned how to create and modify relationships between the tables and set other properties, such as referential integrity and join type. Referential integrity matches data from different tables and helps to ensure data validity. The join type determines which records are to be extracted by a query.

Now you're ready to move on to entering and editing the table data you'll use in later chapters. The next chapter provides details about entering and editing data in tables, including creating lookup lists and customizing data entry. You'll also see how to use the versatile Spelling tool and the AutoCorrect feature that corrects your spelling as you type.

After the information is stored in your database, the world is yours. You can retrieve some or all of the information, display it in forms, and print it in reports. You can even export it to other applications or publish it on the Internet.

Entering and Editing Data

Data errors have a way of burrowing deep into the database, where they're difficult to detect and remove. Trying to prevent errors from getting into the database in the first place makes sense. Access provides many helpful tools to ensure data validity and specify the data type, format, field size, and validation rules discussed in Chapter 4.

This chapter discusses more tools that improve the chances for achieving data validity as well as speeding the data entry process. Techniques such as copying quantities of data from other sources, selecting values from lookup lists, and using shortcut keys all help ease the chore of data entry. Other Microsoft Office tools, such as the spelling checker and AutoCorrect features, also help to keep the database accurate and complete.

Entering New Data

When you open a new table, it appears in Datasheet view, ready for data entry. To add a new record, do one of the following:

- On the Home tab's Records group, click the New command.
- Click the New (blank) Record navigation button.
- Right-click in a record selector box at the left end of the row and choose New Record from the shortcut menu.
- Right-click the Datasheet view button in the upper-left corner and choose New Record from the shortcut menu.
- Scroll down to the blank record at the bottom of the table and start typing.

To navigate among records, use the vertical scroll bar, the navigation buttons at the bottom of the document pane, keyboard shortcuts, or the Go To command in the Find group. To move among fields or columns, use the horizontal scroll bar, the TAB or ENTER key, or keyboard shortcuts. (See Chapter 1 for details about moving around in Datasheet view.)

When the insertion point moves to an empty field, type in the data. If you specified a custom format, the entered value adapts to that format when you move to the next column. If you created an input mask for that field, the mask appears when you enter the field and before you begin to type the data. (See "Adding Input Masks" later in this chapter for details about input masks and how they compare with display format settings.)

Date/time data can be entered in any valid date/time format, and Access converts it to the format you specified in the field property. Don't expect to enter decimal fractions in Number fields that are defined as integers.

NOTE *Entering a large amount of text in a Memo field can be difficult in Datasheet view. One way to see all the text in the field is to use the Zoom box while you're entering the data. Press* SHIFT-F2 *to open the Zoom box and press* ENTER *or click OK to close it after entering the text. If you want to start a new paragraph or enter a blank line of memo text in the Zoom box, press* CTRL-ENTER. *The Zoom box isn't limited to Memo fields. It can be used anywhere text is entered to give you a larger entry area.*

Copying and Moving Data

Access provides some shortcuts for entering repetitive data by letting you copy or move existing data. You can copy or move all the data or individual field values from one record to another. Copying creates exact duplicates of the data in the new location. Moving cuts the data from one location and places it in another, leaving only one copy of the data.

When you collect items by copying or cutting them from their source, they're placed on the Office clipboard, which is shared by all Office programs. The clipboard is a task pane that can hold up to 24 items with previews of the text or pictures that have been copied (see Figure 6-1). You can paste items singly or as a group to a new location. When you reach the twenty-fifth item on the clipboard, the first item is deleted.

If you don't see the Clipboard pane, on the Home tab click the Clipboard Task Pane launcher, the small square next to the Clipboard group name.

Clipboard Task Pane Launcher

If you've copied any items (from Access or another Office program) during the current session, they will appear in the Clipboard pane (see Figure 6-1).

You can display the Clipboard pane and use it while copying and pasting items.

- Click Copy to add the selected item to the clipboard.

- Select one item in the clipboard, move it to the destination, and click Paste.

- Click Paste All to paste all the items on the clipboard to the same document.

To paste an item from the clipboard, place the insertion point where you want to paste the item, click the down arrow next to the item in the clipboard, and choose Paste from the shortcut menu. To delete an item from the clipboard, click the down arrow to the right of the item and choose Delete from the menu. To close the Clipboard pane, click the Close button in the upper-right corner. To display it later, click the Clipboard Task Pane launcher.

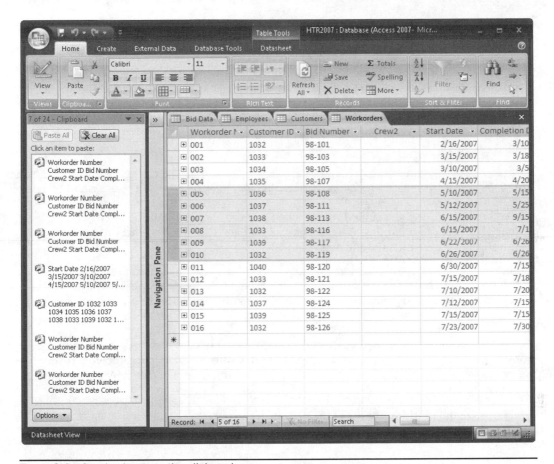

FIGURE 6-1 Copying items to the clipboard

NOTE *You can modify the behavior of the clipboard by clicking the Options button at the bottom of the pane. The options include Show Office Clipboard Automatically, Show Office Clipboard When CTRL-C Pressed Twice, Collect Without Showing Office Clipboard, Show Office Clipboard Icon on Taskbar, and Show Status Near Taskbar When Copying. Only the last two options are usually selected by default. You can also move, resize, or close the pane by clicking the title bar down arrow.*

The items you've collected on the clipboard remain there until you close all the Office programs you have running on your computer. If a number of items are still on the clipboard when you close Access, Access might ask if you want to keep them there for use by another Office program.

NOTE *The Cut, Copy, and Paste commands are also in the shortcut menu accessed by clicking the Datasheet view button.*

Copying and Moving Within the Same Table

To copy a record within the same table, first select the record you want to copy by clicking the record selector—the small gray box to the left of the record. Then on the Home tab's Clipboard group, click the Copy command. This copies the data to the clipboard. Click the record selector in the record you want to replace, and then click Paste. The new record contains an exact copy of the original record. If you want to add the copy as a new record rather than replace an existing one, select the empty record at the bottom of the datasheet, and then click Paste. To remove the data, select the record and click the Cut command instead of Copy.

Tip *Some neat key combination shortcuts:* CTRL-C *(copy),* CTRL-X *(cut), and* CTRL-V *(paste).*

Access tries to save the copied record when you move out of it. If the table has a primary key or a unique index, Access won't let you leave the new record until you replace the duplicate value with a unique one.

Tip *If the primary key field is an AutoNumber data type, Access automatically increments the number rather than copying the original number—just another reason to use an AutoNumber field as the primary key.*

To copy or move more than one record, select all the affected records before choosing Copy or Cut. When replacing records, select the same number of existing records as you placed on the clipboard, and then click Paste. If you want to append the new records to the table instead of replacing existing ones, do one of the following:

- Select the new empty row at the bottom of the datasheet and click Paste.
- Click the down arrow under the Paste command and choose Paste Append.

In either case, Access asks for confirmation when you try to paste multiple records:

If the table has a primary key or a unique index that isn't an AutoNumber, you can't paste multiple records without removing the key or index first. Unlike pasting a single record, Access would have to save all but one of the records and this would create duplicate values in the field. If you try, Access displays an information message:

If you need to paste the value in a single field to the next record while you're entering data, you can quickly copy the value from the corresponding field in the previous record to the new record by pressing CTRL-' (apostrophe).

Copying and Moving from Another Table

To copy or move records from another table, select the records in the source table and choose Copy or Cut. If you choose Cut, you're asked to confirm that you want to delete the record(s) from the source table. Then switch to the destination datasheet and select the blank row at the bottom of the datasheet. When you click Paste, the new records are added to the destination datasheet.

CAUTION *The fields in the copied records are pasted in the same order that they appeared in the original datasheet, regardless of the field names. You might need to rearrange the columns in the destination datasheet before pasting so that they correspond with the incoming fields. Inconsistent data types or sizes between the incoming records and the destination can result in problems.*

If you want to replace certain records in the destination datasheet with records from another table, select the records you want to replace before clicking Paste.

To append records from another table to the existing datasheet, choose Paste Append as described earlier. If the source table has more fields than the destination table, the excess fields aren't pasted.

TIP *If you're pasting records from another application, be sure to check the arrangement of the data before attempting to copy or move it into an Access datasheet. It should be arranged in a spreadsheet, a word-processor table, or as text separated by tab characters before you select it. See Chapter 23 for more information on exchanging data with other applications.*

Fixing Paste Problems

You've heard this warning before, but here it is again—always save a backup copy of your data before attempting anything new. This applies to many of the copying and moving operations, which aren't vulnerable to the Undo button on the Quick Access toolbar. If Access asks for confirmation before executing the operation, it most likely can't be undone once you click Yes.

When errors occur during a paste operation, Access creates a Paste Errors table and displays a message advising you of the errors as each is added to the table. To view the Paste Errors table, double-click the table name in the Tables list in the Navigation Pane.

The problems you might encounter when trying to paste data into a datasheet include the following:

- You might try to paste values of incompatible data types, such as pasting a value that contains letters and numbers into a Currency field.

- The value you try to paste might be too long for the destination field. Compare the Field Size properties of both fields.

- You might have tried to paste a value into a hidden field. Return to the datasheet then right-click and choose Unhide Columns in the shortcut menu to reveal the hidden columns.

- A value you're trying to paste might violate one of the property settings, such as the Input Mask, Validation Rule, Required, or Allow Zero Length settings.

When you open the Paste Errors table, you might be able to correct the problem and paste the data in the destination table field by field.

Inserting Pictures

The Home Tech Repair Employees table has a field reserved for the employee's badge picture. The Badge Picture field is an OLE Object data type and stores a file containing the digitized photograph.

An Object Linking and Embedding (OLE) object is created by an application outside Access and can be inserted into an Access table. Objects can be images, sounds, charts, video clips, or nearly any product of another application. Source applications can include Word, Excel, sound or video recorders, or an image scanner.

The object can either be linked to the Access table or embedded in it. *Linking* is the process by which the object remains in its source application and Access reaches it by means of a link or pointer to the object's location. If the linked object changes in the source application, the Access version also changes. Linking also helps keep database files from getting huge, because picture files can be quite large. The disadvantage is that if you move the database, you have to restore the linkage. *Embedding* an object stores a static copy of the object in the Access table, form, or report. Changes in the original don't reach the Access copy automatically.

Two other definitions are called for here: bound and unbound objects. A *bound object* is stored directly in an Access table as part of the stored data. An *unbound object* is added as an element to a form or report design and isn't directly related to the table data.

The badge picture photos are OLE objects created by a scanner and are contained in image files, such as .tif, .gif, or .pcx files. Because the photos aren't expected to change, they're embedded in the table. In addition, they represent the value stored in the Badge Picture field, which means they're bound objects.

To insert an image in the Badge Picture field:

1. Place the insertion point in the Badge Picture field, right-click the field, and choose Insert Object from the shortcut menu.

2. In the Insert Object dialog box, choose Create From File.

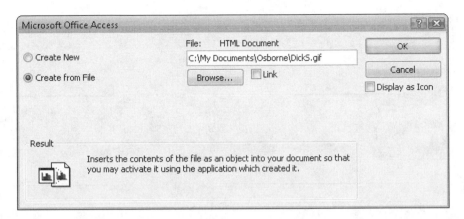

3. Type the path and filename of the image file in the File box, or click Browse and navigate to the object.

4. After entering the filename, click OK to embed the picture in the field.

When you return to Datasheet view, the field now contains the name of the source of the OLE object. Other entries indicate other types of objects. To see the image, on the Create tab's Forms group, click the Form command. Figure 6-2 shows one of the Employee records with the badge picture embedded. If you see the filename instead of the picture, double-click the filename.

NOTE   *The form in Figure 6-2 has been slightly formatted to show the full picture.*

The following other options are also in the Insert Object dialog box:

- Link check box, which creates a link to the object, rather than embedding it.
- Display as Icon check box, which displays only an icon representing the source object, instead of the object itself.

NOTE   *Chapter 10 contains more information about using OLE and other objects when creating form and report designs.*

Inserting Hyperlinks

A *hyperlink* is a connection to an object in the same or another Access database, to a document created in another Office program, or to a document on the Internet or your local intranet. You can link to any OLE or ActiveX application on your computer or local area network (LAN). The *hyperlink field* contains the address of the target object and when you click the hyperlink, you jump to it. If the object is the product of another application, that application is automatically started.

In the Home Tech Repair database, the Workorders table contains a hyperlink field that contains the engineering drawings for that work order. The scanned drawings are saved as .gif files in the same folder as the database itself.

FIGURE 6-2   Viewing a picture inserted into a record

Defining the Hyperlink Address

A hyperlink address can contain up to four parts, separated by the pound sign (#):

displaytext#address#subaddress#screentip

Only the address or, in some cases, the subaddress is required.

- The *displaytext* is optional text to display in the field in place of the actual address. If you don't include display text, the hyperlink address or subaddress appears instead.

- The *address* is either a Uniform Resource Locator (URL), such as a Web address, or a Universal Naming Convention (UNC) path to the document. An *absolute path* starts with a double forwardslash (//) and describes the exact location on the system or LAN. A *relative path* is related to the current path or the base path specified in the database properties. An address is required, unless you added a subaddress that points to an object in the current database.

- The *subaddress* contains a named location within the target object, such as a bookmark in a Word document, a particular slide in a PowerPoint presentation, or a cell range in an Excel spreadsheet.

- The *screentip* is the text that appears when you rest the mouse pointer on the hyperlink. If you don't specify a ScreenTip, the address is displayed.

Here are some examples of hyperlinks and their targets:

- *Presentation#c:\Demos\HomeTech.ppt#Click to preview Home Tech slide* jumps to the first slide in the PowerPoint presentation named HomeTech. Displays *Presentation* in place of the address and shows a ScreenTip.

- *Rhythm&Blues#c:\Favorites\Old Tunes.doc#RandB#Click to see a list of old tunes* jumps to the RandB bookmark in the Word document named Old Tunes.doc in the Favorites folder. Displays *Rhythm&Blues* in place of the address and shows a ScreenTip.

- *Summer Schedule#http://www.va.com/summer/schedule.html#Route* jumps to the location named Route within the HTML file on VA's web site named schedule.html. Displays *Summer Schedule* in place of the address and shows a ScreenTip.

Entering the Hyperlink Address

You can use several ways to enter a hyperlink address that's unique for each record in a form or datasheet, depending on the intended target of the hyperlink:

- Type the hyperlink address directly in the field.

- Copy and paste a hyperlink or hyperlink address from another source.

- Copy and paste text from another Office document.

- Drag and drop an Internet shortcut.

- Use the Insert Hyperlink dialog box.

TIP *If you type the address, you must include the pound signs (#). If you use the Insert Hyperlink feature, Access adds the pound signs to the address for you when it assembles the address parts.*

The scanned drawings for the Workorders Drawing field are stored in the folder with the database. To use Insert Hyperlink to enter the hyperlink address, do the following:

1. Right-click in the Drawing field in the Workorders datasheet and point to Hyperlink in the shortcut menu.

2. Choose Edit Hyperlink. This opens the Insert Hyperlink dialog box.

Up One Folder   Browse the Web   Browse for File

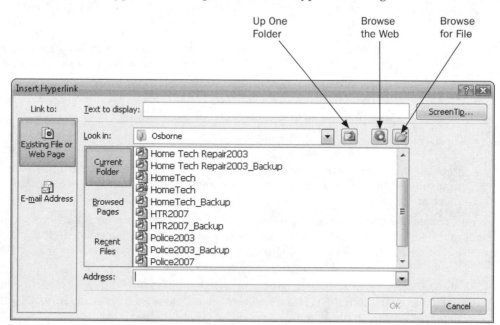

3. Click the Existing File or Web Page button under Link To, if not already chosen. Then do one of the following:

   - Type the path to the drawing file in the Address box. For example, **c:\My Documents\Osborne\fireplace.gif**.

   - If you've accessed the target of this hyperlink before, you can select it from the list of Recent Files or Browsed Pages.

   - Click the Browse for File button (the open folder) and locate the file in the Link To File dialog box. Then click OK.

4. Back in the Insert Hyperlink dialog box, enter the text you want to show in the field in place of the address in the Text To Display box. For example, you could enter **Fireplace**.

5. If you want to show a ScreenTip, click the ScreenTip button and enter the text in the Set Hyperlink ScreenTip dialog box. Then click OK.

6. Click OK to finish inserting the hyperlink and return to the Workorders datasheet where the hyperlink appears in the Drawing field. When you rest the mouse pointer on the hyperlink, you will see the ScreenTip.

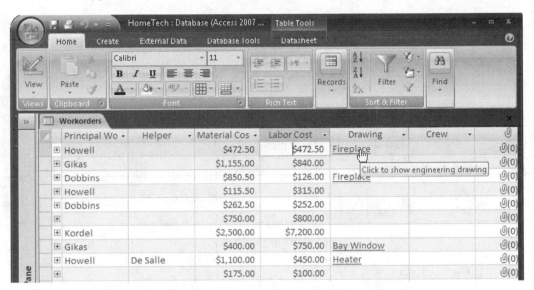

7. Click the hyperlink to test it and Microsoft Picture Library opens displaying the scanned fireplace drawing, as shown in Figure 6-3.

NOTE *If you are using Windows XP, the Windows Picture and Fax Viewer may show up instead of the Microsoft Picture Library.*

Editing and Deleting Hyperlinks

Editing a hyperlink address is a little different from editing normal text, because if you click the address, you jump to the target. You can edit the address in two ways:

- Open the Edit Hyperlink dialog box and edit the address directly.
- Move to the field and press F2 to switch to Edit mode. To see the full address, press SHIFT-F2 to open the Zoom box.

To open the Edit Hyperlink dialog box, right-click the hyperlink, point to Hyperlink in the shortcut menu, and click Edit Hyperlink in the submenu.

Make the changes to the address in the Address box. You can also edit the display text and ScreenTip in the Edit Hyperlink dialog box the same way you specified them.

To edit the complete address in the datasheet, use the keyboard to move to the field. Then press F2 to enter Edit mode and make changes in the address. If you can't read the whole

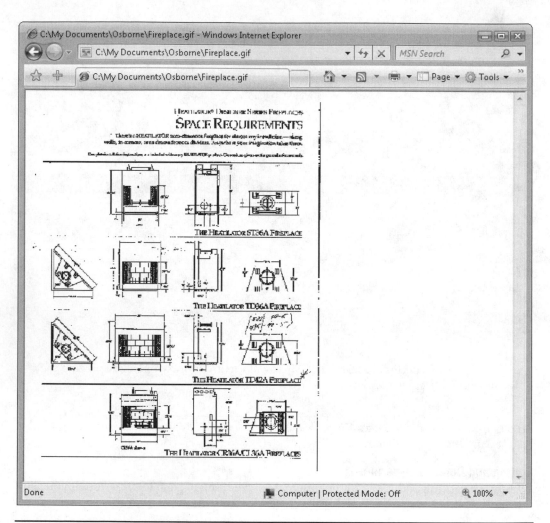

FIGURE 6-3 Viewing the target of the Fireplace hyperlink

address, press SHIFT-F2 to open the address in the Zoom box. You can change all parts of the address this way. The two consecutive pound signs between the address and the ScreenTip indicate no subaddress exists, but its relative position is preserved. Moving to another field saves the changes and completes the edit process.

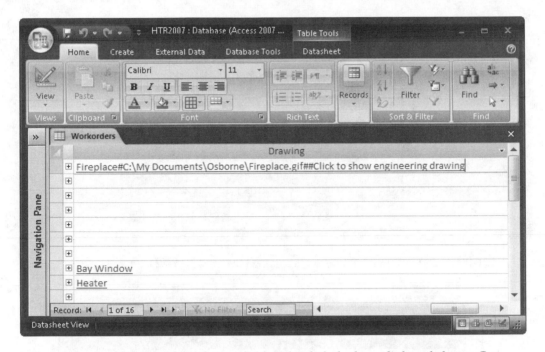

To delete a hyperlink address from a field, right-click the hyperlink and choose Cut from the shortcut menu, or simply use the Tab key to move to the hyperlink and press DELETE. You can also point to Hyperlink in the shortcut menu and click Remove Hyperlink.

TIP *Although Access removes the hyperlink address without asking for confirmation, you can easily restore it by clicking the Undo button on the Quick Access toolbar.*

If you want to delete all the hyperlink addresses you inserted in a field, delete the field from the table design.

NOTE *You can change the hyperlink colors that show whether the link was accessed by clicking the Microsoft Office button and clicking Access Options. Then select Advanced in the left pane and click the Web Options button in the General list. In the Web Options dialog box, select the colors for the Hyperlink and the Followed Hyperlink. See Chapter 16 for more information about customizing the Access workplace.*

Attaching Files to a Table

Suppose you want to add some comments and drawings to the Notes attachment field in a Workorder record. To add a file to the attachment field, open the table in Datasheet view and double-click in the field. Alternatively, you can right-click in the field and choose Manage Attachments in the shortcut menu. The Attachments dialog box appears, displaying a list of files already named as attachments. You use this dialog box to add or remove attachments, open one of the attachments, or save changes you have made to the attachments.

NOTE *You can use the same attachments in more than one table.*

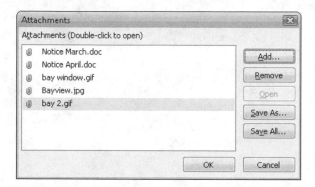

1. Click Add to open the Choose File dialog box.

2. Go through the folders to find the file or files you want to attach to the field. If you know the name of the file, type it in the Search box in the upper-right corner and press ENTER.

3. Select the file or files and click Open to return to the Attachments dialog box.

4. After attaching all the files you need, click OK to return to the datasheet.

Back in Datasheet view, you will see the paper clip icon followed by the number of files currently attached to the field.

NOTE *If you want to look at the attachment directly from the Access table, you will need the program that originated or at least supports the file installed in your system.*

Customizing Data Entry

Data entry is, by nature, a time-consuming task. Access offers many tools to help improve its efficiency, some of which minimize the data entry process, while others assist in navigation in a datasheet or give you access to special symbols. The basic rule is "The more help you can provide, the better."

Adding Input Masks

An *input mask* is a field property similar to the Format property but with a different purpose. An input mask displays a fill-in blank for data entry, while a format is used to display field data with a consistent appearance. Setting the Format property affects how data is displayed after it's entered and offers no control over or guidance for the data being entered. Input masks can be used with Text, Number, Date/Time, and Currency fields.

To decide between a Format property and an Input Mask property, use the following guidelines:

- If you want to make sure the field values look the same when displayed, use the Format property to specify the desired appearance.

- If you want to have some control over data entry, use an input mask to guide data entry and make sure that it's entered properly.

An input mask appears when the insertion point reaches the field, before any data is entered. The mask displays fill-in spaces with literal characters separating them. When you use an input mask, you can be sure the data fits the specifications you set by limiting the number of fill-in spaces. Depending on the characters you use in the mask, you can leave some fill-in spaces blank, but you cannot add more characters than spaces.

An input mask can also specify what kind of values you can enter in each space. Telephone numbers offer a good example to show the difference between Format and Input Mask properties.

- The format (@@@) @@@-@@@@ displays nothing on the screen before data is entered and displays *(619) 555-8867* after you enter this phone number.

- The input mask (000) 000-0000 displays (___) ___-____ before data is entered and displays *(619) 555-8867* after the number is entered.

The format above displays the literal characters and the characters you enter, or it leaves the spaces blank if no character is entered, but only after the record has been saved. The input mask contains zeros, which require that all entries contain the correct number of digits (and only digits) to represent a US telephone number.

Caution *If you set both a display format and an input mask, Access uses the input mask for entering and editing data and the format setting for displaying entered data. If your results don't look quite right, you might have specified conflicting settings.*

You can create an input mask for Text and Date/Time fields with the Input Mask Wizard. If you want an input mask for a Number or Currency field, you must create it manually.

To create an input mask with the Input Mask Wizard, move the insertion point to the field in table Design view and click in the Input Mask property. Then do the following:

1. Click the Build button (…) at the right of the field's Input Mask property. The first Input Mask Wizard dialog box opens (see Figure 6-4), where you can select from a list of 10 predesigned input masks appropriate for commonly used fields. The Try It box shows how the mask works when displayed in Datasheet or Form view. Access might prompt you to save the table design before opening the first dialog box.

2. After selecting the mask similar to the one you need, click Next to move to the second dialog box. In this dialog box, you can make any necessary changes to the mask, such as changing the placeholder that displays as the fill-in spaces (the default is an underline character), and then click Next.

3. Choose to store the literal characters with the data, if desired. This uses more disk space, but the symbols are available when you want to use the value in a form or report, rather than having to specify them in the field format in the form or report design.

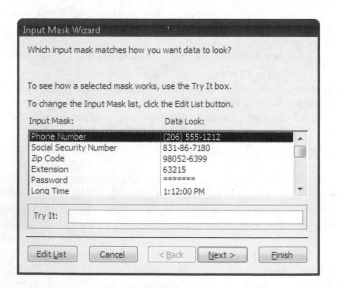

Figure 6-4   Choosing from predesigned input masks

4. Click Finish to close the wizard.

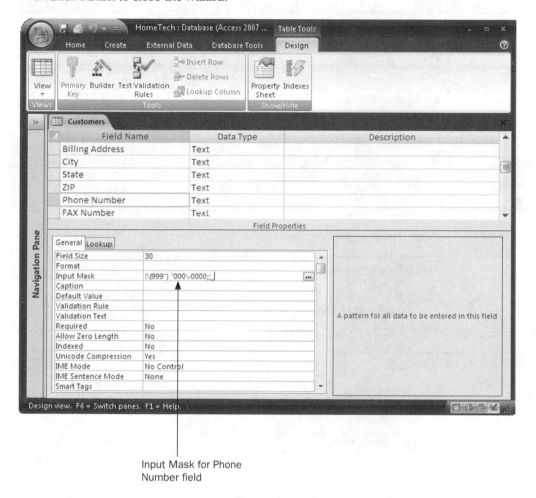

Input Mask for Phone
Number field

If you have a customized field that isn't part of the Input Mask Wizard's repertoire, you can easily create your own mask manually with special symbols. The special symbols are placeholders that specify which entries are required and define what type of characters can be entered at each position in the mask. You can even add a custom mask to the wizard's list of predefined input masks. You cannot create an input mask for a Memo, AutoNumber, Yes/No, OLE Object, Attachment, or Hyperlink field.

To build an input mask manually, enter the desired characters directly in the Input Mask property in Design view. Table 6-1 describes the symbols you can use in an input mask and whether they require an entry in that position.

In addition to the symbols in Table 6-1, you can add any of the characters that represent date and time separators, a decimal point, or a thousands separator. When you add these

Symbol	Entry	Entry Required?
0	Displays a digit (0–9) with no + or – sign. Blanks display as zeros.	Yes
9	Displays a digit with no + or – sign. Blanks display as spaces.	No
#	Displays a digit with + and – signs. Blanks display as spaces.	No
L	Displays a letter (A–Z).	Yes
?	Displays a letter.	No
A	Displays a letter or digit.	Yes
a	Displays a letter or digit.	No
&	Displays any character or space.	Yes
C	Displays any character or space.	No
<	Converts letter to lowercase.	N/A
>	Converts letter to uppercase.	N/A
!	Fills the mask with the characters that the user types into the mask, from left to right. Can appear anywhere in the mask.	N/A
\	Treats the next character as a literal.	N/A
Password	Creates a password entry box. When user types password, the characters are stored but displayed as asterisks (*).	N/A

TABLE 6-1   Input Mask Symbols

characters to the input mask, they appear in the fill-in field where you enter the data. Here are some examples of the effects of using input masks:

Input Mask	Description	Sample Valid Value
00000-9999	Zeros represent required entries, the 9s are optional.	92118-2450 or 92118-
(999) AAA-AAAA	Allows letters or digits; area code is optional.	(301) 555-CALL
!>L0L 0L0	Converts all letters to uppercase; fills left to right.	N0C 1H0
>L<??????????	Converts required initial letter to uppercase; other characters are optional and converted to lowercase.	Henrietta
>LL0000-000	Two required letters converted to uppercase and seven required digits.	BT5430-115

To make a change in one of the wizard's masks, select the mask first in the Input Mask Wizard dialog box, and then click Edit List and proceed to make the desired changes.

Three sections separated by semicolons are available in an input mask definition, as you saw in the Telephone input mask created earlier by the wizard:

!\(999") "000\-0000;;_

- The first section contains the mask itself, which has some interesting features. The exclamation mark tells Access to enter the characters from left to right. The opening parenthesis is preceded by a backslash telling Access that the character that follows is a literal character. The closing parenthesis and the space that follows it are enclosed in quotation marks to indicate that they're also literals. The dash separating parts of the phone number is also preceded by a backslash indicating a literal.

- The second section determines whether to store the literal characters with the data. Enter **0** in this section to store the characters; enter **1** or leave it blank to store only the characters entered in the fill-in spaces in the mask. In this example, the second section is blank.

- The third section specifies the character to use as the blank fill-in spaces in the displayed mask. For example, you would type a plus sign to use + in place of the default underline character. If you want to leave the fill-in spaces blank, type " " (with a space between the double quotation marks).

NOTE *Input masks defined in table Design view are automatically applied to the queries based on the table. They're also inherited by bound controls in forms and reports based on the table, if the form or report was designed after the mask was defined. Input masks for unbound controls must be manually set in form or report Design view. If you want to override the table-defined mask for a query or form (or report) design, change the Input Mask property for the control in the design. Clicking the Build button in the control's property sheet opens the Input Mask Wizard dialog box, where you can make the changes. See Chapter 10 for more information on setting control properties in form and report designs.*

Creating a Custom Input Mask

If you have a field that commonly appears in your tables or forms, such as the Canadian postal code, you can create a new input mask and save it in the Input Mask Wizard's list of predefined masks.

In table Design view, click the Input Mask property for the field, and then click the Build button to open the Input Mask Wizard dialog box.

1. Click Edit List. The Customize Input Mask Wizard dialog box displays the phone number input mask.

2. Click the New (blank) Record navigation button at the bottom of the dialog box to show a blank form.

3. Enter a description of the new mask, the mask itself, the symbol you want to use as the placeholder, and a sample of the data you intend to enter into the field.

4. Then select the Mask Type—Text/Unbound or Date/Time—as the field data type to complete the definition for the Canadian postal code input mask.

5. Click Close. The new definition appears in the list of predefined masks.

Creating Lookup Fields

A *lookup field* is an Access tool that makes entering data quicker and more accurate. A lookup field displays a list of values from which you can choose. The most common type of lookup field, called a *lookup list*, gets its values from an existing table or query. The advantage of this type of lookup field is that the tables are related and, as the source list changes, the current values are available to the lookup field. The lookup table becomes the parent table and its primary key links it to the lookup field, which is the foreign key in the main data table.

The second type of lookup field gets its values from a list you type in when you create the field. This type is called a *value list* and is best used when the list is limited to a few values that don't change often, such as a short list of product categories or employee status. Once you add the list to a field, the list stays with it when you add the field to a data entry form.

You can add either type of lookup field in Design or Datasheet view. If the field already exists in the table design and you want to change it to a lookup field, you must change the data type in Design view. To add a new lookup field to a table, do one of the following:

- In Design view, add a new field row and select Lookup Wizard from the Data Type list.
- In Datasheet view, click in the column to the right of where you want the new lookup field, and then on the Datasheet tab's Fields and Columns group, click the Lookup command.

Either method starts the Lookup Wizard that displays a series of dialog boxes in which you specify the details of the lookup field. In the first dialog box (see Figure 6-5), you decide which type of lookup field to create: a lookup list that relates to a table or query, or a value list that you type in.

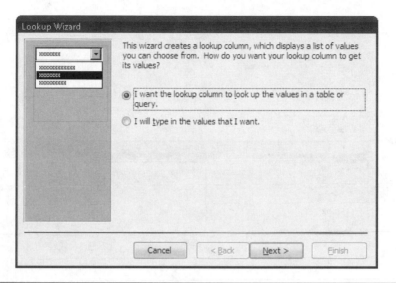

FIGURE 6-5   Starting the Lookup Wizard

If you choose to type in your list of values, the wizard displays a dialog box where you specify the number of columns you want in the list and enter the values. If you choose to get the values from another table, the wizard displays several more dialog boxes in which you do the following:

- Select the source table or query from the current database.
- Select the fields from the table you want to include.
- Specify how you want the columns to look and whether to hide the primary key in the lookup table.
- Specify which field in the table is the key field.
- Enter a name for the lookup field.

Specifying a Lookup Column

To see how you can define a lookup field that gets its values from another table, you'll insert a new field in the Workorders table of the Home Tech Repair database. The Workorders information can be easier to enter and read if a lookup field is used for the Supervisor, Principal Worker, and Helper fields. The list can display the last names of all the employees at Home Tech Repair. Then, rather than requiring the users to remember each employee's ID code, they can select the last name from a lookup column and have Access store the corresponding Employee ID value in the field. The Last Name is displayed, but the Employee ID will be stored. If two employees have the same last name, you can include the first name as well.

To add a lookup field to the Workorders table, follow these steps:

1. Open the Workorders table in Design view and insert a field named Supervisor between Completion Date and Principal Worker, choosing the Lookup Wizard data type.

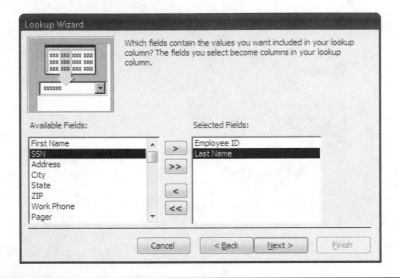

FIGURE 6-6   Selecting the fields for the lookup field

2. In the first Lookup Wizard dialog box, choose the first option, I Want the Lookup Column to Look Up the Values in a Table or Query. Then click Next.

3. Select Employees from the list of tables and click Next. You can also select a query as the source of the values.

4. In the next dialog box, double-click the Employee ID and Last Name fields in the list of available fields in the Employees table (see Figure 6-6). The field names will move to the Selected Fields list. Then click Next.

5. In the next dialog box, you can specify the sort order for fields in the lookup list. For this example, sort by Employee ID, and then click Next.

6. The next dialog box (see Figure 6-7) shows you how the field values will look in the lookup column. If the column width is insufficient or unnecessarily wide, drag the right edge of the column header to change the width. (If no data exists in the lookup table, you won't see any values here, but the relationship is still created.) In addition, check the Hide Key Column (Recommended) option if it is not already checked, so you do not need to view the Employee ID key value, only the last name. Click Next.

7. Accept the name *Supervisor* for the lookup column and click Finish. Access prompts you to save the table so the relationships can be completed. Choose Yes and you will return to the table Design view.

The Lookup Wizard has set the properties for the new field based on your selections in the dialog boxes. You can view them on the Lookup tab of the Field Properties pane.

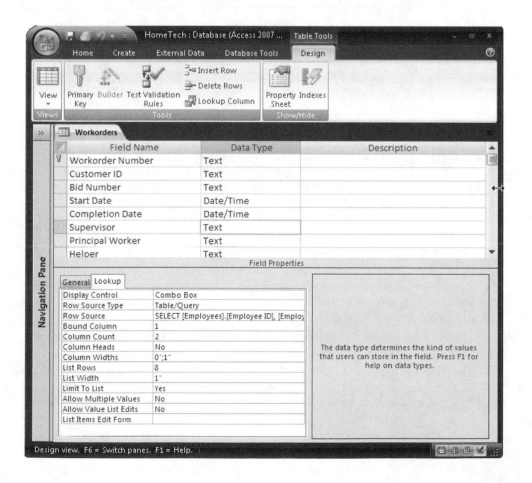

FIGURE 6-7 Changing the lookup column appearance

The *Lookup* properties specify the appearance and behavior of the lookup field when it appears in a datasheet or a form.

- The *Display Control* property determines the type of control implemented. The wizard chose a Combo Box. Other options are Text Box and List Box. (See Chapter 10 for information about different types of controls.)

- The *Row Source Type* indicates where the values come from that are displayed in the lookup column. Here the source is Table/Query. Other Row Source Types are Value List and Field List.

- The *Row Source* property specifies exactly the table and fields that make up the list. To see the entire entry, right-click in the property text and choose Zoom from the shortcut menu. You can edit the statement in the Zoom box, if necessary, or change the font properties. Click OK to close the Zoom box.

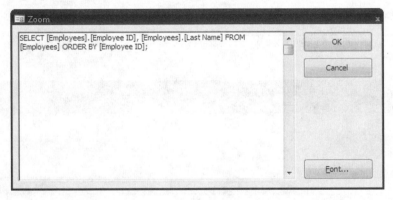

NOTE *The SELECT statement in the Row Source property is a SQL statement created by the Lookup Wizard. See Chapter 9 for more information about creating and using SQL statements.*

- The *Bound Column* indicates which column in the list contains the linking field. The columns are numbered in the order they were selected in the wizard's dialog box. The Employee ID field—selected first—is the primary key in the Employees table, so it is assigned as the bound column for the lookup column.

- The *Column Count* specifies that two columns from the related table are involved. One, Employee ID, is stored in the Workorders table and the other, Last Name, is displayed in the lookup column.

- The No setting for *Column Heads* prevents the captions from the Employees table from displaying in the lookup list.

- The first *Column Widths* setting is 0", which keeps the first column, the Employee ID field, from being displayed. This selection was made when you checked the Hide Key Column option. The Last Name column is set to the width adjusted in the Lookup Wizard dialog box.

- *List Rows* tells Access how many rows to display at once, which indicates the height of the drop-down list. If there are more values in the list, the list will include a vertical scroll bar.

- *List Width* specifies the overall width of the displayed list. If the text to be displayed in the list exceeds the column width in the datasheet or form, you can increase this value.

- The *Limit to List* property prevents the user from entering a value that isn't on the list. This is required in this case because the displayed value must be in the source table for the primary key value (Employee ID) to be retrieved and stored in the foreign key field in the Workorders table.

TIP *With Limit to List set to Yes, you might still be permitted to leave the field blank. The Combo Box accepts null values unless the Required property of the Supervisor field is set to Yes.*

- *Allow Multiple Values* permits more than one entry into the field.
- *Allow Value List Edits* permits the user to make changes in the values in the list.
- *List Items Edit Form* contains the name of the data entry form to use to make changes in the values in the list.

Switch to Datasheet view and click the down arrow in the Supervisor field to see the new lookup field used to locate employee names in the Employees table. You will be asked to save the table first. The lookup field links the Employees table to the Workorders table by the Employee ID field. Although the employee's last name is displayed, the foreign key—Employee ID—is stored in the field but isn't displayed.

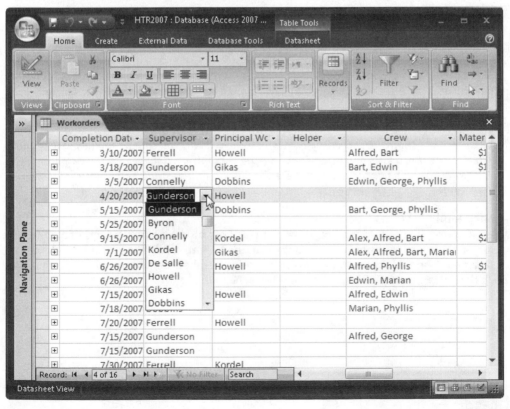

> **NOTE** *If you have specified the field as a multivalued field, you can select more than one value from the list. See the section "Allowing Multiple Values" below for more information.*

Specifying a Lookup List

A static value list can be helpful when entering data in the Employees table. Because only a few valid values are in the Type field, this is a good candidate for streamlining. In the first Lookup Wizard dialog box, choose the second option, I Will Type in the Values I Want, and click Next to move to the next dialog box, where you will enter the values for the column list.

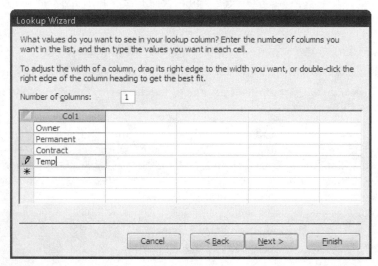

Field properties are inherited by forms and reports, including the lookup fields created in the table design. Figure 6-8 shows the new Type value list in the Employees form.

> **TIP** *When you use the value list in a form, you can set the control properties to allow the user to add values to the list during data entry. Be aware, though, that if you change a value list definition after adding it to a form design, you must modify the control's Row Source property in the form's Design view to include the correct list. See Chapter 12 for more information about customizing form controls.*

Allowing Multiple Values

When you use the Lookup Wizard to create the list of values for the field, you have the option of allowing multiple values to appear in the lookup field. The Workorders table needs a field in which one or more additional crew members can be added. To do this, check the Allow Multiple Values box, and then click Finish.

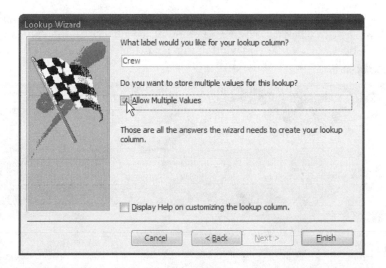

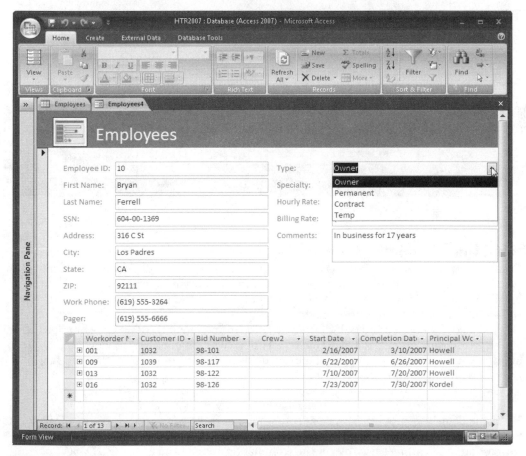

FIGURE 6-8   The lookup field property is inherited by the form

When you open the table in Datasheet view and move to the new multivalued field, you will see a down arrow. Click the arrow and you will see a list of all the values you entered in the value list. Check each value you want in this record and click OK. All the values you choose appear in the field, separated by commas.

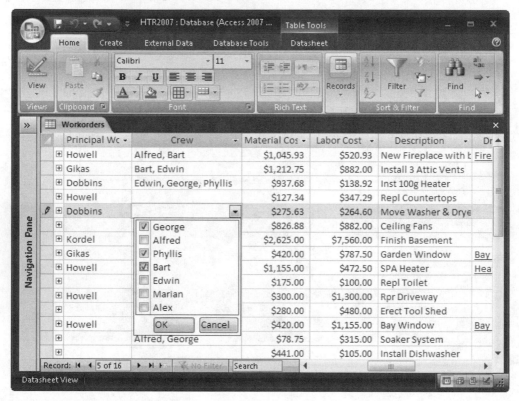

Changing the Datasheet Appearance

Datasheet properties include the layout of the fields and records—the order in which the fields appear, the dimension of the rows and columns, and the column headings. Other properties are the font size and style, the colors of the text and the background, and special cell effects, such as raised or sunken.

You also have the option of hiding some fields from view if the data does not need to be visible to all users of the database. Finally, if you have too many fields to view on the screen at once, you can keep one or more of the key fields on the left of the screen as you scroll right, so you can identify the current record.

Saving the modified datasheet appearance with the table preserves the appearance, so the next time you open the table in Datasheet view, it will look the same.

Some datasheet properties, such as column width, can be changed directly in Datasheet view. Others are accomplished with ribbon commands or dialog box options. Most of the formatting can be done easily by clicking commands on the Datasheet tab's Data Type and Formatting group.

Other appearance settings can be set from the Home tab's Records group with the More command.

Displaying Subdatasheets

After you open a table or query in Datasheet view, you can display a subdatasheet related to a row by clicking the expand indicator (+) to the left of the row. The indicator turns into a minus sign (−) collapse indicator after you click it. To hide the subdatasheet from view, click the collapse indicator.

If the subdatasheet has a subdatasheet of its own, you can expand and collapse it using the same method. You can nest up to eight levels of subdatasheets. Each datasheet or subdatasheet can have only one nested subdatasheet. Figure 6-9 shows the Employees datasheet with three Workorders subdatasheets expanded, all of which are linked to Employee ID Numbers.

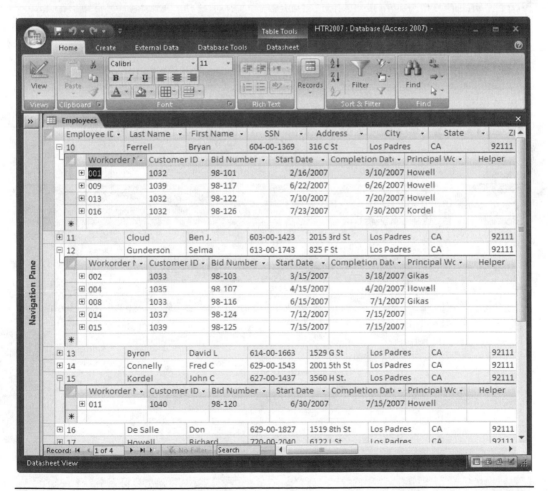

FIGURE 6-9   Expanding nested subdatasheets

> **NOTE** *Hiding and showing the columns in a datasheet or subdatasheet changes only the display and has no effect on the source object of the relationship.*

You can expand the subdatasheets for as many rows as you want. To display all the subdatasheets in the datasheet, on the Home tab's Records group, click the More down arrow and choose Expand All in the context menu. To collapse the subdatasheets, choose Collapse All from the same command group menu.

By default, Access doesn't display the foreign key or matching field in the subdatasheet. The column is hidden from view. If you want to display the field, click the plus (+) sign to expand the subdatasheet and then right-click the minus (–) sign and choose Unhide Columns from the shortcut menu. Then, in the Unhide Columns dialog box, check the column you want to include and click Close. Displaying the column is only temporary. The next time you open the datasheet containing the subdatasheet, the column is hidden again.

> **NOTE** *Notice that the record navigation buttons at the bottom of the Datasheet window refer to records in the active subdatasheet.*

Moving and Resizing Columns and Rows

Access displays the data fields in columns in the same order in which the fields appear in the table design, unless you change the column order. The columns, by default, are all the same width, so you might be unable to see the whole field value or the entire text of some of the field names. Other columns might be wider than necessary and waste screen space. The rows are also a standard height. You can change any of these datasheet properties:

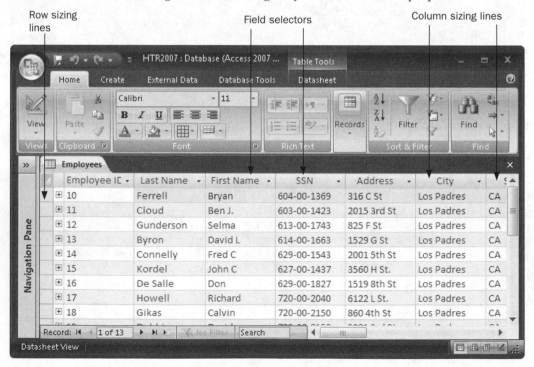

Rearranging the Columns

You might always want some fields in your table to be visible in Datasheet view. If they're far down in the list of fields in the table design, they might be off the screen to the right. One solution is to change the order of the fields in the design, but it's easier to change the column order on the screen. You can move the columns to the left, so that you won't have to scroll to see them.

To move a column, click the field selector and release the mouse button. Click the field again, and when the mouse pointer changes to an arrow shape with a small rectangle, click and drag the column to the desired position. When you begin to move the column, a dark vertical line moves with it, showing you where the left boundary of the moving column is at that moment. The column itself doesn't move until you release the mouse button.

Changing the relative position of a column in the datasheet has no effect on the way the fields appear in the design or the way they're stored on the disk.

Changing the Column Width

Obviously, if all the columns are the same width, but your data and field names are all different widths, some adjustments might make the datasheet look better and make more efficient use of the screen area.

You can change a column width in three ways:

- By dragging the sizing line at the right border of the field selector button.
- By double-clicking the column sizing line.
- By setting the width in a dialog box.

Dragging to a new width with the mouse is the easiest way to change a column width, but it isn't precise. To change the width with the mouse, move the mouse pointer to the column's right boundary line in the field selector. When the pointer changes shape to a plus (+) sign with right- and left-pointing arrows, click-and-drag the boundary to the right to increase or to the left to decrease its width.

TIP *If you drag the right boundary all the way to the left until it reaches the left boundary, the column disappears. This is one way to hide a column. Read more about hiding columns in the section "Freezing and Hiding Columns" in the next section.*

If you want the column just wide enough to fit the contents, double-click the right edge of the column heading.

If you need to be more precise about a column width, you can set the exact width in a dialog box. You can open the Column Width dialog box in two ways after selecting one or more columns:

- On the Home tab's Records group, click More and choose Column Width from the shortcut menu.
- Right-click the field selector and choose Column Width from the shortcut menu.

The Column Width dialog box displays the current column width, measured in characters, in the text box.

To change the width, type a new value in the Column Width text box, click to place a check mark in the Standard Width box to return to the default column width, or click Best Fit. The Best Fit option resizes the selected column or columns to fit the longest data in the field or the text in the column heading, whichever is longer.

NOTE *The only disadvantage to setting the column width to Best Fit is that you might later enter some new data that's longer than anything before and, unless you return to the Column Width dialog box and recheck Best Fit, it won't be fully displayed with the new column width.*

If you want to change several or all column widths at once, so they fit the data and captions, you can select the columns before choosing Best Fit in the Column Width dialog box. Selecting Best Fit adjusts all the selected columns according to their contents.

NOTE *You cannot undo the changes you made in the column width by clicking the Undo button on the Quick Access toolbar. If you want the columns restored to their original width, close the datasheet without saving the changes to the layout.*

Changing the Row Height

You can change column widths individually, but rows are different: they're all the same height and when you change the height of one, you change them all. For example, suppose you have a Memo field that usually contains two or three lines of text and you want to read them in Datasheet view. If you increase the row height to double or triple, you can fit the text in the space allowed. You might be able to combine adjusting the column width with increasing the row height to achieve the proper balance of dimensions.

The row height is modified the same way as the column width: by dragging a sizing line with the mouse or by entering the new height in a dialog box. To change the row height with the mouse, move the mouse pointer to any one of the row sizing lines in the record selector area. The mouse pointer changes shape to a plus (+) sign again, but, this time, the arrow's pointing up and down. Click and drag the line until the rows reach the desired height, and then release the mouse. All the rows will be the same height.

To set a more exact row height, choose Row Height from the More command in the Records group to open the Row Height dialog box. The insertion point can be anywhere in the datasheet when you choose Row Height. To use the shortcut menu, you must right-click in a selected row or any row selector, and then choose Row Height from the shortcut menu. The Row Height dialog box is similar to the Column Width dialog box, except there's no Best Fit option. The height is measured in points and the Standard Height option depends on the default font size.

Freezing and Hiding Columns

Two other properties of a datasheet deal with the display of the data. *Freezing* a column causes the data in it to remain on the screen as you scroll right to see fields in a long record. *Hiding* a column prevents the data from displaying in the datasheet. Neither of these properties changes the way the data is stored, only the way it's displayed.

Freezing and Unfreezing Columns

If your datasheet has more columns than can fit across the screen, some of the information moves off the screen as you scroll right to see the rest of the data. One or two of these fields might contain information, such as the product number or a customer name that identifies the record. When you're editing the table data, keeping this data on the screen is helpful, so you can be sure you're editing the right records. When you freeze a column on the screen, the column and its contents are automatically moved to the left of the datasheet and kept on the screen, even when you scroll right.

To freeze a column, right-click in the column header and choose Freeze Columns from the shortcut menu. To freeze several adjacent columns, select them all by clicking the column headers before choosing Freeze Columns. If you want to freeze nonadjacent columns, freeze them one at a time in the order you want them to appear at the left of the screen. Access then moves them, one by one, to the left side of the datasheet. You can also use the More shortcut menu in the Records group on the Home tab to freeze columns.

To unfreeze the columns, on the Home tab's Records group, click More and choose Unfreeze from the context menu. You can also right-click in one of the frozen columns and choose Unfreeze All Columns from the shortcut menu.

TIP *Unfortunately, Access doesn't return the thawed column to the position it was in before freezing and moving it to the left. You have to move the thawed column back yourself after unfreezing it or close the table without saving the changes in the layout to restore the original arrangement.*

Hiding and Unhiding a Column

If your table contains information irrelevant to the current activity, you might not want this data to take up space on the screen. In this case, you can hide one or more columns from view. Again, this changes only the appearance of the datasheet, not the data stored in the table.

You saw earlier that you can hide a column by reducing its width to nothing. Another way to hide a column is to right-click in a selected column or in the field selector and choose Hide Columns from the shortcut menu. The column immediately disappears from the screen. If you want to hide several adjacent columns, select them all first, and then right-click and make your choice. If you want to hide nonadjacent columns, reposition them so they're adjacent, and then hide them as a group or hide them one at a time. The More shortcut menu in the Records group also provides commands to hide and unhide columns.

NOTE *If you try to copy or move records to a datasheet that currently has hidden columns, the data won't be entered and you'll get paste errors. Be sure to unhide all the hidden columns before attempting to copy or move records.*

To return the hidden columns to the datasheet display, right-click in a column header and choose Unhide Columns from the shortcut menu. The Unhide Columns dialog box appears with a list of all the fields in the datasheet. Check marks next to the field names indicate the fields currently in view. If a field doesn't show a check mark, it's currently hidden. To return a field to the datasheet display, check the box next to its name. You can see the data being restored to the screen behind the dialog box when you click the check boxes. Choose Close after you return all the desired fields to the display.

TIP *You can also use the Unhide Columns dialog box to hide columns by removing the check marks.*

Changing the Font

Access uses 11-point Calibir as the default font for datasheets. The font setting applies to all the characters in the datasheet—data and captions alike. You might want to reduce the font size to get more data on the screen. Or, you might want to enlarge the font size to make it more visible if a group is going to view the screen from a distance. You can also change to any font your computer system supports. The row height and column widths are automatically adjusted to accommodate the font changes.

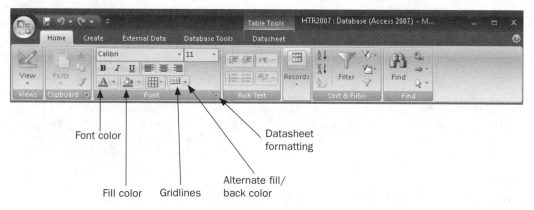

Font color

Fill color   Gridlines

Alternate fill/
back color

Datasheet
formatting

To change the datasheet font, on the Home tab's Font group, click the Font down arrow and choose a font from the drop-down list. To change the font size, click the down arrow and select a size from the list. Changing the font style and size affects both the data and the column headers in the entire datasheet. Clicking the Bold, Italic, and Underline commands also affect the entire datasheet including the column headers.

The remaining commands in the Font group, referring to colors and gridlines, apply only to the data in the table, not the column headers. When selected, the setting affects all the columns and rows in the datasheet.

Changing Gridlines and Cells

Now comes the fun part—making some dramatic changes to the appearance of the datasheet with colors and special effects. The *gridlines*—the horizontal and vertical lines that separate the datasheet into rows and columns—are displayed by default, but you can remove either the horizontal or vertical lines, or both. You can also apply special coloring effects in the datasheet.

You can use two individual commands in the Font group to make quick and simple changes to the datasheet appearance. On the Home tab in the Font group, use the following commands to change the properties:

- Click the Gridlines command and choose to show either or both the horizontal and vertical gridlines or none at all.

- Click the Alternate Fill/Back Color command to select row colors from the palette. Every other row in the datasheet will show the color in the background.

As you make changes in the Font group, the combined effects are shown in the datasheet itself. If you don't like the results, close the datasheet without saving them.

To make more changes in the datasheet format, click the Datasheet Formatting button in the lower-right corner of the Font group. The Datasheet Formatting dialog box opens, where you can choose several other settings such as the cell effect and line styles.

As you make choices, a sample of the results is displayed in the Sample pane. When you are satisfied with the appearance, click OK. To save the new datasheet appearance, save the layout with the table.

Setting Datasheet Default Options

If you want to create a custom datasheet layout for use with all the tables in the current database, you need to change some of the default datasheet options. Click the Microsoft Office button and click Access Options to open the Access Options dialog box. Then click Datasheet in the left pane to see the datasheet view options, as shown in Figure 6-10.

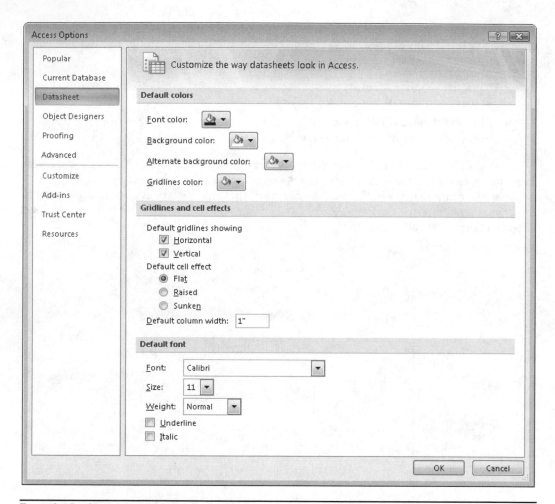

FIGURE 6-10   Setting datasheet default options

The available options are:

- **Default Colors**   Displays a palette of colors you can use for the font, background, alternate background, and gridlines.
- **Default Gridlines Showing**   Displays or hides horizontal and vertical gridlines. Gridlines displayed appear in the color set in the Gridlines Color box.
- **Default Cell Effect**   Lets you choose one of three cell effects: Flat, Raised, or Sunken.
- **Default Column Width**   Sets the standard width for all the columns in the datasheet.
- **Default Font**   Specifies the font, weight, size, and style. The text appears in the color set in the Font Color box.

Changing a Table Definition

Although the best place to modify the table definition is in Design view, you can make some limited changes in Datasheet view, such as removing fields or changing field names or field types.

Inserting a Subdatasheet

If the Subdatasheet Name property for the table on the "one" side of a one-to-many relationship is set to Auto, Access automatically creates a subdatasheet with records from the table on the "many" side. The datasheet and subdatasheet are related by matching the primary key and foreign key fields. To see the table properties, open the table in Design view and right-click anywhere in the table design and choose Properties from the shortcut menu. Or on the Design tab in the Show/Hide group, click the Property Sheet command.

You can add a subdatasheet to any table or query by specifying the source name in the Subdatasheet Name property and setting the linking fields. Click the down arrow next to the Subdatasheet Name property in the Property Sheet and choose the table or query name from the list. The Link Child Fields and Link Master Fields properties are automatically set based on the object relationships.

To remove a subdatasheet from a table or query, open the table or query in Design view and open the Property Sheet again. Go to the Subdatasheet Name property and delete the name. The subdatasheet is removed only from the display. The data isn't affected and the relationship remains intact.

TIP   *If your subdatasheet shows the same data for all the rows in the datasheet, you might not have specified the linking fields.*

Inserting/Deleting a Column

As you saw in Chapter 4, you can create a new table in Datasheet view by entering data directly in a blank datasheet. Access defines the data type to agree with the values you enter. The same principle applies to adding a new field in a table in Datasheet view. Insert a new column, change the caption to the name you want for the field, and then type in the data.

To insert a column, place the insertion point in the column to the right of where you want the new one, and on the Datasheet tab's Fields and Columns group, click Insert. A new blank column appears and the columns to the right move over. Double-click the field selector—usually labeled *Field1*—and rename the column with an appropriate field name.

NOTE   *If you want to change the data type Access assumes for the field, define a validation rule, or change other properties, you must switch to Design view.*

As discussed earlier in this chapter, the commands in the Fields and Columns group offer three special commands: New Field, Add Existing Fields, and Lookup Column.

- **New Field**   Opens the Field Templates pane at the right of the datasheet where you can choose the field template closest to what you need.

- **Add Existing Fields**   Opens the Field List pane where you can choose fields from other tables in the current database.

- **Lookup Column**   Starts the Lookup Wizard.

To delete a column in Datasheet view, click anywhere in the field, and then on the Datasheet tab's Fields and Columns group, click Delete. Access warns you that the deletion will be permanent. This is one of those times where the Undo button on the Quick Access toolbar doesn't work. Choose Yes to go ahead with the deletion or No to cancel. You can delete contiguous columns by selecting them and clicking the Delete command.

NOTE *You cannot delete a field that's part of a relationship without first deleting the relationship. Either open the Relationships window to delete the relationship yourself or accept Access's offer to delete it for you.*

Changing Field Names

You already learned how to create a name for a field in Design view. You also saw how to give a field a new name when you created a table from a blank datasheet. In Datasheet view, you have three ways of renaming an existing column:

- Double-click the text in the field selector and type in the new name.
- Select the column, and on the Datasheet tab's Fields and Columns group, click Rename.
- Right-click the field selector and choose Rename Column from the shortcut menu.

All three methods place the insertion point in the field name text where you can replace or edit the existing name. In addition, any existing field Caption properties are deleted.

Editing Record Data

The standard methods of moving around a datasheet or form to edit record data haven't changed much with Access 2007. You use the Go To command in the Find group of the Home tab or the navigation buttons at the bottom of the datasheet or form to move to another record: First, Previous, Next, Last, or New. The TAB key and the RIGHT ARROW and LEFT ARROW keys can also be used to move to another field.

To change the entire value in a field, select the field and enter the new value. To edit only part of the value, change to Edit mode by clicking in the field or pressing F2. Once in Edit mode, the RIGHT ARROW and LEFT ARROW keys move the insertion point through the characters, instead of among the fields.

The icons that appear in the record selector at the far left of the datasheet row are the indicators that show the status of the current record:

- A colored record selector indicates the current record, not in the process of editing.
- A pencil indicates changes are underway in the current record. Access saves the changes when you move to another record.
- An asterisk indicates a blank row ready for entering a new record.

NOTE *A fourth record indicator, a circle with a diagonal line through it—the international symbol meaning Do Not—shows the record is undergoing changes and is locked by another user. If this appears, you must wait to make your changes to the record.*

To Select	Mouse Action
Characters in a field	Click at the start and drag across the data.
Entire field	Click the left edge of the field when the mouse pointer changes to a hollow plus sign.
Adjacent fields	Click the left edge of the first field and drag to extend the selection.
Column	Click the field selector.
Adjacent columns	Select the first column and, without releasing the mouse button, drag over the adjacent columns.
Record	Click the record selector.
Adjacent records	Select the first record and drag over the adjacent records.

TABLE 6-2   Mouse Actions and Selections

The behavior of the ENTER, TAB, and the arrow keys can be customized, as described fully in Chapter 16. For example, by default, when you press ENTER to move to the next field, the field is selected. You can change this so that the insertion point arrives at the first or last character in the value instead of selecting the field.

Selecting Records and Fields

The mouse is a convenient tool for selecting characters, fields, and records in Datasheet view. Table 6-2 describes the mouse techniques for selecting data.

You can also use many keyboard shortcuts to select data. The results of pressing certain keys and key combinations depend on the current mode in Datasheet view. When viewing a table in Datasheet view, you have a choice between Navigation or Edit modes. In *Navigation* mode, the insertion point isn't visible and you can move between fields and records using the arrow keys. If you're in *Edit* mode, the insertion point appears in a field and the arrow keys move it among the characters in the field.

To switch between Edit and Navigation modes, press F2 or click in the current field. While in Navigation mode, you can switch between selecting the first field of the current record or the entire record by pressing SHIFT-SPACEBAR.

NOTE   *Refer to Help topics for details of the many shortcut key combinations you can use to select table data. You can also see the shortcut key combinations and ScreenTips, if those options are selected.*

If you need to extend a selection often, you can switch to Extend mode by pressing F8 one or more times. Each time you press F8, the extension applies progressively to the word, to the field, to the entire record, and, finally, to all the records. While in Extend mode, the right and left arrow keys extend the selection across the characters in the current field. If the entire column is selected, the arrow keys extend the selection to the adjacent columns in the datasheet. The UP ARROW and DOWN ARROW keys extend the selection to adjacent rows. If you change your mind, cancel the extension by pressing SHIFT-F8. To cancel Extend mode, press ESC.

TIP *You can tell you're in Extend mode by the words* Extended Selector *appearing in the Datasheet view status bar.*

Locating Records

If a table doesn't contain a lot of records, you can probably find the record you want by scrolling down through the records in the datasheet or form, especially if the records are sorted by the field you're searching. If your table contains hundreds of records, however, that method is rather time-consuming. In the unlikely event that you know the number of the record you want to locate, you can find it by using the Search box in the Navigation bar at the bottom of the screen.

Another way to locate a specific record is by the value in a specific field. Access provides the Find feature for this purpose. Just tell Access what you want to find, and where and how to search for the value. The search can apply to the complete value in the field or only to certain characters within the field.

NOTE *If you're looking for values in a datasheet with a subdatasheet or a form with a subform, Access searches only the object that contains the insertion point.*

Finding an Exact Match

To find a record with a specific value in one of the fields, place the insertion point anywhere in the column and on the Home tab's Find group, click the Find command, or press CTRL-F. The Find and Replace dialog box opens, where you can specify the search you want to conduct.

For example, place the insertion point in the Specialty field in the Employees table of the Home Tech Repair database and click the Find command. In the Find and Replace dialog box (see Figure 6-11), enter **Plumbing** as the value to look for in the Find What box, and then click Find Next. The insertion point moves to the next record with that value.

Clicking Find Next again finds subsequent records with the same value in the field. After Access has found the last record that matches the value, choosing Find Next displays an information dialog box indicating no more records exist with that value. Click OK to close the message. The Find and Replace dialog box remains on the screen until you click the Cancel button.

TIP *If you placed the insertion point in the middle of the table, Access searches to the last record, and then begins at the first record until all records have been examined.*

Limiting or Expanding the Search

By default, Access searches only the specified field in all the records. In the Look In box, you have a choice between the field that contains the insertion point or the entire table. You can expand the search by choosing the whole table—for example, Employees—in the Look In box. Access searches for the value in all the Text and Memo fields in the table. This is slower than limiting the search to a single field, but it comes in handy for finding specific values in all fields, especially when you want to replace one value with another globally.

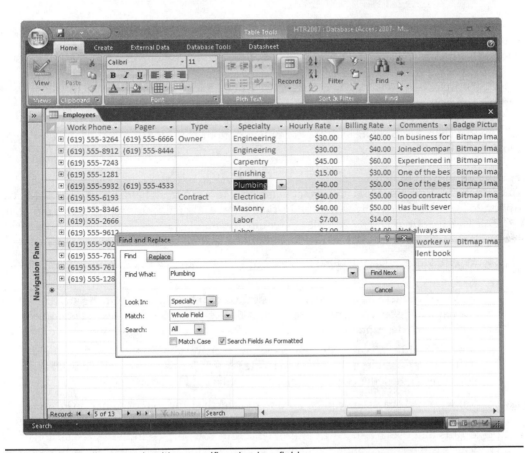

FIGURE 6-11   Finding records with a specific value in a field

---

TIP   *One way to speed up the search process is to index a field if you expect to search it often with Find and Replace.*

Two of the options can be used to limit or expand the search. If you're interested in finding only one occurrence of the value rather than all of them, you can limit the search to a subset of the records. The Search option drop-down list includes the following:

- **All**   This default setting begins at the current record, searches to the end of the table, and then begins again at the first record.
- **Up**   Searches from the current record toward the first record.
- **Down**   Searches from the current record through the remaining records.

TIP   *You can close the Find and Replace dialog box at any time—you do not need to find all the occurrences of the value before you move on to something else.*

The Match Case option, when checked, treats uppercase and lowercase letters as different characters. For example, if you enter the value *plumbing* in the Find What box and check Match Case, Access won't find *Plumbing*. If you check Match Case, the Search Fields As Formatted option is dimmed.

The Search Fields As Formatted option lets you look for the field based on the display format, rather than the stored value. For example, suppose you have a date field displayed in the format 15-May-07, but it's stored as the value 05/15/07. If you want to look for it as 15-May-07, check the Search Fields As Formatted option. This type of search is slower than looking for the stored value.

Finding an Inexact Match

Access offers two ways to find an inexact match in a Text or Memo field: by setting the Match option to limit the search only to part of the field or by using wildcards in the search string.

The Match options specify whether to require a complete and exact match or to accept a match with only part of the field. The Match options include the following:

- **Whole Field**   (Default) Finds only records containing values that exactly match the search string.

- **Any Part of Field**   Finds records whose field contains the search string anywhere in the field. For example, if you want to find all work orders with the word *heater* somewhere in the description, you would ask Access to find a match anywhere in the field.

- **Start of Field**   Specifies the first one or more characters to match with the field values. For example, if you want to locate records for all customers whose last name begins with the letter *A*, you would use the Start of Field option.

Several wildcard characters can be used in the search string to represent one or more characters. For example, if you know only part of the value you want to find or if you want to find records that match a specific pattern, wildcards can be used in the search string.

Wildcards can be mixed and matched to create the string combination you need. Most of them can also be used in queries and expressions, as you will see in Chapters 8 and 9. Table 6-3 describes the wildcard characters and gives examples of how each can be used.

Tip   *While wildcards are intended for use in search strings that locate values in Text and Memo fields, they can sometimes be used with dates and other data types. If you changed the Regional and Language Settings properties for the other data types, the wildcards probably won't work.*

Wildcards can appear anywhere in the search string in the Find What box. For example, you can enter the string **12##[BC]*** to find all addresses in the 1200 block of any street that begins with *B* or *C*.

Tip   *If you included A inside the square brackets, Access would also find addresses on streets with Avenue as part of the street name.*

Finding Blank Fields

As mentioned in Chapter 4 in the discussion of zero-length strings and null values, you can use Find to locate records with blank fields. This is useful when you enter incomplete record data because all the information wasn't yet available. Then, when more data arrives, you can quickly look for the records that need to be filled in.

Wildcard	Matches	Example
*	Any number of characters	**b*** finds "bird," "belt," and "blueberry"
?	Any single character	**b??l** finds "ball," "beal," "bell," "bowl," but not "bali" or "bal"
[]	Any character within the brackets	**b[aeo]ll** finds "ball," "bell," and "boll," but not "bill" or "bull"
!	Any character not in the brackets	**b[!ae]ll** finds "bill," "boll," and "bull," but not "ball" or "bell"
- (hyphen)	Any character in the specified range of characters. The range must be in ascending order	**B[a-d]t** finds "bat," "bbt," "bct," and "bdt"
#	Any single numeric character	**10#** finds "100," "101," "102," and so on, but not "10A"

TABLE 6-3   Wildcard Characters

To find blank fields, enter **Null** or **Is Null** in the Find What text box. When Access finds a record with a blank in the field, the record selector moves to the record, but the field isn't highlighted. When you close the Find and Replace dialog box, the insertion point appears in the blank field, ready for you to enter data. To find a zero-length string, type a pair of quotation marks: "".

If you created a custom format for a Text or Memo field, which specifies a certain display if the field contains a null value and a different display if it contains a zero-length string, you need to watch how you apply the Search Fields As Formatted option.

Looking for Wildcard Characters

The field value you're looking for could include one of the characters Access recognizes as a wildcard, such as an asterisk (*), a question mark (?), a number sign (#), an opening bracket ([), or a hyphen (-). If you use the character directly in a search string, Access treats it like a wildcard.

When you use wildcards in a string to look for one of these characters, you must enclose the item you're looking for in brackets. For example, to find a value that begins with *?B*, you would use the string **[?]B***.

But if you're looking for a hyphen along with another wildcard character, you need to treat it a little differently. Access interprets a hyphen (-) or a tilde (~) as an indication of a sequence of acceptable characters. You must place it before or after all the other characters inside the brackets, not between them. So if you placed an exclamation point (!) inside the brackets to indicate a match excluding the characters within the brackets, you would place the hyphen right after the exclamation point inside the brackets.

If you're searching for an exclamation point or a closing bracket, you do not need to use the brackets at all. Just place the characters in the string with the rest.

In addition, be sure to select Whole Field in the Match box when you're looking for either a null value or a zero-length string.

Finding and Replacing Data

A variation of the Find feature is the Replace tool, which lets you specify a value you want in the field in place of the one already there. The search options are the same. The only difference between the Find tab and the Replace tab is the addition of the Replace With box in which you type the replacement value.

To replace a certain value in a field with another value, on the Home tab's Find group, click the Find command and open the Replace tab.

For example, suppose you want to replace all occurrences of the word *Lost* in the Award Date field of the Bid Data with the words *Not awarded*. Follow these steps:

1. Place the insertion point in the Award Date column.

2. If you already have the Find dialog box open, click the Replace tab.

3. Enter **Lost** in the Find What box and **Not Awarded** in the Replace With box. Notice you have the same search options as with finding records.

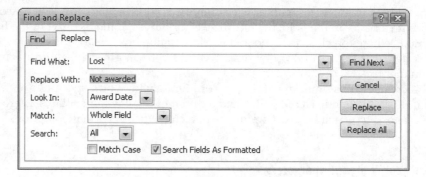

4. Click Find Next, and then do one of the following:

   - Choose Replace to replace this instance of Lost. Access moves automatically to the next occurrence.

   - Choose Find Next to skip replacing this occurrence and move to the next.

   - Choose Replace All to replace all the values without reviewing them individually.

5. Access displays a message when it finishes searching the records. Click Cancel to close the dialog box.

If you have a large amount of data to replace, you can do that faster by using an update query. The only disadvantage is that the update query replaces all the values without your confirmation of individual replacements. If you want to find and replace values in more than one field, the update query isn't as convenient as Find and Replace.

NOTE *As with searching for a value, if the datasheet contains a subdatasheet or the form contains a subform, the replacement occurs only in the object containing the insertion point.*

Setting Edit/Find Options

Many of the Edit and Find options you choose in the Find and Replace dialog box have default settings that can be changed in the Access Options window. Click the Microsoft Office button and then click the Access Options button. In the left pane, choose Advanced to see the Editing group of settings (see Figure 6-12).

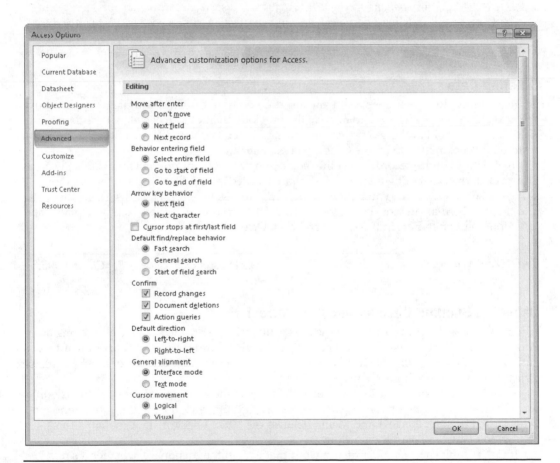

FIGURE 6-12   Setting default Find and Replace behavior

The Default Find/Replace Behavior options present combinations of the Search and Match settings in the Find and Replace dialog box as follows:

- **Fast Search**   Searches the current field and matches the whole field.

- **General Search**   Searches all fields and matches any part of the field.

- **Start of Field Search**   Searches the current field and matches the beginning characters in the field.

CAUTION *The Confirm options specify when Access is to display a confirmation message: before changing records, deleting a document, or running action queries. A good idea is to leave these options all enabled, because these actions cannot be reversed by the Undo button on the Quick Access toolbar.*

Deleting Data

To delete individual characters, place the insertion point in the field and press DEL to remove the next character or BACKSPACE to remove the previous character. To delete all the data in the field, select the field and press DEL or BACKSPACE. Characters deleted from a field can be restored by clicking Undo on the Quick Access toolbar.

To delete an entire record, select the record and press DEL, or on the Home tab's Records group, click the Delete down arrow and choose Delete Record. Deleting a record cannot be reversed, so Access warns you before the deletion. To delete several records, select them all, and then proceed as previously described. To delete a record without selecting it, place the insertion point anywhere in the record and click Delete Record.

TIP *If you need to delete many records, you might be able to use a Delete query. See Chapter 9 for more information.*

Using the Spelling Checker and AutoCorrect

Among the most helpful editing tools is the spelling checker, which can check spelling as you type and offer suggestions for replacing misspelled words. The AutoCorrect feature can automatically correct commonly misspelled words. Access makes full use of these Microsoft Office grammar and editing tools.

After you enter data in a Text or Memo field, select the records, columns, or fields you want to check, and then on the Home tab's Records group, click the Spelling command; or press F7. To check all the Text and Memo fields in the table, select the table name in the Navigation Pane and start the spelling checker.

If the spelling checker encounters a word that isn't in the dictionary, whether it's mis-spelled or simply not recognized, it displays a Spelling dialog box. If the word resembles one in the dictionary, a list of suggestions from which to choose is presented. You can accept one of the suggestions, enter a new word, add the word to your dictionary, or ignore it altogether.

You can specify some of the spelling options, such as what suggestions to make, what types of errors to ignore, and which language dictionary to use as a reference.

If you want Access to correct misspelled words and those you habitually mistype as you enter text, activate the AutoCorrect feature. This feature can also be used to replace abbreviations with longer words. For example, you could speed data entry by having Access convert

Jr to *Junior*. When you type **Jr** and press SPACEBAR, TAB, ENTER, or a punctuation mark, Access automatically replaces it with *Junior*.

To start automatic correction, click the Microsoft Office button and click Access Options. Select Proofing in the left pane then click AutoCorrect Options. The dialog box (see Figure 6-13) offers five options, plus a list of corrections and other replacements it's prepared to make:

- Correct TWo INitial CApitals
- Capitalize first letter of sentences
- Capitalize names of days
- Correct accidental use of cAPS LOCK key
- Replace text as you type

The fifth option contains a list of replacements for many typical spelling errors. You can add more replacements to the list. The AutoCorrect feature is used by all the Microsoft Office programs. Any entries you make in other programs are applicable to misspellings in Access.

You can also specify exceptions to the AutoCorrect rules by clicking the Exceptions button in the AutoCorrect dialog box. The First Letter tab contains a list of common abbreviations, all ending with a period. Normally, Access assumes a period signals the end of a sentence and capitalizes the first letter of the next word. To add to the list of exceptions, type the entry (with the period) in the Don't Capitalize After box and click Add. To remove one from the list, select the entry and click Delete. The INitial CAps tab contains a single entry: IDs. To add more, type the text in the Don't Change box and click Add.

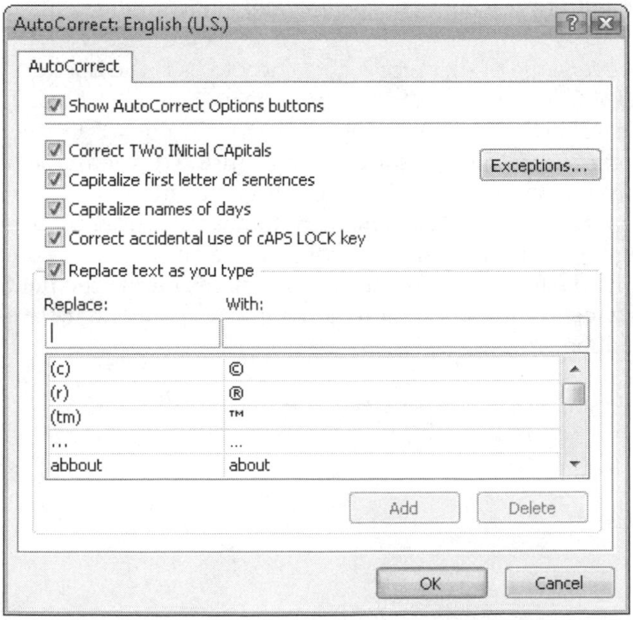

FIGURE 6-13   Setting AutoCorrect options

Caution *Because these tools are shared by all Microsoft Office programs, any changes you make will affect users of other programs.*

Printing Table Data

The quickest way to print table data is to click the Microsoft Office button, point to Print and choose Quick Print in the context menu with the table open or with the table name selected in the Navigation Pane. This sends the data directly to the default printer.

Note *If you want to print the subdatasheet data, expand the subdatasheet before printing.*

If you want to choose other print options, such as printing multiple copies or printing only the selected records, you need to open the Print dialog box. Click the Microsoft Office button and point to Print, and then click Print Preview. This opens the Print Preview window to show you how the printed data looks before you print it. This is a useful way to check whether the data fits across the page with the current page layout. If you want to adjust the page margins, paper size, or the page layout, use the commands in the Page Layout group on the Print Preview tab.

See Chapter 14 for complete information about previewing and printing reports, including changing print options and page setup.

Summary

Access 2007 includes many tools that make data entry and editing quicker and easier. Many of the table field properties can be set to ensure valid and complete data in all the tables in your database.

One of the most versatile of the Access data entry tools is the Lookup Wizard, which helps you create a list from which to choose the proper value for a field. The list can retrieve values from another table or merely specify a set of fixed values. Specifying a default value for a commonly occurring field value can save time during data entry, while adding a field or record validation rule can guard against incorrect data entry.

Access provides many ways to customize the appearance of your Datasheet view, including changing the column width and order, hiding and freezing columns, adjusting the row height, changing the font and cell appearance, and changing the field names.

The next chapter begins the discussion of manipulating table data by sorting and filtering the information.

PART

II

Retrieving and Presenting Information

Sorting, Filtering, and Printing Records

Once you've stored information in the related tables of your database, you need to be able to retrieve specific data and arrange it in meaningful ways. The Access Sort and Filter features help you do that. *Sorting* arranges the records in a specified order, while *filtering* hides records you don't want to see. Combining these two tools gives you the power to display only the records you want in the order you want.

Sorting Records

Access automatically sorts records by the value in the primary key field. During data retrieval and presentation, times will occur when you'll want the records arranged in a different order. For example, you might want to look up all the work orders sorted by the employee who's acting as the supervisor, so you can keep tabs on the workload.

To see records with this information grouped together in Datasheet or Form view, you can sort the records based on the value in a specific field. In Datasheet view, you can sort up to 255 characters in one or more fields to achieve a sort within a sort. The ascending sort order arranges text values in alphabetical order (*A* to *Z*), date/time values from earliest to latest, and number/currency values from lowest to highest. In ascending order, Yes/No fields sort by Yeses first, and then Nos. Use descending order to reverse the order. You can sort on Memo fields using the first 255 characters. Access sorts Hyperlink fields by the Text to Display (if any) or the address. You cannot sort on OLE Object or Attachment fields.

Sorting on a Single Field

To sort by a single field in a datasheet or form, click within the field you want to sort by, and then on the Home tab in the Sort & Filter group, do one of the following:

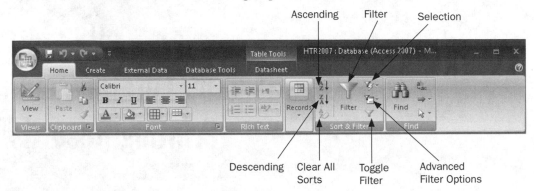

- Click the Ascending command.
- Click the Descending command.
- Right-click in the field and choose Sort A to Z from the shortcut menu.
- Right-click in the field and choose Sort Z to A from the shortcut menu.

To restore the records to their original order, on the Home tab's Sort & Filter group, click the Clear All Sorts command.

NOTE *If the field is a Number field, you will see Sort Smallest to Largest and Sort Largest to Smallest in the shortcut menu. If it is a Date/Time field, the choices are Oldest to Newest or Newest to Oldest. With Yes/No fields, you can choose Selected to Cleared or Cleared to Selected where Selected means "yes" and Cleared means "no."*

To sort records in a subdatasheet, display the subdatasheet by clicking the expand indicator (+) in the left margin, and then proceed as with a datasheet. When you specify a sort order for one subdatasheet in Datasheet view, all the subdatasheets of that level are also sorted accordingly.

When several records have the same value in one of the fields you want to sort by, you can sort on two or more fields at the same time in Datasheet view. In Form view, records can be sorted by only one field with the Sort feature.

Sorting by Two or More Fields

To sort by more than one field, the sorted fields must be adjacent in the datasheet. In addition, Access uses a sort precedence from left to right, so the records are sorted first by the values in the left column. If duplicate values appear in that column, a secondary sort is performed on those records by the values in the next column to the right. If the columns involved in the sort aren't adjacent or are in the wrong relative position in the datasheet or subdatasheet, you must move the columns before sorting the records. When all are in position, select the columns you want to sort on and click one of the Sort commands or choose a command from the shortcut menu.

The Employees Last Name and First Name columns are repositioned and selected, ready to sort by values in those fields. The records are sorted first by Last Name, and then, where these names are the same, by First Name.

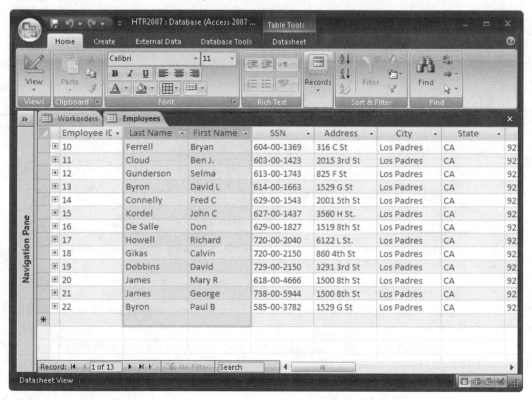

Saving the Sort Order

If you close the table after sorting the records, Access asks if you want to save the changes to the design (this includes the sort order). Responding No saves the table in the original, primary key order. Responding Yes saves the sort order with the table and, the next time you open the table, the records appear in that order. In addition, any new forms or reports you create based on the table inherit the sort order and apply it to the new object.

Filtering Records

When you want to see only certain records in your datasheet, subdatasheet, or form, you can filter out those you don't want to see. The *filter* process screens the records and lets through only those that meet your criteria. The *criteria* is a set of conditions you specify to limit the display to a certain subset of records.

Filtering can help you save time by displaying only the records that are important to you at the moment. Filtering doesn't remove the records from the table, it only removes them from your view of the table. A filter consists of conditions you specify, which can be as simple as "all the records for work orders in October 2007" or as complex as "all bids submitted during June or July that exceeded $750 and were awarded within 30 days of the bid offer."

The difference between finding records and filtering records is this: when Access finds a record, the cursor moves to the record and all the others remain on the screen. With a filter, the nonqualifying records are removed from the screen, leaving only the records you want to see. They all remain in the table, however.

In Access, you have four ways to filter records, depending on the conditions you want to set and whether you want the records sorted in a particular order:

- Common context filters are available in the shortcut menus depending on the field type.

- *Filter By Selection* leaves only the records with the same value as the one you select in one of the records or the records that don't include the same value.

- *Filter By Form* screens records with the criteria you enter into a table skeleton.

- *Advanced Filter/Sort* gives you, in addition to filtering, the capability of specifying a complex sort. With a *complex sort*, you can sort the records by two or more fields using different orders—ascending or descending.

When the records you see on the screen are the result of a filter, Access reminds you in four ways that you aren't viewing the entire table:

- The status bar displays *Filtered*.

- The Record Navigation bar gives you the number of records qualified by the word (Filtered).

- The Toggle Filter command is highlighted and its ScreenTip has changed to Remove Filter.

- A funnel icon in the column header of the filtered field displays a ScreenTip with the condition of the filter.

Sorting Tips

If you stored numbers in a Text field, they're sorted as a character string instead of by numeric value. However, you can get around this by filling out the values with leading zeros, so the strings are all the same length. For example, the result of sorting the values 5, 15, 33, 242 in a Text field would be 15, 242, 33, 5. But, if you store them as 015, 005, 033, and 242, they're sorted properly in numeric order. Better yet, convert the field to a Number data type if you're sure it won't ever contain letters or other characters.

When you sort records by two or more fields, Access performs a "simple" sort, in which the values in the fields are all sorted in the same order, ascending or descending. It won't mix ascending and descending orders. To mix sort orders, you must use the Advanced Filter/Sort operation described in the section "Filtering with Advanced Filter/Sort" later in this chapter.

A filter stays with the table until you remove it or create another one. On the Home tab's Sort & Filter group, you can click the Remove Filter command to see all the records again. You can also remove the filter by clicking the Filtered button in the Record Navigation bar or click the Filter icon in the column header and choose Clear Filter from *field name*.

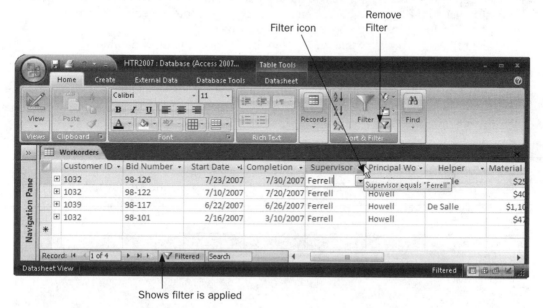

Shows filter is applied

When you apply a filter to a datasheet, the same filter is applied to any subdatasheets within it. When you create a filter on a subdatasheet, the filter is also available when you open the table in Datasheet view.

If you also want the records sorted as part of the filter process, you must use the Advanced Filter/Sort. You can, however, sort the results of the other types of filters after applying the filter by clicking one of the Sort commands in the Sort & Filter group.

Choosing a Filter Type

To decide what type of filter you should use, first think about what you want it to do:

- If you want to search for records that meet more than one criterion at the same time (combined with AND), you can use any of the five types of filters. Using Filter By Selection, you must specify and apply the criteria one at a time.

- If you want to combine criteria with the OR operator or enter expressions as criteria, you must use Filter By Form, Filter For, or Advanced Filter/Sort.

If you also want the records sorted as part of the filter process, you must use the Advanced Filter/Sort. You can, however, sort the results of the other types of filters after applying the filter by clicking one of the Sort commands in the Sort & Filter group.

Filtering by Context

Access 2007 provides many common filter options that are type-specific. These common filters are available in every view that displays data. The set of specific filters that are available depends on the type of data and the values in the selected column. All you have to do is right-click in the field and choose an option from the context menu. You can filter by the displayed value or by a selected partial value in the field.

Context filters are not available for Yes/No, OLE Object, or Attachment fields.

Filtering by Complete Value

As an example of filtering by a complete value, open the Workorders table in the Home Tech Repair database and place the insertion point in a Supervisor field with the value "Ferrell." Then right-click in the field and choose from the four options:

- **Equals**   Limits the display to exact matches.
- **Does Not Equal**   Displays all records without "Ferrell".
- **Contains**   Displays all records in which "Ferrell" is included in the field.
- **Does Not Contain**   Displays all records without "Ferrell" anywhere in the field.

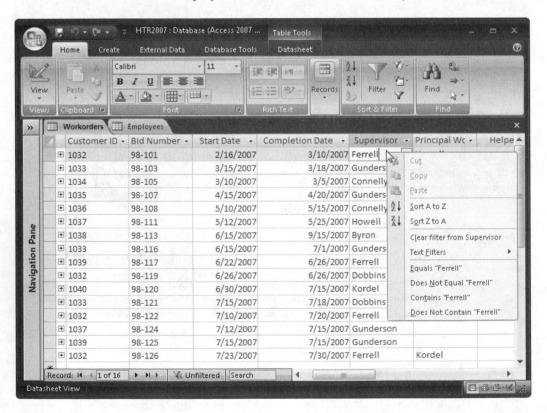

If you want to see additional options, point to Text Filters, and several more choices will appear in the context menu for matching with the selected value.

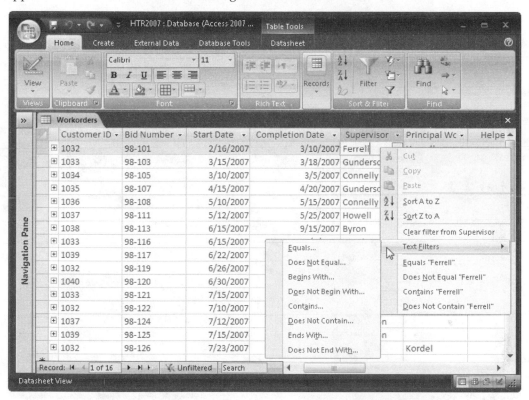

When you choose one of the Text Filter options, such as Equals, a Custom Filter dialog box opens, where you can enter the value you want to use as the filter.

When you filter by a Date field, the context menus offer relevant options. For example, right-click in the Completion Date field and choose from the same four options that applied to the Text field. If you want more options, point to Date Filters to see more type-specific filters.

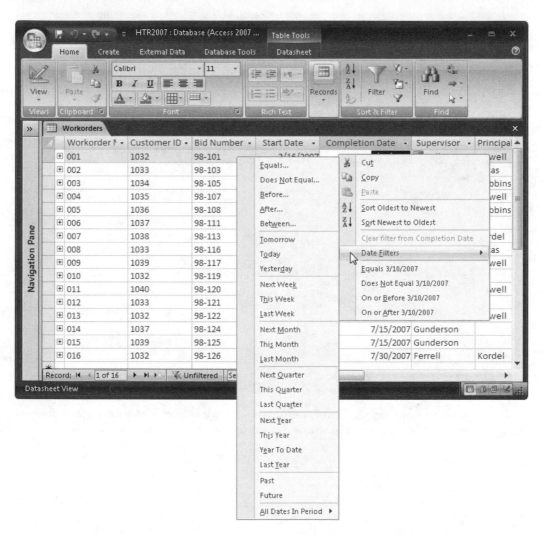

Filtering by Partial Values

If you want to filter on only part of the value in a field, select the characters you want to use and then right-click in the field. You can choose records with the selected characters somewhere in the field or at the end of the field. If you selected characters embedded in the value, you have only the choice of displaying records containing or not containing the selected value.

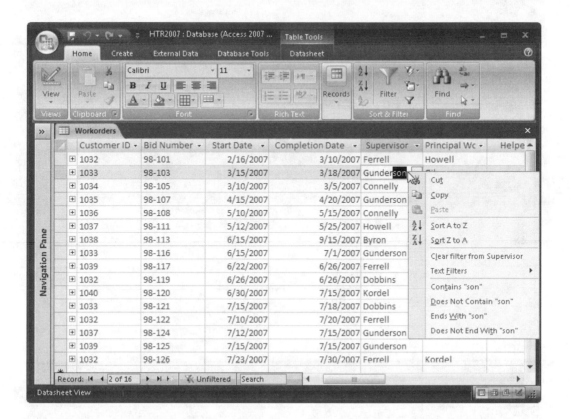

Using the Filter Command

With the insertion bar in a field in the datasheet, you can use the Filter command to limit records by individual values or by the text filters shown in the preceding paragraphs. On the Home tab's Sort & Filter group, click the Filter command. All the values are checked in the list and will be included in the filter unless you uncheck them. You can do that one at a time or, if you only want a short list of values, uncheck Select All and check just those values you want to see. Use the vertical scroll bar to see all the values for the field.

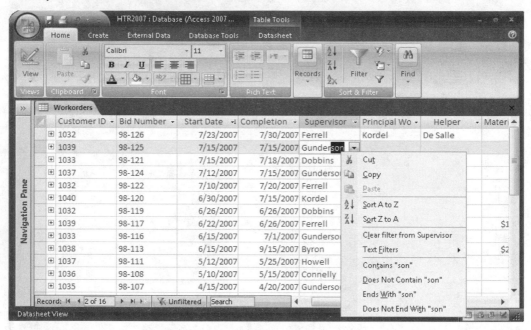

NOTE *You can also click the Filter icon in the column header to see the list of values and other options.*

If the field is a Date/Time data type, you also have the option of screening by date criteria. Rest the mouse pointer on Date Filters to see the options. If it is a Text data type, you can use the Text Filters options.

The Filter command also offers to clear any filters from the selected field.

Filter By Selection

Filter By Selection provides another quick and easy way to limit the records to those with the currently selected value. If you want to filter the Workorders to those for a particular customer, for example, simply click in the row that contains the customer's ID and on the Home tab's Sort & Filter group, click the Selection command. You will see the same choices that appear when you right-click in the field.

Date/Time fields offer more choices. Let's see which work orders will be completed during the month of July 2007.

1. Click in the Completion Date field in any row.
2. On the Home tab's Sort & Filter group, click Selection.

3. Choose Between to open the Between Dates dialog box.

4. Enter the Oldest and Newest dates or use the Calendar buttons to select the dates.

5. Click OK to return to the table now filtered to work orders that are scheduled to be completed in July 2007 (see Figure 7-1).

You can also use the Filter By Selection to filter to a few selected characters or numbers. This works the same as when you use the context filters. The filter choices depend on where the selected characters appear in the value.

- If the characters are at the beginning of the value, the choices are Begins With or Does Not Begin With as well as Contains or Does Not Contain.

- If the characters are within the value, the choices are Contains or Does Not Contain.

- If the characters are at the end of the value, the choices are Ends With or Does Not End With as well as Contains or Does Not Contain.

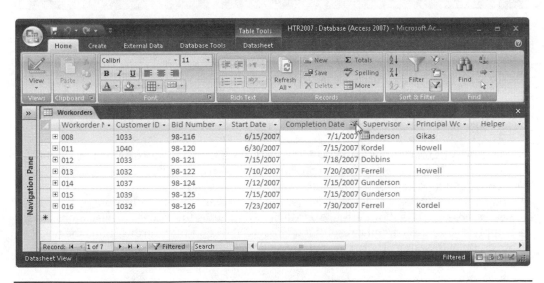

FIGURE 7-1   Filtering to work orders to be completed in July 2007

As an example of filtering to a partial value, filter the Bid Data table so that you see only records that contain the word *heater* in the Description field.

1. In the Bid Data datasheet, select the *heater* part of Replace Waterheater in the Description field of the Bid Number 98-102 record.

2. On the Home tab's Sort & Filter group, click the Selection command and choose Ends with "heater" from the context menu. Two records remain, both with the word *heater* in the Description field.

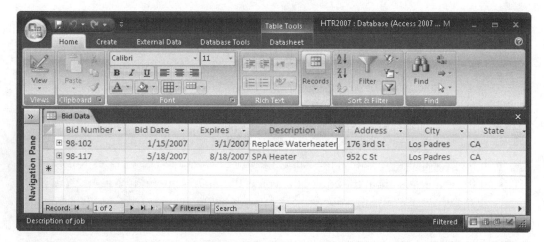

3. To remove the filter, click the Filtered button in the Record Navigation bar.

If the field is a Date/Time field, you also have the option of entering Beginning and Ending Dates.

NOTE *You cannot filter multivalued fields using a partial selection. The selection command is not available for Attachment fields.*

Filter By Selection applies only one filter condition at a time. If you need to filter based on a combination of two or more values, you can apply the second Filter By Selection criterion to the records that remain after the first filter is applied. This is equivalent to combining the filter criteria with an AND operator. For example, you might want to see records for work orders for heater jobs supervised by Ferrell. Apply a filter that limits the records to heater jobs, and then apply a second filter to the results of the first. The second filter further limits the result to records with both values. The order of applying the filters doesn't make any difference; the result is the same either way. When you click the Remove Filter command, the entire filter is removed, not only the last one you applied.

TIP *If you press* TAB *to reach the Drawing field (don't click it or you'll jump to the hyperlink target), and then click Filter By Selection, you can see all the records that refer to the same drawing. For example, the Bay Window drawing is used for three work orders.*

Filter By Form

Filter By Form is one of the choices in the Advanced Filter Options context menu. Filter By Form isn't much different from Filter By Selection. Instead of selecting a value from the datasheet or subdatasheet as a filter criterion, you enter the value in a filter grid. The *grid* is a table skeleton that resembles a blank record showing all the filterable fields in the table with space to enter filter values. One advantage of using Filter By Form is that you can combine filter criteria. You can specify two or more conditions, so a record must meet any one or all of them to survive the filter. The multiple criteria can apply to a single field or to more than one field.

If you want to filter the records in a subdatasheet, click the expand indicator to display the subdatasheet records, and then proceed as with a datasheet filter.

NOTE   *You can't use Filter By Form for Memo, Hyperlink, Yes/No, or OLE Object fields.*

Entering Filter Criteria

When you click the Advanced Filter Options command and choose Filter By Form in the context menu, the table grid similar to the one here appears on the screen. The most recent filter saved with the table appears in the filter grid. Notice that Access has created an expression from your Filter By Selection criterion. The expression *Like "*Heater"* means that all records that have a value in the Description field ending with *heater* will be shown.

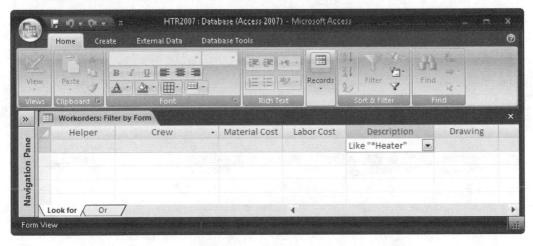

TIP   *The asterisk in front of the word* Heater *in the filter indicates the characters you selected appeared at the end of the value. The filter shows all other records that end with* heater. *If you want records with the value anywhere in the field, add another asterisk, so the filter becomes Like "*Heater*".*

Right-click in the Filter By Form tabbed document to see three useful commands:

- **Apply Filter/Sort**   Runs the filter.
- **Delete Tab**   Removes one of the Or tabs.

- **Clear Grid** Removes the filter that appears in the skeleton, so you do not need to delete every entry individually.
- **Close** Lets you return to the datasheet without applying any filter.

To create a new filter, use the Clear Grid command in the shortcut menu to clear the grid of any existing filter; then move to the field where you want to specify a value. When you move the insertion point to a field in the grid, an arrow appears in the field. Clicking this arrow displays a list of unique values that currently exist in the field, sorted in ascending order—for example, the list of values in the Completion Date field of the Workorders table (as shown next). To filter on one of these values, select the value, and then right-click and choose Apply Filter/Sort from the shortcut menu. This is equivalent to using Filter By Selection.

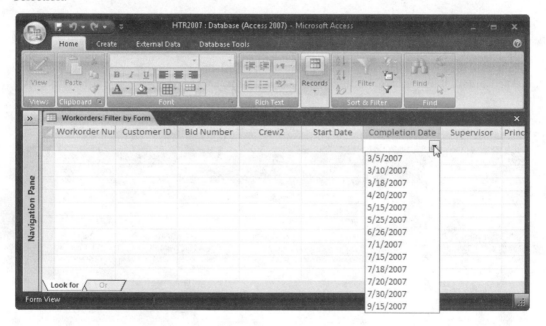

NOTE *If the table has many unique values in a field, Access might not build the list of values. Instead, you see only two choices: Is Null and Is Not Null. See the section "Optimizing Filter By Form" later in this chapter for information about setting the maximum number you want to show in the list. More about customizing your workplace in Chapter 16.*

NOTE *If you display a value list in one of the employee-related fields (Supervisor, Principal Worker, or Helper), you see the values in the lookup table you created in the last chapter. The values in the list are for display only. Access stores the value from the primary key field of the lookup list in the Workorders table. This creates a bit of a problem, as you can see in the section "Filtering with Advanced Filter/Sort" later in this chapter.*

To filter Workorders records to show only those whose scheduled completion date is before July 1, 2007, follow these steps:

1. On the Home tab's Sort & Filter group, click the Advanced Filter Options command and choose Filter By Form from the context menu. The filter grid appears.

2. If entries are in the grid, right-click below the grid and choose Clear Grid from the shortcut menu to remove them.

3. Place the insertion point in the Completion Date field and select 7/1/2007 from the value list. Access automatically adds the date/time delimiter symbols (#) to the date you select from the list.

4. Place the insertion point at the beginning of the date and enter < (less than). You can also press F2 to switch to Edit mode, press HOME, and then enter <.

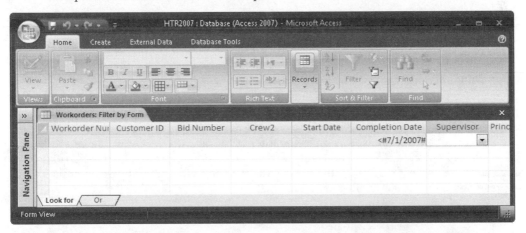

5. Click the Apply Filter command. Only the eight records of Workorders table scheduled to be completed before July 1, 2007, remain on the screen.

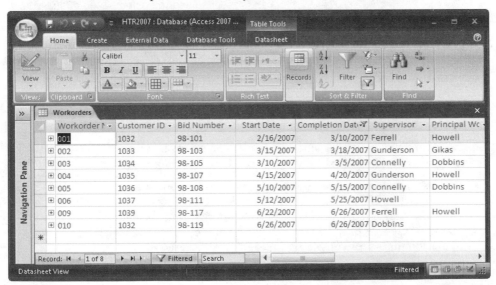

Filtering Memo, OLE Object, and Hyperlink Fields

When you apply Filter By Selection to a Memo, OLE Object, or Hyperlink field, you can see all the records with the same values in the field. But, with the other three filter operations, you can filter based only on whether the field has a value or is empty. When you click the drop-down list in one of these fields, the only available values are Is Blank and Is Not Blank. This filter option is also available for calculated fields in queries.

---

6. To remove the filter, right-click in the column and choose Clear Filter from Completion Date from the shortcut menu.

To remove all filters you have created for the table, on the Home tab's Sort & Filter group, click the Advanced command and choose Clear All Filters from the context menu.

NOTE *The Apply Filter button in the Sort & Filter group is named Toggle Filter until you have created a filter for this object. After the first filter is defined, the button changes to Apply Filter or Remove Filter, depending on whether a filter is active.*

Using Wildcards and Expressions in a Filter

You can use wildcards in filter criteria for Text and Memo fields the same way as in the Find criteria. Wildcards apply only to character strings. (Refer to Chapter 6 for examples of using wildcards.)

You can also enter an expression as the filter criterion, such as the earlier example of < 7/1/07 entered in the Completion Date field in the Filter By Form grid. To use an expression as a criterion, enter it directly in the filter grid. The following table shows examples of expressions you can use as filter criteria.

Address	Like "*3rd*"	Displays records with addresses on 3rd Street or Avenue.
Completion Date	Between #5/1/07# And #7/31/07#	Displays Workorders records for all jobs scheduled to be completed during May, June, and July 2007.
Last Name	>="P*"	Displays records for Customers whose last name starts with letters *P* through *Z*.
Bid Date	Year([Bid Date])=2007	Uses the Year() function to display Bid Data records with Bid Dates in 2007.
Workorder #	Is Null	Displays Bid Data records with empty Workorder # fields.

You need to obey a few rules when entering expressions in a filter condition, whether you're using the Filter By Form or the Advanced Filter/Sort method:

- If a Text field value contains a space, any punctuation, or an operator character, the value must be enclosed in quotation marks. For example, entering **George** is OK, but if the first and last name must be included, it must be entered with quotation marks—**"George Bart"**. If the entry is one of the values in the list, Access adds the quotation marks for you after you leave the filter grid.

- To filter a Memo field, use asterisk (*) wildcards to filter on embedded text.

- For Number, Currency, and AutoNumber fields, don't include characters, such as the currency symbol or the thousands separator. If you do, you'll see a data type mismatch error message. Decimal points and minus signs are OK.

- For Date/Time field values, abide by the options set on the Date tab of the Regional and Language Settings Properties dialog box of the Windows Control Panel. These settings control the sequence of the month, day, and year values within the field. Access encloses the date or time value in pound signs (#).

- For Yes/No fields, you can enter Yes, -1, On, or True to filter for Yes values, or you can enter No, 0, Off, or False for No values.

Combining Filter Criteria with AND

You can use complex criteria that combine two or more filter conditions in the Filter By Form window. If you combine two conditions with the AND operator, you're limiting the records to those that meet both conditions. For example, you could ask Access to limit the Workorders records only to those with a Material Cost less than $1000 and a Labor Cost greater than $500. This would give you a list of labor-intensive contracts.

To combine two filter conditions with AND:

1. With the Workorders table open in Datasheet view, click the Advanced Filter Options command in the Sort & Filter group and choose Filter By Form from the context menu.

2. Right-click in the tabbed document and choose Clear Grid from the shortcut menu to remove the previous filter conditions. Then click in the Material Cost field.

3. Click the down arrow to display the stored values in the Material Cost fields (values appear without the dollar signs, which are part of the display format and not stored with the values).

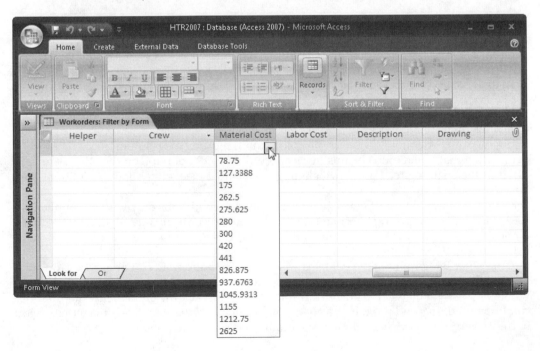

4. Type **<=1000** and press TAB to move to the Labor Cost field, and type **>=500**. Then press ENTER.

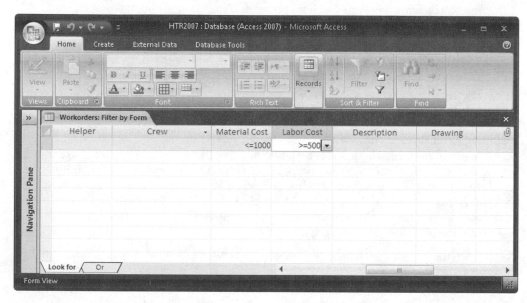

5. Click the Apply Filter command. Four records meet the combined filter conditions that show the labor-intensive contracts.

6. Click the Remove Filter command to restore all the records in the datasheet.

NOTE *The preceding example combined filter conditions in different fields with the implied AND operator. You can also combine filter conditions in the same field with AND by typing AND between the expressions. For example, if you enter the filter condition >=500 AND <=1000 in the Material Cost field, you would see only the records for work orders requiring between $500 and $1000 worth of materials, inclusive. Another way to express the same criterion is to use the BETWEEN…AND…operator: BETWEEN 500 AND 1000.*

Combining Filter Conditions with OR

Using the AND operator to combine filter conditions reduces the resulting record set by demanding that both criteria be met in each record. The OR operator, on the other hand, expands the resulting record set by including records that meet either of the conditions, but not necessarily both.

When you use Filter By Selection, you can combine conditions only with the implied AND operator by imposing a second filter on the set of records already filtered by the first criteria. With Filter By Form, you can apply as many filters as you want in one operation, using both AND and OR operators.

The Filter By Form window contains two tabs at the bottom: Look For and Or. You enter the first filter condition, and any others you want to combine with it, using AND on the Look For page. If you want to add an OR filter condition, click the Or tab and enter the condition on the second page. If you change your mind and want to delete the Or tab, select it, right-click in the grid, and choose Delete Tab from the shortcut menu.

NOTE *Another Or tab appears when you begin to add a filter to the first Or page.*

The OR combination comes in handy when you want to find records with any one of several values in a field. For example, suppose you want to see all the Bid Data records for jobs on B or H Streets. You would enter *** B*** in the Address field in the filter grid on the Look For page and then enter *** H*** in the Address field on the Or page.

TIP *If you don't include a space before the H in the filter criterion, you'll see all records with the letter H anywhere in the Address field. For example, addresses on any numbered street with th, such as 5th or 6th, will appear. The leading space before the H demands that the letter H be the first letter of the word.*

To combine two filter conditions with OR:

1. In the Bid Data datasheet, on the Home tab's Sort & Filter group, click the Advanced Filter Options and choose Filter By Form from the context menu. The Filter window opens with the last filter condition in the grid.

2. Right-click and choose Clear Grid from the shortcut menu; then enter *** B*** (with a space before the *B*) in the Address field on the Look For page, and press ENTER. Access translates the expression to *Like "* B*"*.

3. Click the Or tab. The Or page opens with the same empty grid as the Look For page. Notice a third tab, labeled Or, now showing at the bottom of the window.

4. Place the insertion point in the Address field, enter *** H***, and then press ENTER. The expression is changed to *Like "* H*"*.

5. Click the Apply Filter command. The datasheet now shows the five jobs with addresses on B or H Streets.

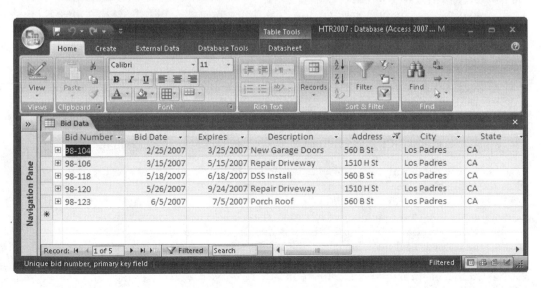

6. Click the Remove Filter command to restore all the records.

AND and OR Can Get Confusing

The logic can get a little confusing when you begin combining filter conditions with both AND and OR. For example, you might want to see all Bid Data records for jobs on B and H Streets that were lost. If the job was lost, *Lost* appears in the Award Date field. Obviously, B and H Streets are combined with the OR operator, but where does the Award Date (Lost) condition go?

The answer is to combine the Award Date filter with both the B and H Street filters using the AND operator in each case. On the Look For page, enter **"Lost"** in the Award Date field in the grid with * B* in the Address field. On the Or page, again enter **"Lost"** in the Award Date field with * H* in the Address field. If you didn't repeat the Lost value in both conditions, you would see all the bids for jobs on B Street that were lost, together with all the jobs bid on H Street, regardless of the outcome.

TIP   If your filter doesn't return any records, you might have set conflicting criteria that were impossible to meet. For example, you might have asked for bids that were for jobs on both B and H Streets, when clearly a job cannot be in two places at once.

Optimizing Filter By Form

In the Filter By Form grid, when you move to a field, you can display the list of unique values stored in that field by clicking the down arrow. To display the list, Access reads all the records and picks out the unique values.

In an extremely large table, the value lists can be quite lengthy and take a long time to display. To improve performance, you can display lists only for indexed fields in the current table and let the user enter the values to look for in the nonindexed fields, instead of choosing from a value list. You can also reduce the number of records to display in the list to less than the default, which is 1000 records.

To make changes in the Filter By Form default settings, click the Microsoft Office button and choose Access Options. Choose Current Database in the left pane and scroll down to Filter Lookup Options for the current database (see Figure 7-2). The Show List of Values In group of options appears:

- **Local Indexed Fields**   Displays value lists for all the indexed fields in the current table.
- **Local Nonindexed Fields**   Displays value lists for other fields in the current table.
- **ODBC Fields**   Displays value lists for linked tables in an external file.

Check only the Local Indexed Fields box to speed up the value list display. If this still takes too long, also clear that option.

The other option that affects Filter By Form is the Default Max Records setting. This represents the maximum number of records Access has to read to come up with the list of unique values. If the number of records exceeds the number in this box, Access stops reading the records and no value list is displayed. The default setting is 1000.

If you checked one or more of the Show List of Values In options and you still don't see a value list for one or more fields in the Filter By Form grid, you might need to increase the number in the Default Max Records field.

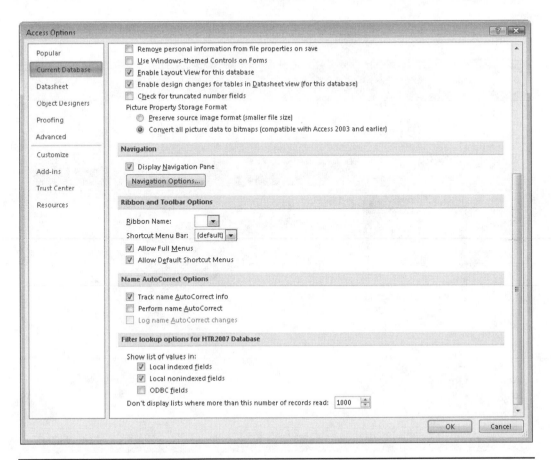

Figure 7-2 Setting the Filter Lookup options for the current database

If you use the same nonindexed field in several filters, you might save time and improve performance by indexing it.

***

Note *Be aware that these option settings apply to the entire database, not only to the current table.*

Filtering with Advanced Filter/Sort

The Advanced Filter/Sort feature is the most flexible and comprehensive of the Access filtering tools. Not only does this feature include all the features of Filter By Form, it also enables you to specify mixed sort orders for different fields in the table. You enter all the filtering and sorting specifications in a single window.

The Advanced Filter/Sort window is divided horizontally into two parts. The upper part contains a box with a list of the fields in the table. The lower part is the design grid where you specify which fields you want to filter, the values to use as filters, and how you want the records sorted in the resulting record set. If you applied a filter recently, the criteria appears in the Criteria row of the grid (as shown next). Right-click and choose Clear Grid from the shortcut menu to remove it.

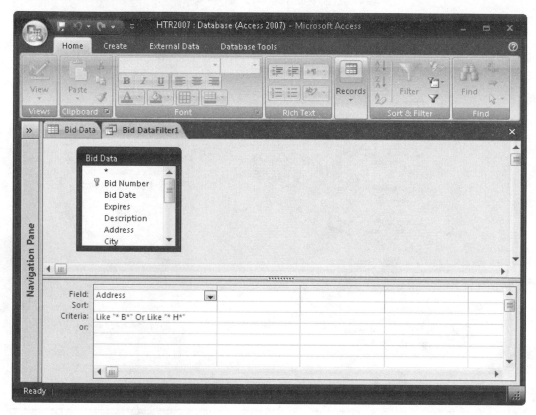

The process of creating an Advanced Filter/Sort is nearly identical to creating a query. See Chapter 8 for the details for creating queries that can be used to create Advanced Filter/Sorts, including the following:

- Selecting fields to filter and sort
- Specifying filter criteria
- Setting sort orders

Applying and Removing the Advanced Filter

Anytime during the design of an advanced filter, you can apply it to see whether you're getting the data you want. Access gives you two ways to apply the advanced filter:

- On the Home tab's Sort & Filter group, click the Apply Filter command.
- Right-click anywhere in the upper section of the Design window and choose Apply Filter/Sort from the shortcut menu.

To remove the filter, do one of the following:

- Click the Remove Filter command.
- Click Filtered in the Record Navigation bar.
- With the insertion point in the filter column, click the filter icon in the column header and choose Clear Filter from *field name*.
- Right-click in a blank area in the filtered table and choose Clear Filter from *field name*.
- To clear all filters for the table, click the Advanced Filter command and choose Clear All Filters from the context menu.

NOTE *You can base a new form or report on a filtered set of records if you create it while the filtered record set is displayed in Datasheet view or if you saved the filter with the table. While the filter and sort properties are inherited by the form or report, you can still override the settings in the form or report property sheets. See Chapter 10 for more information about creating forms and reports and changing their properties.*

Filtering by Lookup Fields with Advanced Filter/Sort

Filtering on a field that gets its value from a lookup list with Advanced Filter/Sort can present a slight problem. When you choose to filter records by values in a lookup field in Filter By Form, you choose from the value list that contains all the values in the lookup list created by the Lookup Wizard. What you don't see in the list are the values actually stored in the field. The value in the primary key field of the lookup list is stored instead of the more informative displayed value.

When you use Advanced Filter/Sort, you don't choose from the lookup list, because only one table is in the Filter window. This means you must enter the stored value in the Criteria row to filter on a lookup field. For example, to filter on *Ferrell* in the Supervisor field of the Workorders table with Filter By Form, you can select Ferrell from the list or type **Ferrell** in the filter grid. To do the same in Advanced Filter/Sort, you must enter **10**, Ferrell's Employee ID number, in the Criteria row.

Modifying a Filter

You use the same techniques to modify a filter that you used to create it. You can add more criteria or change existing ones in any type of filter. You can even switch between Filter windows to see how the filter is progressing or apply the filter during the process to see how the records are selected.

NOTE *When you filter a table, the records you see are limited to those that pass the criteria you set. You still see all the fields in every record. To limit the fields, as well as the records in the resulting set, you need to use a query. Chapter 8 discusses the difference between filters and queries, and suggests ways to help you decide which to use.*

Saving a Filter

The most recent filter is saved with the table—not as a separate object—if you respond Yes to save the table changes. When you reopen the table, the filter is no longer in effect, but you can reapply it by any of the methods discussed earlier. If you create a new filter but want to keep the previous one available with the table, respond No when asked if you want to save the changes. Of course, if you've made other changes you do want to keep, you'll save the filter with them.

If you want to have more than one filter available to a table or want to save a filter permanently, you must save it as a query. Queries are stored as separate Access database objects. When you want to use the filter again, you can bring it back from the query to the Filter window or simply run it as a query.

To save an advanced filter as a query and load it again in the Filter window:

1. With the Filter document tab displayed, right-click anywhere in the design grid and choose Save As Query from the shortcut menu. Access asks for a name for the new query in the Save As Query dialog box.

2. Name the query and click OK.

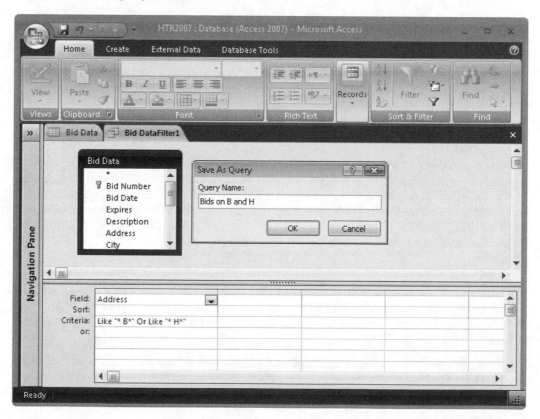

3. To restore the specifications to the Filter window, right-click in an open blank Advanced Filter/Sort window and choose Load From Query from the shortcut menu. The Applicable Filter dialog box shows a list of queries based on the Bid Data table.

4. Choose the query you want and click OK. All the filter parameters are returned to the grid, where you can choose to apply the filter or make changes.

NOTE *If you simply want to filter the records, you can run the query you saved from the filter. If you want to use the query as the basis for a new filter, load the filter from the query and make the changes.*

Removing and Clearing Filters

A difference exists between *removing* and *clearing* a filter. Removing a filter simply returns all the records to the datasheet or form. You can reapply the filter later. Clearing the filter erases the filter criteria and the filter cannot be reapplied without reconstructing it.

Refer to the earlier section, "Applying and Removing the Advanced Filter," for ways to remove a filter from a datasheet or form.

NOTE *When you remove a filter from a datasheet, any filter you applied to a subdatasheet within it is also removed.*

To delete a filter entirely, you need to clear the filter grid and apply the empty filter to the datasheet. On the Home tab's Sort & Filter group, click the Advanced Filter Options command and choose Clear All Filters from the context menu.

Printing Table Data

You do not need to create a fancy report to print your table data. You can print the datasheet as it appears in the Datasheet view or print in the default report format. To print a single copy of the datasheet, click the Microsoft Office button, point to Print, and choose Quick Print from the context menu. If you want to adjust the margin settings, the paper size, or the page layout, use the Page Layout group on the Print Preview tab. If you want to choose other print options—such as multiple copies or selected pages—you need to open the Print dialog box.

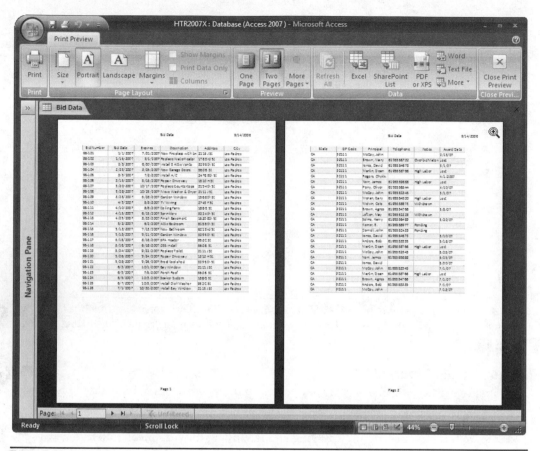

FIGURE 7-3 Previewing the Bid Data datasheet printout

To see how the printed report looks before you print it, click the Microsoft Office button, point to Print, and choose Print Preview from the context menu. This is useful when you think the datasheet might not fit across the page with the current page layout, in which case you can change the page setup before printing the data. For example, Figure 7-3 shows the Bid Data datasheet previewed in two pages.

TIP *The Bid Data datasheet requires three page widths to print all the fields. If the page orientation were changed to Landscape in the Page Setup dialog box, the data would fit on two pages.*

See Chapter 13 for more information about printing data and running the Print Preview and Page Setup features.

Summary

You've now seen how to store information in related database tables and how to retrieve data using different type of filters. Filtering records has some limitations:

- You can limit only the records, not the fields. You can see all the fields of the resulting recordset.

- You can save only one filter or sort order with a table.

- Filtering is limited to records in a single table.

Queries provide an alternative to filters with distinct advantages, such as choosing specific fields from related tables and being stored as separate database objects. The next chapter introduces you to the subject of queries and their applications.

Extracting Information with Queries

When you work with information in an Access datasheet, you can filter and sort the records in many ways, but queries give you even more flexibility. You cannot only limit the records to a specific subset, but you can specify which fields you want to see in the result.

Query is a general term that is synonymous with question, inquiry, or quiz. In Access, to query a database is to ask a question about the information in the database. A query can be about the data in a single table or in multiple related tables.

Access provides several types of queries, ranging from the popular select query that extracts specific data to the more exotic action query that can insert, update, and delete records. This chapter discusses select queries and a few special-purpose queries, while the next chapter covers the more advanced types of queries.

How Do Queries Work?

Several types of queries do quite different things but, in general, an *Access query* is a set of explicit specifications that tell Access exactly what information you want to see and how you want it arranged or manipulated in the results. In the query, you specify the fields you want to include, add selection criteria that limit the records in the resulting recordset, select the desired order for them to appear, and define any summary fields.

With Access queries you can do the following:

- View data from multiple tables sorted in a specific order.
- Perform many types of calculations on selected groups of records.
- Find and display duplicate or unmatched records.
- Update data, delete records, or append new records to a table.
- Create a new table with records from one or more tables.

NOTE *The result of running an ordinary query is called a* dynaset, *which is short for* dynamic subset. *This is called* dynamic *because if you make a change to the data in the dynaset, Access makes the same changes in the data in the tables that provided the basic information. Other types of queries result in a static recordset that cannot be edited, and this result is called a* snapshot.

Access Query Categories

Access queries fall into four general categories: select, special purpose, action, and Structured Query Language (SQL)-specific. A *select query* is the most common category and is used for extracting specific information from one or more tables in a database. The results of a select query are displayed in a datasheet for viewing or editing or are used as the basis for a form or report. With a select query, you can also group records and perform calculations on field values in the groups, such as sum, count, average, minimum, and maximum. Other types of queries can locate duplicate records in a table or unmatched records in a relationship, or they can automatically fill in field data or prompt for criteria.

An example of a *special purpose query* is the *crosstab* (meaning cross-tabulation) query that displays summarized values from one field in the table, grouped in two ways. Other special queries automatically fill in data or prompt for criteria.

Action queries are used to perform global data management operations on tables, such as updating or deleting groups of records, making a new table from an existing one, and appending new records to an existing table.

SQL-specific queries are accessible only through SQL statements. All queries have SQL statements in the background, but SQL-specific queries are constructed with the programming language instead of a design grid like other types of queries.

Access has some query wizards to help create many of these queries. You will learn about the select queries and the special purpose queries you can create with a wizard for now, but you will learn about the more advanced queries in Chapter 9.

When to Use a Filter and When to Use a Query

It might appear that filters and queries do the same thing, but some differences occur in the results. Filters and select queries both retrieve a subset of records from a table or another query. As a rule of thumb, you use a filter to view or edit some records temporarily in a datasheet or form. If you want to return to the subset of records at a later time, you should use a query. Queries are separate database objects that appear in the Navigation Pane, while a single filter is saved with a table.

If you use a query, you do not need to open the table first because a query is an object in its own right. With a filter, you must open the table first before you can view the results of the filter or design a new filter.

You use a query if you want to extract data from multiple tables, control which fields to display, or perform calculations on field values. None of these operations is permitted with filters.

The results of both filters and queries can be used as the source of data for forms and reports. You can also sort the results of both and save the sort order for use in a later work session. Both methods let you edit the data displayed in the results, if editing is otherwise permitted. If you need to extract data from more than one table, select only specific fields to include, or store as a separate object in the database, then you need to use a query. Queries are also required if you want to see the results without opening the underlying table, query, or form, or if you want to include calculated values in the result.

Even if you decide you need to have a query, you can use the easy Filter By Form or Filter By Selection tools to create a filter and then save it as a query. Access translates your filter design into a proper query.

Specific Types of Access Queries
The Access select queries include the following:

- **Simple Select queries**   Display data from one or more tables sorted in a specific order. You can also perform many types of predefined or custom calculations on values in all records or within groups of records.

- **Find Duplicate queries**   Display all records with duplicate values in one or more specified fields. For example, you can query to find customers who have more than one work order. You can include any other fields you want.

- **Find Unmatched queries**   Display records in one table that have no related records in another table. For example, you can query to find customers who have no current work orders.

Special purpose queries include the following:

- **Parameter queries**   Display a dialog box where you enter the criteria for retrieving data or a value to insert into a field. You can apply parameters to other types of queries as well.

- **AutoLookup queries**   Special select queries that automatically fill in certain field values in a new record in one or more tables.

- **Crosstab queries**   Calculate a sum or count and group the results in a spreadsheet format that correlates the data with two types of information—for example, total sales by product and quarter or district.

Action queries include the following:

- **Update queries**   Make global changes to a group of records in one or more tables—for example, raise all labor rates by 15 percent.

- **Append queries**   Add a group of records from one or more tables to the end of one or more other tables.

- **Delete queries**   Remove a specific group of records from one or more tables—for example, remove all records from the Bid Data table with *Lost* in the Award Date field.

- **Make-table queries**   Create a new table out of data from one or more tables.

SQL-specific queries include the following:

- **Union queries**   Combine fields from one or more tables into one field in the result.

- **Pass-Through queries**   Send instructions directly to Open Database Connectivity (ODBC) databases using commands specific to the server.

- **Data-Definition queries**   Create or change database objects in an Access, SQL Server, or other server database.

- **Subqueries**   SQL SELECT or other server statements that form a SELECT query within another query.

Creating Select Queries

If you want to create a select query, you can either start from scratch in the Query Design or choose one of the query wizards to help you. Choosing Query Design takes you directly to the query design window, which looks very similar to the Advanced Filter/Sort window. When you choose a query wizard, you are guided through choices about the basic design of the select query. You can then go to the Design view to customize the query design, if necessary.

On the Create tab's Other group, click either the Query Wizard or the Query Design command.

When you click the Query Wizard command, you can call on the wizards for help with several types of queries. For now, let's create a new query with the help of the Simple Query Wizard.

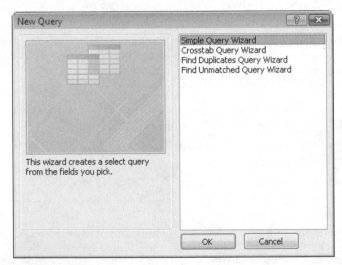

Using the Simple Query Wizard

To start the wizard, select Simple Query Wizard and click OK. The Simple Query Wizard displays a series of dialog boxes in which you specify the fields and records you want to include in the query and enter a name for the saved query. You can include fields from any of the tables or other queries in your database. Figure 8-1 shows the first Simple Query Wizard dialog box.

First, choose the table or query from which you want to see data by clicking the Tables/Queries down arrow and choosing it from the list. To add all the fields from a table, click the double right arrow (>>) to the right of the Available Fields list. To add one field to the Selected

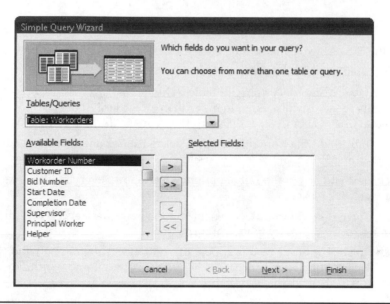

FIGURE 8-1   Choosing which fields to include in the query

Fields list, double-click the field name or select the field in the Available Fields list and click the single right arrow (>). If you change your mind about including a field, double-click it in the Selected Fields list or select it and click the left arrow (<). To add fields from another table, select the table (or query) from the Tables/Queries list box, and then select fields from the new list.

> **TIP** *Double-clicking the field name switches it from one list to the other. The fields will appear in the query result in the order you select them in the first dialog box. You can change the order later in query Design view.*

After you add all the fields you want in the query, click the Next button. The second Simple Query Wizard dialog box gives you two options:

- Create a detail query with all the record data.
- Create a summary query that calculates totals based on the field values. When you choose to summarize field values, you need to specify the summary options in another dialog box, which is discussed later in the section "Summarizing with the Wizard."

> **TIP** *If you haven't selected any Number or Currency type fields, no fields will appear to summarize. The wizard then skips this dialog box and takes you directly to the third and last dialog box.*

In the final wizard dialog box, you enter a name for the query. You also choose whether to view the information immediately or go to the query design window to make modifications to the query.

Let's try the Simple Query Wizard by building a list of current work orders and include information from both the Workorders and Bid Data tables.

To create a Current Workorders query:

1. On the Create tab's Other group, click the Query Wizard command.

2. Select Simple Query Wizard in the New Query dialog box and click OK.

3. Select Table:Workorders from the Tables/Queries list box and use one of the methods previously discussed to move the Workorder Number, Supervisor, Material Cost, Labor Cost, and Description fields to the Selected Fields list.

4. Select Table:Bid Data from the Tables/Queries list box and add the Address, Bid Number, and Principal fields to the Selected Fields list.

5. Click Next and accept the Detail option, which shows every field of every record, and then click Next.

6. Enter **Current Workorders** as the name for the new query and accept the default option to open the query to view information.

7. Click Finish. The query results appear in a datasheet showing only the eight fields you selected, but all the records (see Figure 8-2). The column widths are adjusted in the figure to show all the information.

The wizard has helped you with the basic query definition. Now it's up to you to add the final touches, such as adding selection criteria to limit the records, changing the query and field properties, adding another table, specifying a sort order, or adding calculated fields.

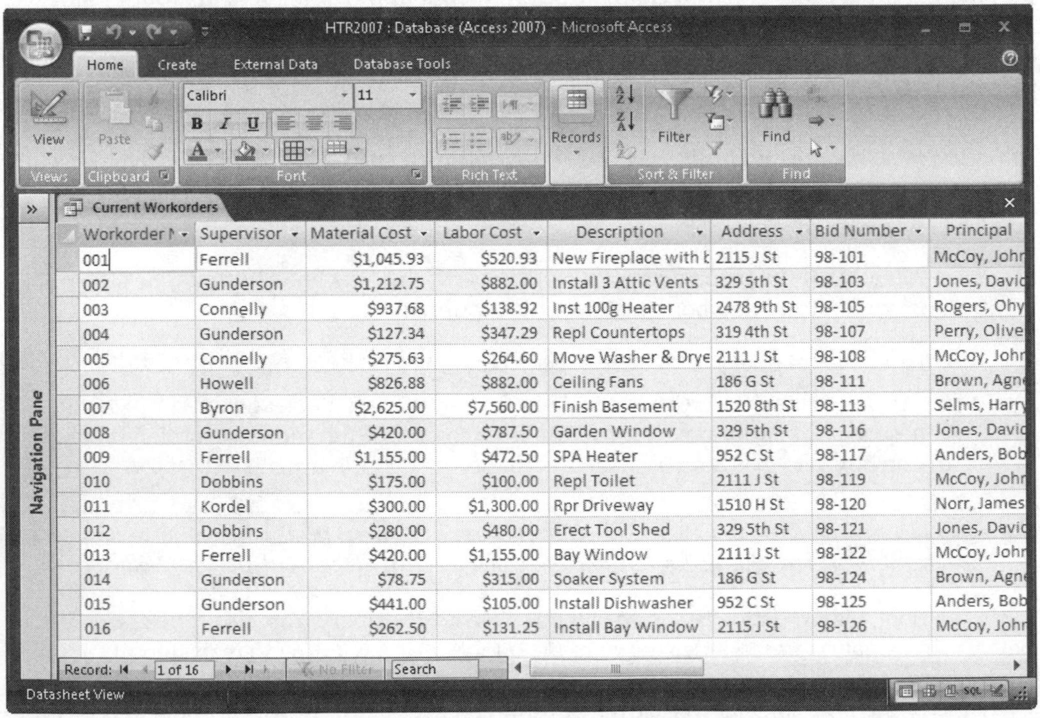

FIGURE 8-2   Viewing the results of the new select query

Touring the Query Design Window

Like most Access objects, a query can be displayed in more than one view. Tables, for example, can be viewed as a datasheet in which you're looking at the data in the table. You can also look at the table in Design view to see the table structure and all the information about the fields, indexes, formats, and so on.

A query, like a table, can be viewed as a datasheet or a design. The *Datasheet view* shows you the data that results when you run the query (refer to Figure 8-2). The *Design view* is where you can look at the query structure and make changes to the query design or even create a new one. The third query view is the *SQL view,* which shows the SQL statements Access creates behind the scenes to implement the query. The SQL view has no counterpart with table objects.

To switch to Design view, right-click the query document tab and choose Design View from the shortcut menu, or on the Design tab's Results group, click the View command and choose Design View from the context menu.

The query design window looks very similar to the Advanced Filter/Sort window with two sections:

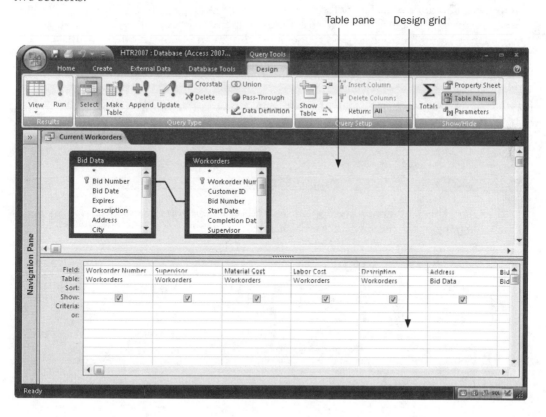

- The upper pane is the table pane, which displays the field lists for all the tables in the query.
- The lower pane is the Query By Example (QBE) design grid, which shows the elements of the query design.

The table pane for the Current Workorders query shows the two tables from which you selected fields: Bid Data and Workorders. Access has accepted the relationship between the tables joining the Bid Number fields.

The design grid shows the field names you selected in the wizard dialog box, including the name of the table (or query) from which they came. The Sort, Criteria, and Or rows are the same as in a filter grid. The check marks in the Show row indicate all the fields are to appear in the result. Clearing the check mark hides the field from the query result. This is helpful when you want to filter or sort the results based on a field that you don't want to appear in the query results.

NOTE *Drag the dividing line between the two panes up or down to change their relative heights. You can also drag the edges of field list boxes in the table pane to enlarge them and see more of the field names. Similarly, you can drag the grid column dividers to change the column width.*

The Query Tools Design ribbon has some new groups and commands. The Results group has commands that change the query view or run the query to see the results before saving the query. The Query Type group offers commands to create all types of queries. The Query Setup group has tools to modify the query design and limit the query results as well as a command to start the Expression Builder. The Show/Hide group includes commands to summarize data, view and change query properties, take the table names off the design grid, and create a parameter query.

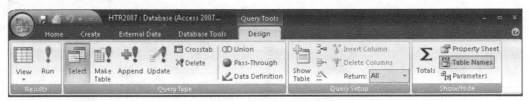

The query shortcut menus that appear depend on where you right-click to display them: in the table pane or the design grid. Right-clicking in the table pane offers these options:

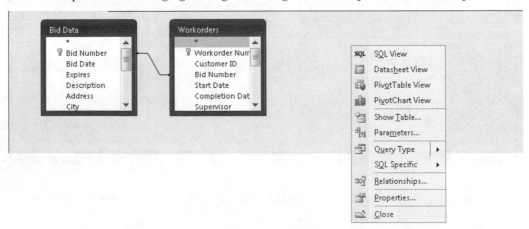

The Parameters command opens the Query Parameters dialog box, where you define the parameters to prompt for when running a parameter query.

The design grid shortcut menu also includes the Parameters option. (See Chapter 9 for more details about creating a parameter query.) When you right-click in the design grid, the shortcut menu offers the following options:

The Build and Zoom commands are available when the insertion point is in the Criteria or Or row that contains an expression.

When a relationship line is selected in the table pane, right-clicking the join line and choosing Join Properties from the shortcut menu opens the Join Properties dialog box. You can change the join properties to get different results with the query. (Refer to Chapter 5 for a description of the types of joins.)

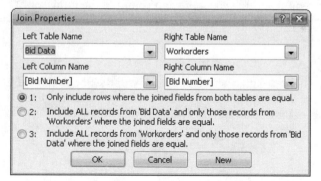

Creating a Query without the Wizard

You can use six basic steps to create a query without the help of a wizard:

1. Select one or more tables and queries that contain the information you want to retrieve, and then add them to the table pane of the new query design.

2. Choose the fields from the field lists in the table pane and add them to the design grid.

3. Specify the sort orders for the field values, if any.

4. Add selection criteria that limits the records in the query results.

5. Add calculated fields that display the results of functions or expressions, if any.

6. Add summarizing expressions, if any.

When you finish with these steps, run the query.

TIP *You can run the query to test the results while you're creating it by switching to Datasheet view or clicking the Run command in the Results group. The query isn't saved until you close it.*

Each of these steps has many features, as you can see in this and subsequent sections.

To bypass the wizard and create your query from scratch, on the Create tab's Other group, click the Query Design command. The Show Table dialog box opens in front of a blank query design, in which you select the tables or queries you want to query. As an example of creating a new query without the wizard, Home Tech Repair needs a list of work orders showing the following fields from the Bid Data and Workorders tables arranged in the following order:

- Bid Number (Bid Data)
- Supervisor (Workorders)
- Job Address (Bid Data)
- Description (Workorders)
- Award Date (Bid Data)
- Start Date (Workorders)
- Completion Date (Workorders)

Later, you'll add the customer's Last Name and Phone Number from the Customers table. In addition, you'll add the cost data and compute the total cost. Then you'll add criteria based on start date, total cost, and other factors to limit the records in the result.

To create this new query, do the following:

1. On the Create tab's Other group, click the Query Design command.

2. The new query design document opens with the Show Table dialog box, which has three tabs that display a list of Tables, Queries, or Both in the current database. (Your lists of tables and queries will be different.)

3. Select Bid Data (if it's not already selected) and choose Add. You can see the field list added to the query table pane behind the dialog box.

4. Double-click Workorders in the Show Table Tables list, and then choose Close. Figure 8-3 shows the query design with the two tables. (Field lists have been expanded in the figure, so you can see the linking fields.)

5. Keep the query design open so you can add fields to the design grid.

The next task is to choose the fields you want to appear in the query result and arrange them in the desired order. But first, look at the relationships Access shows for the two Home Tech Repair tables, and then add a third table to the design.

Relating Multiple Tables in a Query

You begin to see the power of a relational database system when you build a query using more than one table. As you add tables, the query has access to more and more information.

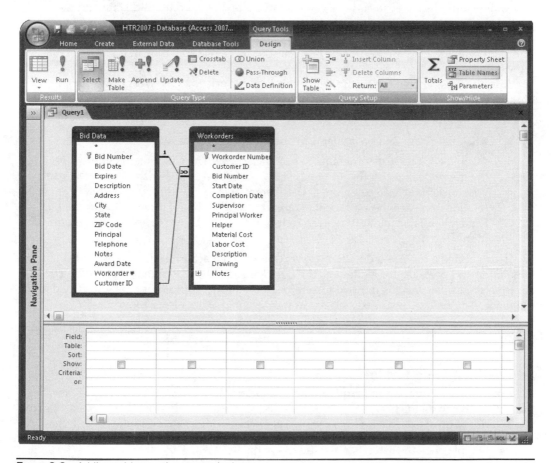

FIGURE 8-3   Adding tables to the query design

To add a table to an existing query, in the Query Setup group, click the Show Table command, or right-click in the table pane and choose Show Table from the shortcut menu. If the tables are already related at the table level, Access automatically displays the join lines when you add the table to the query design. You can tell by the appearance of the line whether referential integrity is enforced and which table is the "one" side and which is the "many" side.

If the tables aren't related before adding them to the query, Access often assumes a relationship between them based on fields with the same name and data type, especially if one of them is a primary key. When Access joins the tables, referential integrity isn't enforced.

CAUTION *If the tables aren't related at the table level and Access cannot join them, you must join them in the query or you'll get what is called a Cartesian product: each of the n rows in one table is matched with every one of the m rows in the second table, resulting in a recordset with n×m records.*

In the Home Tech Repair database, the relationship between the Bid Data and the Workorders table was defined as one-to-many, linked by Bid Number and with referential integrity enforced. The Workorders table is related to the Bid Data table by Customer ID, but referential integrity isn't enforced. You can see these relationships in the query table pane.

Add the Customers table to the new query and include the Last Name and Phone Number in the results, so you won't have to look them up to reach the customer.

To add the Customers table, do the following:

1. Click the Show Table command to open the Show Table dialog box.

2. Double-click the Customers table and click Close. The Customers table is added to the query design and the join lines show the relationships with the Bid Data and Workorders tables (see Figure 8-4). Referential integrity is enforced on the relationship with the Workorders table, but not on the relationship with the Bid Data table. The tables are rearranged slightly in the figure to show the relationships more clearly.

If you added a table and decide that you don't need it after all, click the field list in the table pane and press DEL, or right-click the field list and choose Remove Table from the shortcut menu. The table is removed from the query design, but it remains untouched in the database. Any fields you already placed in the design grid are also removed.

NOTE *You can also add a second copy of the same table and create a self-join.*

Adding/Removing Fields

Adding fields to a query grid is much the same as adding them to an Advanced Filter/Sort grid. You can add all the fields at once, add a selected group of fields, or add one field at a time.

To add all the fields in a table to the grid at once, do one of the following:

- Double-click the asterisk (*) at the top of the field list. This method places the table or query name in the Field row of the column followed by a period and an asterisk (for example, *Customers.**).

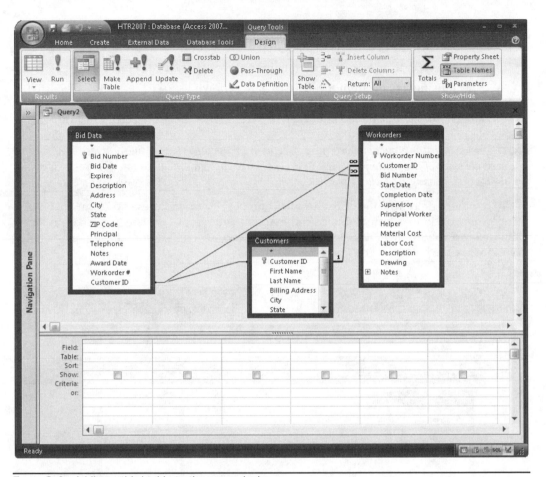

FIGURE 8-4   Adding a third table to the query design

- Drag the asterisk from the field list to an empty column in the grid. This method does the same as the previous one.

- Double-click the field list title bar to select all the fields, and then drag the group to the grid. Access places each field in a separate column across the grid in the order in which they appeared in the field list.

TIP   *Using the asterisk method of adding all the fields to the query can be both an advantage and a disadvantage. The advantage is this: If fields are added or deleted from the underlying table or query, this query automatically makes corresponding changes to the design. The only disadvantage is if you want to sort or filter using one of the fields, it must be added separately to the grid.*

To add a group of fields to the grid at once, select them and drag them as a group. The standard use of SHIFT and CTRL to select adjacent and nonadjacent field names, respectively, works here as with filters. When you drag the block of selected field names to the grid, Access spreads them to empty columns, beginning where you drop the group. If fields are already in the grid, those to the right of where you drop the group move over to make room.

To add fields to the grid one at a time, do any of the following:

- Double-click the field name to place it in the first empty column.
- Drag the field to an empty column or insert it between filled columns.
- Select the field name from the Field row drop-down list (see Figure 8-5). The list in a blank column contains all the fields in all the tables in the table pane, as well as the table names with a period and asterisk. Scroll down the list to see more names.

NOTE *Fields added to a query inherit the properties from the underlying table or query. You can override some of these field properties in the new query design. There is more about this later in the section "Changing Field Properties."*

To remove a field from the grid, click the column selector and press DEL, or in the Query Setup group, click the Delete Columns command. If you remove the check mark from the Show cell in a column with no Sort or Criteria entries, the field is automatically removed from the grid the next time you open the query.

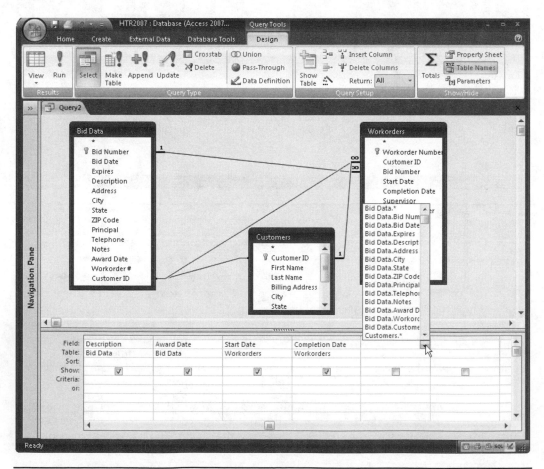

FIGURE 8-5   Selecting a field from the list

You can adjust the column widths and drag a column to a new position, just as in a datasheet or advanced filter. Changing the column width has no effect on the query results datasheet unless you reduce it to zero and the adjustments aren't saved with the query.

NOTE *You can ask Access to adjust a column width to fit its longest visible entry in the design grid, which might be the field name or one of the selection criteria. Move the mouse pointer to the right edge of the column selector and double-click when the pointer changes to a two-way arrow. This sets a fixed column width and, if you enter a longer value in the column later, you'll need to readjust the width to see it all.*

Figure 8-6 shows the new query, still unnamed, with all the required fields in place. The columns have been resized to fit their contents and some are off the screen, out of sight.

When you want to add a multivalued field to a query, you have two ways of displaying it in the query result:

- All entered values in a single cell in the record row.
- Each value in a separate record row.

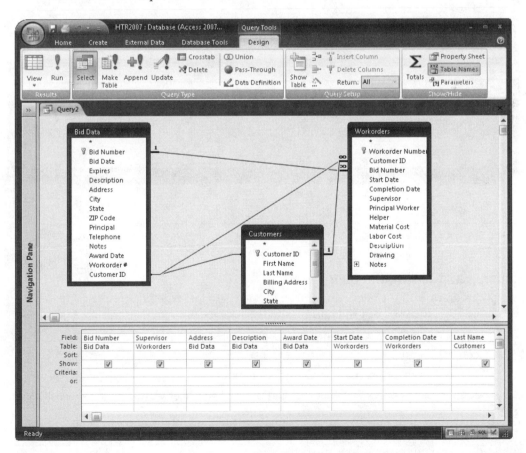

FIGURE 8-6   Adding fields to the query design

If you want all the Crew names for one work order to appear in one cell separated by commas, place the Crew field name in the design grid (see Figure 8-7).

If you want each Crew name to appear on a separate line, choose Crew.Value from the Workorders field list instead.

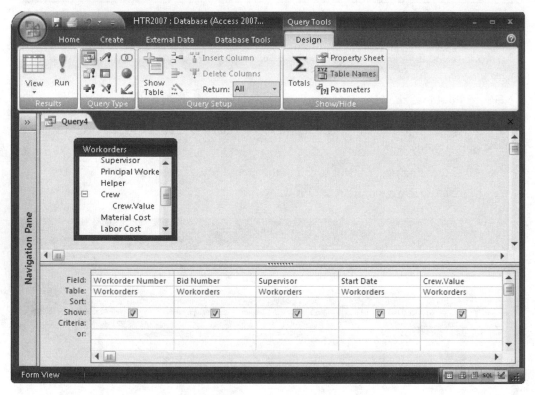

NOTE *You can't choose to sort for a multivalued field when you have chosen the Value version. If you try, you will get an error message when you try to switch to Datasheet view.*

Running and Saving the Query

As you progress with the query design, run the query to test whether or not you're getting the information the way you want it. You can run a query in three ways:

- In the Results group, click the View command and choose Datasheet View from the context menu.

- In the Results group, click the Run command.

- Right-click the query document tab and choose Datasheet View from the shortcut menu.

You do not need to save the query design before looking at the results. Figure 8-8 shows the unfinished query in Datasheet view. The column widths and row heights have been adjusted, so that all the data appears on the screen.

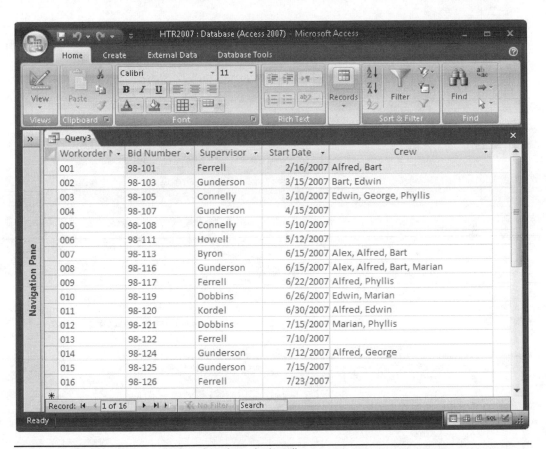

FIGURE 8-7   Placing all the multiple values in a single cell

You can query results in two other arrangements: PivotTable and PivotChart. These provide a shortcut to analyzing the data produced by the query. You can also use the buttons on the right end of the taskbar to change the view.

When you try to close the query either from the Design view or from one of the query result views, Access prompts you to save the design.

Save the new query design before adding the sort order and filter criteria.

1. Right-click in the query document tab and choose Save from the shortcut menu.

2. Enter **Workorder Cost Sheet** in the Save As dialog box, and then click OK.

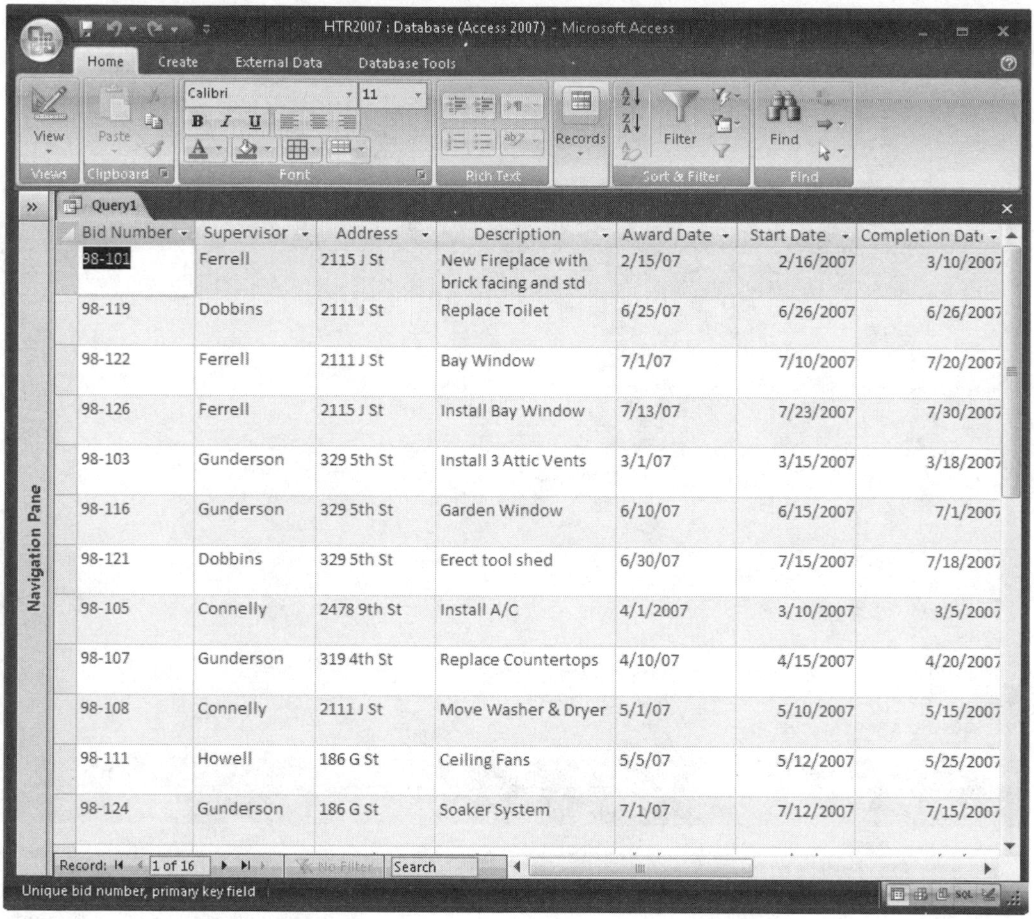

FIGURE 8-8   Viewing query results in Datasheet view

TIP *You can usually cancel a query when it's running by pressing* CTRL-BREAK, *but extremely long queries might not comply.*

Optimizing Query Performance
If you created an important query, but it seems to take a long time to run, you may be able to streamline it to make it run more quickly.

- Make sure all the foreign keys in the related tables are indexed. If a field cannot be indexed, try not to sort on it.
- Include in the design grid only those fields necessary in the results. Extra fields take more time to display.
- Make sure that you aren't using exorbitantly large data fields. Unnecessarily large fields waste disk space and slow processing.

Hiding/Showing Fields

You might want to use one or more fields in filtering or sorting the query results, but you don't want the information to appear in the results. The check box in the Show cell of the design grid determines whether the field values will be displayed. Clear the check mark to hide the field; check it to show the field.

TIP *When you reopen the design of a query in which you hid some of the fields, you might think those fields were removed. Instead, Access moved the hidden fields to the right-most columns in the design grid when you saved the query, and they could be off the screen. However, if no Criteria or Show entries existed, the field has, indeed, been removed from the design.*

Specifying the Record Order

Access lets you sort the results of a query in Datasheet view by clicking one of the Sort commands without having to set the sort order in the design. This gives you flexibility, but if you want to specify that a sort order be saved with the query, you should set it in the query design.

Setting a sort order in a query design is the same as setting it in an advanced filter. You choose Ascending or Descending from the Sort Cell list box in the column containing the field by which you want to sort. If you want to sort on more than one field, make sure that you have the fields arranged in the proper order from left to right. They do not need to be adjacent.

A sort order is saved with the query if you specify it in the design. Any new form or report based on the query then inherits the sort order. It does not need to be applied, but it's an inherited property of the form or report.

Sorting on a lookup field can produce confusing results. For example, Figure 8-9 shows the results of sorting the Workorder Cost Sheet records first by Supervisor and then by Completion date. The lower window shows the underlying query grid with both fields sorted in ascending order.

The Completion Dates are in the correct order within the set of records for a given Supervisor. The Supervisor fields, however, don't appear to be in alphabetical order, either ascending or descending. When you specify a sort in the query grid, Access sorts on the stored value, which in this case is the Employee ID number, not the employee name. If you want the records sorted by the displayed value, you need to sort in the Datasheet view, which has access to the related lookup list values.

NOTE *The same is true when you try to filter records based on a value in a lookup field. You must enter the stored value in the Criteria cell in the query grid only with filtering on a lookup field with Advanced Filter/Sort, as discussed in the previous chapter.*

Like a sort order, you can apply a filter to the query results, instead of making it part of the query design. This has the same effect as adding the criteria to the design, but the filter won't be saved with the query.

Showing Highest or Lowest Values

Limiting the results to the few highest or lowest values in a field can be handy for isolating the more labor-intensive jobs or finding the employees who could use a raise. For example,

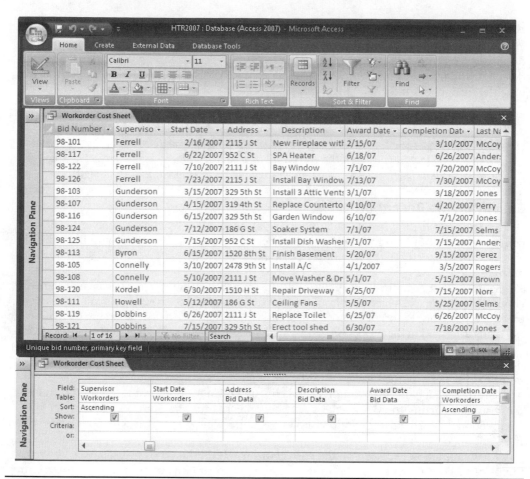

FIGURE 8-9 Sorting records in a lookup field

you can ask Access to display only the records with the 15 highest or lowest values in a field, or the records with the highest or lowest 15 percent of values.

You need to use the Return command in the Query Setup group to specify how many or what percentage of the records to include in the results. The Return list includes 5, 25, and 100 records, and 5 percent and 25 percent of the values to choose from, as well as All. You can also type any percentage or number of values you want directly in the box.

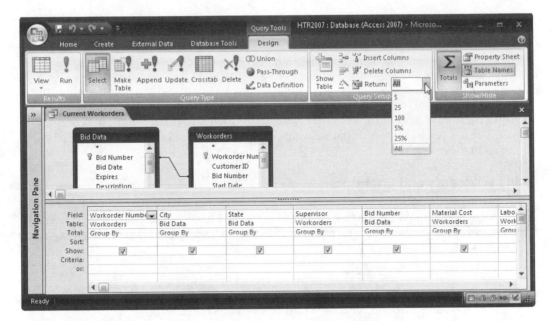

Access selects the records starting from the top of the list, so before you select the Return setting, you must sort in descending order on the field you want to display the highest values. If you want the lowest values, sort in ascending order. If you specified a sort on any other field in the query, make sure the sorted field is to the right of the top values field, so the values will be subordinate to the Top Value list.

TIP *If you specify the number of top values you want to see, all the values that match the last value in the list are also included, so you might see more than you expected. If you don't want to see the duplicate records, change the Unique Values query property in the Query Property Sheet to Yes. You can also use the Top Values query property to limit the records to the top or bottom values. There is more about query properties in the section "Setting Query Properties" later in this chapter.*

Adding Selection Criteria

The last chapter introduced you to the concept of adding selection criteria when filtering records with Advanced Filter/Sort. The selection criteria in queries are also expressions defining a condition that must be met for the record to be included in the subset. An *expression* is a combination of symbols, values, identifiers, and operators used for many purposes, some of which you've already seen, and others you will learn about in later chapters, including the following:

- Establishing field and record validation rules
- Setting default field values

- Defining filter criteria
- Computing calculated field values
- Specifying conditions under which a macro runs

Symbols used in expressions include quotation marks, colons, asterisks, and other special characters. *Values* can be expressed as literal values, constants, the result of a function, or an identifier. *Identifiers* refer to the value of a field, a control in a form or report, or a property. An *operator* is a symbol or word that indicates an operation to be performed on one or more elements in the expression.

Using Wildcards and Operators

If you want to set a criterion for a text field and you want to match only part of the field, you can use the same wildcards that you used in filters: ? to represent a single character and * to represent any number of characters. For example, to find all Bid Data records for jobs on J Street, enter the expression

    J St

in the Criteria cell in the Address column and press ENTER or TAB. Access examines the expression and completes the syntax by adding special characters:

    Like "*J St*"

NOTE *You can also enclose text values in expressions in quotation marks with the wildcards. For example,* Not Like "AB*".

Operators are the key to more flexible expressions. Access has several classes of operators: arithmetic, comparison, concatenation, and logical. Table 8-1 lists the operators you can use in query criteria expressions and gives examples of each.

Operator	Description	Example	Limits Records To
Arithmetic Operators			
+	Addition	=Cost+50	Values equal to 50 more than the value in the Cost field
–	Subtraction	=Cost–50	Values equal to 50 less than the value in the Cost field
*	Multiplication	=Cost*2	Values twice the amount in the Cost field
/	Division	=Cost/2	Values half the amount in the Cost field
\	Integer division	=Cost\2	The integer portion of values that results from dividing the Cost field value by 2

TABLE 8-1 Operators Used in Expressions

Operator	Description	Example	Limits Records To
Mod	Modulo division	=Cost Mod 2	The remainder of dividing the Cost value by 2
Comparison Operators			
=	Equals	=Books *or* ="Books"	Text value Books
>	Greater than	>7/15/07 *or* >#7/15/07#	Dates later than July 15, 2007
<	Less than	<1500	Values less than 1500
>=	Greater than or equal to	>=15	Values greater than or equal to 15
<=	Less than or equal to	<=1/1/08 *or* <=#1/1/08#	Dates on or before January 1, 2008
<>	Not equal to	<>NY	Values other than NY
Between...And	Between two values, inclusive	Between 100 And 500	Numbers from 100 and 500, inclusive
In	Included in a set of values	In("Germany", "France")	Either Germany or France
Is Null	Field is empty	Is Null	Records with no value in the field
Is Not Null	Field is not empty	Is Not Null	Records with a value in the field
" "	Field contains zero-length string	=""	Records with zero-length string in the field
Like	With wildcards, matches a pattern	Like C*	Any text values that begin with *C*
Logical Operators			
And	Both conditions are True	>=10 And <=100	Values between 10 and 100, inclusive
Or	Either condition is True	Books Or Videos	Either Books or Videos
Not	Not True	Not Like AB*	All values except those beginning with AB

TABLE 8-1   Operators Used in Expressions *(continued)*

When filtering on a Date field, you can use one of the date functions in the criteria expression. Table 8-2 shows examples of the date functions included in expressions used as criteria to limit the records in the Workorders table by values in the Completion Date field.

Function	Example	Result
Date()	<Date()+45	Displays work orders with Completion Date less than 45 days from today.
DateAdd()	>DateAdd("m",6,Date())	Displays work orders with Completion Date more than six months from today. The *m* isolates the month value.
Year()	Year([Completion Date]) = 2007	Displays work orders whose Completion Date falls in 2007.
DatePart()	DatePart("q",[Completion Date] = 2	Displays work orders whose Completion Date is in the second calendar quarter. The *q* isolates the calendar quarter.
Month()	Year([Completion Date]) =Year(Now) And Month([Completion Date]) =Month(Now)	Displays work orders with Completion Dates in the current year and month.

TABLE 8-2 Using Date Functions in Expressions

NOTE *If the field name contains a space, a colon (:), or any Access special character, the name must be enclosed in brackets ([ ]) when used in an expression.*

Using a Single Criterion

You add a single selection criterion to a Criteria cell in the query grid, exactly the same as in an advanced filter. For example, if you want to see information from the Workorder Cost Sheet for only those jobs supervised by Gunderson, do the following:

1. Open the Workorder Cost Sheet query in Design view and enter **12** (the Employee ID number for Gunderson) in the Criteria cell of the Supervisor column. Then press ENTER. Access adds quotation marks around *12* because the field is a Text data type.

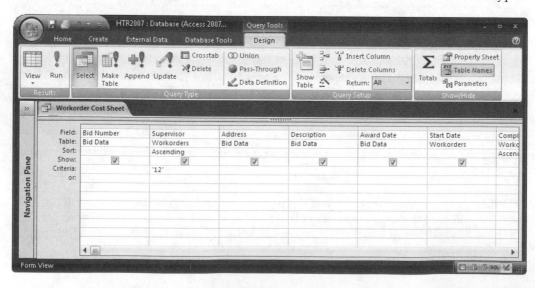

2. Switch to Datasheet view to display the five records for Gunderson's jobs.

3. Now you want to see the records for all jobs started before July 1, 2007, without regard to the supervisor. Return to Design view and delete the Supervisor criteria by selecting the expression and pressing DEL.

4. Enter **<7/1/2007** in the Start Date Criteria cell and press ENTER. Access adds the date delimiters (#).

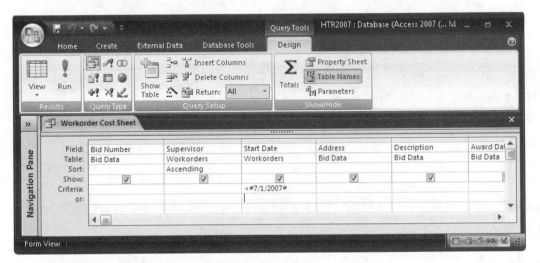

5. Run the query to see the eight records for jobs started before July 1, 2007.

When you move out of the Criteria cell after entering the expression, Access automatically parses the expression and inserts characters to complete the syntax:

- Brackets ([]) around field names
- Number signs (#) around dates
- Double quotation marks ("") around text
- Equal sign (=) before a calculated field expression

Using Multiple Criteria

To apply more than one selection criterion, you combine them with the And or Or operators, using the same logic that is used with filters:

- Use And to require that both criteria be met to include the record in the query result.
- Use Or to return records that satisfy either expression.

NOTE *If you want to select records based on field values, the field must be in the query grid, even if you don't show it in the results.*

Where you enter the expressions in the query grid depends on how you want them to be applied:

- In one field using Or, enter one expression in the Criteria row and the second in the Or row.

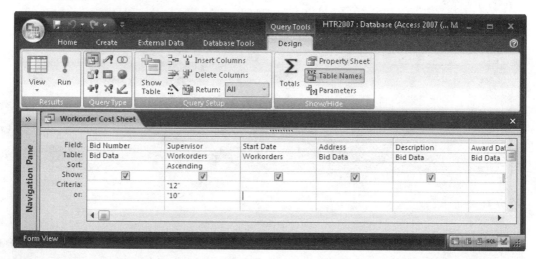

- In one field using And, enter both expressions in the Criteria row combined with the And operator. This combination is seldom used because a field usually can't have two different values at once, but it can be used to find a combination of text strings in a Memo field.

TIP *If the expression is wider than the input area, press* SHIFT-F2 *with the insertion point in the cell where you want to enter the expression. This opens the Zoom box, where you can enter and edit the expression. Even though the text wraps to multiple lines in the Zoom box, the expression is only one line.*

- In two fields using Or, enter one expression in the Criteria row of one column and the other expression in the Or row of the other column. It doesn't matter which is which.

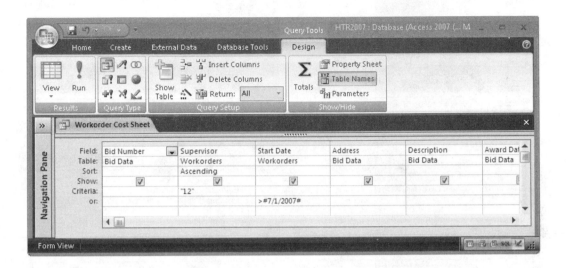

- In two fields using And, enter both expressions in the Criteria row.

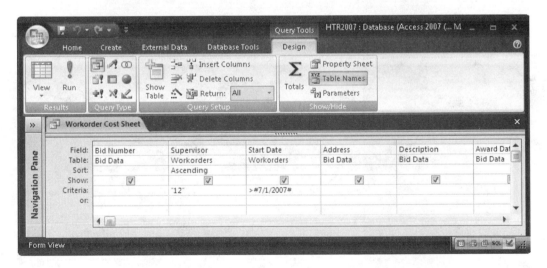

- In three fields using both And and Or, enter one pair of And expressions in the Criteria row and the other pair in the Or row.

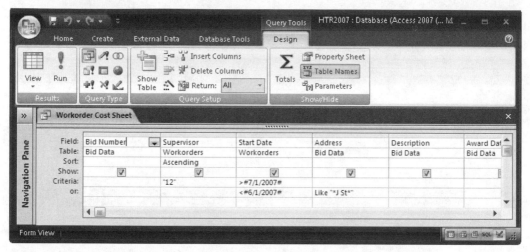

The results of this query are sorted by Supervisor (actually, by Employee ID) and show all work orders by Gunderson (12) that started before July 1, 2007, and other work orders on J Street that started before June 1, 2007.

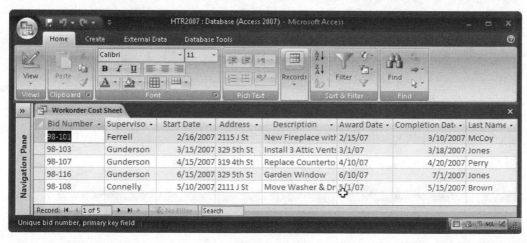

TIP *When working with expressions, you can use the Cut, Copy, and Paste buttons as shortcuts to enter criteria.*

Getting Help from the Expression Builder

When you need to enter a complicated expression in a query design as a selection criterion or you want to construct a calculated field, you can call on the Expression Builder for help. To open the Expression Builder, click in the cell where you want to place the expression, and then in the Design tab's Query Setup group, click the Build command. You can also right-click in the cell where the expression will go and choose Build from the shortcut menu. If the cell already contains an expression, this is copied to the Expression Builder. For example, here the Expression Builder shows the expression with a Start Date criterion leftover from an earlier query:

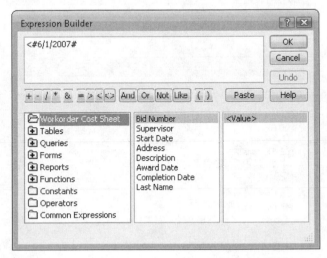

You enter the expression in the upper pane of the Expression Builder. Notice the Workorder Cost Sheet document is selected in the left panel in the lower pane and a list of fields is displayed in the center panel. The lower pane consists of expression elements divided into three levels. The left-most panel contains all the groupings in the current session. When you open a folder in this panel, the contents of the selected item are listed in the middle panel. Selecting an item in the center panel opens a list of individual elements in the right panel. You can add one of these to the expression by double-clicking the name or by selecting it and clicking Paste.

For example, suppose you want to use the Month() function to define a selection criterion on the Start Date field in the Workorder Cost Sheet query to display only records for jobs started in June. To accomplish this, do the following:

1. In the query Design view, right-click in the Criteria cell of the Start Date column and choose Expression Builder from the shortcut menu. Delete any expression that already appears in the upper pane.

2. Double-click the Functions folder to open two subfolders: Built-In Functions and HTR2007, the name of the current database.

3. Open the Built-In Functions folder. A list of function categories appears in the center panel.

4. Choose Date/Time. The right panel shows a list of all the date- or time-related built-in functions.

5. Scroll down the list and select Month, and then click Paste. You can also double-click to add the function to the expression. The Month() function is copied to the upper pane with the correct syntax.

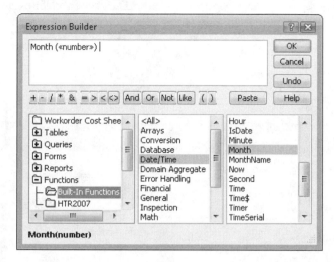

6. The Month() function requires an argument—a number—to tell Access which month you want to specify in the expression. Click to highlight <<number>> in the parentheses and enter **6** (for June).

7. Click OK. You return to the query Design window, where *Month(6)* now appears in the Criteria cell of the Start Date column.

Handling Blank Fields

Fields containing null values and zero-length strings can affect the query results. Consider these aspects when you work with potentially empty fields:

- If the field has been left empty because of incomplete data, it's easy to display those records in a datasheet where you can add the missing data. Use Is Null as the criteria to find null values and "" to find zero-length strings.

- Query results that include data from related tables display only those records in which neither matching field has a null value.

- When you use a field in an aggregate calculation, such as sum or count, Access doesn't include records with null values in that field. If you want to include records with a null value when you count the number of records, use Count with the asterisk (*) wildcard.

- If one of the fields in an expression that uses an arithmetic operator (+, −, *, /, \, ^) has a null value, the entire expression returns a null value.

- You can convert null values to zero-length strings with the Nz() function. If you want to display records with zero-length string values, but no null values, use Like "*" as the selection criterion.

Setting Query Properties

Like all other database objects, a query has a set of properties that controls its appearance and behavior. To open the Query Properties Sheet, place the insertion point in the table pane, and then do one of the following:

- On the Design tab's Show/Hide group, click the Property Sheet command.
- Right-click anywhere in the design window outside the field lists, and then choose Properties from the shortcut menu.
- Click in the table pane and press ALT-ENTER.

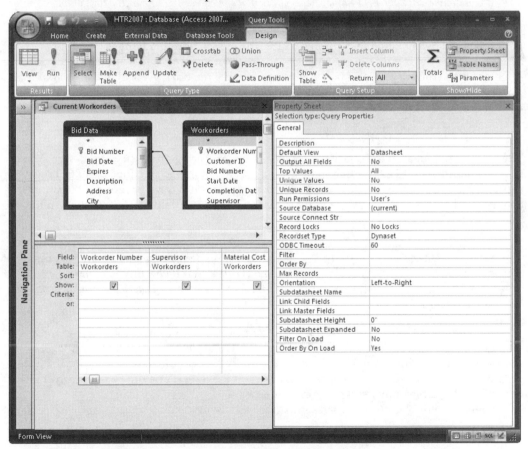

To see an explanation of a query property, click in the property and read the description in the status bar. You can also press F1 to open the corresponding Help topic.

Modifying a Query

To open a query for modifying the design, right-click the query in the Queries group in the Navigation Pane and choose Design View from the shortcut menu. If you want to view the results of the query first, choose Datasheet View, and then switch to Design view later.

You use the query Design document to make changes to the query, just the same as if you were creating it. You can add or delete a field, rearrange the columns, show or hide any of the fields, change the resulting records sort order, and add one or more selection criteria.

Inserting a Field and Changing the Field Order

If you want to add another field to the grid, drag the field name to the Field row of the column where you want the field to appear. The field is inserted and the other columns move over to make room.

TIP *If you double-click the field name, Access puts it at the end of the line in the first empty column.*

Moving a field in the design grid works the same way as moving a field in a datasheet. Select the field by clicking the column selector (the mouse pointer changes to a down arrow). Release the mouse button and click again when it changes to a left upward arrow. Then drag the column to a new position. When you see the dark vertical line appear at the point where you want the column's left margin to appear, release the mouse button. The column moves and the other columns slide over to oblige.

Changing Field Properties

The fields that appear in the query results inherit the properties from the table design. You might want the field to look different or show a different name in the query results, however, especially if you're going to use them as the basis for a custom form or report. You cannot change all of a field's properties, only those that appear in the field's property sheet in the query design.

TIP *When you make changes to field properties in the table design, any new or existing queries usually inherit those changes. The exception to this rule is that if you already changed field properties in the query design, any changes in the table design aren't carried over to override the query customization.*

You might want a field to show a more descriptive name. For example, Access assigns default names to calculated fields, such as Expr1 or CountOfAddress, which aren't very informative. When you change the name in the query design, the new name appears in the datasheet and in any new forms or reports based on the query. The new name doesn't affect the underlying table or any existing forms or reports.

To rename a field in the query design, do the following:

1. Place the insertion point to the left of the first letter of the name in the grid.

2. Type the new name followed by a colon (:). If you're replacing Expr1 or another Access-assigned name, replace only the name, not the expression following the colon.

3. Press ENTER.

TIP *If you want to keep the name in the grid, but show a different name in the datasheet, change the field's Caption property in the Property Sheet.*

To change other field properties, click in the field on the grid and in the Show/Hide group, click the Property Sheet command or press ALT-ENTER. You can also right-click the field name and choose Properties from the shortcut menu. Entries in the field property sheets are blank; they don't contain the settings defined in the table design. Any entries you make in the query Design view override the preset properties.

When you finish with the Property Sheet, click the Close button. Changing field properties in a query design has no effect on the underlying table design.

The field Property Sheet has two tabs: General and Lookup. The General tab shows the properties you can change in the query design, as follows:

- The *Description* is the text displayed in the status bar when you click the field in the Datasheet view. Any text entered here replaces the Description entered in the table definition. You can enter up to 255 characters.

- *Format* shows a list of applicable formats for the field. A Text field has no list, but you can enter a custom format.

- An *Input Mask* property creates a data entry skeleton. You can either type the mask in the box or click Build to start the Input Mask Wizard.

- The *Caption* property specifies the column header for a datasheet, form, or report in place of the field name.

- The *Smart Tags* property specifies which available tags are attached to the field.

- The *Text Format* property offers a choice between Plain Text and Rich Text.

- If the field is a Number field, the *Decimal Places* property also appears in the Property Sheet.

TIP *If you want to change several field properties or even a query property, keep the Property Sheet open and the options will change when you click another object in the query design.*

If the field is a lookup field, the Lookup tab has one option that lets you change the Display Control to a Text Box, a List Box, or a Combo Box. The other properties on the Lookup tab are the same as those in the table design. If the field isn't a lookup field, this tab is blank.

TIP *Calculated fields don't inherit any properties from the table because they didn't exist in the table. The properties must be set in the query design. For example, if the calculated field contains currency data, set the field's Format property to Currency.*

Performing Calculations in a Query

You can perform many types of calculations in a query that are recomputed each time the query is run, so you always have current data. The results of the calculations aren't stored in the table. In a query, two types of calculations can be used: aggregate calculations and custom calculated fields.

The *aggregate calculations* are predefined operations performed on groups of records and provide totals, counts, averages, and other information about field values in all records or in groups of records. Think of these calculations as vertical computations. For example, add up the number of jobs on J Street or calculate the average labor cost for all jobs.

The *custom calculated fields* create new fields in a record by combining the values in other fields in the same record, producing a horizontal computation. You can create new Numeric, Date, or Text fields for each record using custom calculations. For example, use the expression

```
[Completion Date]-[Start Date]
```

to create a new field named Job Time. After creating a calculated field, you can use it to analyze the data further. For example, after finding the job time for each job, you can compute the average time. Or, you can even add a selection criterion to limit the records to jobs in a specific area or supervised by a specific employee.

Adding a Calculated Field

To add a new field that displays the results of a calculation based on other fields in the grid, click the Field row of an empty column and enter an expression. The field names must be enclosed in brackets, so Access recognizes them as fields.

For example, let's add a calculated field to a query of the Home Tech Repair Workorders table that shows the total cost of each current job:

1. In the query Design view, drag the fields you want to see in the result to the grid, including Material Cost and Labor Cost.

2. Click in the Field cell on the first empty column, enter the expression **[Material Cost]+[Labor Cost]**, and then press ENTER. Access adds a default field name to the new field, called Expr1. You can change the default field name to one that's more descriptive.

3. Move the insertion point to the left in the Field cell and replace Expr1: with **Total Cost**:, keeping the colon.

4. Click Datasheet view. Figure 8-10 shows the results of the new calculated field.

If you want to see the total cost of each job, including a 15 percent markup for overhead expenses, add another calculated field using the expression: [Total Cost]*1.15.

TIP   *When you run the query, if you misspell a field name in an expression, Access assumes it's a parameter needed by the query and asks you to enter the value. Click Cancel to close the Enter Parameter Value dialog box and to return to the grid to correct the field name. See Chapter 9 for more information about query parameters.*

You aren't limited to Number and Currency fields in calculated fields. Text fields are easily combined with the concatenation operator (&). For example, if you want to create a new field showing employees' complete names in one field, use the following expression:

```
[First Name]&" "&[Last Name]
```

The quotation marks between the field names add a space.

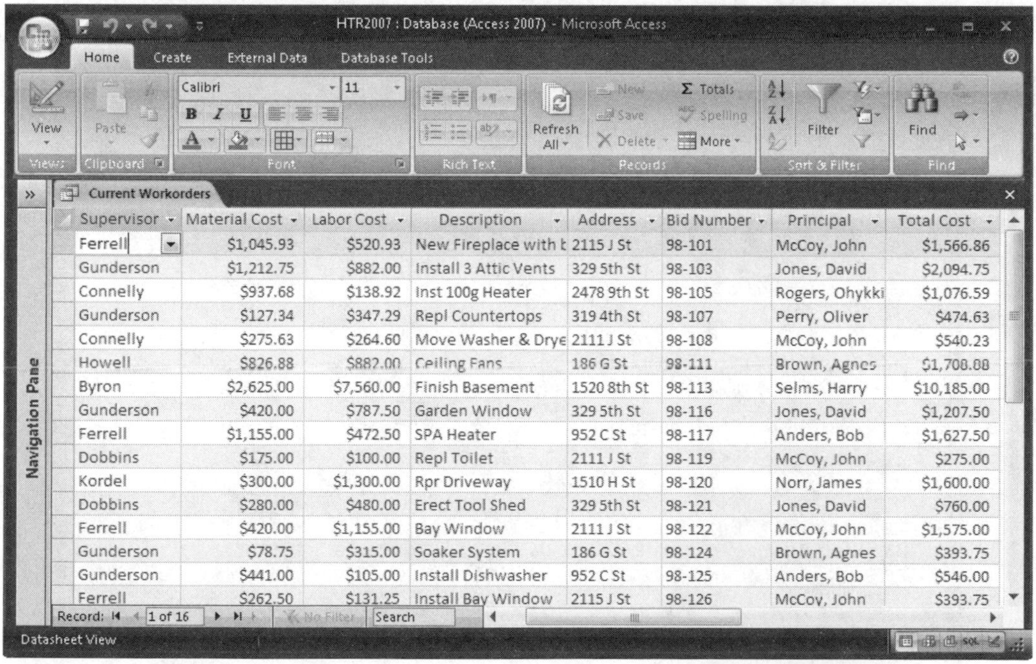

FIGURE 8-10   Displaying the new Total Cost field

If you want to include the employees' full names and add some text to the display, use an expression such as the following:

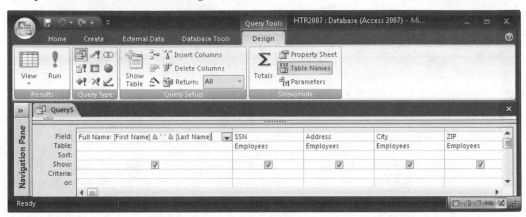

The result of this calculated field looks like this:

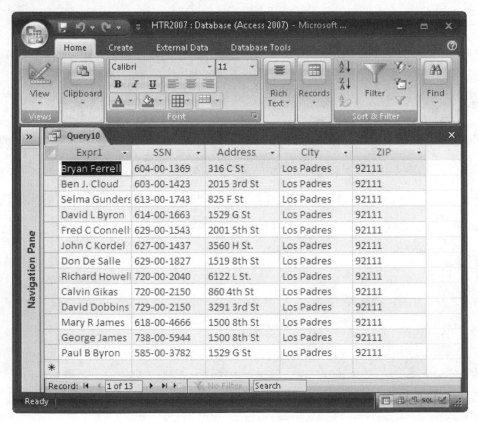

> **NOTE** *If two tables in the query have a field with the same name, you must use the table name as well as the field name in the expression, separated by an exclamation mark (!)—for example, [Customer]![Last Name] or [Employees]![Last Name].*

Once you add the calculated field to the design grid, you can change its properties like any other field in the query. You can also summarize on a calculated field, as well as on a basic table field, as described in the next section. By using more complex functions in expressions, you can create a wide variety of calculated fields using many data types.

> **NOTE** *You cannot edit a calculated field in query Datasheet view. If you want a different value, change one of the fields in the expression.*

Summarizing with the Wizard

As mentioned earlier in this chapter, if the query you're creating with the Simple Query Wizard contains any Number, Currency, or Date/Time fields, you're given the opportunity to create Summary fields.

The second wizard dialog box offers two choices: Detail, in which all records are shown, or Summary. If you choose Summary and click the Summary Options button, the Summary Options dialog box opens, where you can specify the types of summarization you want.

The two currency fields (Material Cost and Labor Cost) are listed with check boxes, where you can choose the type of summary for each field. In addition, you have the option of counting the number of records in each group. After making your choices in this dialog box, click OK and return to the wizard. If any Date/Time fields are in the query, you have an opportunity to group on those values as well, by month, quarter, year, and so on.

Here are the results of choosing to calculate the total and average of both cost fields, as well as to count the number of work orders for each supervisor. When you add summaries to the query design, you can be much more creative.

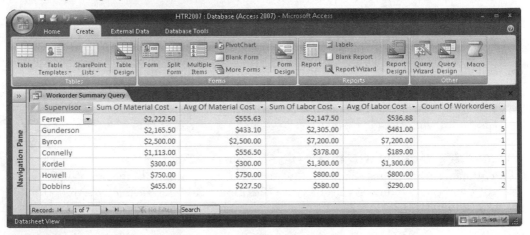

Summarizing with Aggregate Functions

If you want to know the material cost of all the current jobs or the average billing rate for all employees, you can add a summary calculation. The summaries work with values in a field from multiple records. You can summarize all the records in the result or group the records based on a specific field value—such as Supervisor—and calculate the summary value for each group separately.

Summarizing All Records

To summarize field values in a query, start with a select query, add the field you want to summarize, and then specify the way you want the fields summarized. For example, to find the total and average Material Cost for current work orders, do the following:

1. Start a new select query of the Workorders table and drag the Material Cost field to the grid.

2. On the Design tab's Show/Hide group, click the Totals command (the sigma symbol) to add the Total row to the grid. You can also right-click in the grid and choose Totals from the shortcut menu. A new Total row appears in the design grid.

3. Click the Total cell in the Material Cost column and choose Sum from the drop-down option list.

4. To summarize on the same field in two ways, you need another copy of the field in the grid. Drag another copy of the Material Cost field to the next empty column and choose Avg from the Total drop-down list.

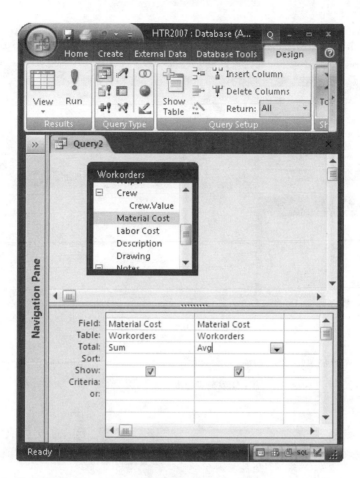

5. Switch to Datasheet view to see the results.

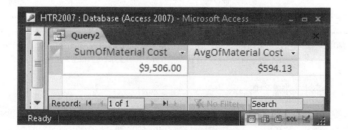

This example is summarized over all the records in the table. You can also base a summary on a subset of records by using the Group By option in the Total cell for the fields that make up the group. For example, you could count the number of jobs assigned to each supervisor.

You have a choice of twelve options in the Total drop-down list, seven of which perform mathematical calculations, two return specific records, and the other three indicate other uses for the field. You can use all the mathematical and selection options with Number,

Date/Time, Currency, and AutoNumber fields. If the field is a Text data type, you can use only the Min, Max, Count, First, and Last options.

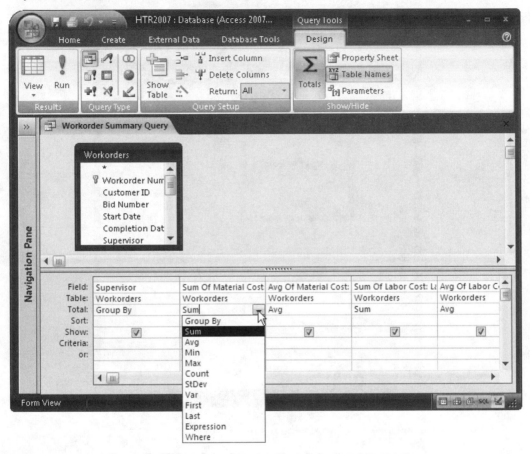

NOTE *If you choose a mathematical selection for a Text field, you will see a "Data type mismatch in criteria expression" message when you try to switch to Datasheet view.*

The other three options are:

- **Group By**   Defines the groups to which you want the calculations to apply—for example, show the average material costs for work orders grouped by supervisor.
- **Expression**   Creates a calculated field with an aggregate function in the expression.
- **Where**   Specifies selection criteria in a field not used in grouping. With this option, the Show check box is cleared by default.

NOTE *Summaries usually don't include blanks, except in the case of Count. If you want to include records with null values, use Count with the asterisk (*) wildcard character: Count*.*

Summarizing by Group

When you add fields to the grid with the Total row visible, the default entry is Group By. To group records with the same value in that field, leave the Group By option in the Total cell. For example, to count the number of work orders under control of each supervisor, do the following:

1. Start a new select query with the Workorders table and drag the Supervisor, Workorder Number, and Labor Cost fields to the grid.

2. On the Design tab's Show/Hide group, click the Totals command. The Totals row is added to the query design.

3. Enter the expression **Avg([Labor Cost]+[Material Cost])** in a blank field and press ENTER.

4. The Total cell still holds the Group By option. Change this to Expression and press ENTER.

5. Change the default Expr1 name to **Average Total**.

6. Choose Count in the Total row for Workorder Number and Avg for Labor Cost.

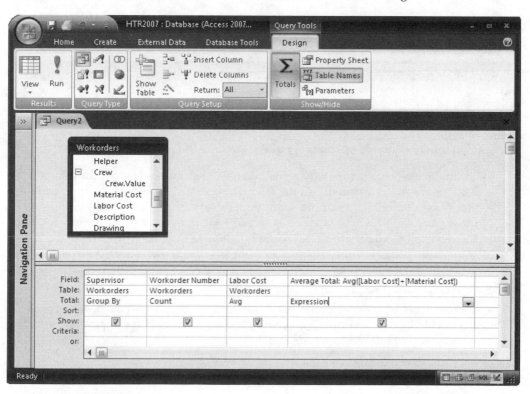

7. Click Run.

The query result shows the new calculated values in the datasheet.

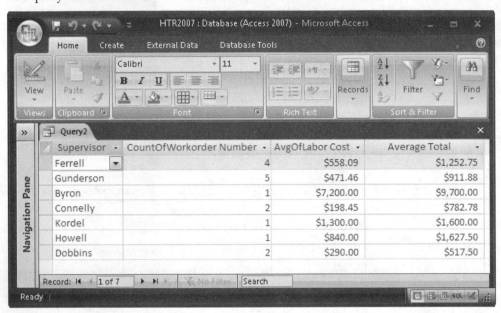

You can also sort the groups by the values computed in the summaries. For example, you could reorder the previous records in descending order of the average total cost of the work orders assigned to each supervisor.

Adding Criteria

You can add selection criteria to summary queries to limit the result in three ways:

- To limit the records before they're included in the group and before the group calculations are performed, add the field whose records you want to limit, and then enter the criterion. For example, in the Supervisor's group, you could include only those work orders whose labor costs exceed $500. If you're calculating any totals in the same query, change the Total cell to Where.

- To limit the groupings after the records are included in the group, but before the group calculations are performed, enter the criterion in the Group By field. For example, you could include a summary for specific Supervisors.

- To limit the results of the group summaries, enter the criterion in the field that contains the calculation. For example, you could display results only for Supervisor groups whose average total cost exceeds $1000.

Adding Customized Expressions

To create your own customized expressions in a summary query, you can use any of the built-in Access functions in the query grid. The most useful functions for summarizing data in a query come in three basic groups:

- *Aggregate Functions,* such as you already saw that calculate statistical values from field data—for example, Avg, Sum, Count, and so on.

- *Domain Aggregate Functions* that compute the same statistical values, but use all the values in the table or query. Domain Aggregate Functions override any grouping restrictions. Examples are DAvg, DSum, DCount, and so on.

- *Formatting Functions* that extract and display parts of the data and combine or format the results in many ways. Examples are Format, Left, Mid, and Right.

TIP *If you use an Aggregate or Domain Aggregate Function that computes the standard deviation or variance with a group containing only two records, the result is a null value.*

You can always get help from the Expression Builder to build a customized expression.

Summarizing in Datasheet View

New with Access 2007 is the ability to add a Total row to the query results in Datasheet view that summarizes values in a column. For example, you can summarize the data in the query built in the previous section:

1. Open the query in Datasheet view.

2. On the Home tab's Records group, click the Totals command. A Total row is added to the bottom of the datasheet.

3. Click in the Total row below the Count of Workorder Number and choose Count in the drop-down list.

4. Move to the Total row below AvgOfLabor Cost and choose Maximum in the drop-down list.

5. Move to the Total row below Average Total and choose Minimum in the drop-down list.

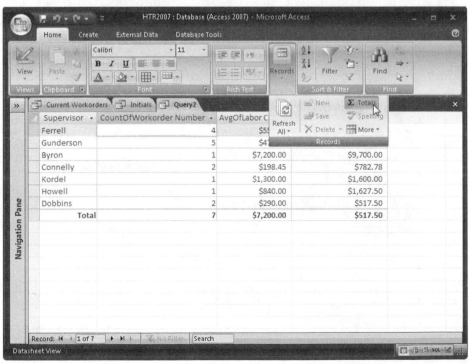

NOTE *You have different choices depending on the field data type.*

To clear the Total row from a column, click in its Total row and select None from the drop-down list. To hide the entire row, on the Home tab's Records group, choose Totals from the context menu.

Creating Special Queries with the Query Wizard

As you saw in the New Query dialog box, more query wizards exist than the Simple Select Wizard. The list includes wizards that create crosstabs, queries that find duplicate records, and queries that find unmatched records in related tables.

Creating a Find Duplicates Query

A Find Duplicates query locates and displays records in which the specified field has the same values. For example, you could use a Find Duplicates query to display all the work orders supervised by a specific employee or all the bids made on jobs at a particular address. The Find Duplicates Wizard can create the query for you using the following steps:

1. On the Create tab's Other group, click the Query Wizard command.

2. Select the Find Duplicates Wizard and click OK. The first dialog box asks you to select the table or query what you want to search.

3. Choose Table:Bid Data and click Next.

4. In the next dialog box (see Figure 8-11), double-click Address in the Available Fields list to add it to the Duplicate-value fields list, and then click Next.

5. Select all the fields you want to display in addition to the field in which duplicates might occur—for example, Bid Number, Bid Date, Description, and Principal. Then click Next.

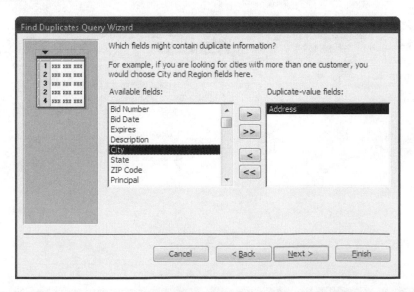

FIGURE 8-11 Adding a value to the Duplicate-value fields list

6. In the last dialog box, enter **Duplicate Addresses** as the name for the query and click Finish.

The resulting datasheet lists only those records that have duplicate Address fields. For example, two Bid Data records apply to 1510 H St. and three records are for 2111 J St.

If you want to sort the results or modify the query in another way, you can choose to modify the query in the last wizard dialog box rather than view the results.

Creating a Find Unmatched Query

With the Find Unmatched Query Wizard, you can locate and display records in one table that have no match in a related table. For example, you can find customers who have no work orders, so you can send a letter to remind them of your services.

To create a Find Unmatched query, do the following:

1. Start a new query with the Find Unmatched Query Wizard.

2. In the first dialog box, choose Customers as the table whose records you want to display and click Next.

3. In the next dialog box, choose Workorders as the table you want to match with the Customers table. If there are any customers with no corresponding work orders, the Customer record is included in the result. Click Next.

4. In the next dialog box, specify the matching fields by choosing the field in each list and clicking the <=> button. If the fields have the same name, Access predetermines the relationship (see Figure 8-12). Click Next.

5. Select the fields you want to see in the result, such as Name, Address, and Phone Number.

6. Accept the query name as Customers Without Matching Workorders, and then click Finish. You can see the three customers that have no work orders in progress.

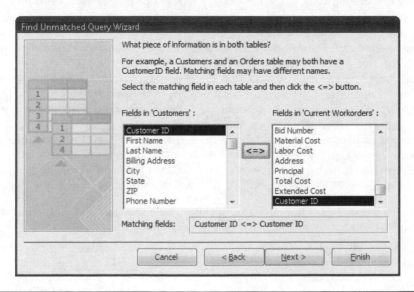

FIGURE 8-12   Choosing fields with unmatching values

If you switch to the query design, you see the wizard has created a left inner join for the two tables, which returns the records from the parent table (the one side) only if no matching records are in the child table (the many side).

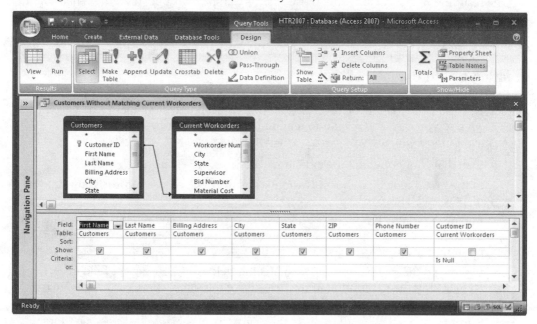

Creating a Crosstab Query

A *crosstab query* is a special type of summary query that correlates summary values between two or more sets of field values, such as sales of types of products within certain sales regions or categories of work order costs correlated with the active supervisor. One set of facts is listed as row headings at the left of the crosstab and the other is listed as column headings across the top. The summarized values, sums, averages, or counts are contained in the body of the crosstab.

To create a crosstab query, you need at least three output fields: row headings, column headings, and values. You can create a crosstab query from scratch or with the help of the Crosstab Query Wizard. The result of running a crosstab query is a snapshot, and none of the data in the results is editable.

As an example of creating a crosstab query, use the table named Workorder Crosstab, which has all the costs in one field, with an additional field that indicates the category of the cost: labor or material. To use the Crosstab Query Wizard to create a crosstab that correlates the category of cost with the job supervisor, follow these steps:

1. On the Create tab's Other group, click the Query Wizard command and choose Crosstab Query Wizard from the New Query dialog box. Then click OK.

2. In the first dialog box (see Figure 8-13) choose the Workorder Crosstab table as the basis for the query, and then click Next. (The table used for a crosstab is a regular table and doesn't need to include the name Crosstab.)

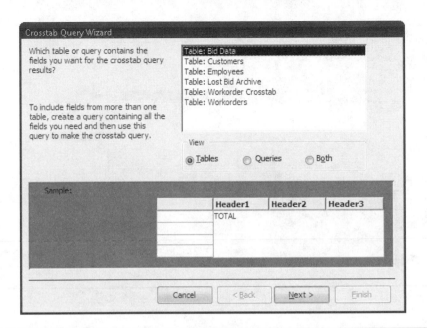

FIGURE 8-13   Working in the first Crosstab Query Wizard dialog box

3. In the next dialog box (see Figure 8-14), double-click Supervisor as the field to use as the row heading. Supervisor will move to the Selected Fields list. Then click Next.

4. In the next dialog box, choose Cost Category as the column heading, and then click Next.

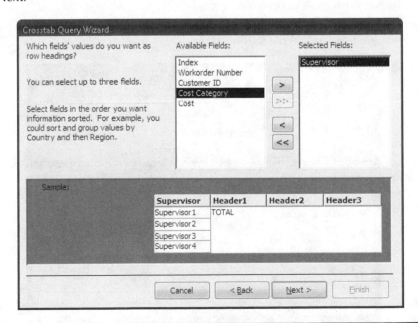

FIGURE 8-14   Choosing the row heading

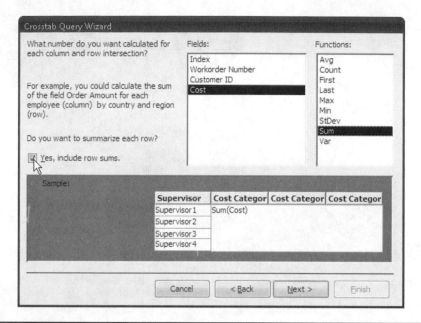

FIGURE 8-15 Choosing the values for the crosstab

5. In the next dialog box, select Cost as the value field and Sum in the Functions list. Clear the check mark next to Yes, Include Row Sums if you don't want to see a Total of Costs column (see Figure 8-15). The sample pane shows how the fields will be arranged in the crosstab. Click Back to return to a previous dialog box to make changes or click Next to finish the query.

6. Enter the query name, **Workorder Crosstab by Category and Supervisor**, in the final dialog box, and then click Finish.

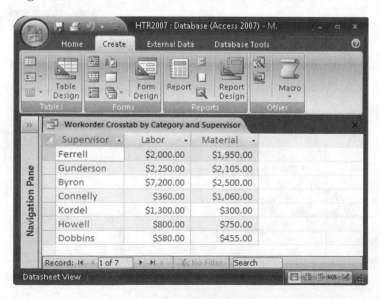

You can make changes to the query design after the wizard is finished with it. For example, you can limit the records included in the crosstab by adding the field on which you want to set the limit and setting the Total cell to Where. Then leave the Crosstab cell blank and enter the expression in the Criteria cell.

If you want to change the column headings in the crosstab, return to the query design and open the query Property Sheet. Enter the titles you want for the columns in the Column Headings property, in the order they are to appear in the result. Separate the headings with semicolons (;) or new line breaks (CTRL-ENTER). You can also type the list of column headings enclosed in double quotation marks separated with commas.

You can have up to three row heading fields. The additional row headings effectively become subgroupings of the data. Each additional row heading multiplies the number of records in the result: two row headings double the records in the result; three headings triple the result.

You can also create a crosstab query from Design view by starting a new query based on the same table. Then on the Design tab in the Query Type group, click the Crosstab command. The crosstab row is added to the design grid. Here is the design of the query created by the Crosstab Query Wizard.

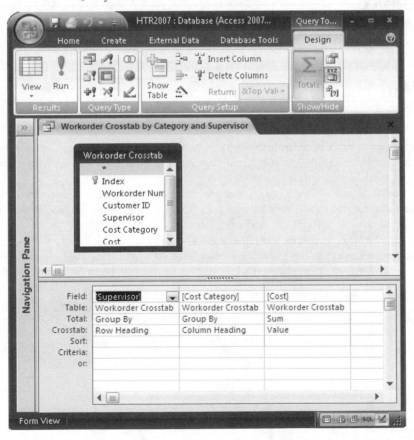

PART II

TIP *If you choose a Date/Time field for a row or column heading, the wizard asks "By which interval do you want to group your Date/Time column information?" You can choose Year, Quarter, Month, Date, or Date/Time. So you can do a crosstab query by month or year, without having to create a calculated field for it.*

Printing the Query Results

After you finish the query design and run the query, you can print the results in the datasheet the same way you print a table datasheet. To send the datasheet directly to the printer, click Print. If you want to select some of the printer options, such as multiple copies or specific pages, click the Microsoft Office button and click Print, and then select options from the Print dialog box.

To preview the datasheet before printing, click Print Preview. You can use all the viewing and zoom capabilities you used with datasheets.

Deleting a Query

To delete a query, right-click the query name in the Navigation Pane and choose Delete from the shortcut menu. Access then asks for confirmation before it deletes the query. Remember that the query will be deleted permanently and you won't be able to get it back after you delete it. But deleting the query doesn't delete any data from the underlying tables—it deletes only the query design.

Summary

You have almost limitless options for extracting and arranging data from one or more tables. This chapter introduced you to the basics of query design and construction with select queries and some special purpose queries.

Query wizards can create queries that can at least get you started with the design you need. Then you can use the query Design view to modify the query to include additional features, such as selection criteria and calculated fields.

The next chapter continues with query development and delves into some of the more advanced queries, such as the Parameter query that prompts for criteria from the user, and several types of action queries that update, append, or delete records in one or more tables.

Creating Advanced Queries

Queries are the primary means of retrieving information stored in an Access database. In addition to the popular select query discussed in the previous chapter, Access offers more flexible ways to retrieve data. Queries also can perform data management operations, such as adding, updating, or deleting data. You can even use an Access query to run a procedure stored in an external database.

In this chapter, you will see how versatile Access queries can be. After examining two special purpose queries, this chapter discusses action queries, including update, append, make-table, and delete queries.

Creating Special Purpose Queries

Data retrieval queries do not need to be static, always extracting the same information. They can be tailored at run time by the user entering the search criteria in a special dialog box. When you want to specify which group of data you want, use a parameter query. A *parameter query* is much the same as a common select query except Access prompts for one or more of the selection criteria before running the query. You can use parameters in other types of queries as well to get last-minute selection criteria.

Another special purpose query is the *AutoLookup query* that automatically fills in certain field values in related tables. The *AutoLookup field* can save you data entry time by looking up the value you enter in the matching field and entering corresponding information into fields in the related tables.

Parameter Queries

Parameter queries are especially useful for looking up such information as activities during a specific time period—for example, sales during the holiday season or work orders started during the month of June. When you enter the starting and ending dates, Access retrieves all records whose values in that field fall between the two dates. You can have as many parameters in the query as you need. Access prompts separately for each one.

Parameters can be set in almost all types of queries, including select and action queries. You can use a parameter in any field in which you can type text in the Criteria row.

NOTE *You can create parameter queries from the design grid, with SQL statements, or in the Record Source property of a form or report.*

To create a parameter query, start with a normal select query and, instead of entering the criteria in the Criteria row, enter the text for the prompt enclosed in brackets ([ ]). The text you enter becomes the prompt in the dialog box, so be sure it's informative enough for the user to know how to respond. You cannot use the field name itself as the prompt, but you can include it in the prompt text.

For example, Home Tech Repair would like a list of a specific customer's current work orders. To allow the user to specify which customer, create a parameter query as follows:

1. On the Create tab's Other group, click the Query Design command.

2. In the Show Table dialog box, hold down CTRL and choose the Workorders, Bid Data, and Customers tables. Then click Add and Close.

3. Drag the following fields to the design grid: Description and Start Date fields from the Workorders field list, and the Address field from the Bid Data field list. Then add the customer's Last Name field, which will be the parameter the user enters.

4. Type **[Enter customer's last name]** in the Criteria row of the Last Name column. This displays as a prompt in the Enter Parameter Value dialog box when you run the query.

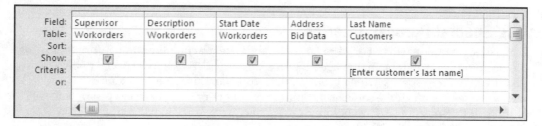

Field:	Supervisor	Description	Start Date	Address	Last Name	
Table:	Workorders	Workorders	Workorders	Bid Data	Customers	
Sort:						
Show:	✓	✓	✓	✓	✓	
Criteria:					[Enter customer's last name]	
or:						

5. In the Results group, click Run and the Enter Parameter Value dialog box appears.

6. Enter the desired Last Name (**McCoy**, in this example) and click OK. When this query is run, the result shows four current work orders for McCoy.

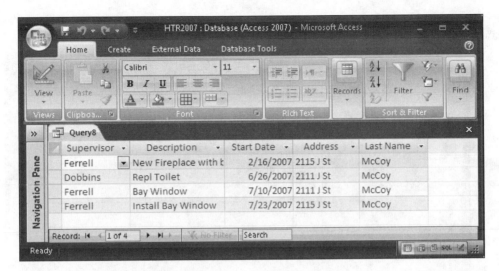

You can also use a parameter query to find records that have a range of values, such as a time period. For example, you can show all the work orders started in the month of June. To do this, include parameters in the Between…And expression in the Criteria row. When you run the query, Access prompts for each parameter in a separate dialog box.

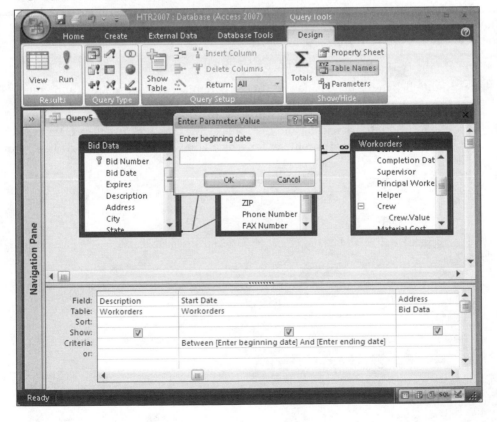

After you enter **6/1/07** in the first prompt box and **7/1/07** in the second, Access runs the query and displays records for the five work orders begun during June.

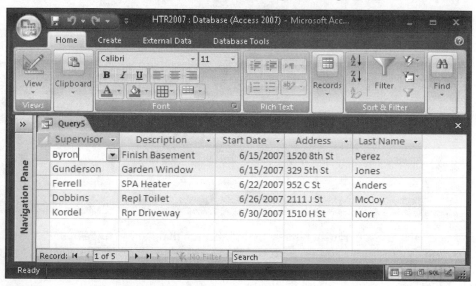

By default, the data type of a parameter is Text. You can specify a different data type, however, by opening the Query Parameters dialog box while in the query Design view using one of the following methods:

- On the Design tab's Show/Hide group, click the Parameters command.
- Right-click in the table pane and choose Parameters from the shortcut menu.

In the Query Parameters dialog box, enter the parameter text exactly as it appears in the Criteria row (without the brackets), and then choose the data type from the Data Type drop-down list. Repeat this for each parameter for which you want to specify a data type, and then click OK.

NOTE *In most cases, Access can tell the data type of the parameter, but you must specifically define the data type for parameters if the field is a Yes/No data type or if it's used in a crosstab query. You must also set the Column Headings property for a crosstab query that prompts for a parameter.*

If you want to display the entered parameter value itself in the query result, add a calculated field with the parameter's name. For example, if you want to see the beginning date in the result of the previous query, enter the following expression in the Field row of an empty column: **Job Start:[Enter beginning date]**. The value will be the same in all the records in the result.

TIP *You can use the Format function to customize the parameter display. For example, use the expression* Job Start:Format([Enter beginning date],"d mmm yyyy") *to display the date as 1 Jun 2007 in the query result, such as a query, form, or report.*

Parameter queries are an excellent basis for reports. For example, you can print monthly reports simply by entering the month of interest and let Access do the rest.

TIP *Sometimes Access prompts for a parameter in a field you haven't designated as a parameter. This can be caused by misspelling the field name or changing the name in the table, but not changing it in other database objects. It also happens if you delete a field from a table but forget to delete it from the query. If you checked the Perform Name AutoCorrect option in the Current Database page of the Access Options dialog box, field name changes are projected to all objects that include that field.*

In Chapter 12, you will see how to create custom dialog boxes that prompt the user for input used in the form.

TIP *If you created a parameter query that extracts fields from a specific set of records, you can also use the same query design to return all the records. Just add a criterion in the* Or *cell for the field used as the parameter and enter the same parameter prompt followed by* Is Null.

You can also use a parameter query to match any part of a field by using the Like keyword with some wildcard characters. For example, build a parameter query to find all records with the word *sink* somewhere in the Description field. The parameter *Like "*" & [Enter job focus:] & "*"* would require that you enter the word *sink* in the Enter Parameter Value box.

You can also use the less than or greater than operator (< or >) to find records with unequal values.

AutoLookup Queries

The AutoLookup query was invented to save time during data entry. This query is not one of the queries listed in the Query Type group on the Design tab but it is quite useful. The query is used as the basis for a data entry form that contains data from more than one table. When you enter a valid Customer ID, for example, the query fills in all the rest of the information in the datasheet or form. An AutoLookup query uses two tables with a one-to-many relationship in which the matching field on the "one" side is either the primary key or a unique index. Referential integrity needn't be enforced.

NOTE *An AutoLookup query is different from a lookup field because the query automatically fills in the data for you, while the lookup field merely displays a list from which you can choose.*

To create an *AutoLookup query*, add the two related tables to the query design, and then drag the join field from the table on the "many" side to the grid. This type of query looks for the related record in the parent table—the "one" side—and retrieves values from other fields in the matching record. The field on the "one" side must be the primary key or have a unique index. But the field on the "many" side can be neither the primary key nor a unique index.

Add any other fields from either table that you want in the form, but don't include the primary key field from the parent table, in this case, Customer ID from the Customers table.

Notice that the Customer ID field in the design grid is from the Workorders table, the "many" side of the relationship.

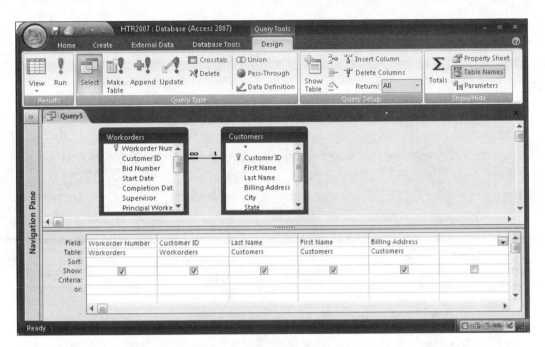

In the query result datasheet, when you add a new record or change the value of the join field on the "many" side, Access automatically looks up and displays the associated values from the table on the "one" side. When you enter a new record such as the Customer ID value—1033—and press the TAB key, the remaining three fields are filled in by Access.

Workorder N	Customer ID	Last Name	First Name	Billing Addre
001	1032	McCoy	John, C	2115 J St
010	1032	McCoy	John, C	2115 J St
013	1032	McCoy	John, C	2115 J St
016	1032	McCoy	John, C	2115 J St
002	1033	Jones	David	329 Fifth
008	1033	Jones	David	329 Fifth
012	1033	Jones	David	329 Fifth
003	1034	Rogers	Phyllis	2478 9th St

CAUTION *Be sure the value entered in the join field on the "many" side exists in the table on the "one" side. If not, Access displays an error message when you try to leave the record. In addition, be sure to include all the required fields and those with validation rules in the query design grid and make sure that their Show boxes are checked.*

You can always update the value of the join field from the "many" side, and Access looks up and displays the associated values from the "one" side. If you want to update the value of the join field from the "one" side, you must have referential integrity enforced with the cascading updates option enabled in the Edit Relationships dialog box for the relationship.

NOTE *Whenever you update the data, Access recalculates any summary totals and expressions using that data.*

Once you design and save an AutoLookup query, it can be used as the basis for a data entry form or a report.

Designing Action Queries

Action queries are used to perform global data management operations on one or more tables at once. The four types of action queries reflect the most common database activities: updating field values, adding new records, deleting records, and creating new tables.

> **NOTE** *The results of action queries cannot be used as a record source for forms or reports. However, if you save the result as a table first, you can use the table as a record source.*

Before undertaking any kind of action query, make a backup copy of the tables that will be involved. If you plan to change several tables, back up the entire database. To create a copy of a table, right-click the table name in the Tables group of the Navigation Pane and choose Copy. Then right-click in the Navigation Pane and choose Paste. Enter a name for the copy in the Paste Table As dialog box and click OK. Accepting the default name Copy of Table *table name* helps keep track of the tables as your database grows. If you plan to make several copies of the table design, you can add the current date to the table name.

> **TIP** *An additional safety precaution you can practice while designing an action query is to switch to Datasheet view to check your progress, instead of running the query. Showing the results in Datasheet view doesn't actually run the query and carry out the intended action, so no data is changed.*

> **CAUTION** *The Editing group in the Advanced set of options in the Access Options list contains three Confirm options, one of which is Action Queries. By default, this option is checked, so Access always asks for confirmation before carrying out an action query. You can clear this option to prevent the display of the confirmation box, but doing so is risky. Running a query inform from the Navigation Pane, even an action query, is so easy. If you clear the Confirm option, you won't even be warned when an action query is about to run.*

Update Query

Update queries are used to change one or more field values in many records at once. You can add criteria that screen the records to be changed, as well as update records in more than one table. Update queries can use most types of expressions to specify the update. Table 9-1 shows some examples.

For example, in the Home Tech Repair database, several bids have expired but can be renewed. To renew the bids, the costs must be increased slightly to reflect inflation and a new expiration date must be set. This involves finding records in the Bid Data table whose Expires date is before August 15, 2007, for example, and then making changes to the related Workorders table to increase the Material Cost and Labor Cost values. If no corresponding work order record exists, the update query doesn't change the Expires value because the

Types of Action Queries

- **Update query**   Makes global changes to fields in a group of records. For example, you can run an update query to raise all the labor costs for jobs in a certain area of the city.

- **Append query**   Adds a group of records from one or more tables to the end of other tables. For example, if you consolidate another contractor's business with your own, you can append his customer list to your own.

- **Delete query**   Deletes a group of records from one or more tables. For example, you can use a delete query to delete records for completed work orders.

- **Make-table query**   Creates a new table from data in one or more existing tables. For example, you can archive outdated information into a new table or make a backup copy of an important table.

relationship is defined as an inner join. Be sure to include one of the identifying fields in the query, so you can tell which records are going to be updated.

To create this update query, start a new query design with the Bid Data and Workorders tables, and then do the following:

1. On the Design tab in the Query Type group, click the Update command. You can also right-click the table pane, point to Query Type, and choose Update Query from the shortcut menu. A new row, Update To, appears in the grid.

2. Drag the Bid Number and Expires fields from the Bid Data field list and Material Cost, and Labor Cost fields from the Workorders field list to the grid.

3. Enter the expression **<8/15/2007** in the Criteria row in the Expires column to limit the records. Access adds the pound sign (#) date delimiters.

4. Enter the following update expressions in the Update To cells:

   - **Bid Number** in the Bid Number column. Access adds quotation marks.

   - **[Expires]+90** in the Expires column.

   - **[Material Cost]*1.05** in the Material Cost column.

Field Type	Expression	Result
Currency	[Material Cost]*1.05	Increases Material Cost by 5%.
Currency	[Workorders].[Material Cost] +[Workorders].[Labor Cost]	Updates the field with the sum of the costs from the Workorders table.
Date	#8/25/2007#	Changes the value to August 25, 2007.
Text	"Completed"	Changes the value to Completed.
Text	"WO"&[Design]	Add characters *WO* to the beginning of the value in the Design field.
Yes/No	Yes	Used with criteria, changes specific values to Yes.

TABLE 9-1   Sample Update Expressions

- **[Labor Cost]*1.05** in the Labor Cost column.

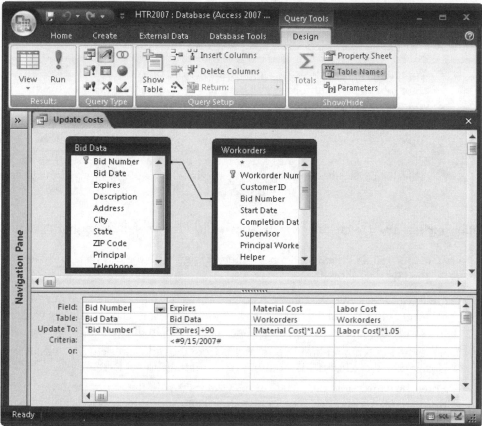

5. Right-click in the table pane and choose Datasheet View from the shortcut menu to see which records will be affected by the update query. If the selection isn't correct, return to Design view and make changes.

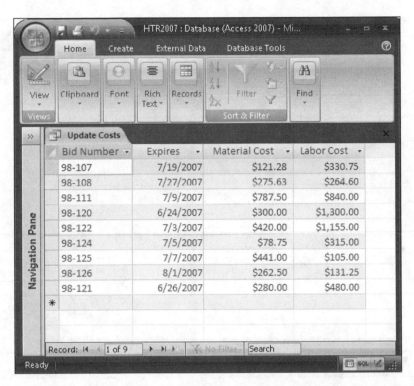

6. Right-click in the table pane and choose Design View to return to the query Design window and save the query as Update Costs, if you haven't already. Then in the Results group, click Run. Access displays a message warning that the update is irreversible.

7. Choose Yes to update the records or No to abandon the process.

To see whether the changes were correctly made, open both the copy of the original tables and the updated version, and then compare the results. Figure 9-1 shows a comparison of the updated Bid Data records with the backup copy. The nine records that appeared in the Datasheet view of the update query now show the Expires date updated in the left-hand datasheet.

As you can see in Figure 9-1, some of the records in the Bid Data table (for example, numbers 98–102 and 98–104) still have an Expires date prior to August 15, 2007. This might seem confusing or an error, but, as mentioned earlier, they aren't updated because no

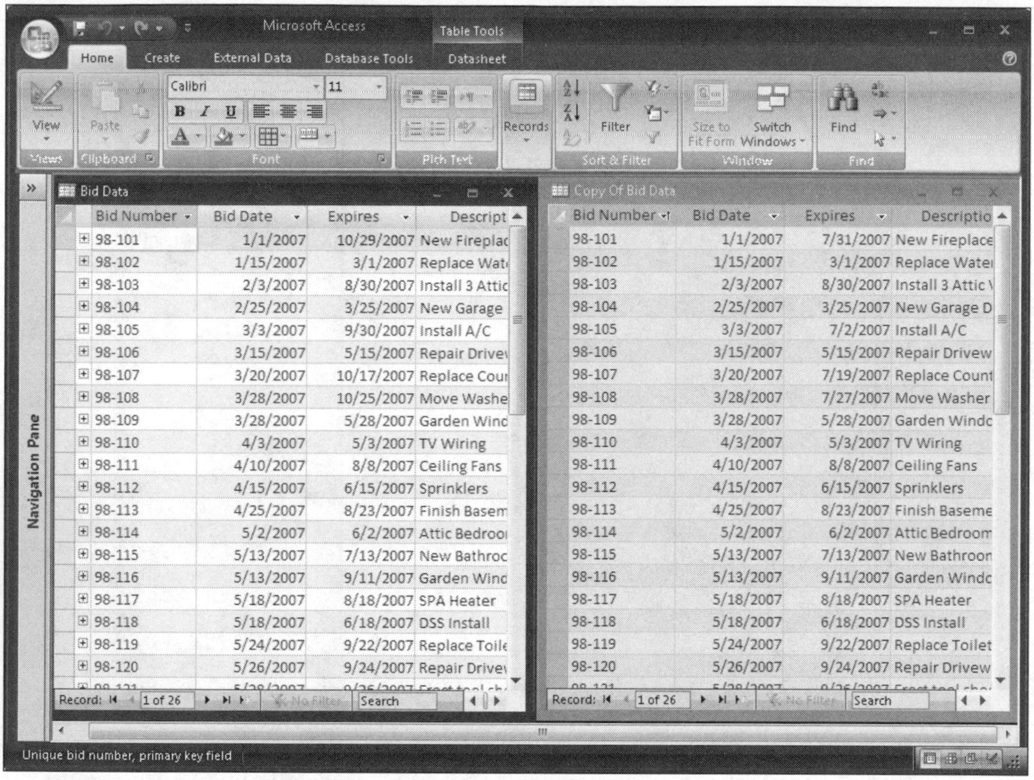

FIGURE 9-1 Comparing updated and backup tables

matching record is in the Workorders record. The join is an inner join, which includes in the result only those records with matching values in the join field.

NOTE *If you enforced referential integrity between related tables in the database and checked the Cascade Update Related Records option in the Edit Relationships dialog box on the "one" side, Access applies the updates to the matching fields on the "many" side, even if they aren't included in the query.*

When you name and save the query, it appears in the Queries group on the Navigation Pane with a warning icon. All the action queries appear with an exclamation point attached to the icon, which warns you that double-clicking this query runs some sort of action. Access displays a confirmation message, however, before running the query, unless you turned off that option (as mentioned earlier).

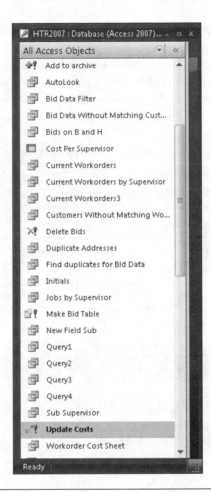

TIP *If you start a new query and decide you want to create a different type, you do not need to scrap the one that you're working on. You can change the query type and proceed. To change the query type while in Design view, choose the type you want from the Query Type group on the Design tab or right-click in the table area of the query window, point to Query Type, and choose the type from the shortcut menu.*

You can create an update query that effectively deletes one or more fields on the "many" side of a one-to-many relationship. To do this, enter either **Null** or **""** in the Update To row for each field you want to delete.

Make-Table Query

The *make-table query* does exactly what it advertises: it makes a new table out of records from one or more tables or queries. Make-table queries are useful in circumstances such as these:

- To export records to another database—for example, to create a table of completed work orders to send to the billing department, which uses another system.

- To export consolidated information from related tables to a nonrelational application, such as Excel or Word.

- To control the information that's exported, such as screening out confidential or irrelevant data.

- To use as a record source for a report of events that occurred during a specific period of time. For example, a report of bids offered during June and July, and the results, including work order information.

- To start the archive table by adding the first set of records, and then using an append query to add more later.

- To replace records in an existing table with a new set.

NOTE *Make-table queries copy the data to the target table. The source tables and queries are unaffected. Use a delete query if you want to remove the records from the original table after you copy them to the new table.*

To build a make-table query, start a new query with the tables and queries from which you want records, and then do the following:

1. In the Query Type group, click the Make-Table Query command. Access displays the Make Table dialog box that requests a name for the table—either a new table or an existing one.

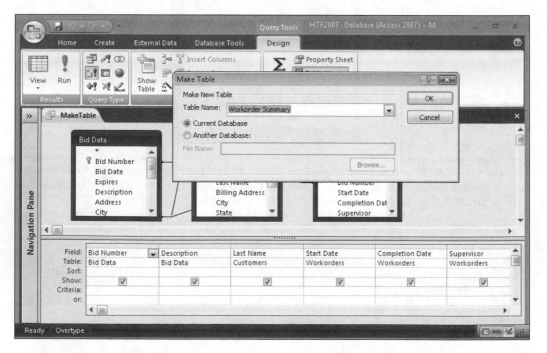

2. Do one of the following:

- If the target table is to be in the same database, enter the table name and make sure the Current Database option is selected; then click OK.

- If the target table is an existing table, choose the table name from the drop-down list. Be aware that the query will replace the records in the existing table.

- If you want the new table to be located in a different database, choose the Another Database option. Then type in the full path and name of the database file in the File Name field, enter the table name, and click OK. If the target isn't an Access database, follow the database name with the name of the application, such as "Paradox." You can also click Browse and look for the other database.

3. Drag the fields from the field lists to the design grid and include record selection criteria, the same as you would with a select query.

4. Right-click in the table pane and choose Datasheet View from the shortcut menu to preview the records to be included in the new table. Return to the query Design view and in the Results group, click the Run command.

5. If you're replacing records in an existing table, Access asks for confirmation before proceeding:

- Respond Yes to continue.

- Respond No to abandon the operation.

- Click No and change the name of the target table by right-clicking in the table pane and choosing Make-Table Query from the shortcut menu. Then choose another table or enter a new table name.

6. Respond Yes or No to the final confirmation box that completes the make-table query.

Although you cannot undo an action query—including the make-table query—if the table isn't what you want, you can delete it and start over.

NOTE *The only field properties inherited by the table created with a make-table query are the field size and data type. All other properties—including the primary key, format, default values, and input masks—aren't inherited and must be reset in the new table or in the form or report that uses the new table as a record source.*

Make-table queries create snapshots of the data as it was at the time it was run and, as such, aren't updateable manually. If the data in the source tables changes, run the query again to update the values.

TIP *If you don't get the results you want with an action query, Access might be able to point you to a solution. Microsoft Office Online Help contains solutions to many of the problems you could encounter, such as appending the wrong records or dealing with key violations.*

Append Query

When you want to add records from one or more source tables to other tables, you first decide which fields you want to append, and then locate the target table and determine which fields in the target table correspond to the fields from the source. The field values are only copied—they aren't moved—to the target table.

Note To be matched, fields do not need to have the same names, but they do need to be of the same data type. The target table also does not need to have exactly the same structure as the source table.

You can append records to a table in the current database or another Access database; establish a path to a FoxPro, Paradox, or dBASE database; or enter a connection string to a Sequential Query Language (SQL) database.

For example, the Home Tech Repair Bid Data table gets large and cumbersome if none of the records are removed. The bids that have been lost are no longer needed in the current table, but they might be useful in an archive history of past bidding. Before you can archive the records, you need to create a new table with the same design as the Bid Data table to hold the records with the following steps:

1. Right-click the Bid Data table name in the Navigation Pane and choose Copy.

2. Right-click in the Tables group in the Navigation Pane and choose Paste.

3. In the Paste Table As dialog box, name the new table **Lost Bid Archive**, choose Structure Only, and then click OK.

The new table name appears in the Tables group in the Navigation Pane. Now you're ready to create the append query that will copy the records with Lost in the Award Date field to the Lost Bid Archive table. If the target table has the same field names as in this case, Access automatically fills in the field names in the query grid. If they aren't the same, you must enter the target field names.

To create the append query, do the following:

1. Start a new query, adding only the Bid Data table from the Show Tables dialog box, and then in the Query Type group click the Append Query command. The Append dialog box appears.

2. Enter the table name, **Lost Bid Archive**, in the Table Name box, choose Current Database, and then click OK.

3. Because you want all the field data in the selected records to be archived, drag the asterisk (*) from the Bid Data field list to the grid. If you don't want all the fields appended, drag the fields individually to the grid.

4. To add the Lost criteria, drag the Award Date field to the grid and enter **"Lost"** in the Criteria row.

5. Remove the field name from the Append To cell, so you won't append two copies of the Award Date field.

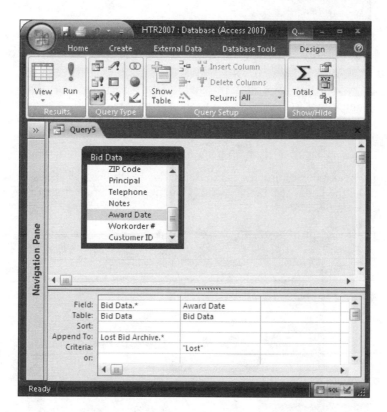

6. Switch to Datasheet view and check for *Lost* in the Award Date field to make sure the right records will be appended, and then switch back to Design view and save the query as Add to Archive.

7. Click Run. Access displays a message asking for confirmation to append six records.

8. Choose Yes to complete the addition or No to cancel the operation.

Once you copy the Lost Bid data records to the archive, the next step is to remove them from the original table.

Delete Query

The *delete query* might be the most dangerous action query of all. Even though no action queries can be reversed, deletion seems to be an even more drastic type of activity—all the more reason to make a backup copy of all the tables before you begin a delete query.

A delete query removes entire records from the table, not only the specified fields. You can remove records from a single table, multiple tables related by one-to-one, or multiple tables related by one-to-many.

Deleting from a Single Table

Deleting records from a single table or several one-to-one tables is straightforward. Add the tables to the delete query design and specify the criteria for deleting the record—for example, the account is paid in full, the work order is completed, or the house has been sold.

To delete records from a single table:

1. Start a new query with the table from which you want to delete records, such as a copy of the Bid Data table.

2. In the Query Type group, click the Delete Query command; or right-click in the table pane, point to Query Type, and then choose Delete Query from the context menu. The Delete row is added to the grid. The only choices in the Delete row are Where and From.

3. Drag the asterisk from the field list to the grid. The Delete row now shows *From*.

4. Drag the field containing the value that indicates the record should be deleted (for example, the value *Lost* in the Award Date field) and enter the criteria expression in the Criteria row.

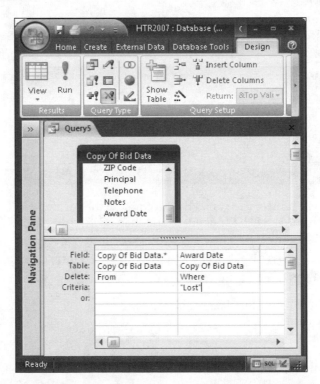

5. Switch to Datasheet view to preview the records to be deleted and make any necessary changes in the query design.

6. Return to Design view and run the query. You will be warned that you will modify data in your table. Respond Yes to proceed or No to cancel the operation.

TIP *If you run a delete query, you may see the message, "Could not delete from the specified table." To fix this, change the query's Unique Records property to Yes.*

> **Warning about Cascade Delete**
> Checking the Cascade Delete Related Records option when enforcing referential integrity can be even more disastrous than checking the Cascade Update Related Records option. With Cascade Delete checked, Access automatically deletes all matching records whether or not the table is included in the query. For example, if you delete a customer, records for all the bids and work orders for that customer would also be deleted.
>
> Before you use a delete query, examine the relationships that you've established between the table and other tables in the database. Of course, if referential integrity is enforced on a relationship without the cascade options, you might not be permitted to delete the records on the "one" side if this would leave orphans on the "many" side.

Deleting from Related Tables

Deleting records from a table or multiple tables that are related with a one-to-many relationship can get complicated, especially if you're enforcing referential integrity and have selected Cascade Delete Related Records for the relationship.

If you have enabled Cascade Delete Related Records for the relationship, all matching records on the "many" side are deleted with the records on the "one" side. If the option isn't selected, you must run two delete queries to accomplish the job. First, delete the records from the tables on the "many" side, and then go after the records on the "one" side.

To delete records from multiple related tables, start a new query with all the involved tables, and then do the following:

1. In the Query Type group, click the Delete Query command.

2. Drag the field to use for criteria to the grid.

3. Drag the asterisk (*) from all the field lists of the tables on the "many" side of the relationships to the grid. Don't drag the "one" table to the grid yet.

4. Switch to Datasheet view to preview the records that will be deleted.

5. Return to Design view and click the Run command.

6. Remove the "many" side tables from the Query window.

7. Drag the asterisk (*) from the "one" table to the grid and run the query again to delete the records from that table.

TIP *You can combine an append query with a delete query using the same query design to create the two-step archive operation that adds the selected records to the history table and deletes the same records from the source table. After making sure that you have selected the correct records to archive, run the append query to add the records to the target table. Then, in the Query Design view, right-click and point to Query Type, and change the query to a delete query. When you run the query again, it deletes the same records from the source table.*

Introducing Structured Query Language

Structured query language (SQL) is the language Access uses behind the scenes to program query operations. SQL is made up of statements, each complying with specific language syntax and conventions. To view or edit SQL statements while working on a query, switch from Design view to SQL view by one of the following methods:

- On the Design tab's Results group, click the View down arrow and choose SQL View from the context menu.
- Right-click in the table pane and choose SQL View from the shortcut menu.

You can enter a SQL statement in most places where you would enter a table, query, or field name, such as the record source for a form or report. If you use a wizard to create a form or report, the record source is a SQL statement created by Access.

> **TIP** *Using SQL statements instead of saved queries as record sources simplifies the database by having fewer objects to store and maintain.*

Looking at SQL Statements

Before going too far into the details of the language, let's look at some simple examples of SQL statements. The SELECT statement is the most common—and the most important—statement in SQL. All select queries start with the SELECT statement. For example, if you create a query that retrieves all the fields in records from the Bid Data table with "Lost" in the Award Date field, the SQL version would look like this:

```
SELECT *
FROM [Bid Data]
WHERE [Award Date]="Lost";
```

- The SELECT * command means that all fields should be included, as does SELECT ALL.
- The FROM clause names the table(s) that contains the records to retrieve.
- The WHERE clause specifies the selection criteria. This is the same value you entered in the Criteria row of the Award Date column. Add the WHERE clause only if you included the FROM clause.
- SQL statements always end with a semicolon (;).

> **TIP** *If you create the query in the design grid and then switch to SQL view, you'll see a lot of extra parentheses that Access adds to keep things straight. You can enter the SQL statement as it's shown here and it will work fine.*

If you don't want to retrieve all the fields, use the SELECT command with a list of field names. The following query displays the Bid Number and Expires fields for Bid Data records in which the Award Date field contains "Lost" or the Expires value is prior to June 1, 2007:

```
SELECT [Bid Number], Expires
FROM [Bid Data]
WHERE [Award Date]="Lost" OR Expires<#6/1/2007#;
```

TIP *A field name that contains a space, such as a Bid Number, must be enclosed in brackets. If no space is in the field name, you do not need to add brackets, but Access usually adds them anyway to be safe.*

All queries result in SQL statements that can be viewed by switching to SQL view. Right-click in the table pane and choose SQL View from the shortcut menu; or on the Design tab's Results group, click the View command and choose SQL from the context menu.

Figure 9-2 shows the SQL views of a few queries in the Home Tech Repair database, including the action queries from the previous section.

Before going into the conventions and syntax of SQL, look at the Customers Without Matching Workorders (shown in the image at the upper-left corner in Figure 9-2). This query was created to locate records in the Customers table that had no matching records in the Workorders table. The entire SQL statement is shown here:

```
SELECT Customers.[First Name], Customers.[Last Name], Customers.[Billing Address],
Customers.City, Customers.State, Customers.ZIP, Customers.[Phone Number]
FROM Customers LEFT JOIN [Current Workorders] ON Customers.[Customer ID] = Current
Workorders.[Customer ID]
WHERE (((Current Workorders.[Customer ID]) Is Null));
```

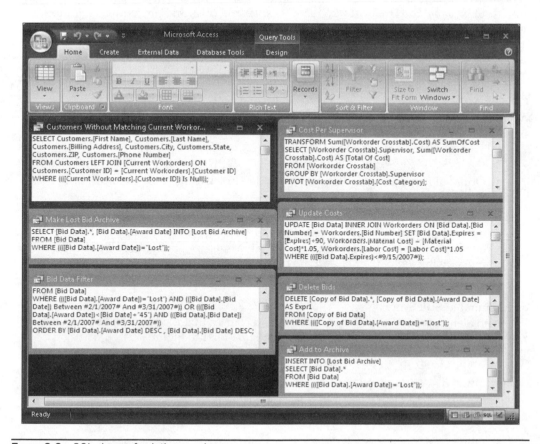

FIGURE 9-2 SQL views of existing queries

This statement has two clauses in addition to the SELECT command: FROM and WHERE.

- The SELECT command determines which fields are included in the query result. Because two tables are involved in the query, field names must be qualified with the table name separated by a period (.).

- The FROM clause shows the table name and also specifies the join type that relates the Customers table with the Workorders table as a left outer join, using the Customer ID as the matching field.

- The WHERE clause sets the criteria that limits the result to Customer records with no matching records in the Workorders table. That is, the Customer ID field has a null value because no matching record exists.

Each clause begins on a separate line for readability; the entire statement is treated as a single line in Access.

SQL Conventions and Syntax

Like all programming languages, SQL has strict conventions and grammatical syntax. The more sophisticated the language, the more complex the rules and procedures. For more details on SQL commands, refer to the many Help topics that Access provides.

The most significant elements in SQL are the statements, clauses, predicates, and declarations. Each statement has a precisely defined syntax that must be followed. The syntax is expressed using typical programming-language conventions.

Reading SQL Conventions

When you look up a SQL command or other element in the Help file, the syntax is expressed using certain conventions:

- All SQL keywords are in uppercase—for example, SELECT, WHERE, and FROM.

- Optional items are in italics and enclosed in brackets ([])—for example, SELECT [*predicate*].

- Choices are enclosed in curly braces ({}) and separated by vertical bars (|)—for example, {* | *table*.* | [*table*.]*field1*[,[*table*.]*field2*[,...]]}, which gives you the choice among including all records in a single table query (*), including all records in a named table (*table*.*), or specifying the fields one at a time, separated by commas. The ellipsis (...) indicates a repeating sequence.

Understanding SQL Syntax

The main elements in SQL are the statements and clauses that accompany the statements. You've already seen examples of the SQL statements (refer to Figure 9-2):

- SELECT retrieves all or specific records from one or more tables or queries.

- SELECT...INTO creates a new table from fields in existing tables (the make-table query).

- INSERT...INTO adds one or more records to a table (the append query).

- UPDATE changes specific values based on specified criteria (the update query).

- DELETE removes records from one or more tables (the delete query).

- TRANSFORM calculates values for a crosstab query.

The following shows the syntax of the SELECT statement. The other statements are similar in structure, using many of the same clauses and options.

```
SELECT [predicate]{*|[table.*|[table.]field1
[AS alias1][,table.]field2[AS alias2][,…]]}
FROM tableexpression [,…][IN externaldatabase]
[WHERE…]
[GROUP BY…]
[HAVING…]
[ORDER BY…]
[WITH OWNERACCESS OPTION]
```

Table 9-2 explains the parts of this SELECT statement.

NOTE *Using the* DISTINCT *or* DISTINCTROW *predicate in a* SELECT *statement is equivalent to setting the query's Unique Values or Unique Records property to Yes.*

The SELECT statement has several clauses, most of which are optional. Only the FROM clause is required; it specifies one or more tables or queries containing the fields listed in the SELECT statement. The FROM clause can include the IN clause to retrieve data from an external database.

The other clauses in the SELECT statements are as follows:

- WHERE contains a criteria expression that specifies which records to retrieve from the tables in the FROM clause.

- GROUP BY combines records with identical values in the specified field. You can specify up to 10 groupings. The order of the field names in the list determines the grouping levels from the highest to the lowest.

Part	Explanation
Predicate	One of the four standard optional predicates: ALL to include all records; DISTINCT to omit records with duplicate data in selected fields; DISTINCTROW to omit data based on entire duplicate records; or TOP*n* [PERCENT] to limit the records to a certain number or percentage of records.
*	Includes all fields from the specified table or tables.
Table	Names the table containing the fields that determine which records to select.
field1, field2	Names the fields containing the data to retrieve.
alias1, alias2	Specifies text to use as column headers instead of the field names.
tableexpression	Names the table or tables containing the data to retrieve.
externaldatabase	Name of database containing the tables, if not in the current database.

TABLE 9-2   Parts of the SELECT Statement

- HAVING specifies which grouped records to display. After the records are grouped in accordance with the GROUP BY clause, HAVING applies a criteria expression to the group.

- ORDER BY sorts the resulting records in ascending or descending order based on the value in one or more specified fields. ORDER BY is usually the last clause in a SELECT statement.

- WITH OWNERACCESS OPTION gives the user running the query the same permissions as the query's owner in a declaration.

You can use any valid expression in a SQL SELECT statement or in WHERE, ORDER BY, GROUP BY, or HAVING clauses. The same rules apply to expressions used in query statements as apply elsewhere.

When included, the INNER JOIN, LEFT JOIN, and RIGHT JOIN commands follow the FROM clause and specify the type of join to be used in the query. The update query created earlier in the chapter resulted in the SQL statement shown in Figure 9-2 (second window on the right side). This query includes this command:

```
UPDATE [Bid Data] INNER JOIN Workorders ON ([Bid Data].[Bid Number] =
Workorders.[Bid Number]) SET [Bid Data].{Bid Number] = "Bid Number",[Bid
Data].Expires = [Expires]+90, Workorders.[Material Cost] = [Material
Cost]*1.05, Workorders.[Labor Cost] = [Labor Cost]*1.05
WHERE ((([Bid Data].Expires)<#8/15/2007#));
```

The INNER JOIN operation establishes the Bid Number as the joining fields in the two tables. The SET operation contains the Bid Number value and the expressions entered in the Update To rows used to update the three fields. The WHERE clause contains the criteria expression that specifies which records to update.

Refer to Chapter 5 for a review of the join types and how they can affect query results.

CAUTION *If you query two or more tables, you must include a WHERE or JOIN clause or you get the Cartesian product of the number of records in the tables. For example, if one table has 50 records and the other 100, the query result will contain 5000 records.*

Creating a Subquery

Subqueries are select queries within other select or action queries. You can use a subquery to specify a criterion for selecting records from the main query or to define a new field to include in the main query. Using subqueries is like layering filters to close in on the data you need, except the subquery runs first and results in a single criterion value that is used in the main query.

Defining a Criterion

To define a criterion, enter the SELECT statement directly in the Criteria cell in the query design grid or in a SQL statement in place of an expression in a WHERE or HAVING clause.

For example, suppose you want to see fields from the Workorders table for all the jobs run by supervisors who have at least one job incurring more than $1000 in material costs. Start a new query and add the Workorders table, and then place the Workorder Number, the Bid Number, Supervisor, and Material Cost fields in the grid.

To place this subquery in the query grid, type **IN (SELECT Supervisor FROM Workorders WHERE [Material Cost]>1000)** into the Supervisor field Criteria cell. Be sure to enclose the SQL statement in parentheses. If you switch to SQL view, you can see both the main query and the subquery created from the criteria:

```
SELECT Workorders.[Workorder Number], Workorders.[Bid Number], Workorders.
Supervisor, Workorders.[Material Cost]
FROM Workorders
WHERE (((Workorders.Supervisor) IN (SELECT Supervisor FROM Workorders WHERE
[Material Cost]>1000)));
```

When you run the query, you see that Supervisor Ferrell has four jobs listed, one of which has a material cost greater than $1000; Gunderson has five jobs, only one of which has material cost of more than $1000; and Byron has only one job listed. You can compare the results of this query/subquery to the full Workorders table to see how it works.

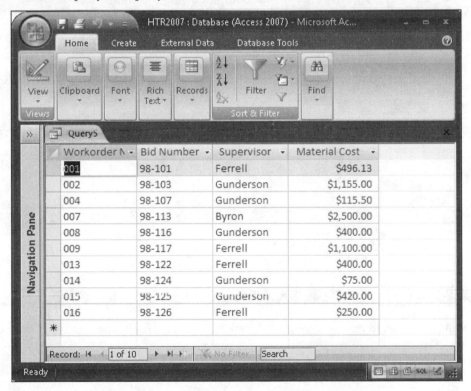

Other predicates you can use with subqueries include the following:

- ANY or SOME, which are synonymous and retrieve records in the main query that satisfy the comparison with any of the records retrieved by the subquery.

- ALL is more restrictive and retrieves only those records in the main query that satisfy the comparison with all the records retrieved by the subquery. For example, all the supervisors' jobs would need to have more than $1000 in material costs for the records to be retrieved by the main query.

- IN retrieves records in the main query for which some record in the subquery meets the comparison.

- NOT IN is the opposite of IN and retrieves records in the main query for which no record in the subquery meets the comparison.

- EXISTS is used in true/false comparisons to determine whether the subquery returns any records at all.

Defining a New Field

To use a subquery to define a new field, type the statement in the Field cell of an empty column. For example, the following subquery adds the Address field from the Bid Data table to the grid.

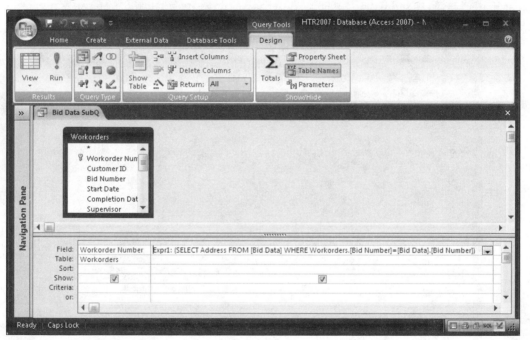

You can return to the Field cell and change the Expr1: default field name to a more informative one, such as Address but be sure to keep the colon (:) in the query design. You can also rename the field later in Datasheet view.

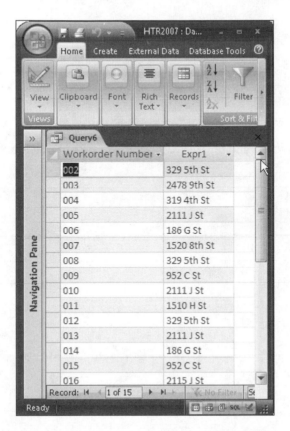

Although this is a simple example, you can see that using subqueries to define fields based on values found in other tables can reduce the number of tables you need in a query. In this case, you didn't have to add the related Bid Data table to the query design to include the job address.

NOTE *You cannot calculate totals with, or group records by, fields defined with subqueries.*

Summary

In the first chapters of this book, you learned how to construct tables and databases and store information efficiently. Now you've seen how to create a wide variety of queries that help you retrieve information. Many queries selectively retrieve information based on carefully specified criteria, while others perform data management operations on records in one or more tables.

Queries have been the mainstays of data retrieval in the past and continue to provide valuable services. One of the principal uses for queries has been as the basis for form and report designs. With the development of the new form and report design capabilities in Access 2007, you might find that you do not need to create a query first, that you can do it right in the object design. The Form and Report Wizards also help select the proper data by filtering records and adding calculated controls.

The next five chapters discuss designing standard and custom forms and reports, including user-interactive data entry forms, special reports used for printing envelopes and mailing labels, and charts and graphs that visually represent trends and other data.

Creating Form and Report Designs

Now that you've seen how to store data efficiently in a relational database and how to retrieve the information you want in exactly the arrangement that will be most helpful, it's time to look at how you can present the information to the world. Information can be displayed on the screen in forms suitable for viewing or editing. These forms can contain data from more than one table, and they have a custom appearance that enhances the understanding of the information and improves the chances for accurate data entry.

If you need to print the information, such as for an annual report or form letter, or simply to transport the information to the outside world, Access offers you a variety of reporting features. You can even create a report that prints on preprinted forms, such as those required by the Internal Revenue Service.

This chapter begins the series that covers form and report development. With Access 2007, designs of the two objects contain mostly the same ingredients, so these common features are discussed in this chapter. Subsequent chapters delve more into features and capabilities that are limited to one object or another.

Deciding the Database Object Type

Access 2007 offers three ways to arrange information for display or distribution. The choice of database object type depends on the specific purpose of the object and how you plan to distribute the information.

- Forms are commonly used for data entry and editing, as well as viewing. You can also print data from a form or save the form as a report for more customizing and printing.

- Reports are used primarily for distributing printed information to recipients within or outside the organization.

- Report snapshots are high-fidelity versions of a report that preserve the two-dimensional layout, graphics, and other embedded objects of the report. A snapshot is stored in a separate file that can be distributed via e-mail to recipients who do not have Access installed on their computers.

This chapter focuses on the design elements common to forms and reports. See Chapter 13 for a discussion on report snapshots, including how they're distributed and viewed.

Common Design Elements

Forms are used mostly for data entry and viewing. They can include user-interactive elements for acquiring additional information and executing user choices. *Reports* are mainly used for presenting information in a static format. Reports are often printed for distribution to other members of the organization.

The design elements common to forms and reports include the record source that contains the data and the graphical objects added to the design. Many of the properties set to control the appearance and behavior of the form or report and their components are also common to both.

Choosing a Record Source

The source of the data you want to include in the form or report can be a table, a query containing fields from one or more tables, or a SQL statement. For example, if you want to display a list of the Home Tech Repair customers, you would choose the Customers table as the record source for the form. If you want to print cost information for the current work orders, you would base the report on the Workorder Cost Sheet query that relates three tables and retrieves data from all three. A SQL statement can also be used in place of a query.

When you create a new form or report with the Form or Report Wizard, the first question asks what the record source is. Similarly, when you create a new object from scratch in the Design window, your first job is to choose the record source from the tables or queries in the current database. The individual fields in the underlying tables and queries become controls in the design.

Any sort orders and filters you saved with the table or query are inherited by the form or report. They aren't applied by default, but they are inherited, so you can easily apply them to sort or filter the information in the form or report.

The record source is one of the properties of every form and report. The only exceptions are special-purpose forms used for user input, such as pop-up forms, or modal dialog forms that present alternative courses of action and don't involve data fields. Forms and reports that don't have a record source are called *unbound* objects.

Understanding Controls

The form or report design is made up of elements called *controls*. All the information shown on a form or report is represented by controls. A control is a graphical object you place on a form or report to display data, perform an action, or enhance the appearance of the form or report. Examples of controls can be boxes that show field values, field labels, lines and rectangles, and command buttons.

Controls come in three basic types, depending on their relationship to values in the tables:

- **Bound control**   Gets its value from a field in the table or query and, as the data changes, the value of the bound control changes with it. The data fields you add to a form design are examples of bound controls.

- **Unbound control**   Has no tie to the underlying table data and retains the value you enter. Examples of unbound controls are lines, rectangles, text, and images.

- **Calculated control**   Gets its value from values in the table and is an expression containing functions and operators, in addition to fields, that produces a result.

The value shown in a calculated control changes as the values in the underlying fields change, but you cannot directly edit a calculated control.

Table 10-1 shows a list of the most common controls used in form and report designs. Most of them can be used in both, but a few are unique to one or another type of design. Although the user-interactive controls, such as command buttons and combo boxes, appear in the report Controls group, they aren't usually used in report designs.

Below is a form with many of the typical controls you can add to your form and report designs. The option group contains a set of option buttons but, in this case, they could also be check boxes or toggle buttons. The combo box is shown expanded to display the value list. Controls are all accessible from the Controls group on the Design tab, which is displayed during the form or report design process.

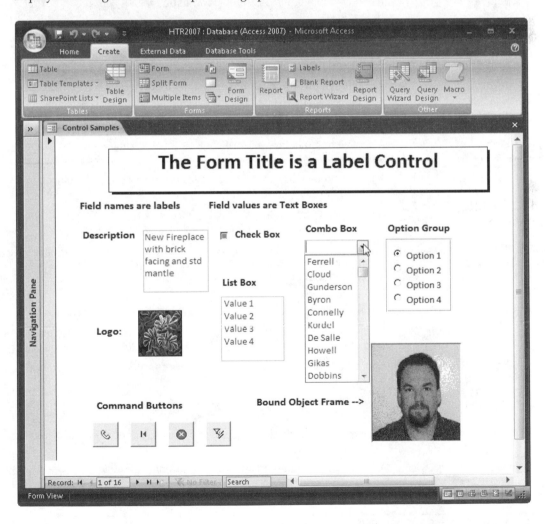

NOTE *In Chapter 12, you will learn about more special controls that you can add to forms, including hyperlinks.*

Control	Description
Bound object frame	A container that displays an Object Linking and Embedding (OLE) object such as an image stored in the record source.
Check box	A control that displays a Yes/No value from the record source. Can be used to represent one of a set of mutually exclusive options in an Option Group control.
Combo box	A control that combines a drop-down list of values with a text box for data entry.
Button	A control that initiates an action, such as opening a linked form, running a macro, or calling a Visual Basic for Application (VBA) procedure. Often shown with an image instead of text.
Image	An unbound picture, such as a company logo.
Label	Descriptive text, such as titles, captions, or instructions.
Line	A straight line used to divide parts of the design.
List box	A control that displays a list of choices, such as values for a field or search criteria.
Logo	A picture to be used as a logo on a form or report. Usually placed in the form or report header section.
Option button	A standalone control that displays a Yes/No value. Can be used to represent one of a set of mutually exclusive options in an option group control.
Option group	A frame with a limited set of alternatives in the form of check boxes, option buttons, or toggle buttons that relate to the same action or type of field value.
Page break	A control that creates a form with more than one page or causes a report to move to the next printed page.
Rectangle	A box that can be drawn for visually grouping fields or other text.
Subform/Subreport	A form or report contained within another form or report that shows data from related tables.
Tab	A control that shows a multiple-page form with tabs at the top of each page.
Text box	A control that displays field data from tables, queries, or calculated fields.
Toggle button	A button that represents an on or off setting.
Unbound object frame	A container for displaying an object not tied to an underlying table.

TABLE 10-1   Access Design Controls

Form and Report Design Properties

You saw in earlier chapters that databases, tables, queries, and fields have properties you can set to customize their appearance and behavior. Forms and reports, as well as all their controls, also have properties. This chapter discusses properties that apply primarily to forms and reports, as well as the controls they contain. Forms and reports have some of the same properties, such as record source, caption, width, and filter, but each has a few unique properties that you will learn about in later chapters. For example, forms have properties that apply to user interfaces and events that occur when a user edits data, clicks a button, or presses TAB. Reports, on the other hand, have properties such as page header/footer text and record grouping for summary reports.

Each type of control also has an appropriate set of properties, such as name, caption, source, format, decimal places, color, filter, position, and size. All the properties relevant to the currently selected control are displayed in a pane called a *property sheet*. You will see how to examine and set these properties in the section "Using Property Sheets."

Working in the Design Window

Similarities also exist in the form and report Design windows. The ribbon tabs and groups are nearly identical and the design surface looks the same. The only difference between them shows up at the beginning of a new design. The report Design window shows the page header and footer sections by default, but in the new form Design window, the form header and footer sections are optional, and only the Detail section is shown at the outset. You can add the headers and footers to the form design, if needed.

Access provides three major contextual ribbon tabs for building forms and reports:

- The Create tab includes four groups for starting new object designs: Tables, Forms, Reports, and Other. The Other objects include queries, macros, and Visual Basic (VB) modules.

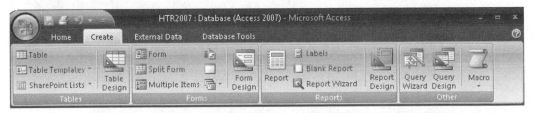

- The Design tab provides five groups for adding fields and controls, formatting, changing properties, switching object views, and other tools. The Report Design tab has an additional group with commands to group and summarize data.

- The Arrange tab has six groups with commands to align and group controls and further improve the design arrangement.

You will see how to use these tabs in this and later chapters. Because the two Design windows are so similar, the following paragraphs focus on the form Design window, pointing out any significant differences in the report Design window.

Touring the Form Design Window

To start a new form, click the Create tab and in the Forms group, do one of the following:

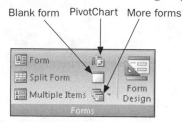

- Click the Form command. This creates a simple form in Layout view. You must have already selected a table or query as the basis for the form.

- Click the Split Form command. This creates a form based on the selected table or query and displays it in Layout view along with a Datasheet view of the underlying data source. You can use the form to enter data into the record selected in the datasheet.

- Click the Multiple Items command. The form resembles a datasheet with data arranged in rows and columns. You must have selected a table or query as the basis.

- Click the PivotChart command. This starts a form with a blank chart for presenting data in a PivotChart format based on data in the selected table or query.

- Click the Blank Form command. This opens a blank form design in Layout view that isn't based on any existing table or query.

- Click the More Forms command. Choose Form Wizard in the gallery to start the Form Wizard. Other options are Datasheet, Modal Dialog, and PivotTable.

- Click the Form Design command. This starts a new form object in Design view not based on a table or query.

In addition to choosing the method of creating the new form, you have the option of selecting a table or query as the basis for the form. This isn't required for either a form or a report unless you plan to add fields to the design. A *modal dialog form* is an example of a form without any data and a cover sheet for a report that does not need to contain any field data.

Access arms you with tools to help create the form, including a new ribbon with a Design tab, a field list from which to choose data, and a group of property sheets. The design surface also has a grid and rulers that help you align and space the controls in

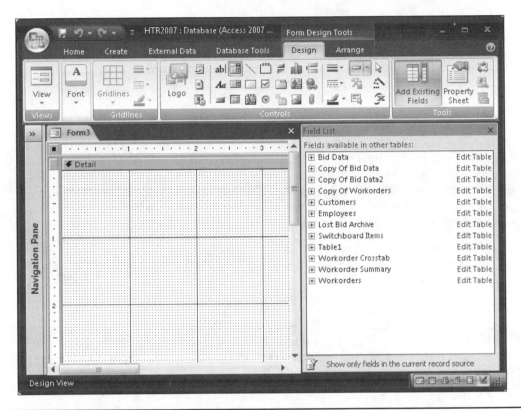

FIGURE 10-1   The form Design window with a few of its tools

the design. Figure 10-1 shows the form Design window with the Form Tools ribbon Design tab and the Field List pane from the Workorders table. Another tool is the Property Sheet, where you can change the properties of the form, a form section, or a control. The next section explains how these tools are used and how to reach them.

To show or hide the Field List pane or the Property Sheet, click the command option again.

The Controls Group

After you've created a new blank form, your next step is to add controls to the design. The Controls group in the Design tab is divided into four sections, the largest of which (second from the right) contains commands for adding 21 different kinds of controls to the form. Hover the mouse pointer over the command icon to see the name of the control.

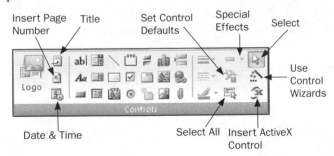

To add a control, click the appropriate command and click in the design where you want the control to appear. You can draw an outline to specify the size of some of the controls.

The first section in the Controls group provides special controls for form and report header sections, such as a logo, a title, page numbers, and the current date/time.

The third section is used for formatting controls by line thickness, type, and color as well as adding special effects such as flat, raised, sunken, and others. One command allows you to change the default properties for specific control types. Another command selects all the controls in the form or report so you can make changes to them all at once.

The fourth section contains three commands. Click the Select command, and you can click one of the control object commands to add the control to the design. The Use Control Wizards command automatically invokes one of the Control Wizards when you add its control to the design. Wizards are available for adding list boxes, combo boxes, option groups, command buttons, subforms, and subreports. If the button is deactivated, a wizard won't be forthcoming when you add one of those controls.

NOTE *When you want to add several controls of the same type, you can lock down the Select control by double-clicking it. This locks the Select command until you click it again or press ESC to unlock the command.*

The Tools Group

You can use the commands in the Tools group to open the Field List pane and property sheets for selected controls or sections. Three other commands open the Visual Basic window so you can view any code attached to the form or report; display the first 10 records in a report preview so you can check the layout; or open the subform or subreport in a separate window to make changes to the design.

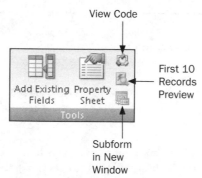

The Font Group

The Font group has all the standard commands for font style, size, color, and alignment as well as the Format Painter and conditional formatting options.

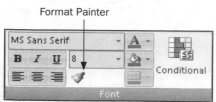

The Gridlines Group

If your controls are contained in a stacked or tabular layout, you can add gridlines with the commands in the Gridlines group to provide visual separation between the controls. You have a choice in the Gridlines gallery of both horizontal and vertical, only one or the other, Cross Hatch, Top, Bottom, Outline, or None. The other three commands set the line thickness, style, and color.

The Property Sheets

Property sheets list all the properties that pertain to the form or the selected form section or control. The properties are grouped by category into four tabs, with a fifth tab showing the entire list. The categories are Format, Data, Event, and Other. As usual, Access gives you more than one way to open a property sheet for the selected object. On the Design tab in the Tools group, click the Property Sheet command, double-click the object in the design, or right-click it and choose Properties from the shortcut menu.

You use property sheets to view properties set for the controls and make any necessary changes. Some properties have drop-down lists of valid settings, while others include the Build option. See "Using Property Sheets" later in this chapter for a complete discussion.

NOTE *If you select more than one control, the Property Sheet shows only those properties the selected group has in common with the title bar, showing Selection Type: Multiple selection. If the selected controls have no properties in common, the property sheet is blank.*

The Field List Pane

The Field List pane resembles the lists you saw in the Relationships window and in a query design, but without the asterisk. To display the Field List pane, in the Tools group, click the Add Existing Fields command. You can use the field list to add fields to a design by dragging the name to the design grid. A text box control in the design displays the field value, and an attached label shows the field caption, which might be different from the field name.

The Alignment Tools

The horizontal and vertical *rulers* at the top and the left side of the form design help you place controls accurately in the design. The *grid* shows as faint dots and lines in the design background. Both are optional, and you can show or hide them by right-clicking anywhere in the form design and choosing Ruler And Grid from the shortcut menu. The single command, Ruler, applies to both the vertical and horizontal rulers.

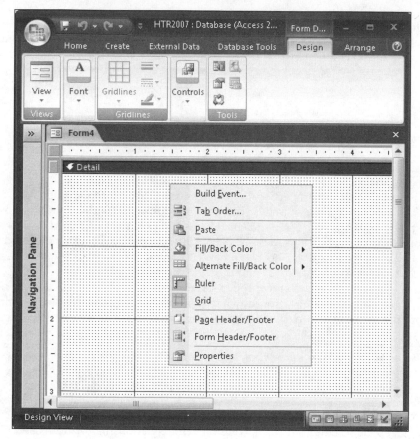

TIP *You can also use the rulers when you want to select more than one control in the design, as you will see later in the section "Selecting Controls and Other Objects" in this chapter.*

One of the settings you can choose from the Control Layout group on the Arrange tab is Snap To Grid. With this setting selected, Access automatically aligns the controls to the nearest gridline. There is more about the commands on the Arrange tab in the "Aligning and Spacing Controls" section later in this chapter.

You can also change the grid granularity to increase or decrease the precision of the control placements. The grid fineness is a property of the form or report design itself and is set in the Format tab of the Property Sheet (see "Using Property Sheets" later in this chapter). The grid is preset to 24 increments per inch horizontally and vertically. You can change either of these settings to any value from 1 to 64 by entering the value in the Grid X (horizontal) or Grid Y (vertical) form property.

Starting a New Design

Let's build a data entry form for Home Tech Repair to enter new work order data. To start the new form, select the Workorders table in the Tables group in the Navigation Pane, and then do the following:

1. In the Create tab's Forms group, click the Form Design command.

2. The blank form shows in Design view and the ribbon changes to the Design tab. In the Tools group, click the Add Existing Fields command or press ALT-F8. The Field List pane opens.

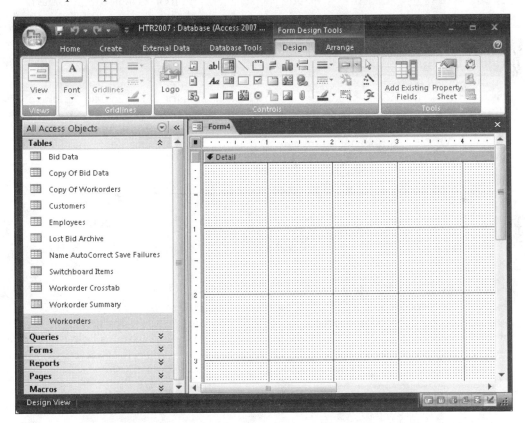

3. Keep the form Design view open for adding fields and other controls.

TIP *If the Field List pane shows no tables or queries, click the message in the pane, "Click to show all tables."*

Other types of forms are available, but for now, let's stick with a simple form that shows one record at a time. (See Chapter 11 for information about other types of forms and how to create them.)

A new form consists only of the Detail section where most of the information is to be displayed one record at a time. If you want some text or other information displayed in a form header or footer, add the section by right-clicking in the form and choosing Form Header/ Footer from the shortcut menu. Both the header and footer are added to the design at the top and bottom of the form, respectively. If you want one and not the other, you can use the mouse pointer to shrink the unwanted header or footer section to nothing. The information placed in the page header and footer appears only when the form is previewed or printed, not when it's open in Form view. To remove the header/footer sections, right-click in the form and choose the command again.

Report designs automatically include page headers and footers in addition to the Detail section. You can add report headers and footers by right-clicking in the report Design view and choosing Report Header/Footer from the shortcut menu.

Adding Controls

You can add all types of controls to the design with the commands in the Tools group, but it's easier to use the Field List pane to add text box controls for the table fields. In the following paragraphs, you will see how to add fields from the Workorders table, a form title and subtitle, and some calculated fields. When you are adding controls to a form design, you have a choice of automatic arrangements that you can use instead of manually adding each control:

- Tabular layout places controls in rows and columns like a datasheet with the labels at the top.
- Stacked layout arranges controls in a vertical list with the labels at the left.

See Chapter 11 for more information about creating a form design using one of the special form design structures.

Adding Controls from the Field List Pane

The Field List pane contains a list of all the tables in the current database. Click the expansion button (+) next to the name of the table you want to use as the basis for the new form. This will show all the fields available in that table. When you drag a field from the list into the design, Access creates a new control that shows field values in the Form view. You can add fields from the list to the design in three ways:

- Drag a field name from the list into the form design. This is much like dragging a field name into the query grid. When you let go of the mouse button, the control appears on the form at that point with an attached label.
- Double-click the field name.
- Press CTRL and select the names of multiple fields to add to the form design. This method can be used only on fields listed in the Fields Available For This View group (see Figure 10-2).

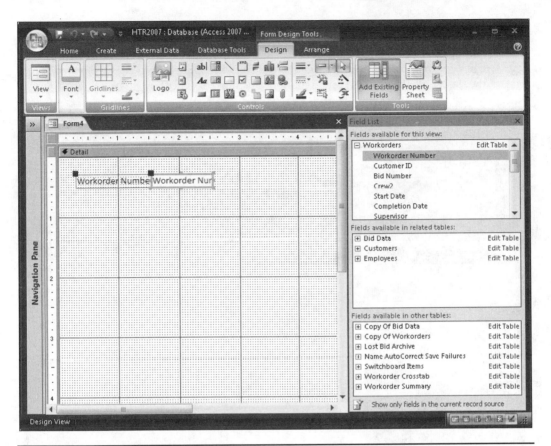

Figure 10-2   Choosing fields from the Field List pane

The Field List pane remains open until you click its Close button, or until you click the Add Existing Fields command again.

Once you have selected a field from one of the tables, the Field List pane changes by grouping the field names (see Figure 10-2) by their availability:

- **Fields Available For This View**   Includes all the fields from the same table you just selected.

- **Fields Available In Related Tables**   Lists the other tables in the database.

- **Fields Available In Other Tables**   Lists other tables not related to the table with which you are working.

To get back to the Home Tech Repair data entry form and add fields from the Workorders table, do the following:

1. Click the Workorder Number field in the Field List pane and drag the button into the design at about the 1½-inch mark on the horizontal ruler.

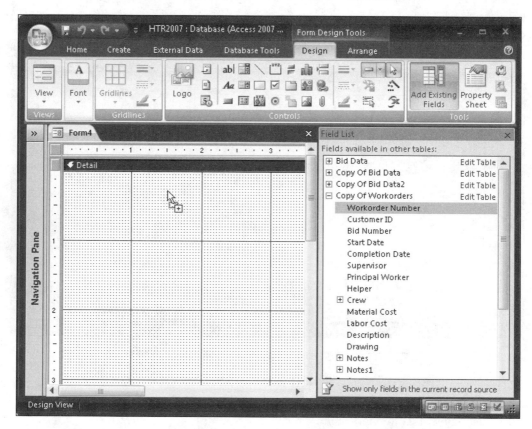

2. Drag the other fields from the list to positions resembling those in Figure 10-3. You need to expand the form design both horizontally and vertically to place the fields as shown.

Once you have added all the fields you want in the design, you can close the Field List pane to make more room on the screen. Next, add a form header, and use the Label command from the Controls group on the Design tab to add a title and subtitle to the header.

Adding Controls from the Tools Group

To add a control, click the appropriate command and draw the control outline in the design. Hover the mouse pointer over the tool's icon to see the name of the control. What happens next depends on the type of control you're adding. If it's a Label control, the insertion point appears inside the outline ready to enter the label text. If you want to add several controls of the same type, you can double-click the tool button to lock it down so you don't have to click it for every control addition.

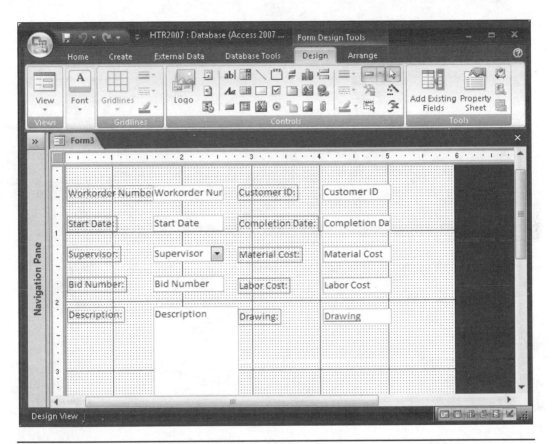

FIGURE 10-3   Workorder fields added to the form design

To add a title in the Workorders form header, do the following:

1. Right-click in the form design and choose Form Header/Footer from the shortcut menu. The new sections are added to the form.

2. Move the mouse pointer to the dividing line between the Form Header and Detail sections, and when it changes shape to a double vertical arrow, click-and-drag the line down ½ inch on the vertical ruler.

3. In the Controls group, click the Label command and draw an outline in the Form Header across the form. The outline appears with the insertion point at the left, ready to type text.

4. Type **Home Tech Repair**, and click outside the label box or press ENTER. If you pressed ENTER, the label control remains selected; otherwise, select the control again.

5. Click the Font group and change the font size to 18-point italic, and centered. Figure 10-4 shows the form with the new header.

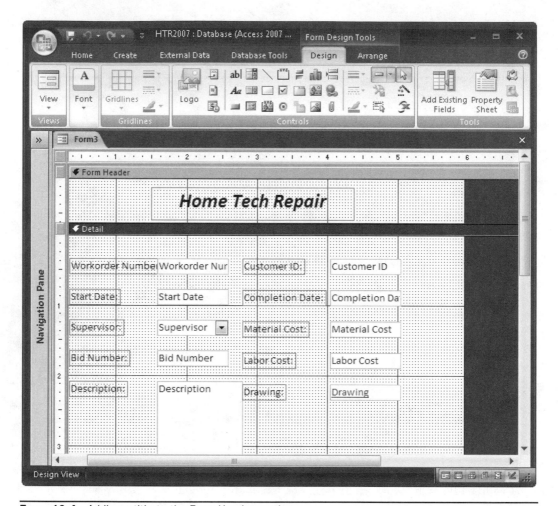

FIGURE 10-4   Adding a title to the Form Header section

TIP   If you see only the Font command and don't see all the font styles and other commands in the Font group, widen your screen to expand the ribbon.

6. Drag the Detail section bar down some to make more room in the Form Header section to add a subtitle.

7. Click the Label command again and draw a box beneath the title. Then type **Data Entry Form—Workorders** in the label control.

8. Use the Font group to change this text to bold and a font size of 10.

9. Right-click the document tab and choose Form View to see how the design looks now.

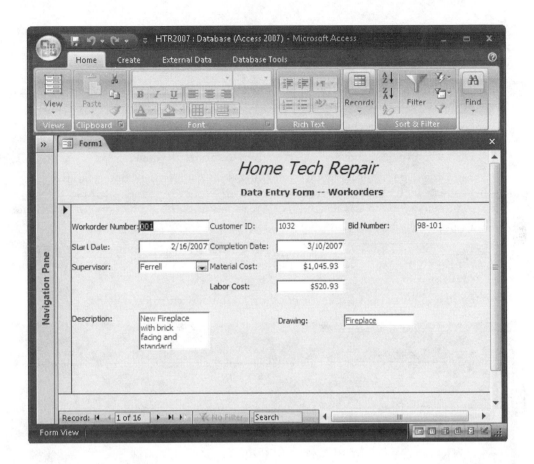

Adding a Calculated Control

A *calculated control* contains values from multiple Text, Number, Currency, or Date fields in the record source. For example, in an earlier chapter, you saw how to combine text values from first and last name fields into a single whole name field. Another example is to create a single field address from separate address, city, state, and ZIP code fields with the expression:

[Address]&", "&[City]&", "&[State]&" "[ZIPcode]

The quotation marks enclose embedded spaces and a comma that separates the values. You can also combine Currency or Date fields—for example:

- **[Birthday]–Date()** displays the number of days until your next birthday.
- **[Price]*1.07+[Shipping&Handling]** computes and displays the sales price, plus 7 percent tax, and adds the shipping and handling charges.

TIP *You can often save processing time by performing the calculations at the query level instead of in the form or report design. Then use the query as the basis for the form or report.*

Now add two calculated fields to the Workorders data entry form that will display the total cost of the job and the number of days estimated to complete the work by doing the following:

1. On the Design tab's Controls group, click the Text Box command and click the area to the right of the Material Cost field. Access adds an unbound text box control.

2. Double-click the new control or click the Property Sheet command in the Tools group to open the Property Sheet for the new unbound text box. You can also right-click a control and choose Properties from the Shortcut menu.

3. Click the Data tab and enter the following expression in the Control Source property box: **=[Material Cost]+[Labor Cost]**. Notice that you must start the expression with an equal sign (=) or Access assumes the expression is a field name.

4. Double-click the attached label that shows Text*n* and type **Total Cost**.

5. Repeat Steps 1 through 4 to add another calculated field to show estimated work time with the expression **=[Completion Date]–[Start Date]** and label it **Work Time (days)**.

6. Switch to Form view to see the design with the new calculated fields.

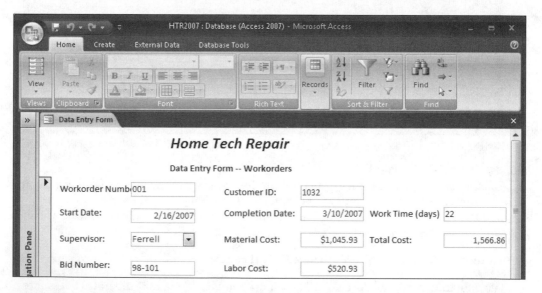

You can see that although the Material Cost and Labor Cost fields retain the currency format with the dollar sign and two decimal places, the Total Cost calculated field does not. You must set the format and other properties separately for calculated fields. In addition, the Work Time control is left-aligned although it is a Number field. The section "Selecting Controls and Other Objects" later in this chapter discusses selecting controls and changing their properties.

> ### Dressing Up with Lines and Rectangles
>
> While they aren't essential, lines are useful in forms and reports for creating a visual separation between parts of the design. A heavy line can help focus attention on a specific area. You can draw a line anywhere in a form or report.
>
> To draw a line, click the Line button in the Design tab's Controls group, and click in the form or report where you want the line to appear, or drag the pointer to draw the line. If you click within the design, Access draws a solid horizontal line, 1-inch long and 1-point thick. When you drag to draw the line, you can drag it in any direction and to any length. To make sure the line is horizontal or vertical when you draw it, hold down SHIFT while you draw.
>
> Rectangles come in handy as boxes that group related data or as a means of emphasizing a control. For example, in a form, you can draw a box around a set of command buttons to set them off from the rest of the design.
>
> To draw a rectangle, click the Rectangle command and drag the cursor to draw the box in the design. After drawing the line or rectangle, you can use the Line Thickness and Line Type commands in the Controls group to change the line or border thickness, choose colors, and add a special effect. You can also use the Property Sheet to change the line or rectangle border style to a dashed or dotted line, for example.

TIP   *A simple calculated control is the current date. To add this control, in the Control Source property, type the expression =**Date()**.*

TIP   *If you draw a rectangle around other controls and add a background color, you might obscure the other controls. To fix this, right-click the rectangle and choose Position in the shortcut menu then click Send To Back in the context menu to place it behind the others. You can also click the Send To Back command in the Position group of the Arrange tab.*

Starting a New Form in Layout View

You don't have to start a new form in Design view. You can use the Layout view instead, which is new with Access 2007. The Layout view is nearly the same as Form view, but you can make changes to the form design in Layout view and see how they will look in Form view. The controls are placed in a stacked or tabular layout as described earlier in the chapter. When you add fields from the Field List pane, they are automatically placed in the layout. Figure 10-5 shows the beginning of a new form in Layout view.

In addition to adding the fields you want, you can add some other controls. The Controls group in the Formatting tab includes Logo, Title, Page Numbers, Date/Time, and options for setting the line thickness, style, and color. No other controls can be added in Layout view, but you can still do all the font formatting and gridline modifications to change the appearance and usability of the form.

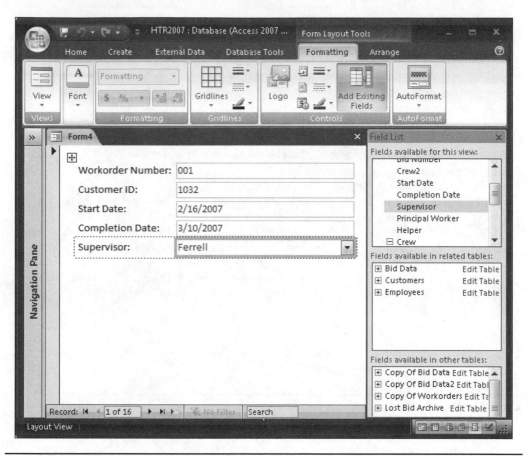

FIGURE 10-5   Starting a new form in Layout view

Modifying Form Sections and Controls

You can customize the controls you add to a form or report design to present information in just the right way. Controls can be moved and resized in the design, and any of their properties can be changed to create the appropriate effect. To change any control, you must first select the control to focus Access's attention on the object.

Selecting Controls and Other Objects

You can select the form or report design, one of the design sections, or one or more of the controls in the design in many ways. The control or object you choose determines the way you select it.

Selecting the Form or Form Section

You can select the form itself in the following ways:

- If the rulers are displayed, click the form selector, the small square in the upper-left corner where the horizontal and vertical rulers meet.

Form selector

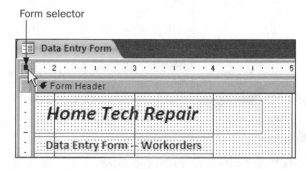

- Click anywhere in the plain background outside the form design.

When the form is selected, the form selector shows a small black square. After selecting the form, you can view and change any of its properties, including the record source, in the form property sheet.

To select a form or report section:

- Click the section selector, the small box in the vertical ruler opposite the section bar.

Section selector   Section bar

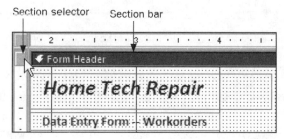

- Click the section bar.
- Click anywhere in the background of the section.

When a section is selected, this horizontal divider that contains the section title appears shaded.

Selecting Controls

That leaves the controls themselves. To select one control, you simply click the control. When you select a control, several small dark squares, called *handles,* appear around the control. You use these handles to move and resize the control. The larger squares are the *move handles* and the smaller squares are the *sizing handles*. (Read more about moving and resizing in the section "Moving and Resizing Controls" later in this chapter.)

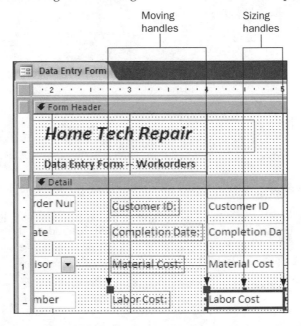

If you want to make the same change to several controls at once, such as moving them or resizing them, you can select them in one of the following ways:

- Hold down SHIFT as you click each control.
- To select a column of controls, click the selection arrow in the horizontal ruler above the controls.
- To select a row of controls, click the selection arrow in the vertical ruler to the left of the controls.
- To select a block of controls, click the selection arrow in one of the rulers and drag to draw a rectangle around the controls. This selects all the controls inside or partially within the rectangle.
- To select a block of controls within the design, but not a complete column or row, click the design outside of any control and draw a rectangle around the controls. If the selected control is a text box, the associated label is also selected.
- To select all the controls in the design, press CTRL-A.

TIP *When you click one of the rulers and draw a rectangle to select a row or column of controls, you can choose to include controls completely or only partially enclosed within the rectangle. This is one of the options you change through the Access Options dialog box. Click the Microsoft Office button and click the Access Options button. Select Object Developers in the left pane and scroll down to the Form/Report options. The Selection Behavior options include Partially Enclosed (the default) and Fully Enclosed.*

To remove the selection, click anywhere outside the selected objects. To remove only a few controls from a group of selected controls, hold down SHIFT and click each of the controls you want to exclude.

A text box control is a special case because it contains two parts that can be treated together or separately: the attached label is usually the field name and the edit region displays the field value. If you click the edit region to select a text box control, you can change the text box properties. If you click the attached label, only the label is selected and you can change its properties. You can move the parts together or separately.

You can tell which element you selected by the size and number of handles that appear around the control. The following shows two text box controls: the edit region of the Labor Cost control is selected, while the label of the Material Cost control is selected.

Once you select the controls you want to work with, you can move, resize, align, space them equally, or change any of their properties.

Grouping Controls

If you want several controls to look and behave alike, you can define them as a single group and format them all at the same time. To create the control group, first select all the controls you want to include, including the labels belonging to the text box controls; then, on the

Arrange tab's Control Layout group, click the Group command. A frame appears around the set of controls, which doesn't show up in Form view. The new form, shown next, contains the cost fields in a single group. When you select one of the controls in the group, they are all selected, including their labels.

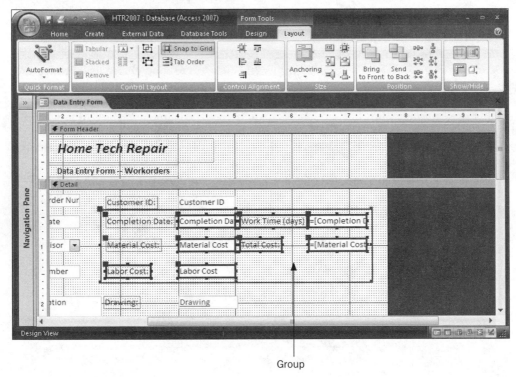

Group

To remove the group designation, click the Ungroup command in the Control Layout group.

Moving and Resizing Controls

One reason you might select a control is to change its size or move it to a different position in the design. As mentioned earlier, when you select a control, handles appear around it. You can use these handles to move and resize a control or a selected group of controls.

Moving Controls

To move a control in the design, move the mouse pointer to the move handle—the larger square in the upper-left corner of a selected control. When the pointer changes shape to a plus sign with arrows at each tip and a larger arrow pointing to its center, click-and-drag the control to the desired position. You can drag it over other controls to place it where you want it.

The text box control is again a special case because it has *two* move handles. If the pointer is directly on the move handle of the edit region, you can move the edit region by itself. If the mouse pointer is elsewhere in the edit region, the control and its label move together. When you move the mouse pointer to the move handle of the attached label, you can move the label by itself. You can't move both parts with the move handle in the label unless you have selected both the label and the edit region.

TIP *Dragging a control by its move handle can be inaccurate, so if you want to move a control a smaller or more precise distance, select the control and hold down* CTRL *while you press the appropriate arrow key on the keyboard. Each keypress moves the control one-fourth of a grid unit in the direction of the arrow. Holding down* CTRL *while you drag a control temporarily turns off the Snap To Grid feature.*

If you selected more than one control, you can drag any one of them and they'll all move together.

Resizing Controls

A selected control has seven sizing handles, one on each side and one at each corner, except the corner with the move handle. Dragging one of the side handles changes the width or height, while dragging a corner sizing handle can change both the height and width at once.

If you selected several controls, they all change to the same size when you drag the sizing handle of one of them.

TIP *If you need to make more precise adjustments in the size of the selected control, hold down* SHIFT *while you click the appropriate arrow key. Each keypress increases or decreases the size of the control by one grid unit.*

The Arrange tab's Control Layout group and the shortcut menu also have options that help you size one control or a group of controls, so they match in length or width. Select the controls you want to resize, and then right-click to open the shortcut menu, point to Size, and choose an option. Or, on the Arrange tab's Size group, click one of the six commands.

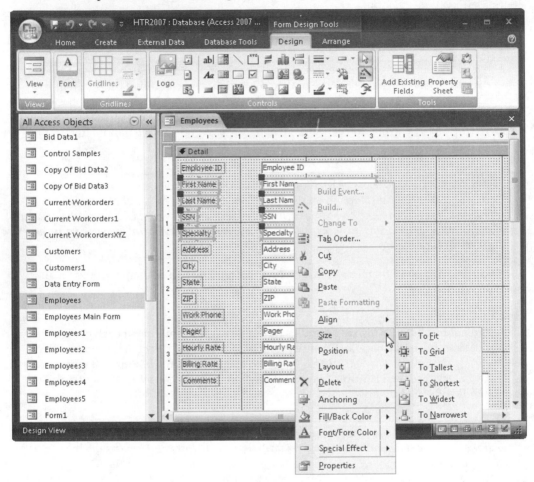

The first command, To Fit, resizes a control to fit its contents. For example, if you've drawn a long label control and entered short text, choose the To Fit command to reduce the size of the control to fit the entered text. The second command, To Grid, automatically adjusts the size of the control, so all four corners fall on the nearest grid points.

TIP *Double-clicking one of the sizing handles automatically resizes the control to fit the contents.*

The remaining four commands adjust the size of each control in a group of controls relative to the tallest, the shortest, the widest, or the narrowest of the group.

TIP *The Snap To Grid command, when checked in the Control Layout group, automatically adjusts the control size when you drag the size handles, so that their boundaries are on gridlines.*

Aligning and Spacing Controls

Having the controls in a form lined up evenly can give the form a professional look. To align a group of controls, first select them, and then on the Arrange tab's Control Layout group, click the Tabular or Stacked command. Tabular arranges all the controls like a datasheet while Stacked puts them in a vertical list. To remove this arrangement, select a member of the group and click the Remove command in the Control Layout group.

If you use the commands in the Control Layout group or right-click and point to Align in the shortcut menu, you are offered several other choices for alignment relative to the members of the group. All members of the group align with the member of the group furthest to the left or right, or closest to the top or bottom.

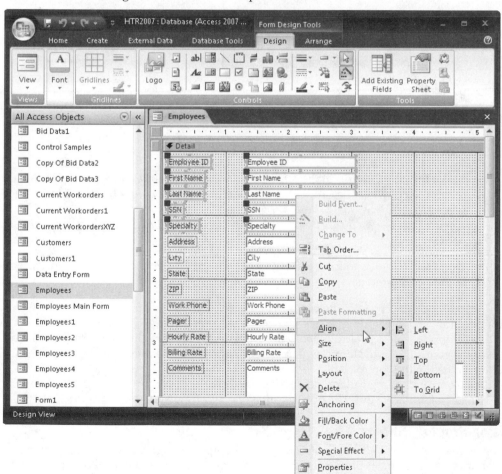

The To Grid command places the upper-left corner of all the selected controls on a gridline. If you have Snap To Grid checked, this is done automatically.

TIP *When aligning controls, be sure to select only those in the same row or the same column. If you have controls in the group from a different area of the form, they will be aligned with the rest, creating a confused appearance.*

When you have a row or column of controls that you want uniformly spaced across or down the form or report, you can use the Horizontal Spacing or Vertical Spacing commands in the Position group on the Arrange tab. These commands are also used to increase or decrease the spaces evenly between the controls.

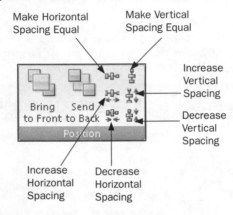

The Horizontal and Vertical Spacing options are as follows:

- **Make Equal**   Controls at the left and right, or the top and bottom of the group remain fixed, while the controls in between are moved to equalize the intervening spaces.

- **Increase**   The left-most or top control remains fixed and the space between the remaining controls is increased by one grid interval.

- **Decrease**   Similar to Increase, except the space between the controls is decreased by one grid interval.

Two more control positioning options are available in the Control Layout group: Control Margins and Control Padding. When you click the Control Margins command, you see a gallery of options: None, Narrow, Medium, and Wide. The None option limits the vertical size of the control to fit the font size. The other options increase the empty space above and below the text in the control.

The Control Padding gallery includes similar options to specify the space between columns in a tabular layout. The options are None, Narrow, Medium, and Wide.

Using Property Sheets

Properties establish the characteristics of form and report design elements. Everything in a form or report design has properties: controls, sections, and even the form or report itself.

Control properties set the structure, appearance, and behavior of the controls. Properties can also determine the characteristics of the text and data contained in a control.

Property sheets contain lists of all the properties that pertain to the selected control or group of controls. To open a property sheet for a control, do one of the following:

- Double-click the control.
- Select the control, and on the Design tab's Tools group, click the Property Sheet command.
- Right-click the control and choose Properties from the shortcut menu.
- Select the control and press ALT-ENTER.

The list of properties depends on the current selection. The All tab of the Property Sheet for the Workorder Number text box control shows all the control's property settings. As you can tell by the scroll bar, quite a few properties are included in the list.

The properties are grouped into tabs in the sheet by type: Format, Data, Event, Other, and All. Click the tab that will show the properties you want to change or stay with All to see the entire list.

To change a property, click the property in the list, and then do one of the following:

- Type the desired setting in the property box (the field to the right of the property name).
- If an arrow appears in the property box, select the desired setting from the drop-down list.
- If a Build button (…) appears, click it to display a builder or a dialog box with a choice of builders, depending on the type of control.

TIP *When you click a property in the Property Sheet, you can see a description of the property in the status bar at the bottom of the screen. If you need more information about the property or how to use it, press* F1.

The calculated field, Total Cost, which we added to the Workorders data entry form earlier, needs to show currency symbols. To set the format property, do the following:

1. In the form Design window, double-click the edit region of the Total Cost text box control. The Property Sheet opens.
2. Click the arrow in the Format property box and choose Currency from the list.

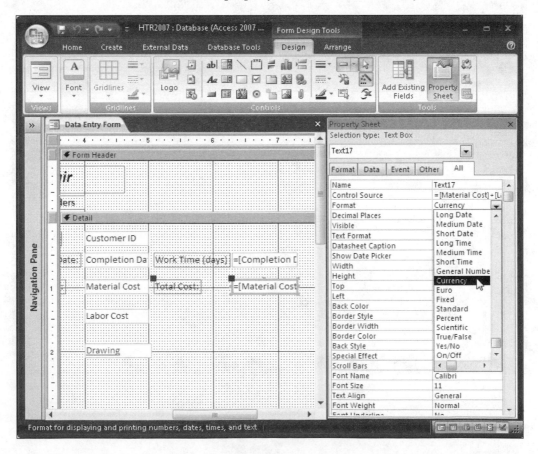

Other items of interest also appear in the Property Sheet for the Total Cost text box. For example:

- Look in the status bar for a description of the Format property.

- The Name property isn't Total Cost, but Text17. Recall that Total Cost isn't a real field name, but is only the label attached to the unbound text box control. Access automatically assigns a name to a new control when it's added to the design. This name is an identifier that Access uses in expressions, macros, and procedures.

- You can see the expression that defines the calculated field. If it's a long expression, right-click the Control Source property line and choose Zoom from the shortcut menu to see the entire expression. You can also click the property box and press SHIFT-F2 to open the Zoom box.

To apply the same property settings to a group of controls of the same type, first select them all, and then open the Property Sheet. Only those properties common to all members of the group are visible in the sheet.

Once you open a Property Sheet, it remains on the screen until you close it. To set properties of a different object in the design, either select the object from the drop-down list at the top of the Property Sheet or select the control in the design.

Assigning a Default Value

When you assign a default value to a bound control in a form or report design, the value you enter overrides any default value set in the underlying table design. Unless you enter a different default value, the one you assign is stored in the field when a new record is entered in the form. For example, if you're entering new bid data and one of the fields in the form is the date, you can assign the current date as the default value. This automatically stores the current system date in the new record.

To assign the current date as the default value, type **=Date()** in the control's Default Value property box on the Data tab of the Property Sheet.

NOTE *Another way to include the current date in a form or report is to use a ribbon command. On the Design tab's Controls group, click the Date & Time command to open the Date and Time dialog box. Then click Include Date and choose a date format. To include the time, check Include Time and choose a time format. If a header section is used in the form or report, Access places the Date/Time text box there; otherwise, it goes in the Detail section. Date and time values added this way are part of the design and aren't stored in the underlying table.*

Specifying a Validation Rule

To apply a validation rule to a control in the form or report, enter the expression in the Validation Rule property box. You can also click the Build button to use the Expression Builder to construct the rule. The validation rule you enter as a control property is enforced, in addition to any that were set in the table design.

If your expression is long, you can press SHIFT-F2 to open the Zoom box, where you can see the whole thing.

Type the message you want displayed when a violation occurs into the Validation Text property box.

Changing Default Control Properties

Access 2007 provides a default set of properties for each type of control. The set specifies the general appearance and behavior of that type of control. For example, the default properties for a text box control determine the font size and alignment of text within the attached label. Another default text box property automatically includes the field name as an attached label. This set of properties is called the *default control style* for that control type.

If you find that you're making the same changes to most of the controls of a certain type, you can change the default property setting. For example, if you usually want a larger font size in your text boxes, change the Font Size from the default size of 8 to a larger size. Or, if you don't want the attached labels for every text box, change the Auto Label property on the Format tab to No. If you're starting a new form, you can save time by setting the default styles before adding the controls.

TIP *When you change a default setting to the one you use most, it saves space. Access doesn't have to store both the default and custom settings.*

To change a default property setting, do the following:

1. Click the tool in the Controls group for the desired control type.
2. In the Tools group, click the Property Sheet command. The Property Sheet for that control type opens, but the title bar indicates that these are the default settings, instead of the settings for a particular control in the design.

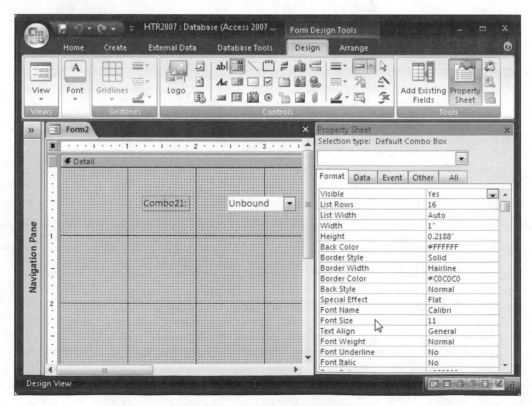

3. Change the setting in the default Property Sheet.

The changes that you make affect only the new controls you add to the design; the existing controls aren't changed. The changes remain in effect for the current design until you change them again.

NOTE *Some of the text box control properties can be set only in the Default Text Box Property Sheet. For example, the Auto Label and Auto Colon properties (on the Format tab) work together. When both are set to Yes, Access automatically adds the field name as an attached label followed by a colon. Label X, Label Y, and Label Align, which position the attached label with respect to the text box, also appear only in the Default Property Sheet. See the Quick Reference on the CD for a complete description of text box and other control default properties.*

If you've already made changes to a control and you like what you see, you can copy the changes quickly to the control type's default style. Any new controls would then use the properties from the existing control as a default control style. Select the control with the characteristics you want as defaults for subsequent controls, and then in the Controls group, click the Set Control Defaults command.

Using the Font Group

The Font group of commands on the Design tab provides a quick way to change the appearance of the text in selected controls. The group has eight commands for formatting text in the design. These commands change the font name, size, and style, and align the text within the control boundaries. Other commands give you a quick way to change the color and style of many elements in the design.

When you click a color command, a color palette is displayed, where you can change the color of the background, the font/foreground, or an alternate fill/back color. The Format Painter command can be used to copy the format settings of a selected control and apply them to other controls.

TIP *If you want to apply the same formatting property changes to a group of similar controls, select them all and then change the common property.*

Formatting Conditionally

You can use conditional formatting with text boxes and combo boxes. With *conditional formatting,* you can specify a default format for the control and up to three additional formats that are applied under special conditions: the current value of the field, when the field gets focus, or when an expression evaluates to True. The expression can refer to the values in other fields in the same record. For example, if a date in a field is more than 30 days past, the value in this field can be underlined and displayed in red on a light green background to highlight it for the Accounting department.

To activate conditional formatting, select the control to which you want to apply it and in the Font group, click the Conditional command. The Conditional Formatting dialog box shows two areas: one for setting the default format and one for specifying a conditional format to be applied under specific conditions.

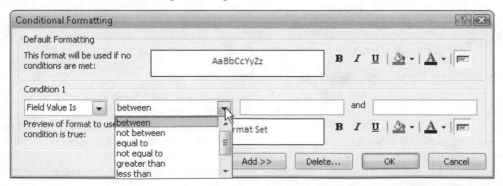

The formatting choices include bold, italic, and underline, as well as Fill/Back and Font/Fore colors. You can also choose to alternate colors in record rows in Datasheet view by setting the Alternate Fill/Back Color. The last option on the right in both sections of the dialog box enables or disables the control if the condition is met. When a control is enabled, you can reach it by pressing TAB. If a control is disabled, it's skipped in the tab order. (There is more about the tab order of controls in a form in Chapter 11.) The box in the middle of the top area displays an example of how the chosen formatting will look.

To set conditional formatting, first set or keep the existing default format, and then move to Condition 1. In the first box, you will have a choice of conditions:

- **Field Value Is** Defines the value or range of values for which to apply the format settings.

- **Expression Is** Applies the formatting if the expression you enter evaluates to True.

- **Field Has Focus** Applies the formatting to the field as soon as it gets focus.

Depending on which selection you make in the first condition box, you can set other specifications in the other boxes. If you choose Field Value Is in the first box, for example, you have a choice of several comparison operators:

If you choose Expression Is, only one box is available in which to enter the expression. Field Has Focus requires no additional criteria.

After defining the condition, use the formatting buttons to set the format to apply if the condition is met.

Click Add to add another condition. You can specify up to three conditional formatting scenarios for each text box or combo box control. The conditions are ranked, with the first one taking precedence. If the first condition isn't met, the second is evaluated, and so on. Figure 10-6 shows the Conditional Formatting dialog box with settings for the Total Cost text box control. The following three conditions are set:

- If the Total Cost exceeds $5000
- If the Total Cost is less than $1000
- If the Labor Cost is greater than the Material Cost

If you want to remove a condition, click the Conditional command again. The Delete Conditional Format dialog box opens, where you can check the conditions you want to delete, and then click OK.

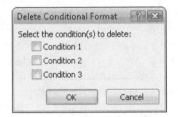

FIGURE 10-6   Conditionally formatting a text box control

Original Control	Permitted Conversions
Label	Text box
Text box	Label, list box, combo box
List box	Text box, combo box
Combo box	Text box, list box
Check box	Toggle button, option button
Toggle button	Check box, option button
Option button	Check box, toggle button

TABLE 10-2 Permitted Control Conversions

Changing a Control Type

When you change your mind about what type of control you want in the form or report, Access lets you change the control type dynamically. Not all types can be converted and you're limited to the types to which you can convert, depending on the original control type.

To change a control type, right-click the control and point to Change To in the shortcut menu. A list appears displaying the list of controls to which the selected control can be changed. Choose the new type of control. If a control type is dimmed in the list, you cannot change the selected control to that type. Table 10-2 describes the types of conversions permitted by Access.

When you change to another type of control, the applicable properties are copied from the original control to the new control. If the original control has property settings that don't exist for the new control, they're ignored. If the new control has properties that were not used in the original control, Access assigns the default settings for the new control.

Deleting Controls

To delete a control, select the control and press DEL, or right-click the control and choose Delete from the shortcut menu. If you change your mind, you can restore the control by clicking Undo on the Quick Access toolbar. With the stacked Undo/Redo, you do not need to act immediately. You can select the action to undo from the Undo drop-down list next to the Undo button on the Quick Access toolbar. You can delete more than one control by selecting them all and then pressing DEL.

Adding Other Objects and Special Effects

One of the important aspects of Access is that you can add objects created by other applications to a form or report. For example, you can add a chart you created in Excel, a picture from Paint, an image from Photo Editor, or a document from Word, to name only a few.

You can add a picture, a sound clip, or another object either as a bound or unbound object, depending on the purpose of the object. A *bound object* is stored in the underlying record source and changes as you move from record to record. For example, a picture of an employee is stored in each record in the Employees table.

An *unbound object* is part of the design instead of the record source and is stored with the design. It remains the same when you move to a new record in the form. A picture of a company logo in a form header or a letterhead is an example of an unbound object.

Linking vs. Inserting Objects

You have two ways to add an object to your design: inserting or linking. When you *insert* a picture or other object in your form or report design, Access stores a copy of the object in your database where it's always available. You can make changes to an inserted object from Access.

When you *link* to a picture or other object, it remains in its original file and location and isn't stored in your database. You can make changes to the object file separately and the changes will show in your form or report.

TIP *One advantage to linking over inserting is that you don't increase the size of your database with large picture files. If the linked object file is moved or renamed, however, you lose the link and must restore it.*

Here are a few examples of using bound and unbound objects and images:

- For an image that doesn't need updating, such as the company logo, insert an image control.
- If you need an Excel chart or a Word document that will change often, use an unbound object frame and link it to the foreign file.
- If you need to see a different image for each record, such as an employee picture, insert a bound object frame.

The advantage of linking objects is that they're updated automatically. Linked objects in reports are updated when the report is previewed or printed. Linked bound objects in forms are updated when the object gets focus in Form view. Linked unbound objects in forms are updated when the form is opened.

NOTE *When you link an object to a form or report, Access creates an automatic link by default. You can change the links to bound and unbound object frames to manual updating. Remember, if the control is a bound object, you must change the link for every record. Background pictures and pictures in image controls are always updated automatically.*

Adding Bound Objects

When you have an OLE Object field in your table, you can add it as a bound object to your form or report. To add the object to the design, drag the field name from the Field List pane into the design. Access creates a bound object frame to contain the field. The frame is part of the design, while the bound object is still part of the underlying record source.

NOTE *You can add a bound object frame control to the design first by using the control command, and then bind it to the field by setting the frame's Control Source property to the name of the OLE Object field.*

To edit a bound object in a specific record, open the form in Form view and locate the record you want to change. Then right-click in the object frame and choose the corresponding command—in this case, Bitmap Image Object—and then click Edit. The image editing window provides drawing tools and color palettes that you can use on the image. In this case, employee photographs don't require editing.

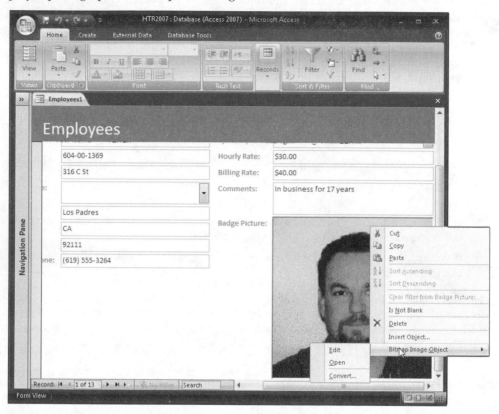

Adding an Unbound Object

You can add an existing object to a form or report design, or you can create a new object using the source program from within the Access Design window. To add an unbound object to the design, begin by doing the following:

1. In the Controls group, click the Unbound Object Frame command and draw an outline of the object in the design. The dialog box opens. (Your Object Type list might be different.)

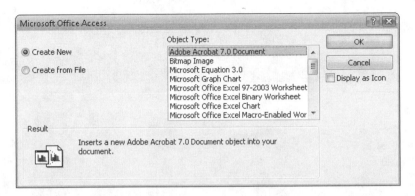

2. Choose Create New to build a new object or choose Create From File to choose an existing object.

3. If you choose to create a new object, select the type of object and click OK. The source program in which you can create the object launches. When you finish creating the new object, close the program and you return to Access.

4. If you choose to get the object from a file, you can enter the filename, including the complete path, in the text box, or click the Browse button to look for the file. Other options in the box include Link, which you can check if you want to link to the file instead of embedding a copy. After entering the filename, click OK.

***

TIP *Another option available to both new and existing objects is Display As Icon, which shows the object as an icon in the form or report, instead of displaying the whole object. The user can either double-click the icon or right-click it and choose Activate Contents from the shortcut menu to see the object.*

When you finish in the dialog box, the object appears in the form or report design. If you want to modify the object later or play a sound in Form view, open the Property Sheet for the new object and change its Enable property to Yes.

To edit an object in Design view, double-click the object, or right-click and point to *name of source program* Object and choose Edit from the Shortcut menu. This launches the source program where you can edit the object.

If you're working in the source program, you can use the standard copy-and-paste procedure to insert the object into the Access form or report. Select the object you want to add and copy it to the clipboard. Then switch to Access, right-click in the design where you want the object, and choose Paste from the shortcut menu.

Adding a Picture

Image controls are used to display pictures or other images. To add a picture to the form or report design, in the Controls group, click the Image command and draw the outline of the picture in the design. The Insert Picture dialog box opens, where you can locate and select

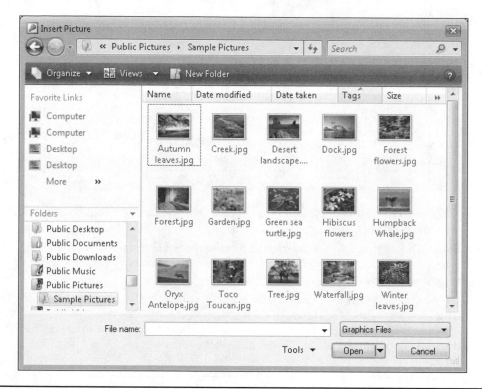

FIGURE 10-7 The Insert Picture dialog box with previews

the picture you want. If you click the arrow next to the Views button in the Insert Picture dialog box and choose Preview, you can see a display of the picture (see Figure 10-7). Once you select the picture, click Open to insert it into the design.

NOTE *If you are using Windows XP, the Insert Picture dialog box looks quite different.*

If you just clicked in the design to add the picture, the form or report design expands to fit the picture. If you created an image control by drawing the outline, the picture is limited to the outline you drew, and you'll probably need to enlarge the frame or change the object's Size Mode property.

The *Size Mode* property sets the size of the image with respect to the frame that contains it. The options are Clip, Stretch, and Zoom. The *Clip* option crops the image to fit the frame, leaving the center portion of the picture in the frame. The *Stretch* setting sizes the image to fit both dimensions of the frame. If the proportions of the image are not the same as the frame, the image might appear distorted. The *Zoom* setting sizes the image to fit either the width or the height of the frame, whichever is the more restrictive, and keeps the original relative height and width. The Zoom setting can leave spaces either on both sides, or on the top and bottom of the frame.

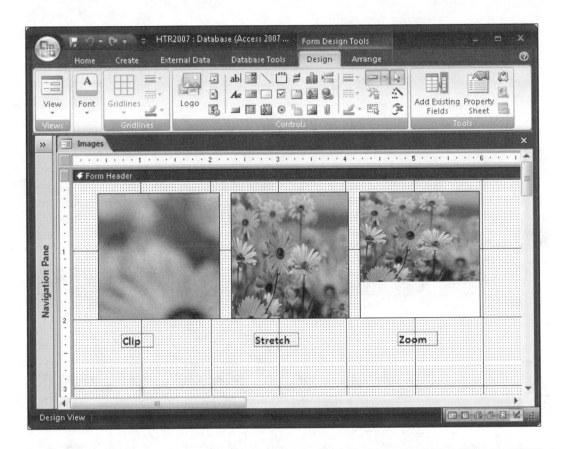

TIP   *Image controls can also be used to display unbound objects. Image controls load much faster than unbound object frames, so unless you want to update the object, insert it as an image control.*

Changing Pictures

If you change your mind about the picture and want to see a different one, you can delete the control and add another one, or you can simply change the Picture property on the Format tab of the control's Property Sheet. The Picture property shows the complete path and filename of the picture in the image control. Click the Picture property box, and then click the Build button to open the Insert Picture dialog box. Then choose another picture to replace the first one and click Open.

Changing Form and Report Properties

Forms and reports have many properties in common, such as Record Source, Filter, Order By, Width, and several event properties. Each of these can be changed in the object's property sheet and some can also be changed in Layout view.

Changing the Record Source

To change a form or report record source, do the following:

1. In the form or report Design view, click the form or report selector. Then in the Tools group, click the Property Sheet command or right-click the selector and choose Properties from the shortcut menu.

2. Open the Data tab and click the down arrow in the Record Source property box.

3. Choose the new record source from the drop-down list of all tables and queries in the current database.

You can also click the Build button to the right of the Record Source property box to start the Query Builder, where you can create a new query to use as the record source.

When you change the record source, some of the text boxes no longer represent fields in the underlying record source. You will immediately see an error tag marker; a small triangle in the upper-left corner.

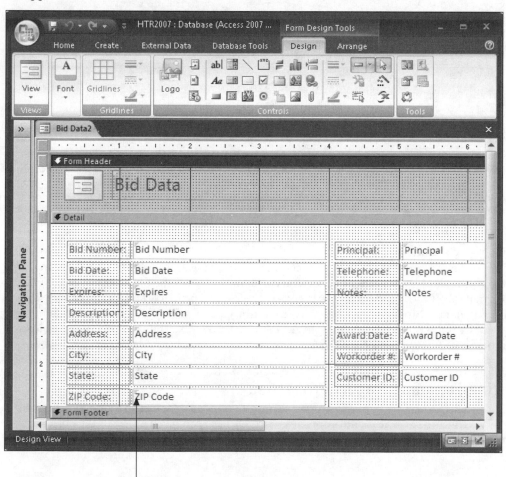

Error tag marker

When you click on the marker and hover the mouse pointer on the exclamation point in the box that appears, you will see a message that the control has an invalid record source. To see how to fix it, click the down arrow next to the marker and choose from the drop-down list of options. This is a big improvement over earlier versions of Access that simply displayed *#Name?* or *#Error?* with no clue as to what was wrong.

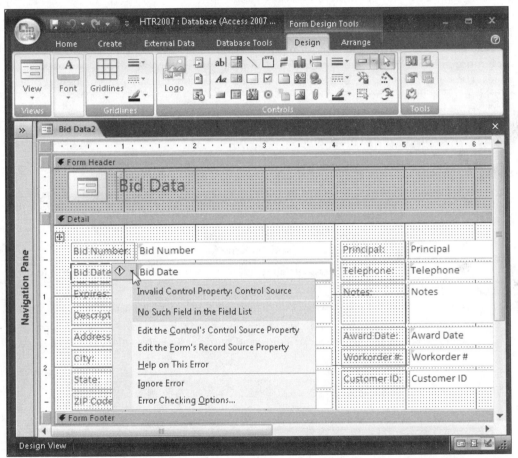

Applying Filters and Sort Orders

When you create a form or report based on a table or query with a filter or a specified sort order, both are included in the object's properties. The sort order is automatically applied, but the filter could or could not be, depending on how you created the form or report:

- If you created the form or report from a table that wasn't open in Datasheet view, the filter is inherited, but not applied. You must apply it when you need it.

- If you created the form or report from a table that was open in Datasheet view and it contained filtered data, the filter is applied every time you open the report. But the filter is applied only the first time you switch to view the form. After you save and close the form, the Filter property is inherited, but you must apply the filter yourself by clicking the Apply Filter command in the Sort & Filter group.

NOTE *If you change the filter in the underlying table or query after the form or report was created, it has no effect on the records in the form or report.*

Resizing a Form or Report

You can change the width of a form or report design in two ways: Drag the right border or, for a more precise setting, change the Width property in the Format tab of the Property Sheet. The height of a report is usually determined by the page setup and the height of a form is usually limited by the screen size.

To change the height of a section in a form or report, drag up or down the section bar below the section you want to change. You can also open the section's Property Sheet and set the Height property to a more precise measure.

Using AutoFormat

Access has provided several attractive formats for forms and reports that add style to the design. To apply the style to a form or report under construction or already completed, do the following:

1. Open the object in Design view and click the form or report selector.

2. On the Arrange tab's Quick Format group, click the AutoFormat command and choose from the gallery of formats.

3. If none fits your needs, choose Use Style at the bottom of the gallery.

4. In the AutoFormat dialog box, you can select from a list of formats. Click Options to see how you can apply the font, color, and border attributes selectively. When you are satisfied with the format, click OK.

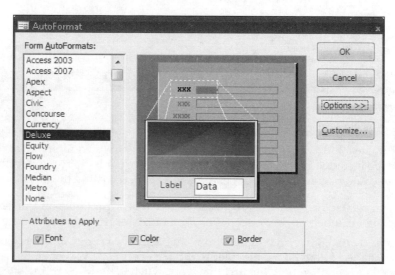

> **NOTE**   *If you want to apply AutoFormat to only one section in the form or report design, click the section selector before you open the AutoFormat dialog box. You can also use AutoFormat for a single control.*

Summary

With the information in this chapter, you're equipped with all the building blocks you need to create substantial forms and reports. This chapter included instructions for applying the tools that Access provides to help with the efforts.

The next chapter discusses the Form Wizard and the way that you can use it to create impressive forms. This wizard lets you choose the form layout and style. After the wizard is finished, you can make changes in the design to get exactly the effect you want. The following chapter continues with form customization.

Using the Form Tools

A rmed with basic information about creating Access forms and reports, you're ready to put the other form tools, including the Form Wizard, to work. With these tools, you can create many types of forms for data entry and viewing. You can build special forms, including hierarchical forms that show data from two or more related tables, forms that display with a datasheet, PivotTables and PivotCharts for summarizing data, and a wide variety of other charts that graphically represent table data.

In this chapter, you will see how to create specially structured forms and use the Form Wizard to create a data entry form based on an existing query. Then you can modify the Form Wizard's finished product in a number of ways.

Creating a New Form Design

Access forms are used for viewing and entering data. You can use Access to design a form that presents data in a way that makes the information easy to understand and nearly foolproof to enter and manage. While the Access Form Wizard can do all—or most—of the work for you, this wizard does only what you ask it to do. It pays to plan ahead and design the form on paper before invoking the wizard.

TIP *If printed data collection forms are already in use, you might want to create a replica of the form on the screen to make computerized data entry look familiar to users who will be entering data.*

Designing the Form

The Home Tech Repair production manager wants a form that shows current work orders with the following information: work order and bid numbers, address, customer's name, supervisor's name, job description, plus all the cost information, including the extended costs that add the overhead expenses. Although she hasn't specified the arrangement of the data in the form, you need to sketch it out and show it to her for approval before starting to create the Access form. Figure 11-1 shows a rough sketch of the new Current Workorders form.

After reviewing and incorporating the comments returned by the prospective users of the form, you must decide on the structure of the form and search for the data that you need in the form design.

Carla: Please review this form design and add your comments:

Current Workorders

Date:
Supervisor   Bid Number

Address   City   State

Bid Date

Principal

Material Cost
Labor Cost
Total Cost
Cost + Overhead

Description

Thanks, G. Prior, ext 583

FIGURE **11-1**   Planning a new form for collecting data

Starting a New Form

As discussed in Chapter 10, you can start a new form on the Create tab by using one of the commands in the Forms group. Most of the form tools require that the table or query you want to use as the basis be open in Datasheet view or selected in the Navigation Pane. The exception is the Blank form, which opens an empty form in Layout view.

Choosing a Form Design Structure

You saw how to start a new form using the Form Design command in Chapter 10. Before getting started with the Form Wizard, take a look at the other predesigned forms available in the Create tab's Forms group. When you start a new form, Access offers several options for the form's structure.

To start one of the automatic form layouts, click one of the commands on the Create tab's Forms group. All the automatic form tools arrange the fields in the same order they appear in the table structure or the query design grid. The table or query name appears in the form document tab and the form adopts the most recently used style.

The Simple Form Tool

When you click the Form command, Access creates a stacked form with the data from the selected table or query. If one table has a relationship with the table or query you chose as the basis for the form, a subform is also displayed as a continuous form below. The form is displayed in Layout view, where you can make form design changes as well as data changes. Figure 11-2 shows a simple form based on the Employees table, with a subform based on the Workorders table. As you can see, some design corrections are needed.

If more than one table or query are related to the table or query you used to start the form, the subform will not be added. You can also delete the subform if you don't want to use it. Notice that the subform shows Workorders records that the current employee is assigned to as the Supervisor.

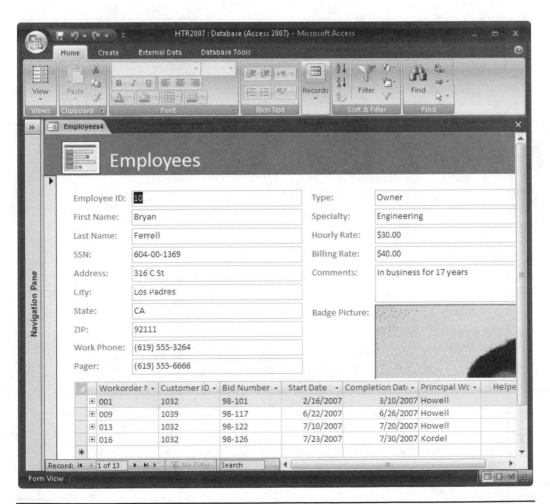

Figure 11-2 A simple form and subform

The Split Form Tool

The split form design is new in Access 2007. It offers the data in two views at the same time. The form Layout view and Datasheet view contain the same data and are synchronized. When you select a field in the datasheet, the same field appears in the form. Then, you can make design changes to the form, form sections, and controls by using commands in the Formatting and Arrange tabs.

You can add, delete, or edit data in either part of the form. To create a split form, select or open the table or query you want as the basis in the Navigation Pane. Then click the Split Form command. Figure 11-3 shows the Employees table in a split form.

If you want to see a form as a split form, do the following:

1. Open the form in Design view.
2. Click the form selector and press F4 to open the Property Sheet.

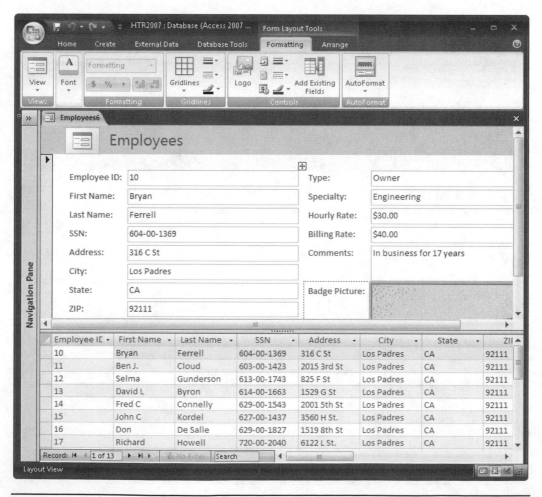

FIGURE 11-3   The Employee data in a split form

3. On the Format tab, select Split Form from the Default View drop-down list.

4. Switch to Form view.

NOTE *You can drag the splitter bar (the divider) to create more space in the form or the datasheet.*

The Multiple Items Form

The multiple items form displays several records in Layout view. As with the split form, you can make some changes to the form design. Figure 11-4 shows the Employees data in a multiple items form.

The PivotChart Tool

The PivotChart command provides the tools you need to create a graphical analysis of the data in a table or query. You can use it to add a chart to an existing form.

The Blank Form Tool

The Blank Form command opens an empty form in Layout view with the Field List pane open at the right. To add fields to the form, expand the field lists for the tables you want to use and drag the fields to the form layout. If you don't see any field lists, click the message Click to Show All Tables.

You can also use the tools in the Controls group to add items to the form, such as a logo, a title, page numbers, and the current date and time.

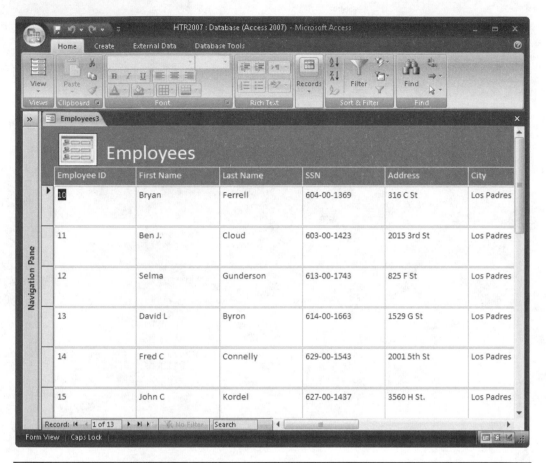

FIGURE 11-4   The Employee data in a multiple items form

The More Forms List
When you click the More Forms command, you'll see four more options for form design:

- **Form Wizard**   Leads you through the form design process.
- **Datasheet**   Opens the table or query that is the basis for the form currently selected in the Navigation Pane in Datasheet view.
- **Modal Dialog**   Guides the construction of a dialog box that is not based on data but includes user-interaction controls such as command buttons, options groups, and drop-down lists.
- **PivotTable**   Summarizes and analyzes data in a table, query, or form similar to the PivotChart but builds a table instead of a chart.

Using the Form Wizard

The Form Wizard guides you through the form design process with a series of dialog boxes. You can choose the table and/or query with the data you want to show as well as select specific fields. Then you choose from a set of layouts and styles.

Selecting the Form Data

In Chapter 8, you designed a query that linked the Bid Data and Workorders tables. The query has most of the fields needed in the Current Workorders form and also has two calculated fields: Total Cost and an additional expression, and Extended Cost that adds 15 percent overhead expenses to the Total Cost value. This query would be a good basis for the new form. If you need to add more fields to the form, you can add them to the query first or add them to the form design after the wizard is finished. If the query is used for other purposes, modifying the form, rather than changing the query design, is a better choice.

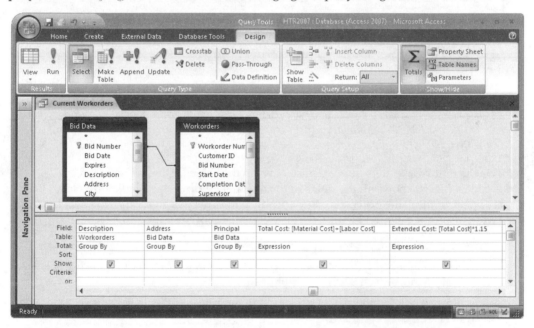

When you use the Form Wizard, you can choose one or more tables or queries as the basis, and then select the fields in the order that they are to appear in the form.

To start a new form design based on the Current Workorders query, do the following:

1. Select the Current Workorders query in the Queries group in the Navigation Pane.

2. On the Create tab's Forms group, click the More Forms command and choose Form Wizard from the context menu. The first Form Wizard dialog box opens (Figure 11-5).

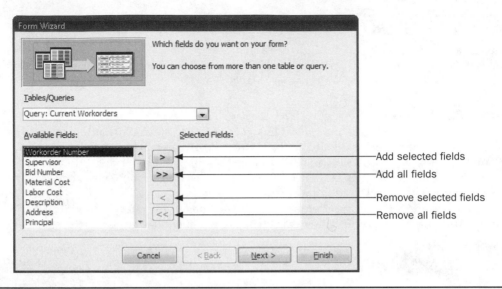

FIGURE 11-5 Choosing fields for the form design

NOTE *If you haven't selected a table or a query before starting the Form Wizard, it automatically selects the first table in the alphabetic list of tables and queries. You can change the record source in the first dialog box, if necessary.*

The Current Workorders query name shows in the Tables/Queries box, and the Available Fields list shows all the fields in the query, including the calculated fields. The fields appear in the same order that they appear in the query design grid. To place the desired fields in the Selected Fields list, do any of the following:

- To add all the fields in the Available Fields list, click the double right arrows.

- To add a single field, double-click the field name in the Selected Fields list or select the field name and click the single right arrow.

- To remove a field, double-click the field in the Selected Fields list or select the field and click the single left arrow.

- To remove all the fields from the Selected Fields list, click the double left arrows.

To continue with the Current Workorders form, do the following:

1. Click the double right arrows to add all the fields from the Current Workorders query to the Selected Fields list.

2. Click Next. The Form Wizard's second dialog box opens.

TIP *If the fields in the Available Fields list are not in the order you want in the form, choose the fields, one at a time, in the order that you want them to appear. You can also insert a field name in the Selected Fields list by selecting the field name above where you want the new one to appear, and then select the field from the Available Fields list and click the right arrow. Selecting them in the right order in the Form Wizard dialog box saves you from having to move the controls around in the form design.*

If you select fields from more than one table, the Form Wizard creates a main form with one or more subforms. Creating hierarchical forms is discussed later in this chapter in the section "Creating a Hierarchical Form from Related Tables."

Choosing the Form Layout and Style

The second Form Wizard dialog box offers a choice of four form layouts: Columnar, Tabular, Datasheet, or Justified (Figure 11-6). When you select a layout, a sample appears in the left pane.

- The Columnar style arranges all the fields on the screen in one or more columns, depending on the number and size of the fields.
- The Tabular style places all the data from one record in a line across the form. If the record has many fields, you must scroll to the right to see them all.

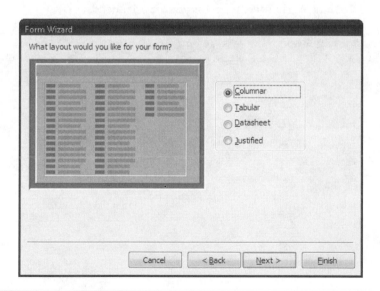

FIGURE 11-6   Choosing a form layout

- The Datasheet style is similar to the table Datasheet view. This style is often used for subforms that show data from multiple records related to the record displayed in the main form—for example, details of the work orders (subform) run by a specific supervisor (main form).

- The Justified layout resembles the Tabular layout, except all the fields appear on the screen without having to scroll. The row of fields is wrapped to multiple lines, as necessary.

Select each layout option and look at the preview pane.

For the Current Workorders form, select the Columnar layout, and then click Next.

NOTE *When working with any of the Access Wizards, you can always click Back and return to the previous dialog box to change a setting. After you click Finish, you cannot return to the wizard to change that design; you must work in the Design window.*

The next dialog box shows a list of 25 styles from which you can choose. These are the same styles that you see when you click the AutoFormat command, as discussed in Chapter 10. Choose a style—we used the Flow style here—and click Next to reach the final Form Wizard dialog box.

In this last dialog box, you name the form and decide whether to view the data in the new form or go directly to Design view to modify the design. After entering the form name, click Finish to save and open the form. Once the wizard is finished, you can go about customizing the Current Workorders form for your special needs.

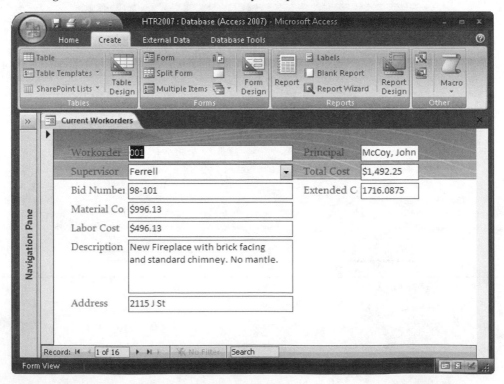

If the Form Is Blank

When you finish with the Form Wizard, the form opens in Form view unless you checked Modify the Form's Design in the wizard's final dialog box. If you only see the style background with no data or field names, one of the following could be to blame:

- You might have based the form on a table that doesn't contain any data. Open the table and see if it has records.

- You might have based the form on a query that doesn't return any data. For example, the criteria could be so strict that it excludes all the records. To see if the query returns data, do the following:

  1. Switch to Design view and double-click the form selector to open the Property Sheet.

  2. Click the Build button to the right of the Record Source property and click Yes to open the Query Builder with the query design displayed.

  3. Click View to run the query.

Modifying the Form Design

While the Form Wizard does a good job of creating a form, you can do much more to improve the result. For example, you can do the following:

- Add a form header with a title.
- Resize the form.
- Change control properties.
- Add special controls, such as the current date.
- Move, resize, and reformat the controls.
- Change the text of attached labels.
- Add lines and rectangles for emphasis.
- Change the progression of the cursor through the controls when the TAB key is pressed (the tab order).

Before starting to modify the new Current Workorders form, look at the form properties to see how they influence the appearance and behavior of the form.

Examining Form Properties

To examine the form properties, switch to Design view and double-click the form selector, or press F4 to open the Property Sheet. These properties affect the entire form.

Other properties can be set to apply to form sections and individual controls on the form. The following tabs appear on the Property Sheet:

- **Format**   Control aspects of the form appearance from the caption in the title bar to the palette source that controls the colors. Scroll down the list to see the rest of the properties.

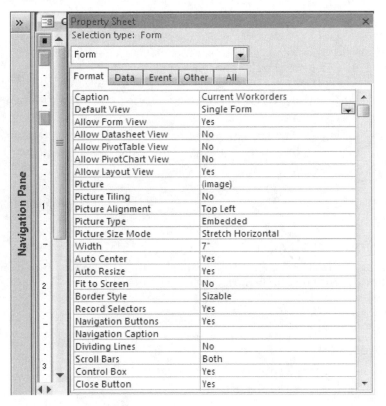

NOTE   A split form includes additional properties relating to the orientation of the form and datasheet, the splitter bar, form size, and printing the form.

- **Data**   Determine what data is displayed and affect how the form handles the data, including the filter and sort order, and whether to use the form for data entry only.

- **Event**   Specify what is to happen when the form opens or closes, or when the user does something such as update a record, press a key, or click a command button. Forms have more than 50 event properties to which you can attach actions when creating an application. Chapter 18 discusses events and event procedures.

- **Other**   Miscellaneous properties such as Pop Up and Modal, which determine the form's behavior with respect to the rest of the work space. Other properties also specify custom ribbons and shortcut menus, and add links to custom help topics.

- **All**   The complete list of form properties.

To see a description of a property, click in the property box and read the text displayed in the status bar. You can see the default setting for the property when you're starting a new form, before you begin to make changes to the properties.

NOTE *For a complete discussion of form and control properties, consult the Quick Reference on the CD that accompanies this book.*

Changing Form Sections

Access forms can contain several sections:

- **Detail**   Contains the record data. You can show data from one record in the Detail section or as many records as can fit on the screen.

- **Form Header**   Contains information to show at the top of the screen for every record—for example, a title, instructions, or command buttons that open another form or print the current form. The information is printed at the top of the first page.

- **Form Footer**   Contains information to show at the bottom of the screen for every record and at the bottom of the last page of the printed form.

- **Page Header**   Contains information such as a title, graphics, or column headings that appear at the top of each page when the form is printed or previewed. This section isn't visible in Form view.

- **Page Footer**   Contains information that appears at the bottom of each page when the form is printed or previewed. This section isn't visible in Form view.

Adding Form Header and Footer Sections

By default, a form created by the wizard from a single table or query has a Detail section and Form Header and Footer sections. The Form Header and Footer sections contain information that appear at the top and bottom of the form. This information remains on the screen as you scroll through records in the Detail section.

In the new Current Workorders form, the Form Header section bar appears above the Detail section with no space between it and the Detail section bar. If you scroll down the form design, you also will see the Footer section. To increase the size of the Form Header section, move the mouse pointer to the top of the Detail section bar. When the pointer changes to a black plus sign (+) with up and down arrows, click-and-drag the bar down.

To add a title to the form header, do the following:

1. On the Design tab in the Controls group, click the Title command. The Form Header section expands and the name of the form is added.

2. Using the Formatting group on the Design tab, you can change the appearance of the title, if you want to.

3. You can drag the Title box to center it in the header, if necessary, or change the text in the title.

Figure 11-7 shows the Current Workorders form design with a title in the new Form Header section.

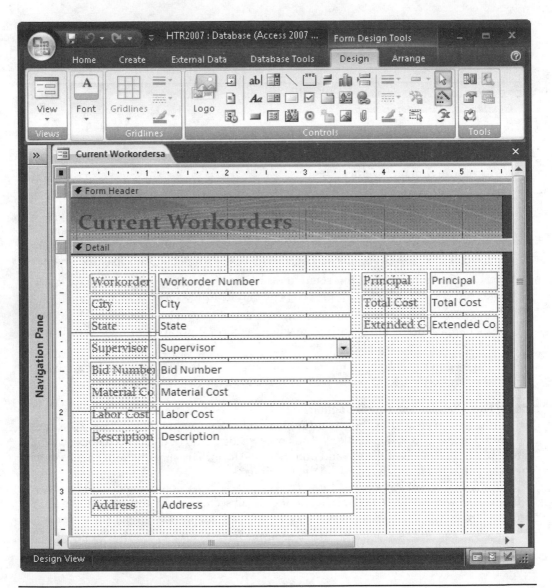

FIGURE 11-7 Adding a title to the Form Header section

TIP *When you choose Form Header/Footer from the shortcut menu, both sections are added to the form design. If you don't have information to put in the footer and you don't want the section to take up room in the form, you can drag the bottom form border up to reduce the footer section space to zero.*

Changing Section Properties

All the sections in a form have the same properties. Double-click one of the section selectors to open the Property Sheet for the section. The sheet shows fewer properties than the form itself. Most of the section properties apply to formatting. There are no Data properties and only six Event properties for form sections.

Four of the important section properties are Visible, Can Shrink, Can Grow, and Force New Page.

- **Visible**   (Default is Yes.) Shows or hides the form section. This is useful when you want to keep information confidential.

- **Can Grow and Can Shrink**   Allows a section to automatically expand or reduce vertically to accommodate all the data in the section. The default settings for these two is No.

- **Force New Page**   Starts printing the form section on a new page rather than on the current page, before or after printing the current section, or both before and after.

Page Header and Footer sections have less properties because the information in them doesn't appear in Form view; it appears only when the form is printed. You can set the height, color, and any special effect for the page sections.

NOTE *The header and footer sections do not need to have the same properties.*

Moving and Adding Controls

The wizard places controls in the form in a straightforward way according to the layout that you choose in the dialog box, not always in the most logical arrangement. When the wizard is finished, you almost always need to move some controls around and resize some that display short values to reduce empty space and add more controls. If the query does not have all the fields you want in the form, now is the time to add them to the record source.

Switch to Design view and select one of the controls. You will see a small orange box with a plus sign in it at the upper-left of the column of controls. This indicates that the controls are grouped. Before you can make changes to individual controls, you must remove the stacking layout that the wizard has imposed on the controls in the form.

First, use the vertical ruler to select all the controls in the Form design. Then, on the Layout tab in the Control Layout group, click the Remove command. The controls are now ungrouped and free to move about the form design.

In the next few paragraphs, you will see how to modify the form by changing and adding controls, including the current date. Refer to Chapter 10 if you need to review how to select controls and how to use the moving and sizing handles.

Moving and Resizing Controls

You can move and resize controls on the form to make them visible.

1. Some of the field names are truncated in the labels. Widen the form to make room for wider labels by dragging the right form boundary to 7-inch on the horizontal ruler.

2. Select the Principal, Total Cost, and Extended Cost controls and drag them as a group to the right.

3. Select the three labels and widen them by dragging one of the sizing handles to the left.

4. Make similar changes to the controls in the left stack so that the labels are complete.

5. Rearrange the text boxes so that the Address and Principal fields are below the Supervisor field, leaving some space below the Principal text box.

6. Drag the Description text box to the right side of the form next to Labor Cost. Resize the Description text box so that it's more square and fits in the space.

7. Select Bid Number in the field list and drag it to the 4-inch mark on the horizontal ruler in line with the Workorder Number field.

NOTE *When you're moving a control past other controls, you can drag it right over the other controls without interfering with them.*

Modifying a Label

When you add a calculated field to a query design, the field is often named Expr1. This is what shows up as the label if you didn't rename the field in the query design grid. Use one of the following methods to change the label *Extended Cost* to *With Overhead*:

- Double-click the label and edit the text.
- Select the label and enter the new text in the Caption property in the Format tab.

Adding New Controls

The Current Workorders query doesn't have all the fields that you want to see in the Current Workorders form. To add more bound text box controls, change the query that's the form's Record Source property and include the additional fields. If you're using a table as the record source, you might need to create a query that includes the fields from the original table, plus the additional fields from related tables.

CAUTION *If you're planning to use a form for data entry, be sure that the design includes all the required fields and that you set the same validation rules in the form as in the tables. See Chapter 12 for information about adding validation rules to a form.*

To add more fields from the related tables used in the query, open the form in Design view and do the following:

1. If the Property Sheet is already visible, click the form selector. If not, right-click the form and choose Properties from the shortcut menu.

2. Click in the Record Source property box on the Data tab, and then click the Build button. This starts the Query Builder, which looks similar to the query design grid except for the words *Query Builder* in the title bar.

3. Hold down CTRL while you select the City and State fields in the Bid Data field list, and then drag the group to the grid. The position in the grid is unimportant right now.

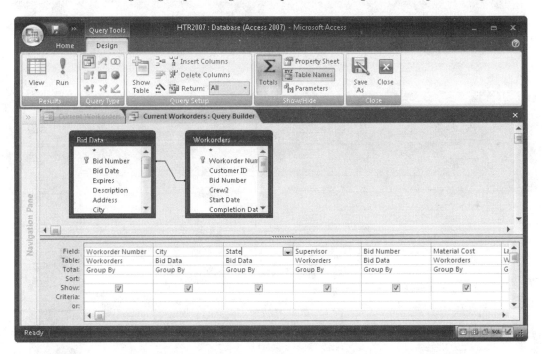

4. Click Save, and then click the Close button to return to the form design.

The additional fields are now available to the form and the field list is displayed. You can add fields to the form in two ways:

- The quickest way is to drag the fields from the field list to the form design.
- You can also add a new bound text box control for each of the fields and set the control source to the field you want to add.

Follow these steps to complete the addition of the City and State fields:

1. Select the City field in the field list and drag it to a position in the design below the Bid Number field; then drag the State field next to the City field.

2. Resize the City and State labels to fit the text, and then resize the State text box because it will contain only two characters. Move the State text box next to its attached label.

3. To make the three address fields all the same height, click the vertical ruler level with the row of text boxes to select all three, and then right-click the group, choose Size in the shortcut menu, and then choose To Tallest.

4. Now align them by right-clicking the group again, pointing to Align, and choosing Top.

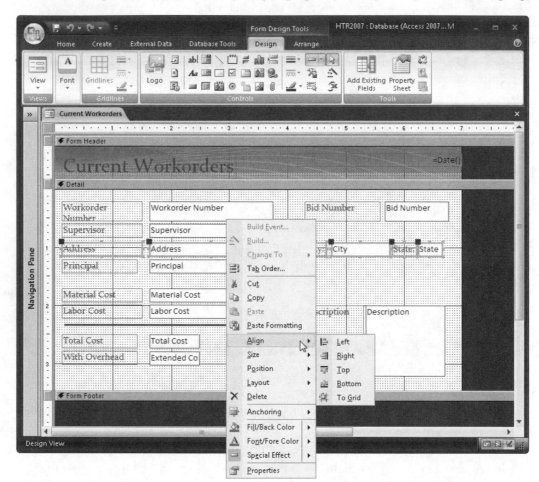

You can also add a line to separate the material and labor costs from the calculated fields that show the total and extended costs. First, move the two calculated fields down a little to make room for the line. Then in the Controls group, click the Line command and draw a line horizontally under the Labor Cost text box. You can change the line thickness, style, and color by selecting them from the Line's properties list in the Controls group on the Design tab.

***

TIP   *While you draw the line, if you are drawing straight across or down the form design, you will not see the line being drawn. If you are drawing the line crooked, you will see the line.*

***

The last control to add to the Current Workorders form is the current date, which appears in the Form Header section. To add the date, do the following:

1. On the Design tab's Controls group, click the Date and Time command. The Date and Time dialog box appears (Figure 11-8).

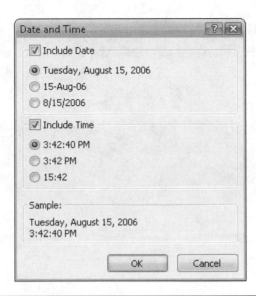

Figure 11-8   Setting the date and time properties

2. Check Include Date (if it isn't already checked), and select the middle date format (Medium Date), which displays dates as *dd-mmm-yy*.

3. Clear the Include Time check box and click OK. The expression = *Date()* appears in the upper-right corner of the Form Header section.

Figure 11-9 shows the completed Current Workorders in Form view.

Sorting and Filtering Data in a Form

When you're viewing data in the form, you can filter the records just as in a datasheet: in the Sort & Filter group on the Home tab, use Filter By Selection, Filter By Form, or Advanced Filter/Sort to limit the records. To sort records in the form, place the cursor in the field you want to sort on and click one of the Sort commands. You can also enter filter and sort expressions in the form's Property Sheet.

If the form is based on a table or query that already has a sort order or filter saved with it, the form inherits both properties. A sort order is automatically applied to the records in the form. Whether the filter is automatically applied to the records in the form depends on the status of the table or query when you created the form.

- If the table or query was open and the filter was applied when you created the form, the filter is automatically applied to the records in the form. The word *(Filtered)* appears to the right of the navigation buttons at the bottom of the form, and *Filtered* also appears in the status bar to remind you of the filter. To remove the filter, click the Remove Filter command on the Home tab's Sort & Filter group, which appears pressed in when a filter is applied.

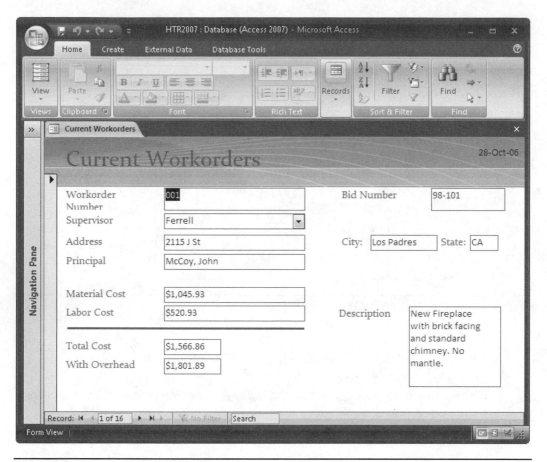

FIGURE 11-9 The completed Current Workorders form in Form view

NOTE The filter isn't saved with the form, so if you close and reopen the form, you will see all the records.

- If the table or query was closed and saved with the filter, the filter is inherited by the form, but it isn't automatically applied. Click the Apply Filter command in the Sort & Filter group.

If you construct and apply a different filter or sort order, the new property replaces the one inherited from the underlying table or query.

NOTE To disable all filtering of records in the form, set the Allow Filters property to No. This disables the Filter By Selection, Filter By Form, and Advanced Filter/Sort.

Using the Form for Data Entry

Forms are the principal user interface with the database information. You can view all of the data, search for specific records, enter new records, and edit existing records. To accomplish these tasks efficiently, you must know how to get around in the form and how to move through the records in Form view.

To open a form in Form view where you can view and edit data, double-click the form name in the Forms group in the Navigation Pane or right-click the form name and choose Open from the shortcut menu. In Form view, you can add a new record by clicking the New Record button to show a blank form. You can also edit existing records using the record navigation tools or the Find group of commands.

Navigating in the Form

As with datasheets, you can operate in two different modes in a form: Navigation and Editing. In Navigation mode, the cursor moves to other fields; in Editing mode, it moves among characters in a field. The keypresses have different consequences, depending on the current mode. For example, in Editing mode, pressing the RIGHT ARROW key moves the insertion point one character to the right. In Navigation mode, this moves the cursor to the next field to the right and usually selects the value.

To change modes, do the following:

- To switch from Editing mode to Navigation mode, press F2 or click in a field label. You can also press TAB or SHIFT-TAB to leave Editing mode and move to another field.

- To switch from Navigation mode to Editing mode, press F2 or click in the text box.

Clicking the record navigation buttons at the bottom of the form moves the cursor to the first, previous, next, or last record. You can enter a specific record number in the record navigation bar and press ENTER to move to that record. On the Home tab in the Find group, clicking the Go To command also moves the cursor to the first, previous, next, or last record. These methods move the cursor to the same field in another record.

Table 11-1 describes the keystrokes that you can use to navigate through records and fields in a form.

NOTE *Remember that the options set in the Editing group in the Advanced Access Options affect the behavior of the TAB, ENTER, and ARROW keys. If you change their default settings, some of the keystrokes in these tables might behave differently.*

The RIGHT and LEFT ARROW keys behave a little differently if you are in the first or last fields in a record:

- If you are in the first field of the record and press the LEFT ARROW key, you will move to the last field in the previous record.

- If you are in the last field of the record and press the RIGHT ARROW key, you will move to the first field in the next record.

Destination	Keystrokes
First field of the first record	CTRL-HOME
First field of the current record	HOME
Last field of the current record or first record in the current record's subform	END
Last field of the last record or first record of the last record's subform	CTRL-END
Current field in the next record	CTRL-PGDN
Current field in the previous record	CTRL-PGUP
Next field	TAB or RIGHT ARROW
Previous field	SHIFT-TAB or LEFT ARROW
Specific record	Enter record number in Record Navigation bar and press ENTER
Previous record or page	PGUP
Next record or page	PGDN

TABLE 11-1   Navigating with Keystrokes

When you're in Editing mode, you need to move around in the field data and insert or delete characters. Many of the same keys are used, but with different results.

Changing the Tab Order

Each time you press TAB in Form view, the cursor moves to another field. The progression of the cursor through the fields in the form is called the *tab order*. Each text box control is assigned a tab index number indicating its position in the sequence. The first control in the order has 0 as the tab index number, the second has 1, and so on. Access sets the tab order to match the order in which the fields were added to the design.

If you open the Current Workorders form in Form view and press TAB several times, you'll that see the order isn't logical. The tab order reflects the way the fields were originally positioned in the query grid and then placed in the form design. Some of the fields have been moved in the design and the tab order doesn't automatically change to match. The three fields added later are at the end of the tab order.

To change the tab order so that the cursor moves more logically through the records, do the following:

1. Open the form in Design view and click the Detail section selector.

2. On the Layout tab's Control Layout group, click the Tab Order command. The Tab Order dialog box opens, showing a list of all of the text box controls in the Detail section.

3. To reposition a control, click the row selector to select the field, then move the mouse pointer to the row selector, and then drag the row to a new position. You can also select a group of rows and reposition them as a group.

4. Repeat step 3 until the order is the way you want it, and then click OK.

Tip *Clicking the Auto Order button in the Tab Order dialog box rearranges the controls in order from left-to-right and top-to-bottom. If this is the way you want the cursor to move through the fields, click Auto Order instead of moving the controls by hand.*

Text box controls have three properties on the Other property tab that involve the tab order:

- **AutoTab**   When set to Yes, automatically moves the cursor to the next field in the tab order when the last character permitted by an input mask or the field size is entered.

- **Tab Stop**   Set to No to keep the cursor from reaching the field by means of pressing TAB. You can still select the field for editing; it just isn't part of the tab order.

- **Tab Index** Indicates the control's position in the order, beginning with 0. For example, if you choose Auto Order in the Tab Order dialog box, the fourth control in the order, Material Cost, has a tab index of 3.

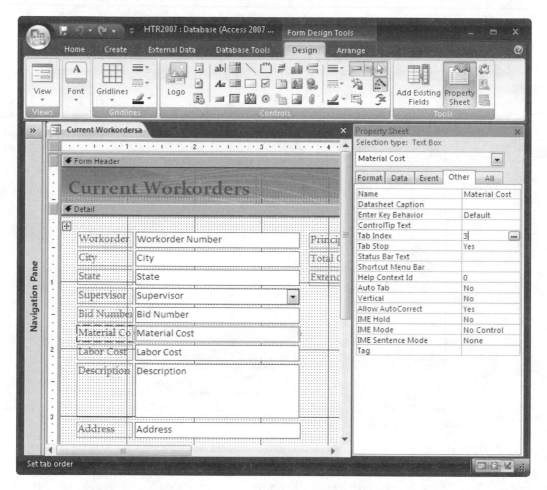

Finding Records

Searching for specific records by examining the value in one or more fields is the same in a form as it is in a datasheet. You use the same Find dialog box to specify the search string and the scope of the match, part, or all of the field.

To display a specific record in the form, place the insertion point in the field you want to look for and on the Home tab's Find group, click the Find command. If you want to replace the current field value with another, click the Replace command. Refer to Chapter 6 for more information about using Find and Replace.

Viewing Multiple Records

If you want to see more than one record on the screen, you can change the form's Default View property from Single Form to Continuous Forms. When you switch back to Form view, the form appears with as many records that can fit on the screen.

Home Tech Repair uses a form named Roster as a quick way to look up employees. When the Roster form is set to Single Form, only one record appears on the screen, as shown in the following:

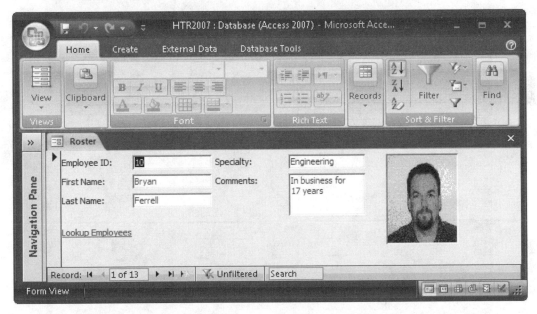

Figure 11-10 shows the same Roster form with the Default view set to Continuous Forms. You might have to drag the lower border of the form to view multiple records.

NOTE *When you use the scroll bar to move through records in a Continuous Forms view, Access always makes sure that a complete record appears at the top of the screen, while only a partial record might appear at the bottom, depending on the size of a single record. Using PGUP and PGDN causes the previous or next set of whole records to appear on the screen. For example, in the Roster form, only three complete records are visible at once with a partial record at the bottom of the screen. When you press PGDN, the partial record moves to the top, where it appears in its entirety with two more complete records below it and another partial record at the bottom.*

Printing the Form

Although forms are used mostly for data viewing, entering, and editing, you can also preview and print the form. Click the Microsoft Office button, point to Print, and choose Print Preview to see how the form will look when printed. See Chapter 13 for information about setting printing options and running the page setup for special print jobs.

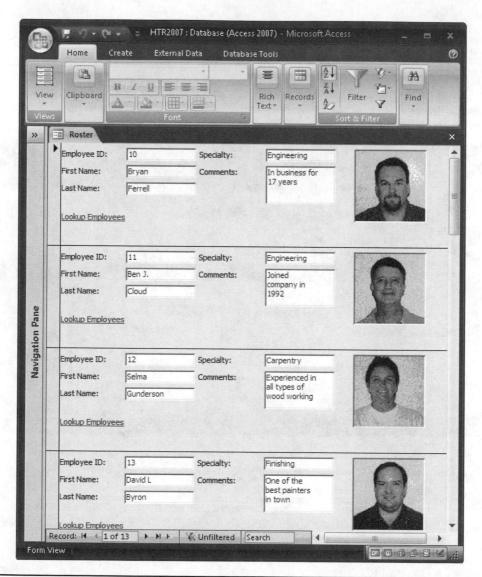

FIGURE 11-10   Showing Roster in Continuous Forms view

Looking at the Other Wizards

Two other wizards are available from the Forms group: the Chart Wizard and the PivotTable Wizard. The *Chart Wizard* converts data in your tables into a variety of charts, including bar charts, pie charts, and line graphs. If you want to illustrate trends over a period of time, you use a bar chart or a line graph. If you want to show relative frequencies or other proportions, use a pie chart. The following pie chart is based on the Home Tech Repair Workorders table and illustrates the percentage of jobs started in each month.

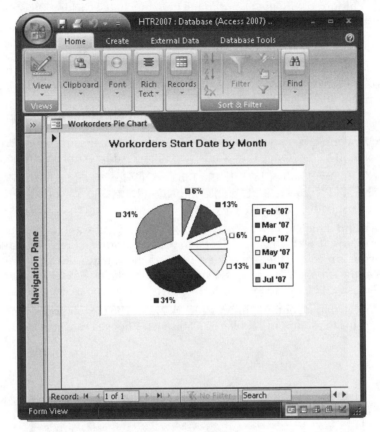

The chart has been added to a blank form, as an OLE Unbound object frame, by the Chart Wizard. To make changes to the chart, such as exploding the pie shown here or adding captions to the pie wedges, switch the form to Design view and double-click the chart.

The *PivotTable Wizard* takes large amounts of data from your tables and summarizes it in rows and columns in a similar, but more flexible, way to crosstab queries. You will need to have Excel installed to modify PivotTables created by the wizard.

Chapter 15 contains more information about creating visual form and report elements containing charts, graphs, PivotTables, and PivotCharts.

Creating a Hierarchical Form from Related Tables

A *hierarchical form* usually consists of a main form and one or more subforms. The main form shows data from records on the "one" side of a one-to-many relationship and the subforms show data from records on the "many" side.

If your main form has many controls and no room exists for a subform, you can link the forms instead. When you click a command button in one form, it opens the other form showing data that's synchronized with the record in the first, much like clicking the subdatasheet expansion button in Datasheet view.

You can create a form and a subform at the same time using the Form Wizard by choosing fields from related tables. For example, to create a hierarchical form showing the list of work orders currently underway for each customer, choose fields from both tables. The Form Wizard can determine how the tables are related and decide which data goes in the main form and which goes in the subform.

To create the Workorders By Customer hierarchical form, do the following:

1. Start the Form Wizard with the Customers table and, in the first dialog box, choose the Customer ID, First Name, Last Name, and Billing Address from the Customers table.

2. Choose the Workorders Table in the Tables/Queries list and add the Workorder Number, Bid Number, Start Date, Completion Date, Supervisor, Material Cost, and Labor Cost fields. Then click Next.

3. The second dialog box (see Figure 11-11) asks how you want to view the data—in other words, it asks which records go in the main form and which go in the subform. Access assumed that the Workorders data (on the "many" side of the relationship) goes in the subform. The other two options in the dialog box let you specify whether the data should be arranged as a form with a subform or as separate, linked forms.

4. Accept the default options, and then click Next. The next dialog box offers two layouts for the subform: Tabular or Datasheet. Choose Datasheet and click Next.

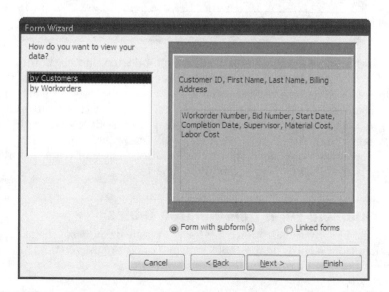

FIGURE 11-11   Creating a form with a subform

5. Choose the style for the form in the next dialog box and go on to the final box, in which you will name the form and the subform. Then choose to view the form or open the form in Design view.

6. Enter the name **Workorders by Customer** for the main form and leave the default name for the subform. Then click Finish.

Figure 11-12 shows the completed hierarchical form with a few modifications, such as a title in the form header. The columns in the subform have also been resized to fit the screen.

You can modify the subform in place. To modify the subform design, open the main form in Design view and click the subform selector or any of the controls in the subform. Modify the subform and its controls the same as you did in the main form. You can also select the subform control, and on the Design tab's Tools group, click the Subform in New Window command to work on the subform in a larger environment.

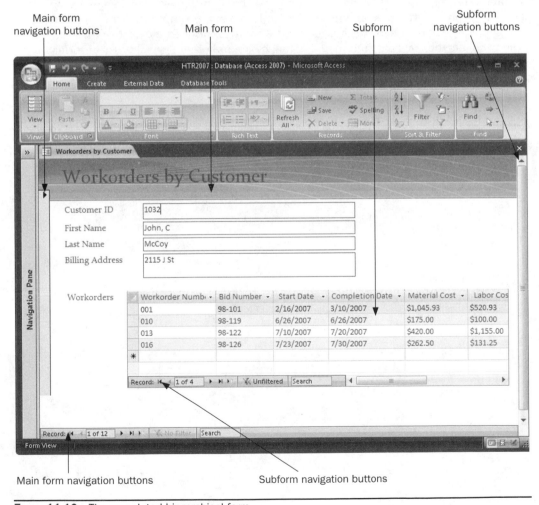

FIGURE 11-12   The completed hierarchical form

You can also add a new or an existing form as a subform within another form by using the Subform/Subreport Control Wizard, or simply drag the form you want as a subform into the Design view window of the main form. If an existing relationship exists between the record sources of the two forms, Access determines which are the linking fields.

NOTE *See the next chapter for more information about creating subforms and linking forms to see related information.*

Summary

This chapter has shown you how helpful the Form Wizard and other form tools can be when you want to create a form. More wizards can help construct the perfect form. Control Wizards can help when you want to add combo boxes, list boxes, option groups, and command buttons. In the next chapter, you'll see how to use these tools in new forms.

When you use Access, you will see pop-up forms that prompt for user action, such as dialog boxes, where you make choices about what to do next. In the next chapter, you'll see how to create your own custom modal dialog boxes and other special types of forms for user interaction.

12

Customizing Forms

With all the building blocks at your disposal, including the help of the Form Wizard, you're ready to explore some of the ways you can make forms more flexible and practical. This chapter offers constructive ideas for creating custom forms. You can add special controls to a form that help with entering data, printing records, or opening another related form to see additional information. Access provides tools that help you add command buttons to perform specific actions as well as improve data entry accuracy and validity.

This chapter continues with examples from the Home Tech Repair database and also introduces you to a real-life, operational database management system in use by law enforcement personnel. The Police database is primarily user interactive and demonstrates some of the special applications of Access forms.

Starting a New Custom Form

When you start a new custom form without the help of the Form Wizard or one of the form tools, you begin with an empty design. If you select a table or query to use as the basis for the form, you can display the Field List pane and drag the fields into the form design. If you haven't already chosen the basis for the form, you can define it in Design view by selecting the table or query from the form's Record Source property list.

No law says that you have to base a form on data. You can create a form that displays courses of action from which to choose or a form that simply displays a welcome screen that times out after a few seconds. The first sections of this chapter dwell on forms that contain data, while later sections discuss special-purpose forms.

Placing and Customizing Data-Related Controls

In the last chapter, you saw how to add bound text box controls to a form design by dragging field names from the Field List pane. In addition to the text box controls in which you enter and edit data, list and combo boxes enable you to choose from a list of values. List boxes limit your choice to values in the list, but combo boxes usually let you type entries or choose from a list. Either of these can be bound or unbound. If *bound,* the selected or entered value is stored in the field to which it's bound. If *unbound,* the value isn't stored in a table but can be used by another control or as a search criterion.

Building a Control Layout

A control layout is a specific arrangement of controls that are either laid out horizontally or stacked vertically on a form. These layouts help give your form a uniform appearance without having to adjust the location of each control individually.

The *tabular* control layout places controls in rows and columns like a datasheet with the control labels at the top. The *stacked* layout arranges controls in a vertical list with the labels at the left. You can mix layouts in a form.

Access automatically builds a stacked control layout when you use the Form or Blank Form command in the Create tab's Forms group and drag the fields from the list into the form design.

You can create your own layouts by selecting all the controls you want to appear in the same layout and then doing one of the following:

- On the Layout tab's Control Layout group, click the Tabular or Stacked command.
- Right-click in the selection, point to Layout in the shortcut menu, and choose Tabular or Stacked.

You can switch from one layout to the other by clicking the orange layout selector in the upper-left corner of the group and repeating one of these steps.

You can also move controls in the layout, move a control to another layout of the same type, and remove controls. To add a control to the layout, select the control or group of controls, and then do one of the following:

- If the form is in Design view, drag the control into the layout.
- If the form is in Layout view, create a new layout with the controls and then drag the new layout into the existing one.

To remove a control(s) from the layout, select the control(s), right-click, point to Layout in the shortcut menu, and choose Remove. If the form is in Layout view, on the Layout tab's Control Layout group, click Remove.

By setting the padding and margin features, you can spread out the controls evenly in the layout, as described in Chapter 11.

Creating List and Combo Boxes

Selecting a value from a list is often quicker and safer than trying to remember the correct value to type. Although list and combo boxes are similar, you must decide which type of control you want to use in the form.

- The values in a list box are always visible, and you're limited to the values in the list. To choose from the list, click the value and press ENTER or TAB. You can also choose one of the values by typing the first letter of the value and pressing ENTER or TAB. (If more than one value starts with the same letter, the first one is selected by default.) You cannot enter a value that is not on the list. List boxes are best when you're limited to a few values, because, otherwise, the list box takes up valuable viewing space.
- The values in a combo box are not displayed until you click the arrow to open it, so these values take up less on-screen real estate than a list box. Like the list box, you

can select one of the values by clicking it or by typing the first few characters of the value into the text box area of the combo box. If the Auto Expand property is set to Yes, the default setting, Access automatically fills in the rest of the value. In addition, you can type in values that are not in the list, unless you set the combo box Limit To List property to Yes.

NOTE *When the characters you type match the first few characters in one of the values, the combo box Auto Expand property specifies whether Access automatically fills in the text box portion of the combo box with a value from the underlying list. As you type, Access displays the first value in the list that matches the characters. If you set the Limit To List property to Yes and the combo box list drops down, Access automatically fills in the matching value as you type in the text box, even if the Auto Expand property is set to No.*

List boxes and combo boxes both consist of rows of data with one or more columns, which can appear with or without headings. One of the columns contains the values you want to store in the field (bound control) or use for other purposes (unbound control); the other columns contain explanatory information.

Figure 12-1 compares examples of list and combo boxes that contain lists of the employee last names from the Home Tech Repair database. The figure also shows a text box for comparison. The list box is always open but is limited to the size you draw in the form design. If the list is wider or longer than the space allowed, Access adds scroll bars. The combo box list is, by default, the same width as the control in the design, but you can change the width to fit the list. Scroll bars are also added to combo boxes, when necessary.

To add a list box or combo box to a form design based on the Employees table, open a blank form in Design view and do the following:

1. Choose the Control Wizard command in the Controls group, and then click the List Box or Combo Box command.

2. Click in the form or draw an outline where you want the control to appear. The wizard's first dialog box opens (see Figure 12-2). The first dialog boxes for the List Box Wizard and the Combo Box Wizard are nearly identical.

3. Choose one of the options (both wizards offer the same options, except instead of using *combo box*, the List Box Wizard uses the words *list box*):

   - **I want the combo box to look up the values in a table or query.** Choose this option and the box displays field values from the table or query you choose.

   - **I will type in the values that I want.** Choose this option and the list contains values you type into the next dialog box.

   - **Find a record on my form based on the value I selected in my combo box.** This option is available if fields already appear on the form. It is used to create a combo/list box that acts as a search string to find a specific record with that value in the field and display the record in the form. This option creates an unbound control.

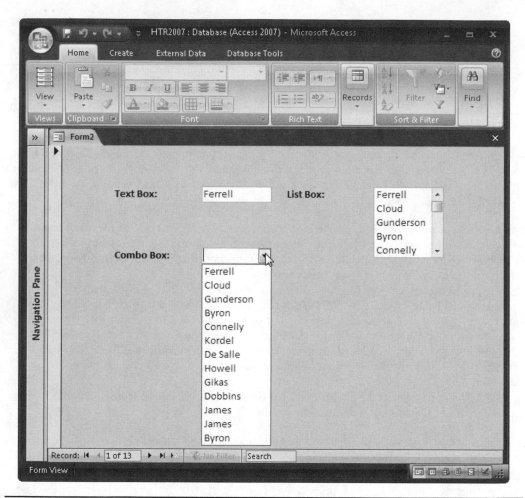

Figure 12-1 Comparing a List Box with a Combo Box

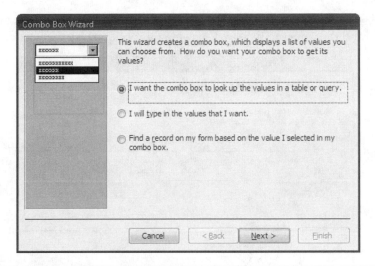

FIGURE 12-2   Starting a new combo box with the wizard

4. After making a choice in the first dialog box, click Next. Depending on your choice in Step 3, do one of the following:

   - If you chose the first option, select the table or query that contains the values that the box will display. Then click Next, select the fields you want to see in the box, and click Next again.

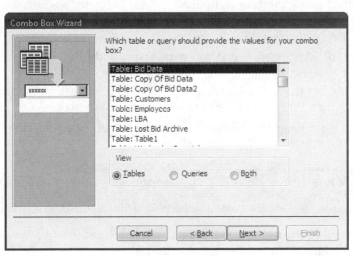

- If you chose to type in the values, enter the number of columns that you want to see and the values to display. Choosing this option skips the next dialog box.

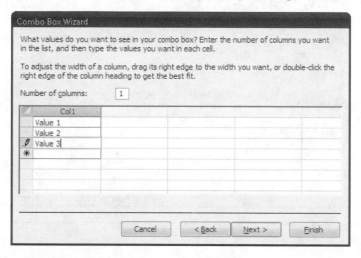

> **TIP** *Press* TAB *to move to the next row in the list of values. If you press* ENTER, *you advance to the next wizard dialog box. In that case, click* Back *to return to the value list dialog box.*

- If you chose the third option, choose the field whose values you want to see. The value you choose in Form view acts as a search value. Then click Next.

5. In the next dialog box (see Figure 12-3), adjust the column widths to show the values and choose whether you want to show or hide the primary key column. Then click Next.

6. The next dialog box asks what you want Access to do with the value you select in the list/combo box:

   - **Remember the Value for Later Use**   Saves the value for use by a macro or procedure. When you close the form, the value is erased.

   - **Store That Value in This Field**   With this option, you select the field in which you want to store the selected value.

> **NOTE** *If you chose to find a record based on the value selected in the combo box, this dialog box is skipped.*

7. If you want a label attached to the box, type it in the last dialog box, and then click Finish.

Changing the Control Type to Combo Box or List Box   If you want to add a list or combo box in place of a text box already in a form, changing the control type is easy. To change the control type, do the following:

1. Right-click the control, and then point to Change To in the shortcut menu and select a control type from the list. The list shows all the control types, but the only types you can use appear in boldface. For example, you can change the following selected text box control only to a Label, a List Box, or a Combo Box:

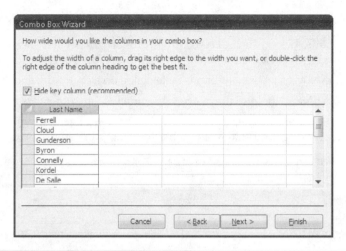

FIGURE 12-3   Adjusting the columns in the combo box

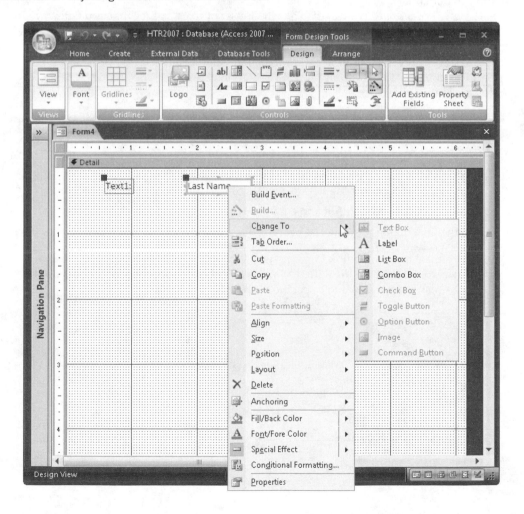

2. After you choose the kind of control you want, the control is changed in the design.

3. Open the combo box or the list box control's Property Sheet and click the Row Source property, and then click the Build (...) button to start the Query Builder.

4. Select the Employees table in the Show Table dialog box, click Add, and then click Close.

5. Drag the Last Name field to the query grid and close the query Design window.

6. Respond Yes to the message about saving the changes. The Query Builder places the following SQL query statement in the Row Source property box:

```
SELECT Employees.[Employee ID], Employees.[Last Name]
    FROM Employees;
```

7. Change other properties as necessary.

NOTE *Refer to Chapter 10 for a list of which controls can be changed to which other types.*

Creating Unbound List and Combo Boxes

An *unbound list* or a *combo box* can display either a set of fixed values that you enter when you create the box or specific values from a table or query. The value you choose from the control list isn't stored in a field in the underlying table. You can use the value for other purposes, such as for looking up a record with that value in a field.

To add a combo box to an Employee form that displays the record for a selected employee, do the following:

1. Start a new form based on the Employees table and add the desired fields to the form.

2. Start the Combo Box Wizard, and in the first dialog box, choose the third option: "Find a record in my Form based on the value I selected in my combo box." Then click Next.

3. Choose Last Name as the field value to show in the list, and then click Next.

4. Choose Hide Key Column and click Next.

5. In the final dialog box, enter **Show record for:** as the control label, and then click Finish.

When you use the combo box in Form view, you will select a value from the list and Access moves to the first record with that value in the corresponding field. This option gives you a quick way to move to a specific record in Form view.

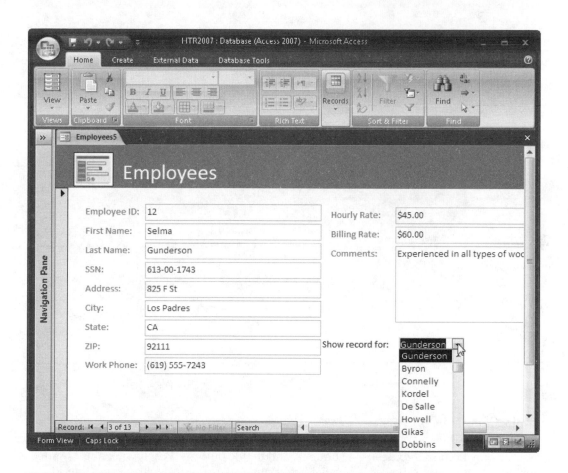

TIP *If you click Back to return to the dialog box where you selected Last Name, you will see that Access added the primary key field, Employee ID, to the list when you were not looking. You chose to hide it in the next dialog box, so it won't appear in the list.*

Setting List and Combo Box Properties

If your form contains a bound list box or a combo box, the control inherits most of its properties from the field properties you set in the table design. When you use a wizard to create a list or combo box, Access sets some other properties for you. You can modify these properties by changing the settings in the Property Sheet to make them work the way you want. To see a description of a property, select the property and read the text in the status bar. For example, the List Rows property sets the maximum number of items to display in the list. The automatic setting in the List Rows property is the number of records in the table.

This property is set to 8 in the following illustration, as you can see, although 16 records reside in the table. A scroll bar was added to this combo box.

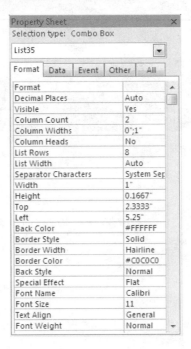

Adding Yes/No Controls

Three different types of controls can be used to view or enter a Yes/No value in the underlying table or query: check boxes, option buttons, and toggle buttons. When you have a limited number of alternative choices in one field, you can also group the controls together in an *option group*. The grouped options work as a single control, and only one of the choices can be selected. The option group can display the list of choices as any of the three types of Yes/No controls.

When you select or clear a check box, option button, or toggle button, Access displays the value in the table or query according to the Format property set in the table design (Yes/ No, True/False, or On/Off). Figure 12-4 shows how the various Yes/No controls appear when the values are Yes and No.

Check Boxes and Option Buttons

A check box displays a check mark in a small box if the value in the underlying field is Yes. The box is empty if the value is No. An option button (also called a radio button) displays a black dot inside a circle if the value in the underlying field is Yes. The circle is empty if the value is No.

Toggle Buttons

When the toggle button appears depressed (selected), the value in the underlying field is Yes. If the button appears raised, the value is No. You can enter a caption for the button by entering text in the control's Caption property box.

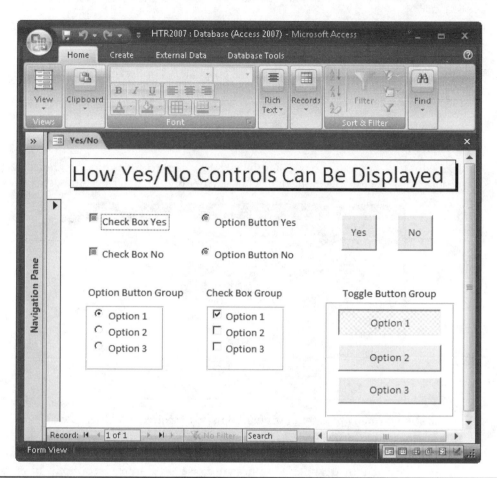

FIGURE 12-4   Examples of Yes/No controls

NOTE   *You can use a picture on a toggle button instead of text to create a more interesting appearance.*

Option Groups

An option group offers a limited set of mutually exclusive alternatives, usually four or fewer. The *option group control* consists of a frame around a set of check boxes, option buttons, or toggle buttons. If the option group is bound to a field, the frame itself is the bound object, not the individual controls in the group. Option groups are used only with number fields, but you can apply them to Yes/No fields by using the numeric values for Yes (–1) and No (0).

When you create an option group, you will specify the values of the options in terms of meaningful numbers to the underlying field. When you select an option in the group, that numeric value is stored in the field.

If Access isn't bound to a field, it uses the value of the option you choose to carry out one of a list of actions, such as print the report you chose or open another form.

Although you can create an option group without the help of the wizard, using the Option Group Wizard makes the job much easier. To create an option group, first choose the Control Wizard command on the Controls group, and then do the following:

1. Click the Option Group command and click the form design where you want the upper-left corner of the group to appear. The wizard draws a 1-inch square box. Then click Next.

2. In the first wizard dialog box, enter the text you want to see as the first choice in the group. Press TAB to move to the next choice. After entering all the values, click Next.

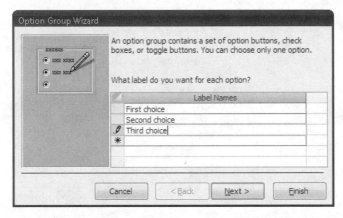

3. In the second dialog box, set the default option, if desired, and then click Next.

4. Specify the Option Value property for each of the options in the group. This property must always be a number. This is the value passed to the field when the option is selected. By default, the values are consecutive integers: option 1 has the value 1; option 2 has the value 2; and so on. For a Yes/No field, set the Yes option to –1 and the No option to 0. Then click Next.

5. The next dialog box asks you in which field you want to store the value (bound) or if you want Access to save the value for later (unbound). If the form doesn't have a record source, the wizard skips this dialog box.

6. Next, choose the type of control and the style you want to see in the option group, and then click Next.

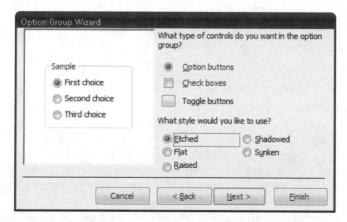

7. In the final wizard dialog box, enter the name you want to appear as the label for the group. This text appears in the group frame. Then click Finish.

NOTE *If each option in a group of options relates to the same type of information but applies to different fields, you can still keep the options together in the form. Arrange the independent options in a group and draw a rectangle around them to resemble an option group. The options won't be automatically set as mutually exclusive.*

Adding User-Interactive Controls

Because a form is often used to enter data, the user is constantly interacting with the form and the controls it contains. Some of the controls are directly associated with table data, such as text boxes, list boxes, combo boxes, and the button types, such as toggles, options, and check boxes with which you can set a Yes/No value. The most common control, unrelated to data is the command button, used in Form view to perform an action. When the user clicks a command button, Access recognizes this event and carries out the response you specified for the event.

Introducing Events and Event Properties

Access is an object-oriented, event-driven application. Nothing happens until the user tells it what to do by pressing a key or clicking the mouse button. An *event* is an occurrence recognized by an Access object. You can define a response to an event by setting the event property of the object or the control.

Following are some examples of events:

- Pressing or releasing a key.
- Opening or closing a form.
- Moving the cursor to or away from a control.
- Applying a filter to records in a form.
- Changing or deleting the value in a control.

Every time that you press a key or click a button, you're initiating an event to which Access will respond. The action Access takes depends on the event property specified. For example, right-clicking a table name in the Navigation Pane and choosing Open (the event) in the shortcut menu opens the selected object (the response). When you move to another record after entering or editing data, the event causes Access to check any validation rules automatically and, if no violation exists, to save the record. These actions are triggered by the system, based on the built-in event properties.

You can set event properties for any of the controls in your form or report design to carry out the appropriate action. When you set an event property, you attach a set of commands to the event. These commands can be in the form of a macro or an event procedure containing Visual Basic statements. Then, when you click that command button or press that key, Access knows what to do.

The Access wizards also provide a number of predefined procedures that you can attach to standard events, such as clicking a command button. The Click event occurs when you quickly press and release the left mouse button on a control. The On Click event property specifies what is to happen when you click the left mouse button on that control.

Another important term when discussing events is *focus*; a control is said to get focus when it's selected or the cursor is resting on it. For example, when you press TAB to move through the controls on a form, focus is shifted from one control to another according to the tab order. See Chapter 18 for information about events and how to make them work for you.

Adding Command Buttons

The Command Button Wizard is on hand to help you create more than 30 different types of command buttons, ranging from commands that move to the next record to those that close the form. The wizard guides you through the selection of the category of action you want and the specific procedure to execute. It also lets you identify the button using text or a picture.

To add a command button to a form, open the form in Design or Layout view and do the following:

1. Choose the Control Wizard command on the Design tab's Controls group, click the Button (Form Control) command, and then click in the form design. The first Command Button Wizard dialog box appears (see Figure 12-5). The list at the left shows the available action categories. The list at the right shows specific actions that fall into the selected category. Each category has a different set of actions. As you highlight an action in the right pane, a sample appears in the left pane.

2. Select the category you want, select the specific action, and then click Next. Depending on your choice of action, the wizard displays additional dialog boxes requesting information, such as the name of the form to open or the report to preview.

3. After choosing the options required by the action you selected, the next wizard dialog box lets you choose between text and a picture for the button. You can accept the default text or enter your own. If you don't like the default picture, click Show All Pictures and choose another one, or click Browse and look in another folder. As you select a picture from the Show All Pictures list, you can see how it looks in the left Sample panel. After making your choice, click Next.

4. Enter a name for the button or accept the default name. Then click Finish.

You can modify the properties of the command button later to change between a picture and text. Of course, you can always move and resize a command button, just like any other control in the form design. Command buttons are included in the tab order of the form design. That is, as you press TAB to move around in Form view, a command button gets focus when its turn comes. Then you can press ENTER to select the button—the keyboard equivalent to clicking the command button.

TIP *If you use a picture on a button instead of text, creating a control tip, which explains what happens when the button is clicked, is a good idea. A control tip automatically displays below the button when you move the mouse pointer over the command button. You can customize the tip the wizard provides by entering the tip text in the ControlTip Text property. If you created a status bar message using the StatusBar Text property, it appears in the status bar when you select the control to which it applies. You can also create your own custom help, as you'll see in the section "Adding Custom Help" later in this chapter.*

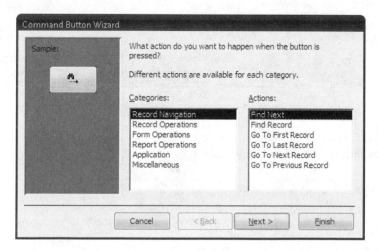

FIGURE 12-5   Choosing the type of command button

When the Command Button Wizard builds the button for you, it builds a macro or an event procedure containing Visual Basic code to store with the form. For example, you can use the wizard to add a command button to print the current record in the Current Workorders form. To add this button, start the wizard, choose the Record Operations category and the Print Record action in the first dialog box, and then click Finish to accept the remaining default options.

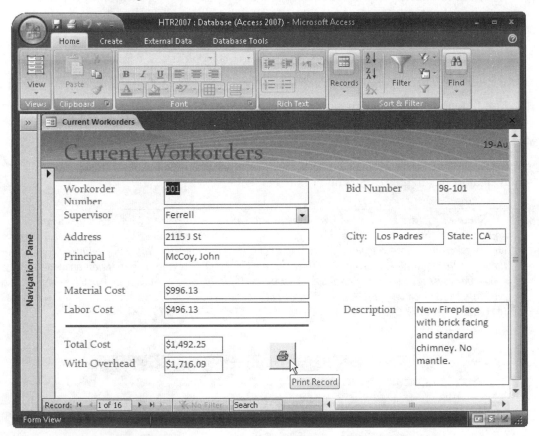

The wizard creates an embedded macro that carries out the action you selected. Look at the button's Event tab on the Property Sheet and you will see *[Embedded macro]* in the On Click property. This indicates the action that will take place when you click the control. See Chapter 19 for more information about creating and using macros.

CAUTION *If you choose Form Operations and Print Form as the action to take, Access prints all the records as one continuous form on multiple pages. If you want to print only the current record, choose Record Operations and Print Record in the Command Button Wizard dialog box.*

Adding Hyperlinks

In Chapter 6, you saw how to add a hyperlink field to a table and how to insert a hyperlink address in the field. You can click a hyperlink in a table to jump to a different address for each record. For example, the Drawing hyperlink fields in the Home Tech Repair Workorders table (shown in Chapter 6) contained addresses of files with scanned engineering drawings.

The hyperlink address you enter in the field in a record appears in Form view, like other fields. To add the field to the form design, drag the hyperlink field name from the Field List pane to the form design.

If you don't need to tie a hyperlink address to a record, you can add it to the form in Design view as an unbound control. You can add a hyperlink to a form design either as a label or an image. Both jump to the target address when you click the control in Form view.

To add a hyperlink as a label to the Home Tech Repair Roster form that will jump to the Employees table, do the following:

1. With the form open in Design view, on the Create tab's Controls group, click the Insert Hyperlink command. The Insert Hyperlink dialog box opens (see Figure 12-6).

2. Enter the path to the file for the hyperlink in the Address text box, using one of the following methods:

   • Select the filename from the list.

   • If the file to which you want to jump is in a folder, type the filename preceded by two periods and a backslash—for example: **..\HTR2007.accdb**.

   • If the file isn't in the current path, type the entire path and filename.

   • Click the Browse for File button (the open folder icon) and select the filename.

3. Next, click Bookmark to open the Select Place in Document dialog box, where you specify the object to which you want to jump.

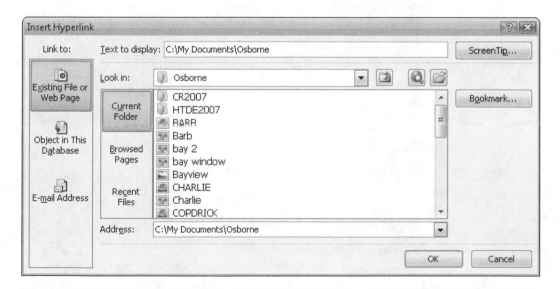

Figure 12-6   Working in the Insert Hyperlink dialog box

4. Click the plus sign (+) next to Tables and select Employees from the list of tables in the database (see Figure 12-7). Then click OK.

5. Enter **Lookup Employees** in the Text to Display box so that will appear in the hyperlink instead of the address.

6. Click ScreenTip and enter Display Employees table in the Set Hyperlink ScreenTip dialog box, and then click OK. The default is the complete hyperlink address.

7. Click OK to close the Insert Hyperlink dialog box.

8. Drag the hyperlink control to the position you want in the form design.

You can test the new hyperlink in the form design by right-clicking, pointing to Hyperlink, and choosing Open Hyperlink from the shortcut menu.

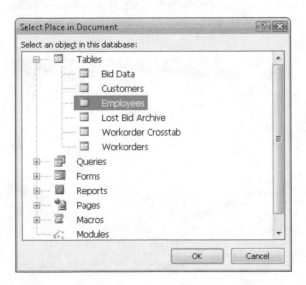

Figure 12-7 Selecting the target of the hyperlink

When you switch to Form view, the hyperlink appears as an underlined label. Rest the mouse pointer on the hyperlink to see the ScreenTip. Click it to open the Employees table in Datasheet view.

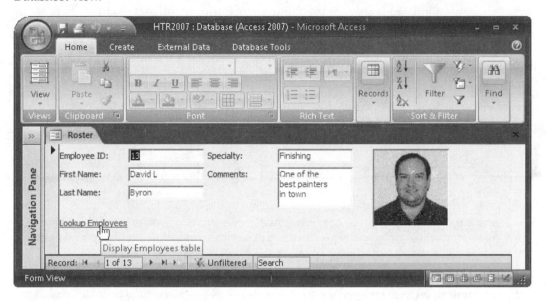

NOTE *If you select a control in the form before inserting the hyperlink, the new hyperlink appears just below the label of the selected control. If no control is selected, the hyperlink appears in the upper-left corner of the form. From there, you can drag the hyperlink to any position in the form design.*

To add a hyperlink that jumps to a picture, add an image control to the design and change its Hyperlink Address and Hyperlink Subaddress properties to specify the target file.

TIP *To add a hyperlink in the form of a command button or an image, unselect the Control Wizard command before adding the button or image control to the form design. After placing it in the design, select the button, and then enter the Hyperlink Address and Hyperlink Subaddress properties. Also, set the Caption property to the text you want to display on the button.*

In Chapter 11, you saw what conditions might cause a blank form to be created by the Form Wizard. If the form you create yourself is empty, one of the following could be the cause:

- The form might not be bound to any record source. Check the Record Source property.
- The form might be in Data Entry mode, in which case a blank record is displayed when you open the form.
- If you added a form header or footer section, they might be so big that the detail section doesn't appear on the screen when you open the form.

Creating a Multiple-Page Form

Access gives you two ways to create a multiple-page form: by inserting a page break control or using a tab control. *Page breaks* are used to separate the form horizontally into two or more pages, each of which is a separate control. To move sequentially among the pages, press PGUP or PGDN. Tab controls produce multiple-page tabbed forms that combine all the pages into a single control. To move between pages in a tab control, you click the desired tab.

Using the Page Break Control

To insert a page break, on the Design tab in the Controls group, click the Page Break command, and then click in the form where you want the split. Access shows a short dotted line at the left border where the break occurs.

CAUTION *Be sure you place the page break between controls. If the page break lines up horizontally within part of a control, the data in the control is then split between the pages.*

Pages are not necessarily full-screen height. If you want every page to be the same size and you want to show only one page at a time, design the form with evenly spaced page breaks. Use the vertical ruler to help place the page breaks.

After placing a page break, change some of the form properties, as follows:

- Change the Cycle property on the Other tab from the current default All Records to Current Page, which keeps you from moving to the next page when you press TAB at the last control in the tab order on one page.

- Change the Scroll Bars property on the Format tab from Both to Horizontal Only to remove the vertical scroll bar. This prevents scrolling to a different page. If the form isn't wider than the screen, you can set the property to Neither and remove both scroll bars.

Switch to Form view, and then press PGDN and PGUP to see if the page breaks are properly placed.

NOTE *Each page is treated as a separate section. If you plan to print the form and want each form page printed on a separate page, change the section's Force New Page property to After Section.*

Adding a Tab Control

Tab controls are easier and more efficient than page breaks because all the tabbed pages belong to a single control. Tab controls are useful for presenting grouped information that can be assembled by category. A tab control has pages, each with a tab of its own. Each tab page can contain all types of controls, such as text boxes, combo boxes, images, and even command buttons.

Tab control pages are also widely used as dialog boxes. For example, the Property Sheet has several tab pages that contain groups of related properties.

To create a tab control, do the following:

1. In Design view, on the Design tab's Controls group, click the Tab Control command and then click in the design where you want the tab control to appear. By default, Access places a tab control with two pages (two tabs).

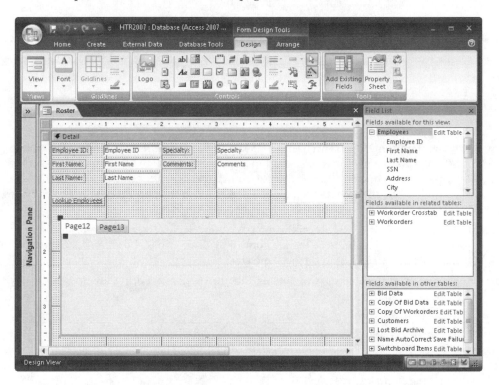

2. You can add controls to each page, as you do with a single-page form, clicking the tab to change between pages. However, when adding controls to a tab page, you can't drag the controls to the page; instead, you need to copy and paste controls from one page to another or from another part of the form to the tab page.

3. Next, do any of the following:

   • Change the default tab page name (Page 1, Page 2, etc.) by double-clicking the page and entering the new name in the Caption property on the Format tab.

   • Add another page or delete a page by right-clicking the tab control border and choosing Insert Page or Delete Page from the shortcut menu. When you delete a page, the last page inserted is removed. If you right-click in a page instead of the tab control border, that page is deleted.

   • Change the order of the tabbed pages by right-clicking the tab control border and choosing Page Order from the shortcut menu. In the Page Order dialog box, select the page in the list and click Move Up or Move Down to reorder the pages; or you can select and drag the page names to change the order.

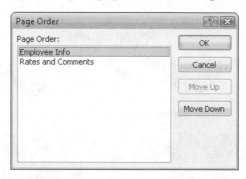

- As mentioned, you can use the TAB key to move among the controls on a page. You can change the tab order of the controls on a page by right-clicking in the page and choosing Tab Order. Rearrange the list of controls in the Tab Order dialog box to indicate the new tab order. To set the control tab order relative to the control locations in the design, choose Auto Order.

4. After placing the controls on the tab pages, check each page to make sure the controls fit. You can resize the tab control by dragging its borders. All pages in the tab control will adjust to be the same size.

5. Save the form with the name **Roster Tab** and switch to Form view to test the new tab control in the form.

TIP *If you are unsuccessful at reducing the size of a tab control, the sizes of controls on one of the tabbed pages could be preventing the reduction. Access doesn't crop any controls to fit a tab control or page. You might need to move or reduce a control object on one of the pages before you can reduce the entire tab control.*

Figure 12-8 shows two copies of the Roster form, showing both pages of the tab control.

To create the two-page tab control shown in Figure 12-8, do the following:

1. Open the Roster form in Design view and drag the lower detail section boundary down.

2. On the Design tab's Controls group, click the Tab Control command and draw a tab control frame horizontally across the lower half of the form design.

3. Use the vertical ruler to select all the controls in the upper half, right-click, and choose Copy from the shortcut menu.

4. Right-click in the tab control and choose Paste from the shortcut menu. The controls from the Roster form appear in the first page of the tab control.

5. Click the second page tab and drag the other fields from the Field List pane.

6. Double-click in a page to open the Property Sheet and change the Caption property to Employees Info. Then click in the other page and also change its Caption property to Rates and Comments.

Figure 12-8   Creating a two-page tab control

7. Delete the controls from the upper half of the form and reduce the form height to show only the tab control, and then switch to Form view.

NOTE *You might have to change some control properties. For example, change the Badge Picture Size Mode property to Zoom.*

Customizing a Tab Control

Two property sheets are used to customize a tab control: the Tab Control Property Sheet and the Page Property Sheet. To customize the tab control, double-click the control border outside of a page to open the Property Sheet. For example, you can change the style to show tabs or buttons, specify multiple rows of tabs, or set the height and width of the tabs.

To set individual page properties, double-click in the page area. You can enter the text you want to show on the page's tab or even add a graphic to it.

Adding Special Controls

In addition to images, unbound option groups, lines, and rectangles, you can add other special controls to a form design to enhance its appearance or provide additional information. Calculated controls can combine data from more than one field into processed or summary information. Remember that one of the rules of relational databases is that you don't include a field in a table that could be derived from fields already in the table.

Other special controls fall into the category of *ActiveX controls,* which were called *OLE (Object Linking and Embedding) Custom Controls* in earlier versions of Access. The Insert ActiveX Control command mentioned in Chapter 10 opens the list of all the ActiveX controls available in your system.

Adding Calculated Controls

Including a calculated control in a form or report is often helpful for users. For example, in the last chapter, a query was used to add two calculated controls to the Current Workorders form. One field totaled the labor and material costs, and the other added a 15 percent overhead cost. You can also add a calculated control to a form directly without using a query. An *unbound text box control* is usually used for a calculated control, but you can use any control that has a Control Source property, which tells Access where to get the information to display. Combo boxes, list boxes, bound and unbound object frames, toggle buttons, option buttons, and check boxes all have a Control Source property.

The calculation in the control is based on an expression you enter in the Control Source property box of the Property Sheet. An *expression* always begins with an equal sign (=). The expression contains operators and functions, in addition to the names of the fields or other controls involved in the calculation. Three types of operators are available for use in expressions:

- *Arithmetic operators,* such as +, –, *, ^, /, \, and Mod, which are used to compute results.
- *Comparison operators,* such as = <, >, <, >=, <>, and Between, which are used to create criteria expressions.
- *Logical operators,* such as And, Eqv, Imp, Not, Or, and Xor, which produce a Yes or No value.

NOTE *See the Quick Reference on the CD for a compete list of operators used in Access expressions and many examples of useful expressions.*

Access also provides more than 150 built-in functions to help create the expression you want for the calculated control. Each function is followed by parentheses, which enclose the arguments of the function. *Arguments* identify the values that the function uses to come up with a value.

Brackets around an identifier in an expression indicate the name of an Access object, such as a table, query, field, form, report, or control. If you type in the expression, you must include the brackets if the name includes a space or special character, such as an underscore. Otherwise, Access automatically adds the brackets.

NOTE *When you create a calculated control, Access gives it a default name, such as Textnn, where nn is a sequential number created as Access adds the controls. If you change the Name property to another name, be sure that you don't use the name of any of the controls already in the expression.*

Here are some examples of expressions you can use as the Control Source property for a calculated control:

- **=[Labor Cost]/[Total Hours]**   Computes the average hourly cost.
- **=Format(Now(),"ww")**   Displays the week number in the current year.
- **=IIF([Award Date]="Lost", "Review bid", "Create workorder")**   Tests the value in the Award Date field. If the field contains the word *Lost*, the value of the calculated control is *Review bid*; otherwise, it displays *Create workorder*.
- **=Count([Bid Number])**   Displays the number of records with a value in the Bid Number field.
- **=Sum([Qty]*[Price])**   Displays the total of the values obtained by multiplying the Qty and Price values in each record.

TIP *You can use the name of a calculated control in another expression if the expression doesn't use an aggregate function, such as Avg or Sum. You can use only field names from a table, query, or SQL statement in aggregate functions.*

To add a calculated control to a form design, do the following:

1. In Design view, on the Design tab's Controls group, click the Text Box command, and then click in the form design to place the control.
2. Enter the expression using one of the following methods:
   - Type the expression directly into the calculated control box. Be sure to precede the expression with an equal sign (=).
   - Type the expression, again preceded by an equal sign, in the Control Source property box in the Property Sheet.
   - For more complex expressions, click Build next to the Control Source property to open the Expression Builder.
3. Switch to Form view to test the new calculated control.

TIP *If you created an expression in a query that you can use in a calculated control in a form, copy and paste it in the Control Source property of the calculated control. Then place an equal sign in front of the expression.*

Using the Expression Builder

The *Expression Builder* is a dialog box, also known as a *modal form*, which will not let you do anything else until you close the form by clicking either OK or Cancel or, of course, the Close button. The dialog box is divided into two major parts: the upper part contains the expression under construction; the lower part contains all the elements you can add to the expression. Between the two parts is a row of buttons that you can use to add operators to the expression.

The lower half of the form contains three columns, the left-most of which lists all the different groupings of elements, such as database objects, functions, constants, operators, and common expressions. The following illustration shows the Expression Builder as it appears when you click Build (...) in the Control Source property of a new calculated control in the Current Workorders form. Notice the Current Workorders folder appears open in the left column and the center column displays all the elements of the form design. The objects and functions available in the Expression Builder depend on where you were when you launched it.

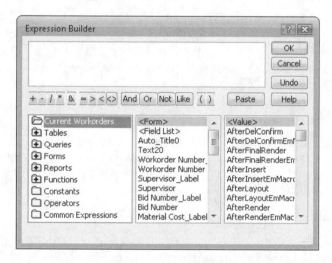

Double-click any item in the list that shows a plus (+) sign to expand it and show all the elements in the group. When you select an item in the left-most column, the elements in the item are listed in the center column. The right-most column lists elements from the selected item in the center column. If you select a field or control name in the center column, the right column shows *<Value>*, plus an alphabetical list of related properties. To add the item to the expression, double-click it in the right column or select it and click Paste.

TIP *You can always edit the expression that you're building by clicking in the upper part of the Expression Builder.*

To add the expression *[Total Cost]*1.15* in the Expression Builder, do the following:

1. With the Current Workorders folder open in the left column, scroll down the center column and double-click the Total Cost control name. Notice that Access automatically encloses the control name in brackets.

2. Click the asterisk (*) operator button to add it to the expression.

3. Type **1.15** to finish the expression and click OK. The Expression Builder dialog box closes and you will return to the form design.

NOTE   *If you look at the Control Source property for the calculated control, you will see that Access has added the equal sign at the beginning of the expression.*

If you want to add a function to an expression, in the left-most column of the Expression Builder, double-click Functions to open the folder, and then choose Built-In Functions. Next, choose the function category from the center column and the function itself from the right column. Each function has a set of arguments of various data types—some required and others optional. The message at the bottom of the Expression Builder dialog box shows the function syntax. (See the Access Help topic about an individual function for information about the proper use and the exact requirements.)

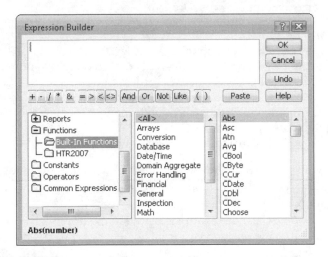

Adding Common Expressions

One of the folders in the left column of the Expression Builder dialog box is Common Expressions. When you click the folder to open it, you will see a list of six Common Expressions dealing with page numbers, date/time values, and current user.

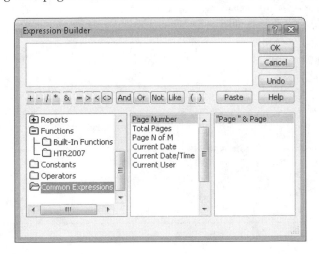

ActiveX Controls

ActiveX controls extend your reach to products supplied by third-party developers. Each control is a separate file with all the code, methods, events, and properties necessary to function in an Access environment.

Some ActiveX controls are installed with Access 2007 and others can be installed later. After you install the control using its installation program, all that you need to do is register it, so Access knows that the program exists in your system and knows where to find it. Some ActiveX controls are automatically registered during installation, while others must be registered manually.

After adding an ActiveX control to a form design, you can open the Property Sheet for the control and change its properties as necessary.

Adding a Calendar Control

The *Calendar control,* one of the most popular ActiveX controls, displays dates graphically on a calendar. The custom control has properties that enable you to set and retrieve dates in a table. For example, Figure 12-9 shows the Workorders form with a Calendar control that displays the start dates of the work orders in the Workorders table.

As you navigate among the records, the month changes to show the value in the Start Date as a highlighted date in the calendar.

To add a Calendar control to a form, do the following:

1. Start a new form based on the Workorders table and add the fields to the design.

2. With the form open in Design view, on the Design tab's Controls group, click the Insert ActiveX Control command and then select Calendar Control 12.0 from the list and click OK. The Calendar control is placed in the upper-left corner of the form. You can drag it to the position you want and change the size, if necessary.

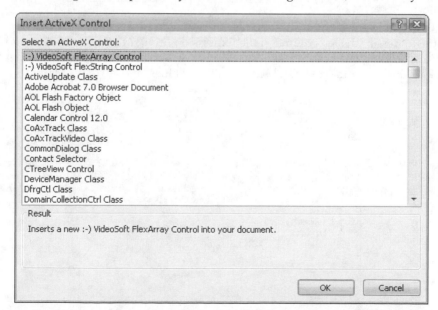

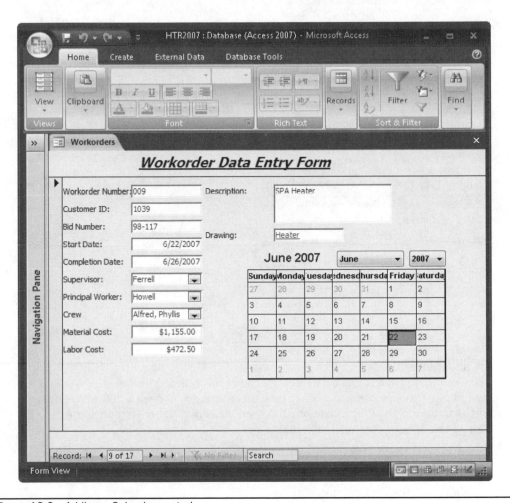

FIGURE 12-9   Adding a Calendar control

3. Open the Property Sheet for the Calendar control, click the arrow next to the
   Control Source property, and choose Start Date from the list.

The Calendar control has many properties that you can set to create a custom appearance.
In addition to the individual properties in the Property Sheet, you can open the Calendar

Properties dialog box to make changes. To open this dialog box, click Build (...) next to the Custom property on the Other tab of the Property Sheet.

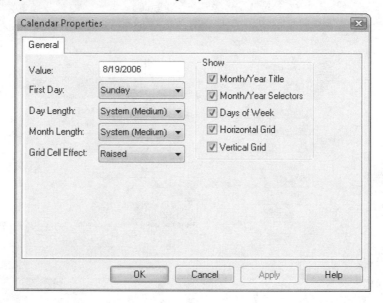

Adding an AutoDial Control

Use the Command Button Wizard to create a command button you can click to dial a selected phone number automatically. To use this feature, you need a dial-up modem connected to your computer and a regular telephone connected to the same line.

To add this special control, do the following:

1. Open the form in Design view.

2. Make sure the Control Wizards command in the Controls group is selected, and then click the Button command.

3. Click in the form where you want the button to appear. The Command Button Wizard starts.

4. In the first dialog box, click Miscellaneous in the Category box, and then click AutoDialer in the Actions box. Click Next.

5. Accept the picture of a telephone or click Show All Pictures and select a different image.

6. Enter a name for the new control and click Finish.

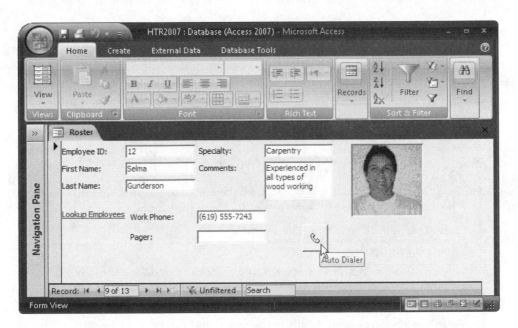

When you click the button in Form view, the AutoDialer dialog box opens. If you moved the cursor to a telephone number field before clicking the button, the number appears in the box. If not, you can enter a number in the empty Number box. Click OK to dial the number.

The Setup button in the AutoDialer dialog box opens a new dialog box, where you can set the modem properties.

Introducing the Police Database

The Police database is used 24 hours a day by a local police department in support of law enforcement and on behalf of its citizens. This is a mostly user-interactive data management system that tracks incidents and maintains records of all of the people who report, or who are involved in, activities that require police attention—for example, people who have been victims or perpetrators of crimes such as burglaries, auto theft, vandalism, and spousal abuse; people involved in traffic collisions, with or without injuries; and even people who come in to be fingerprinted as a requirement for employment.

The users of this database include the following:

- Police officers in the field who call the station to find out whether the person that they've stopped for speeding has a previous violation. The dispatcher at the station looks in the database for prior contacts.

- Victims of traffic accidents who need case information to send to their insurance companies.

- Parents of missing children who want to know if the child has been located.

The database consists of four tables: two main tables and two collateral tables used mainly for lookup.

The *Alpha Card table* lists all the people who have filed a report or called in an incident, or those who might be a suspect in some sort of incident, for example:

- A rental car agency reports a stolen vehicle.

- A home owner reports a burglary.

- A police officer responds to a two-car injury accident and identifies both drivers and one passenger. This report results in three separate records in the Alpha Card table, one for each civilian involved in the accident.

The *Alpha Entry table* contains details of the report and is related to the Alpha Card table with a one-to-many relationship. The Alpha Card table is on the one side and the Alpha Entry table is on the many side, because one person may be involved in more than one incident. The Index primary key field, an AutoNumber, in the Alpha Card table links to the Index field, the foreign key, in the Alpha Entry table. Here are the relationships between the four tables in the Police database:

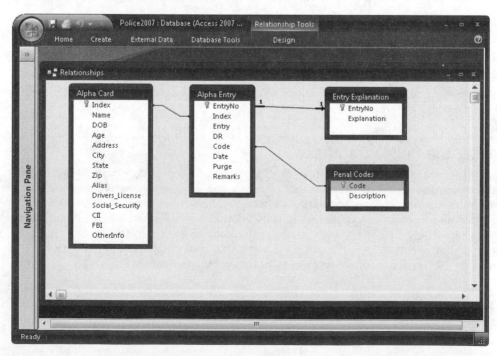

The third table, *Entry Explanation,* contains a more understandable explanation of the police shorthand descriptions in the Entry field on the Alpha Entry table. This table is related one-to-one with the Alpha Entry table with a left outer join. Referential Integrity has also been enforced, so Cascade Delete could be enabled. This has been found to be convenient because when the Alpha Entry record is deleted, the corresponding Explanation record is also deleted and the user doesn't have to look for the Explanation record to delete it.

The last table, *Penal Codes,* is a list of penal code numbers and their descriptions used as a lookup list.

The Police database is built in a different work environment to show that you can use Access 2007 in various ways. Settings have been changed to show overlapping documents instead of tabbed documents and the ribbon is hidden when it is not needed. To change the document settings, click the Microsoft Office button and click Access Options. In the Current Database set of Application options, check Overlapping documents. The Tabbed Documents and Display Document Tabs options are automatically cleared. Click OK to return to the database and then restart it to activate the changes.

You cannot replace the ribbon with toolbars and menus from previous versions, but you can hide the ribbon to give you more room to work. When you want to hide the ribbon, press CTRL-F1. Press it again to restore it.

The principal user interface is the Alpha Card form (see Figure 12-10), which shows all the entries linked to a particular individual. The main form in the upper half shows the data from the Alpha Card table. The lower half is a subform that shows all the related entries from the Alpha Entry table. Both the main form and the subform have record navigation buttons. The printer command button prints the current record and the Explanation button opens a pop-up form displaying an explanation of the entry. These special controls are discussed in subsequent sections in this chapter.

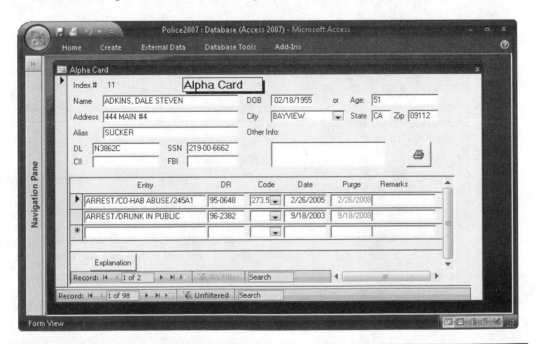

FIGURE 12-10   The Police Alpha Card form

Another major form in the Police database is the Alpha Entry form, which is a tabular form showing all the records in the table. The Alpha Entry form also includes a command button that opens the Alpha Card form at the same index number, so the officer can see the identity of the person involved as well as any prior entries for that person.

Adding a Subform

The main form and subform in a hierarchical form are synchronized so the subform displays only the records related to the record currently displayed in the main form. You can enter new records in either the main form or the subform. A main form can have as many subforms as you need and you can even nest subforms up to two levels, which means you can place a subform within a subform.

In the last chapter you saw how to create a main form and a subform at the same time using the Form Wizard. Simply create a new form with fields from two or more related tables. If the relationship is one-to-many, the wizard shows fields from the one side in the main form and fields from the many side in the subform. If you already have a main form and want to add a subform to it, you can use the Subform/Subreport Wizard available in the Controls group on the Design tab.

With the Subform Wizard

You can use the Subform Wizard to create and insert a new subform or to insert an existing subform into a main form. To use the wizard to add the Alpha Entry subform to a copy of the Alpha Card form, do the following:

1. Open the copy of Alpha Card form in Design view. Press CTRL-F1 to restore the ribbon.

2. Make sure the Control Wizards command is selected and click the Subform/ Subreport command in the Controls group.

3. Click in the form design and draw an outline where you want the subform to appear. You usually want the subform to span the width of the detail section in the form below the information in the main form. After the wizard starts, do one of the following:

   • If creating a new subform, click Use Existing Tables and Queries, and then click Next. Then choose from the Tables/Queries list and fields lists, just as you do when creating a regular form with the Form Wizard. Then click Next.

   • If you already created and saved the form you want to insert, choose Use an Existing Form, and select the Alpha Entry Subform from the drop-down list (see Figure 12-11); then click Next.

4. In the next dialog box, you can choose from a list of field links assumed by Access or choose to define your own. If you choose to define your own fields, the dialog box includes boxes where you can choose the fields that link the main form to the subform (see Figure 12-12). Choose the Index field in both forms, and then click Next.

5. Enter a name for the subform or accept Alpha Entry Subform, and then click Finish.

6. Open the Property Sheet and click the subform border (not the label), if it is not already selected.

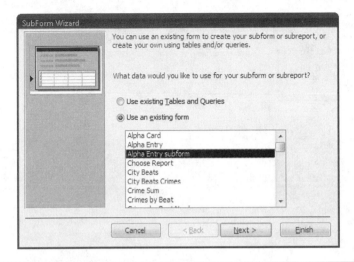

FIGURE 12-11 Choosing an existing form as the subform

7. Click the Data tab and make sure the Link Child Fields property refers to the foreign key (Index) in the subform and the Link Master Fields property refers to the linking field (Index) in the main form.

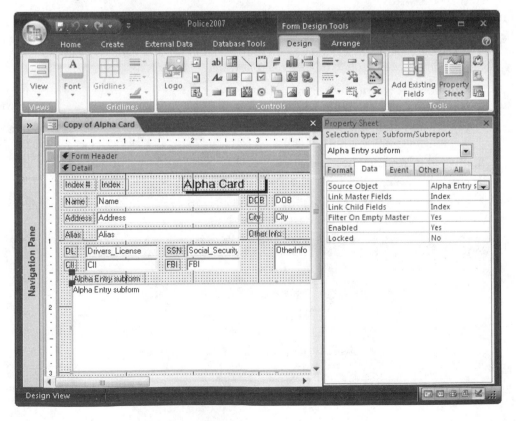

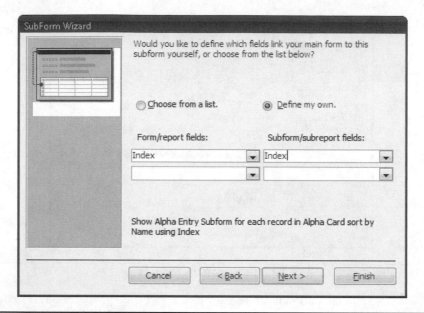

FIGURE 12-12   Setting the linking fields

Without the Subform Wizard

If you have already created and saved the form that you want to insert into the main form as a subform, the easiest way to do this is to drag the subform to the form design from the Navigation Pane. To accomplish this, do the following:

1. Open the main form in Design view.

2. Select the Alpha Entry Subform form in the Navigation Pane and drag it to the lower part of the Copy of Alpha Card form. As you drag the form name, it becomes a subform icon (see Figure 12-13).

3. Open the Property Sheet and click the Data tab.

4. Click the subform border and check that the Source Object is Alpha Entry Subform.

5. Click the Build button in the Link Child Fields property to open the Subform Field Linker dialog box to check the linking fields.

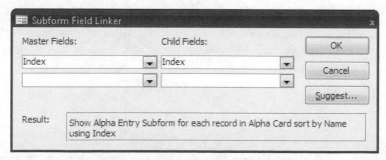

6. Click OK and close the Property Sheet.

Using the Hierarchical Form

To move from the main form to the subform in Form view, click in the subform, usually in a record selector or an editable area. To return to the main form, click an editable control in the main form or click its label. When you work in Navigation mode, some special key combinations move the cursor from the subform back to the main form:

- Pressing CTRL-TAB moves the cursor through the sequence of editable controls in the main form, and then moves to the first record in the subform. Pressing this key combination again moves to the first control of the next record in the main form.

- Pressing CTRL-SHIFT-TAB moves the cursor to the previous control in the main form or, if the cursor is anywhere in the subform, it moves the cursor to the last control in the tab order of the main form.

- Pressing CTRL-SHIFT-HOME moves the cursor to the first editable field in the main form, even if the key combination was pressed while the cursor was in the subform.

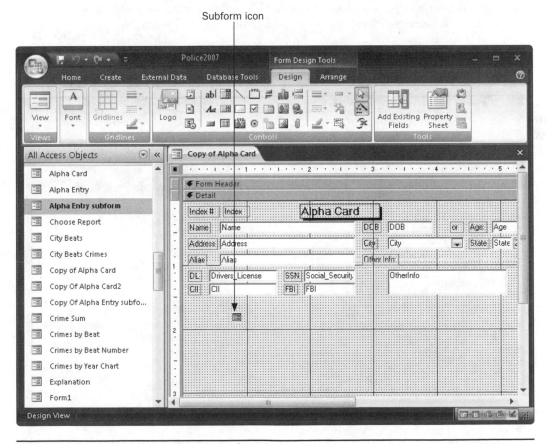

FIGURE 12-13   Dragging the subform to the form design

Each form has its own set of navigation buttons that you can use to move among the records. The subform also has a vertical scroll bar to move other records into view. You can add new records or edit or delete existing records in either the main form or the subform using the standard data entry techniques.

CAUTION *Make sure that the cursor is in the right place—in the main form or the subform—before you try to add or delete records.*

You can also sort records and set filters to limit records in either the main form or the subform using standard sorting and filtering methods.

Modifying a Subform

The complete subform design is included with the main form design. You can make changes to it in place. Select the control in the subform you want to change, and then change it as usual. If you want to work on the subform in its own window, right-click the subform frame and choose Subform in New Window from the shortcut menu. You can also choose the Subform in New Window command in the Tools group on the Design tab.

Subform in
New Window

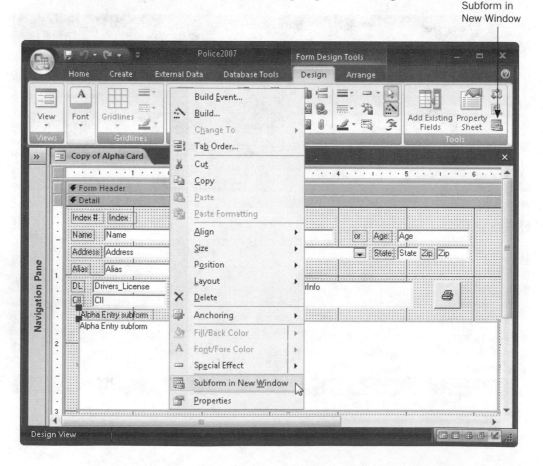

> **TIP** *The subform control in the main form is a separate control and has different properties than the subform object. To select the subform control, click one of the subform boundaries. To select the subform object for making changes in the subform itself, click the form selector in the subform.*

Linking and Synchronizing Forms

Each month, the Los Padres Police Department purges entries from the database that have been kept for the required period of time. To do this, the user opens the Alpha Entry form, a tabular form showing all the entries in Daily Report (DR) number order. One of the fields is Purge, which contains the date when the record should be removed from the file. If this entry is the last one connected to the individual, the Alpha Card should also be removed.

To view the related record in the Alpha Card file, use the Command Button Wizard to add a command button at the right end of the Alpha Entry record that opens the Alpha Card form for the same Index number.

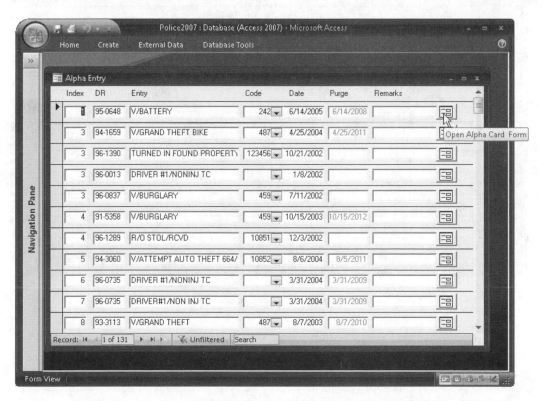

When you click the command button in Form view, the Alpha Card form opens showing only that single record. The record navigation bar shows Record 1 of 1 and the word *Filtered*, indicates that only one record has been extracted. Figure 12-14 shows the Alpha Entry form and the resulting Alpha Card record with the windows tiled vertically. The record for Index 3 is the current record in the Alpha Entry form and the Alpha Card form shows the related record.

FIGURE 12-14 Viewing the Alpha Card record for a specific entry

The Police database includes another form that is linked to the Alpha Entry subform. The *Explanation form* is a pop-up form displaying additional information about the entry that appears in the Alpha Entry subform. To add this feature, first create the pop-up form. A *pop-up form* is a special-purpose form that can be kept on the screen while you're doing other things. The pop-up form remains on the screen until you close it.

In contrast, a dialog box doesn't let you do anything else until you respond to the options presented in the box and click OK, Close, Cancel, or another button in the box. In Chapter 21, you will see how to create custom forms that can be used as dialog boxes. For now, let's work with a pop-up form.

To create a pop-up form that displays an explanation of the entry selected in the Alpha Entry subform, start a new form based on the Entry Explanation table. Add both fields to the design and resize the form to the smallest possible height and width.

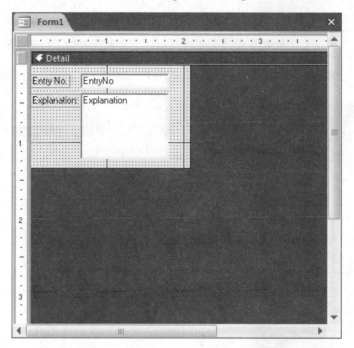

Then open the Property Sheet for the form, and on the Format tab change the following properties:

- Set Scroll Bars to Neither.
- Set Record Selectors, Navigation Buttons, Dividing Lines, Auto Resize, and Auto Center all to No.
- Set Border Style to Thin.
- Set Min Max Buttons to None.
- Then, on the Other tab, set Pop Up to Yes.

Now add a command button to the form footer of the Alpha Entry subform that opens the Explanation form for the selected entry by doing the following:

1. Open the Alpha Entry subform in Design view.
2. The form already has a header and footer section. Drag the lower border of the form down to make room for a command button, if necessary.
3. Make sure the Control Wizards command is selected and in the Controls group, click the Command Button command. Then click in the left end of the form footer section.
4. In the first Command Button Wizard dialog box, choose Form Operations from the Categories list and Open Form from the Actions list; then click Next.

5. Choose Explanation as the form to open, and then click Next.

6. In the next dialog box, choose Open the Form and Find Specific Data to Display, and then click Next.

7. Select EntryNo as the linking fields in both tables. Then click Next.

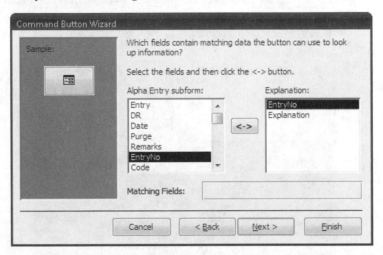

8. Choose Text instead of Picture for the button, enter **Explanation** in the box, and click Next.

9. Enter **Explanation** also as the name for the command button and click Finish.

Figure 12-15 shows the explanation of the entry selected in the Alpha Entry subform. The pop-up form remains on the screen until you close it.

NOTE *The way the form is designed, when you move to another entry, you must click the Explanation button again to see the explanation for that entry. If you want to synchronize the two forms so that the Explanation form follows the subform selection, you need to add a macro or an event procedure to one of the event properties. Chapter 19 discusses creating and using macros.*

Adding Custom Help

You've already seen some of the ways you can get help from Access. When you move the mouse pointer over a ribbon command, a ScreenTip pops up, displaying the name of the command and often additional information. The status bar displays messages related to the current activity or object, including the description you entered for the fields in your table design.

Then, in nearly every window, you can click the Help button or press F1 to open the Access Help window.

When you design your own application, you might appreciate a quick reminder to help with entering data, creating a filter, or printing a report. Access lets you create your own custom tips and status bar messages as properties of a form or report.

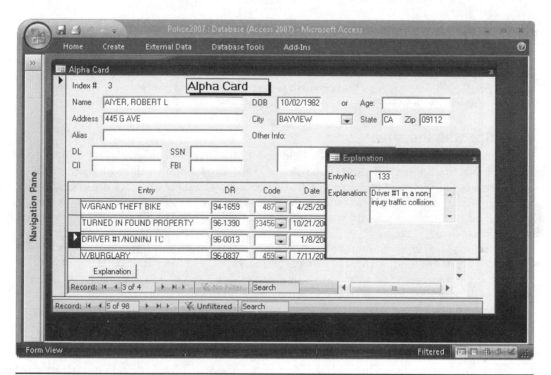

FIGURE 12-15   Explaining the current entry

Custom Control Tips

The *ControlTip Text property* specifies the message that appears when you move the mouse pointer over a control in the form. Short tips are best, but you can enter up to 255 characters. To create a control tip, open the form in Design view and select the control; then type the message in the ControlTip Text property box on the Other tab.

Status Bar Messages

A *status bar message* is a good way to display instructions for entering data in a control or explaining the options in an option group. *Status Bar Text* is a control property available for any control on a form that you can select. The message displays when the control gets focus.

To specify a message to display in the status bar, type the text in the Status Bar Text property box on the Other tab. Again, you can enter up to 255 characters, but the amount of text displayed is limited by the physical space across the status bar. This depends on the size of the window and the font that you use for the message.

TIP   *Try to keep the status bar messages brief. A lengthy message can be truncated and could cause some confusion on the part of the user.*

Validating or Restricting Data in Forms

Access gives you several ways to validate or restrict data entered in forms. You can create controls, such as check boxes, that limit the data to Yes/No values or a list box that requires a value be chosen from the list. You can also set certain form and control properties that limit or restrict data entry.

Validating with Properties

When you designed your tables, you set field properties to help ensure valid data. You created input masks, entered validation rules, and specified default values for some of the fields. This is the preferred way to validate data because you have to do it only once. Any bound control you add to a form inherits the properties you set in the table design. If you wait and add the validations and restrictions to a form, you need to do it for every form that refers to that data.

Sometimes, however, you might want to superimpose more validation in the form. For example, you might want to display different error messages when the data is invalid or prevent any data from being entered in a field. If you want to validate unbound controls, you must do it in the form design because they have no ties to a table. The validation rules for controls in a form are created the same as for a field in table design. You can get help from the Expression Builder if you need it.

The Default Value, Validation Rule, Validation Text, and Input Mask properties are the same as for table fields.

Three form properties determine the liberties the user can take with data in the form: Allow Edit, Allow Additions, or Allow Deletions. Set these to Yes or No. You can also set the Data Entry property to Yes so that the user sees only an empty form with no existing data.

Each control has two additional properties: Enabled and Locked. If the control is enabled, it can receive focus. If the control is locked, the control becomes read-only and you can't change it in Form view.

If you set one of these properties in the table design and set the same property to a different value in the form design, the bound control property in the form overrides the field property in the table. For example, if you want to set the default value for a date field to today's date in the form instead of the value set as the field property in the table design, type **=Date()** in the control's Default Value property box. This takes precedence over the setting in the field property.

Validation rules are applied in the following order:

1. Rule specified by a macro or event procedure that responds to the Before Update event.
2. Rule specified as the control Validation Rule property.
3. Rule specified as the field Validation Rule property.
4. Rule specified as the table Record Validation Rule property.

CAUTION *If you change any of the validation rules in table Design view, these changes are enforced on controls based on those fields, even if you added the controls to the form before making the changes.*

You can combine property settings to accomplish specific purposes. For example, if you want the form to be read-only, set Allow Edits, Allow Additions, and Allow Deletions all to No.

Combining the Enabled and Locked property settings for a control can create custom results, as shown in Table 12-1.

You can also combine the Enabled and Tab Stop properties. If you set Enabled to Yes and Tab Stop to No, the control can't be selected by pressing TAB, but it can still be selected by clicking the control or its label.

Validating with Events

Attaching macros or event procedures to form and control event properties can give you additional flexibility and power over data entry. For example, you can require that at least two of three fields must be filled in before you can save the record. You would also use an event procedure if the validation refers to controls on other forms or if the control contains a function.

If you want to validate the data before the whole record is updated, add the procedure to a form event. To validate the data before moving to the next control, add the procedure to a control event. Table 12-2 shows a few of the form and control events that you can use for data validation.

See Chapter 18 for more information about events and their sequence of occurrence, and how to make the macros that will carry out the actual validation.

Enabled Setting	Locked Setting	Results
Yes	Yes	Control can receive focus. The data is displayed normally and can be copied but can't be edited.
Yes	No	Control can receive focus. Use this combination to allow editing of objects in unbound object frames. The data is displayed normally and can be copied or edited.
No	Yes	Control cannot receive focus. Data is displayed normally but can't be copied or edited.
No	No	Control cannot receive focus. Control and data both appear dimmed and are disabled.

TABLE 12-1   Combining Enabled and Locked Properties

Event	Description
Before Update (form)	Rule enforced before saving new or changed data in a record.
On Delete (form)	Rule enforced before deleting a record.
Before Update (control)	Rule enforced before saving new or changed data in a control.
On Exit (control)	Rule enforced before leaving control.

TABLE 12-2   Data Validation Events

Summary

You might never want to add hyperlinks or a calendar to a form, but if you do, this chapter contains all the information you need to add these and other special controls. The most important question regarding form design isn't "What new and exotic things can I add to it?" but, rather, "What does the user need to see and know to do his or her job?"

One of the most flexible features of form design is the ability to link subforms to a main form to show related data from more than one table. You saw examples of using subforms in this and the preceding chapter where records from a table on the many side of a one-to-many relationship were displayed in a subform with the data from the one side in the main form.

Starting with the next chapter, you will learn how to create reports for distributing information to outside users. You also make further use of the Police database introduced in this chapter and continue to see examples using the Home Tech Repair database. You create reports first with the help of the Report Wizard, and then from scratch in report Design view. Chapter 14 then discusses special reports that group and summarize data or print envelopes and mailing labels.

Using the Report Wizard

T he Access Report Wizard helps you prepare many types of reports—from simple reports that contain complete information from one or more tables to reports that calculate and summarize information and present it in a variety of visual representations. You can also create multiple column reports to be used for printing mailing labels of all kinds and use Access tables for mail merge applications with Microsoft Word.

In this chapter, you will see examples of reports using different databases: the Access Northwind Traders sample database, as well as the Home Tech Repair and Police databases introduced in earlier chapters. No single database has all the elements necessary to display the versatility of Access report writing.

In this chapter, the Report Wizard guides you through creating a simple report based on one table, a more complex report based on two tables, and finally, a summary report that groups records and calculates summary values. After using the Report Wizard, you can then modify the design to add special features and set report properties. Chapter 14 continues the discussion of reports by addressing customization, subreports, and mailing labels.

Creating a New Report Design

Although you can create Access reports using the same techniques that you use for creating forms, major differences exist between forms and reports with respect to the design concepts. *Forms* deal with data and the processes of data management, such as data entry, validation, and retrieval. *Reports,* on the other hand, deal with information derived from the data. For example, the numbers 999900000 are simply data and mean nothing to you until you turn the sequence into information: 999-90-0000, which indicates a Social Security Number.

Forms are used primarily by people who are acquainted with computers and database management systems, so forms can be somewhat abbreviated, assuming that the user understands the process at hand. Reports are much more widely distributed and need to be designed for the needs and understanding of their intended audience.

What Is the Purpose of the Report?

The differences between forms and reports necessitate a much wider range of report design features, which, in turn, creates a more complex design problem. As with form design, you start the process by defining what you want from the report. Concentrate first on the intended recipients and the level of detail they want to see. For example, managers want to see information to help them make strategic decisions, such as trends in sales and summary economic data. Operational personnel want more detailed information relating to ongoing business, such as stock levels and employee performance.

Figure 13-1 shows examples of three types of reports. You can see these reports and others in the Northwind Traders database.

The top report shows a summary of sales by product category, complete with a chart illustrating the information. This type of report is suitable for a manager who makes decisions based on product popularity. The second report shows a detailed list of all products in the store in alphabetic order. This kind of report is used by operational personnel to look up an item when a customer calls to ask if the product is in stock. If you want to carry this kind of report into the stockroom to check current inventory levels, you might want to add the storage location field, and then sort or group the records by that value instead.

The lower report is an example of a special purpose report used for printing invoices. This report is based on a query that extracts information from several related tables containing shipper, customer, order, product, and salesperson data.

Tip *A report can be designed to print on a preprinted form, which can be scanned and saved as a report template. See Chapter 14 for information on printing reports on preprinted forms.*

Consulting the future users of the report is essential to the design process and drawing a sketch of the proposed report for review by the intended users is helpful. Unfortunately, even experienced business people don't always predict everything they want in a report until they see the finished product; then they identify other things they need in the report. For this reason, you should plan on the design process being an iterative one that continuously improves the product.

Selecting, Sorting, and Grouping the Data

Once you collect the requirements for the report content and appearance, you can begin to locate the required data in the database. It might be stored in a single table or distributed among several related tables. If the data is stored in several tables in the database, make sure the tables can be linked, if they aren't already related.

Sorting Records

Define the sort order for the records in the report. For example, do you want the records sorted in chronological order or by some identifier, such as the primary key? If a sort order is saved with the table, you can apply it automatically in the report. For example, if you have a mailing list for sending promotional material to your customers, you might want to sort the outgoing mail by ZIP code to save on postal costs.

Filtering Records

At times, you might want to limit the records in a report based on a certain filter criterion. For example, you might want to prepare a report for the ordering clerk to use in placing orders. The report would include only those products that have fewer items in stock than the minimum number recommended. You can base the report on a query that extracts only the data you want or apply a filter to the report later. To complete the report, you could also include the name and telephone number of the supplier of each product.

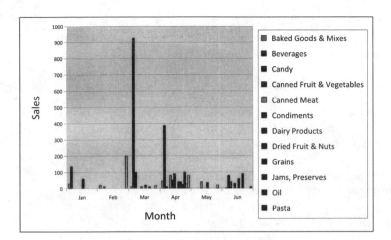

Alphabetical List of Products

Product Name	Category	Quantity Per Unit	List Price
Northwind Traders Almonds	Dried Fruit & Nuts	5 kg pkg.	$10.00
Northwind Traders Beer	Beverages	24 - 12 oz bottles	$14.00
Northwind Traders Boysenberry Spread	Jams, Preserves	12 - 8 oz jars	$25.00
Northwind Traders Brownie Mix	Baked Goods & Mixes	3 boxes	$12.49
Northwind Traders Cajun Seasoning	Condiments	48 - 6 oz jars	$22.00
Northwind Traders Cake Mix	Baked Goods & Mixes	4 boxes	$15.99
Northwind Traders Chai	Beverages	10 boxes x 20 bags	$18.00
Northwind Traders Cherry Pie Filling	Canned Fruit & Vegetables	15.25 OZ	$0.00
Northwind Traders Chicken Soup	Soups		$0.00
Northwind Traders Chocolate	Candy	10 pkgs	$12.75
Northwind Traders Chocolate Biscuits Mix	Baked Goods & Mixes	10 boxes x 12 pieces	$9.20
Northwind Traders Clam Chowder	Soups	12 - 12 oz cans	$9.65
Northwind Traders Coffee	Beverages	16 - 500 g tins	$46.00
Northwind Traders Corn	Canned Fruit & Vegetables	14.5 OZ	$0.00
Northwind Traders Crab Meat	Canned Meat	24 - 4 oz tins	$18.40
Northwind Traders Curry Sauce	Sauces	12 - 12 oz jars	$40.00
Northwind Traders Dried Apples	Dried Fruit & Nuts	50 - 300 g pkgs.	$53.00
Northwind Traders Dried Pears	Dried Fruit & Nuts	12 - 1 lb pkgs.	$30.00
Northwind Traders Dried Plums	Dried Fruit & Nuts	1 lb bag	$3.50
Northwind Traders Fruit Cocktail	Canned Fruit & Vegetables	15.25 OZ	$39.00
Northwind Traders Gnocchi	Pasta	24 - 250 g pkgs.	$38.00
Northwind Traders Granola	Cereal		$0.00
Northwind Traders Green Beans	Canned Fruit & Vegetables	14.5 OZ	$0.00
Northwind Traders Green Tea	Beverages	20 bags per box	$2.99
Northwind Traders Hot Cereal	Cereal		$0.00
Northwind Traders Hot Pepper Sauce	Sauces	32 - 8 oz bottles	$21.05
Northwind Traders Long Grain Rice	Grains	16 - 2 kg boxes	$7.00
Northwind Traders Marmalade	Jams, Preserves	30 gift boxes	$81.00
Northwind Traders Mozzarella	Dairy Products	24 - 200 g pkgs.	$34.80
Northwind Traders Mustard	Condiments	12 boxes	$13.00
Northwind Traders Olive Oil	Oil	36 boxes	$21.35
Northwind Traders Peaches	Canned Fruit & Vegetables	15.25 OZ	$0.00

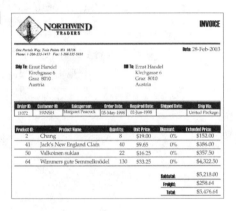

Figure 13-1   Some typical useful reports

Grouping Records

Records are often grouped in a report. This is a good way to relate data from several records and convert it into meaningful information. For example, you could group sales by quarter in an attempt to predict future inventory requirements. You can include charts and graphs in your report that illustrate the information more visibly.

Specifying Summary and Calculated Fields

After the records have been grouped, summaries and calculated fields can add an important element to reports. They can save the reader time by doing much of the data evaluation work for them. For example, the first report shown in Figure 13-1 is intended to compare the sales of various beverage products. The manager is considering eliminating some of these product lines and needs information to decide which ones are no longer popular. If the report summarizes sales data over a period of time and presents it in a report, the manager then has all the required numeric information already summarized.

Starting a Report

You can create a report in several ways, depending on the type of report you need:

- Use the Access Report tool.
- Use the Report Wizard.
- Create your own design in the Report Design view.
- Create a report for printing Labels.
- Start with a Blank Report.

Using the Report Tool

The *Report tool* creates a quick report of all the data in a table or query and displays it in Layout view. The report isn't fancy, but it's useful for checking and verifying the data in a table. When you print the records from Datasheet view, the data appears in a tabular layout resembling the datasheet itself. The report created by the Report tool includes all the data in the table or query you used as the basis in a columnar layout with the field names in the left column and the field values in the right column. When completed, the report is displayed in Layout view, where you can make changes to the report design. For example, you can adjust column widths, rearrange columns, and add grouping levels and totals. You can also add fields to the report design and set properties for the report and its controls.

NOTE   *The Report tool places all of the fields in the same order in which they appear in the table or query and uses the table or query name as the report title. When you try to close the report, Access asks if you want to save the report.*

After creating the report, you can print it as it appears or switch to Design view and make changes. This report method is so quick and easy, that unless you plan to use a report quite often, you need not bother to name and save it; you can easily recreate it later. To close the report without saving the design, right-click the document tab, choose Close from the shortcut menu, and respond No when asked if you want to save the changes.

Using the Report Wizard

The *Report Wizard* is similar to the Form Wizard. It presents a series of dialog boxes that guide you through the design process. Most of the dialog boxes present the same kinds of options presented for forms, but the Report Wizard includes a couple of new options for sorting, grouping, and summarizing specifications. The examples in the remainder of this chapter use the Home Tech Repair database as well as the Police database introduced in the previous chapter.

Creating a Single-Table Report with the Report Wizard

In the first example, the Report Wizard creates a report based on the Alpha Entry by Code Query that limits the data in the Alpha Entry table of the Police database only to those with a numeric incident code. This screens out the employment fingerprint and traffic collision reports that don't involve a crime.

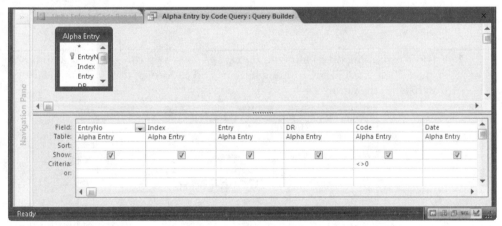

To create this new report with the help of the Report Wizard, do the following:

1. Select the Alpha Entry by Code Query in the query group on the Navigation Pane, and on the Create tab's Reports group, click the Report Wizard command.

2. The first dialog box is the same as the box that appears in the Form Wizard, in which you choose the fields you want to include in the report from the tables and queries in the database. Make sure that the Alpha Entry by Code query appears in the Tables/ Queries box. Then click the double arrows (>>) to select all the fields, and click Next.

3. In the second dialog box, the wizard asks if you want to group the records by any of the field values. Select Code as the name of the field you want to group by and click the right arrow (>), as shown in Figure 13-2.

    If you change your mind, select the field name and click the left arrow (<) to remove the group designation. The up and down Priority arrows change the group order.

Add grouping field

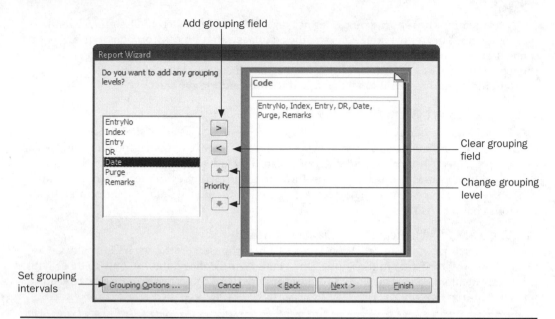

Clear grouping field

Change grouping level

Set grouping intervals

FIGURE 13-2 Choosing the grouping level

- If you're grouping on a field with numeric values, you can group by an interval such as 50 or 100. Click Grouping options and choose an option from the drop-down list in the Grouping Intervals dialog box.

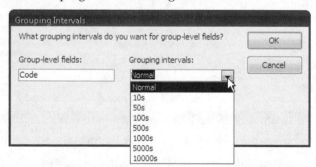

- If one of the fields that you're grouping on is a number or currency field, the Summary Options button becomes available. (More about adding summaries is discussed later in the section "Creating a Summary Report with the Report Wizard" and in Chapter 14.)

4. Click Next to move to the next dialog box, which is also unique to the Report Wizard. The wizard asks if you want to sort your records within the groups in other than primary key order. The groups are automatically sorted in ascending order by the group field value. Figure 13-3 shows a sort specified by Date in ascending order. You can sort on up to four fields by clicking the arrow next to the sort box and choosing the field from the list. If you want to sort in descending order, click the Ascending button to the right of the sort box. When you are done, click Next.

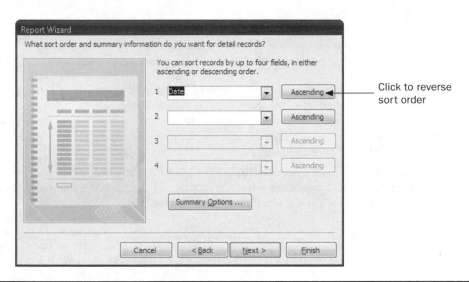

FIGURE 13-3   Specifying the sort order

TIP   *The fields do not need to all be sorted in the same order. You can sort one field in ascending order and the next in descending order, for example.*

5. In the next dialog box (see Figure 13-4), you can select the layout you want for the report and the print orientation. If you selected a lot of fields, you might want to change the orientation to landscape so that they all fit on the page. Select a format and look at the sample in the left pane. For this report, select Stepped and Portrait, then click Next.

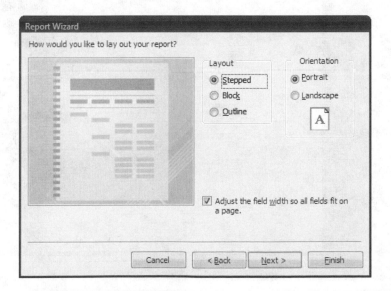

FIGURE 13-4   Choosing the report layout and orientation

TIP *Another option tells the wizard to adjust the width of the fields so that they all fit on the page. This might result in losing characters in the column headings or currency symbols in the field data, but you can adjust the column widths later in Design view.*

6. The next wizard dialog box offers 25 different styles from which to choose. The styles apply to the font size and style, the line spacing, and color—much like with the Form Wizard—but these are more suited to printed output. As you select each style, an example is displayed in the sample pane on the left. Select the desired style (the Civic style was chosen in this example) and click Next.

7. The final dialog box is the same as that of the Form Wizard: You name the report and choose whether to view the report or go directly to Design view. Enter **Alpha Entry by Code Report** as the report name and click Finish.

Figure 13-5 shows a Print Preview of the Alpha Entry by Code Report generated by the Report Wizard. If you also want an interpretation of the code to appear with the code number in the group header, add the Description field from the Penal Codes table to the query.

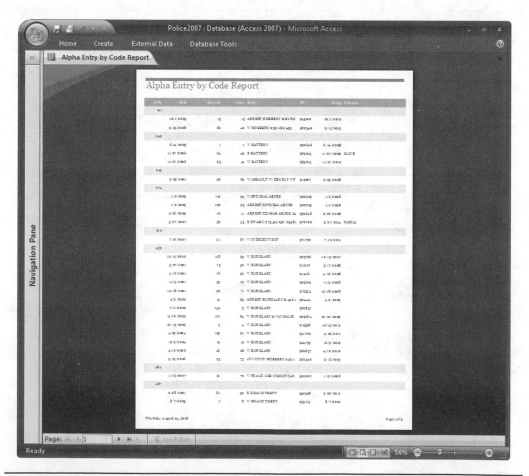

FIGURE 13-5 The Alpha Entry by Code Report in Print Preview

Creating a Three-Table Report with the Report Wizard

When you use the Report Wizard to create a report based on two or more tables or queries, you can specify which table contains the main data and which contains the subordinate data. In the example in this section, the Alpha Card table is specified as the parent table and the Alpha Entry table as the related child table. The Entry Explanation table, which is related one-to-one to the Alpha Entry table, is also included. The resulting report shows multiple Alpha Entry records for a single Alpha Card record.

TIP *When you choose fields from one or more tables, the Report Wizard automatically creates a query that is run every time to open the report. The query is a SELECT statement that appears as the report Control Source property. If the query is complex, you can save processing time by creating the query yourself and using it as the basis for the report.*

To create the three-table report, do the following:

1. Select the Alpha Card table in the Navigation Pane, and then on the Create tab's Reports group, click the Report Wizard command.

2. In the first dialog box, choose the Index and Name fields from the Alpha Card table. Then select the Alpha Entry table in the Tables/Queries box and choose the EntryNo, Entry, Code, and Date fields. Finally, select the Entry Explanation table and choose the Explanation field. Then click Next.

NOTE *If you select fields from two or more tables that are not related, Access displays a message box asking if you want to quit the Report Wizard and edit the relationships. Click OK to open the Relationships window and the Show Table dialog box. After relating the tables, you must restart the Report Wizard. If you don't want to relate the tables, click Cancel and you will return to the first wizard dialog box, where you can remove the unrelated fields.*

3. In the second dialog box (see Figure 13-6), the wizard asks how you want to view the data. This dialog box appears only if you chose fields from more than one table or query. Access assumes that the parent table of the relationship is to appear as the main data—in this case, the Alpha Card table. Accept the wizard's choice and click Next.

TIP *The Show Me More Information button opens the Report Wizard Tips window where you can ask to see several examples of how the wizard can group your data in the report. If you open this window, you can click Close to return to the Report Wizard.*

4. The next dialog box, similar to the one shown in Figure 13-2, shows the Alpha Card fields in the upper box and the Alpha Entry and Entry Explanation fields in a list below. Select any grouping levels you want in this dialog box. Click Next twice to skip this and the Sort Options dialog box to reach the Layout dialog box, in which you select a layout.

5. Choose Outline, keep the Portrait orientation, and click Next twice.

6. In the last dialog box, name the report **Alpha Card with Entries** and click Finish.

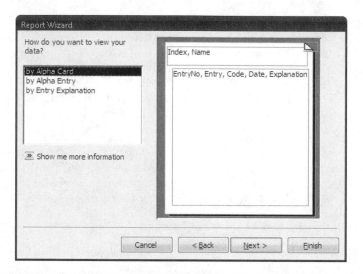

FIGURE 13-6 Choosing the table containing the main data

TIP *Don't use any special characters, such as an* ampersand (&), *in the report title. Although the filename may include the character, when the title appears on the first page of the report, the character is converted to an* underscore (_).

Figure 13-7 shows the printed first page of the new Alpha Card with Entries report. As you navigate through the pages, you will see that several improvements could be made. For example, the column headers might appear on one page and the corresponding Alpha Entry data is carried over to the next. To correct this, you can group on the Index field and specify that the group not be broken between pages. In addition, the Entry field needs to be widened to reveal the full values. The next chapter discusses these and other modifications that you can make to improve the report design. You might also like to see a group divider appear between the index lists in addition to the alternate background color feature.

Troubleshooting the Report

If the relationships among the three tables used in this report are not set properly, the report might not contain complete information. For example, the default relationship uses an inner join. An *inner join* includes only records for which both parent and child have the same value in the linking field. So, if an Alpha Entry record is related to the Entry Explanation table with an inner join, you won't see any Alpha Entry records that have no corresponding Entry Explanation record.

To solve this problem, edit the relationship and change it to the second option in the Edit Relationship dialog box, a left outer join. This will include all the records from the Alpha Entry table and only those from the Entry Explanation table that match.

Another useful feature of this relationship is the ability to enforce referential integrity and choose Cascade Delete. This automatically cleans up the database by deleting the explanation records when the entry record itself is deleted.

Alpha Card with Entries

Index	1				
Name	ALLEN, FRANK ROGER				
EntryNo	**Entry**		**Code**	**Date**	**Explanation**
1	V/BATTERY		242	6/14/2005	Victim of battery

Index	3				
Name	AIYER, ROBERT L				
EntryNo	**Entry**		**Code**	**Date**	**Explanation**
134	V/BURGLARY		459	7/11/2002	Victim of house burglary
133	DRIVER #1/NONINJ T			1/8/2002	Driver #1 in a non-injury traffic collision.
132	TURNED IN FOUND P		123456	10/21/2002	Turned in jewelry found in store parking lot.
2	V/GRAND THEFT BIKE		487	4/25/2004	Victim of grand theft. Bicycle was stolen.

Index	4				
Name	AILLEM, PAUL CALVIN				
EntryNo	**Entry**		**Code**	**Date**	**Explanation**
3	V/BURGLARY		459	10/15/2003	Victim of burglary
135	R/O STOL/RCVD		10851	12/3/2002	Registered owner of recovered stolen vehicle.

Index	5				
Name	AIZENBAUM, ESTELA				
EntryNo	**Entry**		**Code**	**Date**	**Explanation**
4	V/ATTEMPT AUTO TH		10852	8/6/2004	Victim of an attempted auto theft.

Index	6				
Name	AKEN, HAILESILASSIE B				
EntryNo	**Entry**		**Code**	**Date**	**Explanation**
5	DRIVER #1/NONINJ T			3/31/2004	Driver #1 in non-injury traffic collision

FIGURE 13-7   Printed Alpha Card with Entries report

Creating a Summary Report with the Report Wizard

The Report Wizard's summarizing abilities are useful when you create reports involving numeric or monetary information. When you choose to group records, the wizard makes summarizing options available with which you can compute the total value; determine the average, minimum, and maximum of the group of values; compute a grand total; and calculate the percent of the grand total represented by each of the groups. The wizard might not create the report exactly as you want to see it, but it can save you a lot of time with the arithmetic. You can always modify the report appearance later.

For this example, turn back to the Home Tech Repair database. This database has some currency fields that can demonstrate the summary options by creating a report that summarizes the work orders grouped by supervisor. When you choose to group the Workorders records by Supervisor, the next dialog box in which you set the sort order now has the Summary Options button available. Clicking this button opens the Summary Options dialog box, which shows the names of all the fields in the report that contain number or currency data. Both the Material Cost and Labor Cost fields are from the Workorders table.

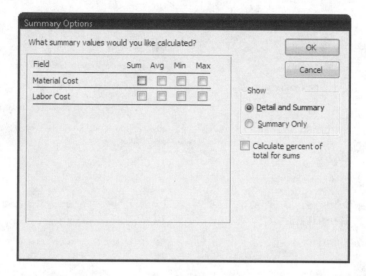

Click the check boxes for all the summary values that you want the wizard to calculate for you. In the Show option group, you can choose to include the detail records with the summaries or show only the summary values. The other option, Calculate Percent of Total for Sums, includes the relative size of each group sum compared to the Grand Total, which is calculated and printed at the end of the report.

The wizard finishes the report in Print Preview. Right-click the document tab and look at the report in Report view (see Figure 13-8). The report groups the Home Tech Repair work orders by supervisor and computes the sum, average, minimum, and maximum of the Material Costs and Labor Costs for each group of work orders. The Report Wizard also automatically counts the number of detail records in each group and displays it at the top of the summary section. Another background color has been added to the group header to separate one supervisor's work orders from the next.

You can see that some small changes need to be made in the report. For example, you could format the summary values to show currency symbols and widen some of the controls to show the entire name or value.

Modifying the Wizard's Design

All the small changes to the report the wizard constructed can be made in Layout view. There is no need to switch to the report Design view.

1. Click in the Material Cost column header and drag the left border to widen the column enough to see all the values.
2. Click in the Labor Cost column header and drag the right border to widen the column.
3. Individually, click the Sum, Avg, and Standard labels in the summary section and widen each one to see the full text.

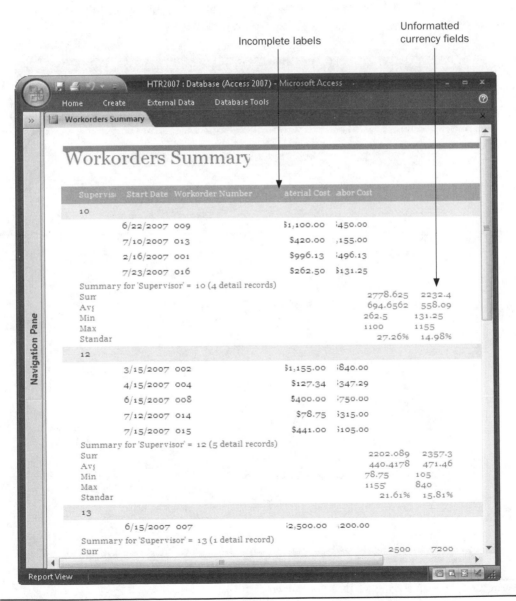

FIGURE 13-8 Summarizing work order costs by supervisor

4. Hold down SHIFT while you select all eight of the summary values in one group section.

5. Right-click in the group and choose Properties from the shortcut menu.

6. On the Format tab of the Property Sheet, click the Format property and choose Currency from the drop-down list. Then set the Decimal Places property to 2.

7. Widen each of the summary columns to show the currency symbols, as necessary.

Figure 13-9 shows the finished Workorders Summary report in Report view.

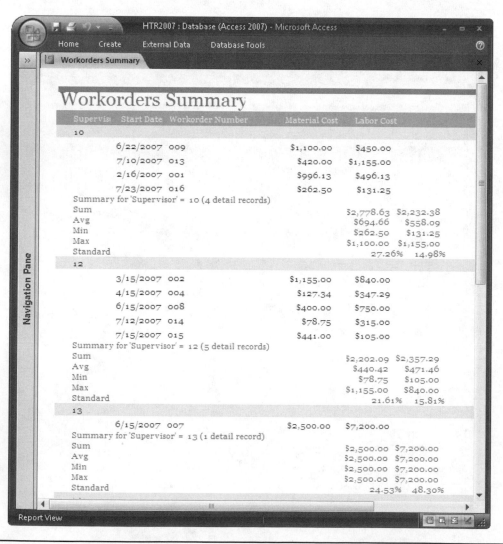

FIGURE 13-9 The finished Workorders Summary report

> **TIP** *If you look at the report in Print Preview, you will see that the group containing work orders headed by Supervisor 17 is split between pages 1 and 2 in the report. One of the properties of a group section is Keep Together, which can be set to Yes or No. Set this property to Yes if you want to keep the group header, the detail section, and the group footer together on the same page. Chapter 14 contains more information on grouping records in a custom report and setting group properties.*

Previewing the Report

When the Report Wizard finishes creating the report design, you have a choice of going directly to the report Design view or previewing the report as it will be printed. If you haven't used the Report Wizard or you want to preview an existing report, right-click the report name in the Reports group in the Navigation Pane and choose Print Preview from the shortcut menu.

If the report is already open, right-click the document tab and choose Print Preview from the shortcut menu.

Working in the Print Preview Window

The Access Print Preview window offers you many ways to view the report, including moving around a single page and among pages, looking at several pages at once, and changing the magnification so that you can see the details more clearly. Returning to the Police database, Figure 13-10 shows the first page of the Alpha Card with Entries report in Print Preview.

To close the Print Preview window, do one of the following:

- Click the Close button in the report header.
- On the Print Preview tab's Close Preview group, click Close Print Preview.
- Right-click the document tab and choose Close from the shortcut menu.

To change to a different view, you can use the task bar buttons to change to Report view, Layout view, or Design view.

> **TIP** *When you close the Navigation Pane, the ribbon reverts to the Home tab. So if you don't see the Print Preview tab, right-click the report document tab and select Print Preview from the shortcut menu.*

Navigating in the Preview

The navigation buttons at the bottom of the Print Preview window let you move among pages in the report. Click one of the buttons to move to the first, previous, next, or last page of the report. You can also enter the page number in the page number box and press ENTER to move to a specific page.

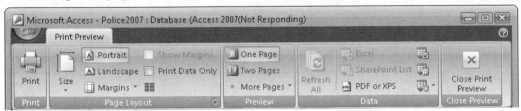

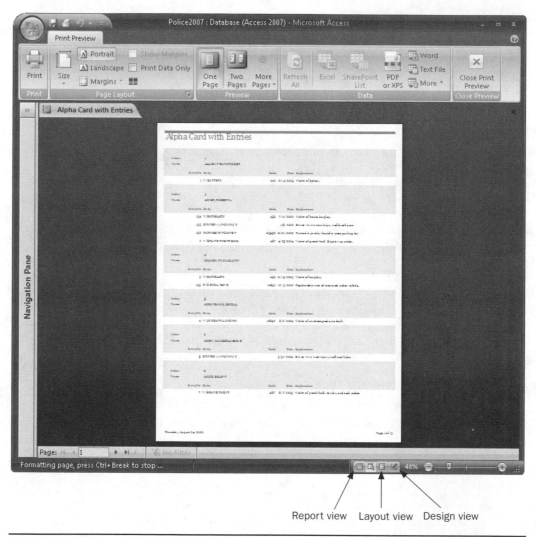

Report view   Layout view   Design view

Figure 13-10   Viewing the new report in Print Preview

You can use many shortcut keys to navigate in a report preview. See the Access Help topic "Keyboard Shortcuts for Access" for a list of all of the combinations that you can use in Print Preview.

Viewing Multiple Pages

Using the Print Preview commands, you can view two pages adjusted to fit the screen or up to twelve pages arranged in three rows of four pages each.

To view one complete page at a time, do one of the following:

- On the Print Preview tab in the Preview group, click the One Page command.

- Right-click and choose One Page from the shortcut menu.

To view two or more complete pages adjusted to fit the screen, right-click, click Zoom, and choose Fit from the drop-down list; then use one of the following methods:

- On the Print Preview tab in the Preview group, click the Two Pages command. Right-click and click Multiple Pages and drag the mouse pointer over the grid to select the number of pages and the arrangement that you want. You can choose up to six pages with this method.

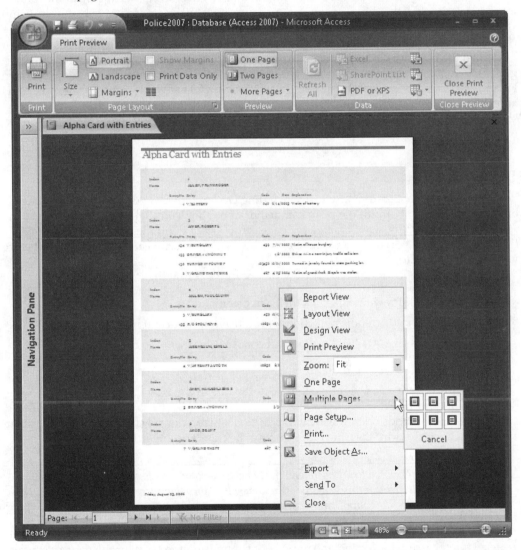

- On the Print Preview tab in the Preview group, click the More Pages command and choose the number of pages from the list: four, eight, or twelve pages.

To return to previewing a single page, click the One Page command in the Preview group.

Changing the Magnification

When you first open the Print Preview window, the report is automatically displayed with the Fit option, which sizes the page in the window vertically. You can increase or decrease the degree of magnification to almost any value or ask Access to adjust the report to fit on the screen.

Right-click in the Print Preview window and choose Zoom from the shortcut menu to toggle between Fit and the last magnification that you set. To change the magnification more precisely, click the down arrow next to Zoom and choose a percentage between 10 and 1000 percent from the list, or enter a value and then press ENTER. The number of pages you choose to preview at once determines the degree of magnification when you choose Fit.

When the mouse pointer passes over the report preview, it changes to a magnifying glass with a plus (+) or minus (–) sign, which you can click to alternate the preview between Fit and the last percentage (%) that you chose. When the glass shows a minus sign, clicking zooms out, making the preview less magnified. Clicking the magnifying glass with a plus sign zooms in on the area where the pointer was when you clicked it. This provides a quick way to zoom in on a specific part of the report—for example, a group summary field.

Printing the Report

You can print the report from any view, including Design view, or you can print without opening the report at all. All the print commands open the Print dialog box, where you can select other print options and change the page setup. It is a good idea to print from Print Preview, because if you make any changes to the page setup, you can see the changes before you commit to print.

To print the report from Print Preview, do one of the following:

- On the Print Preview tab, click the Print command.
- Right-click in the report and choose Print from the shortcut menu.
- Click the Microsoft Office button and choose Print from the context menu.
- Press CTRL-P.

If the report is not open, right-click the report name in the Navigation Pane and choose Print from the shortcut menu.

All of these methods open the Print dialog box, where you can change some of the print options or choose to print the data only, without the titles and other features.

NOTE *You can also click the Print button on the Quick Access toolbar to send the report directly to the printer. If you print in this way, the Print dialog box does not open and you cannot change any print options before committing to print.*

If you want to change any of the printing or page layout options, such as the margins, the page layout, the printer selection, the number of columns on the page, or the page size, you can use the commands in the Page Layout group or run Page Setup. The Page Layout group offers common settings for margins and paper size, and the Page Setup dialog box lets you specify custom settings. After setting the page specifications, you can choose the print options in the Print dialog box, such as the number of copies and the range of pages to print.

Changing the Page Settings

When you switch to Print Preview, the Print Preview tab becomes active with several printing and layout command groups. You can change many of the settings from other views, but if you use Print Preview, you can see how the changes affect the report. You can scroll through the pages to make sure that the changes are appropriate.

The Page Layout settings are stored with the report, so you need to set them only once and they'll be in effect every time that you print the report. The Page Layout group offers tools to set many of the report features:

- **Size**   Displays a gallery of letter and envelope sizes.
- **Portrait and Landscape**   Changes the orientation.
- **Show Margins**   Offers a gallery of three preset vertical and horizontal margin settings including Normal, Wide, and Narrow.
- **Print Data Only**   Leaves out the labels and other unbound controls.
- **Column**   Opens the Columns tab in the Page Setup dialog box, where you can specify a columnar report. This is used mostly for printing mailing labels on predesigned sheets. Access offers ready-made layouts for most of the commercially available label sheets. There is more about columns in reports in Chapter 14.

TIP *If you want to change the default page margins, so that you don't have to change them for each report separately, click the Microsoft Office button and click Access Options. In the Advanced group of options, scroll to Printing. Specify the margins in the margins group and click OK. This affects only new forms and reports, not existing ones. See Chapter 16 for more information about customizing the Access work place.*

You can also use the Page Setup dialog box to make changes in the report page settings. You must be in Print Preview to open Page Setup from the report. On the Arrange tab in the Page Layout group, click the Page Setup command or click the tiny arrow below the command to open the Page Setup dialog box. You can also right-click in the report and choose Page Setup from the shortcut menu. The Page Setup dialog box has three tabs containing the same tools that appear in the Page Layout group on the Print Preview tab.

- Use the Print Options tab to set margins and choose to print data only.
- Click the Page tab to set the orientation of the print on the page, set the paper size and source, and select a different printer if you have more than one on your system. The choice of paper sources depends on the printer that you're using.

- Use the Columns tab to choose the number of items across the page, their row and column spacing, their size, and the layout on the page.

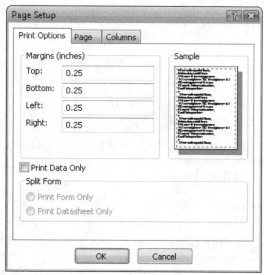

If you want to print using a printer other than the default printer, click Use Specific Printer on the Page tab, and then click the Printer button. This opens a dialog box that displays a list of the printers currently installed in the system. Select the printer and click OK to return to the Page Setup dialog box.

After you make all desired changes to the page setup, click OK to return to the previous view of the report or the Database window.

NOTE *You can also open the Page Setup dialog box from the Print dialog box, but this version has only two tabs: Print Options and Columns.*

Modifying the Report Design

The method you use to open a report in Design view depends on where you start:

- If the report is not open, right-click the report name in the Navigation Pane and choose Design View from the shortcut menu.

- With the report open, on the Home tab click the View command and choose an option from the context menu.

- Right-click the document tab and choose Design View from the shortcut menu.

Working in the report Design view is almost identical to working in the form Design view. The controls are the same, although you include fewer types of controls in reports. You select sections and controls and change their properties using the same techniques that you use with form designs. Placing, positioning, and sizing controls in the report design also use the same techniques.

Touring the Report Design Window

The report Design window is similar to the form Design window. The Design ribbon is the same, except a new group of commands called Grouping & Totals appears, which you'll learn about in Chapter 14. The View command on the Design tab shows a context menu containing Report View, Print Preview, Layout View, and Design View.

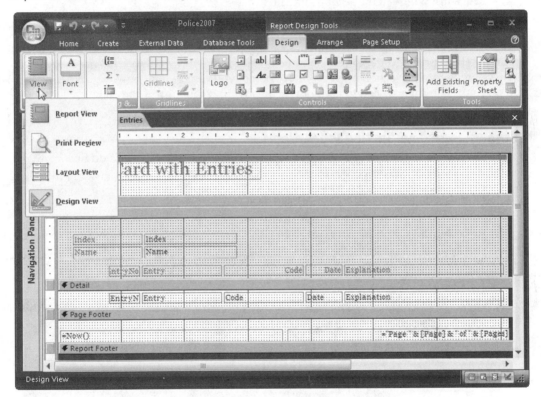

The Arrange tab in the report Design window is also the same as the tab in the form Design window. The Page Layout group on the Page Setup tab is the same as the group on the Print Preview tab, as described earlier in this chapter, and contains the same tools to let you specify the report page layouts.

Examining Report Sections

If the report design looks more cluttered than the form designs you worked with in the last chapter, it's probably because of the extra Page Header and Footer sections. The wizard automatically adds these sections when it creates a report. The Page Header section contains information to be printed at the top of each page, such as the field names used as column headings. The Page Footer section contains information to be printed at the bottom of each page, such as the current date and the page number.

The Report Header and Footer sections contain information to be printed only once, at the beginning or the end of the report. The Detail section contains the bulk of the data in the report.

Two optional sections, the Group Header and Footer sections, contain information to be printed at the top and bottom of each group of records. These sections are used when you group the records by the values in a specific field, such as by Code as in the Alpha Entry by Code Report shown earlier.

You select a section in a report design the same way you do in a form design:

- Click the section selector at the left of the section label line.
- Click anywhere in the section label line.
- Click anywhere in the section, outside of any control.

To change the size of a report section, select the section and drag the lower boundary up or down. The report and page sections come in pairs, so if you want to remove one, reduce its height to zero. The section must be empty before you can do that, however. When you add a group, you do not need to use both the header and footer. You can choose whether you want a group header or footer, or both, by setting the group properties.

Setting Report and Section Properties

You open and use the property sheets in a report design the same way you do in a form design, and many of the properties are the same. Three report format properties apply to the Report Header and Footer sections, as well as the grouping of records in the report: Force New Page, New Row Or Col, and Keep Together.

Four report Data properties relate to sorting and filtering the records: Filter, Filter On Load, Order By, and Order By On Load. Two Other properties specify whether records are locked while the report is being previewed or printed and how you want to group dates in the report. Click in the property and read the descriptive text in the status bar to find out more about a property.

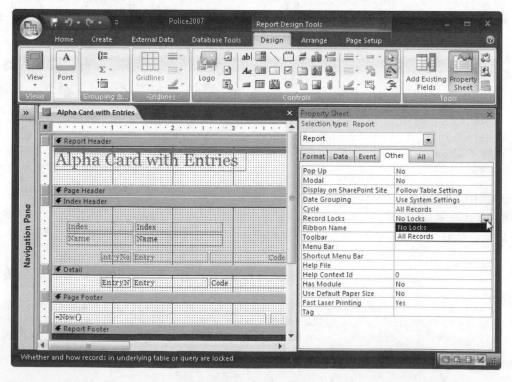

When you create a report with a special title page and you don't want to print the page header or footer information on the same page, set the Page Header and Page Footer report properties to Not With Rpt Hdr. Then set the report header Force New Page property to After Section to continue printing on a new page.

If you want the report footer information also printed on a separate page at the end of the report, set both the report Page Header and Page Footer properties to Not With Rpt Hdr/Ftr, and then set the report footer Force New Page property to Before Section.

When you create a report based on a table or query saved with a sort order or a filter, the report inherits both properties. If you look at the report properties, you can see the Filter and Order By expressions saved with the table. The Order By On Load property is set to Yes and the records are sorted by the inherited sort order. The inherited filter isn't applied. To apply the filter, set the Filter On Load property to Yes. To remove them both, change the settings to No. If you want to change the filter or sort order, type a new expression in the Filter or Order By property box.

Each of the report sections also has a list of properties that you can set to get exactly the appearance and behavior you want. For example, the section name, whether the section is visible or not, the height, back color, and special effect, and a tag that stores extra information about the section.

Page headers and footers have no additional properties, but the remaining sections—Report Header and Footer, Group Header and Footer, and Detail sections—share several other properties:

- **Force New Page**   Specifies whether report sections are printed on a separate page, rather than on the current page.

- **New Row Or Col**   Specifies whether a section is printed in a new row or column within a multiple-column report.

- **Keep Together**   Specifies whether a section prints all on one page or prints across two pages.

- **Can Grow and Can Shrink**   Allows the section to grow or shrink vertically, depending on the amount of data in the section.

The Group Header section has one more property unique to that section: Repeat Section, which is used to specify whether a group header is repeated on the next page or column when a group spans more than one page or column. The default setting is No. If the group header contains column headings and other relevant information, you might want to change that to Yes to print it at the top of each page or column.

Placing and Adjusting Controls

You can place controls in a report design using the control commands in the Design tab, just the same as with a form design. To resize and move controls, you can drag the handles and use the commands on the Arrange tab. All the methods are the same as with form design.

Changing the Report Style

One of the Report Wizard dialog boxes showed you a list of styles from which to choose. If you don't like the style you selected there, you can change to one of the other styles in the list by clicking the report selector (the small square at the intersection of the report rulers), and then on the Layout tab's Quick Format group, click the AutoFormat command and choose from the gallery of formats. You can also click the Use Style button at the bottom of the gallery to open the AutoFormat dialog box. If you want to reformat a report section rather than the entire report, select that section before opening the AutoFormat dialog box.

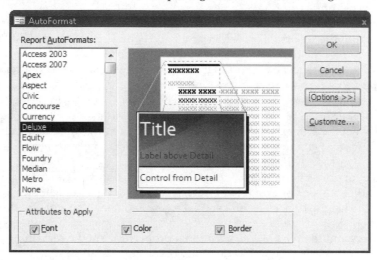

Customizing a Report AutoFormat

By clicking the Customize button in the AutoFormat dialog box, you can create a custom format and add it to the list of AutoFormats available to your reports. You have three options:

- Create a new AutoFormat based on the one used in an open report.
- Modify the AutoFormat selected in the AutoFormat dialog box with the changes you made to the format of the open report.
- Delete an AutoFormat from the list.

Before starting to customize a format, click the Options button, check the attributes you want modified, and then click Customize to open the Customize AutoFormat dialog box.

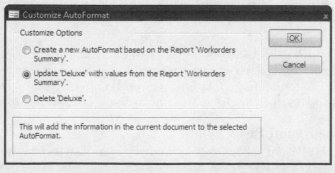

As you select an option, an explanation is displayed in the lower panel of the dialog box. Select one of the three Customize Options, and then click OK, or click Cancel to return to the AutoFormat dialog box. If you choose to create a new AutoFormat, Access asks you to enter a name for the new style. Once you save the new AutoFormat, it's available to use with any new reports.

You can use the options to apply the font, color, and border formatting selectively. By default, all three options are checked. If you clear them one at a time, you can see the difference in the displayed sample.

Adding Page Numbers and Date/Time

The Report Wizard automatically added page numbers and the current date/time to the Page Footer section of the Alpha Card with Entries report. A *page number* is an unbound text box control that you can add to a report design and format in several ways. A *date/time field* is also an unbound control and is based on your current system date/time settings.

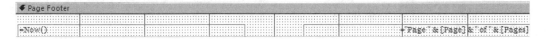

Adding a Page Number

If you haven't used the Report Wizard and you want to add a page number to your report, on the Design tab's Controls group, click the Insert Page Number command to open the Page Numbers dialog box. You have several options regarding the page number format, position, and alignment. You can also suppress printing the page number on the first page of the report.

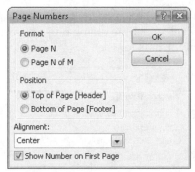

The Page Numbers dialog box offers two page number formats: *Page N* and *Page N of M*, where *N* is the page number and *M* is the total number of pages.

NOTE *You can see that the Report Wizard used the* Page N of M *option in specifying the page numbers in the Alpha Card with Entries report. The expression that appears in the page number text box control is* [="Page "&[Page]&" of "&[Pages]. *This expression concatenates alphabetic characters with the Page (current page number) and Pages (total number of pages) field values. The characters enclosed in quotation marks appear in the page number field. Notice that spaces follow the word* Page *and are on both sides of the word* of *to separate the words from the numbers. The ampersands (&) are the concatenation operators. The result is, for example, Page 12 of 25 pages.*

You can position the page number either in the page header or footer by selecting from the Position options:

- **Left**   Places the text box at the left margin.
- **Center**   Places the text box centered between the right and left margins.
- **Right**   Places the text box at the right margin.
- **Inside**   Places the text box at the left margin on odd pages and at the right margin on even pages.
- **Outside**   Places the text box at the right margin on odd pages and at the left margin on even pages.

If you don't want to print the page number on the first page of the report, clear the check mark in the Show Number on First Page box.

Changing the Page Numbers Format

The Page Numbers dialog box gave you a choice of two formats for the page number text box. You can also enter a custom expression in the Control Source property of the page number text box, which includes characters with the values. Some other expressions you might want to use for page numbers are these:

Expression	Displays
=[Page]	1, 2, 3
="Entry Report: Page "&[Page]	Entry Report: Page 1, Entry Report: Page 2, Entry Report: Page 3
=[Page]&"/"&[Pages]&"Pages"	1/3 Pages, 2/3 Pages, 3/3 Pages

Adding a Date/Time Control

To add the current date and time to the report, on the Design tab's Controls group, click the Date & Time command. The Date and Time dialog box lets you include the date and/or the time and gives you a choice of formats for each.

If the report design has a Report Header section, the date/time control is automatically placed there. If not, the control goes in the Detail section. You can drag it to any place you want in the design.

NOTE   *The Report Wizard added the expression =Now( ) to the Page Footer section of the Alpha Card with Entries report. This prints the current system date at the bottom of each page. You could also use the expression =Date( ) to insert the current system date. Many other built-in date/time functions are available from the Expression Builder; these return the date and time components (day, month, year, hour, week, and so on) in a variety of ways.*

If you look at the properties of the date/time control in the report, you can see the Control Source property is the expression =*Now( )* and the Format is *Long Date*. This displays the day of the week as well as the date—for example, Tuesday, January 1, 2008. You can change the Format property in the Property Sheet to one of the other date/time formats.

Adding Page Breaks

If left to its own devices, Access starts a new page when a page fills up. You can add a page break control within a section to tell Access where you want a new page to begin. For example, suppose you have a report title and an abstract of the report's contents all in the Report Header section, but you want them printed on separate pages. To accomplish this, on the Design tab's Controls group, click the Page Break command and place the control in the Report Header section between the controls you want to appear on the first page and those you want on the second page. Access displays the position of the page break as a short dotted line at the left edge in the report design.

Saving the Report Design

When you create a report with the help of the Report Wizard, the report is saved for you using the name that you entered in the final wizard dialog box. If you don't use the wizard, you should save the report design frequently as you refine it. This guards against catastrophe and gives you a recent starting point if something goes wrong. To save the report design, do one of the following:

- Right-click the document tab and choose Save from the shortcut menu.
- Click Save on the Quick Access toolbar.
- Press CTRL-S.
- Click the Microsoft Office button and click Save.

To close the report design, right-click the document tab and choose Close from the shortcut menu.

You have two other options when saving a report design with the Microsoft Office button:

- Choose Save As, which opens the Save As dialog box, where you can save the report design to the current database with the same or a new name. If you use the Save As pointer, you have an additional option to publish the report as a PDF or XPS document. More about exporting Access objects in Chapter 23.

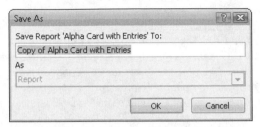

- Choose E-mail, which opens the Send Object As dialog box, where you can choose the output format for the form.

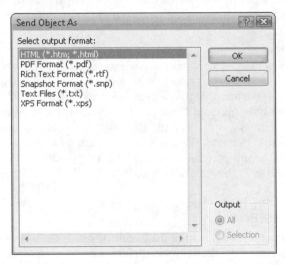

Using Report Snapshots

Access 2002 began offering a new type of report called a *report snapshot*, which is a separate file with the .snp extension that contains a copy of every page of an Access report. The copy includes high-fidelity graphics, charts, and pictures, and it preserves the colors and the two-dimensional layout of the report.

The advantage of a report snapshot is that you can save time and money by distributing the report electronically as an e-mail attachment, rather than photocopying and mailing the printed version. The recipients can then preview the report online and print only the pages that they want.

To view, print, or e-mail a report snapshot, you need the Snapshot Viewer program installed. The *Snapshot Viewer* is a standalone executable program that comes with its own control, help file, and related files. By default, the Snapshot Viewer is installed by Access the first time you create a report snapshot. You can use the Snapshot Viewer to view a snapshot from Internet Explorer versions 3.0 and later or from any application that supports ActiveX controls.

NOTE *While you need Access 2007 to create a report snapshot, the recipients don't need it to view the snapshot. They only need a combination of the Snapshot Viewer and another program, such as Windows Explorer, a web browser, or an e-mail program, such as Microsoft Exchange or Outlook.*

Creating a Report Snapshot

To create a report snapshot from an existing report, do the following:

1. Select the name of the report in the Navigation Pane, and on the External Data tab's Export group, click the More command and choose Snapshot Viewer in the gallery.

2. The Export – Snapshot Viewer dialog box opens (see Figure 13-11), where you specify the destination filename and format.

3. If you don't want to use the same name as the Access report, enter the filename in the File name box or click Browse to locate a destination.

4. You can also choose to open the destination file after the export is complete.

5. Click OK. You will see another dialog box that offers to save the export steps you just used. This can save you a little time by not having to go through the steps again.

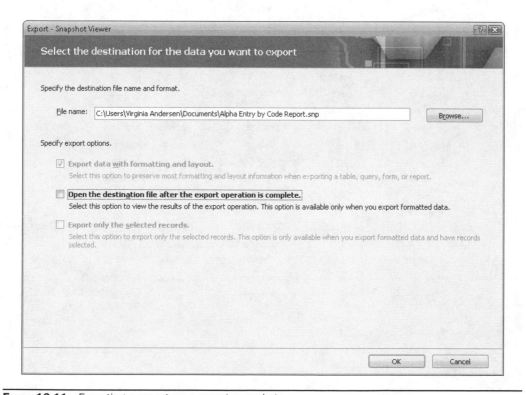

FIGURE 13-11   Exporting a report as a report snapshot

The Snapshot Viewer usually automatically starts and displays a preview of the report snapshot. The new report snapshot inherits any current sort order and filter settings in the underlying recordset.

NOTE *If the Snapshot Viewer does not start, you will need to download it. Go to Microsoft Office Online and choose Viewers for Access 2002. Select Snapshot Viewer for Access 2003, 2002, 2000, and 97 and choose Download.*

Viewing the Report Snapshot

The Snapshot Viewer window (see Figure 13-12) has a standard menu bar with commonly used File, View, Window, and Help menus. It also shows a navigation bar at the bottom of the window that you can use to move among the pages in the report snapshot. The Print button in the navigation bar opens the Print dialog box.

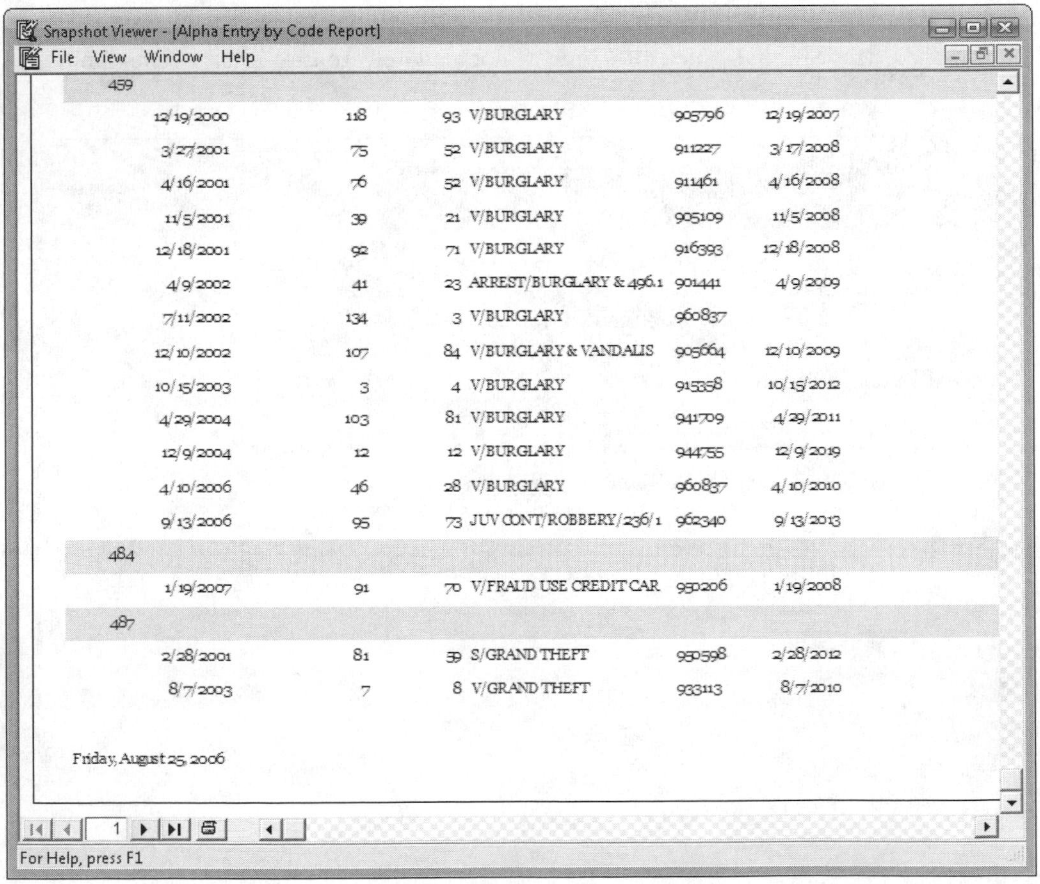

FIGURE 13-12   Previewing the new report snapshot

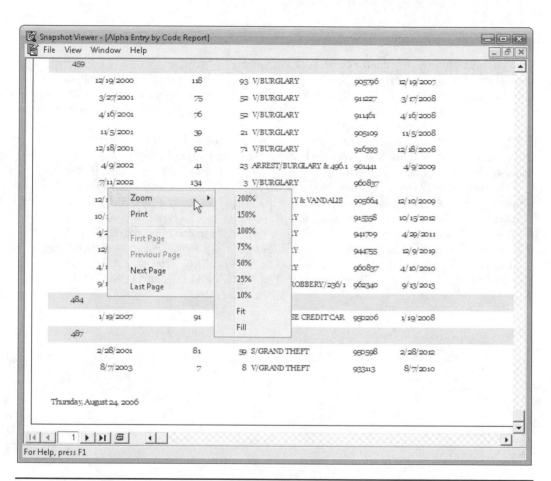

FIGURE 13-13   Changing the Print Preview magnification

The Snapshot Viewer works much like the Print Preview window in Access. You can change the magnification by clicking in the page. If the whole page shows on the screen, clicking it increases the magnification. If already magnified, clicking reduces the preview to its former magnification.

You can right-click in the report and choose from the same options available on the navigation bar in addition to the Zoom command (see Figure 13-13). You can zoom to a magnification from 10 percent to 200 percent or choose Fit to show one complete page in the window. The Fill command widens the page to fill the width of the window.

Sending the Report Snapshot

You can send the report snapshot to others in e-mail by using the Send command in the Snapshot Viewer. With the report snapshot open in the Snapshot Viewer, choose File | Send.

Summary

This chapter only begins the discussion of the variety of printed material Access and the Report Wizards can produce. So far, you have learned the fundamentals of report construction and how to use the Report Wizard for creating standard detail and summary reports. You also had a glimpse of the advantages of using report snapshots for electronic distribution of Access reports.

The Report Wizard can create reports from several related tables and arrange the information in almost any way you choose. You have the opportunity to summarize any numeric or currency field values in several ways to include more useful, analytic information.

The next chapter delves deeper into customizing reports and creating special purpose reports, such as a report based on a parameter query that requests information from the user. You will see how to create a report from scratch and add special types of controls, including a subreport that contains the detail data related to the data in the main report. The chapter also describes how to create columnar reports for such purposes as printing mailing labels.

Chapter 15, the final chapter in this trio of chapters dealing with printed Access products, also looks at the analytical tools provided by the Chart, PivotTable, and PivotChart Wizards.

Customizing Reports

When you create reports with Access 2007, you're limited only by your imagination. Because Access offers so many tools and features for creating custom reports, you can design and print information any way you like.

In addition to printing table or query data grouped and arranged in special orders, you can create reports that print data in columns on the page. A special type of columnar report can be used to print mailing labels or labels for other purposes, such as book plates or CD labels.

This chapter discusses creating custom reports from Design view, as well as printing labels with the help of the Label Wizard. Most of the examples deal with data in the Police database introduced in Chapter 12. You might want to keep the Police database open as you work through this chapter.

Creating a New Report Design

Using the Report Wizard is by far the easiest way to start a custom report, but you can also start from an empty report design or in Layout view. In the Create tab's Reports group, you simply click either the Blank Report or the Report Design command. If you have selected a table or query in the Navigation Pane, the associated Field List pane appears at the right.

Figure 14-1 shows a new report in Layout view when you use the Blank Report command. The Field List pane opens on the right where you can expand the Alpha Card table to add its fields to the report. Notice the active ribbon tab is Formatting, which includes tools for grouping and formatting the report. You can also add controls to the report in Layout view.

The Field List pane shows all the fields in the table selected in the Navigation Pane, plus it lists of the other tables in the database. As you drag fields from the Field List pane to the report, they are stacked with one record per row and one field per column, with the field

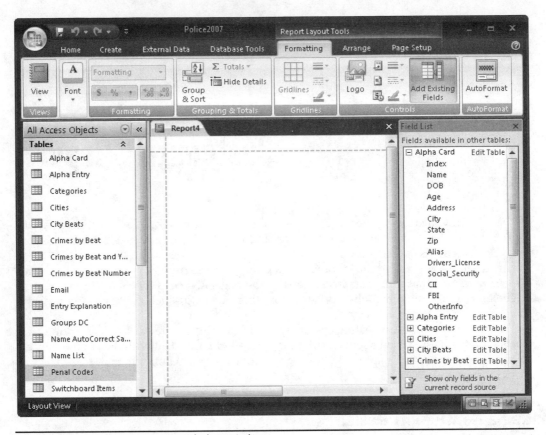

FIGURE 14-1   Starting a new report in Layout view

names at the top. After adding all the fields you need, you can remove the applied layout and rearrange the controls the way you want.

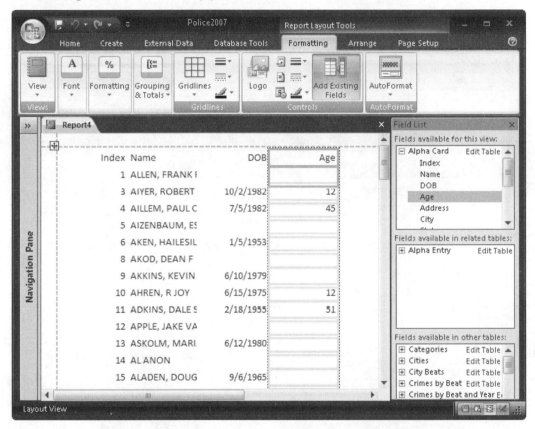

You can also start a new report by choosing the Report Design command. Figure 14-2 shows the start of the report in Design view. The active ribbon tab is Design, which contains the tools you need to finish building the report design.

As you add fields to the report design, they are arranged in a tabular layout with the field names at the left. The easiest way to add fields is to double-click the field name in the

Field List. Notice that the Page Header and Page Footer sections are automatically added to the design with the Detail section, unlike a new form design that contains only the Detail section by default.

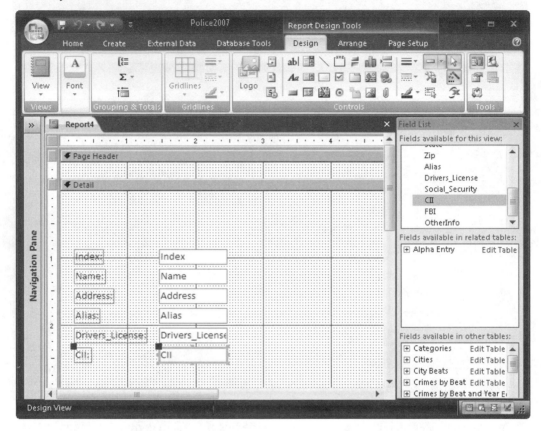

NOTE *If the report isn't based on table or query data, you can insert only unbound controls, such as labels, lines and rectangles, and unbound objects. You can also include hyperlinks to other objects.*

Figure 14-3 shows the Design view for a report based on the Alpha Card table in the Police database.

After opening the report in Design or Layout view, you can drag more fields to the design from the field list. Then use the Controls commands on the Design tab to place other controls in the report design and open the Property Sheet to create the appearance you want.

NOTE *If the Field List pane doesn't appear when you open the report in Design view, on the Design tab's Tools group, click the Add Existing Fields command.*

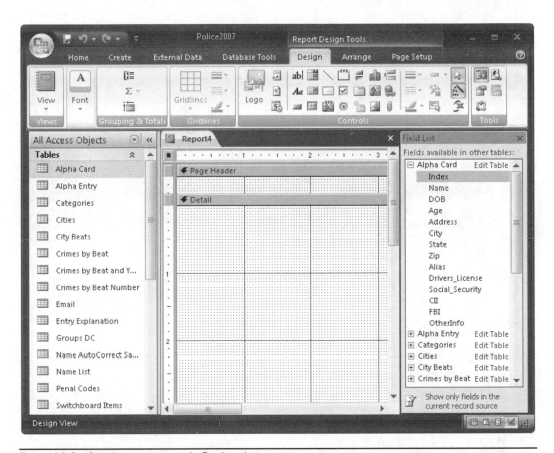

FIGURE 14-2   Starting new report in Design view

Adding Headers and Footers

A report design can include pairs of header and footer sections: Report Header and Footer for printing information at the beginning and end of the report, and Page Header and Footer for printing information at the top and bottom of each page. To add a header/footer pair, right-click in the report design and choose Page Header/Footer or Report Header/ Footer from the shortcut menu. To delete the header/footer pair, repeat the shortcut choice. If any controls are in the section you try to delete, Access displays a message asking if you want to delete all the controls in the sections. Click Yes to delete them or No to abandon the deletion.

CAUTION   *All deletions are permanent. Always save a copy of the report design before you delete controls or sections so that you have a design to fall back on. Then, if you change your mind, you don't have to start over. You can also close the design without saving the changes and open it later in its original condition before the deletions.*

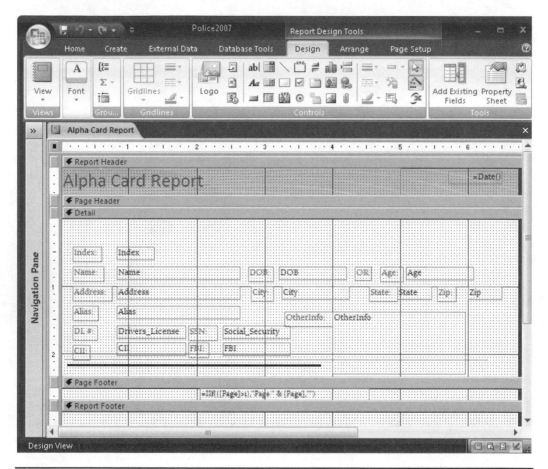

FIGURE 14-3   The Alpha Card Report in Design view

To change the height of a section, drag the lower section boundary up or down. If the section contains controls, you can't shrink it beyond the control borders. To keep from having too much blank space when you print a report with no information in the header or footer, shrink the height by dragging the lower boundary up or by setting the Height property to 0. You do not need to select the section first to drag the boundary.

TIP *If you selected the section and the Property Sheet is open when you resize the section, you can see the Height property value change as you drag the boundary.*

To suppress the printing of a section that contains information, set the section's Visible property on the Format tab of the Property Sheet to No. The section still appears in Design view; it just doesn't print.

The Page Header and Page Footer report properties on the Format tab of the Property Sheet specify whether to print the information on the first page with the report header or on the last page with the report footer. Following are the settings for both properties:

- **All Pages**   Prints the information on every page.
- **Not with Rpt Hdr**   Prints on all but the first page.
- **Not with Rpt Ftr**   Prints on all but the last page.
- **Not with Rpt Hdr/Ftr**   Prints on all pages except the first and last.

The Report Header section contains a title and the current date. The title was added by clicking the Title tool in the Controls group on the Design tab. The page header has been reduced to zero height and the page number has been added in the center of the page footer. You need to scroll down the report to see the page footer. (To review how to insert dates and page numbers, see Chapter 13.) A line control was added to the bottom of the Detail section to separate the detail information of each record. Finally, the Flow style was chosen from the AutoFormat dialog box.

You may notice a slightly different page number control in the page footer. This is the result of choosing not to print the page number on the first page. The expression is

=IIf((([Page]>1), "Page " & [Page], "")

This means that if the page number is greater than 1, print the word *Page* followed by the page number. If the page number is not 1, leave the page number blank.

Figure 14-4 shows the report in Print Preview.

Customizing with Special Controls

Reports are not user interactive, so they can contain fewer types of special controls. Command buttons and option groups, for example, have no place in reports. But you can add calculated fields, graphics, and images to a custom report, either bound or unbound. You can also add hyperlinks, although they are not "live" within the report.

Adding Calculated Fields

Reports often include calculated fields contained in an underlying query. You can also add calculated controls, as described in Chapter 10. A *calculated control* is a text box whose Control Source property is set to an expression that produces the desired value. The expression can contain combinations of text, number, currency, or date/time fields from the record source.

Calculated controls are often used to show summary information in reports with grouped records. Later in this chapter, the section "Filtering, Sorting, and Grouping Records in Layout View" discusses grouping records and summarizing data with expressions and aggregate functions.

Adding Graphics and Images

As discussed in Chapter 10, you can insert a graphic or an image in a report in two ways: as an image control or as an OLE object in an unbound object frame. The advantage of using an image control is that it loads quicker than an OLE object in a frame. If you think that you might need to edit the OLE object, embed it in an unbound object frame where you can double-click to open the application that created the object.

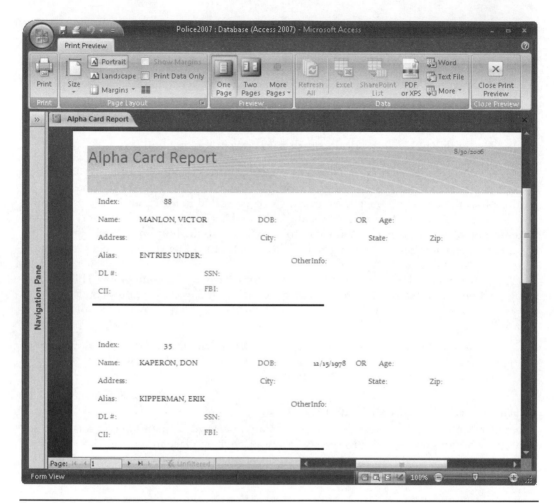

FIGURE 14-4   A Print Preview of the Alpha Card Report

To add an image control to a report, do the following:

1. On the Design tab's Controls group, click the Image Control tool and click in the report design where you want to place the upper-left corner of the image. Access draws a square frame for the image and opens the Insert Picture dialog box.

2. Locate and select the image that you want, and click OK. The frame expands to accommodate the full size of the image.

3. Resize the image frame by dragging the sizing handles.

4. Change the image control Size Mode property to Stretch or Zoom.

To insert the image in an unbound object frame, click the Unbound Object Frame tool and draw the frame in the report design. A dialog box opens, in which you can choose Create New or Create From File. Then you can locate and select the image that you want in the report.

If the object you want to insert in the frame is an existing Office document or other file originated by an application that supports OLE, choose Create From File and type in the path of the file you want to insert.

Figure 14-5 shows a report design with a photograph of plumeria flowers embedded as an image and a Word document embedded as an OLE object in an unbound object frame. If you want to edit the Word document, double-click the object in Design view and edit it in place. The photograph in the image control isn't editable.

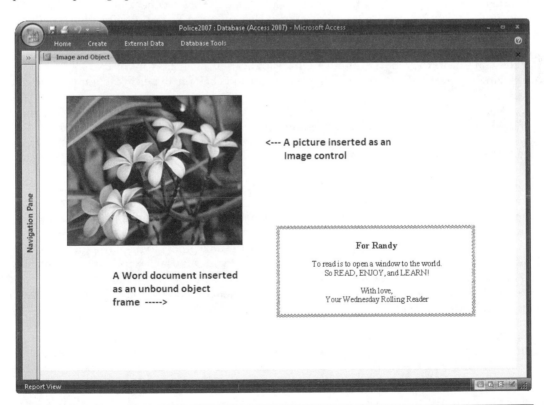

Figure 14-5   An image and an unbound object embedded in a report design

---

NOTE *You can link an OLE object to a report design or embed it by choosing Link in the dialog box. Linking leaves the object in the host application and provides a path to the object in the report. This saves disk space and ensures that the latest version of the object is used, but problems can result if the path to the linked object is changed.*

Adding a Bound OLE Object

Bound OLE objects are OLE Object data type fields from the underlying table or query. To add a bound object to the report design, simply drag the field name from the field list to the design. Access automatically draws the bound object frame for the object.

NOTE *An OLE Object data type is only a pointer to the object. Such a field cannot be used to sort or index records.*

You can also draw the bound object frame first by using the control tool and then binding it to the field in the underlying record source by setting its Control Source property to the name of the field.

Adding a Hyperlink

You can add a hyperlink to a report design the same way as to a form design by clicking the Insert Hyperlink command in the Controls group. After you specify the target of the hyperlink, you can test it in the report Design view by right-clicking the hyperlink, pointing to Hyperlink in the shortcut menu, and choosing Open Hyperlink.

The hyperlink isn't live in the report in Access Print Preview, but it does become active when you export the report to another Office application, such as Word or Excel. From the receiving application, you can open the document and click the hyperlink to jump to the address.

When you add a hyperlink to a report design, Access places it in the upper-left corner of the Detail section. You can move it to any position you want in the report design.

Adding an Attachment

To add an attachment field to a report, open the report in Design view and drag the field name from the Field List pane into the report. Drag the entire field—both the parent and child items—if you want to see all the attachments in the field. Right-click the attachment control and choose Properties from the shortcut menu if you need to change some of the properties to match your report format.

When you open the report in Report view, click the attachment to display a toolbar above it. The toolbar has forward and backward buttons that you can use to scroll through the files in the attachment field in the table. If the attachment contains an image, the control renders the file. If it is another file type, such as a Word document or a PowerPoint presentation, the appropriate icon is displayed.

Adding a Background Picture

Pictures can serve a special purpose in a report other than as an illustration—for example, a picture can be used as a company logo watermark that appears behind the text. When you add a background picture to a report, it applies to the whole page and is a report property.

To add a watermark to the Alpha Card Report design, enter the path and filename of the picture you want to use in the report's Picture property, and then set the other report properties:

- The Picture Type property specifies whether the picture is embedded or linked.
- The Picture Size Mode property can be set to one of the three size modes: Clip, Stretch, or Zoom. Refer to Chapter 10 for a description of the effects of setting size modes.
- The Picture Alignment property determines the position of the picture in the report. The available settings are Top Left, Top Right, Center, Bottom Left, and Bottom Right.
- When the Picture Tiling property is set to Yes, the picture is repeated across and down the page, beginning at the position specified by the Picture Alignment property, and it spreads in four directions. For example, if you set the alignment to Center, a complete picture appears in the center of the page, perhaps with incomplete versions fanning out from it. If you choose to tile the picture, use the Clip size mode setting.
- The Picture Pages property specifies on which pages to print the background picture: All Pages, First Page, or No Pages.

Basing a Report on a Parameter Query

Basing a report on a parameter query enables the user to set the criteria for the report at run time. For example, suppose the police department would like to see a list of incidents reported during a specific time period. When you try to preview the report based on the parameter query, you're prompted to enter the parameters, the same as you would when you try to run the query itself.

Access also gives you the tools to print the entered parameters in the report, usually in the Report Header section.

Creating the Parameter Query

To create a parameter query that extracts Alpha Entry records having a date within an arbitrary time period, do the following:

1. On the Create tab's Other group, click the Query Design command.
2. In the Show Table dialog box, choose Alpha Entry Table and then click Add and Close.
3. Double-click the asterisk (*) in the Alpha Entry field list to add all of the fields to the query.
4. Double-click the Date field to add it to an empty column in the grid and clear the check mark in the Show row, so that the value won't appear twice in the report.
5. Type the following in the Criteria row of the Date field:

   Between [Type beginning date] And [Type ending date]

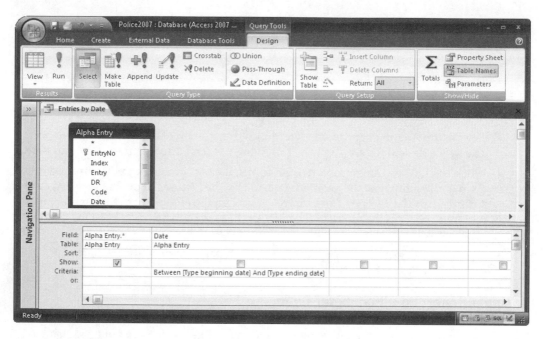

6. Save the query as Entries by Date.

If you run the query, Access displays two parameter prompts: one requesting "Type beginning date" and the other "Type ending date." Enter the desired dates and click OK to see the list of Alpha Entries reported within that time period. See Chapter 9 for more information about parameter queries.

Creating the Report

A report based on the parameter query also prompts for the parameter values when you open the report in Print Preview. To create a simple report based on the parameter query, do the following:

1. Select the Entries by Date query in the Navigation Pane and on the Create tab's Reports group, click the Report command.

2. Because Access immediately starts to open the new report in Layout view, it prompts for the parameters:

3. Enter the desired beginning date in any valid date format and press ENTER or click OK.

4. Repeat Step 3 to enter the ending date. When you click OK, the report opens in Layout view.

TIP *The report design has automatically added date and time controls in the report header. You are prompted twice to enter the start and end dates. To fix that, in the report Design view, delete the Date and Time controls and save the report.*

5. Click Close to switch to Design view, where you can modify the report design as required.

Printing the Parameters in the Report Header

Access treats the prompt expression as a valid control source for a text box. The selection parameters can be printed with the report by adding text box controls to the design. You can add two text boxes: add one text box for each parameter, or combine the parameters in an expression in a single text box. To print the parameters in the report header as one text box, do the following:

1. On the Design tab's Controls group, click the Text Box tool and place the control in the Report Header section.

2. Click outside the new control, and then select the attached label and press DELETE to remove the attached label.

3. Double-click the new text box control to open the Property Sheet and enter the following expression in the Control Source property box:

="Between "&[Type beginning date]& " and " &[Type ending date]

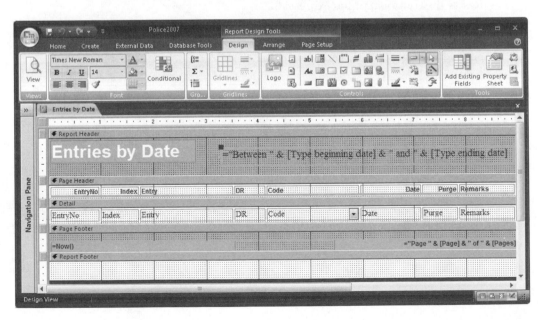

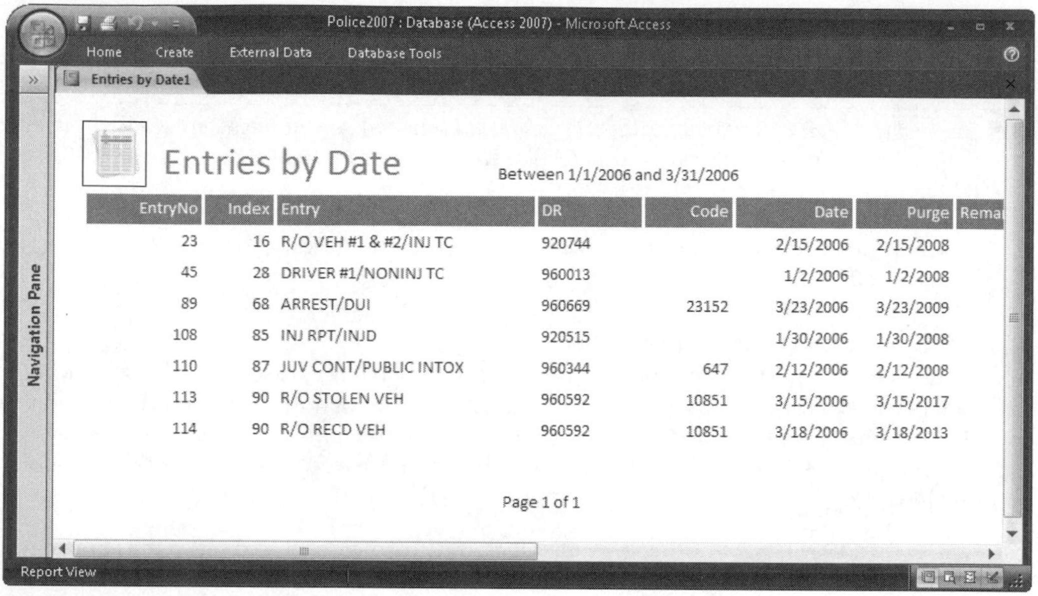

FIGURE 14-6   Viewing the Entries by Date report

(For more about combining text and field values in report designs, see the section "Manipulating Text Data" later in this chapter.)

4. Resize the control to fit the expression.

5. After making the final touch-ups, save the report and switch to Print Preview. Figure 14-6 shows a preview of the report displaying Alpha Entries reported between January 1, 2007 and March 31, 2007.

NOTE *If you choose to add the parameters as two separate text box controls, you can edit the attached labels to read* Between *and* and. *This method requires more alignment and size adjustments than adding both parameters to one text box.*

TIP *If you're unexpectedly prompted for parameters when you try to print or preview a report, you might have misspelled a field name in the report design, so that the name in the design doesn't match any in the underlying table or query. If you created an expression using field names, one of them could also be misspelled. Another possibility is that you used a control name instead of a field name in an aggregate function, such as Sum or Count. Aggregate functions must use field names, not control names.*

Troubleshooting Custom Reports

When you design a report, several problems can occur. For example, when you print the report, you might see too much white space. To solve this problem, reduce the size of the controls to fit the values they contain and move them closer together.

If every other page is blank when you preview or print the report, the width of the report exceeds the available width of the paper and "spill-over" pages result. The total width of the report plus the right and left margin settings must not exceed the width of the paper. To correct this problem, either reduce the width of the report or change the margin settings with Page Setup. You can also change the page orientation to landscape.

If the report prints a blank page at the end, you might need to reduce the size of the report footer. If no controls are in the report footer, reduce its height to zero by dragging the lower boundary or by setting the Height property to 0.

If data spills over to the next page, reduce the overall height of the report or decrease the top and bottom margins.

If you don't see all the data that you expected, the report may be filtered. When you apply a filter before saving the new report for the first time, the filter is saved with the report and can't be turned off. So be sure to remove the filter before saving the report for the first time. To remove such a saved filter, you will need to change the Record Source property.

Filtering, Sorting, and Grouping Records in Layout View

As you saw in the previous chapter, some of the most useful features of Access reports are the ability to filter, sort, and group records based on the value in one or more fields. After using one of these features, you can summarize the information in many ways to illustrate trends and draw conclusions. Such summaries are often critical to business decision-making processes, and Access can do most of the arithmetic for you. You can perform all these tasks with the report in Layout view, where you can immediately see the results.

If you have a report based on a query that sets criteria for the records, you can use that filter or set a new one later in Layout view. You can apply the filter by setting the report's Filter On Load property to Yes while in Design view. But you can also filter the record while you are viewing the report in Report or Layout view.

You can change the sort order that the report has inherited from the underlying record source. Records can be grouped on Text, Number, Date/Time, Currency, or AutoNumber field types or expressions containing those field values. Access can nest up to 10 sorting and grouping levels, each group subordinate to the previous group.

Depending on the data type of the field you are using to group the records, you can choose different options for how to group the records. For example, if the field is a Text field, you can group on the entire value or the first few characters of the value. Date/Time values can be grouped by each value or any time increment of the value—year, day, hour, minute, and so on.

Filtering Records in Layout View

To filter on the value in a single field, right-click the value and choose a filter from the shortcut menu. For example, suppose you want to filter the Alpha Card Report to show only reports from Nevada. Right-click the field with that value, point to Text Filters in the shortcut menu, and choose Equals. If you want all the records except Nevada, choose Does Not Equal in the shortcut menu. If you filter on a number or date field, you will see other options for criteria. These are the same choices you saw when filtering table data in Datasheet view in Chapter 7.

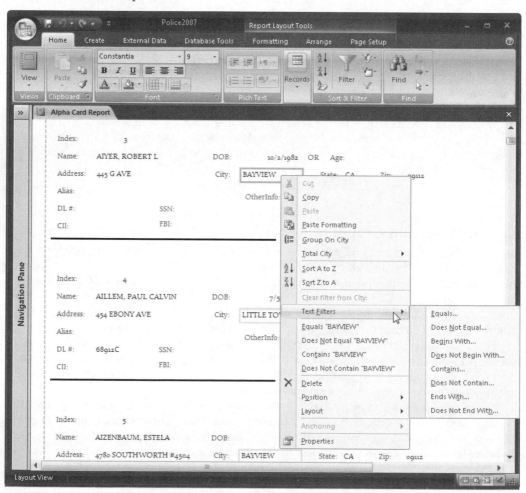

NOTE   *If you are told that Layout view is not available for this report, go to the report Property Sheet and change the Allow Layout View property to Yes.*

If you want to filter on the values in more than one field in the report, you need to use the Filter tool as follows:

1. Select one of the text box controls in the report. Then, on the Home tab's Sort & Filter group, click the Filter command. A drop-down menu appears listing all the fields in the report with check marks indicating that they will all appear in the report.

2. Click the Select All button to clear the check marks from all of the fields.

3. Check the boxes next to the fields you want included in the report and click OK. This menu also gives you a choice of sorting on the value in the field or sorting on the fields you filter by.

You can create a more detailed filter by choosing the Text Filters command from the drop-down menu. Rest the mouse pointer on Text Filters to see a list of options, each of which opens a dialog box where you can specify the filter criteria. These are the same options that you see if you right-click the field and choose Text (or Date or Number) Filters from the shortcut menu.

If you save the report with the filter still in place, the filter is saved with the report, but when you open the report in Report or Layout view, the filter is not applied. You can click the Toggle Filter command to apply the same filter. The Toggle Filter command turns the filter on and off; it does not remove it.

To remove the filter instead of just turning it off, select one of the filtered fields and click the Filter command again. In the drop-down menu, choose Clear Filter From *Field Name*: Button. You can also simply right-click the field and choose the same command from the shortcut menu. If you want to change the filter, select the filtered field again, click the Filter command, and make the changes in the drop-down menu.

Changing the Sort Order

You can remove or reapply the sort order inherited from the record source by setting the report's Order By On Load property. Choose No to remove the sort order or Yes to reapply it. If you want to use the inherited sort order, you must also set the Filter On Load property to No.

You can also change the sort order in Report or Layout view to a different field or to more than one field.

Working in Layout View

To sort by field values while in Layout view, right-click any value in the field and choose the Sort option from the shortcut menu. If the field contains text, your options are *Sort A to Z* or

Sort Z to A. A date field has the options to Sort Oldest to Newest or Newest to Oldest. Numbers can be sorted Smallest to Largest or Largest to Smallest.

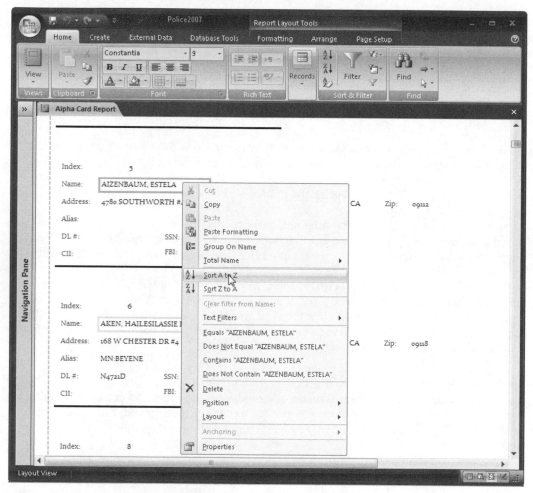

You can sort on only one field with this method. If you want to sort on more than one field, use the Order By property or the Group, Sort, and Total pane, as described later in the section "Adding Group Sections."

Setting the Report Sort Property

To sort the records in the report in an order that differs from that of the underlying table or query, set the report's Order By On Load property to Yes and its Order By property as follows:

- To sort the records by values in one field in ascending order, type the field name enclosed in brackets followed by *ASC*—for example, **[Code] ASC**.

- To sort the records by values in one field in descending order, type the field name enclosed in brackets followed by *DESC*—for example, **[Last Name] DESC**.

- To sort the records by values in more than one field in ascending or descending order, type each field name enclosed in brackets, followed by *ASC* or *DESC*, and separated by commas. For example, the setting **[Code] ASC, [Last Name] DESC** sorts first by the Code field in ascending order, and then by the Last Name field in descending order.

If you don't specify *ASC* or *DESC*, Access automatically sorts in ascending order. The new setting overrides the inherited sort order without affecting the data source. Be sure to set the Order By On Load property to Yes to affect the new sort order.

NOTE *If you create the report with the Report Wizard and specify a sort order, it overrides the inherited sort order. You can still change the order in the Layout view if you change your mind.*

Adding Group Sections

To illustrate grouping records in a report, create a new report based on the query created in Chapter 13 that extracts only those records with a value in the Code field. This eliminates Alpha Entry records not related to a potentially criminal offense. The Alpha Entry by Code query contains the expression *<>0* in the Criteria row of the Code column in the grid. After dragging the relevant field names from the Field List pane to the Detail section of the new Entries by Year Report, delete the labels and drag the text boxes closer together. You can place the labels in the Group Header section later. Now you can proceed to group the records by the year that the incident was reported.

To add a group section to an existing report, switch to Layout view, and on the Formatting tab's Grouping & Totals group, click the Group & Sort command. This opens the Group, Sort, and Total pane below the report layout, where you can set the sort order and choose the field or expression on which you want to group. You can also specify totals in this pane.

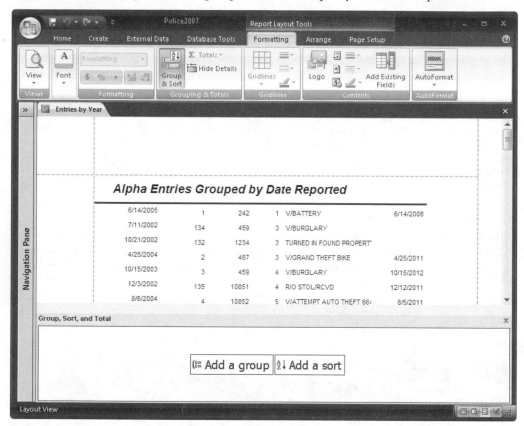

To group the records, do the following:

1. Click the Add a Group button to add a new list to the pane that can display a list of available fields.
2. Click the Group On button and select Date from the drop-down menu.
3. Click the From Oldest to Newest button and then click More.

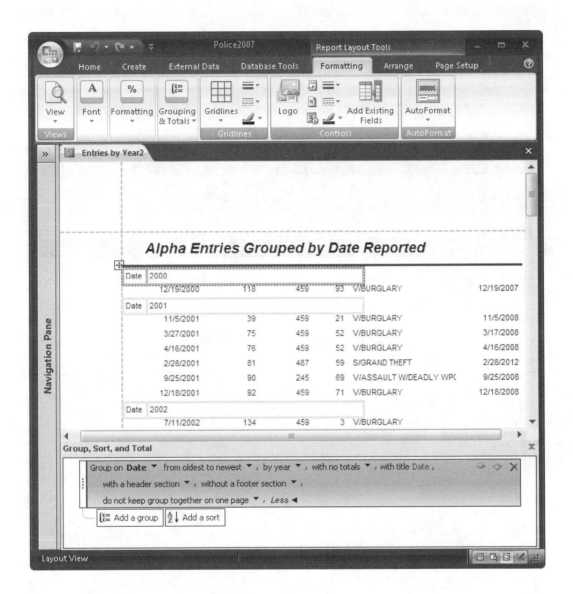

NOTE *The Group, Sort, and Total pane has up and down arrows in the upper-right corner that can return to a previous selection.*

4. To set the grouping interval, click the By Entire Value down arrow, choose By Year from the drop-down menu, and click in the Group, Sort, and Total pane to close the list. If you are grouping by a text or number field, the options will match the data type. You can also create a custom grouping by clicking Custom and choosing from

the By: options. With a Date field, you have a choice of minutes, hours, or days and can specify how many to include in the group.

5. Click the With No Totals down arrow, choose EntryNo in the Total On drop-down list, and accept Count Records as the Type. Then Check the Show Grand Total and Show in Group Footer options.

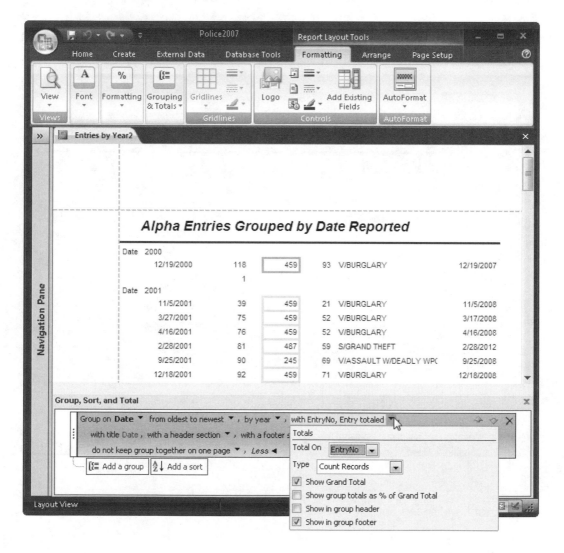

NOTE *If you want the group totals represented as a percentage of the total, select Show Group Totals as % of Grand Total.*

6. If you want a special title for the field being summarized, click the blue text following the words *with title* and enter **Year Reported:** in the Zoom box; then click OK.

7. The other options are:

- With or Without Group Header Section.
- With or Without Group Footer Section.
- Keep Group Together On One Page, Don't Keep Group Together On One Page, and Keep Header And First Record Together On One Page.

8. Choose to include a group header and group footer, and then click Less when you are through setting grouping options.

9. To sort the records within the group, click the Add A Sort button and choose Date from the drop-down list; keep the from oldest to newest sort order.

10. If you want to add another group within the one you build, click the Add A Group button again.

11. Click the Close button in the Group, Sort, and Total pane to return to the report Layout view to see the results of the grouping.

NOTE *If you want to delete the selected group level, click the* Delete (X) *button in the Group on pane.*

Before looking at the report in Layout view, use the Label control to add titles in the Report Header and Page Header sections. Then add the field labels to the Page Header section with the font set to Bold. Figure 14-7 shows the completed report in Design view.

Now switch to Print Preview to see how the report will look when printed (see Figure 14-8).

As you saw in the previous steps, the grouping options vary with the field type selected or the expression entered in the Select Field list. The number entered in the Custom option in the Group Interval setting specifies the interval or the number of characters on which to group. For example, you might want to group records by values in a currency field in $50 increments. Select Custom in the Group Interval drop-down list and type **50** as the interval. The first group will include values from $0 to $49, the second from $50 to $99, and so on.

NOTE *The Group Header and Footer Sections also have Keep Together properties, set in the Property Sheet in Design view, which are a little different from the group properties set in the Group, Sort, and Total pane. The group properties refer to the entire group, while the section properties refer only to a section. However, if you want the group Keep Together property to take effect, the group section Keep Together properties must also be set to Yes.*

The Group On options in the Group, Sort, and Total pane vary with the field type selected or the expression entered in the Group On drop-down list.

Numbering Items in a Report

Sometimes numbering each of the items in a report is handy, so you can refer to an item using a unique number—for example, numbering items can help keep track of the topic

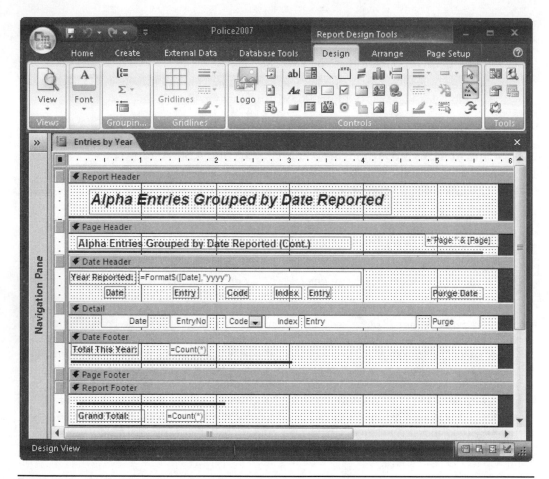

FIGURE 14-7   The Entries by Year report design

if you're taking part in a teleconference call and need to be sure that you are all talking about the same item. To number the items, do the following:

1. Add a calculated text box control to the Detail section in a prominent position at the left of the record data.

2. Remove the new text box label.

3. Double-click the new control to open its Property Sheet and change the Control Source property to the expression **=1**.

4. Set the Running Sum property to Over All, which increments the calculated text box value by 1 for each record in the Detail section.

This works for grouped records as well. To number the records in each group separately, add the calculated control to the Detail section, but set the Running Sum property to Over Group instead of Over All.

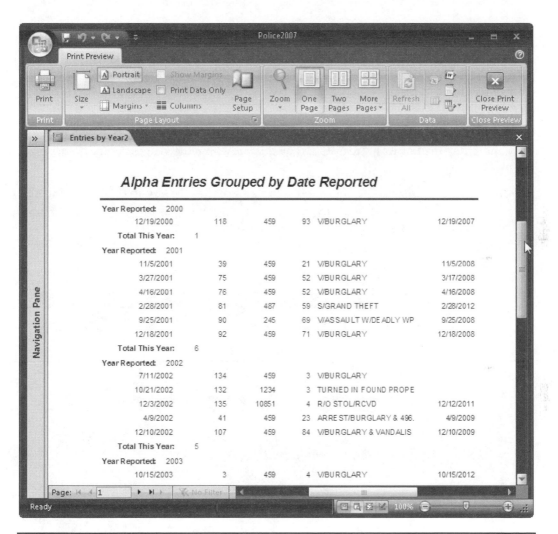

FIGURE 14-8   Entries by Year report in Print Preview

Modifying and Adding Groups

To change the sort order of the records in an ungrouped report or of the groups in a grouped report, open the report in Layout view and on the Formatting tab's Grouping & Totals group, click the Group & Sort command to open the Group, Sort, and Total pane.

If you want to change the grouping levels of existing groups, click the row selector of the group you want to move. Then click the Move Up or Move Down buttons in the group row selector. You can also drag the row to the desired position in the list of groupings. If the groups you move have headers or footers, Access moves them and all the controls they contain to the new positions in the report design. The controls might need some adjustment after repositioning.

To change the field or expression the records are grouped by, select it and choose another field from the drop-down list or enter a different expression. If you want to add a grouping level, click the next empty Field/Expression row and choose the field from the drop-down list or enter an expression.

To remove a grouping, click the Delete button on the row selector or press DELETE. If the group header or footer contains controls, you will see a warning message asking if you want to continue.

Adding a Second Level Grouping

To see how you can add a second grouping level, open the Entries by Year report in Design view and group the Entries by Year Report by quarter within the year group by doing the following:

1. On the Design tab's Grouping and Totals group, click the Group & Sort command.

2. Then on the Group, Sort, and Total pane, click the Add a group button and choose Date from the drop-down list of available fields.

3. Choose to Group by Quarter and leave the By interval set to 1.

4. Click More and choose to show the group header but not the group footer.

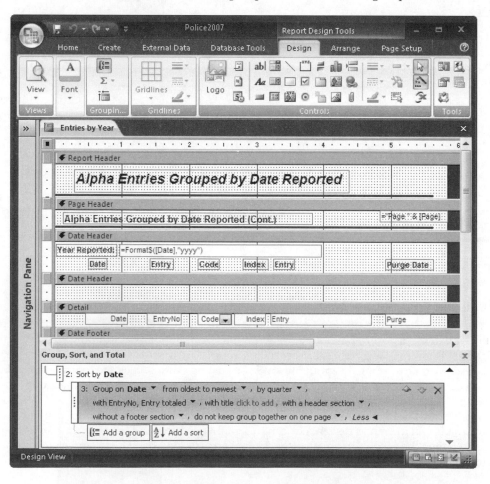

5. Close the Group, Sort, and Total pane.

6. Add an unbound text box to the left end of the Detail section and enter the expression **="Qtr: "& DatePart("q",[Date])** in its Control Source property box.

7. Open the Property Sheet and on the Format tab, change the Hide Duplicates property to Yes. Then delete the new control's attached label.

8. Save the report as **Entries by Quarter** and switch to Print Preview to view the changed report.

Figure 14-9 shows a preview of the report that now groups the Alpha Entry records by the year the entry was reported, and then by quarter. You can also edit the report title accordingly.

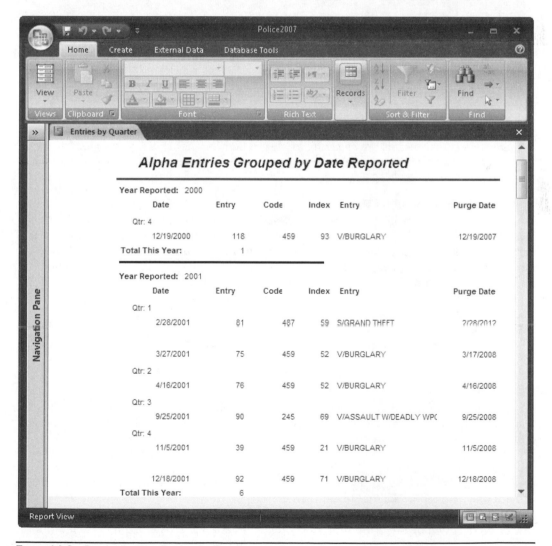

FIGURE 14-9   Previewing the Entries by Quarter report

TIP *The DatePart function extracts a specific part of an existing date value. See "Custom Formatting Symbols" in the Quick Reference on the CD for more details.*

Printing an Alphabetic Index

By combining the Group On and Group Interval settings, you can create an alphabetic list of items grouped by the leading character. For example, to create a list such as the one shown in Figure 14-10, do the following:

1. Select the Member List table in the Navigation Pane, and on the Create tab's Report group, click the Report Design command.

2. Place the LastName field in the Detail section and delete the attached label.

3. Shrink the Detail section to show only the LastName control.

4. On the Design tab's Grouping & Totals group, click the Group & Sort command.

5. In the Group, Sort, and Total pane, click the By Entire Value down arrow and choose By First Character.

Figure 14-11 shows the completed report design, as well as the Group, Sort, and Total pane.

CAUTION *Be careful not to use the word* Name *as a field name. Access reserves that word as the name of the current object. If you use the expression* Left([Name],1) *in the group header, you will see* M *(the first letter of the report name) in every group header. Many more words are reserved in the Access language, such as field, form, report, table, and query.*

Hiding Duplicates and Other Tips

Duplicate values appearing in the detail Section can clutter up a report. For example, a report grouping the Alpha Entry records by code would show multiple records with the same code value. You have two ways to alleviate such a problem: move the Code field to the Group Header section where it will be printed only once, or leave it in the Detail section and change the control's Hide Duplicates format property to Yes.

Two other properties are useful when printing reports containing Memo fields that might contain a varying amount of data or, possibly, none at all. Changing the Can Shrink property to Yes prevents blank lines from showing when there is no value in the field. Changing the Can Grow property to Yes lets the field value expand, if necessary.

Adding a Subreport

A *subreport*, a complete report in its own right, is inserted into another report, called the *main report*. A main report can be either bound or unbound. A *bound main report* is based on a table or query and its subreports contain related information. For example, the main report can contain details about the year's business, while the subreport can show charts and graphs summarizing and illustrating the numbers in the main report. A bound main report might also have two or more subreports that provide parallel information but relate only to the main report and not to each other.

An *unbound main report* isn't based on a table or query but can serve as a container for one or more subreports—for example, an annual report in which the main report is a title

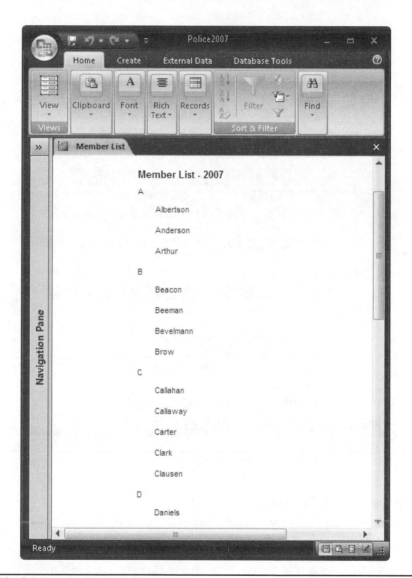

FIGURE 14-10   Printing an alphabetic Member List

page with some introductory information, and the subreports contain parallel information unrelated to each other about the business during the previous year.

A main report can include as many subreports and subforms as necessary. You can also add up to two levels of subreports. A first-level subreport can contain another subreport or a subform. If the first level is a subform, it can contain only another subform, not a subreport, as the second level.

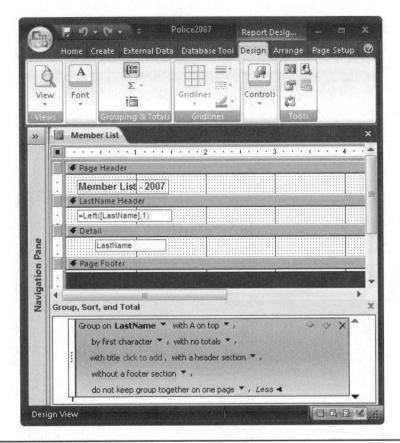

FIGURE 14-11 Reviewing the Member List report design

Creating a Subreport Control

You can use the Subform/Subreport Control tool in the Create tab's Reports group to create a new subreport in the current report design. The Subform/Subreport Wizard creates the subreport based on your selections in a series of dialog boxes. It also saves the finished subreport as a separate report whose name appears in the Reports tab of the Database window.

As an example of creating a new subreport, let's add the Alpha Entry information to the Alpha Card Report, relating the two reports by the Index field. To be safe, save the Alpha Card Report with a different name before adding the subreport as follows:

1. Select the Alpha Card Report name in the Navigation Pane.
2. Click the Microsoft Office button and choose Save As. In the Save Database Object As group, click the Save Object As button.
3. Enter the new name, **Alpha Card with Entries Subreport**, in the Save As dialog box and click OK.

To create the subreport containing related Alpha Entry information, do the following:

1. Open the Alpha Card with Entries Subreport report in Design view.

2. Increase the height of the detail section by dragging the Page Footer bar down and move the line to the bottom to make room for the subreport in between.

3. On the Design tab's Controls group, click the Subform/Subreport command and click in the report design between the last row of controls and the line at the bottom of the detail section. Access draws a square frame in the report design and opens the first dialog box, where you can select an existing report or form as the subreport or create a new one using an existing table or query.

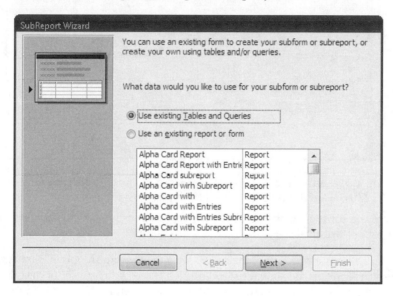

NOTE *You can also draw a custom subreport frame to the desired size before releasing the mouse button and starting the wizard.*

4. Choose Use Existing Tables and Queries to create the new subreport, and then click Next.

5. In the next dialog box, select Alpha Entry from the Tables/Queries drop-down list, click the double right arrow (>>) to select all the fields, and then click Next.

6. Accept the link the wizard suggests, which links the report and subreport by the Index field. Then click Next.

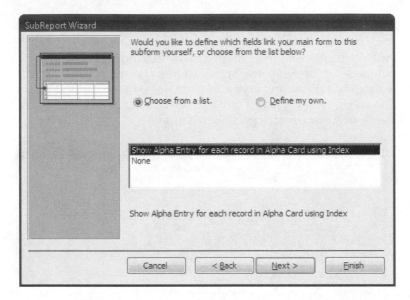

7. Accept Alpha Entry subreport as the report name or enter a different name, such as **Alpha Entries**, and then click Finish to return to the main report Design view.

8. Delete the subreport label, if necessary, and then move and resize the subreport control as appropriate.

Figure 14-12 shows a preview of the report with the new subreport. The style adopted for the subreport depends on the style most recently accessed. Your subreport's style could be different. As you can see in the preview, you can make several refinements in the subreport to improve its appearance. For example, you can hide the Index field and spread out the remaining controls to make room for the Entry information. In addition, the Code field doesn't need that much room so you can adjust that here as well.

Inserting an Existing Subreport

To use an existing report as a subreport, make sure that the underlying tables or queries are properly related to the main report, and then open the Subform/Subreport Wizard. Instead of choosing Table/Query in the first wizard dialog box, choose Reports or Forms, and then select the desired report or form from the drop-down list of all the reports and forms in the current database. Follow the instructions in the remaining wizard dialog boxes.

Linking the Report and Subreport

If you insert the subreport in a bound report, the underlying tables must be linked, so both reports contain corresponding data. You need to set the links in the Relationships window before trying to insert the subreport.

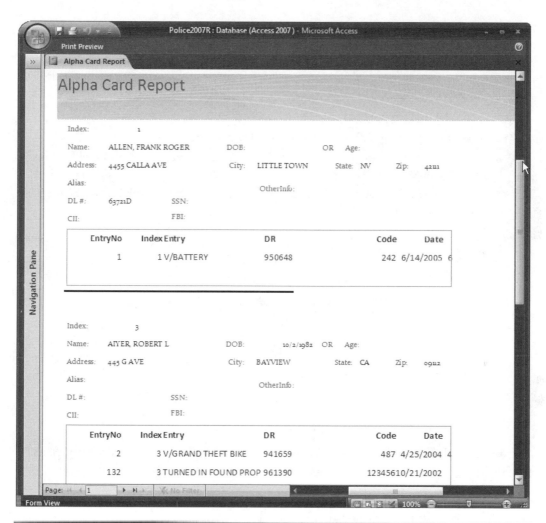

FIGURE 14-12 Previewing the new subreport

When you use the wizard to create a subreport or drag the name of an existing report or datasheet from the Navigation Pane, if one of the following conditions is met, Access automatically links the main report and subreport:

- The reports are based on related tables.
- The main report has a primary key and the table in the subreport contains a field with the same name and the same or compatible data type.
- Both reports are based on queries whose underlying tables meet either of those same conditions.

The linking fields must be included in the underlying record source, but you don't have to show them in either report. The wizard automatically includes linking fields, even if you don't select them from the Field List.

If, for some reason, the wizard hasn't linked the tables properly, you can set the properties yourself by doing the following:

1. Open the main report in Design view.

2. Select the subreport control and open the Property Sheet.

3. Enter the name of the linking field in the subreport in the Link Child Fields property box.

4. Enter the name of the linking field in the main report in the Link Master Fields property box.

TIP *You must use the field name, not the name of the control. If you are not sure of the field names, click the Build button (...) next to one of the linking properties to open the Subreport Field Linker dialog box. Click Suggest to see the same link suggestions presented by the Subreport Wizard.*

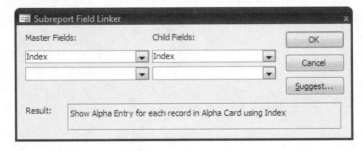

You can link on more than one field by entering the field names in the Property Sheet, separated by semicolons, or by selecting the field names in the Subreport Field Linker dialog box.

Modifying a Subreport Control

The first thing you might want to do with a new subreport control is to edit or delete the attached control label. You do this in the main report Design view. Then make changes in the subreport design to match the style and arrangement of the controls in the main report.

You can make modifications to a subreport design just like any other report. You can work on it in the main report Design window, or on the Design tab's Tools group, click the Subreport in New Window command to work on it alone.

Subreport controls share many of the properties with other types of controls—for example, the position and size properties, as well as the Special Effect and border properties. By default, the Can Grow property is set to Yes and the Can Shrink property is set to No. In addition to the link field properties, the subreport has a Name property on the Other tab, set to the name you gave the file or the name you entered in the Subform/Subreport Wizard dialog box.

The Source Object property is unique to subforms and subreports and contains the type and name of the object—for example, the Source Object property of the subreport in the Alpha Card with Subreport is Report.Alpha Entries subreport.

Designing a Multiple-Column Report

You can also arrange information in a report by using columns. When information is arranged in a tabular layout, it's easy to scan down a column of data and compare values in different records. Arranging the information in columns makes focusing on individual records easy because all of the data for one record is grouped together.

The Report Wizard gives you a choice of Tabular or Columnar layout in one of the dialog boxes. Choosing Columnar creates a report with the fields arranged in a single column on the page. Using Page Setup, you can change the layout to include as many columns that can fit across the page. For example, if you rearrange and resize the controls in the report design, you can reduce the width of a column to 2 inches, and then specify three columns on the page. Figure 14-13 compares the columnar report created by the Report Wizard with the same data in a newspaper column report.

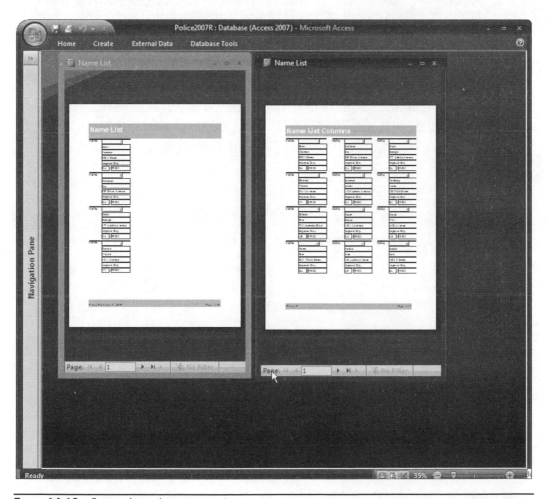

FIGURE 14-13 Comparing columnar reports

You can place controls anywhere in the page or in the Report Header and Footer sections because they span the entire width of the page when you print the report. If you grouped the records, the group header and footer, as well as the detail section, span only the width of the column. So, place the controls that you want in the group sections within the width that you allow for the column.

When designing a multiple-column report, use the following formula as a guide to the page layout:

```
(Column width * Number of columns) + (Column spacing * (Number of columns -1)) +
Right margin + Left margin <= Paper width
```

First, create the Name List report from the Name List table with the Report Wizard, choosing the Columnar layout. Then do the following to create this three-column report:

1. With the report open in Layout view, on the Page Setup tab's Page Layout group, click the Columns command. The three-tab Page Setup dialog box opens.

2. Click the Columns tab and change the Number of Columns to **3**.

3. Leave the Column Spacing at the default **.25"**. If you left some space between the bottom control in the Detail section and the lower boundary of the section, you can also leave the Row Spacing at **0**.

4. In the Column Size group, set the Width to **2"**. You can also set the Height here or use the height drawn in Design view.

5. Click OK. If you were in Print Preview, the report shows the new layout. If not, switch to Print Preview to see how the report looks.

TIP *If the report design exceeds the page width, Access displays a warning when you try to switch to Print Preview. Then you can either enter a smaller column width, reduce the column spacing, or reduce the size of the side margins. If you reduce the column width, be sure to change the controls in the group and Detail sections to fit.*

The Columns tab of the Page Setup dialog box also shows the Column Layout option group, where you can choose the order in which the records are laid out on the page. The default is Down, Then Across, which places records down the page in the first column to the bottom of the page, and then moves to the second column, and so on. The alternative choice is Across, Then Down, which places the records across the first row to the right margin of the page, and then moves to the second row, and so on.

Grouping Records in a Multiple-Column Report

When you create a multiple-column report with grouping levels, you keep the groups together in a row or column, depending on the Column Layout setting, when printing the report. You can also have a group start in a new row or column by setting combinations of group and report properties.

Starting a Group in a New Row or Column

If you grouped the records in the report and want to set each group apart when the report is printed, you can ask Access to start a new column or row with each new group by setting the Group section (header or footer) New Row Or Col property. Your choices are as follows:

- **None**   Lets the setting in the Page Setup dialog box and the available space on the page determine the row or column breaks.

- **Before Section**   Starts printing the group section (usually the header) in a new row or column, and then prints the next section (usually the Detail section) in the same row or column.

- **After Section**   Starts printing the group section in the current row or column, and then prints the next section in a new row or column. This option can be used to print the group headers alone in the first row or column, and then print the Detail section in the second row or column.

- **Before & After**   Starts printing the group section in a new row or column, and then prints the next section in a new row or column. This option can be used to cause the information in the Group Header section to stand apart from the information in the Detail section.

You might have to play around with combinations of the Column Layout options in the Columns tab of the Page Setup dialog box and the New Row Or Col group section property settings to get the effect you want in the report.

Keeping Groups Together in Rows or Columns

Earlier in this chapter, you saw how to keep data together on a page by the setting group properties in the Group, Sort, and Total panes, and by setting report properties in the Property Sheet. If you arranged the records in columns and you want to keep the group together, do the following:

1. In Design view, on the Design tab's Grouping & Totals group, click the Group & Sort command to open the pane.

2. Click the group level you want to keep together and set the Keep Whole Group Together On One Page option.

3. Open the report Property Sheet and change the Grp Keep Together property to Per Column.

NOTE *If you set the Column Layout in the Columns tab of the Page Setup dialog box to Across, then Down, the group is kept together in a row. The Down, then Across setting keeps the group together in a column.*

Printing Mailing Labels and Envelopes

Labels are used for many purposes: mailing addresses, name tags, disk labels, and bookplates (such as "From the library of…"). Because labels are usually smaller than a sheet of paper, you can print many of them on one page. This leads to a multiple-column-per-page report layout. Label printing is so common that Access provides a special Label Wizard to help with the layout.

After you create the label design, you can use it to print addresses on envelopes as well, by making a few changes to the page layout. Using the Label Wizard, you can create your own custom label size and layout, and then save it to use again.

Using the Label Wizard

In one of the Label Wizard's series of dialog boxes, you can select from a long list of predefined label layouts that match commercially available label stocks. You can prepare labels for printing on continuous-feed or sheet-feed printers. The Label Wizard helps with every stage of the label design, including choosing the layout, changing the text appearance, adding field data
to a prototype label, and even offering to sort the labels for you before printing.

As an example of printing mailing labels, the local police department keeps the names and addresses of the Retired Senior Volunteer Program (RSVP) members in the Name List table in their Access database, so monthly notices can be mailed to the members.

To create mailing labels for the volunteers, do the following:

1. Select the Name List in the Navigation Pane, and on the Create tab's Reports group, click the Labels command.

2. In the first dialog box, set the following options:

   - Select the desired Unit of Measure: English or Metric.
   - Select the Label Type: Sheet feed or Continuous.
   - Choose the brand of label from the Filter By Manufacturer drop-down list.
   - Choose the desired label from the Product Number list. The dimensions are specified as height × width.
   - If you want to create a custom label size, click the Customize button.

- If you have already created some custom label sizes, you can choose Show Custom Label Sizes to see that list.

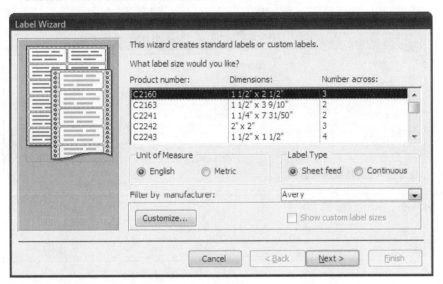

3. Click Next to open the second dialog box, where you can select the font name, size and weight, and text colors. Italics and underlining are also options here.

NOTE *These settings apply to all the text in the label. You can change individual lines of text later in Design view. For example, you might want the addressee's name to be in boldface text, but not the address.*

4. Click Next to continue. The next Label Wizard dialog box displays a blank label prototype, where you arrange the data.

   - To move a field to the prototype label, double-click the field name in the Available Fields list or select it and click the right-pointing arrow (>).
   - To remove a field from the prototype label, select the field and press DELETE.
   - To move to the next line, press ENTER.
   - Enter spaces, punctuation, and other characters as necessary as you place the fields.

5. After you enter the first name, middle initial, and last name, press ENTER to move to the next line in the label.

6. Access automatically concatenates the values in the fields and trims the spaces from the names and addresses. Notice the spaces entered between the field names and the comma entered between the City and State fields.

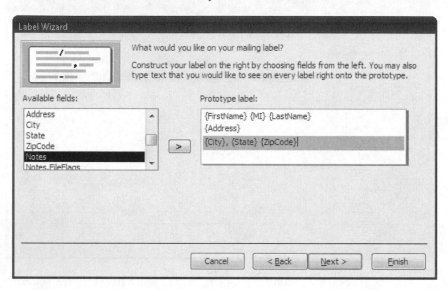

7. Click Next to move to the next dialog box, where you can choose to sort the records before printing the labels. Then click Next to move to the last Label Wizard dialog box, where you enter a name for the label design.

***

NOTE *If you don't specify a sort order, the labels are arranged in the same order as the source table, ascending, based on the first field in the table. If the label report is based on a query, the labels are arranged in ascending order based on the left-most field in the grid.*

Figure 14-14 shows a preview of the new labels for the Labels Name List, using the Avery 5160 label size. The labels are sorted by last name.

***

TIP *It's a good idea to print one page of the new labels on plain paper and compare it with your label stock before committing to print many pages of labels on expensive label sheets.*

Manipulating Text Data

In the Formatting tab's Views group, click View, and choose Design View to see the new Labels Name List in Design view.

You can see how the Label Wizard created the calculated text box controls. The Label Wizard combined the text values in special expressions using the concatenation operator (&) and the Trim function. The *concatenation operator* serves to combine the values in the field with any other characters you want, enclosed in quotation marks. The *Trim function* displays the field value without leading or trailing spaces.

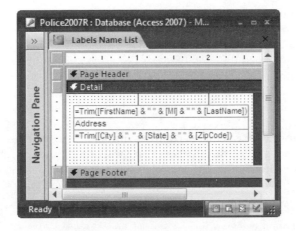

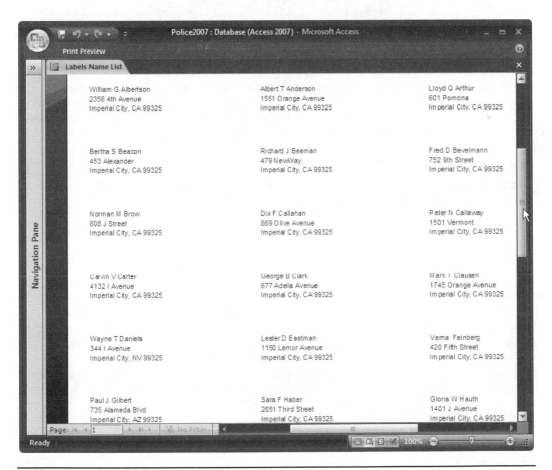

FIGURE 14-14   Preview of the new labels

Other text functions are also useful when combining text values. In addition to the Trim function, the *LTrim function* removes only the leading spaces, while the *RTrim function* removes only the trailing spaces. Be sure to add a space between the field names and literal characters in the same line in the prototype label or all of the characters will run together.

The Left function used earlier when creating the alphabetic list report lets you display only the first few characters of the text value. The number of characters to display is specified as the second argument in the function statement. The Right function displays the last few characters.

You can create your own calculated control expressions to combine text values by using these tools and functions. Type the expression in the Control Source property box of the calculated text box or directly into the control in the design. Always begin the expression with the equal sign (=). Here are some examples of expressions that you can use in calculated controls placed in forms and reports:

- **="None"**   Displays *None*.
- **="Mr/Mrs " & [First Name] & " " & [Last Name]**   Displays the first and last names preceded by *Mr/Mrs* and separated by a space.
- **=Trim([City])**   Displays the City field with no leading or trailing spaces.
- **=Left([Last Name],3)**   Displays the first three characters in the Last Name field.
- **=IIf(IsNull([MI]),[FirstName]&" " &[LastName],[FirstName] & " " & [MI] & " " & [LastName])**   Uses the IIf function to test the MI field for a null value. If the field is null, only the first and last names are displayed. If the field is not null, all three field values are displayed. All the values are separated by spaces.

Printing Addresses on Envelopes

You can use the same report design you created for printing the labels to print the addresses on envelopes. All you need to do is change the Page Setup options to reflect the different size and arrangement of the controls. First, save the report you created for printing labels with a different name, and then open the report in Design view and make any changes to the text in the report.

Summary

This chapter covered designing custom reports for many purposes, but an almost unlimited number of features and tools are available in the Access repertoire. As you work with report designs and begin to realize how versatile Access can be in presenting information in a variety of ways, you'll gain an even greater appreciation for the program.

The last remaining piece of information retrieval and presentation involves graphically presenting information in such a way that the viewer can perform analyses and detect trends in the underlying data. The next chapter discusses three tools for doing this: the Chart Wizard, the PivotTable Wizard, and the PivotChart Wizard. The Chart Wizard helps create charts and graphs from Access table data, which you can edit using the Microsoft Graph applet. The PivotTable Wizard helps create spreadsheet-like tables from Access table data that you can edit using Excel. The PivotChart Wizard presents a graphical analysis of data in a table, query, or form.

Creating Charts and Graphs

C harts and graphs enhance the data presented in forms and reports by summarizing the information and illustrating it in easily understood ways. With these tools, the reader can analyze trends and make comparisons. Access offers a wide variety of chart types including column, bar, line, pie, XY scatter, area, and many others. Many of the types can also be shown in three dimensions. If you want the chart to reflect the values in the currently displayed record, you can also link the chart to a field in the underlying table or query.

Creating a New Chart

When you decide to add a chart to a form or report, you must first understand the purpose of the chart. Do you want to point out trends over a period of time or compare the relative values summarized by groups? For example, suppose the local police department is interested in the increase or decrease of violent crimes over the last four years. This type of chart would involve tabulating the number of crimes reported during each year and displaying the results as a column chart or a line chart.

The police are also concerned with the crime rates in different areas of the city. Such a comparison can be illustrated with a bar or column chart, as well as a pie chart in which each area is represented by a slice of the pie.

Other decisions that must be made during the planning stage are whether to embed the chart in the form or report or to create a freestanding chart that can be available to more than one form or report. If you embed the chart in the form or report, you can link the chart to data in the underlying table or query and the chart then changes for each record. If you want the chart to remain the same as you move through records, leave the embedded chart unlinked.

If you create a chart in another application, such as Excel, you can import the chart to your form or report. On the External Data tab's Import group, click the Excel command and specify the source and destination of the data. You can also click the Unbound Object Frame command in the Controls group to place the frame in the form or report and then copy the chart to that.

TIP *The fundamental rule when you design a chart or any other user-oriented object is to keep it simple. Just because Access and the other Office applications offer all kinds of bells and whistles, this doesn't mean that you need to clutter your products with a lot of items that may obscure the point that you're trying to make. Keep the purpose of the chart in mind as you look at the tools Access and Microsoft Graph offer.*

The Anatomy of a Chart

A chart is composed of *elements*, some of which relate to the data, while others relate to the structure of the chart itself. Figure 15-1 shows a typical chart based on data taken from the Northwind sample database that came with Access. This chart compares the sales of eight categories of products during the year 2006.

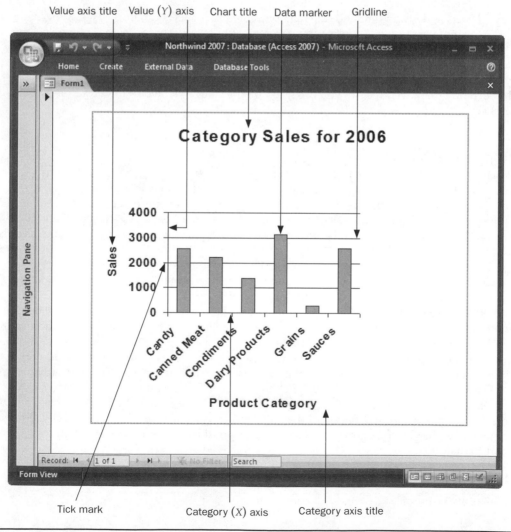

Figure 15-1 A typical Access column chart

Many other types of charts can show comparisons among data groups. For example, Figure 15-2 shows the same data displayed in an exploding pie chart. Many of the same elements appear in this chart, in addition to a few new ones: a legend, a slice, and data labels. Data labels can be displayed with the percentage of the whole that the group represents, as the figure shows or with the data name or both.

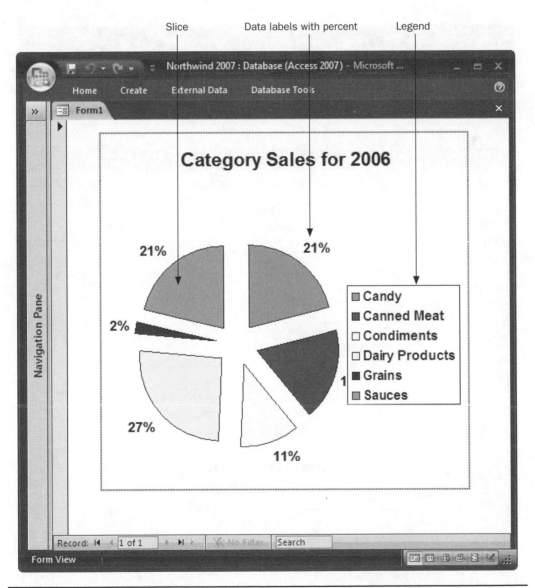

Figure 15-2   An exploding pie chart with data labels

Another reason to include charts in a form or report is to visually show trends over a period of time. Figure 15-3, which uses data from the Police database, shows a line chart that tracks the number of crimes reported over a four-year period. The crimes are grouped as violent or nonviolent and a legend is included that identifies the lines. This chart includes data labels, which show the number of crimes at each data point on the lines. The legend that appears to the right of the chart identifies the individual categories of information.

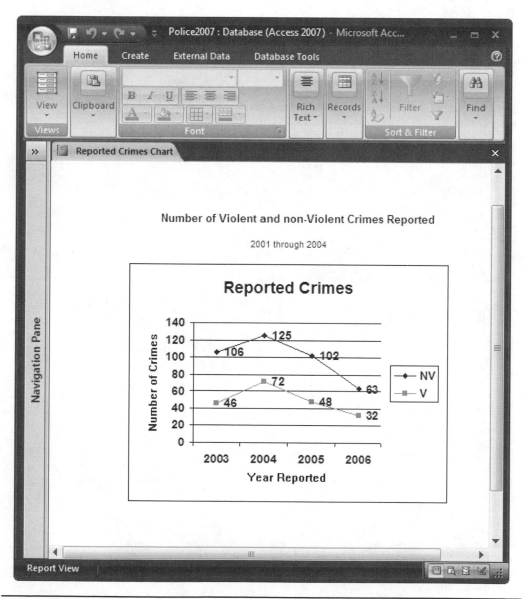

FIGURE 15-3   A line chart showing a trend

NOTE *The lines appear in different colors when displayed on the screen or printed with a color printer, but when they're printed in black and white, you must rely on the shape of the data points to identify the data series.*

The line chart has been embedded in a simple report with a title and subtitle added to the page header. The report could be much more comprehensive in real life.

Before moving on, be sure that you understand each of the main elements in a standard chart (refer to Figures 15-1, 15-2, and 15-3):

- **Category (X) axis**   The horizontal line at the bottom of the chart that usually identifies the data in the chart. For example, when you plot sales by product, the product name appears on the Category axis.

- **Value (Y) axis**   The vertical line that measures the values in the chart data—for example, the sales in dollars or other currency.

- **Z axis**   Optional, appears in 3-D charts and also measures values. The Z axis appears to project outward from the chart.

- **Series**   A group of related data values from one field in the underlying record source. For example, in a sales by product chart, each year's sales total would represent one of a series of values. The values are grouped together in one category: the product type. A series is a further partitioning of grouped field data, which adds more detail to the chart.

- **Titles**   Explain the purpose and scope of the chart. Titles are optional and can appear at the top of the chart and by each axis.

- **Tick marks**   Short lines that appear on the axes to mark evenly spaced segments. They help you read the values and determine the scale of the chart.

- **Gridlines**   Horizontal or vertical lines that appear across or up and down the chart at the tick marks.

- **Scale**   Defines the range of values in the chart and the increments marked by tick marks on the axes. This is usually determined by the Chart Wizard, but you can change the scale and spacing of the tick marks.

- **Slice**   A wedge of a single field in a pie chart, which represents the relative value of one data point with respect to the whole.

- **Data markers**   The elements that show the value of the data—for example, bars, columns, slices of a pie chart, or small icons on a line chart.

- **Data labels**   The actual values that can be displayed above or near the data markers. Figure 15-2 shows percentage data labels with each slice of the pie.

- **Legend**   The list that identifies the members of a series of data values. For example, in Figure 15-3, the legend next to the chart indicates which line represents which type of crime.

Selecting the Data for the Chart

After you decide what you want the chart to accomplish, you can begin locating the data that the chart will require. If the data is all contained in one table, you can use the table as the basis for the chart. If not, you can create a select or crosstab query that groups and summarizes the data for the chart. With a select query, you can combine data and add calculated fields such as an extended price, as well as add totals that summarize field values.

You can use up to six fields of any data type, except Object Linking and Embedding (OLE), Memo, and Attachment. Only two requirements exist:

- You must include at least one field for categorizing data, such as the year the crime was reported or the area of the city where it occurred.

- You must also include a field or a calculated field that you can add up, average, or count, such as the number of violent crimes or the sales during the third quarter of 2004.

TIP *If you include a date/time field in the chart, you can group the values with the wizard instead of creating a query to do the job.*

A simple chart might contain only two fields—one as the category and the other as the data or value that corresponds to the category. For example, in Figure 15-1, only two fields exist: Product Category used as the category; and Sales, which was summed to form the value.

Using the Access Chart Wizard

The way you begin to create a new chart depends on the type of chart you want. Do you want a standalone chart in its own form or report design, or a chart embedded in an existing form or report? In either case, you will eventually use the Chart Wizard to create the chart. The chart is built in a chart control in the form or report.

To create a new chart, start the Chart Wizard by doing one of the following:

- If you're creating a freestanding chart, start a new blank form or report, and then on the Design tab's Controls group, click the Insert Chart command. Then draw a box in the form or report design. The Chart Wizard begins.

TIP *You can also use one of the other methods you learned in the preceding chapters to open the New Form or New Report dialog box.*

- If you want to create a new chart in an existing form or report, open the form or report in Design view and click the Insert Chart command. Then click in the design where you want to place the chart and the Chart Wizard opens.

In the first Chart Wizard dialog box, select the table or query you want to use as the basis for the chart. Once you specify the underlying record source, follow the instructions in the wizard dialog boxes as follows (this example uses the Crimes by Beat Number table in the Police database):

1. Choose the fields you want to use in the chart—for example, Year, CrimeType, and Number of Crimes. You need at least one field as the category and one as the data. You can choose up to six fields. Then click Next.

2. In the next dialog box, select the type of chart you want to create (see Figure 15-4), and then click Next. You can click each type of chart and read a description in the right pane.

3. The next dialog box (see Figure 15-5) shows you the Chart Wizard's interpretation of the arrangement of the fields in the layout of the sample 3-D column chart.

4. Access has guessed which field you want to use as the category, but this isn't always what you had in mind. Click Preview Chart to see how this arrangement would look.

   The preview doesn't show what the chart is meant to present—the number of crimes by type reported in each year. It shows the number of years in which violent and nonviolent crimes were reported. To change this layout, close the Preview window and do the following:

5. Drag the SumOfYear label to the area below the chart to replace the CrimeType label. The label changes to *Year* because it represents a category on the X axis, rather than a numeric value on the Y axis.

6. Drag the Number of Crimes field button to the Data area below the Preview Chart. The label changes to SumOfNumber of Crimes.

7. Drag the CrimeType field button to the Series area.

8. To remove a field from the Preview Chart, drag it off the chart. The field name is replaced by Series, Data, or Axis, depending on the chart area. Figure 15-6 shows the new layout.

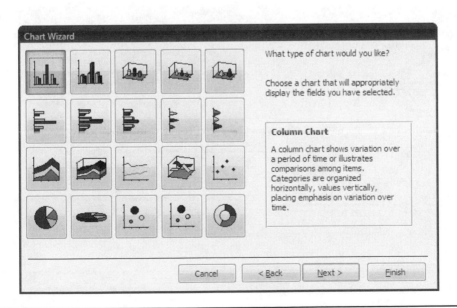

FIGURE 15-4   Select the type of chart

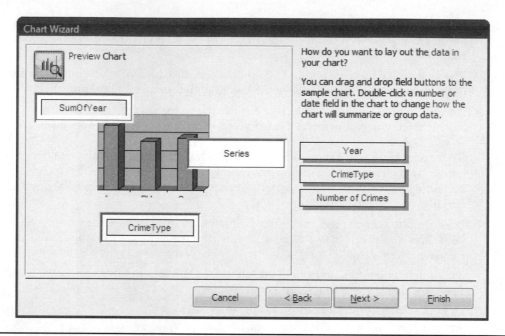

FIGURE 15-5 Working in the Chart Wizard's layout dialog box

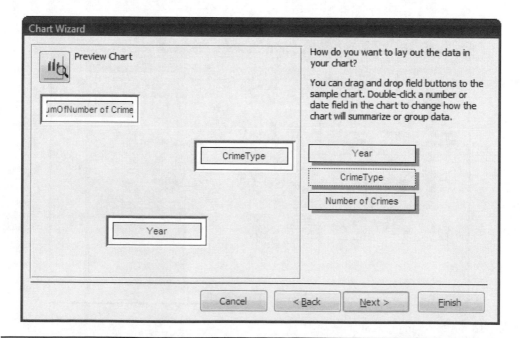

FIGURE 15-6 Modified chart layout

9. Click the Preview Chart button again to see the effects of the changes.

10. Close the Preview window and click Next.

11. In the final Chart Wizard dialog box, you can enter a name for the chart, such as Crimes by Year Chart, or accept the name of the table or query you used as the basis. You also have the option of displaying a legend explaining the series data. When you close the dialog box, you can open the form or report and display the chart, or you can go directly to Design view to edit the form or report.

12. Click Finish to see the chart in the new form. You may have to resize the form or the chart control to get the appearance you want.

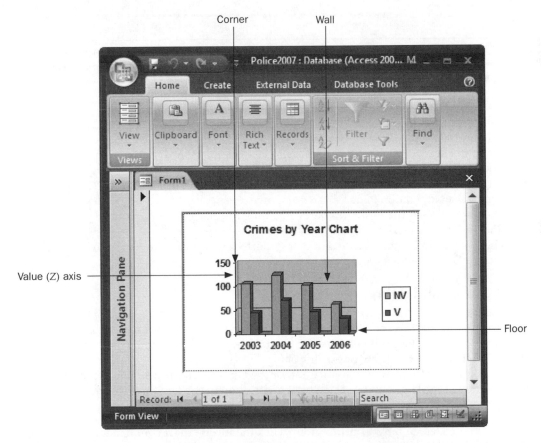

A *3-D chart* has a third dimension, *depth*, that creates a back wall, an end wall on the left, side walls, and a floor. The back wall and end wall meet at the corner. You can set the pattern and color properties of each of these features to get the appearance that you want in the chart.

You don't have to go to the trouble of creating a query to summarize the data for the chart. You can create the chart and let the Chart Wizard do that for you. When you drag a field to the Value area in the sample chart, the Chart Wizard assumes that you want to use the Sum aggregate function to create the value, but you can change to another function by double-clicking a number field, choosing from the Summarize dialog box, and then clicking OK.

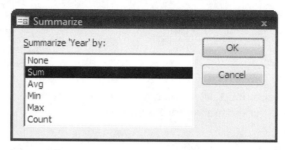

NOTE   *When you first create a chart, it shows sample data rather than the data you asked it to process. Don't worry, though, because the chart will show the real data the first time you view the form in Form view or the report in Report view or Print Preview.*

Printing and Saving the Chart

In the final Chart Wizard dialog box, you assigned a title to the new chart, but you haven't yet named the host form or report, as you can see from the Form1: Form name that appears in the document tab. To name and save the form or report containing the chart, right-click the tab, choose Save from the shortcut menu, and enter the desired filename. The new name is added to the Navigation Pane.

When you reopen the form or report containing the chart, it contains the current data from the underlying record source.

When you preview the chart in Form or Report view or Print Preview, you can print it or switch to Design view to make changes.

Linking to Record Data

When you start a new chart from within a form or report design, Access assumes that you want to link the chart to one of the fields in the underlying record source, so that different data appears in the chart with each record. To do this, you first create the host form or report and then insert the new or existing chart.

For example, let's create a columnar form based on the City Beats table, which contains only two fields: the beat number and a brief description of the territory. Then switch to Design view and create a new chart by doing the following:

1. On the Design tab's Controls group, click the Insert Chart command and click in the design just below the text box controls in the form. Be sure you have made room in the section for the embedded chart.

2. In the first Chart Wizard dialog box, choose the Crimes by Beat Number table as the basis for the chart and click Next.

3. In the second dialog box, select the fields you want to appear in the chart. For this chart, choose Year, BeatNo, Crime Type, and Number of Crimes from the field list, and then click Next.

4. In the next dialog box, choose a simple column chart and click Next.

5. In the layout dialog box, drag the Year field to the Axis area, the Number of Crimes to the Data area, and the CrimeType to the Series area. Then click Next.

6. In the next dialog box (see Figure 15-7), the wizard suggests BeatNo as the linking fields in both the form and chart because they have the same name. If no matching names exist between the tables, the wizard makes no suggestion. You can change the linking field names or choose not to link the chart to the form at all by choosing <No Field>. Click Next to move to the final dialog box, and name the form **City Beats Crimes**.

NOTE   *The linking fields do not need to have the same names, but they must have the same kind of data and be of the same or compatible data types.*

Figure 15-8 shows the finished form with the linked chart. As you move through the records, the heights of the data column markers change to reflect the number of crimes reported in that beat area.

TIP   *Reconstructing the chart when you move to the next record may take a few seconds, so be patient.*

If you open the form in Design view and look at the properties of the chart control, you will see that the Link Child Fields and Link Master Fields are both set to the BeatNo field.

NOTE   *If you already created the chart and want to embed and link it in a form, you can set the Link Child Fields and Link Master Fields properties yourself in the chart control Property Sheet.*

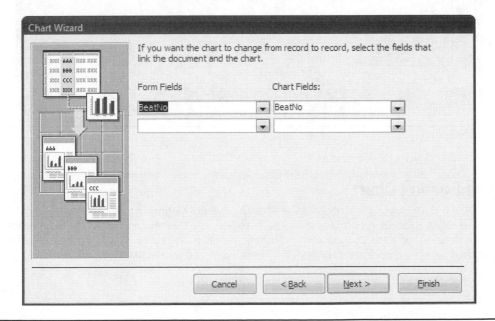

FIGURE 15-7   The Chart Wizard offers to link the chart to records in the form

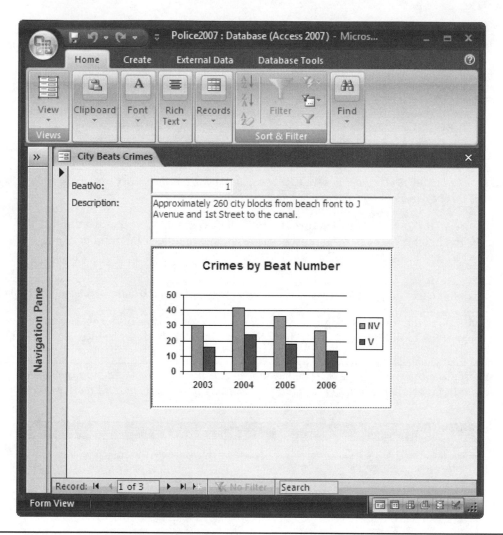

FIGURE 15-8 The new form with a linked chart

Adding an Existing Chart

You can insert an existing chart created within the current database or in another Access database into a form or report. To add a chart created in the same or another Access database, you can drag or copy the chart from one form or report to the other. To use, drag-and-drop to insert the chart from another database, you must have two instances of Access running.

To insert a new chart created with Microsoft Chart, another Office program, open the form or report in Design view and do the following:

1. On the Design tab's Controls group, click the Unbound Object Frame command and click where you want the chart to appear. You can also draw the frame in the design.

2. In the Microsoft Office Access Insert Object dialog box, click Create From File and enter the path to the file, or click Browse to locate the file if you don't know the path.

3. If you want to link the chart to the form or report, choose Link. If you want the chart to appear as an icon instead of the full chart, choose Display As Icon. Then click OK.

Modifying the Chart

The tools you use to modify a chart depend on the kind of changes that you want to make. If you want to change any of the properties or the position of the control, you can do so in Access. If you want to change the underlying data, you can create a new query and change the Row Source property of the chart within Access. You can also edit the SQL statement in the Row Source property rather than create a new query.

However, if you want to change any of the chart's elements, such as the axis titles or the chart type, or change the appearance of the chart, you must activate Microsoft Graph for in-place editing.

Modifying with Access

To modify the chart with Access, open the host form or report in Design view and select the chart control frame. With the frame selected, you can do the following:

- Drag the frame to a different position in the form or report.
- Drag the sizing handles to change the frame size. This resizes only the frame. Double-click the chart object to activate Microsoft Graph in the background and change the size of the chart itself. When Microsoft Graph is running, the chart is framed with a grilled border with move and size handles. By default, the chart frame's Size Mode property is set to Stretch. Click outside the chart to return to the Access object then open the Property Sheet and change the property to Clip or Zoom if you need to resize the frame.
- Open the chart's Property Sheet and change any of the control properties, including the frame's fill color, border color and width, and special effect. You can also change the Row Source, Link Master Fields, and Link Child Fields properties.

For example, to unlink the Crimes by Beat Number chart from the form, do the following:

1. Open the City Beats Crimes form in Design view.
2. Right-click the chart control and choose Property Sheet from the shortcut menu.
3. Delete the BeatNo field names from both the Link Master Fields and Link Child Fields properties.

When you return to Form view and move through the records, you can see the chart no longer changes with each record. Instead, it shows the total crimes for all beats with each record.

TIP *If disk space is a concern, you can save space by converting the unbound object control to an image control. Right-click the chart in form or report Design view and choose Change To from the shortcut menu. Then select Image, the only option available to an unbound OLE Object control. The data shown in the chart won't be updated with changes in the underlying record source. Use caution with the transformation because it can't be undone.*

Editing the Row Source Property

If you created the chart in Access with the Chart Wizard, it creates a query whose SQL statement becomes the row source for the chart. You can modify the row source using the query grid or by editing the SQL statement itself.

To change the row source, do the following:

1. Open the Sum Crimes report in Design view and open the Property Sheet for the chart control.

2. Click the Build button next to the Row Source property to open the Query Builder dialog box with the Sum Crimes query.

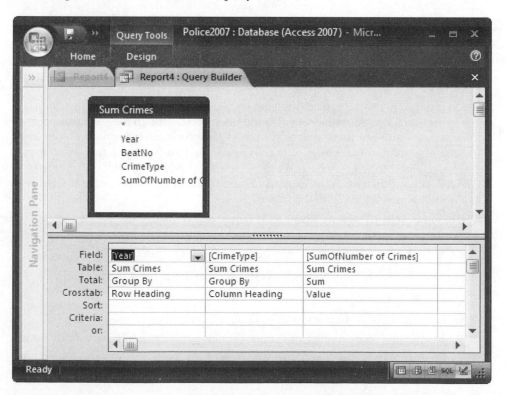

3. To limit the chart to crimes occurring in specific years, enter **Between 2003 And 2005** in the Criteria row of the Year column.

4. Close the Query Builder dialog box and respond Yes to save the changes. Then switch to Report view.

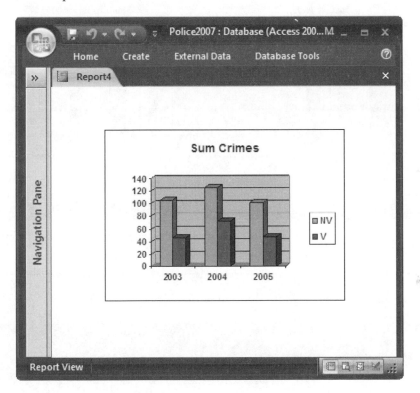

NOTE *If you plan to limit the time interval before finishing with the wizard, you can also set the chart interval in the Chart Wizard dialog box.*

Editing the Chart Legend

When you add a series to the chart layout that summarizes data within the category, as shown in Figure 15-9, the legend isn't always as informative as possible. The two charts illustrate the same data and are based on tables that contain the same data, but they use different table structures.

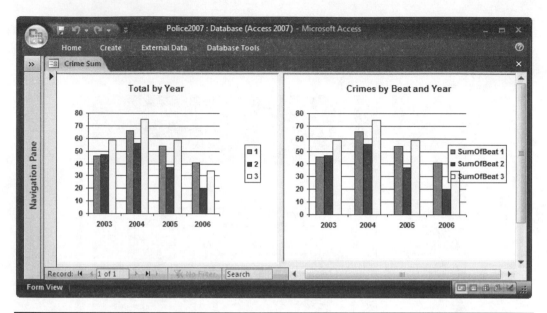

FIGURE 15-9   Two charts illustrating the same data

The chart on the left is based on the Crimes by Beat Number table:

When you built the chart, the Chart Wizard created a crosstab query that totaled the number of both types of crimes reported for each beat. The chart legend in the chart on the left takes its values from the value of the field whose Crosstab row shows Column Heading, which is BeatNo (1, 2, and 3). The legend would be more informative if you edited the query design grid to read Beat 1, Beat 2, and Beat 3.

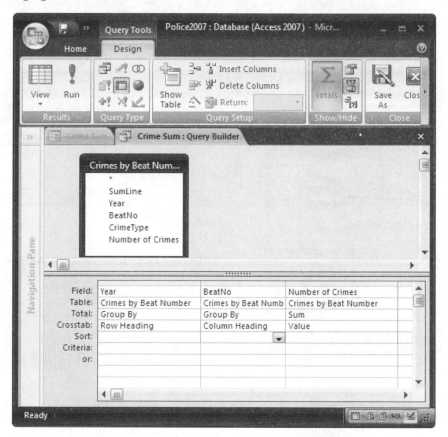

To fix this, open the Crime Sum report in Design view and select the chart. Then open the Property Sheet and click the Build button in the Row Source property. You have two ways to change the legend in the Row Source property:

- You can change the BeatNo field in the query grid to the expression **"Beat "&[BeatNo]**. Be sure to include a space after **Beat** within the quotation marks to separate it from the number. Then close the Query Builder and save the change.

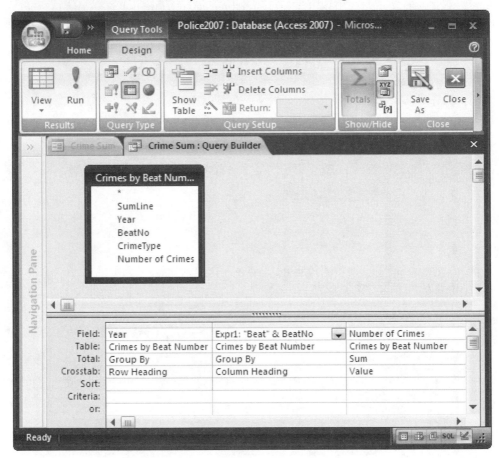

- Or you can right-click the document tab and choose SQL View from the shortcut menu and change the PIVOT clause from

  PIVOT [BeatNo];
  to
  PIVOT "Beat "&[BeatNo];

Tip *If you make the change in the grid, the SQL statement changes to match, and vice versa.*

The legend in this chart now reads Beat 1, Beat 2, and Beat 3.

The chart on the right in Figure 15-9 is based on the more compact Crimes by Beat and Year table.

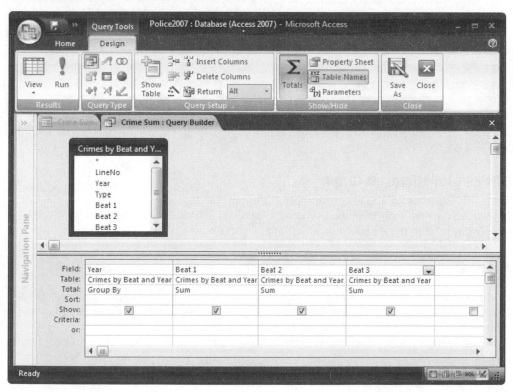

For this chart, the Chart Wizard created a select query that sums the value in each of the Beat*n* fields by year. The legend shows SumOfBeat 1, SumOfBeat 2, and SumOfBeat 3. You can use the same two methods to change the legend text, add expressions to the Field row of the query grid, or edit the SQL statement.

Open the form in Design view and start the Query Builder as before. Then do one of the following:

- Type **Beat 1:** before the Beat 1 field name. Type **Beat 2:** and **Beat 3:** for Beat 2 and Beat 3 field names, respectively.

- Switch to SQL view and edit the AS clauses by deleting *SumOf* from each clause.

CAUTION *Be sure to leave the brackets around the field names in the SQL statement because they contain spaces.*

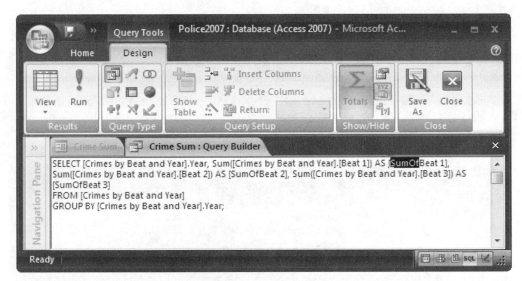

Save the changes and switch to Form view. Figure 15-10 shows the two charts with their new legends.

Editing with Microsoft Graph

Microsoft Graph is an applet (a small program) you can use from within Access to edit the charts you created with the Chart Wizard. When you activate Microsoft Graph, special toolbars appear in the Access window that you can use to edit the chart in place.

NOTE *Access 2007 uses Microsoft Graph 2003 as of this writing.*

Microsoft Graph serves many programs and not all its features apply to Access charts. This chapter covers the main features that help you modify charts that you included in Access forms and reports, you can experiment with others.

To activate Microsoft Graph, double-click the chart control in the form or report Design view. Figure 15-11 shows the Crimes by Year form in the Access window when Microsoft Graph is active. In addition to the Form window containing the chart, a Datasheet window appears containing the related data. Notice the crosshatched border around the chart that indicates Microsoft Graph is currently running.

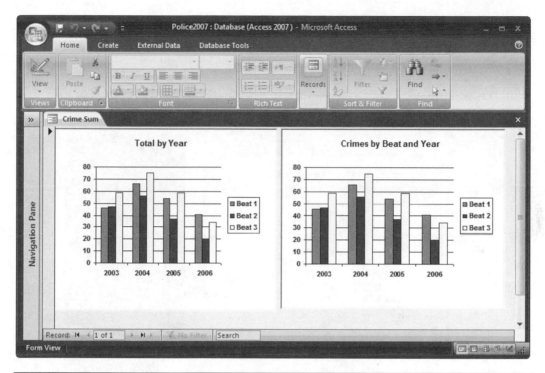

FIGURE 15-10   Charts with legends edited in Access

The title you entered in the Chart Wizard dialog box appears as the chart title in Microsoft Graph, and the data shown in the datasheet is from the row source table or query. To show or hide the datasheet, do one of the following:

- Choose View | Datasheet, which toggles the Datasheet window off and on.
- Right-click the Chart window and choose Datasheet from the shortcut menu.
- Click the Close button to close the Datasheet.

To leave the Microsoft Graph window and return to the Access form or report Design view, click anywhere outside the chart object. The changes you made to the chart in Microsoft Graph appear in the Access chart. You must save the form or report design to save the changes.

Looking at the Microsoft Graph Toolbars

The Microsoft Graph window normally has two toolbars: Standard and Formatting. Three other toolbars are available on demand: Drawing, Picture, and WordArt, which you can use to add special objects to the chart. To display a toolbar, right-click in any toolbar and select the one you want to use. You can also choose a toolbar from the View | Toolbars menu.

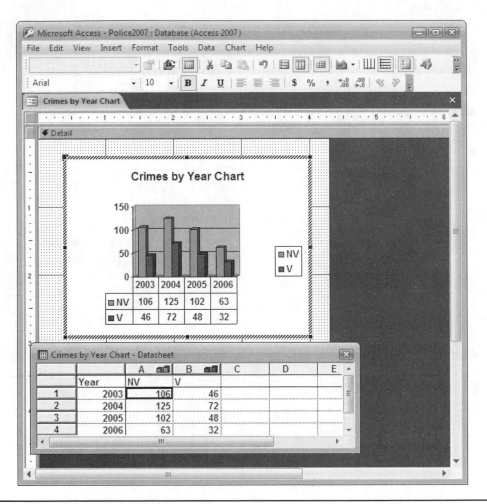

FIGURE 15-11 A typical Microsoft Graph window

The first combo box on the Standard toolbar is used to select a chart object. The By Row and By Column buttons change the display of the series. Click Chart Type to change to a different type of chart. The Gridlines buttons display or hide the horizontal or vertical gridlines.

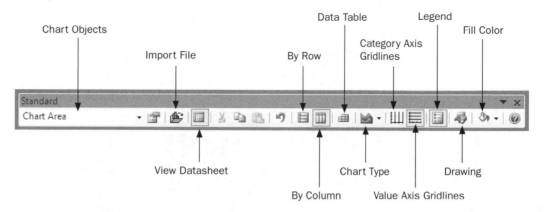

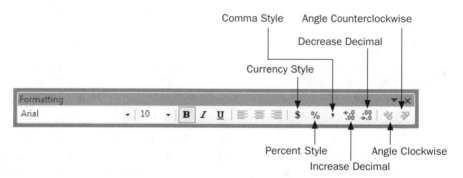

The *Graph Formatting* toolbar has many of the common font name, size, weight, and alignment buttons, in addition to a few that are unique to Microsoft Graph. All these formatting activities are available by selecting the chart element and choosing Format | Selected *chart element* (*chart element* is replaced by whatever object you selected).

The Increase Decimal button adds one decimal place to the right of the decimal point. The Decrease Decimal removes the right-most point. The three Style buttons add a currency symbol, a percent sign, or a comma thousands separator to numeric values.

Changing the Chart Appearance

To change the size of the chart, select the chart border and drag the sizing handles until it reaches the size you want.

NOTE *You may find that some changes in the chart appearance depend on the relative sizing of the chart and the frame in the form or report. You may have to experiment to reach the desired appearance.*

Formatting Text Elements   You have the same options when formatting most of the text elements in the chart. Select the element and choose the Format | Selected *chart element* to open the Format dialog box. You can also press CTRL-1 to open the Format dialog box for the selected element. The Format Chart Title dialog box has three tabs: Patterns, Font, and Alignment.

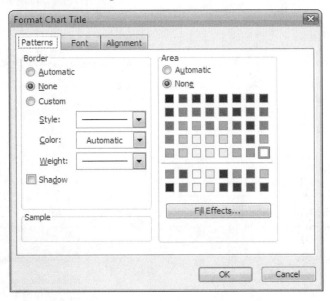

NOTE *Select Fill Effects in the Format dialog box to open another dialog box, where you can choose gradients, fill textures, or patterns, and even select a picture to use as a background.*

The Font tab contains the standard font name, size, weight, colors, and effects, such as underline, strikethrough, superscript, and subscript. When you select the chart title or one of the axis titles and choose the Format | Selected *chart element*, the Alignment tab appears, where you can choose the text alignment, plus the orientation. You can have the text displayed vertically or at a specific angle by clicking the arc in the Orientation area.

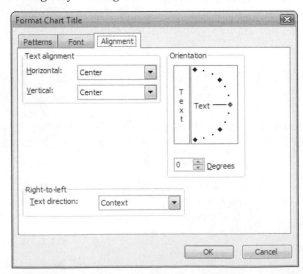

If you select the legend and choose Format | Selected Legend, the Alignment tab is replaced by the Placement tab, in which you can choose to display the legend at the bottom, corner, top, right, or left of the plot area.

Formatting Other Chart Elements   When you select one of the axes and choose Format | Selected, the Format Axis dialog box shows five tabs: Patterns, Scale, Font, Number, and Alignment. The Patterns, Font, and Alignment tabs are the same as for text elements. The other tabs offer the following options:

- The options in the Scale tab depend on which axis you select. If you select the Value (Y) axis, you can choose to set the minimum and maximum values manually for the axis, as well as the major and minor units for the gridlines and tick marks. The alternative is to let Microsoft Graph set these values automatically. You can also specify where the Category (X) axis is to cross the Value axis and whether to arrange the values in reverse order.

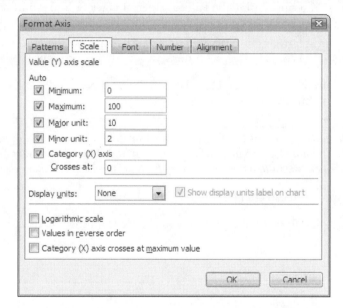

- The Number tab gives you a selection of number categories and specific formats for the values on the Value (Y) axis. Also, a check box links the values to the source data. Clear this to create a snapshot chart that doesn't update with changes in the underlying data.

- When you select the Category (X) axis, the formatting options are slightly different. The Scale tab contains options that relate to data categories instead of values.

When you format the data series by clicking one of the columns, bars, or another representation of the data, the Format dialog box contains four or five tabs, depending on the type of data series. For example, the column and line series Format dialog box shows five tabs: Patterns, Axis, Y Error Bars, Data Labels, and Options. The 3-D column Format dialog box shows four tabs: Patterns, Shape, Data, and Options. The pie series Format dialog box also shows four tabs: Patterns, Axis, Data Labels, and Options.

The Patterns tab offers the same color, border, and fill options as before. The other tabs offer the following options:

- The Axis tab specifies whether to plot the series on the primary or secondary axis. The secondary series is plotted against values placed in a Value axis on the right side of the plot area. A sample chart illustrates the choice.

- The Y Error Bars tab gives you the option of displaying the statistical error estimation or the standard deviation in the values either as values or percentages. You can choose to display plus errors, minus errors, or both. This option is handy for presenting the results of statistical survey for which you need to express the level of confidence.

- In the Data Labels tab, you can choose to display the data values and labels with the data series. You can display the values as percentages or in the unit of the value itself.

- In the Options tab for a column data series, you can choose to have the series overlap and set the amount of overlap, as well as specify the amount of space between the sets of data series. Options vary with the different types of data series.

The Shape tab in the 3-D column chart Format dialog box includes other 3-D figures such as pyramids, cylinders, and cones.

TIP *You can add graphics, such as lines, arrows, and shapes, to the chart in Microsoft Graph by displaying the Drawing toolbar and clicking the appropriate button. You may need to use the Format | Placement menu to move the shape in front or in back of the chart elements.*

Changing Chart Type   You can change the chart type in two ways:

- Click the Chart Type toolbar button and choose from the palette containing 18 chart types.

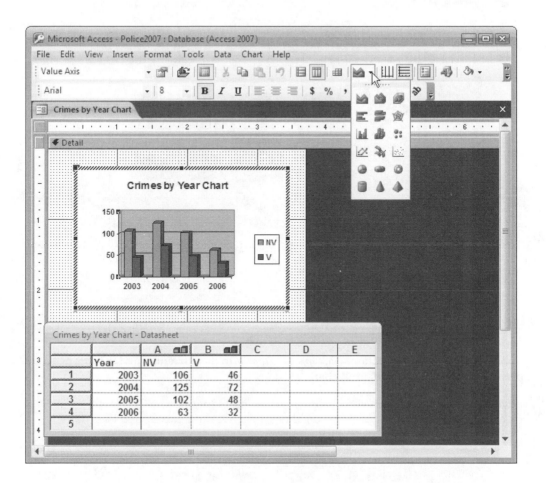

- Choose Chart | Chart Type and choose from the Chart Type dialog box. The Standard Types include 14 types with many subtypes for each. In the Standard Types tab, press and hold the button below the Chart subtype pane to see a sample of the selected chart. The Custom Types tab shows an additional 20 chart types from the built-in list of charts and, if you created any custom chart types, they're displayed when you choose Select from User-Defined.

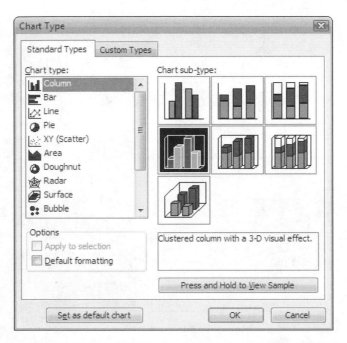

After making your selection, click OK to apply it to the current chart. You can also specify a chart type as the default chart.

Setting Chart Options   When you choose Chart | Chart Options, the Chart Options dialog box opens with six tabs: Titles, Axes, Gridlines, Legend, Data Labels, and Data Table.

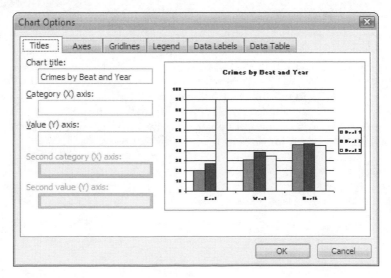

The tabs offer the following options:

- **Titles**   Enter the text you want to display as the chart title and the axes titles. You can specify a primary and secondary title for each axis, but only one for the chart itself. If the chart is 3-D, you can provide only primary titles.

- **Axes**   Specify whether to display the axes and choose the method by which to display the Category (*X*) axis.

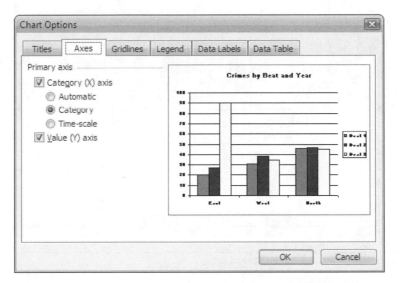

- **Gridlines**   Specify whether to display the gridlines on one or both of the axes. You can choose to display both major and minor gridlines on each axis.

- **Legend**   Choose whether to display the legend with the chart. The tab also gives you the same options as the Placement tab of the Format dialog box for placing the legend: Bottom, Corner, Top, Right, or Left.

- **Data Labels**   Choose from the same options as the Data Labels tab in the Format Data Series dialog box.

- **Data Table**   Choose whether to display the data in the underlying data source in a grid attached to the bottom of the chart. When you choose to display the data table, you can also display the legend keys with it. Figure 15-12 shows the Total by Year chart with the corresponding data table. If you choose not to display the legend keys, then the colored squares at the left of the data table row headings don't appear. The Data Table option isn't available for several of the chart types, such as pie, XY scatter, and surface.

NOTE   *If you need a statistical analysis of the data over time, you can add a trendline. The Add Trendline option in the Chart menu draws a line in the chart, which can be used in regression analysis of a large sample of recorded data. Once a trend is established, the line can be extended to predict future performance. Trendlines are also used to create a moving average, which smoothes out fluctuations in data and shows the pattern or trend more clearly.*

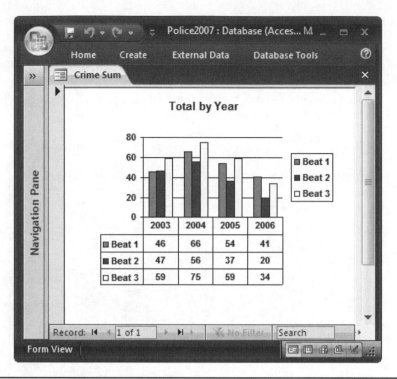

Figure 15-12   Adding the data table to the chart

Troubleshooting Charts

Sometimes the changes you make in Microsoft Graph fail to show up in the chart when you switch to Form view or Print Preview in Access, even though they appeared in Design view. For example, you can change the column headings in the Microsoft Graph datasheet to display the text you want to appear in the legend. When you return to Access, the new labels appear in the design, but not in Form view or Print Preview.

The reason for this seeming inconsistency is that you have several places in which to specify the chart information, and Access must set an order of precedence to decide which values to use. The order is as follows:

1. The data in the underlying table or query—for example, the field names or the expressions in the Field row of the query grid.

2. The contents of the Row Source property.

3. The data entered in Microsoft Graph.

So, if you set the legend text in Microsoft Graph, but the underlying query column headings are different, they override the Microsoft Graph settings.

If the columns don't appear in the order you want in the chart, open the Query Builder and rearrange the fields, left to right, in the order that you want them sorted. Then choose the Sort order for each.

Summary

This chapter concludes the discussion of customized output from Access and brings to a close the part of the book devoted to retrieving and presenting information. Trying to anticipate what every reader needs in the area of information storage and retrieval is impossible, but this chapter attempts to provide a wide view of the capabilities within Access. The many Help topics can expand on the information presented in the last nine chapters.

The next chapter begins the discussion of improving the Access work place. The topics covered include changing the workplace options, setting startup options, and adding commands to the startup sequence. Later, in the next part of the book, you will learn about creating and using macros to automate the database application even further.

PART

Improving the Workplace

Customizing the Workplace

This chapter covers all the workplace customization options in one place for easy reference. Using the many Access and Windows options, you can change the default appearance and behavior of a database application, keyboard action, hyperlink, search and filter routines, editing, and form and report design windows, among many other aspects of your workplace. Many of the features discussed in this chapter were mentioned in previous chapters, and some are covered later.

In addition to the changes you can make that affect the current Access database, you can change many startup options, such as displaying a startup form, opening a specific database, and changing language settings.

Personalizing the Workplace

You can customize the layout and behavior of the Access environment in a personal way that works best for you. The Access developers attempted to design a workplace that would be appropriate for most users, but changing some aspects is easy to do. For example, if you have a large monitor, you might want to use a larger font size. You can, of course, change each of these factors every time you work with Access, but changing the default settings saves time.

Working with Objects in the Navigation Pane

You can choose a specific sort order for the list of Access objects in the Navigation Pane. You can also change the appearance of the object names. If you don't want an object type to appear in the list, you can choose to hide that group. To set these options, right-click any of the group title bars and choose an option from the shortcut menu.

Sorting Objects

In the shortcut menu, point to Sort By to see the Sort options:

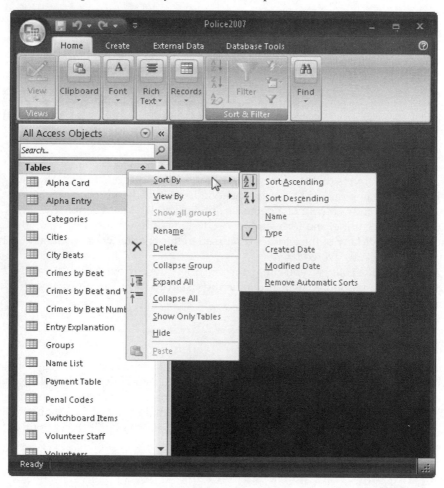

- Choose Sort Ascending (the default) or Sort Descending.
- Choose the means of sorting: Type is the default, but you can choose to sort by Name, Created Date (date it was created), or Modified Date (the date it was last modified).
- The final choice, Remove Automatic Sorts, removes the automatic sorts you can move the object names in the order that you want. This clears the check marks from the other choices. To return to automatic sort, choose one of the other sort options.

Changing Object Appearance

You can include detailed information about objects with the names in the Navigation Pane or add a larger object icon. To see the options in the shortcut menu, after right-clicking a group title bar, point to View By and choose from the list:

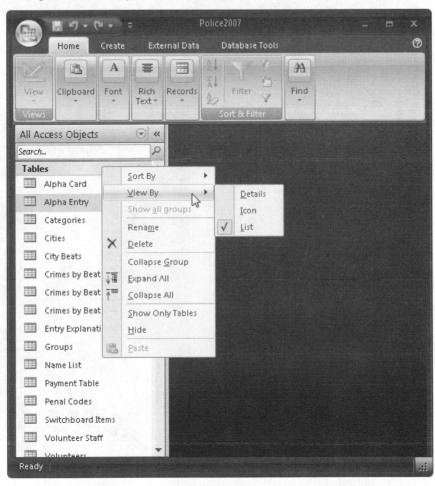

- The Details option shows the date of creation, date of the latest modification, and the object type name. Tables and queries are called *datasheets* while the others are called *forms, reports, macros,* and *modules.*

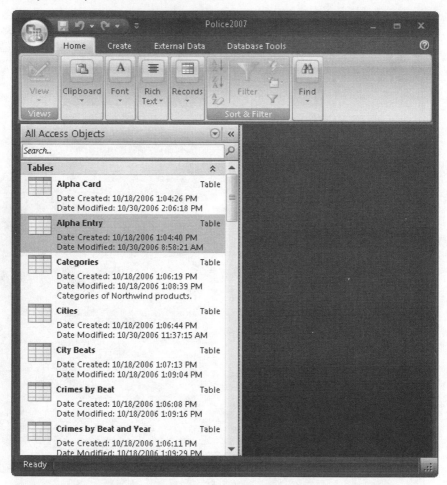

- The Icon option adds a larger object type icon to the names in the lists.
- The List option, the default, displays the names as a list with smaller icons.

Other Navigation Pane Options
Several more options are available in the object header shortcut menu.

- Expand Group applies to the selected group and shows all objects in that group. This produces the same result as clicking the down arrow in the group header. It toggles to Collapse Group if the group is already expanded.
- Expand All opens the lists of all object groups.

- Collapse All leaves only the group headers with no object lists.

- Show Only Tables leaves the object list in the selected group but closes all other object lists, leaving only the group headers.

- Hide removes all the objects of that type along with the group header. To restore the objects, right-click the Navigation Pane title bar and choose Navigation Options. In the Navigation Options dialog box, check the object group that you have hidden and click OK.

Using the Ribbon

As you have probably noticed while working with Access 2007, the ribbon changes content depending on the current activity. The ribbon also changes configuration based on the size of the current window. With the window maximized, the ribbon appears with two rows of commands with all of their labels. With the window resized and narrowed, the ribbon can change to three rows of commands that can lose many of their labels.

When the window is very narrow, the ribbon removes the right-most commands and adds a right arrow that you can click to scroll through the ribbon. If the window is even more narrow, for example to show only the Navigation Pane, the ribbon is removed from view.

If you want more room to work on your database, you can hide the ribbon by pressing CTRL-F1. To restore the ribbon, press CTRL-F1 again.

Creating a Shortcut

If you use an Access object regularly, you can create a shortcut that launches Access and opens the database object directly from the Windows desktop. The easiest way is to drag the object from the Navigation Pane to the Windows desktop. You must first resize the Access window so that you can see the area where you want to place the shortcut icon. When you double-click the shortcut, Access opens the database that stores the object and displays the object.

NOTE *To delete a shortcut, click it and press* DEL. *This doesn't delete the object itself, only the shortcut.*

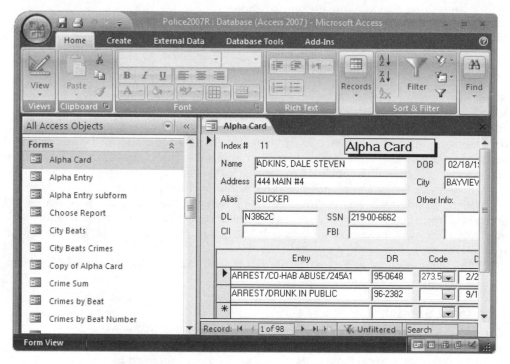

Shortcut to Alpha Card in Police2007R.a ccdb

NOTE *If you moved the database that's the destination of a shortcut, remove the shortcut and create a new one with the new path.*

Setting Access Options

Access is installed with certain characteristics set as defaults. For example, the width of the print margins, the default database folder, the color of hyperlinks, the gridlines, and the font styles in a datasheet are all set by default. If you change specific default values often when you work with a database, you can reset the default value to the one that you use the most. All default values can be overridden later, if necessary. To make changes in the default settings, click the Microsoft Office button and choose Access Options.

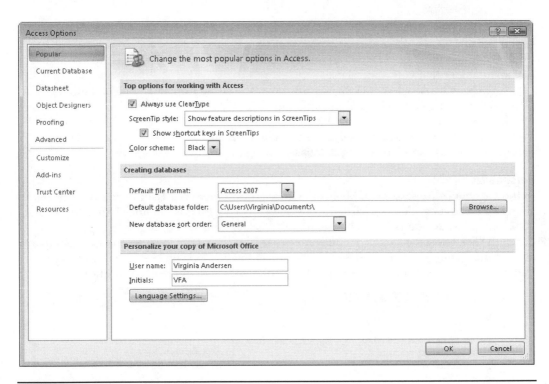

FIGURE 16-1   The Access Options dialog box

In the left pane of the Access Options dialog box are 10 categories of options that you can change (see Figure 16-1). Many of the options relate to settings for all Microsoft Office programs, not just Access.

NOTE   *If you want to see an explanation of the options, click the* Help *button (?) in the upper-right corner of the dialog box. The Help window opens with descriptions of all of the options in the current dialog box.*

Setting Popular Options

These options relate to the basic characteristics applied when you start Access.

Setting Top Options

You can set up the ScreenTip Style to show ScreenTip descriptions (the default) or not. Clear the Show Shortcut Keys In ScreenTips check box if you don't want to see ScreenTips when you rest the mouse pointer on a command. In the Color Scheme setting, choose between Blue, Silver, and Black.

Creating Database Options

In the Default File Format option, you can choose between Access 2007, 2002–2003, or 2000. Enter the folder pathname in the Default Database Folder text field or click Browse and locate the folder that you want to use.

In the New Database Sort Order setting, you can choose from a list of 33 language settings that change the default alphabetic sort order for new databases. The General setting applies to English, French, German, Italian, Portuguese, and modern Spanish. To change the sort order for an existing database, select the language, and then compact the database.

You must close and reopen the database for these options to take effect.

Personalize Office

In the Personalize Your Copy of Microsoft Office group, enter your User Name and Initials. To change the Language Settings, click the button to open the Microsoft Office Language Settings 2007 dialog box, where you can choose from the list of Available Editing Languages. Scroll down the list, select the language you want to use, and click Add. You can choose more than one language, but when you choose one other than English, you will see a warning message that the language has limited support in Microsoft Office and will require additional support.

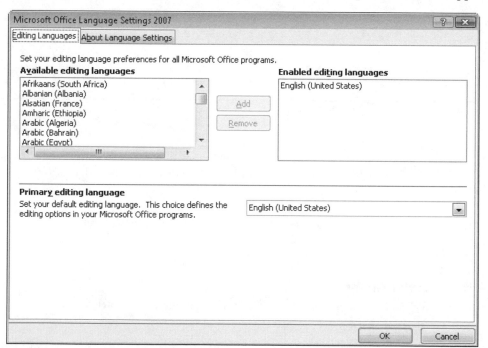

Setting Options for the Current Database

A wide range of options are available for the current database, including application, navigation, toolbar, name autocorrect, and filter lookup limitation options (see Figure 16-2). All of these options are applied only to the current database. For most of these options to take effect, you need to close and reopen the database. To use the same settings for another database, you must open the other database and choose the settings.

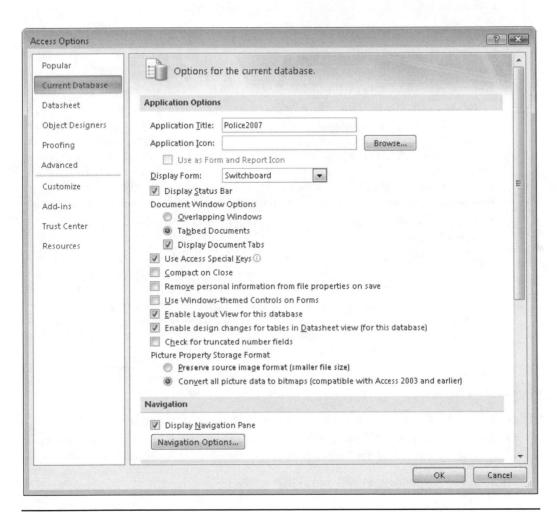

FIGURE 16-2   Setting options for the current database

Application Options

Most of the changes in the Application Options group take effect the next time you open the database. Only the Application Title and Application Icon options take effect as soon as you close the dialog box.

- **Application Title**   To display a custom title in the Windows title bar, enter the text that you want to display.

- **Application Icon**   To add a custom icon to the title bar in place of the default Access icon in the Windows title bar, type the name of the bitmap (.bmp) or icon (.ico) file. If you don't know the name of the file that you want to use, click the Browse button next to the box and use the Icon Browser to locate the file.

TIP *If you're creating an application to be distributed to multiple users, you should place the icon file in the same folder as the host application.*

- **Use as Form and Report Icon**   Check this to place the application icon in the tabs above the form and report documents.

- **Display Form**   Many applications display a special form when opening—either as a welcoming screen or as a switchboard with a list of choices of actions to take next, such as enter/edit data or preview a report. After you create the special form and save it in the current database, you can use it as the startup form. To choose a form for display at startup, click the drop-down arrow in the Display Form box and choose the form from the list of forms in the current database. The default is None.

- **Display Status Bar**   Clear this option to prevent displaying the status bar at the bottom of the window.

- **Document Window Options**   These options are new to Access 2007. They allow you to change the structure of the document pane. Overlapping Windows allows you to open and view more than one Access object at a time. If you hide the Navigation Pane and use this option, it looks like earlier versions of Access. The Tabbed Documents option is the default in this set, which applies the single-document interface to display only one object at a time. The Display Document Tabs check box shows and hides the tabs that appear above the documents. The default setting is to display them.

If you choose to show overlapping windows with no tabs, a new group of commands appears on a Home tab. The Windows group includes two commands:

- **Size to Fit Form**   Reduces the window to fit the currently displayed form.
- **Switch Windows**   Offers a list of the currently open objects from which you can choose. You also have the option of tiling or cascading the objects in the window.

The next seven options are check boxes that set the following actions:

- **Use Access Special Keys**   When selected, you can use the special key combinations that display the Navigation Pane or Immediate window, open the Module window, or interrupt a server. The Immediate and Module windows are used when working with Visual Basic for Applications (VBA) code. The special keys are as follows:
- F11   Shows or hides the Navigation Pane.
- CTRL-G   Displays the Immediate window in the Visual Basic Editor.
- ALT-F11   Starts the Visual Basic Editor.

- CTRL-BREAK   In a project, stops Access from retrieving records from the server.

- **Compact on Close**   Automatically compacts and repairs the database when you close it, if the size will be reduced by at least 256K.

- **Remove Personal Information from File Properties on Save**   Automatically deletes your name, the name of your company, and any other personal information you entered in the Database Properties dialog box.

- **Use Windows-Themed Controls on Forms**   Applies the Windows theme to the controls on forms and reports in place of the standard theme.

- **Enable Layout View for This Database**   Shows or hides the Layout View option in the status bar and in the shortcut menus that appear when you right-click the object tab. If you have set the Allow Layout View property to No, this check box might not be available.

- **Enable Design Changes for Tables in Datasheet View (For This Database)**   Permits changes in the table design while in Datasheet view.

- **Check for Truncated Number Fields**   When set, if the control is not wide enough to show the number value, ##### appears in the control. If not set, you will only see part of the number. The default is unchecked, but it is a good idea to check this option when designing new forms and reports.

In the Picture Property Storage Format section, you can choose these options:

- **Preserve Source Image Format**   Stores images in their original format. This option reduces the size of the database.

- **Convert All Picture Data to Bitmaps**   This default setting creates a copy of the original image file in Windows Bitmap or Device Independent Bitmap format. With this option, you can view images in databases from Access 2003 and earlier.

Navigation Options

The Display Navigation Pane option shows (when checked) or hides the Navigation Pane. You can also press F11 to show or hide the pane. The other option is the Navigation Options button that you can use to create custom categories for listing the objects in the Navigation Pane. See Chapter 20 for more information about customizing grouping in the Navigation Pane.

PART III

Ribbon and Toolbar Options

Scroll down the Current Database window to see more options:

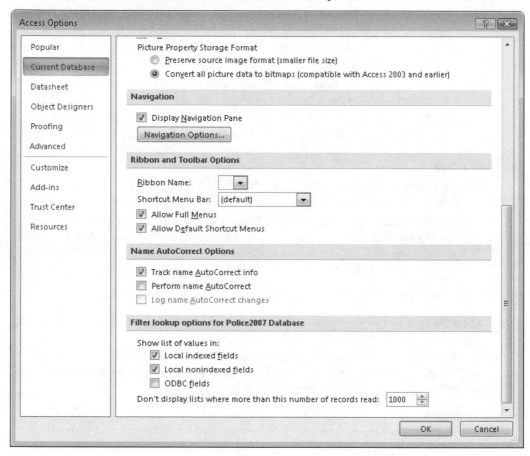

For these options to take effect, you need to close and reopen the database:

- **Ribbon Name**   Select the name of the custom ribbon from the drop-down list. If you have not created a custom ribbon, the list is empty.
- **Shortcut Menu Bar**   Choose from the list of custom shortcut menus in the database or leave it set to default.
- **Allow Full Menus**   Expands the menu list to include all commands. If you clear this option, Access hides certain menus that give the user the power to open an object in Design view and make changes.
- **Allow Default Shortcut Menus**   Leave this option checked to allow access to the built-in shortcut menus that appear when you right-click an object, a toolbar, or a menu bar. Clear the option to disable all shortcut menus.

Name AutoCorrect Options

The Name AutoCorrect options help Access propagate name changes to objects that refer to the renamed object. The group offers three options that help fix common side-effects that occur when you make changes in an object via a user interface. Access stores the identifier for each object and tracks naming information. When Access notices an object has been changed since the last Name AutoCorrect action, it runs it again for all items in that object. For example, if you added a text box to a form that is bound to the Alpha Card table and you change the Alpha Card table name to Alpha Card Plus, Access can track down all of the items from the original Alpha Card and change their names to match the new table name.

The three options you can check for Name AutoCorrect are as follows:

- **Track Name AutoCorrect Info** Stores information it needs to correct naming errors but doesn't immediately correct them. You can also look at object dependencies, so that you're aware of potential renaming problems. Keeping this option checked is a good idea.

- **Perform Name AutoCorrect** Tries to update references to objects that you renamed. This doesn't cover references in macros and Visual Basic modules.

- **Log Name AutoCorrect Changes** Creates a log named AutoCorrect Log that contains the changes it makes to the database each time it runs Name AutoCorrect. This option becomes available when you check the second option.

Filter Lookup Options

The Filter Lookup options group limits or extends the size of the value list displayed in the Filter By Form window and sets the maximum number of records to read in order to build a value list for a given field. The more fields you include in the filter operation, the longer it takes to filter the data. This group also specifies whether to display values for indexed or nonindexed fields and for a linked table in an external file. These settings apply only to the current database.

- **Local Indexed Fields** Limits the value list to the indexed fields in the current database.

- **Local Nonindexed Fields** Includes the fields in the current database that are not indexed.

- **ODBC Fields** Includes fields in a linked table in an external source.

- **Don't Display Lists Where More Than This Number of Records Read** Enter the maximum number of records you want to read to build the list of unique values for the field. If the number of records exceeds this amount, no values at all are displayed for the field in the Filter By Form window. You see only Is Null or Is Not Null. The default is 1000.

Setting Datasheet Options

The Datasheet category of options (see Figure 16-3) includes default value settings.

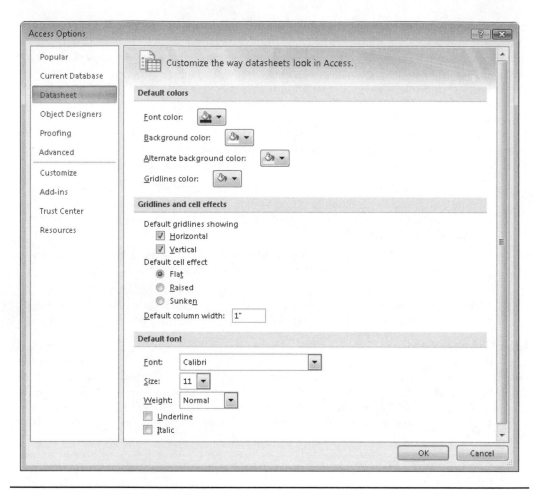

FIGURE 16-3 Setting options for datasheets

Default Colors
Default Colors settings enable you to specify the default font, background, alternate background, and gridline colors for the datasheet. When you click the drop-down arrow next to one of the options, the color palette appears, where you can choose the desired colors.

Gridlines and Cell Effects

- **Default Gridlines Showing** Determines whether to show or hide the horizontal and vertical gridlines in the datasheet.

- **Default Cell Effect** Normally set to Flat, but you can change this to Raised or Sunken to create a special effect in the datasheet.

- **Default Column Width** Specifies the width of the columns in a new datasheet. You can change the width easily in the datasheet by dragging the column dividers. Type a new default width in the box. The default width uses the system unit of measure. The default setting is 1 inch.

Default Font

Default Font settings enable you to select the font name from a list of fonts installed on your system. You can also choose from nine font weights ranging from Thin to Heavy; the default setting is Normal.

- **Size** Choose the font size from the drop-down list that contains font sizes ranging from 8 to 72 points, or enter a number in the box.
- **Italic and Underline** Sets that style as the default.

Object Designers Options

The groups of options in this set (see Figure 16-4) specify many default settings for creating Access objects. One group offers several methods of checking for many types of data entry and keyboard errors.

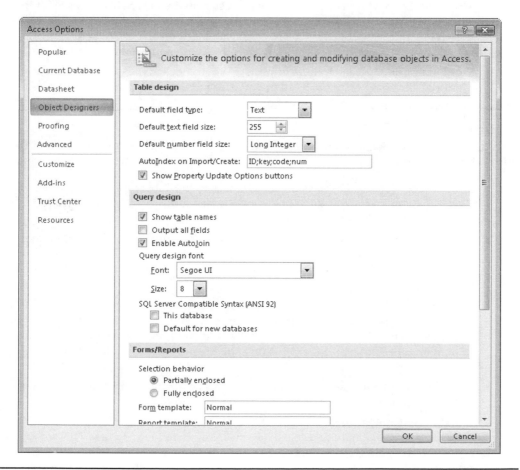

FIGURE 16-4   Setting options for object designers

Table Design

The Table Design group includes default field size and type choices, as well as prefixes to use for automatically indexing fields.

- **Default Field Type**   Usually set to Text, but you can select any of the nine field types as the default, including Object Linking and Embedding (OLE) Object, Hyperlink, or Memo.

- **Default Text Field Size**   Includes the default size for text data type fields. You can enter any number in the text box, but 255 is the maximum as well as the default.

- **Default Number Field Size**   Includes a drop-down list from which to choose the default. The number choices are Byte, Integer, Long Integer, Single, Double, Decimal, and Replication ID. The default is Long Integer.

- **AutoIndex on Import/Create**   Used when you import a table from an external source or create a new table in Design view. This setting tells Access to index on all fields automatically that begin or end with the characters that you type in the box. Multiple entries are separated by semicolons. For example, the entries in the AutoIndex box shown in Figure 16-4 instruct Access to create an index on all fields whose names begin or end with the characters ID, key, code, or num. These are also the default choices.

- **Show Property Update Options Buttons**   When checked, this gives you the option of propagating property changes that you made in a table or query to controls bound to that field. Checked by default.

Query Design

In the Query Design options group, you can choose to remove the table names from the design grid and show all the field values in the recordset. You can also change the font type and size.

- **Show Table Names**   Displays the table names in the Table row of the query grid. This helps you keep track of the field source when multiple tables are used in a query. The default setting is checked.

- **Output All Fields**   Displays all the fields in a query's underlying tables and queries when you run the query. The fields are not added to the query grid, only to the result-ing datasheet. When you check this option, only new queries are affected. Unchecked by default.

- **Enable AutoJoin**   Automatically creates an inner join between two tables in the query grid. If you want to define the relationships yourself, clear the check box. For two tables to be autojoined, they must have fields with the same name and of the same data type, and one of the fields must be the primary key field for that table. Checked by default.

- **Query Design Font**   Sets the default font and size for the query results. The default setting is Segoe UI size 8.

- **SQL Server Compatible Syntax (ANSI 92)**   Tells Access to format queries for the current or all new databases exclusively in ANSI 92 standard syntax. This setting ensures Structured Query Language (SQL) Server compatibility. Default is unchecked for both.

Forms/Reports

The settings in the Forms/Reports group in the Object Designers window all relate to working on a form or report in Design view.

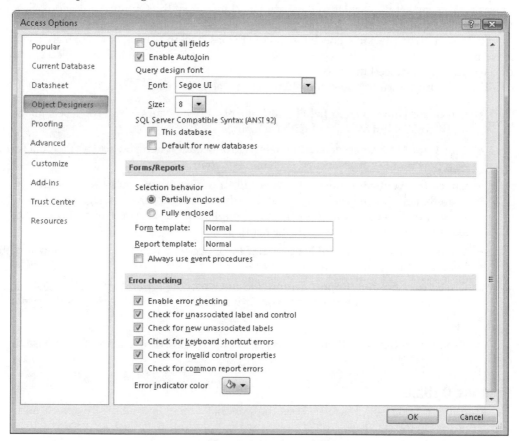

- **Selection Behavior**   Relates to the results of drawing a rectangle in the design to select controls. Partially Enclosed, the default, selects all controls with any part within the drawn rectangle, while Fully Enclosed selects only those controls totally within the drawn rectangle.

- **Form Template and Report Template**   Enable you to specify an existing form or report as the template for new designs. Type the name of the form or report you want to use as the default template. The default is Normal for both.

- **Always Use Event Procedures**   When selected, takes you directly to the VB Editor window when you click the Build button in a property sheet, bypassing the Choose Builder dialog box. With the check box cleared, the default, the Choose Builder dialog box appears, offering the choice of Expression Builder, Macro Builder, or Code Builder.

Error Checking

Automatic error checking identifies errors in form and report designs and offers suggestions for correcting them. You can choose to apply automatic error checking to five general types of errors. You can set these rules in the Error Checking tab of the Options dialog box. See Chapter 10 for examples of how error checking can help with form and report design.

To request error checking, check the Enable Error-Checking check box. Then choose a color for the error indicator button, the small triangle that appears in the upper-left corner of the control that caused the error.

The categories of rules you can specify include the following:

- **Check for Unassociated Label and Control**   Error occurs when you select a label and a control not associated with each other.
- **Check for New Unassociated Labels**   Error occurs when you add a label to a form or report that is not associated with another control.
- **Check for Keyboard Shortcut Errors**   Error occurs when you select a control on a form that shows an invalid shortcut key (the underlined character you can use with ALT to move focus to the control)—for example, an unassociated label, a duplicate shortcut key, or a space used as the shortcut key.
- **Check for Invalid Control Properties**   Error occurs when you select a control with invalid values in one or more properties.
- **Check for Common Report Errors**   Occurs when the report has an invalid sorting and grouping definition. Can also occur when the report width exceeds the paper width.

You can also set the default error indicator color. Click the down arrow and choose the color from the palette.

Proofing Options

The Proofing options (see Figure 16-5) set the way that Access automatically detects and corrects errors in the database. You can also use these options to choose a custom dictionary that includes special words and terms related to your workplace.

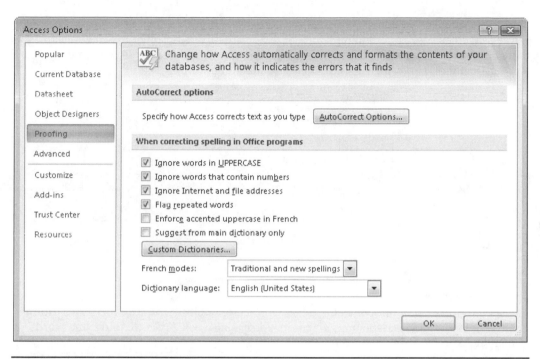

FIGURE 16-5   Choosing options for document proofing

AutoCorrect Options

You can choose the method Access uses to correct typos and commonly misspelled words as you enter the data. Click the AutoCorrect Options button to see the choices.

In the AutoCorrect dialog box, you can choose to apply AutoCorrect to certain types of errors as well as specify certain replacement text or characters for other misspellings. If there are some combinations of text or abbreviations that would normally be caught by the AutoCorrect tool, you can click Exceptions and make some changes.

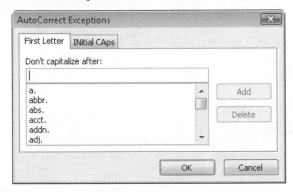

Spelling Corrections

The spelling correction options in the When Correcting Spelling in Office Programs group offer choices of which misspellings to ignore. You can also ask Access to underline words that are repeated in case they shouldn't be.

Since French is a commonly used language, you can choose to Enforce Accented Uppercase in French. If you are not using any special terms or unusual words, you can choose the option Suggest From Main Dictionary Only.

You can also choose to use a custom dictionary rather than the default main dictionary. A custom dictionary can contain proper names, technical terms, or acronyms that are used in the application but don't appear in the main dictionary. You can build a custom dictionary, click the Custom Dictionaries button and choose from the list in the dialog box.

The next option in this group is the French Modes, which has three choices:

- Traditional and New Spellings, the default
- Traditional Spellings
- New Spelling

The drop-down list in the final option, Dictionary Language, offers a variety of country-related English, French, and Spanish dialects.

Advanced Options

The Advanced set of options (see Figure 16-6) includes editing, display, printing, and some general and advanced settings.

Editing

The large group of Editing options includes settings for keyboard behavior and the edit and find options. Some international options specify the direction and alignment of text as well as cursor movement.

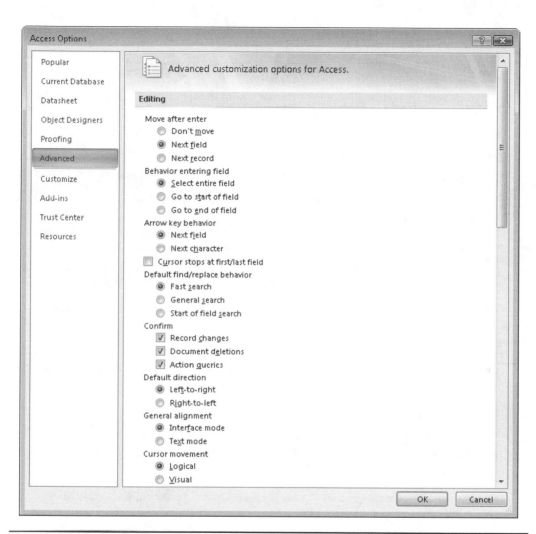

FIGURE 16-6   Choosing advanced options

The first set of options determines the consequences of pressing certain keys such as ENTER, TAB, RIGHT ARROW, and LEFT ARROW.

The Move After Enter options refer to the behavior of the insertion point (cursor) after pressing ENTER:

- **Don't Move**   Keeps the insertion point in the current field.
- **Next Field**   Moves the insertion point to the next field. This setting works with the Behavior Entering Field settings to complete the behavior.
- **Next Record**   Moves the insertion point to the next record in the table or form.

The Behavior Entering Field group determines what happens when the insertion point enters a field:

- **Select Entire Field**   Selects all the characters in the field.
- **Go to Start of Field**   Places the insertion point in front of the first character in the field without selecting any characters.
- **Go to End of Field**   Places the insertion point at the end of the field after the last character without selecting any characters.

The Arrow Key Behavior settings specify what occurs when you press RIGHT ARROW and LEFT ARROW.

- **Next Field**   Moves the insertion point to the next or previous field when you press the RIGHT ARROW or LEFT ARROW keys, respectively. To move the insertion point within the field, press F2 to enter the Edit mode, and then use the arrow keys.
- **Next Character**   Moves the insertion point to the next or previous character in the current field when you press the RIGHT ARROW or LEFT ARROW keys, respectively.

The Cursor Stops At First/Last Field check box locks the insertion point within the current record and prevents the RIGHT ARROW and LEFT ARROW keys from moving the insertion point to the next or previous record.

The second set of editing options set find and replace features.

The Default Find/Replace Behavior settings determine the extent of the search. These options are also available on an immediate basis in the Find and Replace dialog box.

- **Fast Search**   Searches the current field only and matches the entire field.
- **General Search**   Searches all the fields and matches any part of the field.
- **Start of Field Search**   Searches the current field and matches only the beginning characters in the field.

The Confirm group requires that Access display a message asking for a confirmation of the current operation under specific conditions, such as when a record changes (Record Changes), when you delete a database object (Document Deletions), or when you run an action query (Action Queries).

The final set of Editing options deal with the direction and alignment of text and the movement of the cursor through the data.

The Default Direction group offers the choice between Left-to-Right and Right-to-Left.

- **Left-to-Right**   Starts entering data in the left-most column and places the next data in the column to the right, and so on.
- **Right-to-Left**   Places the first field in the right-most column and places the next in the column to the left, and so on. To apply this option, you must have Right-To-Left language enabled by Microsoft Office Language Settings.

In the General Alignment, you can choose between Interface mode and Text mode:

- **Interface Mode**   Sets the general alignment consistent with the user interface language. For example, if the direction is left-to-right, the text is aligned left.

- **Text Mode**   Sets the general alignment according to the direction of the first language-specific characters it encounters.

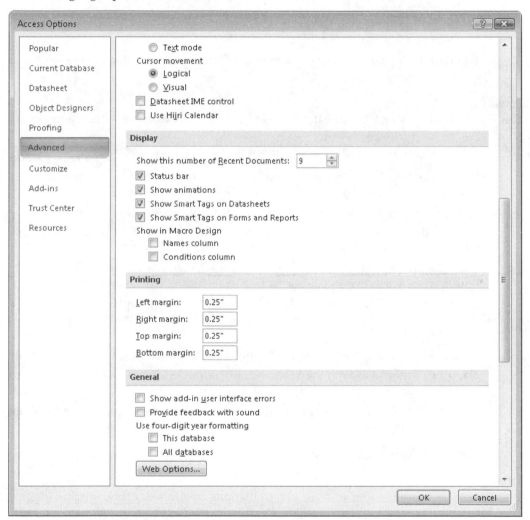

In the Cursor Movement group, you have several choices:

- **Logical**   Tells the cursor to move within bidirectional text, according to the direction of the language it's encountering. For example, if you use English and Arabic words in the same sentence, the insertion point moves left-to-right in the English text, and then starts at the right-most character of the Arabic word and continues to move in a right-to-left direction.

- **Visual**   Tells the cursor to move within bidirectional text by moving to the next adjacent character. For example, if you use English and Arabic text in the same sentence, the insertion point moves left-to-right through the English text, and then continues at the leftmost character of the Arabic word and continues in the left-to-right direction.

- **Datasheet Input Method Editor (IME) Control**   Sets the East Asian IME Mode to No Control when entering data in a table datasheet.

- **Use Hijri Calendar**   Changes to the Islamic lunar calendar instead of the Gregorian calendar.

Display

The Display options all relate to what you see at startup, while working in the Database window, or when creating a macro.

In the Display group, you can choose to show or hide the following items:

- **Show This Number of Recent Documents**   Sets the number of filenames that appear in the Open Recent Database pane on the Getting Started page.

- **Status Bar**   Displays the status bar at the bottom of the Access window.

- **Show Animations**   When checked, shows movement in the datasheet. For example, when you insert or delete a column, the other columns slide over.

- **Show Smart Tags on Datasheets**   When checked, displays the Smart Tag Action button when you move to a datasheet field that has a Smart Tag attached.

- **Show Smart Tags on Forms and Reports**   When checked, displays the Smart Tag Action button when you move to a form or report field that has a Smart Tag attached.

In the Show in Macro Design group, both options relate to creating and editing macros:

- **Names Column**   Displays the Macro Name column by default in the macro design grid where you can enter an optional macro name.

- **Conditions Column**   Displays the Condition column by default in the macro design grid where you can enter the conditions under which the macro action is to take place.

See Chapter 19 for more information about creating macros.

Printing

You can set the default margin sizes for all four margins. You can enter any number in the Print Margins group that's compatible with your printer and paper size, ranging from 0 to the height or width of the printed page. The default setting for all margins is .25 inch. Override the default settings established here by running Page Setup before printing a form or report.

General

The General group of options shows the following options:

- **Show Add-In Interface Errors**   Shows errors in your user interface customization code.

- **Provide Feedback with Sound**   Lets you activate sounds to accompany such tasks as a print job completion or an alert notification. You can customize sounds for this option through the Sounds dialog box in the Windows Control Panel.

CAUTION *The sound option affects all Office programs.*

- **Use Four-Digit Year Formatting**   These options apply the format to the current database or to all databases, even if the Format property of the field or control is set to show a two-digit year.

- **Web Options button**   Opens a dialog box in which you can specify the default appearance of new hyperlinks. You can choose the text colors for hyperlinks, one color before you have clicked it to jump to the target and a different color after you have jumped to it. You can also include underlining with the address.

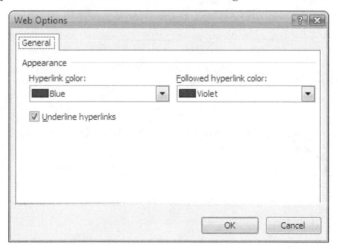

PART III

Advanced

The last group of settings in the Advanced page apply to the performance of the database and restricting time spent interfacing with outside sources.

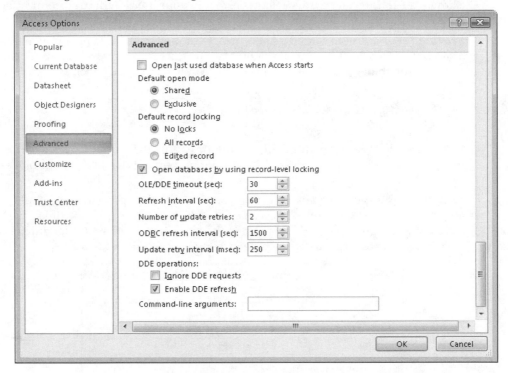

- **Open Last Used Database When Access Starts**   Opens the most recently used database instead of the Getting Started page.

- **Default Open Mode group**   Choose between Shared, which allows others to open the database at the same time you have it open, and Exclusive, which gives you sole access to the database. See Chapter 24 for more information about running Access in a shared environment.

- **Default Record Locking**   Set to No Locks, which doesn't lock records while they're being edited; All Records, which locks all the records in a form or datasheet (and the underlying tables) as long as the form or datasheet is open; or Edited Record, which locks only the record currently being edited.

- **Open Databases by Using Record-level Locking**   Makes record level locking the default for the open database. When you check this check box, only one row or record is locked at a time instead of locking an entire page that might include several records.

The next group of selections in the Advanced group deals with shared databases and interactions with external sources.

- **OLE/DDE Timeout (sec)**   Sets the period of time after which Access retires to perform an OLE or DDE operation that failed. Enter a number between 0 and 300 seconds. Default is 30 seconds.

- **Refresh Interval (sec)**   Relates to the Enable DDE Refresh option and specifies the time after which Access automatically updates records in a Datasheet or Form view. Enter a number between 1 and 32,766. Default 60. Set to 1 prevents updates.

- **Number of Update Retries**   Refers to the number of times Access tries to save a changed record locked by another user. Enter a number between 0 and 10. Default is 2.

- **ODBC Refresh Interval (sec)**   Set to a number between 1 and 32,766 to specify the interval after which Access automatically refreshes records that you're accessing through ODBC. This is used only if the database is shared on a network. The default is 1500 seconds.

- **Update Retry Interval (msec)**   Sets the time (in milliseconds) after which Access automatically tries to save a changed record locked by another user. Enter a number between 0 and 1000. The default is 250 milliseconds.

- **DDE Operations group**   Sets the behavior of the database when dealing with other applications. Ignore DDE Requests does just that—it ignores DDE requests from external sources. Enable DDE Refresh allows updating DDE links at an interval specified in the Refresh Interval setting. See Chapter 23 for more information about interacting with external applications.

- **Command-Line Arguments**   Enter the name of one or more values you want the Command function to return in this text box. The command-line arguments customize the way Access starts up. For example, open a database automatically, run a macro, supply a user account name or password, or open a database for exclusive access or as read-only.

Customizing the Toolbar

The Customize page (see Figure 16-7) is used to add buttons to the Quick Access toolbar that will perform specific actions. You can click one of the buttons from the File list and click Add to include it in the Quick Access toolbar.

To see the list of all the commands on all the ribbon tabs and groups, click the Choose Commands From down arrow. Figure 16-8 shows the list of available ribbon commands. You can choose the actions from the list at the left and click Add. If the toolbar is hard to see above the ribbon, you can choose to move the toolbar below the ribbon.

You can also drag a command from the ribbon to the Quick Access toolbar without using the Access Options. See Chapter 20 for examples of customizing the Quick Access toolbar.

Viewing and Managing Add-Ins

Add-ins are described as application extensions because they go beyond the built-in capabilities of the Access program. For example, customized templates, smart tags, and

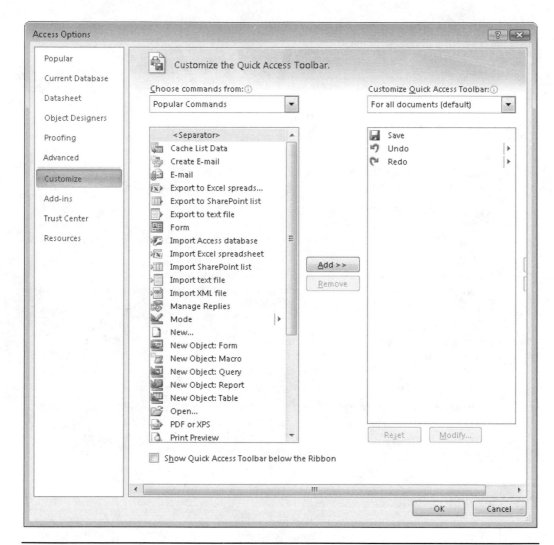

Figure 16-7 Adding actions to the Quick Access toolbar

XML Schemas are add-ins. The Add-ins page (see Figure 16-9) shows the name, location, and type of add-in in four groups.

- **Active Application Add-Ins**   Currently registered and running in Access. There are no currently active add-ins in this database.

- **Inactive Application Add-Ins**   Registered but not currently loaded.

- **Document Related Add-Ins**   Template files currently referenced by open documents.

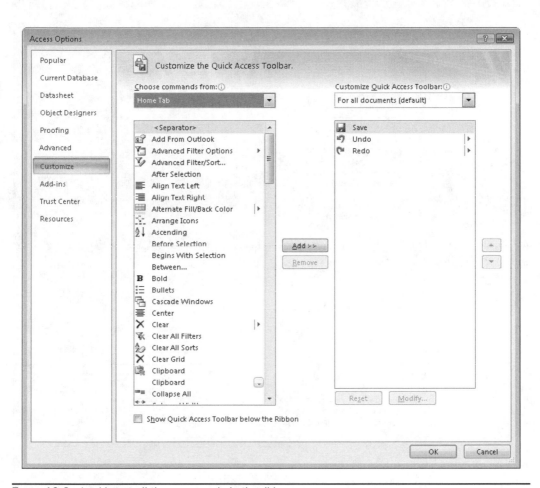

FIGURE 16-8 Looking at all the commands in the ribbons

- **Disabled Application Add-Ins** Automatically disabled because they caused programs to crash.

To choose more add-ins, click the Manage field down arrow and choose from the list of available add-ins. Then click Go and choose the options that you want.

Choosing Trust Center Options

The Microsoft Office Trust Center (see Figure 16-10) was designed to protect against hackers that can do harm with add-ins. Microsoft has designed specific criteria that add-ins must meet to be accepted. Click the hyperlinks to see more information about the criteria.

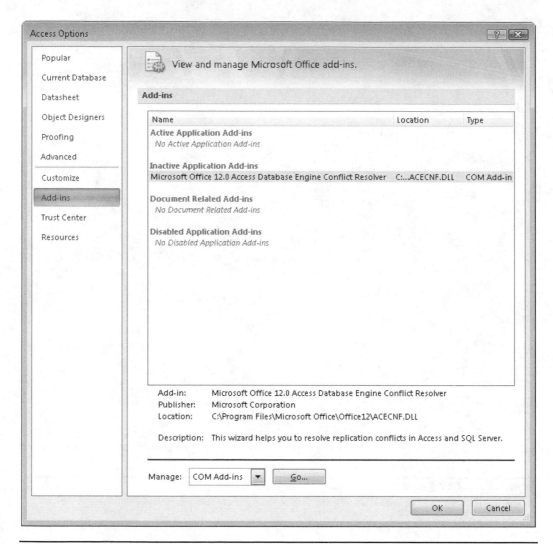

Figure 16-9   Viewing and managing add-ins

Click the Trust Center Settings button and click one of the options in the left pane to change any of the settings. The Message Bar is the security message that you will see when you open a database that includes macros, VBA code, or add-ins that are not certified. There is more about database security in Chapter 25.

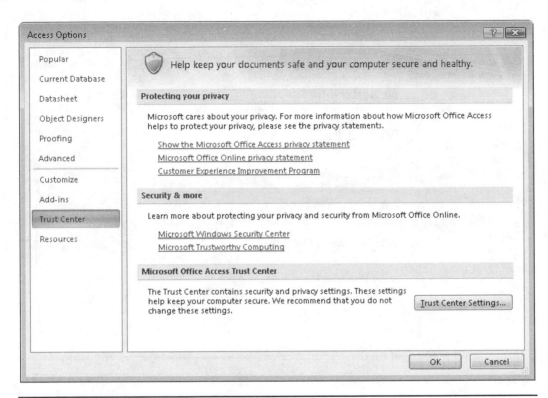

FIGURE 16-10   Finding security information

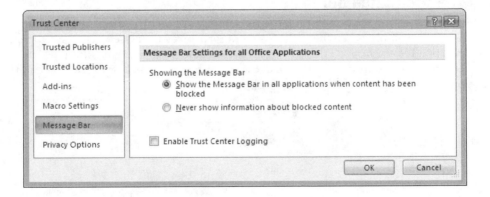

Searching Additional Resources

The Resources page in Access Options (see Figure 16-11) provides many ways for you to keep up to date with the latest improvements and get help with problems. You can use this page to activate Microsoft Office and register for online services.

FIGURE 16-11 Using additional resources

Customizing the Status Bar

The Access status bar at the bottom of the screen displays many indicators of current activities. For example, when the CAPS LOCK or NUM LOCK key is pressed, its name appears in the status bar. It also shows "Filtered" when the current object contains filtered data.

To change these settings, right-click in the status bar and check or uncheck the options that you want.

Improving Database Performance

In this hectic information age, we're always looking for ways to speed up operations and improve the accuracy and consistency of the results. Optimization is the ultimate goal, and stacking up performance improvements is a way to get close to that goal. Access helps you create efficient databases by offering many tools, including the Analyzer wizards, which examine the organization of your database and suggest ways that you can improve the distribution of information among the tables and speed overall database performance.

One of the most important goals of a database is to maintain accurate and complete information. A tool that was new in Access 2003 helps you to prevent errors by publishing the interdependencies among your database objects. So, for example, if you rename or delete an object, you can determine what else is affected by the change.

For security and reliability, Access tools let you back up and restore databases in case of emergency. Other tools compact the database to take up less disk space and repair damaged databases.

Optimizing a Database

Access provides two analytical tools that can save you a lot of time and help you optimize a new database. You can also help to optimize the performance of a database, without using the analyzers, by focusing on each of the elements that make up the database—for example, the user's access to the database, and the features of the database, including the filters and indexes, as well as the objects themselves.

Using the Analyzer Wizards

The *Table Analyzer Wizard* examines the distribution of data among the tables and presents suggestions and ideas for further improvements. The *Performance Analyzer* looks at any or all of the objects in the database and makes suggestions for improving their performance. The Performance Analyzer can also examine the relationships that you've established in the database and the set of all Visual Basic code modules in the database, including class and standard modules.

Both of these tools are available on the Database Tools tab's Analyze command group.

Table Analyzer

When you design a new database, you do the best that you can to reduce the redundancy of data by creating a set of related tables. If you notice that your database has a table showing repeated values in a field, you can use the Table Analyzer to help you split the table. The Table Analyzer can look at the data distribution, and perhaps, make suggestions for additional optimization, including adding more indexes and further normalization.

To start the Table Analyzer, on the Database Tools tab's Analyze group, click the Analyze Table command. The first two dialog boxes provide a good description of the process of table optimization by first describing the problem and then showing possible solutions to the problem. Each dialog box also offers a look at examples of the problems and the solutions. Figure 17-1 shows the first of the two introductory dialog boxes. Click one of the Show Me An Example buttons to get a picture of what the Table Analyzer can do.

The second Table Analyzer dialog box shows how it plans to solve the problem by splitting tables, so each piece of data is stored only once.

The third Table Analyzer dialog box shows a list of tables in the current database (see Figure 17-2). Select the table that contains repeated data and click Next. In the next dialog box, you can choose to let the wizard decide how to split the data or do it yourself. If you let the wizard decide, the next dialog box presents a diagram of the suggested redistribution of information.

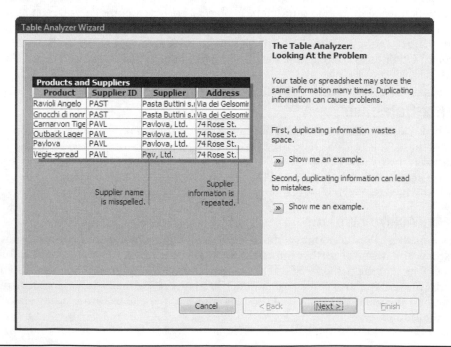

Figure 17-1 Starting the Table Analyzer Wizard

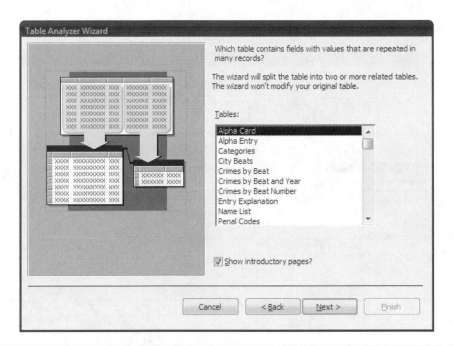

Figure 17-2   Selecting the table to analyze

TIP *If you expect to use the Table Analyzer often and don't want to see the two introductory dialog boxes each time, clear the check mark next to Show Introductory Pages? in the dialog box showing the list of tables. If you want to see those boxes again, open the Table Analyzer and check the check box.*

In Figure 17-3, the Table Analyzer found that the values in the ZipCode and City fields are repeated many times in the Police database Name List table. It suggests that you create a lookup table for each field with a link from the new Table2 to the original Name List table and an additional link from the new Table3 back to Table2. Notice the wizard hasn't changed any table names: changing the table names is only a suggestion.

TIP *Click the Tips button (the light bulb icon) to get instructions about how to handle the wizard's suggestions.*

To change a table name, select the table, and then click the Rename Table button in the dialog box and enter a new name. When you change the name of the related table, the wizard changes the table name in the linked field in the primary table to match. If you change your mind about the new name that you entered for a table, click the Undo button next to the Rename Table button, and then enter a different name.

If the way the fields are grouped doesn't make sense to you, drag the field names from one table to the other to change them. Click Next to move to the dialog box in which

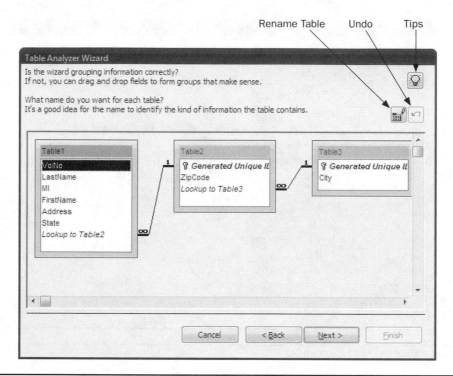

FIGURE 17-3 The Table Analyzer has suggestions

you verify the primary key fields are correct (see Figure 17-4). The wizard has, by default, added a unique field to each new table and corresponding linking fields.

Each of the new tables has a designated primary key field, but Table1 (Volunteer Staff) has no primary key field. You can specify a primary key for Table1 in two ways:

- Select an existing field that you know has unique values and click the Set Unique Identifier button. The key symbol appears next to the field name.

- Select the table and click the Add Generated Key button. A new Generated Unique ID field is added to Table1.

After adding key fields, click Next. In the final dialog box (Figure 17-5), the wizard offers to create a query for you that uses the same name as the original table and looks like the original table. Allowing the wizard to do this lets you work with the data all in one place and guarantees that all of the forms and reports that you created using the original table as a basis will continue to work properly. You can also choose to create this query yourself, if you prefer.

If you choose to decide which fields to place in which tables (refer to Figure 17-3), the next dialog box shows only the original table without the new Table2. You can create the new table by dragging a field name from the list in Table1. You can also rename the tables and define the primary key field for the new table using buttons in the dialog box. After you click Next, the wizard offers to create a query for you as before.

Set Unique Identifier   Add Generated Key

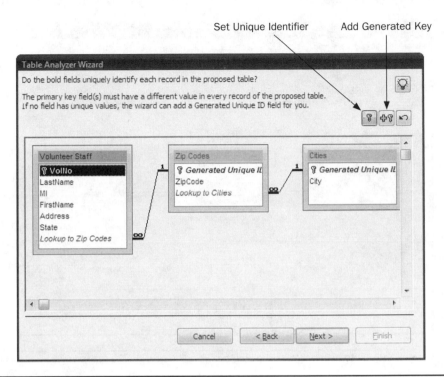

FIGURE 17-4   Verifying the primary key fields

Performance Analyzer

The *Performance Analyzer* looks at any or all of the objects in the database and suggests ways that you can improve the application's performance. When you finish using the Performance Analyzer, many of the suggestions can be implemented automatically. To start the Performance Analyzer, on the Database Tools tab's Analyze group, click the Analyze Performance command. The first dialog box includes a tab for each type of database object. Each tab contains the names of all those objects in the current database. The Current Database tab contains the Relationships and Visual Basic for Applications (VBA) Project options. The All Object Types tab contains all the names in one place. You can tell by the leading icon what kind of object it is.

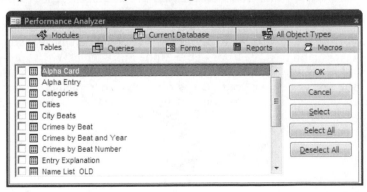

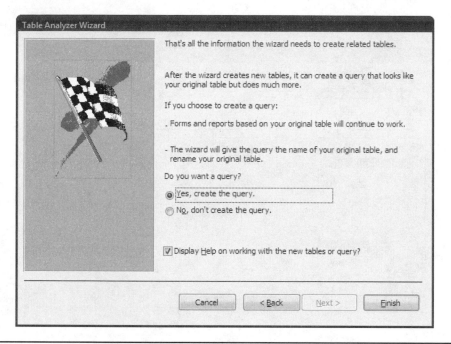

> **Table Analyzer Wizard**
>
> That's all the information the wizard needs to create related tables.
>
> After the wizard creates new tables, it can create a query that looks like your original table but does much more.
>
> If you choose to create a query:
>
> . Forms and reports based on your original table will continue to work.
>
> - The wizard will give the query the name of your original table, and rename your original table.
>
> Do you want a query?
>
> ⦿ Yes, create the query.
>
> ○ No, don't create the query.
>
> ☑ Display Help on working with the new tables or query?
>
> [Cancel] [< Back] [Next >] [Finish]

FIGURE 17-5   The final Table Analyzer Wizard dialog box

To choose which objects you want to examine, select the appropriate tab and choose the object names. Click Select All to choose all the objects. To analyze the entire database, click the All Object Types tab, choose Select All, and then click OK. A message box keeps you informed about the progress of the analysis, and after all the objects are inspected the wizard displays a dialog box with a list of recommendations, suggestions, and ideas (Figure 17-6). Any problems that were fixed are also noted. The Analysis Results pane describes the general overall findings. When you select one of the items in the list, additional explanations are displayed in the Analysis Notes pane.

TIP   *If you include queries in the objects to analyze, be sure that you have enough data in the tables to give the query a good workout.*

In our example in Figure 17-6, the Analyzer has recommended that we add an index to the Daily Report (DR) and the Date fields of the Alpha Entry table. When you select one of these recommendations, the Analysis Notes pane shows that, if you index on this field, it benefits the Alpha Entry table and your queries run faster. To implement a recommendation, select it, and then click Optimize. After considering all of the items in the list, click Close to close the Performance Analyzer.

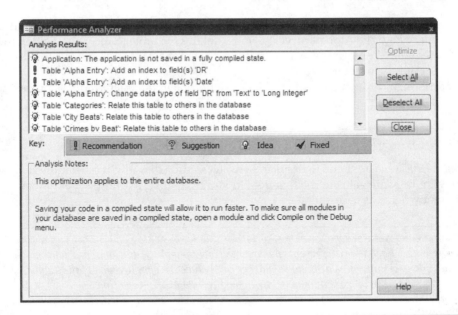

FIGURE 17-6   The findings of the Performance Analyzer

CAUTION *The Performance Analyzer doesn't always have the whole picture. Accept its recommendations and suggestions only after careful consideration. For example, adding indexes might improve query performance, but more indexes increase the disk space needed for the database and could slow the process of entering and editing data.*

Optimizing Tables and Queries

After you do all you can to normalize the database and distribute data efficiently among the tables, you can do a few other things to speed data processing. Following are some examples:

- Choose the appropriate data type for each field to save space and improve join operations. In addition, if you know the range of values to be stored in the field, choose the smallest field size that the data type will accept. You have no choice with Date/Time fields, but you can reduce the default 255-character field size for Text fields if the data is, for example, a ZIP code.

- Make sure that the fields on either side of a relationship are of the same or a compatible data type.

Optimizing with Indexes

In addition to the primary key, which is automatically indexed, one or more fields can be indexed to help you find and sort records faster. Indexes can speed queries if the fields on both sides of the join are indexed. In a one-to-many relationship, the primary table is already indexed on the primary key field, but creating an index for the field in the related table helps when the query is run.

For example, in the Police database, the Alpha Entry table has two indexes in addition to the primary key. The Alpha EntryCode index relates the table to the Code field in the Penal Codes table. The Alpha EntryIndex index related the Alpha Entry table to the Index field in the Alpha Card table.

In addition, indexing any field used in a criteria rule in the query reduces processing time for the query.

NOTE *Refer to Chapter 4 for information about creating indexes.*

Multiple-field indexes help distinguish between records that might have more than one record with the same value in the first field. If you're creating a multiple-field index, use only as many fields as necessary.

NOTE *While indexes can speed searches, sorts, and queries of related tables, they can also add to the database size. Each index represents a condensed lookup table. Additional problems can occur in a multiple-user environment because indexes can reduce the concurrency of the database, thereby limiting the ability of more than one user to modify data at the same time.*

Optimizing Queries

Among the guidelines for optimizing queries are the following:

- Include only the fields that you need in the query. If a field isn't needed in the result set, but you're using it as a criterion, clear the Show check box in the query grid.

- Avoid calculated fields in a query as much as possible. If you nest the query in another query as a subquery, you slow the operation considerably. If you need an expression in the result of the query, you can add a control to the form or report and use the expression as the control source. If necessary, prompt the user to enter a value required by the expression in a parameter query.

- Use Between…And… in a criteria expression rather than the > and < operators.

- If you want to count all the records in the recordset, use Count(*) instead of Count([*fieldname*]).

- Don't use domain aggregate functions, such as DSum, in a query. Access must retrieve all the data in the linked table before running the query, even if the data isn't included in the query.

- When grouping records by values in one of the joined fields, be sure to place the Group By aggregate function in the field that's on the side of the join containing the values that you want to summarize. If you place Group By in the joined field, Access must join all the records and then calculate the aggregate using only the necessary fields.

- Use as few Group By aggregates as possible. You might instead be able to use the First function in some cases.

- Try not to use restrictive criteria on nonindexed or calculated fields.

- If you need to place criteria on one of the fields used to join two tables in a one-to-many relationship, you can place it on either field in the grid. Run some tests to see which placement results in a faster query.

- If you're working with fairly static data, consider running a make-table query and using the resulting table instead of the query as the basis for forms and reports. You can always run the make-table query again if the data changes. Be sure to add indexes to the resulting table.

- When you create a Crosstab query, try to use fixed column headings to avoid the time it takes to update them.

TIP   To save even more time running queries, always save the query in a compiled state. When you simply save the query after making modifications in Design view, you're saving the query file. A query isn't compiled until it's run. To save the compiled query, run it by opening it in Datasheet view, and then save it. The query is optimized if it's compiled with the same amount of data that your application will have.

Working with Linked Tables

Although linked tables look just like your own tables when you use them in forms and reports, they're stored in another database file. Every time that you access a linked table, Access must retrieve the records from that file, which takes time. If the linked table is on a network or in a SQL database, this might take even more time because of network traffic.

You can reduce the time it takes to retrieve the records from a network or an SQL database in these ways:

- If you don't need to see all of the records from the linked table, use filters or queries to limit the number of records and reduce the transfer time.

- Paging up and down among records causes Access to load the records into memory, which takes time. If you want to add new records to the linked table, on the Home tab's Records group, click the New command. This avoids loading all the records into memory, and then having to page through them to the end of the recordset to add new records when the table first opens in Datasheet or Form view.

- If you usually add new records to the linked table, create a data entry form and set the form's Data Entry property to Yes. This also avoids loading and displaying all the records from the linked table.

- When you need to query a linked table, don't use functions in the criteria. And, especially, don't use domain aggregate functions, which require that Access load all the data in the linked table before executing the query.

- You can also create problems for the other users on the network who want to use the same data. Lock the records no longer than necessary.

Optimizing Filter By Form

The Filter By Form defaults for filter lookup options for the current database can improve the performance of all tables and queries, as well as all text box controls that use the Database Default setting in the Filter Lookup property. As discussed in Chapter 16, the Filter lookup group of options can limit the displayed list of values to indexed fields only or include local indexed and nonindexed fields. You can also set a limit on the number of values to display in the list in the displayed filter form.

If the list of field values takes too long to display, you can optimize the Filter By Form for a single text box control on a form by setting the control's Filter Lookup property (on the Data tab) to Never. This suppresses displaying the field values on the drop-down list in the Filter By Form window.

Optimizing Forms and Reports

Most of the optimization strategies can be used on both forms and reports, as well as on subforms and subreports. You can also apply techniques to individual text box and combo box controls to improve their performance in forms and reports.

The following tips apply to both forms and reports:

- Base the subform or subreport on a saved query that includes only the required fields and with a filter that results in only the required set of records.

- If the record order isn't important, you can save time by not sorting records in an underlying query, especially if the query uses fields from multiple tables.

- Try not to sort or group on expressions.

- Make sure that the underlying query is itself optimized before loading the form or report.

- Index on the fields you use for sorting or grouping.

- Don't overdo the design with bitmaps and graphics objects. If you need to add graphics, convert the unbound object frame controls to image controls, which take less time to load.

- Save disk space by using black-and-white bitmaps rather than color.

- Don't overlap controls unless absolutely necessary. Access must draw the controls in the form or report window twice to place overlapping controls.

- Use subforms and subreports sparingly; they occupy as much space as the main form or report. Base all subforms and subreports on queries instead of tables. Include only the necessary fields because more fields decrease performance.

- Index all fields in a subform or subreport linked to the main form or report. In addition, index all fields used in criteria.

- When you need to include data from an external table, you can save time by importing the table, rather than linking. This does take more space, however.

- If the form or report has no event procedures associated with it, make sure that the form or report Has Module property (on the Other tab) is set to No. The form or report can load faster and takes less disk space without the reserved class module space.

For Reports Only

When you're opening a report from a procedure, you can test the Has Data property to see if the underlying recordset is empty. If it has no records, you can save time if you branch to the next operation and avoid opening the useless report.

To do this, open the report in Design view and open the Property Sheet. On the Event tab, select the On No Data event property and attach a macro that cancels the print operation if there is no data in the report. See Chapter 19 for information about creating macros.

Before printing a report, set the Fast Laser Printing property (on the Other tab) to Yes if you're using a laser printer. If you're using a nonlaser printer, printing in landscape orientation can take more time because of the mechanical motion across the page.

For Forms Only

A few more strategies that apply only to forms:

- Don't leave a form open if you are not using it. Access must still refresh the window whether or not you're working in it.

- Design a form with as few controls as possible. More controls reduce the efficiency of the form. If you need a lot of controls, consider adding a tab control to create a multiple-page form with controls grouped logically on the pages.

- If the underlying record source contains many records and you're planning to use the form primarily for data entry, change the form's Data Entry property to Yes. When the form opens, it automatically moves to the end of the recordset and displays a blank record in the form. If you open the form with records showing, Access must read every record before it can display a blank new record.

- If you don't expect to edit the records in a subform, you can save time by setting the subform's Allow Edits, Allow Additions, and Allow Deletions properties all to No. An alternative is to set the Recordset Type to Snapshot, instead of the default Dynaset. These are properties of the subform object itself, not the subform control on the main form.

- Use a hyperlink instead of a command button to open a form. Command buttons added with the help of the Command Button Wizard result in an event procedure written in VB code. Without VB code, you can eliminate the class module and save space and time.

Optimizing Controls

List box and combo box controls all show field values from which you can choose. They're bound to a field in the underlying record source. When you use a wizard to create the list box or combo box control, it automatically constructs an SQL statement and assigns it to the control's Record Source property. You can save time by basing the control on a saved query instead of the SQL statement, which must be evaluated each time that you activate the control.

To convert the wizard's SQL statement to a saved query, do the following:

1. Open the control's Property Sheet and click the Build button next to the Row Source property. The SQL statement appears in the Query Builder window.

2. On the Design tab in the Close group, click the Save Object As command and enter a name for the query in the Save As dialog box.

3. When you close the Query Builder window, Access asks if you want to save the query with that name and update the property with the query name. Respond Yes.

You can optimize the behavior of these controls in several more ways:

- Include only the necessary fields in the query that you specify as the Row Source property for the control. Adding extra fields slows the display of the list.

- If different fields are used, be sure to index on both the first field displayed in the combo box or the list box, as well as on the bound field in the underlying table.

- Set the AutoExpand property of the combo box control to No if you don't require the fill-in-as-you-type feature.

- If you do use the fill-in-as-you-type feature by setting the AutoExpand property to Yes, be sure that the first field in the displayed list is a Text data type, rather than a Number data type. Access converts the numeric value to text to find a match for completing the entry. Using text in the first field eliminates the need for this conversion.

- You usually include the bound field in a lookup combo box list, but if you don't do this, don't use expressions for the bound field or the displayed field. Also, use single-table (or query) row sources and don't add restrictions to the row source.

- If you don't expect the data to change, base the control on imported, rather than linked, data.

- Use the default format and property settings for the controls. Access saves only the exceptions to the default settings with the form. If you find that you're changing the same property frequently, you can change the default setting for the control.

Avoiding Errors

The *Name AutoCorrect* feature can help you avoid those pesky #Error# messages where you wanted to see data. These errors occur when you rename a table, query, or one of the fields. Name AutoCorrect creates name maps that store interdependency information between database objects. The name maps apply to tables, queries, forms, and reports in an Access database.

TIP *You must have Track Name AutoCorrect Info checked to view dependency information. Click the Microsoft Office button and choose Access Options. On the Current Database window, check all the Name AutoCorrect options.*

The *Object Dependencies* feature works both ways: you can look at all the objects that depend on the object with which you're working, as well as look at all the objects on which your current object depends. Being able to look at these lists helps you maintain the database and keeps it free of errors caused by a missing or renamed object. The Object Dependencies list appears in the pane at the right of the screen.

NOTE *You must have permissions to open an object in the database in Design view to look at the dependency information.*

Before you can view the current dependencies, you must close the table, query, form, or report that you're working with. This ensures the most accurate and current information. To view the dependencies, do the following:

1. Select the object name in the Navigation Pane.
2. On the Database Tools tab's Show/Hide group, click the Object Dependencies command.

3. The Object Dependencies pane lists the objects that rely on the object that you selected in the left pane (see Figure 17-7). You might see a dialog box warning you that dependency information needs to be updated before you can view object dependencies. This could take several minutes. Click OK.

4. If you want to see the list of objects that use the one that you selected, click the Objects That I Depend On radio button.

5. Click an expand icon (+) to see the elements of that object (see Figure 17-8).

To view the types of objects and how they depend on one another, see the Help topic "About object dependencies" for a complete list of objects and their dependencies.

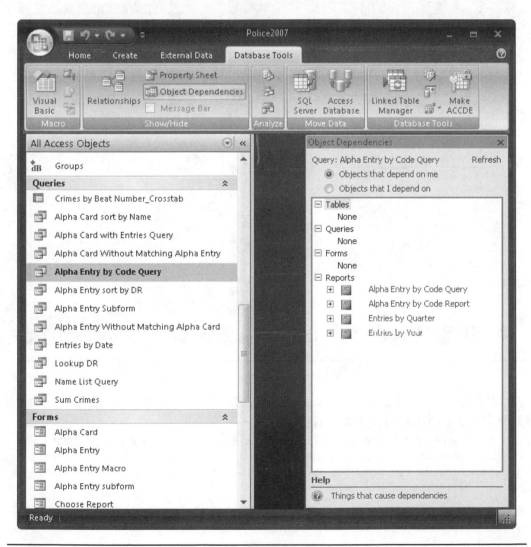

FIGURE 17-7 Looking at what depends on me

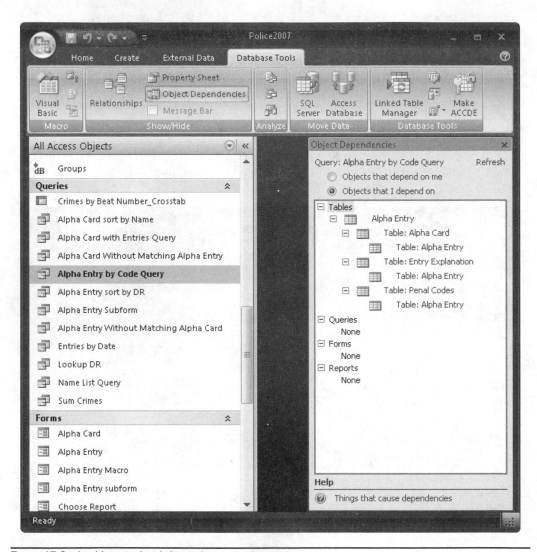

FIGURE 17-8 Looking at what I depend on

Backing Up and Restoring a Database

To reduce the risk of losing data, it's a good idea to create a backup copy of your database. The database must be closed before you can back it up. If you're working in a multiple-user environment, make sure that all the users have closed the database before you start the backup process. You can make a backup copy in several ways:

- Double-click the My Computer shortcut and open successive folders until you locate the folder that contains your database. Drag the filename in the Windows Explorer list from the hard disk to another disk drive.

- Right-click the filename or database shortcut in Windows Explorer and point to Send To in the shortcut menu, and then click the drive to which you want to copy.

- Use Microsoft Windows 2000 or later Backup and Recovery Tools, the MS-DOS Copy command, or other third-party backup software. Some programs also offer the option of compressing the files.

You can also use Access to create a backup database. This creates a regular copy of the database with no compression or other reformatting. To restore the database, simply copy it back to where you want to use it. To back up the database with Access, do the following:

1. Click the Microsoft Office button and then rest the mouse pointer on Manage and choose Backup Database.

2. In the Save As dialog box, enter the name and location for the backup copy.

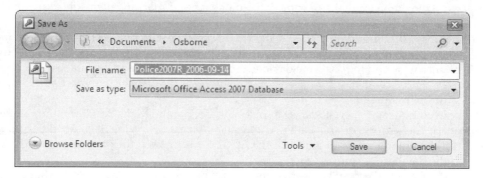

NOTE *If you are using Windows XP, the Save As dialog box looks slightly different.*

3. Click Save.

If you're working in a multiple-user environment with user-level security, also be sure to make a backup copy of the workgroup information file. You won't be able to start Access if the file is damaged or missing. See Chapter 24 for more information about workgroups and shared databases.

You can also back up individual objects of your database without copying the entire file. To do this, create a new, blank database and import the objects into it from the original database. See Chapter 22 for information about importing database objects.

To restore the database from a copy, use the recover feature of the same method you used to make the backup copy. If you used Windows Explorer, drag the filename from the floppy disk list to the database folder on the hard drive.

CAUTION *If the backup copy and the existing database in the database folder have the same name, you can replace the existing database when you restore the backup copy. If you want to save the original database, rename it before restoring from the backup copy.*

Compacting and Repairing a Database

Access provides some useful tools for managing databases. One of these tools converts databases to or from previous versions of Access. Another creates an ACCDE file from the current database. An ACCDE file contains compiled versions of all the code in the database with none of the source code. ACCDE databases run faster, but the user cannot access the source code for viewing or editing.

NOTE *See Appendix A for information about converting databases to and from Access 2007.*

Another utility repairs and compacts a database to use disk space more efficiently. As you delete tables and queries, your database can become fragmented as it is stored on various parts of the hard disk, with useless small blocks of storage space between data. Compacting the database makes a copy of the database and rearranges the file to make better use of the disk space.

If a database becomes damaged in some way, Access usually detects this when you try to open the database or if you try to compact, encrypt, or decrypt it. When damage is found, Access offers the option to repair the database at once. If, however, your database begins to act strangely, and Access hasn't noticed any damage, you can use the Compact and Repair Database utility manually.

You can compact an open database in place by clicking the Make ACCDE command in the Database Tools group on the Database Tools tab. Access opens the Save As dialog box, where you can enter a different name for the ACCDE file or keep the original name. Click Save and the database is compacted.

If the database isn't open, you can compact it using the same filename or a different name, drive, or folder. To compact and repair a closed database, do the following:

1. Close all databases. From the Getting Started window, click the Microsoft Office button, choose Manage, and click Compact and Repair Database.

2. In the Database to Compact From dialog box (Figure 17-9), select the name of the database that you want to compact and click Compact.

NOTE *If you are using Windows XP, your dialog box will look slightly different.*

---

3. In the Compact Database Into dialog box, specify the drive and folder for the compacted database and enter a name for the copy, or choose a name from the list.

4. Click Save. If you choose the same name as the original database, Access asks for confirmation before replacing the file.

TIP *You can stop the process at any time by pressing* ESC *or* CTRL-BREAK.

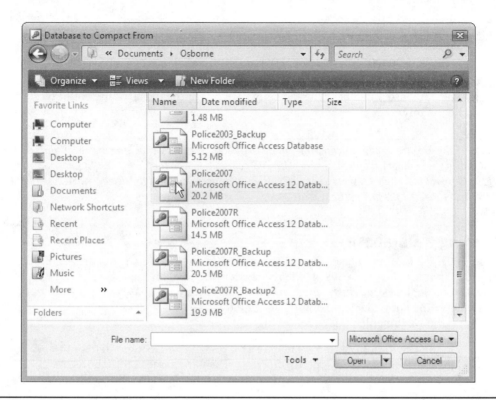

FIGURE 17-9   Selecting the database to compact

If the compaction was successful, and you chose to use the same name and path for the compacted file, Access replaces the original database file with the compacted version. If Access isn't successful with compacting a database, one of the following reasons might be to blame:

- Another user could have the database open.
- Your disk didn't have enough free space for both the original copy and the compacted copy of the database. To remedy this, delete as many unnecessary files as possible and try compacting the database again.
- You might not have permission to copy all the tables in the database. You need both Open/Run and Open Exclusive permissions to make copies of the data. If you are not the owner of this database, find the owner and try to obtain permission. If you are the owner, update the permissions for all of the tables.

- Some earlier versions of Access allowed the back quote character (') to be used in a database object name. This is no longer permitted. Open the database in the previous version and change the object name and all the references to the object in queries, forms, reports, macros, and code.

- The database might be on a read-only network or the file attribute could be set to Read Only.

NOTE *If the file size would be reduced by more than 256K, you can save time by specifying that the database be compacted automatically when you close it. Check the Compact On Close option on the General tab of the Options dialog box. If another user has the database open, Access won't compact it until the last user closes it.*

Documenting a Database

One of the most important tasks in a database management system is documentation, especially if many people are involved with its development and use. One of the Access analysis tools is the *Documenter*, which analyzes the current database and prints a report of the details of the entire database or only specified parts.

To run the Documenter, do the following:

1. On the Database Tools tab's Analyze group, click the Documenter command. The Documenter dialog box opens, showing nearly the same eight tabs as the Performance Analyzer. Each tab displays a list of objects in the database.

2. Select the items on each tab that you want to document or choose Select All on the All Object Types tab to select everything in the database, including the relationships and the database properties.

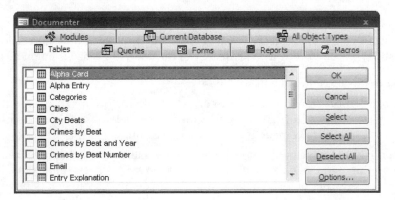

3. If you want to limit the amount of information to print in the table definitions, click Options, and then check the desired options in the Print Table Definition dialog box (Figure 17-10). Click OK after you have made your choices.

4. To limit the information in another object type, select the object and click Options. Each object has a list of details from which to select.

5. After making all your selections, click OK twice to start the Documenter.

TIP *You can stop the Documenter at any time by pressing* CTRL-BREAK *or* ESC.

The status bar shows the progress of the analysis with messages and odometers. When the Documenter is finished, the report is opened in Print Preview. Figure 17-11 shows the first page of the Documenter's analysis of the Alpha Card table in the Police2007 database.

TIP *You might want to look at how many pages the definition report contains before you start to print it. Some definitions, even with small databases, are quite lengthy. If you want to save the report, you can output the definitions to one of several file formats. On the Print Preview tab's Data group, choose PDF or XPS, Word, Text File, or click More and choose to export to another Access database, an XML file, the Snapshot Viewer, or an HTML file.*

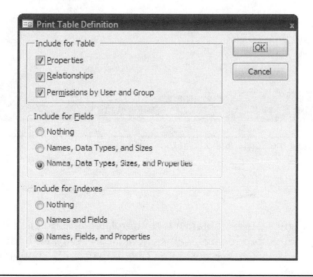

FIGURE 17-10   Choosing the features to print

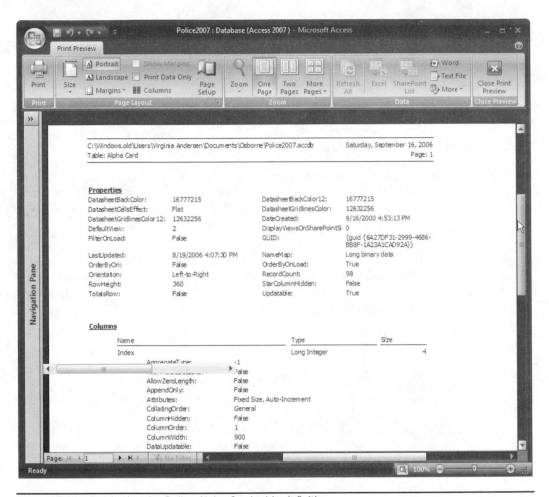

FIGURE 17-11 Previewing the Police Alpha Card table definition

Summary

While this chapter might seem to contain a lot of unrelated and detailed information, all the suggestions are relevant to producing an efficient database. Because both time and space have visible effects on efficiency, whatever you can do to optimize both factors can help you create a better database.

Access provides many tools for optimization. Each of the Access database objects can be optimized by following the rules and guidelines presented in this chapter.

Access provides the means to compact and repair a database to improve disk storage efficiency. This chapter also addressed the issue of backing up a database to ensure the retention of important information.

The next chapter begins to explore the world of creating an application that can be controlled by the user. In an event-driven program—such as Access—understanding the concept of events and learning when and in what sequence events occur is important. After you become familiar with events, you can proceed to create macros and event procedures that carry out specified actions when events occur.

PART III

Understanding Events and the Event Model

Although you can manage a database adequately using the Access wizards and other tools without knowing anything about events, when you begin to build a customized application that the user can control, you need to understand events and know when and in what sequence they occur. Then you can create macros to carry out appropriate responses to all of the user's actions. When you decide to work with Visual Basic for Applications (VBA) to create VBA procedures, this information will also be useful.

This chapter contains most of the details about events that are necessary to create a basis for subsequent chapters that discuss writing macros to automate an Access application. Skim through this chapter to get enough of an understanding of events, and then refer to it while reading the later chapters to find specific information.

What Are Events?

An *event* is something that happens to a certain object, a recognized action that occurs and triggers some type of response. For example, when you click a command button, the *Click* event occurs and the command button's event property specifies a response. Access is an *event-driven program,* which means it responds to a variety of events as they occur. In fact, if no event occurs, nothing happens at all.

Events are usually triggered by the user, but Access also responds to events resulting from system changes or external influences. For example, a specified timer interval expires, data in the table changes, linked data is updated, or a filter finds no records that match the criteria. When an event occurs, you can have Access respond with a specific action by running a macro or executing a VBA procedure.

The macro or VBA procedure is attached to an event property of the object to which the event occurs. For example, suppose that when the user clicks a command button, you want the Alpha Entry form to open. You would create a macro or VBA procedure that opens the form and specifies it as the On Click event property for the command button.

> ***TIP*** *When you create a command button using the Command Button Wizard, the wizard automatically creates a VBA procedure and adds it to the button's On Click property.*

The next chapter discusses creating macros that respond to events. For now, let's take a close look at events and when they occur.

Types of Events

Events are grouped into eight categories, depending on the effects of the event. For example, some events relate to the data, others to filters, and still others to keyboard actions. The following sections describe each type of event and list the commonly used events that fall into each classification.

Each event corresponds to a property of the object to which it applies. The property usually has the same name or a name similar to the event (but with spaces and sometimes beginning with *On*). For example, the Change event corresponds to the On Change property of several controls. You can set the property to respond to the event in a specified way.

Data Events

A *Data event* occurs when data is entered, edited, or deleted in a datasheet or a form. For example, when the user enters data into a text box control in a form or selects a value from a combo box, a Data event occurs. In addition, when the entry focus moves from one record to another, this is classified as a Data event. A control has focus when it can receive user input by means of the mouse or keyboard action. Table 18-1 describes some of the more common Data events and the Access objects to which each applies.

Here's some additional information about Data events and their uses:

- The BeforeUpdate and AfterUpdate events don't occur when the value in a calculated field changes.

- You can use the BeforeUpdate record event to validate data, especially with complex validation rules that involve more than one value. You can display different error messages for different data, giving the user the opportunity to override the rule violation, if desired. Use the Validation Rule property for controls in a form, as well as the Validation Rule and Required properties specified in the table design for fields and records in forms.

- The BeforeUpdate event can also be used to cancel updating the record before moving to another record in case of an error. It can also check to see whether a value was already entered in the control.

- You can use the AfterInsert event to requery the underlying recordset (the datasheet result of running the query) to incorporate new data when a record is added to the form.

- The Change event can be used to coordinate data among several controls in the form.

A problem can occur when you use the NotInList event to enable the user to add a value to the combo box list. If you set the AutoExpand property for the combo box control to Yes, Access selects matching values from the list as you enter characters in the text box part of the control. So, if you want to add the name John to the list, but Johnston is already on the list, the AutoExpand property fills out the complete Johnston value and the NotInList event doesn't occur. The cure for this is to enter a space after you enter the new value, so it no longer

Event	Applies To	When It Occurs
AfterInsert	Forms	After a record is added to the database.
AfterUpdate	Forms, controls	After a control or record is updated with modified data. Also occurs when the control or record loses focus or you choose Save in the Records group on the Home tab to update the current record without moving to another. Occurs for both new and existing records.
BeforeInsert	Forms	When you begin to type the new data in a new record, but before you add the record to the database.
BeforeUpdate	Forms, controls	Before a control or record is updated with modified data. Occurs when the control or record loses focus or you choose Save in the Records group on the Home tab. Occurs for both new and existing records.
Change	Controls	When the contents of a text box control or the text box portion of a combo box control changes. When you type a character in the control or change its Text property with a macro or procedure.
Current	Forms	When focus moves to a record and it becomes the current record. When the form is first opened and when the focus moves from one record to another in the form. Also when you requery the form's record source by removing the filter or the sort order, or with a macro action.
NotInList	Controls	When you enter a value in a combo box that isn't in the combo box list.

TABLE 18-1   Common Data Events

matches a value in the list. You can also simply delete the extra *ston* characters. Then the NotInList event occurs when you move to the next control.

CAUTION   *The Change event can result in cascading events—a never-ending loop. If the Change event procedure alters the contents of the control, the Change event occurs again, which triggers the Change event procedure again, and so on. If you plan to use the Change event, don't create two or more controls that affect the contents of each other.*

Error and Timer Events

One error event, *Error,* is important in an application for handling errors during operation. The Error event is often used to intercept Access error messages and replace them with more helpful messages that relate to the application.

The other error event, *Timer,* is used for synchronizing data on forms and reports by refreshing the data at regular intervals. This event occurs when the interval specified in the form's Timer Interval property has elapsed.

Filter Events

Filter events apply only to forms and occur when you apply an existing filter or create a new filter for the form. The *ApplyFilter event* occurs when you apply or remove a filter using any of the filter commands. The ApplyFilter event can be used to change a form display, so it hides or disables controls, depending on the filter criteria.

The Filter event occurs when you choose one of the filter methods to create a new filter. You can use the Filter event to remove an earlier filter, so extraneous criteria are not carried over to the next filter. To do this, set the form's Filter property to a zero-length string using a macro or an event procedure that completely clears the filter criteria.

Focus Events

Focus events (see Table 18-2) occur when a form or control gets or loses focus. Two Focus events apply to both forms and reports, and they occur when the object becomes active or inactive. Some other Focus events apply only to forms or controls in forms.

The Enter event occurs before focus moves to a control, so you can use the event to display instructions for entering data in the control or other information.

You can use the GotFocus and LostFocus events to set the control's Visible and Enabled properties. These events are also used to display a message in the status bar when a control, such as an Option button, has focus. The message clears when the control loses focus.

Keyboard Events

All *Keyboard events* apply to forms and controls that have focus. A form can receive focus only if it contains no controls or if all visible controls are disabled and cannot get focus. The object with focus receives all the keystrokes. When the Key Preview form event property is set to Yes, the Keyboard events are invoked for the form before they're invoked for the controls on the form. The default setting is No.

- The *KeyDown event* occurs when you press any key on the keyboard while the form or control has focus.

Event	Applies To	When It Occurs
Activate	Forms, reports	When a form or report becomes the active window by opening it, by clicking it, or by clicking a control on a form.
Deactivate	Forms, reports	When a different Access window replaces the form or report as the active window, but before it becomes the active window. Doesn't occur when focus moves to a window in another application, a dialog box, or a pop-up form.
Enter	Controls	Before a control receives focus from another control or as the first control in a newly opened form. Occurs before the GotFocus event.
GotFocus	Forms, controls	When a control receives focus or a form with no active or enabled controls receives focus.
LostFocus	Forms, controls	When a form or control loses focus.

TABLE 18-2 Common Focus Events

- The *KeyPress event* occurs when you press and release a key or any key combination that produces a standard ANSI character while the form or control has focus.

- The *KeyUp event* occurs when you release a pressed key while a form or control has focus. The object that has focus receives the keystrokes.

Holding the key down causes repeated KeyDown or KeyPress events. If you're using the KeyUp event, holding the key down causes the KeyUp to occur after all the KeyDown and KeyPress events have occurred. All these key events occur when you send a keystroke to a form or control using a macro with the SendKey action. KeyUp and KeyDown are often used to recognize function keys; navigation keys; key combinations that use CTRL, SHIFT, or ALT with another key; and number keys from the keyboard or the number keypad. KeyUp and KeyDown don't occur when you press ENTER if the form has a command button whose Default property is Yes. Pressing ENTER is the same as clicking the command button. KeyUp and KeyDown also don't occur when you press ESC if the Cancel property is set to Yes.

The KeyPress event doesn't indicate the physical state of the keyboard; it indicates only the character pressed. The event accepts any printable character, CTRL combined with a character, ENTER, or BACKSPACE.

TIP *Pressing* BACKSPACE *results in an ANSI character and triggers the KeyPress event, but pressing* DEL *does not.*

Mouse Events

All the mouse events (see Table 18-3) apply to both forms and controls. Again, a form itself can receive focus only if it contains no controls or if all visible controls have been disabled and cannot get focus.

Event	When It Occurs
Click	When you click and release the left mouse button on a control or its label. When you click a record selector or an area outside a section or control in a form.
	When you select a combo box or list box by pressing TAB or an arrow key, and then press ENTER.
	When you press SPACEBAR while a command button, check box, option button, or toggle button has focus.
	When you pass the mouse pointer over a hyperlink and click the left mouse button when the pointer changes to a pointer hand.
DblClick	When you click and release the left mouse button twice on a control or its label.
	When you double-click a record selector or a blank area in a form.
MouseDown	When you click a mouse button while the mouse pointer is on a form or control. It also happens when the SHIFT, ALT, or CTRL key is pressed while the mouse button is pressed down.
MouseMove	When you move the mouse pointer over a form, form section, or control.
MouseUp	When you release the mouse button while the pointer is on a form or control.

TABLE 18-3   Common Mouse Events

PART III

The Click event, one of the most common events, occurs when you click the left mouse button. Click and DblClick apply to the left mouse button only. Any other mouse buttons don't trigger the Click or DblClick event. You can use the MouseUp or MouseDown event to differentiate between the mouse buttons.

NOTE *The mouse events don't apply to attached labels; they apply only to freestanding labels. Clicking or double-clicking an attached label triggers the event for the associated control.*

The result of the DblClick event depends on the type of control you clicked:

- If the control is a text box, double-clicking selects the entire word.
- If the control is an OLE object, the source application starts where you can edit the object.

If you don't double-click quickly enough, the action is treated as repeated Click events.

CAUTION *The MouseMove event can occur when a form moves under the mouse pointer, even if the pointer doesn't move. If you run a macro or event procedure that moves the form, you can generate unexpected MouseMove events.*

Print Events

Print events apply only to reports and they occur for each section of the report when the report is either being printed or formatted for printing.

The *Format event* occurs when Access determines what data goes in each report section, but before the section is formatted for previewing or printing. You can use the data in the current record to change the page layout by creating a macro or VBA procedure for this event. Depending on the section of the report, the Format event applies to a different set of data:

- In the Detail section, Format occurs for every record.
- In the group header, Format applies to all the data in the Header section, plus the first record in the Detail section.
- In the group footer, Format applies to all the data in the Footer section, plus the last record in the Detail section.

The *NoData event* occurs when a report has an empty recordset. If the report isn't bound to a table or query, it doesn't occur, and it doesn't occur for empty subreports. If you want to hide an empty subreport, you can attach a macro or event procedure that suppresses previewing or printing to the subreport's HasData property.

The *Page event* occurs after the page is formatted, but before it's printed. You can use it to draw a border around a page or add a graphic to the report. This can save disk space that would otherwise be used for storing the graphic with the report design.

The *Print event* occurs after formatting, but before printing the report. A macro or event procedure attached to it can be used to perform calculations, such as running page totals after the data is prepared for printing on a page.

Window Events

Window events occur when you open, close, or resize a form or report window.

The *Load event* occurs when the form is opened and records appear on the screen. You can use the Load event to specify default control settings or to display calculated data in the form.

The *Open event* occurs when you open a form, but before the first record is displayed. You can use the Open event to display a message asking if the user wants to add new records. If the response is Yes, the form can go quickly to a blank record at the end of the recordset. If not, it continues to display the first record. With a report, the Open event occurs when the report opens, but before it begins printing.

Forms and reports behave differently when based on an underlying query. When you open a form, the query runs before the form is displayed. When you open a report, the Open event occurs before the query is run, giving you the opportunity to enter query parameters or other criteria.

The *Resize event* occurs when you change the size of a form or when the form is first displayed and expanded to its previously saved size. You can use the Resize event to cause certain controls on the form to be repositioned or resized to accommodate the change in the form size.

Understanding the Sequence of Events

Many types of events can happen to an object in a short period of time. When you begin to create macros that will govern how an application operates, you need to understand not only when events occur, but also the sequence in which they occur. This is especially important if you intend to have two or more macros executing in response to events and want them executed in a specific order. You must know to which events to attach the actions.

Form Control Events

Two types of events occur when you're moving about the controls in a form. When focus moves from one control to another, *Focus events* occur. When you add or change data in a control, *Data events* occur.

Moving among Controls

When you move to another control on the same form, the *Enter* and *GotFocus* events occur, in that order.

NOTE *An exception to this rule exists: The Enter event doesn't occur for the items grouped in an option group, it occurs only to the option group control. The Exit event also applies only to the option group control. The toggle buttons, check boxes, or option buttons in the option group experience only the GotFocus and LostFocus events.*

If you're opening a form that has one or more active controls that get focus at opening, certain other events occur before those two:

```
Open(form)→Activate(form)→Current(form)→Enter(control)→GotFocus(control)
```

Conversely, when you move to another control, the control loses focus, and the Exit and LostFocus events occur in that order.

If you're closing a form that has one or more active controls, other *Form events* occur as well:

```
Exit(control)→LostFocus(control)→Unload(form)→Deactivate(form)→Close(form)
```

Working with Data in a Form

When you enter new data or change existing data, and then move focus to a different control, the BeforeUpdate and AfterUpdate events occur in that order. Then the Exit and LostFocus events for the changed control follow immediately after.

Whenever the content of a text box or combo box control changes, the Dirty and Change events occur before either the BeforeUpdate and AfterUpdate events occur. The Dirty event occurs when the current record has been changed since last saved. In fact, the Change event occurs in conjunction with keyboard events every time you press a key to enter or edit data. The sequence for each time you press a key while in the text box or the text box portion of a combo box is this:

```
Key→DownKeyPress→Dirty→Change→KeyUp
```

In the special case when you enter a value in the text box portion of a combo box control that isn't in the displayed list of values, the NotInList event occurs after the Change event, but before any other Control or Form events. If the Limit To List property for the combo box control is set to Yes, this also triggers an Error event. The sequence is as follows:

```
KeyDown→KeyPress→Dirty→Change→KeyUp→NotInList→Error
```

NOTE *This sequence of events is often used to display a message box asking if you want to add the value to the list, even though the property specifies limiting the values to those in the list.*

Form Record Events

Events occur for records in forms on several occasions:

- When the record gets focus
- When you update the data in a record by moving to the next or previous record
- When you delete one or more records
- When you add a new record

When you move from one record to another in a form or save the current record by clicking Save on the Quick Access toolbar, the update events apply to the current record in the form. By contrast, when you move from one control to another within the same record in a form, the update events apply to the individual controls in the form. Only when you move to another record do the form update events occur.

Moving Focus and Updating Data

At the top level are the Form events that occur when you move focus to a record on the form, enter or edit the data in the record, and finally, move to another record. The following Form events occur:

```
Current(form)→BeforeUpdate(form)→AfterUpdate(form)→Current(form)
```

If you changed the data in a record and leave the record, the Exit and LostFocus events occur for the last control that got focus in that record, before you enter the next record. The form itself becomes current when you are moving to the next record. The events occur after the AfterUpdate event for the form and before the Current event for the form as follows:

```
AfterUpdate(form)→Exit(control)→LostFocus(control)→RecordExit(form)→Current(form)
```

As you move among the controls within the same record on a form, several events occur for each control that gets focus. When you open a form and change the data in a control, the following events occur:

```
Current(form)→Enter(control)→GotFocus(control)→BeforeUpdate(control)→
AfterUpdate(control)→Exit(control)
```

Then, if you move focus to another control, the events reflect the shift in focus:

```
Exit(control1)→LostFocus(control1)→Enter(control2)→GotFocus(control2)
```

When you finish working in one record and move to the next, the following events occur in which the record is updated and the form itself becomes current until another control gets focus with the Enter event:

```
BeforeUpdate(form)→AfterUpdate(form)→Exit(control2)→LostFocus(control2→RecordExit(form)→
Current(form)
```

NOTE *When moving between records, the BeforeUpdate and AfterUpdate events apply to the form. When moving between controls in the same record in the form, they apply to the controls.*

Creating New Records

To add a new record, you move to the blank record on the form and type data in a control. Creating a new record triggers the following sequence of events:

```
Current(form)→Enter(control)→GotFocus(control)→BeforeInsert(form)→(control update
events)→AfterInsert(form)
```

The BeforeUpdate and AfterUpdate events for the controls and for the new record occur between the BeforeInsert and AfterInsert form events.

Deleting Existing Records

When you delete a record from the form, Access displays a dialog box asking for confirmation of the deletion and the following events occur:

```
Delete→BeforeDelConfirm→AfterDelConfirm
```

The confirmation dialog box is displayed after the BeforeDelConfirm event. If you cancel the deletion with a macro or event procedure with the Delete event, the dialog box isn't displayed at all, and the BeforeDelConfirm and AfterDelConfirm don't occur.

Form and Subform Events

Events occur when you work with forms, whenever you open or close a form, move between two forms, move between a main form and a subform, or work with the data displayed in the form.

Opening or Closing a Form

When you open a form, the sequence of events depends on whether the form has any active controls. If it does, the sequence of Form events is this:

```
Open→Load→Resize→Activate→Current
```

These events are followed by the Control events. If no active controls are on the form you open, the GotFocus event occurs for the form between Activate and Current.

When you close a form, the following events occur for the form:

```
Unload→Deactivate→Close
```

If no active controls are on the form, the LostFocus event occurs for the form between Unload and Deactivate.

NOTE *Open occurs before Load, so you can cancel Open, but you can't cancel Load. Conversely, Close occurs after Unload, so Unload can be canceled, but Close cannot.*

Moving to Another Form

More than one form can be open at a time, but only one form can be the active form. When you switch between two open forms, the Open, Load, and Resize events occur for the second form while the first is still active. Then the Deactivate event occurs for the form, that you're leaving and the Activate event occurs for the form to which you're switching and it becomes current.

Deactivate also occurs for the form when you switch to another open window unless the window is one of the following:

- A dialog box
- A form whose Popup property is set to Yes
- A window in another application

When you move to a form that's already open, the Open event doesn't recur for the form.

Changing Data in a Form

When you work with data in a form, the Form and Control events occur in a sequence as you move between records and edit the data in them. The Form events occur first as you open the form and move to the first control, and then the Control events take over. The following events occur when you first open the form:

```
Open(form)→Load(form)→Resize(form)→Activate(form)→Current(form)→Enter(control)→
GotFocus(control)
```

When you finish entering data in the last control in the form and close the form, the following sequence of events occurs:

```
Exit(control)→LostFocus(control)→Unload(form)→Deactivate(form)→Close(form)
```

If any of the data in a control in the form is changed, the BeforeUpdate and AfterUpdate events for both the form and the control occur before the Exit event for the control takes place and starts the form-closing sequence.

Using Subforms

All the events that occur for a form also occur for a subform. The subform and its data are loaded before the main form, using the same sequence of events. The exception is the *Activate event,* which occurs only for the main form.

When you close a form that contains a subform, a similar sequence of events occurs, but in reverse order: the form and its records are unloaded before the subform and its records. Also, the *Deactivate event* occurs only for the main form. To summarize, the closing events for the main form, the subform, and the controls occur in the following order:

1. The events for the controls on the subform, including Exit and LostFocus

2. The events for the controls on the main form, including the subform control

3. The events for the form, including Deactivate and Close

4. The events for the subform

Keystrokes and Mouse Events

Keyboard and mouse events are initiated by the user while working in a form or with controls in the form. *Keyboard events* occur when you press a key or a key combination while the form or control has focus. A keyboard event also occurs if you use a SendKey macro action or a procedure to send the ANSI character keystroke equivalent to the control.

Mouse events occur for forms, form sections, and controls on the form when you manipulate the mouse or press one of its buttons. Releasing a mouse button also triggers an event.

Using the Keyboard

The following events occur when you press a key on the keyboard while a control has focus:

```
KeyDown→KeyPress→KeyUp
```

If you press the key and hold it down, the KeyDown and KeyPress events alternate repeatedly until you release the key. Then the KeyUp event occurs.

If the key you press isn't an ANSI character, the KeyDown and KeyUp events occur, but not the KeyPress event. Pressing and holding down a non-ANSI key causes the KeyDown and KeyUp events to alternate repeatedly.

If the key you press changes the data in a text box control, the Change event occurs between the KeyPress and KeyUp events.

If the keystroke moves focus from one control to another, the KeyDown event occurs for the first control, while the KeyPress and KeyUp events occur for the second control. For example, if you edit the data in a text box control, and then press TAB to move to the next control, the following sequence of events occurs:

```
KeyDown(control1)→BeforeUpdate(control1)→AfterUpdate(control1)
```

```
→Exit(control1)→LostFocus(control1)→Enter(control2)→GotFocus(control2)
```

```
→KeyPress(control2)→KeyUp(control2)
```

Using the Mouse

When you place the mouse pointer on a control in a form and click the mouse button, the following events occur.

```
MouseDown→MouseUp→Click
```

TIP *Notice the Click event doesn't occur until after the MouseUp event.*

If you use the mouse to move focus from one control to another, the sequence of events is as follows:

```
Exit(control1)→LostFocus(control1)→Enter(control2)→GotFocus(control2)→
MouseDown(control2)→MouseUp(control2)→Click
```

If you move to another control by other means, such as pressing TAB, and then click the mouse button, the Current event for the form occurs between the LostFocus event for the first control and the Enter event for the second.

When you double-click a mouse button on a control other than a command button, both the Click and DblClick events occur, each with a corresponding MouseUp event, as follows:

```
MouseDown→MouseUp→Click→DblClick→MouseUp
```

If the control is a command button, a second Click event follows the second MouseUp event.

The *MouseMove event* is independent of the other mouse events and occurs when you pass the mouse pointer over the form, a form section, or control. The MouseMove event is often used to display ScreenTips and other comments explaining parts of a form.

Report and Report Section Events

Report and *Report section events* occur when you open or close a report. Opening a report for previewing and printing both trigger the same sequence of events. Some of the Report section events occur during or after section formatting and before printing the section.

The following events occur if you open a report for previewing or printing, and then close the report or switch to a different Access document:

```
Open→Activate→Close→Deactivate
```

If you have two reports open and you switch between them, the Deactivate event occurs for the first report, followed by the Activate event for the second. The Deactivate event doesn't occur for the report if you switch to a dialog box, a pop-up form, or a window in a different application.

When the report you open is based on a query, the Open event occurs before the query is run. This is useful for entering the criteria for the query in a procedure that responds to the Open report event. The procedure could open a dialog box in which the user is prompted to enter a value to be used in the parameter query.

When you preview or print the report, each section is formatted individually and prepared for printing after the Activate report event and before the Close report event. When all the sections are formatted for printing, the report is closed and deactivated. The sequence is as follows:

```
Open(report)→Activate(report)→Format(section)→Print(section)→Close(report)→
Deactivate(report)
```

Some special events can occur while a section is being formatted or after formatting is complete, but before printing:

- **Retreat**   Occurs when Access returns to a previous section to make changes during formatting. For example, if you set a group's Keep Together property to Whole Group or With First Detail, Access must return to the previous report section to determine whether the controls can all fit on the page. The Retreat event is also useful for maintaining the positioning of report items on a page.

- **NoData**   Occurs if no records are in the report.

- **Page**   Occurs after formatting, but before printing. If you want to add special formatting to customize the report's appearance, you can attach a procedure to this event.

Setting Event Properties

Event properties are used to run a macro or a VBA procedure each time the associated event occurs. The tables in an earlier section of this chapter describe the events and indicate to which objects each applies. When an event applies to a form, control, or report, that object has an event property that corresponds to the event. This is the property that you set to create the appropriate response to the event.

For example, enter the name of a macro in the On Click property of a command button and it will run when you click the button.

To set an event property, open the Property Sheet for the object, and then click the Event tab. Figure 18-1 shows the Event Property Sheet for a form. The maxView macro maximizes the Alpha Card form when it opens in Form view.

Depending on how you intend to create a response to the event, do one of the following:

- To set the property to an existing macro, choose the macro name from the drop-down list in the event property.

- To set the property to a macro in a macro group, choose the name from the drop-down list. The name then appears in the list as *macrogroupname.macroname*.

- To set the property to an existing VBA procedure, choose [Event Procedure] from the drop-down list. Only one event procedure can exist for each event property, named with the name of the property.

- To set the property to an existing user-defined function, enter an equal sign (=) followed by the function name, and then empty parentheses: *=functionname()*.

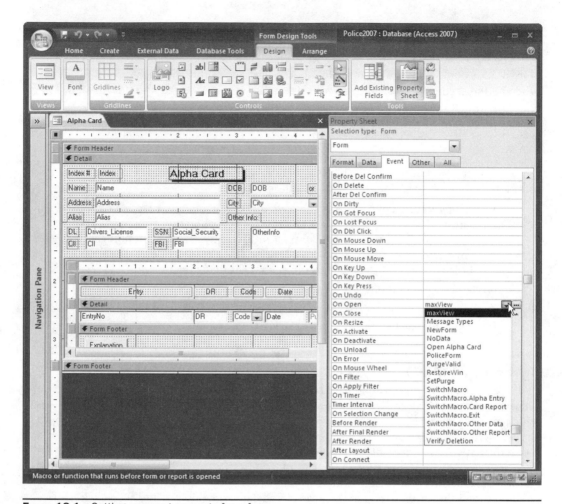

FIGURE 18-1   Setting an event property for a form

NOTE *The status bar displays a brief description of the event property when the insertion pointer is in the property box. Press F1 to open the Help topic for that event property.*

If you want to create a new macro, VBA procedure, or function for the event property, click Build (the ellipses: ...) to the right of the property box or right-click the property and choose Build from the shortcut menu. In the Choose Builder dialog box, do one of the following:

- Select Macro Builder to create a new macro for the property or to edit the already specified macro. See Chapter 19 for information about creating and editing macros and macro groups.

- Select Expression Builder to choose a built-in function or create a user-defined function for this property.

- Select Code Builder to open the Module window where you can create a new VBA procedure or edit one that is already specified for this property.

Summary

This chapter presents an overview of events and how they can be harnessed to customize an application. In addition, it lists many of the common types of events and the objects to which they apply, as well as the sequence in which they occur. Once you understand events, you're ready to proceed to creating your own macros, so the application responds properly to each user action and system event.

As you're building macros in the next chapter, you can refer to the event details in this chapter. Attaching the macro action to the proper event for it to execute at the intended time and operate on the intended object is important.

The next chapter launches into automation with macros and gives many useful examples of macros that display message boxes, filter records, and even change the flow of operations.

Automating with Macros

Macros provide a quick and easy way for you to program your Access application to do just what you want. With macros, you can specify customized responses to user actions, such as clicking a button, opening a form, or selecting an option in an options group. Macros can also respond to system conditions, such as an empty recordset. In addition, frequently performed tasks can be automated using macros.

Although the Access control wizards offer an easy way to add user interaction to a form or report, they don't always create exactly the right response. Creating a macro as a response to an event is an alternative to using a control wizard. Writing event procedures in Visual Basic is another alternative, but it requires some skill in programming with precisely constructed commands written in established syntax. Visual Basic for Applications (VBA) procedures are stored with the form or report that activates them, or they're stored as modules that are available from the Modules group in the Navigation Pane. Macros are easier, because you select the actions and their arguments from predefined lists, which virtually precludes any errors in construction. Macros can also be either embedded in the form or report or available as separate Access objects in the Navigation Pane. You might as well start with a macro, because you can always convert the macro to a VBA procedure later, if necessary.

This chapter discusses how to create macros and how to attach them to events to get the desired response. The Police database introduced earlier in the book is used as the sample database in this chapter. In subsequent chapters, you'll see how to use macros to find records, display custom dialog boxes, and create an opening home document for an application.

How Macros Work

A *macro* is a list of one or more actions that work together to carry out a particular task in response to an event. Each *action* carries out one particular operation. You create the list of actions in the order in which you want them to execute. In addition to selecting the action to be taken, you can specify other details of the action called *arguments*, which provide additional information, such as which form to open or how to filter the records to be displayed.

You can also set conditions under which the macro action is to be performed, such as to display a message box if a field contains a certain value or is blank. The macro runs only if the condition evaluates to True. If the condition is False, the action is skipped. Then, if another action is in the macro, it's executed. If not, the macro stops.

To run a macro, you assign it to the event property of a form, report, report section, or control. Once the event occurs, the macro automatically executes, beginning with the first action in the list. For example, a macro that opens a form and moves to a blank record for data entry can be assigned to the On Click event property of a command button in a dialog box or another form. When you click the button, the macro executes.

Standalone vs. Embedded Macros

In previous versions of Access, all macros were individual database objects that could be used in event properties. Now with Access 2007, you can embed the macro directly in the event property without adding the macro to the object list in the Navigation Pane.

If you do not expect more than one form or report control to need the macro, simply create it from the Property Sheet. If other form or report controls may be able to use the macro, save it as a standalone macro.

Standalone macros are individual Access objects listed in the Macros group in the Navigation Pane. Once you create and save a macro, it's available for attaching to an event property of any object in your database. Not all macro actions are appropriate for all objects, however, just as not all events occur on all objects. For example, if you create a macro that opens a form, you would probably attach it to the On Click event property of a command button or an option group, but not to a control in a report.

The process of using macros to automate an application is a simple one, composed of these steps:

1. Open the form or report to which the macro applies in Design or Layout view and select the specific control.

2. Open the Property Sheet for the control and click the Event tab.

3. Click the desired event property and do one of the following:

   • Choose the macro name from the drop-down list.

   • Click the Build (…) button and use the Macro Builder to create the embedded macro.

4. Save the form or report and switch to Form or Report view to try it.

Creating a Macro

The section "Choosing Actions," later in this chapter, describes categories of macro actions and how they're used. But first we'll take a look at the two ways you can build the macro and how you can use it.

The first step in creating a macro is to design the macro carefully by listing the actions you want performed when the event occurs. Each action might require specific arguments or need to be performed only under certain conditions.

Next, verify that you're choosing the correct event to which the macro will respond. Refer to Chapter 18 for information about events and when they occur.

When you complete the planning and design of the macro action list, you're ready to open the Macro window. You have two ways to start the Macro Builder:

   • On the Create tab's Other group, click the New Object: Macro command.

- Go to the Property Sheet for the control that needs the macro, click the Build button in the Event property box, and choose the Macro Builder in the Choose Builder dialog box.

Touring the Macro Design Window

The Macro Design window opens, showing a blank macro. The drop-down list in the Action column (Figure 19-1) contains a list of actions from which to choose. The Arguments column displays a list of arguments to select for each macro action. As you enter arguments in the lower pane, they are listed in the Arguments column. Entries in the Comment column are optional but highly recommended as a reminder of what the macro is meant to accomplish.

TIP *Comments are especially useful when macros are stored as separate objects, not embedded with a particular form or report. The comments can explain how the macro is used and to which events it's attached. This can also be important if you rename the macro. You need to find all the references to the macro and change the name there, as well.*

Once you select an action from the list, the lower pane displays the associated arguments. Some are required, while others are optional, depending on the action.

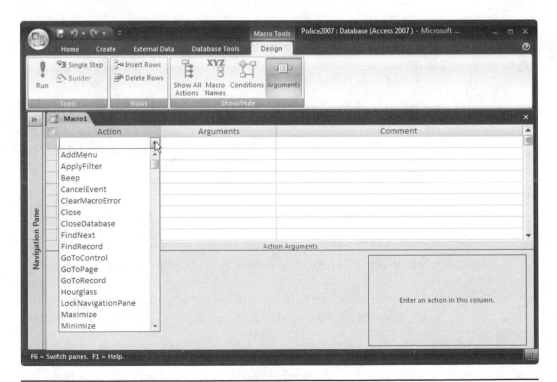

FIGURE 19-1   Working in the Macro Design window

The Macro Tools ribbon includes some new groups and commands:

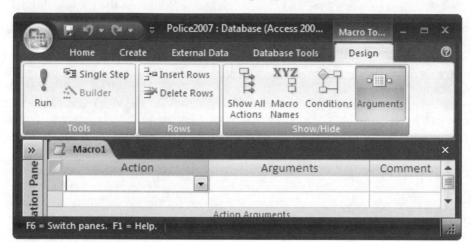

In the Tools group:

- The Run command runs the macro.
- The Single Step command runs the macro one action at a time and displays intermediate information.
- The Builder command starts the Expression Builder for help in creating an expression.

In the Rows group:

- The Insert Rows command inserts one or more blank rows in the grid above the selected row. If you select more than one row, that number of rows is inserted. You can also right-click in the macro design and choose Insert Rows from the shortcut menu.
- The Delete Rows command deletes the selected row or rows. You can also choose this command from the shortcut menu.

In the Show/Hide group:

- The Show All Actions command expands the list of actions to include those that may require trusted status. If the command is dimmed, the only macro actions available for use are those that do not require trusted status to run.
- The Macro Names command shows or hides the Macro Name column in the macro design.
- The Conditions command shows or hides the Condition column in the macro design.
- The Arguments command shows or hides the Arguments column in the macro design.

The lower pane is the Action Arguments pane, and it displays information about the current row of the macro. The lower-right pane in the Macro window displays information about the currently active part of the macro sheet. For example, in Figure 19-1, the first row is selected and the message "Enter an action in this column" is displayed in the information pane. As you work in the macro sheet, the pane shows other information and comments.

Creating a Simple Macro

Here you'll create a macro in the Police database that opens the Alpha Card form in read-only mode by doing the following:

1. Open the Macro window from the Create tab or start the Query Builder from the Property Sheet. The Macro window appears.

2. In the first row of the macro, click the Action drop-down arrow and choose OpenForm from the list.

   The Action Arguments pane now contains the arguments for the OpenForm action and the information pane describes the selected OpenForm action. The required arguments are also displayed in the Arguments column. The Form Name argument is required. Other required arguments show default selections. The optional arguments are blank in the Action Arguments pane and skipped in the Arguments column.

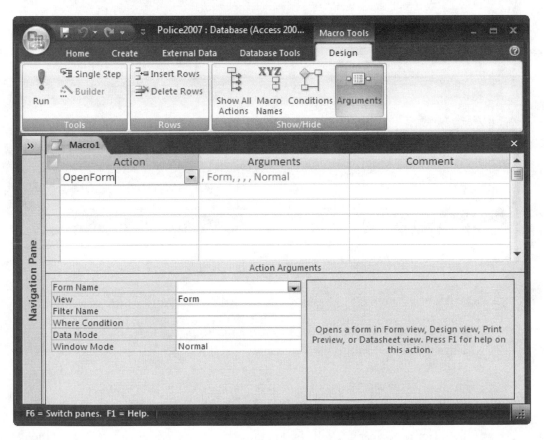

> **NOTE** *You can remove the Arguments column by clicking the Arguments command in the Show/Hide group.*

3. Click the Form Name box in the Action Arguments pane and select the Alpha Card form from the list of the forms in the current database.

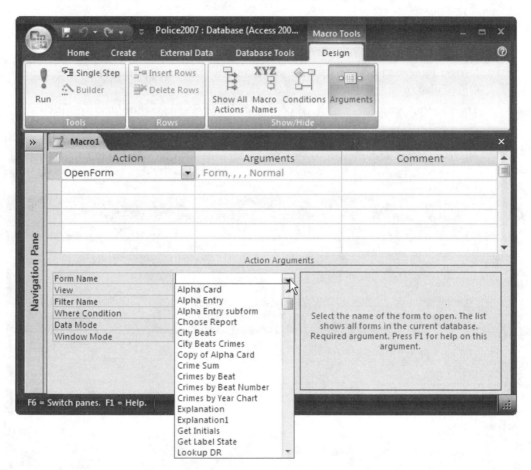

4. Set the other arguments as follows:

- **View (required)**   Choose from the list of options including Form (default), Design, Print Preview, Datasheet, PivotTable, or PivotChart. For this example, leave the default setting as Form view.

- **Filter Name (optional)**   Enter the name of the filter to limit or sort the records in the form. This can be a query or a filter saved as a query. For now, leave this blank because you want all the records.

- **Where Condition (optional)**   Enter a SQL WHERE clause that limits the records in the form. You can click the Build button next to the argument box to start the Expression Builder if you need help. Again, you want all the records with this example, so don't add a Where Condition.

NOTE   *See "Introducing Structured Query Language" in Chapter 9 for information about the SQL WHERE clause.*

- **Data Mode (optional)**   Choose from the list of data entry modes: Add, to allow adding new records; Edit, to allow editing of existing records; or Read Only, to prevent any additions or editing. Choose Read Only from the list for this example.

- **Window Mode (required)**   Choose from the list of window modes, including Normal (default); Hidden, which hides the form; Icon, which displays the form minimized; or Dialog, which sets the form Popup and Modal properties both to Yes. Leave the Window Mode with the default Normal setting for now.

5. If you started the Macro Builder from the Create tab, close the Macro window, enter a name for the macro in the Save As dialog box, and then click OK. When you return to the Macros group in the Navigation Pane, you'll see the name of the new macro. If you started the Macro Builder from the Property Sheet, you will not be asked to name the macro. It is saved with the form or report design.

Choosing Actions

Access offers actions that cover data management activities, such as opening forms and reports, printing reports, filtering data, validating data, moving among records in a form, playing sounds, displaying message boxes, and even exchanging data with other programs.

To add an action to a macro, you can either choose an action from the Action drop-down list or type the name yourself. As with many lists offered by Access for choosing an item, if you begin to type the name of the action, Access automatically fills in the remaining characters for you.

NOTE   *See "Programming with Macros and SQL" in the Quick Reference on the CD for a complete description of all the macro actions and their arguments.*

- To navigate between controls or records, use the FindNext, FindRecord, GoToControl, or GoToRecord actions.

- To modify an Access window, use the Maximize, Minimize, MoveSize, or Restore actions.

- To open an object, use the OpenForm, OpenModule, OpenQuery, OpenReport, or OpenTable actions.

- To set the value of a field or control, or a property of a form, control, or report, use the SetValue or SetProperty actions.

- To print a report, use the OpenReport action and set the View argument to Print Preview. If you want to print the report without previewing, set the View argument to Print.

- To run a query, use the OpenQuery action and set the View argument to Datasheet.

NOTE   *If you don't see SetValue in the list of macro actions, click the Show All Actions command in the Show/Hide group on the Design tab.*

Setting Action Arguments

Most macro actions have a list of associated arguments that give Access more information about how you want to carry out the action. Some arguments are required and others are optional. When you add an action to a macro, the argument list appears in the Action Arguments pane and the Arguments column.

You can usually type the value that you want in the field next to the argument, but many fields offer drop-down lists. If you enter a value, some arguments require that the value be included in the list. A description of the current argument is displayed in the information pane to the right of the argument list. If you need more help, press F1 with the insertion point in the argument field.

TIP *In some cases, choices for one argument can determine which choices are available for an argument farther down in the list. For this reason, setting the arguments in the order that they're listed in the Action Arguments pane is best.*

If the argument requires an object name, you can enter the name or drag the object from the Navigation Pane to the argument field. When you drag an object from the Navigation Pane, Access automatically sets the appropriate arguments for that action.

Instead of selecting from a list or entering a value, you can enter an expression that evaluates to the argument value that you want to use. Always precede the expression with an equal sign (=) so Access recognizes it as an expression instead of an identifier. For example, the expression = *[EntryNo]* sets the argument to the value in the EntryNo control.

TIP *The equal sign rule has two exceptions: The Expression argument of the SetValue action and the RepeatExpression argument of the RunMacro action give unexpected results if you use an equal sign. They evaluate the expression twice.*

If you want help from the Expression Builder, click the Build button, which appears at the right of the argument field when you select an argument that accepts an expression.

Not all arguments accept expressions. For example, you must select from the list for the ObjectType argument. If you use an expression where one isn't permitted, you'll get an error message.

NOTE *If you want to refer to a control on another form, you must use the full object identifier syntax: [Forms]![formname]![controlname]. The ! symbol indicates what follows is an object named by the user. If the reference is to something named by Access such as a control property, you would use a period (.) to separate the object names. In addition, both forms must be open. See the Access 2007 Help topic "A guide to expression syntax" for more information.*

Testing and Debugging a Macro

After you complete the macro, you can run it to see if it behaves as planned. You have a choice of running the complete macro at once or stepping through the macro one action at a time. If an error occurs in the macro or you don't get the results you expect, use the Single Step method of running the macro to see what went wrong.

Starting the Macro

After you finish adding the actions and setting the arguments, you can run a macro in several ways. While still in the Macro window, on the Design tab's Tools group, click the Run command. After you name and save a standalone macro, you can run it from the Navigation Pane by one of the following methods:

- Double-click the macro name.
- Right-click the macro name and choose Run from the shortcut menu.

If your macro is embedded in a particular form or report, open the form or report in Form or Report view and perform the task that activates the macro. You can also open the Macro window from the form or report event property and run it by clicking the Run command.

If an error occurs during the operation, Access displays an error message explaining the reason for the error. In this case, we left out the required Object Name argument. Read the message, and then click OK to open the Action Failed dialog box. This tells you which action in the macro failed and the arguments being used at the time. The following Arguments box shows that the second argument is missing from the GoToRecord action. You can tell by the two commas with no argument between them. It also shows any conditions that were in effect. Your only option in this dialog box is to click Stop All Macros to stop the macro. Before closing the dialog box, note the action name, error number, and other data about where the fault occurred. Then, it's up to you to switch to the Macro window to correct the problem.

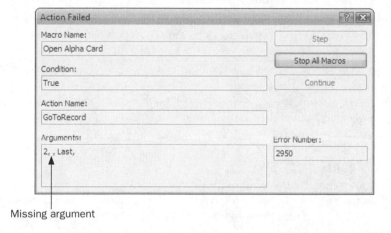

Missing argument

NOTE *The error number shown in the Action Failed dialog box is new to Access 2007. You can use it to create a macro or procedure that can respond to that particular type of error.*

Stepping through a Macro

If you create a macro with many actions and it contains an error, you can use the Single Step method to move through the macro, one action at a time. You must be in the Macro window to step through the macro actions. To start stepping through the macro, click the Single Step command in the Tools group, and then click the Run command to carry out the first action. A Macro Single Step dialog box opens showing the details of the first step in your macro.

NOTE *The Single Step mode remains in effect until you turn it off by clicking the Single Step command again, or choosing Run and clearing the Single Step command.*

Your options in this dialog box are as follows:

- **Step (default)**   Moves to the next action.
- **Stop All Macros**   Stops macro execution.
- **Continue**   Stops Single Step mode and runs the rest of the macro without stopping. If another error occurs, the macro stops and an Action Failed dialog box appears.

NOTE *Your macro might cause other macros to run. For example, an OpenForm action in a macro might open a form that has other macros assigned to the OnOpen, OnLoad, or other event properties. If other macros run as a result of the macro that you're testing, their steps are also displayed in the Macro Single Step dialog box. You can tell it's a different macro by the name that appears in the Macro Name box.*

Modifying a Macro

After you see how a macro runs, you might decide to make some changes to it, such as adding another action, changing the order of the actions, adding a condition to the action, adding a Where Condition argument to limit the records, or creating additional macros to include in a macro group.

To open a standalone macro for modification, right-click the macro name in the Navigation Pane and choose Design View. If the macro is embedded, open the form or report in Design or Layout view and open the Macro window by clicking the Build button in the Property Sheet and choosing Macro Builder.

Use the Insert Rows and Delete Rows commands in the Rows group, or right-click in the macro design and choose a command from the shortcut menu to add or delete actions. You can also use the standard cut, copy, and paste operations to edit a macro. The Undo button is available on the Quick Access toolbar to reverse the recent changes, as well.

TIP *If the macro operates on important data, make a temporary copy of the data to work with during the modification process. This way, if anything goes wrong, you haven't destroyed valuable information.*

After making the changes to the macro, save it again. If you save it with a different name, be sure to change all of the references to the macro accordingly.

Adding Conditions to a Macro

When you want a macro to run only under specific circumstances, you can add a condition to one or more of the macro actions. The macro condition states this effectively: If this condition is true, run this action. If it is not true, go to the next action, if any. This is a highly useful tool when programming an application. You can use conditions to set values of controls or control properties and even run additional macros. Note that such test comparisons are not case-sensitive.

The following are some examples of using conditions:

- If the balance of an account is negative, change the color of the number to red.

- If a student's grades are exemplary, print a congratulatory message.

- If the inventory level of an item is low, display a message to remind you to reorder.

- If the order exceeds a specific total, calculate the amount due with a volume discount.

NOTE *Don't confuse the macro condition that determines whether the action takes place with the Where Condition that limits the records in the form or report. The macro condition is entered in the Condition column of the macro sheet and the Where Condition is an argument of many macro actions.*

To add the Condition column to the macro sheet, in the Show/Hide group, click the Conditions command. Type the logical expression for the condition in the row with the action that you want to carry out if the condition is True. If you want to use the Expression Builder to help with the expression, right-click in the Condition column and choose Build from the shortcut menu. You can also click the Builder command in the Tools group.

Normally, a condition applies only to the action on the same row in the macro sheet. If the condition isn't met, the next action is executed. To continue the condition to the next action, enter an ellipsis (…) in the Condition column of the next row. You can apply the condition to several sequential actions.

TIP *When you're debugging a macro, you can temporarily disable an action by entering* False *in the Condition column. This can help to isolate the problem.*

You can also use conditions to create an If…Then…Else structure in a macro. This conditional logic runs one or more actions if the condition is met and a different set if the condition evaluates to False.

NOTE *You cannot use a SQL expression as a condition in a macro. SQL expressions are used only in Where Condition arguments.*

Running a Macro with a Condition

When you run the macro, Access evaluates the condition and does the following:

- If the condition is True, Access runs the action on that row, and all actions directly following it that have an ellipsis (…) in the Condition column. Then Access runs any additional actions that have blank conditions until it encounters another condition, a macro name in the Macro Name column, or the end of the macro.

- If the condition is False, the action is ignored as are any additional actions with an ellipsis (…) in the Condition column. Then Access moves to the next action, if any.

Table 19-1 shows some examples of expressions that you can use as conditions with macro actions. All the fields in the expressions are in the form from which the macro originates, unless otherwise specified.

NOTE *Notice the use of identifiers to specify a control in a form other than the one from which the macro was launched. The referenced form must be open at the time the macro runs.*

Choosing between Two Actions

You can use a macro to make one thing happen if a condition is true and make something else happen if it's false: you simply create two versions of the same condition. If you follow the conditional action with another action without using the opposite condition, the second action is always carried out.

For example, you want to do one thing if the Start Date is empty and carry out a different action if it shows a date. You could use the IsNull function in both conditions as follows:

- **IsNull("Start Date")**   Carry out the action when the Start Date is empty.

- **Not IsNull("Start Date")**   Carry out the action for a Start Date value.

Expression	Evaluates to True If:
[State]="CA"	CA is the value in the State control.
Forms![Alpha Entry]![Purge]<Date()	The Purge field on the Alpha Entry form is earlier than the current date.
[State] In ("CA","AZ","NV","NM") And Len([ZipCode])<5	The State value is one of those in the list and the value in the ZipCode field contains fewer than five characters. Combines two conditions into a single expression.
DCount("*","Alpha Entry", "[Index]=Forms![Alpha Card]![Index]")>5	More than five records are in the Alpha Entry table whose Index value matches an Index value in the Alpha Card table. Uses the DCount aggregate function.

TABLE 19-1   Examples of Conditional Expressions

Assigning a Macro to an Event Property

Access responds to all kinds of events that occur when you're working with a form or report, including mouse clicks, changes in data, changes in focus, and opening or closing a form or report. Chapter 18 contains a description of commonly used events, including when they happen and in what sequence. Assigning the macro to the right event in a sequence is important. If you have not embedded the macro in an event property, you need to decide when you want the macro to run.

After you decide when you want the macro to run, you set the corresponding event property of the form, report, or control to the name of the macro. For example, if you want to run a macro that sounds a beep when a form opens, assign the macro to the On Click property of a control on a form.

To attach a macro to an event property, do the following:

1. Open the form or report in Design or Layout view, and then select the form, report, section, or control to which you want to attach the macro.

2. Open the Property Sheet and click the Event tab to see a list of events that can occur for the selected object.

3. Click the property whose event you want to run the macro and choose the macro name from the drop-down list.

4. Save and close the form or report design.

Note If you select a macro name and then click Build (…) *next to the property box, you open the macro Design window, where you can view and edit the selected macro.*

When the event occurs, the built-in response, if any, occurs first, and then the macro runs. For example, when you click a button, the built-in response occurs and the button appears pressed. If you attach a macro to the On Click event property, the macro runs next.

Tip If you want the macro to occur when you click either the control or its label, select them both before opening the Property Sheet. Then choose the macro name in the On Click event property for the multiple selection.

Deciding Which Event to Use

Although the Property Sheet shows quite a long list of event properties for forms and controls, you'll use a few of them more often than others. Here are some of the commonly used form and control event properties:

- **On Open**   Occurs when the form opens, but before the first record is displayed. Use this property to open, close, or minimize other forms or to maximize this form.

- **On Current**   Occurs when the form is opened and focus moves to a record or the form is refreshed or requeried. Use this to synchronize data among forms or to move focus to a specific control.

- **Before Update**   Occurs after focus leaves a record, but before the data is saved in the database (also after a control loses focus, but before the control is changed). Use to display a message to confirm the change before it's completed.

- **After Update**   Occurs after the record changes are saved in the database (also after a control loses focus and after the control is changed). Use to update the data in other controls, forms, or reports or move focus to a different page, control, or record in the form.

- **On Click**   Occurs when you press and release the left mouse button over a control.

- **On Enter**   Occurs when you move to a control, but before it gets focus. Use to display information about data to enter in the control or a request for user password.

Reports and report sections have fewer event properties because little user interaction occurs with a report. Some of the more common event properties used to attach macros and event procedures to reports are as follows:

- **On No Data**   Runs a macro when the report has an empty underlying recordset. Use to cancel the print event.

- **On Open**   Runs a macro when the report opens, but before printing begins. Use to prompt for a filter for the records to be included in the report.

- **On Page**   Runs a macro after the page is formatted, but before printing begins. Use to add a graphic or border design to the report.

Report sections also have a few event properties to which you can attach a macro or event procedure.

Some Common Uses for Macros

When you work with a database, Access causes many things to happen in response to your actions. You might be unaware that you can customize the database with macros to accomplish many similar operations according to your designs. Here are some of the more common applications for macros.

Displaying a Message Box

The *MsgBox action* is one of the most useful macro actions when interacting with the user. You can use it to display warnings, alerts, and other information. The MsgBox action has four arguments: Message, Beep, Type, and Title. Table 19-2 describes the values that you can enter in each of the arguments.

TIP *Don't enclose the message in quotation marks unless you also want the marks displayed with the message.*

If you like the format of the built-in Access error messages, you can create the same effect with your own messages. The Message action argument can contain three sections separated by the @ character. The first section is text displayed as a boldface heading and can be used as an alert. The second section appears in plain text below the heading and is used for an explanation of the error. The third section appears below the text of the second section, also in plain text, with a blank line between. For example, the message,

Argument	Description
Message	Enter the text of the message you want displayed when the macro runs. You can enter up to 255 characters; the box expands accordingly. You can also enter an expression preceded by an equal sign (=) that evaluates to a text message.
Beep	Specifies whether to sound a beep signal when the message box opens. Set to Yes (default) or No.
Type	Sets the type of message box, each of which displays a different icon. Choices are None (default); Critical (a red circle with an *X*); Warning? (a bubble with a question mark); Warning! (a yellow triangle with an exclamation mark); or Information (a bubble with a lowercase *i*).
Title	Text that displays in the message box title bar. If left blank, the box is titled Microsoft Office Access.

TABLE 19-2 MsgBox Action Arguments

"Invalid Code@Look up the correct code in the log @Should have less than 6 numbers" displays this dialog box when a code of more than 5 numbers is entered:

Validating Data

Usually, you ensure that valid data is entered in a form by specifying a validation rule for the control in the form or by setting record and field validation rules in the underlying table design. For more complex data validation, use a macro or an event procedure to specify the rule.

The recommendation is that you use a macro or an event procedure if any of the following situations are present:

- You want to display different error messages for differing errors in the same field. For example, if the value is above the valid range, display one message; if the value is below the valid range, display another.

- You want the user to be able to override the rule. In this case, you can display a warning message and accept the user's confirmation or cancellation.

- The validation refers to controls in other forms or contains a function.

- The validation rule involves conditions based on more than one value. For example, if the user checks Credit Card as the method of payment, be sure that the number and expiration date are also entered in the form.

- You have a generic validation rule that can be used for more than one form. When you want to apply it to a control on a form, run the SetValue macro action that sets the Validation Rule property for the control.

One example of using a macro to validate data is checking to make sure that certain reports of serious criminal activity in the Police Alpha Entry table are never purged from the database. The macro is based on a condition that compares the Code value, which identifies the crime, with the value in the Purge field. The Purge field contains the date when the record could be erased from the file. The report of certain crimes is never to be erased. If the Code is in a certain range, no date should be entered in the Purge field.

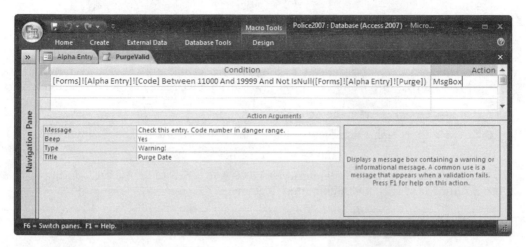

Figure 19-2 shows the results of the macro that accomplishes this data validation. A date value was entered in the record that has a code between 11000 and 19999. The macro has been embedded in the Before Update event property of the text box control that contains the data in question.

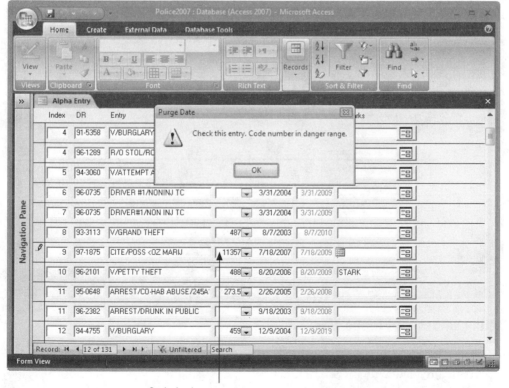

Code in danger range

FIGURE 19-2 Validating data entry with a macro

Filtering Records

You can create a macro to limit the records you want to print by adding a Where Condition to the OpenReport action. For example, suppose that you want to preview the Alpha Entry records for all incidents with a Code in the danger range, 11000 to 19999. Start a new macro with the Macro Builder from an Event property or from the Create tab and do the following:

1. Choose OpenReport in the Action column.

2. In the Report Name argument, select Alpha Entries from the list of available reports.

3. Choose Print Preview as the View argument.

4. Enter **[Alpha Entry]![Code] Between 11000 And 19999** in the Where Condition argument or click the Build button to get help from the Expression Builder.

TIP   Don't use an equal sign in the Where Condition argument.

5. Save the macro and then click Run.

You can see in the Print Preview that only three of the incidents reported fall within the danger range.

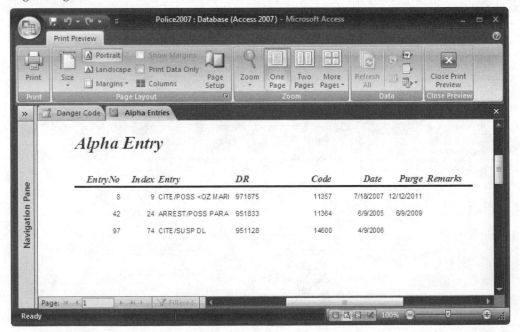

Setting Values and Properties

SetValue is a useful macro action that sets the value of a field, control, or property of a form, a form datasheet, or a report. You can set a value for almost any control, form, and report property in any view with the SetValue action.

NOTE *If you don't see the SetValue action in the drop-down action list, on the Design tab's Show/ Hide group, click the Show All Actions command.*

The action has two arguments, both required: Item and Expression.

- The *Item* argument contains the name of the field, control, or property whose value you want to set. When you enter the name in the Item argument box, you use the control name if the control is on the form or report from which the macro is called. If the control is on another form or report, you must use the full identifier including the form or report name: *[Forms!] formname!controlname*. If you're setting the value of a property, add the property name to the identifier preceded by a period: *[Forms!] formname!controlname.property*. If it's a form or report property, omit the control name and the preceding exclamation point (!).

- The *Expression* argument contains the value you want to set for the item. Again, use full syntax when referring to any Access objects in the expression. Use the Expression Builder if you need help. Don't precede the expression with an equal sign.

Setting Control Values

In addition to entering the value itself, you can set the value of a control based on the value of another control in the same or a different form or report. You can also use the result of a calculation or the value returned by an option group to set the value of a control.

For example, when you're adding new records to a person's file in the Alpha Entry recordset in the subform of the Alpha Card form, you can compute the value of the Purge field. Depending on the Code value, the entry might be purged from the person's file after a certain length of time—seven years in this example. To save data entry time, you can write a macro that examines the Code value and uses the DateAdd function to set the Purge date by adding a specified number of years to the Date field value.

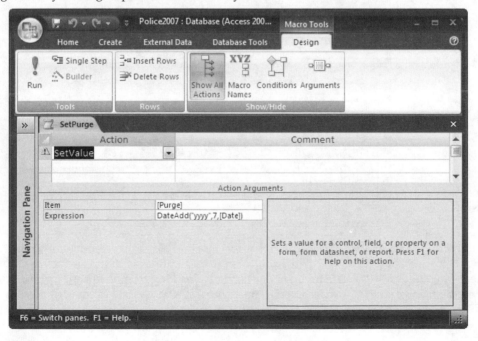

NOTE *The first argument in the DateAdd function, yyyy, indicates that the interval you want to increment is the year part of the date value. The second argument is the number of years to add, and the third names the control that contains the original date.*

Setting Control Properties

Many of the properties of forms, reports, and controls can be set by running a macro. For example, you can hide a control from view on the form or disable it so that the user can't enter data in it. You can also change colors, fonts, and other appearance properties.

As an example of setting a property with a macro, in the Police database, you can disable the Drivers_License control if the subject of the Alpha Card report is younger than age 16. To do this, set the Enabled property to No. When a control is disabled, it still appears on the screen, but it's dimmed and you can't reach it by pressing TAB or by clicking it.

To make sure that you enter the correct identifier, you can use the Expression Builder. After adding the SetValue action to the macro, click Build (…) next to the Item argument to open the Expression Builder, and then do the following:

1. Double-click the Forms folder, and then double-click the All Forms folder in the left panel to open the list of forms in the current database.

2. Choose the Alpha Card form. A list of all controls and labels in the form appears in the center panel.

3. Choose Drivers_License. A list of all the properties that apply to the Drivers_ License text box control appears in the right-most column.

4. Choose Enabled from the list of properties and click Paste. When you click OK, the expression is placed in the upper panel in the Expression Builder.

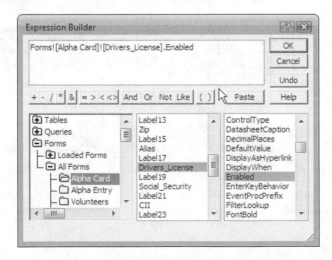

To complete the macro, click OK to return to the macro design window and enter No in the Expression argument and add a condition to the action row that runs the macro only if the Age value is less than 16. If you are not already working from the Property Sheet to embed the macro, attach the macro to the Age control's After Update event property.

You will probably want to add another macro to reenable the Drivers License control when you move to the next record.

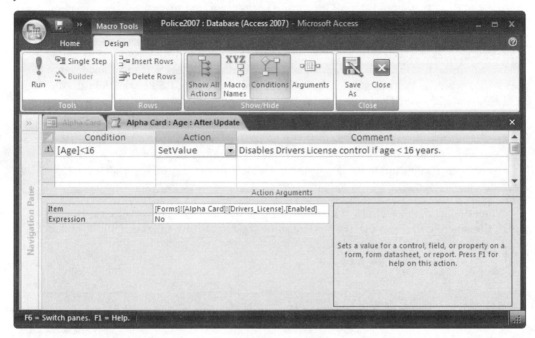

If you want to hide a control, set its Visible property to No.

If the property value is a string expression, enclose it in quotation marks in the Expression argument box.

To set report section properties, refer to the section by its number.

Changing the Flow of Operations

You can control the flow of operations by adding conditions that determine whether a macro action is carried out. If the condition evaluates to True, the corresponding action takes place. You can add the MsgBox function to a macro condition to let the user decide which action to carry out.

The MsgBox *function* is similar to the MsgBox *action* with the exception that the function returns one of seven different values, depending on which button the user clicks in the message box. The MsgBox function displays a message box containing the message and waits for the user to click a button indicating a choice.

The MsgBox function has three main arguments; only the first is required:

- *Prompt* is a string expression displayed in the dialog box. You can display up to 1024 characters, depending on the font size.

- *Button* is a number equal to the sum of three values that specify the visual characteristics of the message box, such as the number and type of buttons, the default button, the icon style, and the modality of the message box.

- *Title* is a string expression displayed in the dialog box title bar.

Two additional optional arguments can specify a Help file and context number in the file where you can find context-sensitive help.

You can display seven different buttons in various arrangements, as well as a choice of four icons. You can also specify which of the buttons is the default. Table 19-3 lists these button arrangements and dialog box features with their numeric values. The buttons are placed in the message box in the order—from left to right—that they're listed in the table.

For example, if you want the message box to display the Yes, No, and Cancel set of buttons (3) with the Warning Query icon (32) and set the Yes button as the default (0), enter **35** (3 + 32 + 0 = 35) as the second argument in the MsgBox function.

NOTE *The message box normally opens as an application modal, which requires the user to respond to the message box before continuing. Additional argument settings can be used to change that. For example, if you want to make it system modal, which suspends all applications in the system until the user responds, add 4096 to the other values in the second argument.*

When the user clicks a button in the message box, the corresponding value is returned, which the macro condition can use to determine the next action to take. Table 19-4 lists the values returned by each type of button.

Value	Buttons to Display:
0	Display only the OK button.
1	Display the OK and Cancel buttons.
2	Display the Abort, Retry, and Ignore buttons.
3	Display the Yes, No, and Cancel buttons.
4	Display the Yes and No buttons.
5	Display the Retry and Cancel buttons.
	Icons to Display:
0	Display no icon.
16	Display the Critical Message icon.
32	Display the Warning Query icon.
48	Display the Warning Message icon.
64	Display the Information Message icon.
	Specify the Default Button:
0	Set the first button as default.
256	Set the second button as default.
512	Set the third button as default.
768	Set the fourth button as default.

TABLE **19-3**   MsgBox Function Button Argument Settings

Button	Returned Value
OK	1
Cancel	2
Abort	3
Retry	4
Ignore	5
Yes	6
No	7

TABLE 19-4   Values Returned by MsgBox Function

When you use the MsgBox function in a macro condition, you can compare the returned value to a specific number and carry out the action if the comparison is True. For example, you can use the MsgBox function to display a confirmation message before deleting a record. The box contains three buttons: Yes, No, and Cancel. If the user clicks the Yes button, the function returns 6, so if any other value is returned, the user didn't click Yes. This shows a macro that uses the MsgBox function in a condition that evaluates to True if the function returned any value except 6 (Yes). If the value isn't 6, the deletion event is canceled. You could add other conditions that carry out actions as a result of the other button selections.

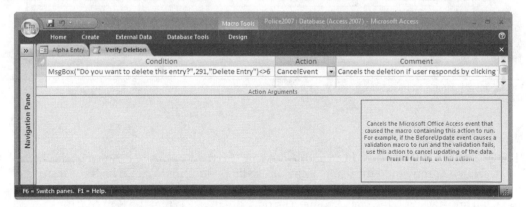

The Verify Deletion macro should be embedded in or attached to the form's Before DEL Confirm event property. The message box displays when you select a record and press DEL. In Figure 19-3, the Alpha Entry record for Index 35 was selected before pressing DEL. You can see it's been deleted from the Form view, but isn't confirmed yet. If you respond by clicking Yes, Access displays another confirmation message if the deletion can result in cascade deletions of other records or interfere in some other way with the relationships in the database.

NOTE   *The Button argument in the MsgBox function in Figure 19-3 is 291, the sum of the Yes, No, Cancel button arrangement (3), the Warning Query icon (32), and setting the second button (No) as the default (256).*

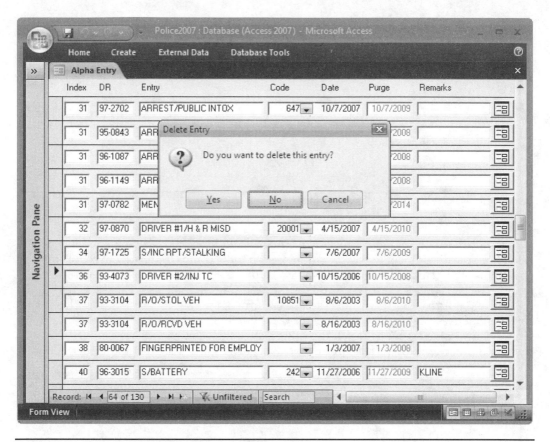

FIGURE 19-3   Using the MsgBox function in a macro condition

Nesting Macros

If you want to run one macro from another macro, use the RunMacro action and set the Macro Name argument to the name of the macro that you want to run. The RunMacro action is similar to clicking the Run Macro command in the Macro group on the Database Tools tab and selecting the macro name. The only difference is that the Run Macro command runs the macro only once. With the RunMacro action, you can repeat the macro many times.

The RunMacro action has two arguments in addition to the Macro Name:

- **Repeat Count**   Specifies the maximum number of times the macro is to run.

- **Repeat Expression**   Contains an expression that evaluates to True (−1) or False (0). The expression is evaluated each time the RunMacro action occurs. When it evaluates to False, the called macro stops.

The Repeat Count and Repeat Expression arguments work together to specify how many times the macro runs.

- If both are blank, the macro runs only once.
- If Repeat Count contains a number, but the Repeat Expression is blank, the macro runs the specified number of times.
- If the Repeat Count is blank, but the Repeat Expression contains an expression, the macro runs until the expression evaluates to False.
- If both arguments contain entries, the macro runs the specified number of times or until the expression evaluates to False, whichever occurs first.

When the called macro is finished, Access returns to the calling macro and runs the next action after RunMacro.

NOTE *You can call a macro in the same macro group, as well as a macro in another group. If you enter a macro group name as the Macro Name argument, the first macro in the group runs.*

You can nest macros to more than one level. The called macro can, in turn, call another macro, and so on. As each macro finishes, it returns control back to the macro that called it.

Create a Macro Group

If you create several macros that apply to controls on the same form or report, you can group them together as one file. Using macro groups offers two advantages:

- It reduces the number of macro names in the Navigation Pane.
- You can find all the macros for a single form or report in one place, where they're easy to edit, if necessary.

To create a macro group, open the macro sheet as usual and in the Show/Hide group, click the Macro Names command to display the Macro Name column. Add a macro to the sheet and enter a name for it in the Macro Name column of the first row of the macro. Add the rest of the actions to the macro.

To add another macro, enter the name in the Macro Name column and add the actions that you want to occur.

When Access runs a macro in a group, it begins with the action in the row that contains the macro name and continues until it finds no more actions or encounters another macro name. After adding all the macros to the group, close and save it as usual with the group name.

TIP *The macros in a group are much easier to read if you leave at least one blank row between the macros. You can also leave several rows blank at the top of the macro and add information in the Comment column that explains the purpose of the macro and where it's called from. Then the macro starts on the next row, where the Name and first Action appear.*

When you assign macros from a group to an event property, you need to use the group name as well as the macro name. In the Property Sheet for a control, the drop-down list in an event property shows compound names for all of the macros in a group, as well as the names of all of the single macros. The group name and the macro name both appear separated by a period: *macrogroupname.macroname*. Figure 19-4 shows the macro group Choose Report, which you will meet in Chapter 21 when you see the Choose Report dialog box.

Assigning AutoKeys

You can create a special macro group named *AutoKeys*, in which you can assign an action or a set of actions to a specific key or key combination. These act like the shortcut key combinations that you can use to carry out a ribbon command. Pressing the key or combination of keys carries out the action that you specify. You can add as many individual macros to the group as you need, each one named with the key or key combination that runs it.

For example, the following macro opens the Alpha Card form when the user presses CTRL-F.

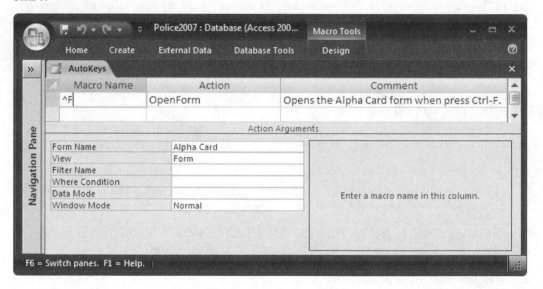

CAUTION *If you use a key combination that Access already uses, such as CTRL-C for Copy, your actions will replace the Access key assignment. Also be warned that resetting to default assignments will remove all custom assignments.*

Table 19-5 shows a list of valid AutoKeys key combinations. These combinations are part of the set that can be used by the Visual Basic SendKeys statement. The SendKey syntax form is used as the macro name. The carat symbol (^) represents CTRL and the plus sign (+) represents SHIFT. Function keys and other key names are enclosed in curly brackets ({}).

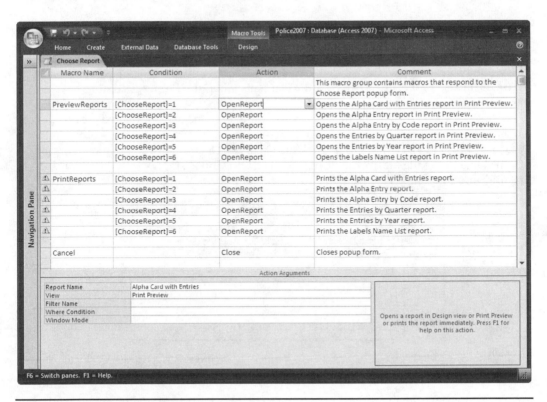

FIGURE 19-4 The Choose Report macro group

Key Combination	Macro Name
CTRL-Any letter or number key	^A, ^4
Any function key	{F1}
CTRL-Any function key	^{F1}
SHIFT-Any function key	+{F1}
INS	{INSERT}
CTRL-INS	^{INSERT}
SHIFT-INS	+{INSERT}
DEL	{DELETE} or {DEL}
CTRL-DEL	^{DELETE} or ^{DEL}
SHIFT-DEL	+{DELETE} or +{DEL}

TABLE 19-5 AutoKeys Key Combinations

Documenting Macros

Because macros are database objects, they're listed in the database Properties dialog box on the Contents tab. To view the list, click the Microsoft Office button, point to Manage, and choose Database Properties. Then click the Contents tab in the Properties dialog box and scroll down the list until you reach the macro section.

If you want to keep documentation for the standalone macros and macro groups in your database, you can print the macro description by using the Database Documenter. On the Database Tools tab's Analyze group, click the Database Documenter command. Select the Macros tab, choose the macro you want, and click OK. Choose Options, and in the Print Macro Definition dialog box, check the categories of information that you want to print:

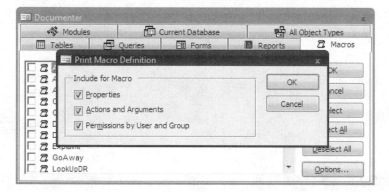

- **Properties**   Includes the container, date created, date of last update, owner, and user.

- **Actions and Arguments**   Lists all the actions with their conditions, if any, and the values of all the arguments.

- **Permissions by User and Group**   Lists user permissions, such as admin, and group permissions, such as Admins and Users.

Then click OK again to see the macro definitions in Print Preview.

Creating an AutoExec Macro

You can create a special macro that runs when you first open a database. The AutoExec macro can carry out actions such as opening a form for data entry, displaying a message box prompting the user to enter his or her name, or playing a sound greeting. The Northwind database opens with one of two forms depending on the current project security status.

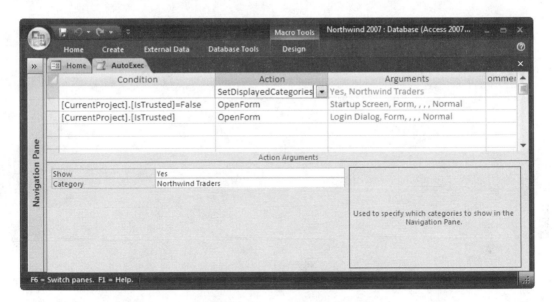

All you need to do is create the macro with the actions that you want carried out at startup and save it with the name AutoExec. A database can have only one macro named AutoExec.

When you open a database, all the startup options that you set in the Current Database group of Access Options take place first. You can see these by clicking the Microsoft Office button and choosing Access Options. Then Access looks for a macro named AutoExec, if one exists, and executes the actions in it.

You can bypass both the startup options and the AutoExec macro by pressing SHIFT when you open the database.

CAUTION   *Many of the same options can be set in the AutoExec macro as in the Startup dialog box. Be careful not to include conflicting settings in the macro. See Chapter 16 for information about the startup settings.*

Summary

Properly constructed macros carry out actions when you want them to and in the way that you want. They're useful for responding to user input and manipulating data. They are easy to construct and test and provide a degree of automation to your database. As you work with macros, you can begin to see their potential.

In the next two chapters, you will investigate modifying the ribbons and customizing the Quick Access toolbar. The Navigation Pane can also be customized to provide groups of special database objects that relate to the purpose and structure of the database. Macros are also used in later chapters for building custom dialog boxes.

Customizing the User Interface

The ribbon, the new user interface with activity-oriented tabs and groups of commands, presents a flexible portal for using Office Access 2007. Even though the ribbon has been designed to make every action available to you as you work, you can make some changes to it—for example, if you print reports frequently, you can add a print button to the Quick Access toolbar. You can also move the ribbon and the Quick Access toolbar to make more room in the active window.

You can also create customized dialog boxes for entering or retrieving specific information from the database and keep your startup options from a previous version of Access.

Working with the Ribbon

Although you can't customize the commands on the Access 2007 ribbon, you can manipulate them to fit your needs. The commands shown in the ribbon relate specifically to the current activity, but the way they are displayed depends on the current width of your Access window.

Resizing the Ribbon

The ribbon is designed to fit the maximized Access window. When the window is maximized, you will see the commands widely spaced with their names displayed.

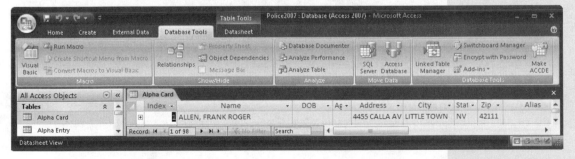

If you are using Access in a narrower window, the ribbon is resized to fit. The icons may not appear in the order that they appear in the maximized window. The commands might also appear compressed horizontally, and many of the command names are removed, leaving only the icon. They can also appear stacked in a column of three icons without command names instead of in a row with command names. For example, consider the commands in the Macro and Analyze groups:

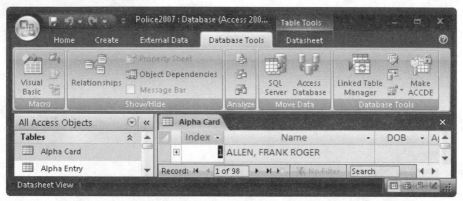

Shrinking the window width further reduces the ribbon and eventually hides it altogether. Some groups, for example, the Show/Hide group, will then be represented by a single icon with a down-arrow that you can click to display the commands within the group in a context menu.

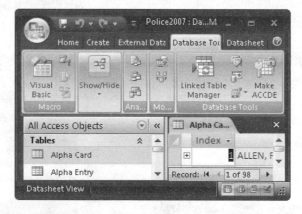

NOTE   *If you have created a custom ribbon using XML, you can use it with your database. In the Current Database page of the Access Options window, select Ribbon Name in the Toolbar Options and choose the ribbon from the drop-down list.*

Hiding and Restoring the Ribbon

If the ribbon is taking up too much of your work space, you can hide it, either briefly or for the whole session. You can hide the ribbon in three ways:

- Press CTRL-F1.
- Double-click an active ribbon tab.

- At the right end of the Quick Access toolbar, click the Customize Quick Access Toolbar button and check Minimize the Ribbon in the context menu.

When the ribbon is hidden, the tabs still appear, so you can use the commands by clicking a tab to restore the ribbon temporarily. After you select a command, the ribbon automatically withdraws again. To restore the ribbon to its normal appearance, repeat the action you used to hide it.

Using Keyboard Shortcuts for Ribbon Commands

Access 2007 uses a set of KeyTips to provide a way for you to use any command in the ribbon with only a few keystrokes. To see the keys available in the current view, press ALT or F10. The Microsoft Office button shows the KeyTip *F* and the Quick Access toolbar buttons are numbered *1, 2, 3*. Each tab also has a KeyTip: the Home tab shows *H*, Create is *C*, External Data is *X*, and Database Tools is *A*. When you press one of the tab KeyTips, the commands on that tab show additional tips.

For example, press C to open the Create tab and display the KeyTips for the commands in the tab. The Table command in the Tables group now shows *TN* and the Forms command in the Forms group shows *FN*. You can use these KeyTips to carry out complete Access tasks without using the mouse. If a ribbon command is not currently active, the KeyTip is also inactive.

To cancel the action that you are taking and hide the tips, press ALT or F10 again.

NOTE *Access 2007 uses the same key combinations that were used in earlier versions to carry out specific commands. So if you are used to using keystrokes for common actions, you can continue using them. For example, you can press* CTRL-P *to open the Print dialog box for the current datasheet, form, or report.*

Table 20-1 lists the keyboard actions that you can use to move around in the groups and commands in a ribbon.

Customizing the Quick Access Toolbar

Unlike the ribbon, the Quick Access toolbar is independent of any current activity and can be customized to fit your requirements. If you prefer to have the toolbar more accessible or wider so that it can hold more commands, you can move it below the ribbon. Then you can add frequently used commands to it. For example, if you print reports often, you can add the Quick Print or Print Preview command to the toolbar.

Moving the Quick Access Toolbar

To place the toolbar below the ribbon, click the Customize Quick Access Toolbar button and choose Show Below the Ribbon. To restore the toolbar to its original position, choose Show Above the Ribbon from the Customize Quick Access Toolbar context menu. You can also right-click in the toolbar and choose the command from the shortcut menu.

PART III

Adding Commands to the Toolbar

The Customize Quick Access Toolbar context menu displays a list of common commands that you can add to the toolbar. The commands that are already in the toolbar are checked. Check the commands you want to add.

To Do This	Press
Select the active tab and show access keys	ALT or F10
Move to another tab	LEFT or RIGHT ARROW
Minimize or restore the ribbon	CTRL-F1
Move focus among areas of the window: active ribbon tab, status bar, and current document	F6
Move focus to command in the ribbon, forward or backward	ALT or F10, then TAB or SHIFT-TAB
Move up, down, left, or right among items	UP ARROW, DOWN ARROW, LEFT ARROW, RIGHT ARROW
Activate selected menu command or control	SPACEBAR or ENTER
Open context selected menu or gallery	SPACEBAR or ENTER
Activate a command or control so you can make changes	ENTER
Complete changes and move focus back to the document	ENTER
Get help with command or control	F1

TABLE 20-1   Using Keystrokes to Access Ribbon Commands

The commands New, Open, Quick Print, and Print Preview have been added to this toolbar below the ribbon:

If the commands that you want to add are not in the short list in the Customize Quick Access Toolbar menu, click More Commands to open the Customize page of the Access Options dialog box. Figure 20-1 shows the list of available commands in the Popular Commands list. The right pane lists the commands already on the toolbar.

To add more commands, select them one at a time and click Add. To remove a command, select it in the right pane and click Remove. The <Separator> command at the top of the list places a vertical line between the commands to group the commands visibly on the toolbar.

NOTE *The default setting is to apply the changes to the Quick Access toolbar to all documents. If you want changes to apply only to the current database, click the Customize Quick Access Toolbar down arrow and choose this option from the drop-down list.*

The Choose Commands From drop-down list offers more sources for commands (see Figure 20-2).

Click each of the command categories to see what is available.

- Popular commands are just that—commands that are often used during database management.

- The Commands Not in the Ribbon list includes commands found on the status bar, title bar, and Quick Access Toolbar.

- The All Commands list includes commands from earlier versions of Access as well as all current commands.

- The Macros list includes macros available in the current database.

- The Office Menu list includes commands to open or close a database and other database file commands.

- The remaining lists can copy commands from specific ribbon tabs or tab groups.

When you are finished adding the commands to the toolbar, click OK.

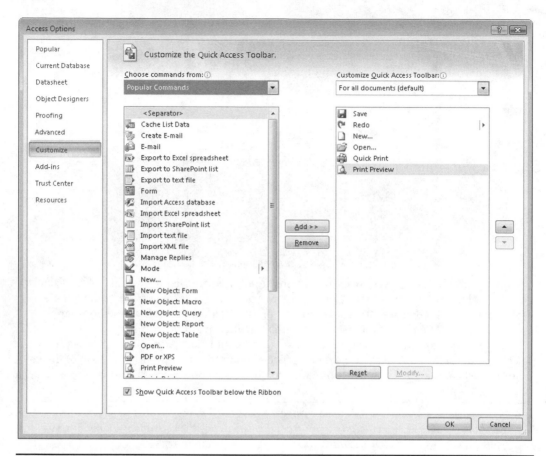

FIGURE 20-1   Choosing commands to place on the Quick Access Toolbar

Adding Commands from the Ribbon

Another way to add a command to the Quick Access Toolbar is to bring it directly from the ribbon. Simply right-click the command that you want to add, and choose Add to Quick Access Toolbar from the shortcut menu.

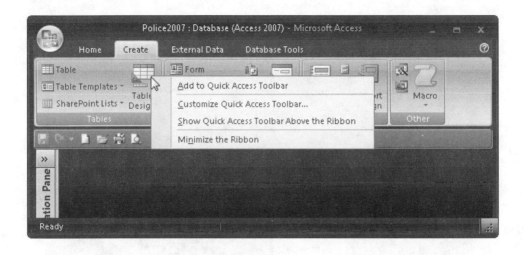

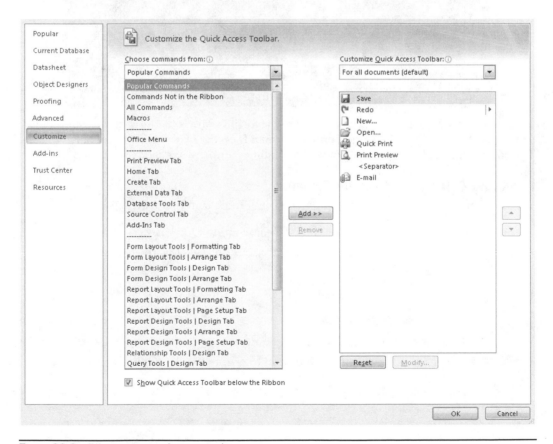

FIGURE 20-2 Other sources of commands

Many of the lists and galleries in the ribbon can also be added to the toolbar. In the following example, the More Forms and Table Templates commands were added to the toolbar:

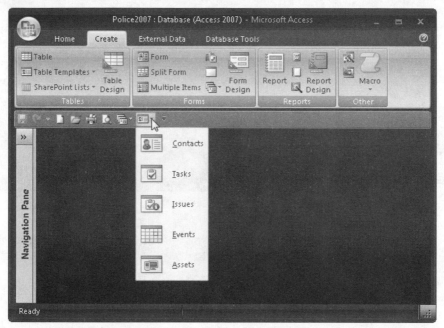

Not all ribbon commands can be added to the toolbar. The contents of some command groups, such as the Data Type and Format commands on the Datasheet tab, are not available. The other commands in the Data Type & Formatting group are available, however.

Removing Commands from the Toolbar

You can remove a command from the Quick Access Toolbar in two ways:

- Right-click the command and choose Remove from Quick Access Toolbar.
- Click the Customize Quick Access Toolbar button and clear the check mark from the command in the list.

To restore the toolbar to its original settings, do the following:

1. Click the Microsoft Office button and choose Access Options.
2. On the Customize page, click the Reset button.
3. A message asks if you are sure you want to restore the default buttons. Click Yes.

4. Click OK to close the Access Options dialog box.

Using Existing Customization

If you are updating from Access 2003, you don't have to give up all your custom settings. For example, you can still have your main switchboard form show at startup. You can also use the custom toolbars and menus you built in Access 2003.

Showing a Startup Switchboard

If a switchboard appeared at startup in your Access 2003 database, you can use it in Access 2007 as well. All you need to do is change the Current Database option to display the form at startup, as follows:

1. Click the Microsoft Office button and choose Access Options.

2. Go to the Current Database page, and choose the name of the form—Switchboard, in this case—from the Display Form list (Figure 20-3).

3. Click OK to close the dialog box.

4. Close and restart the database.

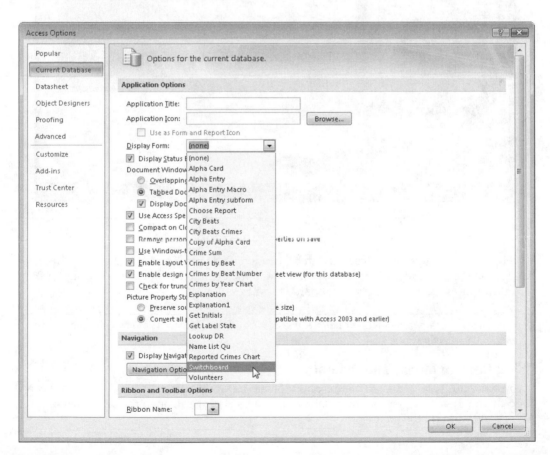

PART III

FIGURE 20-3   Choosing the startup form

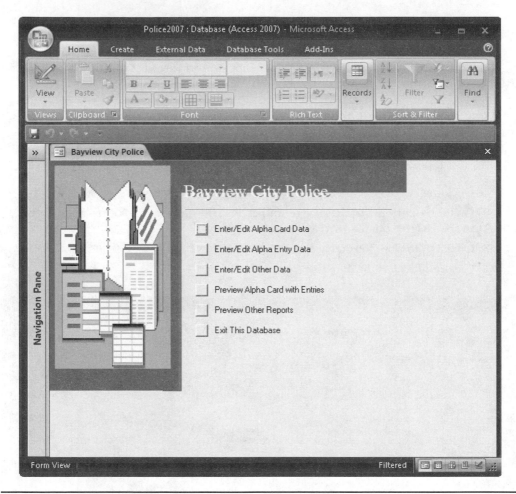

FIGURE 20-4   Starting the Police database with the switchboard

Figure 20-4 shows the Police2007 database when it restarts. The switchboard form may need some changes so that it doesn't spread out in the document window. See Chapter 21 for information about creating switchboards for Access 2007.

TIP   *Be sure to remove any unsupported actions such as Open Database Window from the converted switchboard before designating it as the startup form.*

Using Custom Menus and Toolbars

If you have built some custom menus and toolbars for your Access 2003 database, you can keep them when you work on the database in Access 2007. First, open the database in Access 2003 and do the following:

1. Choose Tools | Startup.

2. In the Startup dialog box, select your custom menu bar from the Menu Bar list.

3. Clear the Allow Built-In Toolbars check box and click OK.

4. Save and close the database.

Next, open the Access 2003 database (Access 2007 refers to it as a "legacy" database) with Access 2007 and do the following:

1. Click the Microsoft Office button and click Access Options.

2. Open the Current Database options page.

3. In the Ribbon & Toolbars Options group, clear the Allow Full Menus check box.

4. Click OK.

The custom menus and toolbars from the Access 2003 database appear as groups in the Add-Ins ribbon tab. If your database does not have a custom toolbar, the Add-Ins tab does not appear.

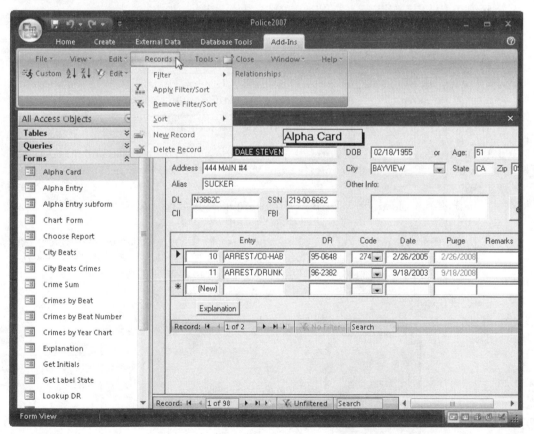

Creating a Custom Dialog Box

A dialog box is a special type of window that pops up and stays on the screen until the user makes a selection, even if it is only to cancel the box. To create a dialog box, you start with a blank, unbound form and add controls that you can select to carry out specific actions. After completing the form, you create macros or event procedures and attach them to the corresponding controls on the form.

Designing the Form

In this section, you will learn how to create a dialog box that offers a choice of police reports when the user clicks the Print button on the new dialog box form. Creating this custom dialog box involves four major steps:

1. Create the form.
2. Add an option group control and command buttons.
3. Create the macros.
4. Attach the macros to the command buttons.

NOTE *It may help to open the Navigation Pane to show the report names. Then you don't have to remember the exact wording of the report titles to enter them in the wizard dialog box.*

Here's how to create the Choose Report dialog box for the Police database:

1. On the Create tab in the Forms group, click the More Forms command and choose Modal Dialog from the context menu. Make sure the Use Control Wizards command is selected.
2. In the Controls group, click the Option Group command and draw a frame in the empty form design to start the Option Group Wizard.
3. In the first wizard dialog box (shown next), enter the report names as the Label Names for the options in the group. After entering a name, press the DOWN ARROW or TAB to move to the next line. If you press ENTER, you move to the next dialog box and must click the Back button to continue. After entering all the option labels, click the Next button.

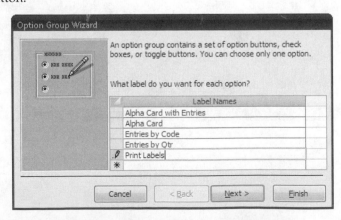

4. In the next wizard dialog box, accept the first option as the default returned value and click Next.

5. In the next dialog box, accept the default values and click Next.

6. The next wizard dialog box (as shown) displays a variety of styles for the option group and the options in it. Choose Option Buttons as the type of control and Raised as the frame style, and then click Next.

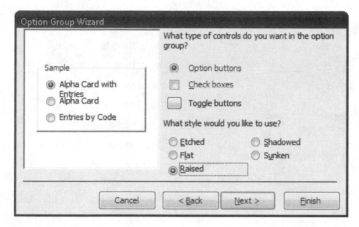

7. In the final wizard dialog box, enter **Choose Report** as the caption for the group that will be displayed at the top of the group frame; then click Finish.

8. Back in the form Design view, select the option group frame, if it's not already selected, and open the Property Sheet. Choose the Name property on the Other tab and enter **Choose Report** as the name for the option group.

9. Right-click the form tab and choose Save in the shortcut menu.

10. Enter the name **Choose Report** in the Save As dialog box and click OK.

Table 20-2 lists the property settings that the Modal Dialog Wizard set for the form. This wizard is new to Access 2007. In previous versions, you had to set these properties yourself.

The next step is to add the command buttons to display the selected report in Print Preview, to print the selected report, and to close the form. Do this without the help of the Command Button Wizard because you want to attach macros to the buttons instead of using the default operations offered by the wizard. To add the three command buttons, make sure that the Use Control Wizards button in the Controls group is not pressed, and then do the following:

1. In the Controls group, click the Button command and then click in the form design. Repeat twice more, spacing the buttons as desired. Each button will display the default caption: Command*n*.

2. Select the first button, and then click in it and type **Preview**. Press ENTER to save the new caption.

3. Repeat step 2 to change the default captions on the other two buttons to **Print** and **Cancel**.

Property	Setting	Purpose
Pop-Up	Yes	Form will remain on top of other windows.
Modal	Yes	Form retains focus until it is manually closed.
Caption	Choose Report	Displays this text in the title bar in Form view instead of the form name. Enter the name.
Allow Form View	Yes	Permits the form in Form view.
Allow Datasheet View	No	Prevents switching to Datasheet view.
Allow PivotTable View	No	Prevents switching to PivotTable view.
Allow PivotChart View	No	Prevents switching to PivotChart view.
Allow Layout View	Yes	Permits switching to Layout view.
Scroll Bars	Neither	Removes scroll bars from the form.
Record Selectors	No	Removes record selectors from the form.
Navigation Buttons	No	Removes navigation buttons from the form.
Dividing Lines	No	Removes horizontal lines from the form.
Auto Center	Yes	Centers the form automatically when it opens. If you want the form to appear in a special place, set to No.
Border Style	Dialog	Adds thick border to form with only a title bar with a control menu box at the right and the Close button at the left.
Control Box	Yes	Displays the control menu box in the title bar in Form view so that the user can close the form.
MinMax Buttons	None	Prevents the user from resizing the form in Form view.

TABLE 20-2   Property Settings for a Modal Dialog Form

4. If the buttons are not evenly spaced or accurately aligned, select all three and use the Control Alignment commands on the Arrange tab to adjust the buttons.

5. If the buttons are not the same size, use the Size group commands to adjust them.

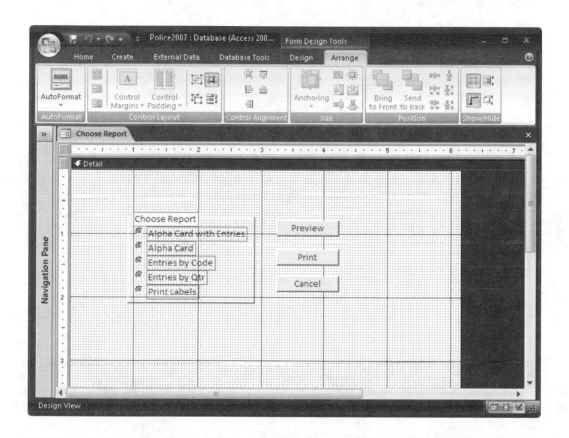

> **NOTE**   *You can also use the sizing handles in the group of controls to size them all at once.*

So far, the command buttons on the Choose Report form do not carry out an action. You must create the macros that will run and perform the intended action when the user clicks the button.

Creating and Attaching the Macros

You need to create a macro for each of the command buttons in the form. In addition, you must convey to the Print and Preview macros which report to open. The macros that you attach to the Preview and Print buttons must distinguish among the reports and open the one that you select from the option group.

The option group returns a value depending on which item in the group is selected. As you saw earlier, the Option Group Wizard set default return values so that if you click the first item, the group value is 1; if you click the second item, the value is 2; and so on. You can use this value in the macro condition to choose the specific report to preview or print.

Creating the Macro Group

The best way to respond to a selection from an option group is to build a set of macros that you can attach to each option in the group. Here's how to build a macro for the Preview button:

1. On the Create tab's Other group, click the Macro command.

2. On the Design tab's Show/Hide group, click the Macro Names and Condition commands to show the two optional columns, and then click the Arguments command to remove it from the design to save space.

3. Type **PreviewReports** as the name of the first macro, and choose OpenReport as the Action.

4. In the Action Arguments pane, choose Alpha Card with Entries from the drop-down list of Report Names and choose Print Preview as the View argument.

5. In the Condition column, enter the condition under which to preview the report: **[Choose Report]=1**. *Choose Report* is the name of the option group control, and *1* is the value of the group when you select the first item in the group.

TIP *It is a good idea to add comments in macro commands so that you will know what actions are attached to the macro.*

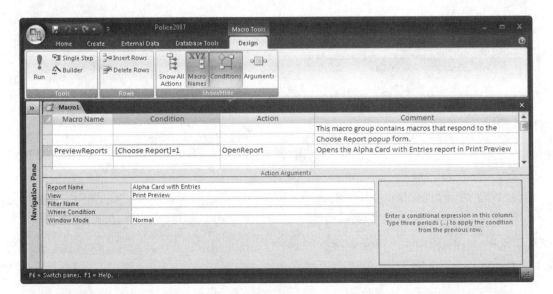

TIP *If you are in doubt about the name of the control, look at the Name property on the Other tab of the control's Property Sheet.*

6. Move to the next row and repeat steps 4 and 5 to open the Alpha Entry report in Print Preview with the condition that the Choose Report group value is 2.

7. Continue to define macro actions to open the remaining reports in Print Preview. You should have five actions in the PreviewReports macro, each opening a different report in Print Preview.

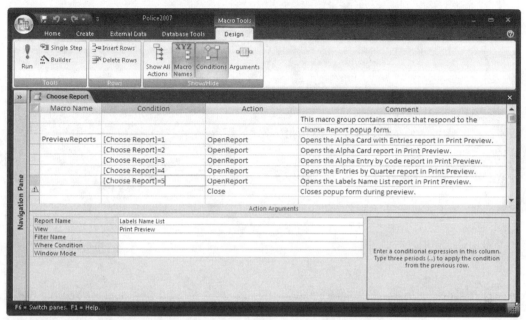

8. You could add a final action to the macro that closes the Choose Report form so you can see the Print Preview window without the pop-up dialog box in the way. Set the following arguments for the Close action:

   - Object Type: Form
   - Object Name: Choose Report
   - Save: No

9. Leave an empty row and create a new macro named PrintReports to print each of the reports using the same conditions. Do not include the Close action with the second macro, so the pop-up dialog box remains on the screen for further selections in case you want to print other reports.

TIP *An easy way to add the conditions to the PrintReports macro is to copy the* [Choose Report]= *part of the condition and paste it in subsequent lines, and then add the values.*

The macro command for the Cancel button can be simply *Close* with the Choose Report form name as the Object Name argument. You can accept the default Prompt as the Save argument or choose No to close the form without a prompt. Figure 20-5 shows the completed macro group for the Choose Report form.

NOTE *The alarm icons in the left margin of the macro design indicate that the action will not be allowed if the database is not from a trusted location.*

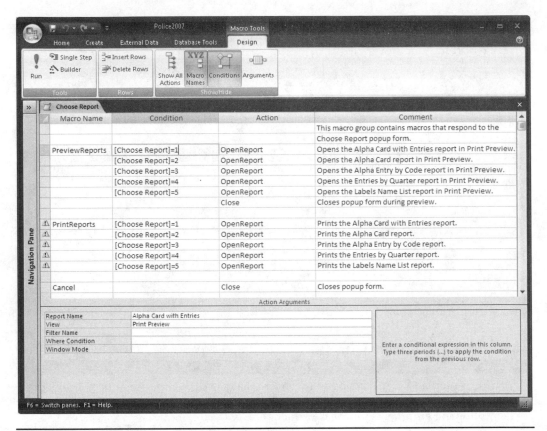

FIGURE 20-5   The macro group for the Choose Report form

Attaching the Macros to Form Controls

Once you have created the macros, your next step is to indicate when they should execute by attaching them to the event properties of the controls. Here's how to attach the macros to the command buttons:

1. Return to the form in Design view, select the Preview command button, and open the Property Sheet.

2. Click the Events tab and choose the macro name from the drop-down list next to the On Click event property. Figure 20-6 shows the PreviewReports macro in the Choose Report macro group as the action to carry out when the button is clicked.

3. Repeat steps 1 and 2 to attach the Choose Report.PrintReports macro to the Print button and the Choose Report.Cancel macro to the Cancel button.

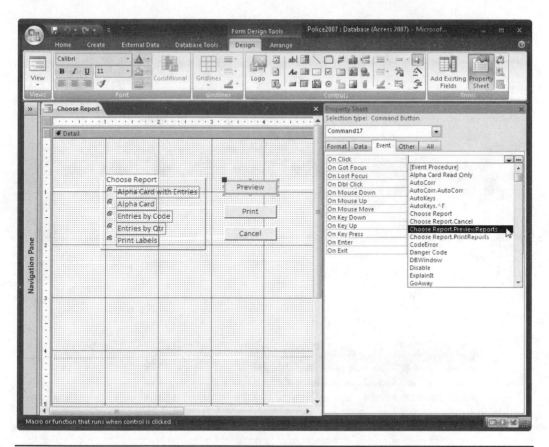

Figure 20-6   Attaching a macro to the Preview command button

A dialog box created by the wizard is a *pop-up modal form*. *Pop-up* means that it opens and stays on top of other windows even when it is no longer the active window. *Modal* means that you must hide or close the form before you can work in any other object or menu command. The Form Wizard sets these properties for you.

Now you need to shrink the form to show only your option group and the command buttons. When you try to move the right border, it doesn't move. The Modal Form Wizard has added two command buttons to ensure that you had a way to close the modal form.

Scroll down the form in Design view and locate the OK and Cancel buttons in the lower-right corner.

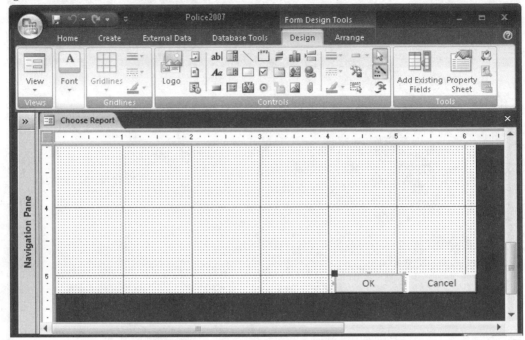

Select them both and press DELETE. Then resize the form to fit the option group and the command buttons.

NOTE *To switch from Form view to Design view, right-click within the form and choose Design from the shortcut menu. Right-clicking the form tab only closes the form.*

Two additional features that help turn a form into a dialog box are the default and Cancel button properties:

- The command button specified as the default button is pushed automatically when the user presses ENTER.

- The command button specified as the Cancel button is pushed automatically when the user presses ESC.

You can assign any one button in the form as the default button and another as the Cancel button by setting the Default or Cancel control property to Yes.

While you are working with the command button properties, you can add ScreenTips that will appear when you rest the mouse pointer over the button. To add ScreenTips, type the text in the button's ControlTip Text property box on the Other tab of the Property Sheet. In this case, enter Open the selected report in Print Preview as the ControlTip.

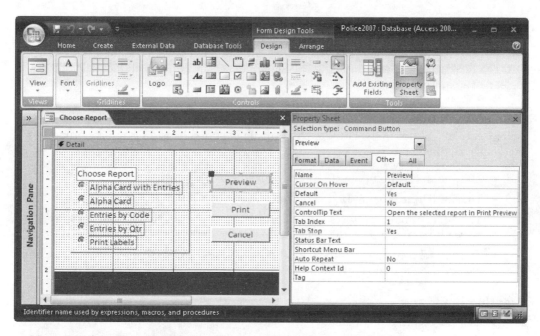

Now switch to Form view to see the new Choose Report dialog box, ready for previewing and printing Police reports.

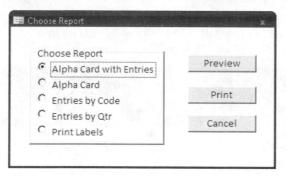

Creating a Dialog Box for User Input

In Chapter 8, you saw how to create a parameter query that prompts the user to enter the criteria for the query. You can use a custom dialog box to accomplish the same thing. For example, the dialog box shown in the following illustration prompts the user to enter the DR value of the Alpha Entry record that the user wants to see. It includes instructions to ensure a valid input value.

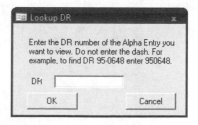

After the user enters the DR value and clicks OK, a parameter query runs using the value as the criteria for the DR field and displays the more descriptive Detail Report for the Alpha Entry. For this example, make a copy of the Alpha DR Query and name it **Lookup DR**. You can change the criteria of the DR column to get the value from the dialog box instead of a parameter prompt.

Setting the Input Form Properties

Several special features in the Lookup DR form are included in addition to the properties that make it a dialog box:

- The DR box is an unbound text box named FindDR.
- The FindDR text box is first in the tab order with a Tab Index property of 0.
- The OK command button's Default property is set to Yes so the user can simply press ENTER after typing the DR value to run the query.
- The Cancel command button Cancel property is set to Yes so that the user can press esc to close the dialog box.

Creating the Macros

The LookUpDR macro group contains two macros, one for each command button:

- The CloseForm macro attached to the Cancel button closes the Lookup DR form without running the query.
- The Run Query macro attached to the OK button contains two actions: OpenQuery, which runs the Lookup DR query in Datasheet view in read-only mode, and Close, which closes the Lookup DR form after running the query.

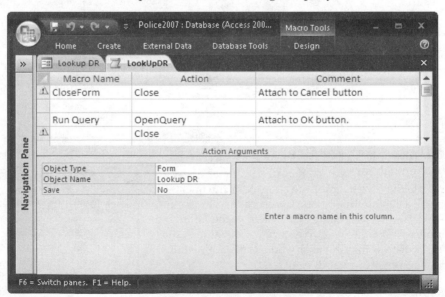

Modifying the Query

To pass the DR value from the form to the query, the Criteria must be set to the unbound text box control in the form. To do this, type **[Forms]![Lookup DR]![FindDR]** in the Criteria row of the DR column in the query grid.

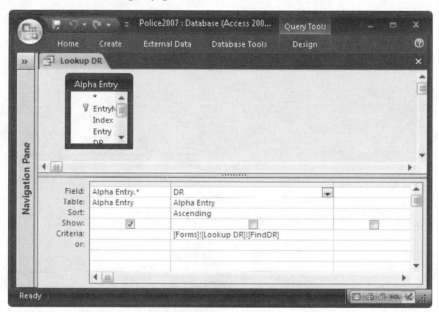

Each of the three parts of the statement is enclosed in square brackets to indicate that it is an identifier that refers to an object or control. The first element defines the object type, Forms; the exclamation point (!) indicates that the element that follows was named by the user. The second element identifies the specific form, Lookup DR; and the third identifies the unbound text box control, FindDR, in the form.

NOTE *Be sure to clear the check box in the Show Row of the DR column in the query grid; otherwise, the query results will include two copies of the DR values.*

Summary

The new Access 2007 user interface offers much flexibility in its appearance and usage. You can move through the commands in different ways. The Quick Access toolbar is a prime place for frequently used commands, where they are immediately accessible. You can create your own dialog boxes for special uses such as choosing from a list of options or entering data search criteria.

The next step in creating a unique operating environment for your application is to customize the Navigation Pane to focus on relevant actions. Another user-interactive tool is the switchboard form that can be displayed at database startup.

In the next chapter, you will discover how to create custom groups and categories in the Navigation Pane to build the Access 2007 equivalent of a switchboard. If you don't want to customize the Navigation Pane, you can still create a switchboard for the user to choose the desired activities.

Customizing the Navigation Pane and Creating Switchboards

The Navigation Pane, new to Access 2007, is the point of entry to your database. You can use it as presented or create your own custom access to the database objects. The Navigation Pane replaces the switchboards in earlier versions, which appeared at startup and offered a choice of actions to perform within the current database. You can still use switchboards if you want to, however. In fact, Access 2007 provides the Switchboard Manager that lets you create and use switchboards instead of customizing the Navigation Pane.

Viewing Objects in the Navigation Pane

You were introduced to the Navigation Pane in earlier chapters, but in this chapter, you will learn how to make it work for you. By default, the pane displays a list of all the objects in the database in predefined categories and groups. For example, with categories set to Object Type and groups to All Object Types, you can see all the objects in each group by clicking the expand button in the group title bar.

You can open and close the Navigation Pane itself by clicking the shutter bar Open/Close button at the right end of the title bar. You can also press F11 to open and close the pane.

Changing Categories and Groups

You can categorize the database objects in the Navigate to Category list (see Figure 21-1) in five ways:

- **Custom**   Arranges objects in specially designed categories and groups that you create for your database.
- **Object Type**   (Currently selected.) Groups objects by a specific type or by all types.
- **Tables and Related Views**   Lists all objects related to the table you choose in the Filter By Group below.
- **Created Date**   Lists objects created within the time period that you choose in the filter group.
- **Modified Date**   Lists objects modified within the time period that you choose.

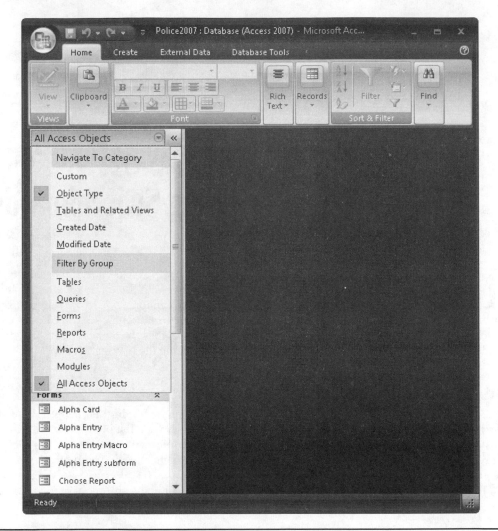

FIGURE 21-1   Choosing a category and group

You have been working with the Object Type category so far in this book. After deciding how you want to categorize the objects, you can choose how to group them within the category. You will learn how to create customized categories and groups in later sections.

Categorizing by Tables and Related Views

When you choose the Tables and Related Views category and select a table from the Filter By Group list, you will see the names of all the forms, reports, queries, and other objects that use that table as a source for data. For example, to see all the objects related to the Alpha Entry table, do the following:

1. Click in the Navigation Pane title bar and choose Tables and Related Views in the Navigate to Category list.

2. Click again in the Navigation Pane title bar and choose Alpha Entry from the list of tables in the Filter By Group list (Figure 21-2).

NOTE *If you don't see the table that you want in the list, click More to open the Filter by Table dialog box, where you can choose from the entire list of tables in the current database.*

The resulting list of objects includes the Alpha Entry table, with all the queries, forms, and reports related to the table. You can tell what type of objects they are by the accompanying icons. Figure 21-3 shows the list of objects currently related to the Alpha Entry table.

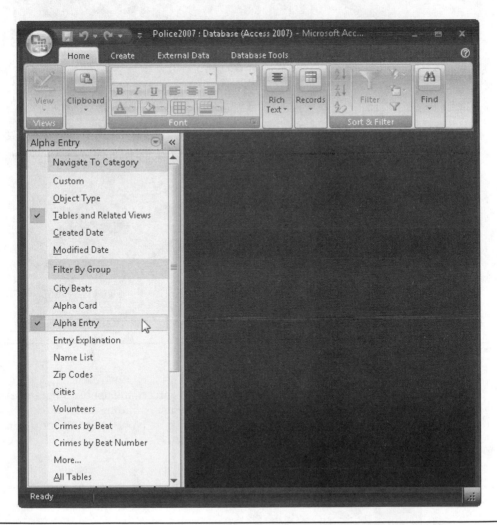

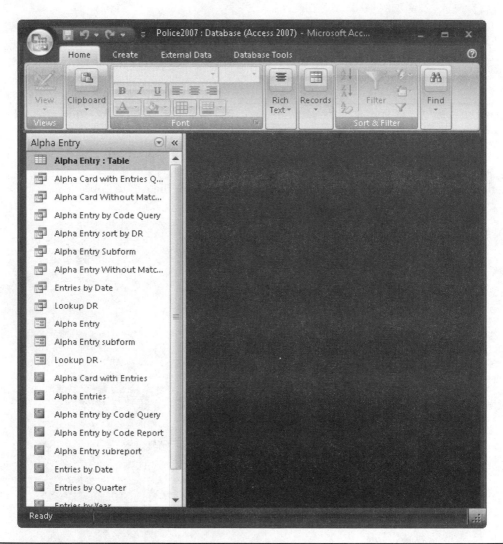

FIGURE 21-3 Viewing the objects related to the Alpha Entry table

If you choose All Tables in the Filter by Group list, you can see the list of all the tables in the database with their related objects. You can shorten the list by hiding some of the repeated objects. For example, if a form uses data from more than one table, the form name will appear in both the table groups. You can right-click the object in the group and choose

Hide in This Group from the shortcut menu to hide the object; the object is not deleted, just hidden from the list.

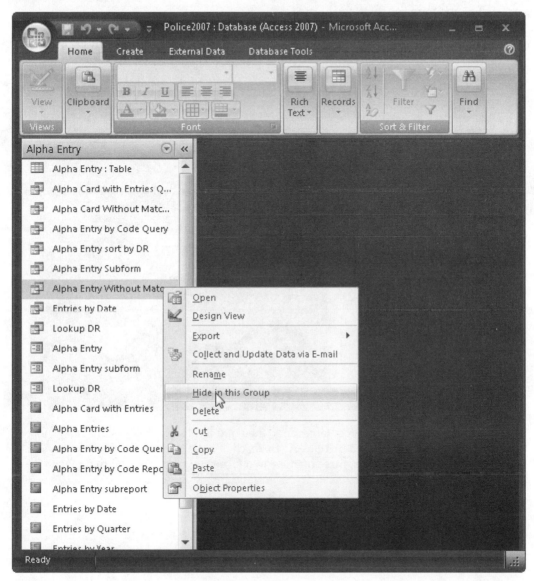

NOTE *The Navigation Pane Options setting Show Hidden Objects determines whether hidden objects are completely removed from the list or simply displayed dimmed. See the section "Hiding and Restoring Groups and Objects" for information about the difference.*

Grouping by Created or Modified Date

Both date filters offer the same criteria with respect to the filter's time frame. You can choose a specific time frame or choose All Dates.

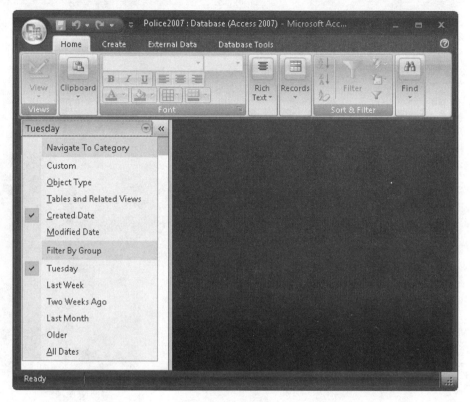

The objects are listed by type: tables first, then queries, forms, reports, macros, and modules; the list is then sorted by date. Again, each object's icon tells you what it is. The following list shows six tables, three queries, two forms, two reports, and two macros.

Hiding and Restoring Groups and Objects

You probably don't need to see all the groups and objects in the Navigation Pane all the time. You might want to hide some for security reasons or because of you don't use them often and you'd like to make the list shorter.

You can hide the group or object or simply have it displayed as dimmed in the Navigation Pane list by setting or clearing the Show Hidden Objects in the Navigation Options dialog box.

Hiding/Restoring a Group

To hide a group in the Navigation Pane, right-click the group name and choose Hide from the shortcut menu. The complete group is hidden in the pane, including the group's title bar.

To restore the hidden Queries group, for example, do the following:

1. Right-click the Navigation Pane title bar and choose Navigation Options from the shortcut menu.

2. In the Categories list in the left pane, select Object Type as the category that contains the Queries group. In the Groups for "Object Type" pane, check the box next to Queries.

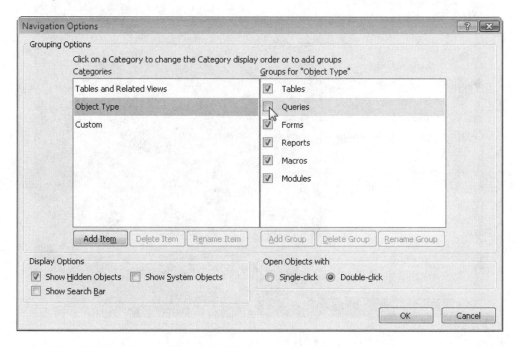

3. Click OK. The Queries group will be restored to the Navigation Pane.

Hiding/Restoring an Object

You can choose to hide the object only from its parent group or from all the groups in which it may appear. To hide the object from its parent group, right-click it in the Navigation Pane and choose Hide in This Group from the shortcut menu.

If you want an object, such as the Lookup DR form, hidden from all categories and groups, do the following:

1. Right-click the Lookup DR form in the Navigation Pane, and click View Properties from the shortcut menu.

2. In the Lookup DR Properties dialog box, check the Hidden check box.

3. Click OK.

To restore the hidden object, you need to reopen the Navigation Options dialog box.

1. Right-click the Navigation Pane title bar and choose Navigation Options.

2. In the Display Options group at the bottom of the Navigation Options dialog box, check Show Hidden Objects.

3. Click OK.

When you return to the Navigation Pane, you'll see the hidden object names dimmed in the list. To complete the restoration, do one of the following:

- If the object is hidden only from its home group and category, right-click the object and choose Unhide in This Group from the shortcut menu.

- If the object is hidden from all groups and categories, return to the object's Properties dialog box and clear the Hidden check box.

Searching for an Object

If your database is quite large and complicated, it may not be easy to find a particular form or report with which you want to work. The Navigation Pane provides a Search Bar to help you find any database object quickly. It actually filters the objects to display only those with all or part of the text that you enter in the search bar.

The search bar is a text box just beneath the Navigation Pane title bar. If you don't see it, right-click the Navigation Pane title bar and choose Search Bar from the shortcut menu.

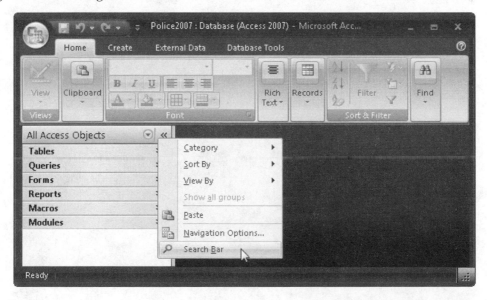

Enter part or the entire name of the object you want and press ENTER. The list of groups in the pane changes to hide all the groups except those that contain an object with the name that

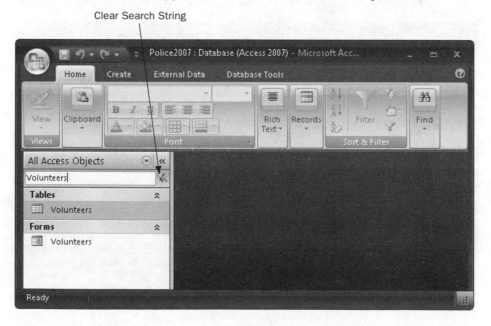

FIGURE 21-4 Hiding a form in the Lookup DR Properties dialog box

you entered. For example, suppose that you want to find all objects relating to Volunteers in the Police database. You would type **Volunteers** in the search bar and press ENTER.

To stop the search and restore the Navigation Pane groups, delete the search text or click the Clear Search String button.

Customizing the Navigation Pane

After all your forms, reports, and queries have been completed, your final piece of database development is to create the customized user interface. You can accomplish this in two ways: by customizing the Navigation Pane to include special categories and groups, or by creating a switchboard that branches to the database activities. This section describes the process of creating a custom Navigation Pane. The next section covers using the Switchboard Manager to build user interactive forms for your database.

If daily users are devoted to a few specific database activities, they don't need to scramble through all the objects in the database to get their jobs done. You can create a custom Navigation Pane with a category focusing on the department activities. Within the category, you can place custom groups relating to certain jobs so that each group contains only the objects required for that job.

You can always revert to the default Navigation Pane if the IT staff needs to work on the database itself. To do that, open the Navigation Options dialog box and choose one of the native categories, such as Object Type or Tables and Related Objects, and then click OK.

Planning the Custom Groups

Here's a look at how to map out the database and arrange activities based on the business at hand. To plan the arrangement of objects in the custom groups in the custom category, you need to look at what users do on a regular basis. For example, in the Bayview Police Department, staff users enter incident reports and other reports about people who are involved in some way with police activities on a daily basis. The incidents are recorded in the Alpha Card table while the public activities are stored in the Alpha Entry table. Each of these tables has a data entry/edit form that you can place in a custom group. Other data entry forms can also be included, as necessary.

On a weekly basis, users print reports for distribution of the information within the department. If mail is regularly sent to personnel, you can also include a report that prints labels.

It makes sense to create two custom groups for these two activities. As a start, place the following forms in the first group, named *Data Entry*:

- Alpha Card
- Alpha Entry
- Volunteers

The second group, named *Print Reports*, includes the following:

- Alpha Entry by Code
- Alpha Card with Entries

PART III

- Alpha Card Report
- Alpha Entries
- Entries by Date
- Entries by Quarter
- Entries by Year
- Labels Name List

Creating the Custom Category

To start a new category, do the following:

1. Right-click in the Navigation Pane title bar and choose Navigation Options from the shortcut menu.

2. In the Navigation Options dialog box, under the Categories list, click Add Item.

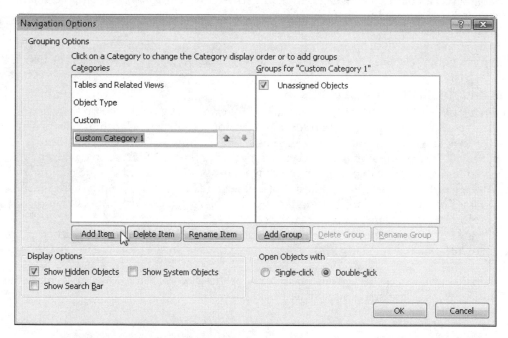

3. Enter **PoliceDesk** as the name for the new category and press ENTER. The Groups For pane now shows the new category name with a single item in the list of groups: Unassigned Objects.

4. Under the Groups For pane, click Add Group and enter the name of the first group,
   Data Entry, and then press ENTER.

5. Click Add Group again and enter the name **Print Reports** as the new group name.

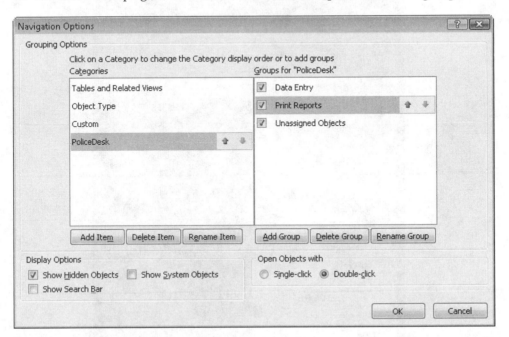

6. Press ENTER and click OK.

The next step is to open your new groups and add objects to them.

Adding Objects to the Custom Groups

To add objects to your new groups, click the Navigation Pane title bar and choose the new
category from the list in the upper section. The groups that you added to the category

PART III

appear in the lower section with the Unassigned Objects group, from which you will get the objects for each new group.

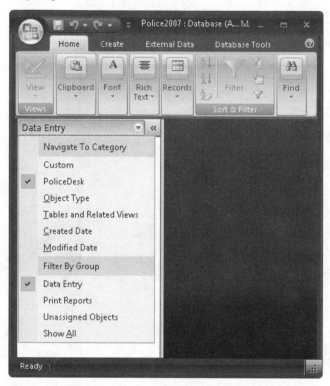

To be able to create shortcuts from the Unassigned Objects group to your new groups, check Show All in the lower section. Then you have three ways to move objects to the new groups:

- Drag the objects one at a time from the Unassigned Objects list to the new group.
- Select multiple items as you hold down the ctrl key, and then drag the set to the group.
- Right-click an item, point to Add to Group, and then click the destination group.

To add Alpha Card, Alpha Entry, and Volunteers forms to the Data Entry group, do the following:

1. Scroll down the list of objects in the Unassigned Objects list and select the Alpha Card form. Drag it to the top of the list and drop it on the Data Entry group name.
2. Scroll down again to select the Alpha Entry form. Press CTRL and scroll down to select the Volunteers form. Drag the selections to the Data Entry group name.

You can repeat these steps to move the eight reports from the Unassigned Objects group to the Print Reports group or use a third method:

1. Select all the objects you want to add to the group.
2. Right-click a selected object and point to Add to Group in the shortcut menu.
3. Select Print Reports.

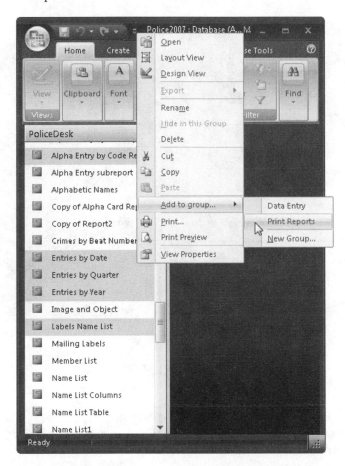

You can leave the Unassigned Objects group in the Navigation Pane if you think that you may need to add more objects later, or you can hide it. To hide it, do the following:

1. Go to the Navigation Options dialog box again and select the PoliceDesk custom category.
2. Clear the check box next to Unassigned Objects in the Groups For pane, leaving only the two custom groups checked.
3. Clear the Show Hidden Objects check box in the lower-left section of the dialog box.

4. Click OK.

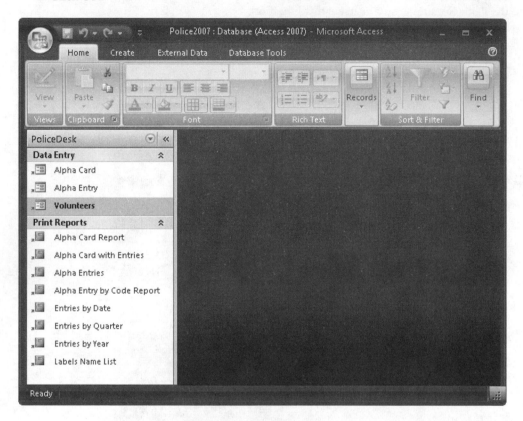

___

NOTE *You can tell by the icons accompanying the object names that these are shortcuts, not the objects themselves.*

Hiding/Restoring Custom Groups and Objects

Sometimes you won't need to see all the custom groups in a custom category. You can make them completely invisible or have them show up in the Navigation Pane as dimmed features.

Hiding/Restoring Custom Groups

To hide a custom group, right-click the group in the Navigation Pane and choose Hide from the shortcut menu. To restore the group, you need to use the Navigation Options dialog box:

1. Right-click the Navigation Pane title bar and choose Navigation Options from the shortcut menu.

2. Choose the category that includes the group that you want to restore, and, in the Groups for that category pane, check the group that you want to restore.

3. Click OK.

Hiding/Restoring Objects in Custom Groups

Even though you placed all the tables, forms, and reports in just the right custom groups when you created the database, things can change and some of the groups might need to be reorganized.

You can remove an object from a custom group or simply give it a different name. To remove an object from the custom group, right-click the object name in the Navigation Pane and choose Remove from the shortcut menu. If you want to hide it, choose Hide from the shortcut menu.

TIP *Custom groups contain shortcuts to the actual objects, not the real thing. So choosing Remove removes only the shortcut, not the object itself.*

To rename the object, right-click the object and choose Rename Shortcut from the shortcut menu. Enter the new name in the text box and press ENTER.

To restore the hidden or removed object shortcut to the custom group, do the following:

1. If you don't see the Unassigned Objects group in the Navigation Pane, right-click the Navigation Pane title bar and choose Navigation Options.

2. In the Navigation Options dialog box, select the category, and, in the Groups for that category, check Unassigned Objects. Click OK.

Then, back in the Navigation Pane, you can drag the object that you want from the Unassigned Group into your custom group.

Creating Switchboards

A *switchboard* system for a database consists of a hierarchical arrangement of switchboard *pages*, including a main switchboard page that usually branches out to two or more subordinate pages. Each page contains a set of items with commands that carry out a specified activity. Most items also include an *argument* that specifies which form to open, which report to preview, which macro or procedure to run, and other particulars.

The Difference between the Navigation Pane and a Switchboard

Both types of user interfaces offer particular advantages. You can decide which to use based on your preferences.

The Navigation Pane is always available, even when closed. It keeps objects visible but you can limit the objects in a view by creating special categories and groups of objects that focus on specific activities. When you create custom groups of objects, you don't need to build macros or write Visual Basic for Applications (VBA) code.

A switchboard is a small screen that is easy to reach and has buttons that you can click to take an action, such as open a data entry form or print a report. The switchboard is hidden while you are working with an object. You can hide objects that you don't want others to use by limiting their availability. For example, a switchboard may not allow access to object designs.

When the Access 2003 Database Wizard created a new database, it always added at least one switchboard for the user interface. Figure 21-5 shows the Main switchboard page for the Order Entry database created in Access 2003.

In addition to the main switchboard page were two other switchboard pages in the user interface within the Order Entry database:

- The Forms Switchboard, reached by clicking the Enter/View Other Information item.

- The Reports Switchboard, reached by clicking Preview Reports.

The ellipses (…) following each of those items tell the user that the choice opens secondary switchboard pages.

Access 2007 includes the Switchboard Manager to help create your own. Notice that one of the items on the Main Switchboard in Figure 21-5 is Change Switchboard Items, which launches the Switchboard Manager.

Using the Switchboard Manager to Create Switchboards

To start the Switchboard Manager, on the Database Tools tab's Database Tools group, click the Switchboard Manager command. If your database already has a switchboard system, the Switchboard Manager window lists all the existing switchboard pages. If your database does not already have a valid switchboard, the Switchboard Manager displays a message asking if you want to create a new one. Click Yes.

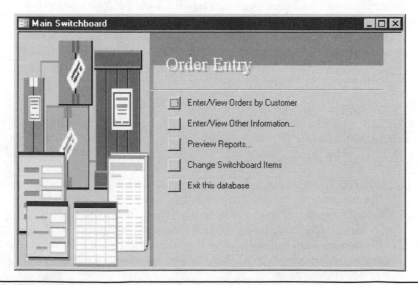

Figure 21-5 The Order Entry database Main Switchboard page

The first Switchboard Manager dialog box starts with the mandatory default main switchboard page.

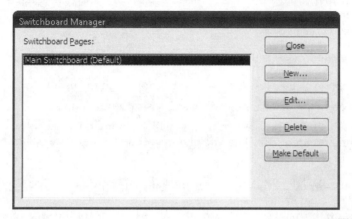

Adding Items to the Page

If you are creating a new switchboard system, your first step is to add items to the main switchboard by selecting the page in the Switchboard Manager dialog box (if not already selected) and clicking Edit. This opens the Edit Switchboard Page dialog box.

No items appear in the main switchboard for the Police database yet. Before adding them to the switchboard, enter **Bayview City Police** as the Switchboard Name in place of Main Switchboard. Then begin to add a list of items that you want to appear when the database starts up, and click New to open the Edit Switchboard Item dialog box.

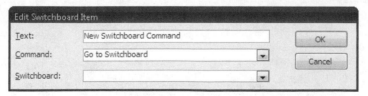

TIP *You'll need to include an item at the end of each subordinate switchboard page's item list that allows the user to return to the main switchboard. The item moves control back up the switchboard tree to the main switchboard. In addition, the opening switchboard should have an item that closes the database.*

Three entries define a switchboard item; they are created by doing the following:

1. In the Text box, enter the text you want to appear in the list of items.

2. In the Command box drop-down list, choose a command.

3. In the Switchboard box, depending on which command you choose in step 2, enter the command argument. The title of the box and the arguments vary with the command chosen.

Table 21-1 describes the available commands and the arguments that they require, if any. To create an efficient switchboard system, place the buttons for the most commonly performed tasks on the main switchboard, and place buttons for the secondary or subordinate activities on other pages. The most frequent activity performed in the Police application is to look up or enter Alpha Card information in the Alpha Card form. This form also displays the Alpha Entry information in a subform.

Start with the Police switchboard system:

1. Type **Enter/Edit Alpha Card Data** in the Text box in the Edit Switchboard Item dialog box.

TIP *You can use the [ampersand (&)] character in the item's Text box to specify shortcut keys for the items in the switchboard. You place the ampersand directly in front of the letter that you want to use as the shortcut key. For example, typing Enter/Edit &Alpha Card Data would indicate that user can either click the item or press* ALT-A.

Command	Description	Argument
Go to Switchboard	Opens another switchboard and closes this one.	Name of destination switchboard
Open Form in Add Mode	Opens a form for data entry with a blank record showing.	Form name
Open Form in Edit Mode	Opens a form for viewing and editing data.	Form name
Open Report	Opens a report in Preview mode.	Report name
Design Application	Opens Switchboard Manager to make changes to the current switchboard.	None
Exit Application	Closes active database.	None
Run Macro	Runs a macro.	Macro name
Run Code	Runs a Visual Basic procedure.	Procedure name

TABLE 21-1   Commands Offered by the Switchboard Manager

2. Click the drop-down arrow next to the Command box and choose Open Form in Edit Mode from the list of eight commands.

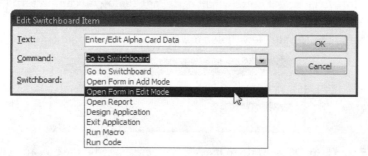

3. Click the drop-down arrow next to the Form (formerly Switchboard) box.

4. Choose Alpha Card from the list and click OK.

5. You return to the Edit Switchboard Page dialog box, where the new item appears in the Items on This Switchboard list. Repeat the same steps to add the following two items to the main switchboard:

- **Enter/Edit Alpha Entry Data**, which opens the Alpha Entry form in Edit mode.

- **Preview Alpha Card with Entries**, which opens the Alpha Card with Entries report.

Adding a New Switchboard Page

The Police database user might also want to open several more forms and reports, but less frequently than those already added to the main switchboard. The less frequently used forms and reports can be grouped on secondary switchboard pages.

Here's how to add a new page to the switchboard system:

1. Click Close to close the Edit Switchboard Page dialog box and return to the Switchboard Manager dialog box.

2. Click New. The Create New dialog box opens, in which you can start a new page.

3. Type **Enter/Edit Other Data** in the Switchboard Page Name box and click OK. Include an ampersand if you want to specify a shortcut key for this item.

4. The new page name is added to the list in the Switchboard Manager dialog box. Select the Enter/Edit Other Data switchboard page and click Edit to open the Edit Switchboard Page dialog box.

5. Click New to open the Create New dialog box, and type **Enter/Edit City Beats**. Choose Open Form in Edit Mode from the Command list and choose City Beats from the Form list.

6. Repeat step 5 to add the following items to the list:

   - **Enter/Edit Name List**, which opens the Name List form in Edit mode.

   - **Enter/Edit Description**, which opens the Explanation form in Edit mode.

7. Finally, add the item that returns to the main switchboard by typing **Return to Main Switchboard** in the Edit Switchboard Item dialog box. Choose Go to Switchboard from the Command list and choose Bayview City Police from the Switchboard list. Figure 21-6 shows the completed Edit/Enter Other Data page.

NOTE *As you add pages to the switchboard hierarchy, remember to add items to the main switchboard to branch to the page and add the item to the page that moves back up the hierarchy. Otherwise, the user has no way to move from one page to another in the switchboard.*

FIGURE 21-6   Items added to the Edit/Enter Other Data switchboard page

The items are added to the page in the order in which you define them. If you need to rearrange them, select an item in the Edit Switchboard Page dialog box and click Move Up or Move Down to change its position in the list. Each click moves the item up or down one position.

To complete the Police switchboard system, create another page titled Preview Other Reports and add the items to it that will open other reports as specified in the item text:

- Alpha Entry
- Entries by Code
- Entries by Qtr
- Entries by Year
- Print Labels
- Return to Main Switchboard

When all the pages have been completed for the switchboard system, close the Switchboard Manager. The Switchboard form now appears in the Forms group in the Navigation Pane. Double-click the form name (Switchboard) to open the main switchboard form in Form view. Figure 21-7 shows the completed main switchboard for the Police database. The Switchboard Manager has added a colored border to the switchboard template.

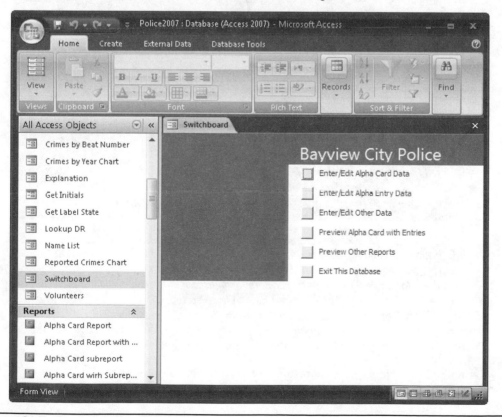

FIGURE 21-7   The new Police database main switchboard

Adding a Logo

The new switchboard looks a little bare. You can add a logo to the form header and other markers to the detail section. Open the switchboard in Design view, and in the Design tab's Controls group, click the Logo command. Browse in your computer to find the logo that you want and select it. Access places the image in the upper-left corner of the Form Header section.

To add a character for each of the items in the switchboard, in the Design tab's Controls group, click the Text command and place the new control in the Detail section, opposite the switchboard item. Then type the character that you want—an asterisk (*) in this case. Change the font size and color as desired.

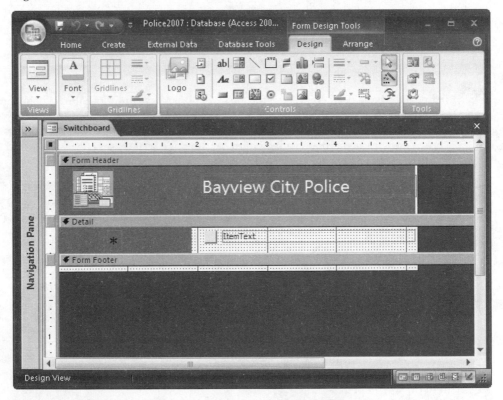

NOTE *You'll notice a major difference between a switchboard created by the Access 2007 Switchboard Manager and one created with earlier versions. The Default View property of earlier versions is set to Single Form with a maximum of eight items in the list of actions in the Detail section. The title and any pictures are also in the Detail section instead of the form Header section. The 2007 switchboard is, in contrast, a Continuous Form with each item maintained as a separate record. So when you add a picture to the switchboard form design, such as in the 2003 Police database, it appears with each record in the 2007 version.*

Switch to Form view to see the results of the added art (Figure 21-8).

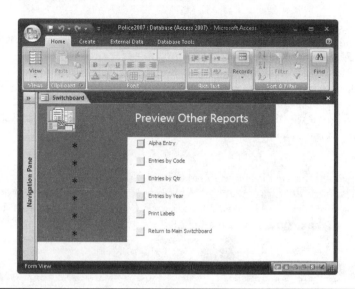

FIGURE 21-8   The completed Enter/Edit Other Data switchboard

NOTE   *The picture used here can be found at Office12 Bitmaps\Dbwiz\ledger.gif .*

Displaying the Switchboard at Startup

When you select a switchboard in the Switchboard Manager dialog box and click Make Default, you designate that page as the one to display when the Switchboard form opens. You must still tell Access to display the default switchboard by setting the Display Form option in the Access Options dialog box.

Click the Microsoft Office button and choose Access Options. In the Current Database page, click the arrow next to the Display Form box, choose Switchboard from the list, and click OK. The change takes effect the next time you start the database. To bypass the switchboard display after setting it as the default startup form, hold down SHIFT while the database opens.

Modifying the Switchboard

To edit any item on a switchboard page, open the Switchboard Manager and use the Edit button, as follows:

- Choose the switchboard page you want to change and click Edit.
- To add an item, click New and enter the text in the Create New dialog box. Then choose a command and an argument in the Switchboard Manager.
- To change an item, select it and do one of the following:
  - To change the displayed text, the command, or the argument, click Edit.
  - To delete the item, click Delete.
  - To move the item in the list, click Move Up or Move Down.

Close the Switchboard Manager when you're done.

You can also delete an entire switchboard page by selecting it in the Navigation Pane and clicking Delete. You will be asked if you are sure you want to delete it. The switchboard page and all the items on it are deleted.

To change the switchboard that displays when you start the database, open the Switchboard Manager and select the switchboard you want to display. Then click Make Default. The startup option is still set to display the Switchboard form, but the Switchboard Manager has designated a different screen as the default switchboard that will appear the next time you open the database.

Changing the Switchboard Mode

To make the new switchboard look more like a dialog box, you can change a couple of the form's properties. With the form open in Design view, open the Property Sheet. Then, on the Other tab, change both the Pop-Up and Modal properties to Yes. This makes the switchboard similar to the dialog box you saw in Chapter 20. It remains on the screen until you close it.

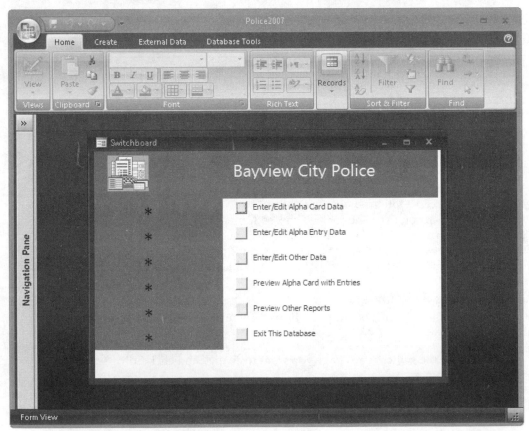

Viewing the Switchboard Items Table

When you use the Switchboard Manager to create a switchboard, Access creates a new table named Switchboard Items. Each record in the table represents an item in one of the switchboard pages, and each field in the record describes what command the button carries out and the argument it uses. Figure 21-9 shows the table created for the Police database switchboards.

Table 21-2 describes the contents of the Switchboard Items table. You can widen the columns in the table, but don't make any other changes in the table design.

NOTE   *The first row of each switchboard contains 0 in both the ItemNumber and the Command fields, indicating that the ItemText is the switchboard caption and is to be displayed in the title bar. The main switchboard has a 0 only in the ItemNumber column.*

The Argument field needs a little explanation. The first row contains Default in the Argument field, indicating the Bayview City Police switchboard has been specified as the default switchboard to be displayed at startup if the Display Form/Page option is set to Switchboard. A number in the Argument field represents the ID number of the switchboard

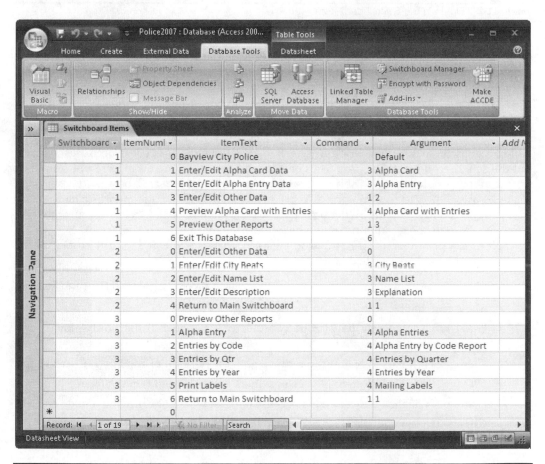

FIGURE 21-9   The Switchboard Items table

Field	Contents
SwitchboardID	A sequential number assigned to the switchboard page.
ItemNumber	A sequential number assigned to each item on a page, beginning with 1. Together with the SwitchboardID, it forms the primary key that uniquely identifies the item and switchboard page. Switchboards have ItemNumber 0.
ItemText	Text entered in the Text box of the Edit Switchboard Item dialog box.
Command	Number representing the command selected from the Command list in the Edit Switchboard Item dialog box. Commands are numbered sequentially in the order that they appear in the drop-down list. For a switchboard page itself, the Command value is 0.
Argument	Number of the switchboard; the name of form, report, macro, or procedure to be used by the command in the Command list in the Edit Switchboard Item dialog box.

TABLE 21-2   Fields in the Switchboard Items Table

as the goal of the command *Go to Switchboard*. For example, the fourth row shows 2 in the Argument field, indicating that the command is to display switchboard number 2, Enter/ Edit Other Data.

Creating a Switchboard without the Manager

To create a switchboard from scratch, start with a blank form not bound to an underlying table or query; then add command buttons that trigger macros or event procedures to carry out the actions you want. The properties of a switchboard form are quite different from the normal data entry form, which shows record navigation buttons, scroll bars, and other data-related features. You are not creating a "real" switchboard with a corresponding table or one that you can modify with the Switchboard Manager; you are instead creating a form that works like a switchboard but one over which you will have a lot more control.

Before you place command buttons on the form, change some of the form properties so it will appear more like a switchboard:

- Enter the text you want to see in the switchboard title bar in the Caption property box.
- Make sure the Default View property is Single Form.
- Leave the Allow Form View property as Yes and change the other four Allow… properties to No.
- Change Scroll Bars to Neither to remove both the horizontal and vertical scroll bars.
- Change Record Selectors to No because there will be no data on the form.
- Change Navigation Buttons to No because the user will not be moving among records.
- Change Dividing Lines to No because the form won't display records.
- Set Auto Resize to Yes so the form will always appear the same size in Form view.
- Set Auto Center to Yes to ensure that the form opens in the middle of the window, and thus will be easier to view and use.

The next step is to add to the form the command buttons and labels that will carry out the desired actions:

- If the switchboard item is designed to carry out a single action, such as open a form in Form view, you can use the Command Button Wizard to add a command button.

- If the item must carry out two or more actions, you must add the button without the Command Button Wizard and create a macro or Visual Basic event procedure to attach to the button's On Click event property.

Summary

Modifying the Navigation Pane and creating custom switchboards can add significantly to the efficiency of an end user application by presenting interfaces tuned to the goals of the application and to the level of the intended user.

Grouping objects in the Navigation Pane can help the user perform the tasks required of the application by offering a customized list of object categories from which to choose. A switchboard can serve as the main entry point into an application when it first starts.

In the next section, you will learn about sharing Access data and objects and how to maintain a secure system.

Exchange Data with Others

Exchange Database Objects and Text

Your application development can proceed more rapidly when database objects are reused or modified, rather than being developed from scratch. Access provides a number of useful functions and tools that enable you to exchange database objects between Access databases and that support the exchange of Access objects with other types of databases, such as dBase, Paradox, or SQL tables, and databases that support the ODBC protocol. You can also exchange Access data in the form of text files.

This chapter and the next cover the exchange of information between Access and the outside world. This chapter concentrates on exchanging information between Access databases and other database programs as well as text files. The next chapter expands the discussion of data exchange by including other programs, such as word processors and spreadsheets, and covers e-mailing data to another destination.

Access database objects include tables, queries, reports, forms, macros, and modules. This chapter describes techniques for exchanging many of these database objects by

- Copying objects among Access databases
- Importing or linking Access data
- Importing or linking other database formats
- Using linked or imported tables
- Exporting to Access databases
- Exporting objects to other database formats
- Importing and exporting text files

You can get your development work done faster if you don't have to create everything from scratch. Access provides a number of useful functions and tools that enable you to exchange database objects between Access databases. You can even exchange Access objects with other types of databases such as dBASE, Paradox, or SQL tables and databases that support the Open Database Connectivity (ODBC) protocol. You also can make use of text files in Access or send Access data out as text.

Copying Objects among Access Databases

It is often easier to copy and modify an existing object than it is to develop a table, form, or report from scratch. The first step in the modification of existing Access database objects is to copy the objects that you want to edit. Standard copy-and-paste operations and drag-and-drop techniques can be used to copy objects from one Access database to another.

Copy-and-Paste

To copy and paste an Access database object, first select the object that you want to copy in the Navigation Pane. With the Office 2007 clipboard, you can copy up to 24 objects before you need to paste them into their ultimate destination and clear space for more copied objects.

For example, suppose you want to make a copy of the Alpha Card table in the Police database:

1. Select the Alpha Card table in the tables group in the Navigation Pane.
2. Do one of the following to copy the table to the clipboard:
   - On the Home tab's Clipboard group, click the Copy command.
   - Right-click the table name and choose Copy from the shortcut menu.
   - Press CTRL-C.

If you want to copy the table to the same database, you can paste the table in one of three ways:

- Click the Paste command in the Clipboard group.
- Right-click in the Navigation Pane and choose Paste from the shortcut menu.
- Press CTRL-V.

When you copy a table, the Paste Table As dialog box asks for a name for the table and presents the following options:

- Paste the structure of the table (without its data).
- Paste the structure of the table and its data.
- Append the data to an existing table.

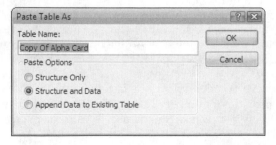

TIP *If you choose to paste the data to an existing table, you might have problems with duplicate primary key fields or unique index values. You also need to consider differing table structures. See Chapter 9 for information on solving problems with append queries.*

If you want to copy an object to another Access database instead of within its own database with a different name, do the following:

1. Start up a second instance of Access and open the destination database.

2. Resize the two Access windows to show both instances in a split-screen format.

3. Copy the object in the source database.

4. Open the object group in the destination Navigation Pane and paste it into the destination database.

If you don't want to use two instances of Access, close the source database after you copy the object, and then open the destination database and destination group in the Navigation Pane and paste.

NOTE *Copying an object generates a copy of all the properties of that object. For example, when a form is copied, the format, source data, event specifications, filters, and all other properties are copied with the form.*

Drag-and-Drop

A drag-and-drop technique can also be used to copy objects among databases. To use drag-and-drop, two instances of Access must be active at the same time.

To drag an object from one window to another:

1. Make sure both database Navigation Panes are open to the same group, and then select the object you want to copy in the source database.

2. While holding down the left mouse button, drag the item to the destination database.

3. Release the mouse button and the table appears in the destination Navigation Pane.

4. Enter a new name, if necessary, choose the desired Paste option, and click OK.

NOTE *If an object with the same name exists, you will be asked if you want to replace the existing object with the new one.*

Importing or Linking Access Data

Two other important techniques for adding Access data to an Access database are *importing* and *linking*. Importing is used to copy Access data or other objects from one Access database into another Access database. Importing has advantages when compared to copying database objects:

- Importing can copy all the database objects in one operation.
- Table relationships are also copied with importing.
- When you import a table, you can also import its related objects.

Linking is a way of connecting to and using data in an Access database without actually copying the data from the other database. You can link data between databases if they need to share table data.

You can import or link data from earlier Access MDB files or Access 2007 ACCDB files to Access 2007 databases. If the source file is an MDE or ACCDE file, you can't import forms, reports, or modules.

NOTE *If you are importing or linking a database that requires a password, you must enter the password before you can proceed.*

Importing Objects

You can import every object in a database. Let's start with the simplest case. First, we'll import a couple of objects from one Access database to another:

1. On the External Data tab's Import group, click the Access command. The Get External Data dialog box opens (Figure 22-1), where you can locate and select the database file that contains the objects you want to import. You can also right-click in the Navigation Pane, select Import from the shortcut menu, and click Access Database.

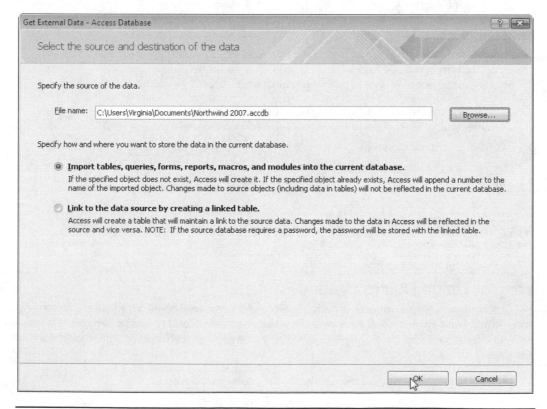

FIGURE 22-1 Choosing the source of the file

> **Import vs. Link**
> You should choose to import data into an Access database if you expect to use the data only in Access and will not depend on another program to maintain the data. Access is more efficient when working with its own tables and you can modify the data just the same as native-grown data.
>
>   You should link with data in another program if you rely on the source program to update the information. Linking is also useful in a multiuser environment where you split an existing database and place the data on a network server. Users can then share the database and create their own forms, reports, and other objects.

  2. Enter the name of the source database file or click Browse to look in the File Open dialog box.

  3. After locating the database file from which you want to import objects, choose the option Import Tables, Queries, Forms, Reports, Macros, and Modules Into the Current Database, and click OK. The Import Objects dialog box opens, where you choose the objects to import. In this example, the Northwind database is selected from sample Access applications, and the Products and Customers tables will be imported to the Police database.

  4. To choose objects to import, click the tab of the type of object you want to import and select each object name individually, or click Select All to select all the objects. To remove an object from the import list, select it again, or click Deselect All to remove all selected objects.

5. Repeat steps 3 and 4 to select all the desired object types.

6. After selecting all the objects that you want to import, click OK to return to the Navigation Pane, where you can see the objects that have been imported. You are asked if want to save the import procedure for later use. Doing so is helpful if you intend to do a lot of importing. You can also save export procedures.

Figure 22-2 shows the Police database Navigation Pane with the newly imported Customers and Products tables. The imported tables are now part of the Police database and do not appear different from the native tables in the Navigation Pane.

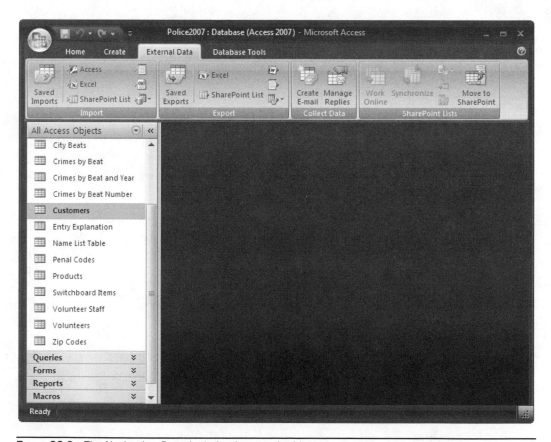

FIGURE 22-2   The Navigation Pane includes imported tables

> **TIP**   *If you import a table that includes Lookup fields, you must remember to import the tables or queries to which the fields refer and from which they get their values. If you don't want to or can't import the supporting value tables or queries, you can change the imported table design by changing the field Display Control property on the Lookup tab to Text Box for each Lookup field.*

> **NOTE**   *If you try to import a table that is already linked to another table, you will link to the source table data instead of importing it.*

Setting Import Options

You can set several options to customize the import process. When you click Options in the Import Objects dialog box, the box expands to show a lower pane with three sets of import options.

The first set of options, Import, presents other table features that can be imported:

- **Relationships**   Selected by default and includes the relationships that you have already defined for the tables and queries you import.

- **Menus and Toolbars**   Includes all the custom menus and toolbars in the database from which you are importing. Imported menus and toolbars are displayed on a tab named Add-Ins. Refer to Chapter 16 for information about custom menus and toolbars from earlier versions of Access.

- **Import/Export Specs** Includes all the saved import and export specifications set for the source database. (See the section "Importing and Linking Text Files" later in this chapter for information about setting import specifications.)
- **Nav Pane Groups** Includes custom Navigation Pane groups from the source database.

The second set of options, Import Tables, determines whether to import both the table definition and the data (default) or only the definition. This is useful for creating a copy of the table structures for a new database without including any existing data.

The third set of options, Import Queries, applies to any queries that you have selected to import and specifies whether to import queries as queries (the default setting) or run the query and import the resulting recordset as a table.

Once opened, the Options pane remains open as you click other object tabs. Click OK when you're finished choosing import options, and click Yes to save the details of the import operation. This saves time when you want to do it again.

CAUTION When choosing which objects to import, consider the options carefully. For example, importing a form without importing its underlying tables or queries can result in problems that might be difficult to resolve. Logical, useful groupings of objects should be imported together. This means that tables should be imported to provide the field definitions and data for all the forms, queries, reports, macros, and modules that you choose to import.

Linking Access Tables

Linking to tables in another Access database makes them available without your having to copy them into the active database. Linking saves space and reduces the need to maintain redundant data. Linking also ensures that you always have access to current information. However, linking also means that the data is dependent on an object that resides in another environment, where it can be renamed, moved, or deleted.

CAUTION If you're linking to a table in a database that is password-protected, you must enter the correct password to continue. When you enter the password, it's stored in an unencrypted form with the link information, and any user who can open your database can also open the linked, password-protected database. See Chapters 24 and 25 for more information about multiple users and security.

To link to a table in another Access database:

1. Open the destination database—in this example, Police.
2. To start the linking process, on the External Data tab's Import group, click the Access command.

3. In the Get External Data dialog box, select the database that you want to link to your active database. We are using the Northwind Traders database as the source in this example.

4. Choose the second option, Link to the Data Source by Creating a Linked Table, and click OK. The Link Tables dialog box opens, showing only a Tables tab, because tables are the only Access objects to which you can link.

5. Select one or more of the available tables and click OK.

In this example, the Suppliers table is linked to the Police database, as shown by the arrow next to the table icon.

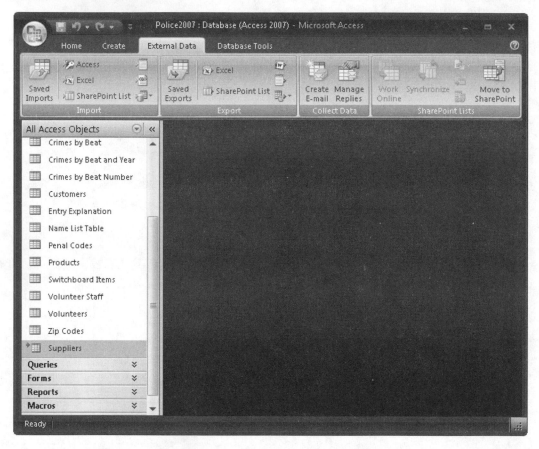

NOTE *If you link two related tables from the same database, the relationship is retained.*

Importing from or Linking to Other Data Sources

Access can import data or link to existing tables in other database management systems. Access provides specific recognition of some database table formats. Acquiring data and other objects from foreign databases is not much different from importing or linking Access databases.

You can both import and link dBASE III, IV, 5, and 7 files as well as Paradox 3.x, 4.x, 5.0, and 8.0 files. For version dBASE 7 and Paradox 8.0, you need the updated ISAM drivers available from Microsoft Technical Support.

You can also import and link data from ODBC data sources such as the Microsoft SQL Server and Visual FoxPro. You will need a connection to the appropriate ODBC data source and the data source defined.

Data types are generally compatible among these database management systems, although they are not labeled consistently. For example, dBASE Character and Paradox Alphanumeric data types both become Text fields in Access. dBASE Float and Paradox Currency types become Number fields in Access with the Field Size property set to Double. dBASE calls Yes/No fields Logical.

Using Data from dBASE or Paradox

Importing a dBASE table or a Paradox file into an Access database is similar to importing a table from an Access database. For example, to import a dBASE table:

1. On the External Data tab's Import group, click the More command, and select dBASE File from the context menu.

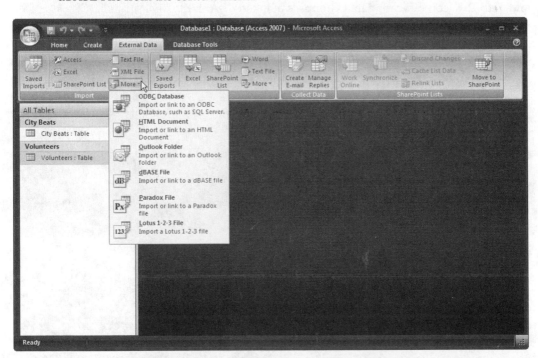

2. In the Get External Data dialog box, locate and select the file that you want to import—Groups.dbf, in this example—and click Import.

After the table is imported, it looks and behaves just like an Access table. You can use the same procedure to import Paradox files.

Another approach to making use of data from a dBASE or Paradox database is to use the Link Tables operation by choosing the linking option in the Get External Data dialog box. When you import a dBASE file, Access creates a table with the same name as the .dbf file and imports the data. Conversely, when you link to a dBASE file, Access also requires that the associated dBASE index files be linked. If you choose to link to a dBASE file, the Select Index Files dialog box may appear, in which you can choose the indexes (.ndx and .mdx files) that are associated with the .dbf file.

- If there are no index files, click Cancel and proceed with the link operation.
- If you select one or more index files, the Select Unique Record Identifier dialog box prompts you to select the corresponding index field. Your index must have a unique value for each record, or difficulties might occur when you try to update records.

After importing or linking a dBASE file, you can set field properties for the table. If you import a file with no primary index, you can set the index in Access. When you update the file with Access, the index is also automatically updated. If you use dBASE to update the file, you must also update the corresponding index in dBASE before trying to open the file in Access.

Figure 22-3 shows a linked dBASE file in the Database window by displaying the arrow and a dBASE icon indicating that Groups is a linked dBASE file.

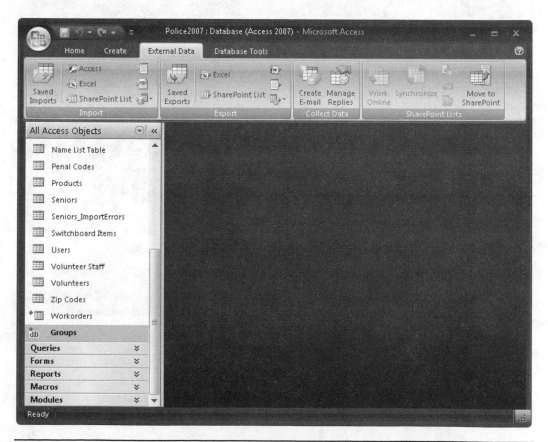

FIGURE 22-3   A linked dBASE file in the Access Navigation Pane

---

NOTE *If you select a Paradox table to link to, you need the index (.px) file and the memo (.mb) file (if the table has any). Without these files, you will not be able to open the linked table in Access. If the Paradox table does not have a primary index, you must create one in Paradox to be able to update the table in Access.*

Using Linked or Imported Tables

You can use linked or imported tables the same way you use any other Access table, with some precautions. Imported tables essentially become new tables within your Access database. However, linked tables still reside within the environments in which they were created. Thus, issues such as renaming the table or changing its characteristics have implications for relating the linked table to its original source environment.

Renaming a Linked Table in Access

The linked table might have a name that is not very meaningful in your Access database. You can give it a more relevant name without disturbing the link. Right-click the table in the Navigation Pane and choose Rename from the shortcut menu. Then edit the old name or enter a new name.

Changing Linked Table Properties

The database that owns a table usually sets the table properties of linked tables. The source database also sets the field properties and validation rules. Data entered in the table from within Access must conform to most of the properties set for the originating database fields such as default values, minimum or maximum values, field format, text options, and any other validation requirements.

Field properties that you can change in a linked table from within Access include Format, Decimal Places, Input Mask, and Caption. If you want to change other field properties in a form, set them for the controls that are bound to the fields.

Changing the basic properties or validation rules of a linked table requires access to the table through its original database application. If the table is in a database environment other than Access, that database management system must be available to support efforts to change the table properties.

Updating Links with the Linked Table Manager

When the location of a linked table is changed, use the Linked Table Manager database utility to reestablish the proper path or link to the table. The Linked Table Manager does not physically move files; it simply updates the path leading to the file location. The Linked Table Manager can be consulted for two reasons:

- To examine or refresh links
- To change the path or location of linked tables

NOTE *The Linked Table Manager doesn't move database or table files; it simply updates the path to the object. If you want to move the file to a new location, use one of the Windows commands. After you move the file, you can use the Linked Table Manager to refresh the link.*

To refresh links:

1. On the Database Tools tab's Database Tools group, click the Linked Table Manager command. The Linked Table Manager dialog box displays a list of all tables linked to the current database with the table name and the current path.

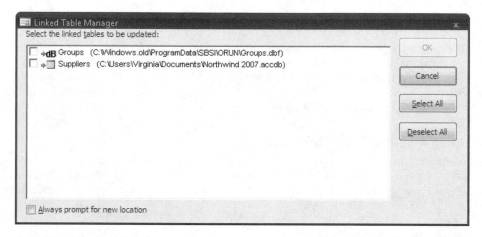

2. Click Select All or check only the table links you want to refresh, and then click OK.

3. If the Linked Table Manager is successful in locating and refreshing the file, it displays a message to that effect. If not, the manager prompts for the location of the table by displaying a Select New Location of *Tablename* dialog box, where you can locate the file and change the path.

NOTE *The Linked Table Manager has no way of refreshing links to tables whose names were changed in the source database after linking. In that case, you must delete the current link and start over.*

To change the path to a linked table, open the Linked Table Manager and do the following:

1. Select the Always Prompt for New Location option at the bottom of the Linked Table Manager dialog box.

2. Check the tables whose links you want to change, and then click OK.

3. Designate their new location in the Select New Location of *Tablename* dialog box, and then click Open. The Linked Table Manager verifies that all selected tables were successfully refreshed.

4. Click OK to close the message box, and then click Close.

TIP *If more than one of the tables that you selected were moved to the new location, all the links are updated at once.*

Unlinking Tables

Unlinking a table removes the linkage only to a table in another (source) database. The procedure for unlinking a table is identical to that for deleting a table; however, the Delete function does not actually delete the linked table—it deletes only the link to the database.

CAUTION *If your intention is to delete a link to a table in another database and not to actually delete a complete table and its data, be sure to select a table name with the arrow indicating that it is a linked table. If you inadvertently select a regular table (as opposed to a linked table) and perform a Delete, the table and its data will be lost. (Another good reason to back up your files on a regular basis.)*

Importing and Linking Text Files

Text files are useful when you import or link data to Access tables. If no other common data format exists between the source of the data and Access, you can create a text file with the source program and then import that file into Access. Most relational, hierarchical, or network-oriented database management systems can generate a text version of the data using some kind of record selection function.

Text files are either *fixed-width* (files consisting of rows of data of the same length) or *delimited* text files (files containing records that use special characters to indicate the separation between data fields). Most delimited text files also use a *text qualifier*—usually double quotation marks—to delimit strings. You can use any character that does not appear in field values. After you have generated text files, you can import or link them to an Access database using the same external importing and linking functions used for data from any source.

Using Delimited Text Files

Importing or linking a delimited text file begins with the same sequence used by other importing and linking operations. However, prior to starting the importing/linking process, you must specify that a table is ready to receive the data—either a new table structure with the appropriate field definitions or an existing table to which this new data can be appended.

NOTE *You can create a new table to receive the data from delimited text files by using basic table design techniques (see Chapter 4) or by copying the table structure from an existing table. Be careful to account for the proper number of fields, field length, and data type selection to import text data correctly.*

To import a text file, do the following:

1. On the External Data tab's Import group, click the Text File command.
2. Locate and select the text file (see Figure 22-4) that you want to import and choose how you want to store the data: as a new table, appended to an existing table, or as a linked table. Then click OK.

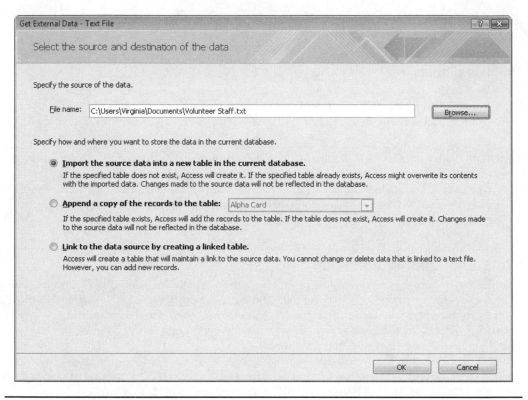

FIGURE 22-4   Choosing the text file and how to store it

3. The Import Text Wizard dialog box appears, displaying sample data from the selected text file. The Import Text Wizard analyzes the selected file and determines whether it is a fixed-width text file or a delimited file. Figure 22-5 shows that the text file we are importing, SENIORS.TXT, is a delimited text file.

4. Click Next to see how the file is formatted. In the case illustrated in Figure 22-6, the wizard has determined that the fields in this file are delimited by commas, text fields are bounded by quotation marks, and the first row does not contain field names.

5. Do one of the following:

   • If you agree with the results of the Import Text Wizard's processing, click Next.

   • If you do not agree, adjust the selections (for the delimiting character, the text qualifier, and whether the first row contains field names) until you are satisfied that they are accurate. Then click Next.

6. The Import Text Wizard asks you to specify information about each field in the file (Figure 22-7).

7. Enter or verify the field name, data type, whether the field is indexed, and whether you want to import or skip that field. The wizard names the fields Field1, Field2, and so on, but you can rename them. Click in the field column to make changes.

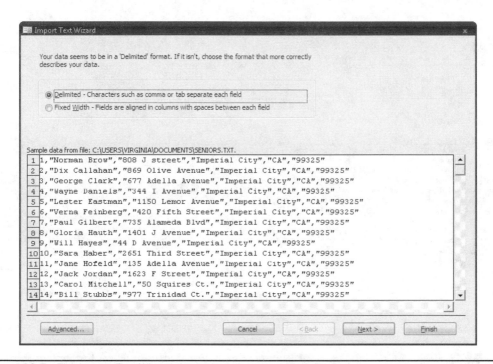

FIGURE 22-5   The Import Text Wizard determines the type of text file

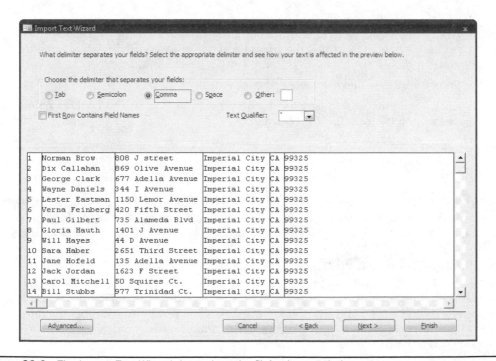

FIGURE 22-6   The Import Text Wizard determines the file's characteristics

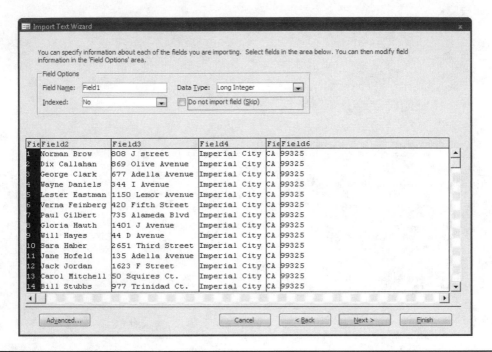

FIGURE 22-7   Setting imported field information

8. After completing the field information, click Next; the wizard suggests specifying a primary key field by letting the wizard add one or by specifying an existing field, or you can choose not to have a primary key (Figure 22-8). Click Next.

9. Enter a name for the new table and click Finish.

10. Click Yes if you want to save the import process for later use and enter a name and description for the import specifications.

***

TIP   *If the import process seems to be taking a long time, errors could be occurring. Press* CTRL-BREAK *to cancel anytime during the process.*

Linking delimited text files with the Link Text Wizard is the same as importing, with two exceptions: you are not asked if you want to link to an existing table or create a new one, and you are not prompted for a primary index because you are not creating a new table.

Using Fixed-Width Text Files

The Import Text Wizard reacts a little differently once fixed-width text files are detected. The second wizard dialog box (Figure 22-9) shows the fixed-length data with vertical lines between fields and a ruler at the top. The wizard asks you to confirm whether the lines indicate the proper separation point between fields and provides guidance for how to move or reposition the lines:

About Import Errors

It is possible that improperly defined data or data of an improper length could cause errors. If this occurs, Access creates an Import Errors table containing descriptions of the errors that occurred while importing the text file or spreadsheet into an Access database. The table shows the field names and row numbers of the data that caused the error.

Some of the possible import errors are shown here:

- **Field Truncation**   Occurs when the text value is longer than the Field Size property setting for the destination field.

- **Type Conversion Failure**   Occurs when a value is the wrong data type for the destination field.

- **Key Violation**   Occurs when a duplicate primary key value appears.

- **Validation Rule Failure**   Occurs when a field value breaks the rule defined in the Validation Rule property for the destination field.

- **Null in Required Field**   Occurs when the Required property of the destination field is set to Yes and a Null value occurs.

- **Null Value in AutoNumber Field**   Occurs when the data intended for an AutoNumber field contains a null value.

- **Unparsable Record**   Occurs when a text value contains a character specified as the text delimiter character.

If the problem is with the data, edit the file. If you're trying to append data to an existing table, you may need to change the table definition. After correcting the problems, import the file again. When a value contains the delimiter character, edit each field to repeat the character twice. When you finish, check the destination files to make sure that some of the records are not duplicated.

- To create a line, click at the position where a field separation is desired. Two lines have been added in Figure 22-9.

- To delete a line, double-click the line to remove the field separation.

- To move a line, click and drag the line to the proper position.

Once adjustments are completed, the process of identifying the destination table and completing the import or link is the same as with delimited files.

Changing Import Specifications

You can change the import specifications for a text file using the Advanced features of the Import Text Wizard. Click the Advanced button in the Import Text Wizard dialog box to display the Import Specification dialog box (Figure 22-10), which enables you to specify a number of table characteristics, including the following:

- The file format (delimited or fixed-width).

- If delimited, the field delimiter and text qualifier characters.

PART IV

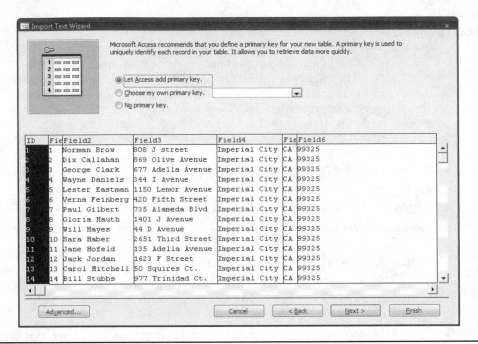

FIGURE 22-8   Adding a primary key

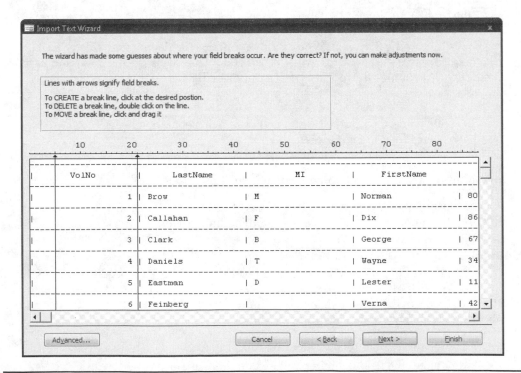

FIGURE 22-9   Adjusting a fixed-width text file

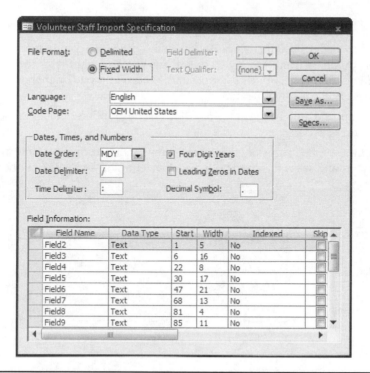

FIGURE 22-10   Setting the import specifications

- The language and code page.
- The specifications for dates, times, and numbers.
- Information for each incoming field such as name, starting and ending position in the record, data type, whether the field is to be indexed, and whether to omit the field from the import.

Click the Specs button to see a list of import specifications that you have saved from which you can choose.

Once the text file characteristics have been satisfactorily specified, clicking the OK button returns you to the Import Text Wizard dialog box, where clicking the Finish button will complete the text import action and place the table in your Access database.

Exporting to an Existing Access Database

Exporting data or database objects to another Access database has the same functionality as copying and pasting. Once in their destination database, the objects look and behave like the native objects. The same data formats are supported as with importing.

To export a table:

1. On the External Data tab's Export group, click the More command and choose Access Database from the context menu. You can also right-click the table name in the Navigation Pane, point to Export in the shortcut menu, and choose Access Database in the context menu.

2. In the Export dialog box, locate and select the destination database, and then click OK (Figure 22-11).

3. Accept the existing name or enter a new name for the destination table in the Export dialog box and select to export both the table definition and data or only the definition.

4. Click OK.

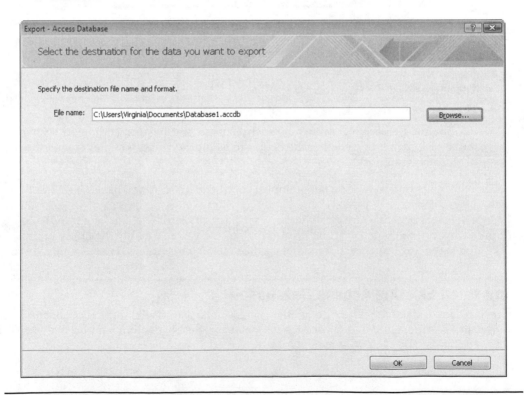

FIGURE 22-11 Choosing the destination file for the table

When you are exporting database objects other than tables, the basic steps are the same with the exception that the final step is not required, because you are exporting only an object design without any data.

TIP *You can export only one database object at a time. If you need to export multiple objects to an Access database, it might be quicker to open the destination database and use the Import group of commands that can be used to import multiple objects at once.*

Exporting to Another Database Format

Access supports exporting data to the same database, and text formats are acceptable for importing and linking. Access can also export data in the proper formats for other applications such as spreadsheets (Excel and Lotus 1-2-3) and text files such as Rich Text Format (RTF) and Word files, as discussed in the next chapter.

CAUTION *When you export data to older database programs such as dBASE or Paradox, both of which limit table names to eight characters (not including the file extension), the longer table names are truncated to comply with the limitation. This can result in duplicate table names. To prevent this, make a copy of each affected table with a shorter name before exporting the copy.*

To export data to these formats:

1. Select the table in your active database, and on the External Data tab's Export group, click the More command and choose from the list of files; or right-click the table name in the Navigation Pane and choose Export from the shortcut menu.

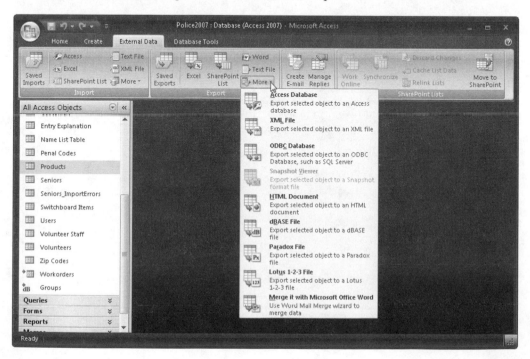

2. Choose dBASE file or Paradox file in the context menus.

3. In the Export dialog box, enter the destination and file format. You can choose dBASE versions III, IV, or 5. With Paradox, you have the choice of 3, 4, 5, or 7–8.

4. Enter the destination filename in the File Name box and click OK.

Exporting to Text Files

When you want to export data from an Access database to a text (.txt) file, call upon the Export Text Wizard, which works much like the Import Text Wizard. The wizard helps you specify the format of the exported Access file and determine where to store the output.

To export data to a text file using the Export Text Wizard:

1. In the Navigation Pane, right-click the table, query, form, or report containing the data that you want to export to a text file. Then point to Export and choose Text File from the context menu.

NOTE *If the form or datasheet contains subforms or subdatasheets, only the main form or datasheet is exported. If you want the subs exported as well, you need to export them separately. Reports including subforms or subreports are all exported at once.*

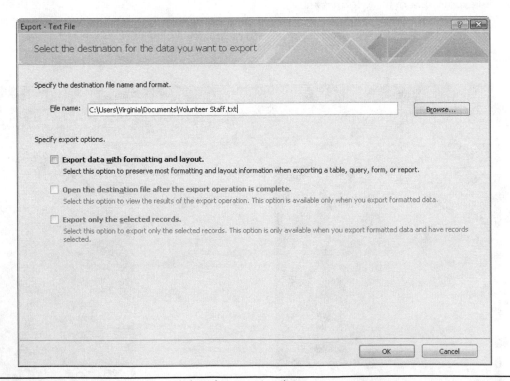

FIGURE 22-12 Specifying the file and choosing export options

2. In the Export–Text File dialog box, accept the default name or enter a new one. You have three export options (Figure 22-12):

   - Export Data with Formatting and Layout
   - Open the Destination File After the Export Operation Is Complete
   - Export Only the Selected Records

NOTE *If you choose to export the data with formatting and layout, you can choose the encoding: Windows (default), MS-DOS, Unicode, or Unicode (UTF-8).*

3. For now, choose no export options and click OK.

4. The Export Text Wizard dialog box (Figure 22-13) displays data from the selected table similar to the Import Wizard. You can choose between saving the data as a fixed-width or a delimited text file.

5. Click Next.

6. If you choose Delimited, the next dialog box (Figure 22-14) contains the specifics of the delimiters, text qualifiers, and other features of each field.

7. If you agree with the default settings, click Next.

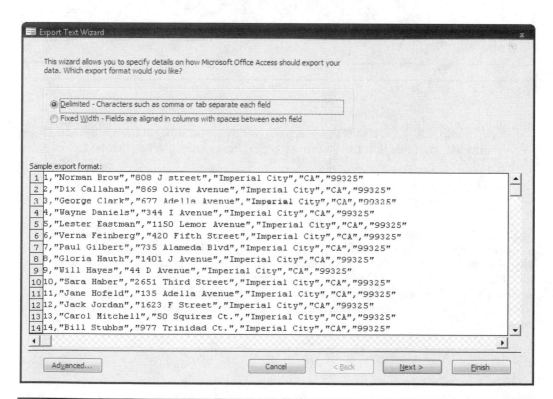

FIGURE 22-13   Selecting the text file type with the Export Text Wizard

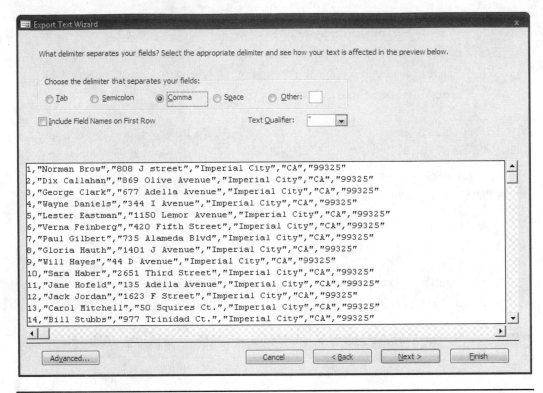

FIGURE 22-14 Setting the text file characteristics with the Export Text Wizard

8. If you do not agree, adjust the selections (for the delimiting character, the text indicator, and whether the first row contains field names). When finished, click Next.

9. If you choose Fixed Width, the next dialog box asks for verification of the field lengths. Figure 22-15 shows the same table being exported as fixed-width. You can drag the divider lines left or right to adjust the width of the fields.

10. Click Finish to complete the export.

You can also use the Export Text Wizard to customize the export specifications for a text file the same way you set the import specifications with the Import Text Wizard. When you click the Advanced button in the Export Text Wizard, an Export Specification dialog box appears, allowing you to specify the file format (fixed-width or delimited); the language and code page settings; the specifications for dates, times, and numbers; and field information. The options are the same as those for importing.

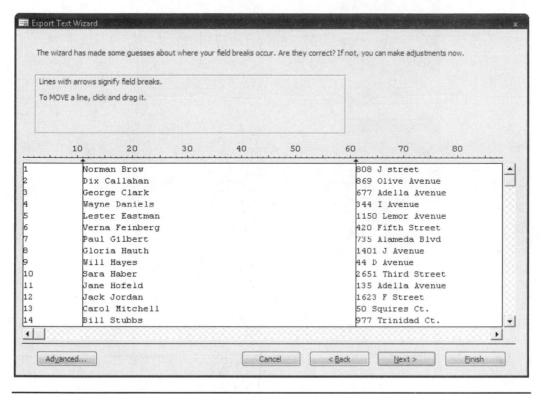

FIGURE 22-15   Exporting the text as fixed-width

Summary

Importing, linking, and exporting data are important ways of sharing data between Access databases, as well as with other applications. These data exchange functions are essential tools in sharing data with applications in Microsoft Office 2007, as well as Paradox, dBASE, and other database management systems. The External Data commands that support these data exchange operations have a number of options and should be the subject of considerable experimentation to ensure that your results are useful and reliable.

In the next chapter, you will learn about the issues of exchanging data with outside sources and sharing data with multiple users.

PART IV

Exchanging Data
with Outside Sources

C hapter 22 focused on exchanging data within the Access management realm, with other database management systems, and with text files. In this chapter, you will learn how to exchange information between an Access database and an outside source—data from a word processor, a spreadsheet, or an HTML document. A successful exchange of data with these outside sources involves a sequence of steps that are intended to ensure that the end result is useful. For example, records moved into Access from a word processor or a spreadsheet need to be evaluated and, in some cases, edited to be compatible with the table's data structure.

This chapter describes the procedures that you can use for data exchange operations with outside data sources. Procedures are described for the following:

- Copying or moving records from word processors and spreadsheets
- Saving Access objects as external files
- Working with Microsoft Word
- Working with Microsoft Excel
- Working with HTML
- Mailing Access database objects
- Importing Outlook Contacts
- Collecting data via e-mail

Copying or Moving Records

To copy or move records from other applications to Access, make sure that the data is arranged in an appropriate format, and then use the selection, copy, and paste functions in Access to move the records that you want. The following sections describe specific approaches for moving data from word processors and spreadsheets.

Copying or Moving Data from a Word Processor

You can use two approaches to copy or move records from a table created with a word processor. The first approach is to save the desired records to a text file with fixed length or delimited records, and then import them into either an existing table or a new one. Procedures for importing these text files to an Access table are described in Chapter 22.

The second approach to moving records from a word processor to Access is to perform a copy-and-paste operation. For this approach to work properly, you must be aware of these two major points:

- The records in the word processing file must already be in a table or properly separated by tab characters.
- The columns in the word processor table should be in the same order as the fields in the Access table that you're targeting.

When you copy data, you place a copy of that data in the destination file and leave the original data alone in the source file. When you move data, you delete it from the source and place it in the target file.

When performing copy or move operations, the Access database must be open to receive the new data. You can add new records to a datasheet or a form. If you're adding records to a datasheet, the columns are not required to have the same names as the fields, but the data being copied or moved should be the same data type.

If you're adding records to a form, the data is copied or moved to text box controls, which are bound to table fields and have the same names as the incoming data columns. If the column names don't match the control names or the columns have no names, the data is moved or copied to the form in the tab order.

On the receiving end, you can replace existing records or add to the records already in the datasheet or form. When you replace records in a datasheet, you select the same number of records to eliminate that you selected to bring in from the word processor. In a form, you can replace only the current record.

To move or copy word processing data, do the following:

1. In the word processor application, select the records that you want to move or copy using the selection method provided by the application. In Microsoft Word, this can be as simple as clicking the left mouse button on the first record that you want, and then holding the left mouse button down as you drag the cursor down the file until the last desired record is highlighted (see Figure 23-1).

2. Then, do one of the following, both of which place the selected records on the clipboard:

   - If you want to move the records from the word processing document to the Access database, do one of the following: on the Home tab's Clipboard group, click the Cut button; right-click the selected text and choose Cut from the shortcut menu; or press CTRL-X.

   - If you want to copy the records, as opposed to moving them, do one of the following: on the Home tab's Clipboard group, click the Copy button; right-click the selected text and choose Copy from the shortcut menu; or press CTRL-C.

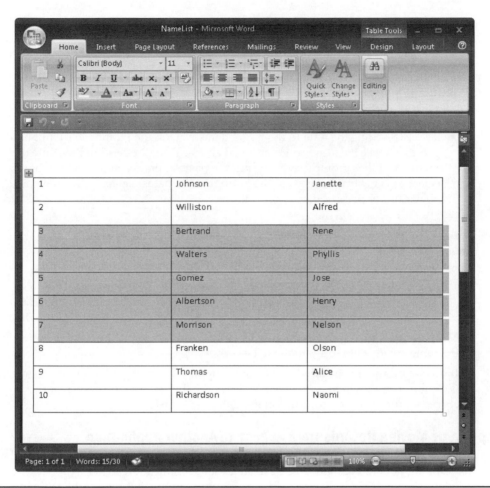

FIGURE 23-1   Selected records in a Word document

3. Open the datasheet or form into which you want to paste the records, and then do one of the following:

- If you're replacing records in Datasheet view, select the records that you want to replace, and then do one of the following: on the Home tab's Clipboard group, click the Paste command; right-click and choose Paste from the shortcut menu; or press CTRL-V. If you select less records in the target (Access) than in the source (Word) table, the selected records are replaced and the excess records from the source table are ignored. If you select more records in the target table, they're replaced with the records selected in the source table beginning at the top of the table. The excess selection in the target table is untouched.

- If you're replacing a record in a form, move to the record that you want to replace and click the record selector (the pale blue bar along the left side of the form), and then either click the Paste command in the Clipboard group of the Home tab or press CTRL-V.

NOTE *If you included the column labels when you copied or moved the records to the clipboard and they don't match the field names in the form, Access asks if you want to paste the field names in the order that you defined as the Tab Order.*

- If you're adding the data to the target datasheet, on the Home tab's Clipboard group, choose the Paste command and choose Paste Append in the context menu. You'll be prompted to confirm the paste append action. You can also select the new blank record at the bottom of the datasheet and click the Paste command or press CTRL-V.

Copying or Moving Data from a Spreadsheet

The process for copying or moving records from a spreadsheet is similar to the process for copying or moving records from a word processor. The advantage in the case of the spreadsheet is that the data does not need to be arranged in or converted to table form because it's already in tabular form on the spreadsheet. The same cautions apply as in the case of the word processor:

- The columns in the spreadsheet must be in the same order as the data elements in the table for the data copy/move to be useful.
- If the records are to be added to a form (as opposed to being added to a datasheet), the column names in the spreadsheet should be the same as the names of the corresponding text box controls on the database form.

Copying or Moving Records from Access to Another Application

Copying or moving records from a datasheet or a form to another application is much the same as bringing new records into Access from a source application. When you paste Access records to a different application, the field names appear in the first row of the table in a word processor or a worksheet in a spreadsheet.

TIP *If you're copying from a datasheet that has subdatasheets, only one level is copied at a time. To copy the subdatasheet, you must open it, and then perform the same copy or move operation.*

Use the same four basic steps:

1. Select the Access data you want to copy or move, and then copy or cut it to the clipboard.
2. Open the other application.
3. If you're replacing existing data, select that data. If you're adding to existing data, place the insertion point where you want to begin pasting the data.
4. Use the other application's command to paste or append the Access data.

If you're pasting Access records into a Word document, place the insertion point where you want the records to appear. The data is pasted in the document as a table. If you're copying from a form, Access includes the form and column names, as well as the data.

If you're pasting to Excel, place the insertion point in the cell where you want the first column heading to be located. The rest of the Access data fills out columns and rows to the right and down in the Excel worksheet.

TIP *You can also use the drag-and-drop method to move database objects among applications. You must have both applications running, and then click an Access table or query in the Database window, and drag it to a Word document or Excel worksheet. Going in the other direction, you can create an Access table by dragging-and-dropping a range of cells from an Excel worksheet to the table group in the Navigation Pane.*

Saving Access Output as an External File

Chapter 22 discussed saving Access data and objects in other database management systems or in a text format. You can also export the data from Access tables, queries, forms, and reports to a number of other file formats both within and external to Microsoft Office. The export commands are on the External Data tab's Export group. Click the More command to nine additional file formats.

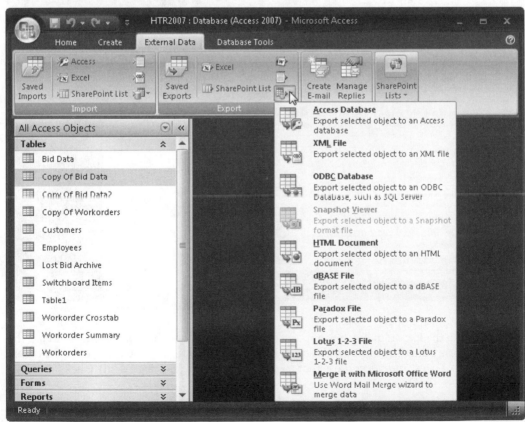

PART IV

NOTE *The list of available formats depends on the type of object that you are trying to export.*

NOTE *You can also use the SharePoint Team Services and Windows SharePoint Services to export Access objects.*

To save the data from an Access table in one of these file formats, do the following:

1. In the Navigation Pane, select the table containing the data that you want to export.
2. Right-click and point to Export in the shortcut menu, and then choose the type of file format that you want to create from the context menu; or click the appropriate command in the Export group of the External Data tab.

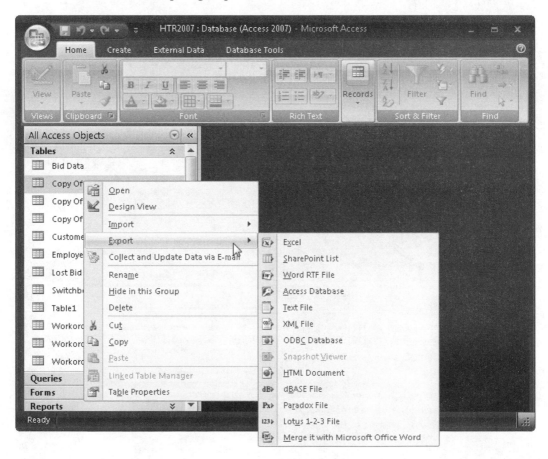

3. When the Export dialog box appears, select the filename. You may also want to use the Browse button to select the directory where you want to save the file. Notice the three check boxes, and select those that meet your needs (as described next). Click OK.

Some file types allow you to use some or all of the three export options check boxes on the Export dialog box:

- **Export Data with Formatting and Layout**   Preserves as much of the formatting and layout as possible.

- **Open the Destination File After the Export Operation Is Complete**   Launches the destination application and opens the exported file for viewing or editing when you click Export.

- **Export Only the Selected Records**   If you have selected records before giving the Export command, you can choose to export the whole object or only the selected records.

Working with Word

You have two ways to use Access data in Word:

- Save the Access data as Rich Text Format (RTF) and then open it with Word.

- Send the Access data to Word as a mail merge source file.

Saving in Rich Text Format

RTF is a standard format used by Word and other word processing and desktop publishing programs for Windows. Settings such as text fonts and styles are kept intact when files are saved as RTF files.

To save the output of an Access datasheet, query, form, or report as an RTF file, select the object in the Navigation Pane, and then on the External Data tab's Export group, click the Word (Export to RTF File) command. Alternatively, right-click the object you wish to export in the Navigation Pane, point to Export, and choose the Word RTF File from the context menu. The Export–RTF File dialog box opens (Figure 23-2). When you export to the RTF file type, the Export Data with Formatting and Layout option is automatically selected and cannot be cleared. The second option (Open the Destination File After the Export Operation Is Complete) becomes available, and, if checked, launches Word for editing the file when you click OK to close the Export dialog box.

After selecting the export options, click OK. Figure 23-3 shows the Alpha Card table as an RTF file in the Word 2007 window.

NOTE   *The arrangement of the data in the RTF file in Word reflects the field sizes and formats of the original Access table. If this doesn't look right—for example, if the field label row or a data column is too large—go back to the Access table to make adjustments. Then export the table again.*

Using Merge It with Microsoft Office Word

An Access database is often an ideal place to store addresses and names of customers, business associates, or friends. Being able to use these names and addresses in correspondence is a valuable capability. Once the link between Access and Word is established, you can open Word at any time to print form letters, envelopes, or labels using the current data from Access.

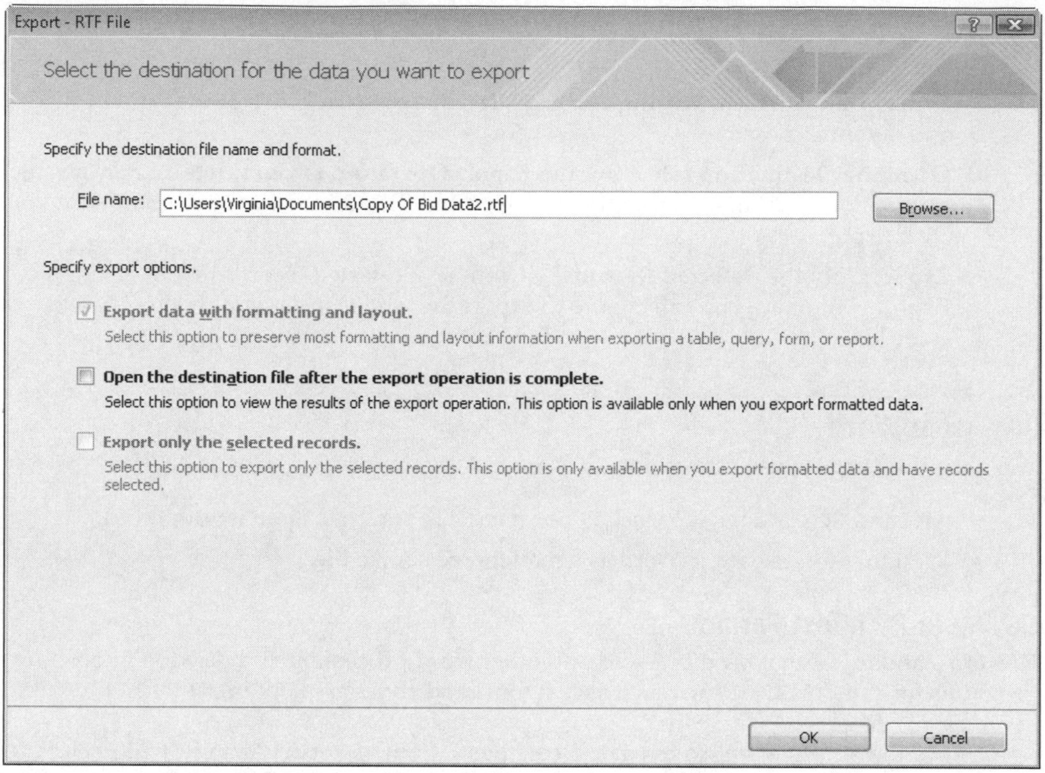

FIGURE 23-2   Exporting an Access table to a Word RTF file

A query might be the ideal way to simplify Access data structures for this mail merge function. Your table with customer names and addresses might have a number of other fields, such as a telephone number or date of last order, which you do not need to pass on. A query that selects only those fields relevant to addressing correspondence (that is, Name, Title, Company, Street Address, City, State, and ZIP code) can be designed to support mail merge actions. The Word mail merge feature can do this after receiving the table data as well, but you might as well not clutter the exchange of data with unnecessary fields.

To merge data from an Access table or query using the Microsoft Word mail merge functions, follow these steps:

1. In the Navigation Pane, select the table or query containing the data.

2. On the External Data tab's Export group, click the More command to display the context menu. Then click Merge it with Microsoft Office Word to begin the export. Alternatively, right-click the object you wish to export in the Navigation Pane, and point to Export and choose Merge it with Microsoft Office Word from the shortcut menu.

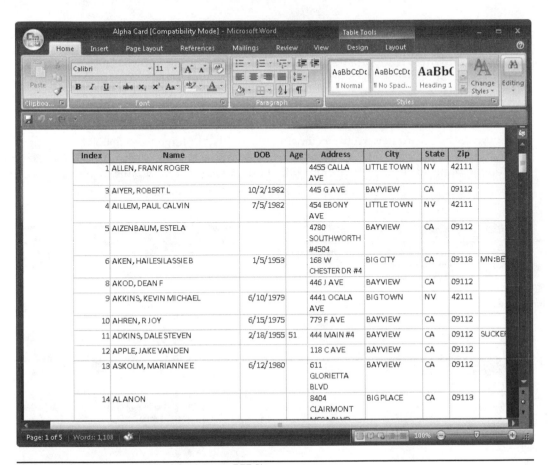

FIGURE 23-3   An Access table saved as an RTF file

3. The Microsoft Word Mail Merge Wizard dialog box appears, giving you a choice of linking your data to an existing Microsoft Word document or creating a new document.

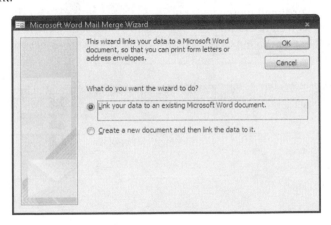

4. Select one of these options and click OK. Word starts and opens either a new document or the document that you selected.

5. In Word, the Write and Insert Fields group of the Mailings tab has an Insert Merge Field button. Click this button to display a list of fields from the Access table.

6. Select the specific fields that you want to insert in your document, and then place them in the document.

Figure 23-4 shows a new Word document with an Insert Merge Field dialog box listing the fields from the Alpha Card Access table as the data source. Notice also the Mail Merge pane on the right side of the Word window that can guide you through the merge process.

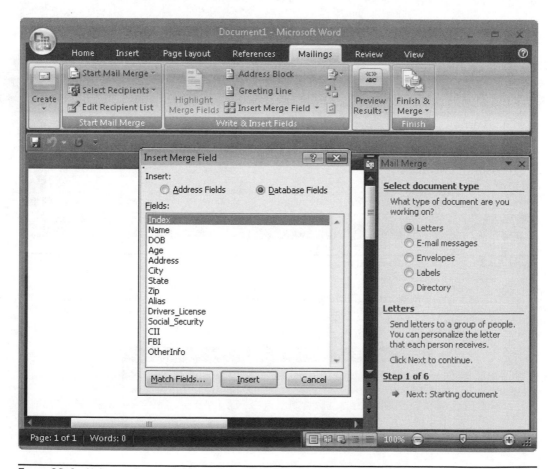

FIGURE 23-4   Using an Access table as the mail merge data source

For further information about how mail merge works, consult the Microsoft Word documentation.

Working with Excel

You can make use of Excel data in Access by importing or linking, and you can export data from Access to Excel. You can make use of Access data in Excel or another spreadsheet program in three ways:

- Export the Access datasheet as unformatted data.
- Save the output of a datasheet, form, or report as an Excel file or worksheet.
- Load the output of a datasheet, form, or report directly into Excel.

When you use either one of the last two methods, most of the formatting is preserved. A form is saved as a table of data. If you're saving a report that includes grouped data, the group levels are saved as outline levels in Excel.

Importing from and Linking to Excel Spreadsheets

Before you try to import or link to data from an Excel or other spreadsheet, make sure that the data is arranged in a tabular format. The spreadsheet must also have the same type of data in each column as the target Access datasheet, and the rows must contain the same field in each position.

You can choose to import or link an entire spreadsheet or only the data from a named range of cells within the spreadsheet. Usually, you create a new table from the imported or linked spreadsheet data, but you can also append the data to an existing datasheet if the spreadsheet column headings are the same as the table field names.

Tip *Access tries to assign appropriate data types to the imported data fields, but it doesn't always make the correct assumption. Before you do any work on the new table, make sure the field data types are what you want. You should also check the assumed field properties and set additional properties, such as formatting, to fit the intended table use in Access. Number field formatting might differ between Excel and Access.*

If you're importing from Excel version 5.0 or later, you can select one or more of the worksheets in the workbook. You can't import multiple spreadsheet files from Excel 4.0 or from Lotus 1-2-3. If you want to import one of these spreadsheets, you must open the program and save each spreadsheet as a separate file before importing.

To import or link an Excel spreadsheet, invoke the Import Spreadsheet Wizard by doing the following:

1. On the External Data tab in the Import group, click the Excel command. You can also right-click the object in the Navigation Pane and point to Import and choose Excel from the shortcut menu.

PART IV

2. In the first dialog box's File Name box, select the path of the source spreadsheet file. Use the Browse button if necessary.

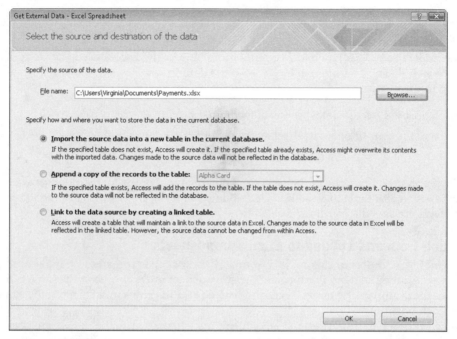

3. Choose what you want to do with the Excel data: Import it to a new table, append a copy of it to an existing table (select the table name from the list of tables in the current database), or link to the Excel data so that changes in the Excel file are reflected in Access. Then click OK.

4. In the first Import (or Link) Spreadsheet Wizard dialog box, choose to import a specific worksheet or a named range of cells. Then click Next.

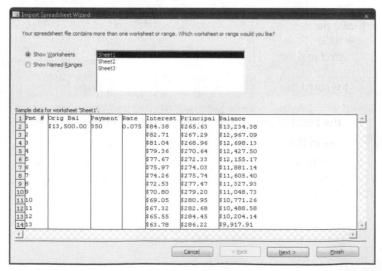

5. In the next wizard dialog box, check First Row Contains Column Headings (if this is true of your data), and then click Next. Clear the check box if the first row contains field data instead of column headings.

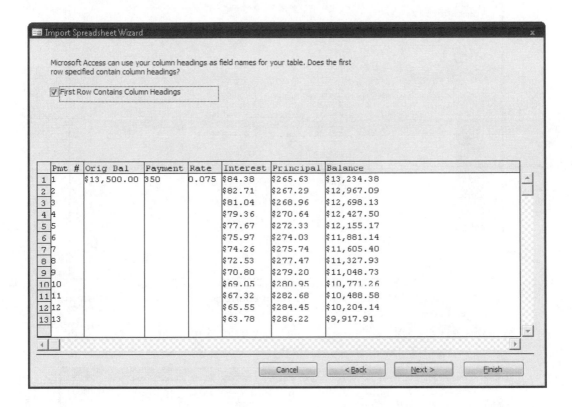

NOTE *If you indicate the first row contains column headings and some headings contain data that can't be used for valid Access field names (for instance, the heading is blank), Access displays a message to that effect and automatically assigns valid field names.*

6. In the next wizard dialog box, you can set the field options for each field in the worksheet:

   • Click in the Field Name box and enter a new name for the field.

   • Choose Yes in the Indexed box to create an index on that field.

   • Change the data type, if applicable, in the Data Type box.

PART IV

- Check the box to choose to skip the field when importing the spreadsheet.

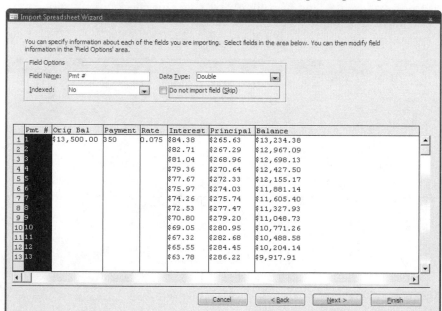

7. Click the next field header and make other changes. After making the desired changes to each field, click Next.

8. In the next dialog box, choose a primary key field. You can also let Access add a field as the primary key or choose not to have a primary key at all. Then click Next.

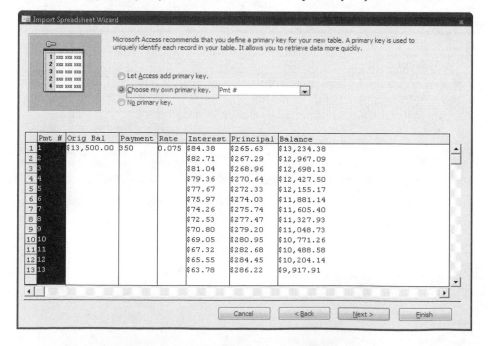

9. In the final wizard dialog box, you can accept the name that Access provides or enter a new name for the Access table, and then click Finish. An option in this dialog box lets you run the Table Analyzer with the new table to see if it can be made more efficient.

10. When the import is complete, Access asks if you want to Save the import steps. If you think you will repeat this import, select the Save Import Steps check box and click Close.

The new table in Access contains the data located in the Excel range of cells (Figure 23-5).

Exporting a Table or Query to Excel

Exporting all or part of a table or query datasheet to an Excel spreadsheet is similar to exporting to other file types. On the External Data tab's Export group, click the Excel command. In the Export dialog box, use the File Name box to locate the folder in which you want to store the exported data and name the file. If you're adding the data to an existing spreadsheet, select that name; otherwise, enter a new file name in the File Name box, and select the desired Microsoft Excel version or other spreadsheet file type from the File Format list.

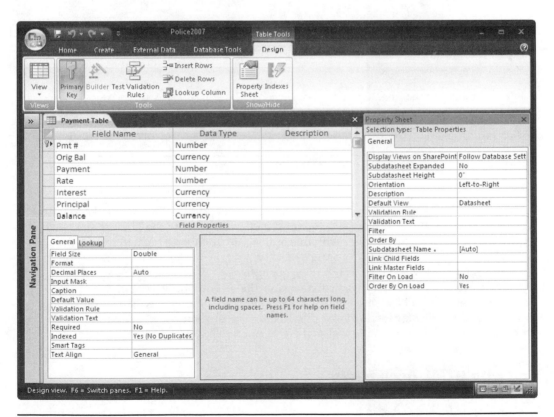

Figure 23-5 The Payment Table imported from Excel

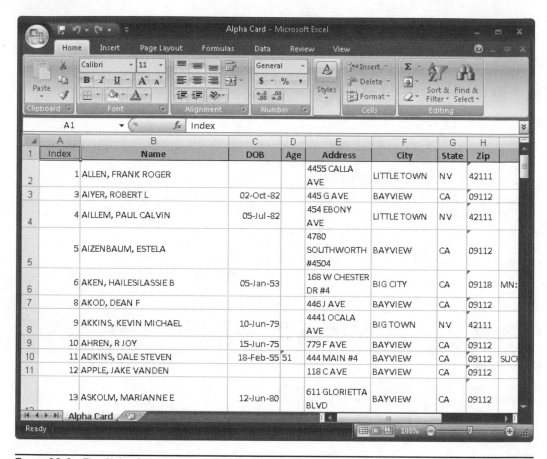

FIGURE 23-6   The Alpha Card table exported to Excel

Check the Export Data with Formatting and Layout option if you want to keep the same fonts and field width, as well as preserve the data that displays in the Lookup fields. The export process takes a little longer with this option, but you won't have to restore the formatting in the spreadsheet. The spreadsheet file created by Access contains the field names in the first row and data in the subsequent rows.

When you choose the Save Formatted option, the second option becomes available (Open the Destination File After the Export Operation Is Complete), which automatically launches Excel to display the exported data on the screen when you click Export. Figure 23-6 shows how the Alpha Card table looks when exported to Excel.

Working with HTML Documents

Hypertext Markup Language (HTML) is the standard markup language used to create documents on the web—better known as *web pages*. HTML uses tags, which the web browser interprets to display page elements, such as text and graphics, and to respond to user actions.

While HTML dictates how the document should look, it falls short of defining the data and the data structure.

Importing Data from HTML Documents

You can use the same Get External Data routine to import HTML lists and tables:

1. On the External Data tab's Import group, click the More button and choose HTML Document from the context menu.

2. Locate and select the file that you want to import, and then click Import. On the Get External Data dialog box, select whether you want to Import, Append, or Link to the data.

The Import HTML Wizard dialog boxes are the same as those of the Import Spreadsheet Wizard, except for the first box, where you choose between a worksheet and a named range in Excel.

The following are a few exceptions to watch for when importing or linking to an HTML document:

- Access doesn't import any .gif or .jpg image files embedded in the HTML document.
- If a table is embedded within a table cell in the HTML file, Access creates a separate table for it.
- If data spans rows or columns in an HTML table, Access duplicates the data in each cell.

Exporting Data to HTML Documents

To begin exporting an Access datasheet or form to an HTML document, right-click the table, query, or form in the Navigation Pane, and point to Export and choose HTML Document. (Or open or select the object and on the External Data tab, click the More button in the Export group, and then click HTML Document from the context menu.)

The Save Formatted and Open the destination file options work as explained. If you checked Export Data with Formatting and Layout, the HTML Output Options dialog box appears when you click Export. You can enter the path of the HTML template or click Browse and look for the one you want.

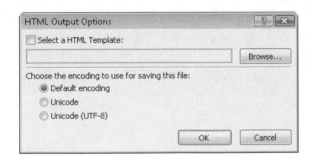

NOTE *An HTML template includes the tags and tokens unique to Access. These markers indicate where to put output and other information in the HTML files. If you don't specify a template, Access provides a default scheme.*

When you want to export a report to an HTML document, Access exports the report as multiple HTML files—one for each printed page. The first file is named with the report name, and subsequent files use the report name followed by *Page1*, *Page2*, and so on.

All the controls and features of the report, including any subreports, are exported correctly except for lines, rectangles, and Object Linking and Embedding (OLE) objects. You can still use an HTML template file to include images in the report header or footer.

Using Outlook to Get Data

Access 2007 includes strong integration with Microsoft Outlook. You can use an import command to move Contacts from Outlook to Access. You can also use e-mail messages to collect data for your Access database.

Getting Contacts from Outlook into Access

To import contacts from Outlook to Access, do the following:

1. Right-click a table and point to the Import and choose from the shortcut menu Outlook Folder, or, on the External Data tab's Import group, click the More command and choose the Outlook Folder from the context menu.

2. Choose whether to Import, Append, or Link To the data on the Get External Data dialog box, and then click OK.

3. Choose whether you want to import your Outlook Address Book or your Contacts folder.

4. Click Next to see the data.

The Import Outlook Contact boxes are the same as those of the Import Spreadsheet Wizard—you can choose your data and rename it as necessary.

Using E-mail to Collect Data

Access 2007 lets you collect data via e-mail messages. To use this feature, follow these steps:

1. If necessary, create a table or query to hold the data that you will collect with the e-mail messages. Outlook will use the fields in this object to create the fields for the user to fill out in the e-mail. Alternatively, you may use an existing table or query.

2. Open the table or query that will be filled with data collected from e-mail messages.

3. On the External Data tab's Collect Data group, click the Create E-mail command. A wizard leads you through the steps of creating an e-mail that will collect data. This first page lists the major steps that you will go through. Click Next.

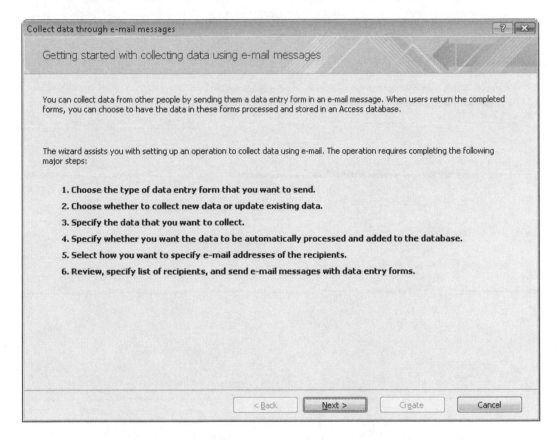

4. In the next wizard dialog box, choose to create an HTML form or an InfoPath form. The HTML form can be used by nearly all recipients, as long as their e-mail software supports HTML. The InfoPath form requires that the user have Outlook 2007 and InfoPath 2007. However, the InfoPath form supports more features than the HTML form. Click Next.

5. Select the fields that you want to include in your e-mail form, then click Next.

6. In the next dialog box, choose to collect new information or update existing information. Note that you can update existing information only if the recipients' e-mail

addresses are stored in the database. Click Next to set the collection processing options.

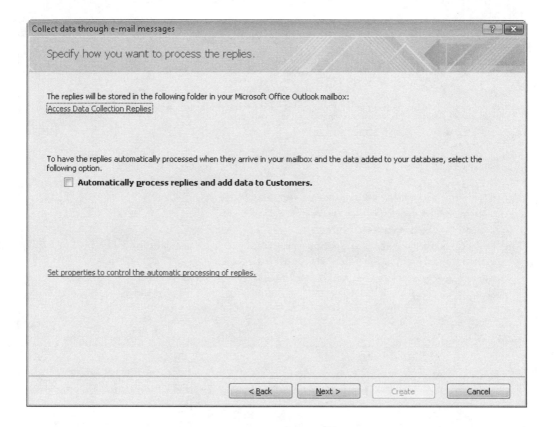

7. If desired, change the location of the arriving e-mails by clicking the Access Data Collection Replies link near the top of this dialog box. Determine whether you want to process replies automatically (which automatically adds data to your database if it is open) or manually process them one at a time by selecting (or not) the Automatically Process Replies and Add Data to *Tablename* check box. You can also set properties to control the automatic processing of replies by clicking the lower link. Click Next.

8. Determine how you want to specify recipients' e-mail addresses. If e-mail addresses are in the database, you can use the second option. Otherwise, select the first option: Enter the E-mail Addresses in Microsoft Office Outlook. Click Next.

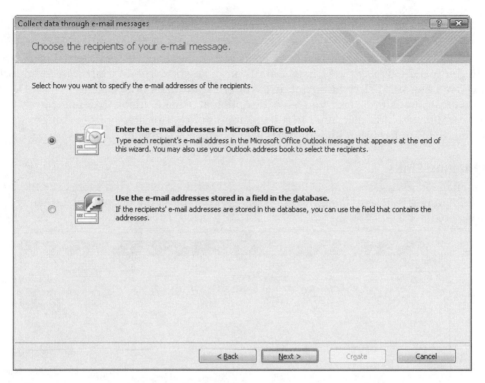

9. If you are using addresses from the database, the next dialog box asks you to specify the table and field containing the addresses. Otherwise, you are asked to customize the e-mail message. Explain why you need the data. It is helpful to tell users that they need to use the mouse to click the next field, since pressing TAB does not work. You can also customize the message in Outlook if you are selecting e-mail addresses there. Click Next.

10. Click Create to create the e-mail message. Once in Outlook, you can edit the message and add recipients before sending it.

Use the Manage Replies button in the Collect Data group of the External Data tab to see a summary of the data collection e-mails that have been sent from this database.

***

NOTE *If you have chosen to process replies manually, you need to view the replies in Outlook: right-click the Reply and choose Export Data to Microsoft Access.*

Managing Links and Saved Import/Export Definitions

Access 2007 allows you to repeat imports and exports if you save the definitions. Also, if you link to data, you may need to manage the links (for instance, if the source file moves).

Using Saved Definitions

Access gives you the option of saving import and export definitions so that they can be reused using the Saved Imports and Saved Exports commands on the External Data tab. Both commands display the Manage Data Tasks dialog box with two tabs: Saved Imports and Saved Exports. Select the operation to run it, create an Outlook task from it, or Delete it. If you create an Outlook task, you have the option of using Outlook to define dates when the operation should occur. You can run the import or export directly from Outlook by clicking the Run Export or Run Import button on the tasks ribbon.

Managing Links

To manage links, use the Linked Table Manager. On the Database Tools tab, click the Linked Table Manager button in the Database Tools group to open the Linked Table Manager dialog box.

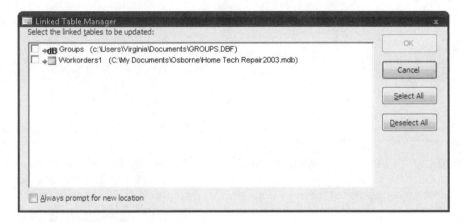

Select links to be updated. If the linked table is not found, Access asks you to name the file and select its location on the Select New Location Of Groups dialog box.

If you want Access to always prompt for the location of files before updating data, select the Always Prompt for the New Location check box in the lower left corner of the dialog box.

Mailing Access Objects

You can send Access tables, queries, forms, reports, report snapshots, and even modules attached to an e-mail message. When you attach objects or data to an e-mail message, the attachments can be converted to several versions of Excel, RTF, MS-DOS text, HTML, or report snapshot formats as part of the e-mail operation.

NOTE *To e-mail an Access database object, you must install an electronic mail application that supports Messaging Application Programming Interface (MAPI), such as Microsoft Outlook, Microsoft Exchange, or Eudora.*

To attach an Access object to an e-mail message, do the following:

1. Select the object you want to send in the Navigation Pane. If you want to send only some of the records from a table or query, open the table or query in Datasheet view, and then select the records you want to send.

2. Click the Office button and choose Email from the drop-down menu. The Send Object As dialog box opens. Choose the file format you want to use for your e-mail attachment, and then click OK. If you selected only part of the datasheet in step 1, two output formats options become available: All, which attaches the entire datasheet to the e-mail message, and Selection, which attaches only the selected data.

3. If you choose HTML, the next dialog box gives you the opportunity to attach an HTML template. You can accept the filename displayed in the HTML Output Options dialog box (shown earlier), enter a different name, and then choose Browse to locate another file. Or you can clear the template box and not use a template. Click OK.

Your e-mail client program opens an e-mail message form, where you can address your message, add text to the message, and send it out. The object you selected to send is automatically attached to the message.

Summary

In this chapter, we expanded the concept of exchanging data with outside sources by looking at the use of Office Links to exchange data with Word, Excel, and HTML documents, and collect data from Outlook. In addition, you looked at the challenges in importing text and e-mailing database objects. As you saw in this chapter and in Chapter 22, a large number of options and techniques are available for exporting data from Access and importing data into Access from outside sources. These techniques have many variations and, in some cases, require analysis and preparation of the data being exchanged.

PART IV

Both this chapter and Chapter 22 emphasized that the use of these techniques is a challenge in terms of selecting the most efficient and effective method for accomplishing the data exchange. With outside sources, this is an even greater challenge because the effort to identify the data structure and accomplish a useful and accurate transfer can be significant.

The next chapter discusses creating an application to be shared among users in a workgroup. Multiple users can add complications, as well as advantages, to the process. Security, data integrity, and validity all become issues.

Sharing with Multiple Users

Creating and maintaining a database in a multiple-user environment isn't a simple task. You can share data in several ways, depending on the environment and the location of the users. Several users can share a single Access file by placing the database on a central server and accessing it from workstations. The database can also be split into two pieces—a front-end containing the database objects and a back-end containing all the data. Using this method, users can run different versions of Access and also create their own custom database objects to use locally.

When you open the database to multiple users, you may confront a whole new set of complications. Some users may not have the latest information; other users may try to update the same information at the same time, causing conflicts. Access provides several tools that can help ensure the integrity and security of the database and provides other means of resolving conflicts. This chapter explains how to share an Access database among multiple users and how to ensure integrity and security of the database.

Sharing a Database on a Network

When several users need access to the same data, you can share a single database with others in several ways. Rather than each user keeping a complete copy of the database, you can provide opportunities for sharing that can also improve data reliability and consistency. The following options are available for sharing an Access database:

- Placing the database in a central location where all users have access to all objects in it.
- Splitting the database so the users share only the table data.
- Publishing the entire database or part of the database on a SharePoint Services site.

Sharing an Entire Database

The easiest way to share data is to put the entire database—tables and all—on the network server or in a folder that can be shared. All users then have access to all the data and use the same database objects. If everyone uses the database for the same activities and you don't

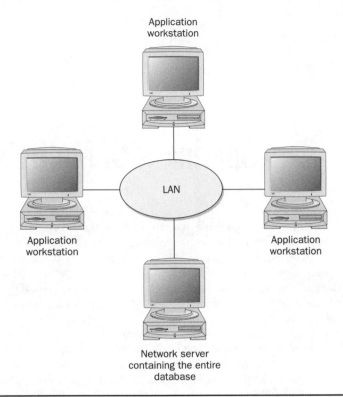

FIGURE 24-1 Sharing a database among multiple users

want the users to customize their own objects, this is the best strategy. Figure 24-1 shows the model for sharing the entire database among multiple users. The entire database is stored on the network server, and the workstations access all the objects via the LAN.

To share an entire database on a network server, copy the database to the shared folder, and then use the Advanced page of the Access Options dialog box (as shown later in this chapter) to set the Default Open mode to Shared. Access must be installed on each workstation on the network to share Access databases this way.

Splitting the Database

A faster method of sharing a database is to put all the tables on the network server and let the users keep the other objects on their own workstations. Only the data is transmitted over the network, thus reducing network traffic. This strategy is useful when the users' jobs and activities are different or the users don't all use the same version of Access. The users maintain only those objects on their computers that pertain directly to their own activities.

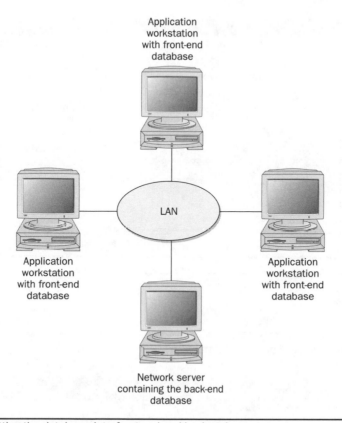

Figure 24-2 Splitting the database into front-end and back-end

The database containing the tables is called the *back-end* database and the one containing the other objects is the *front-end* database. The front-end database contains links to the tables in the back-end database. Access provides the Database Splitter Wizard to separate the tables from the rest of the database. Figure 24-2 illustrates the front-end/back-end models for sharing an Access database. All tables are stored on the network server. The application workstations store all of the other objects—queries, forms, reports, macros, and modules.

Tip *Undoing what the Database Splitter Wizard does isn't easy, so be sure to make a backup copy of the database before you attempt to split it.*

To split a database into the front- and back-end elements, do the following:

1. Open the database and make sure no objects in the database are open. On the Database Tools tab's Move Data group, click the Access Database command. The Database Splitter Wizard opens with a message describing the process (Figure 24-3).

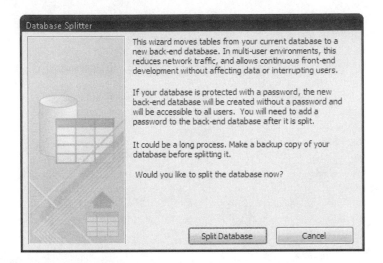

FIGURE 24-3   Starting the Database Splitter

2. After reading the message, click Split Database. The next dialog box lets you specify where to place the back-end database.

NOTE   *If you are using Windows XP, this dialog box looks quite different, but it will do the same thing.*

3. Click the Browse Folders down arrow and the dialog box shows more information. Look for the network server.

4. Click the Folders down arrow on the left pane and choose Network in the list (Figure 24-4).

5. Select the network server and enter a filename for the back-end database, or accept the default name: the name of the current database with _be added.

6. Click Split. When the process is completed, a message appears, announcing the successful split. Click OK to close the message box.

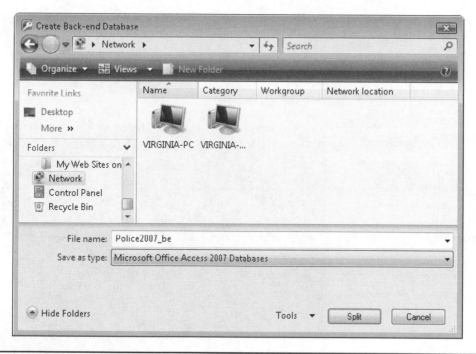

FIGURE 24-4   Choosing the network server

Splitting a large database might take awhile. The wizard is deleting the tables from the current database, creating a new database with the tables, and then linking the current database to the new back-end tables.

When you look at the list of tables in the Navigation Pane of the current database after splitting, you can see that the tables listed are all links to another database (Figure 24-5) by the link icons next to the names in the list. If you open the new back-end database, you can see all the tables listed in the tables group in the Navigation Pane, but all the other groups are empty.

To customize the distributed database environment further, you can reduce network traffic even more by moving relatively static tables, such as lookup tables containing data that doesn't change often, back to the front-end databases. If the data in the lookup table changes, you can make the changes in the back-end version and alert the users to copy the data to their own lookup tables. Temporary tables should also be stored locally to prevent conflicts and reduce network traffic.

If you need to change the link to any of the back-end tables, on the Database Tools tab's Database Tools group, click the Linked Table Manager command. In the Linked Table Manager dialog box, choose the affected tables and check the Always Prompt for New Location check

PART IV

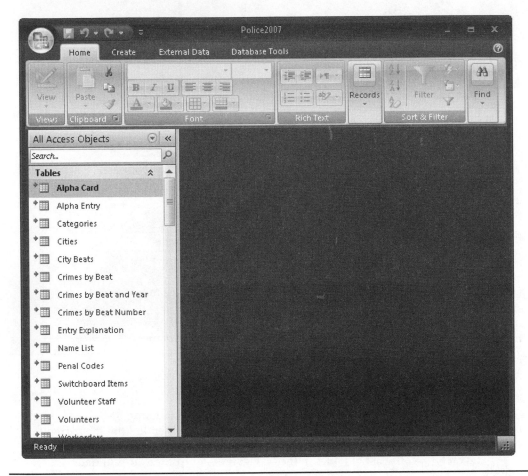

FIGURE 24-5   Tables are linked to the back-end database

box (Figure 24-6). Then, when you refresh the link to the table, you will have the opportunity of changing the location of the linked table in the standard file location dialog box.

CAUTION   *When you link tables, you can leave a security hole, unless you secure both the front-end and the back-end tables.*

Preventing Exclusive Access

When multiple users are sharing a database, competition for data access can occur. If one user opens the database with exclusive access, no other user can work with it at the same time. To prevent, or at least discourage, this from happening, Click the Microsoft Office button and choose Access Options to open the Access Options dialog box, and on the Advanced page, set the Default Open Mode to Shared. Then instruct all the users not to open the database in Exclusive mode. See Chapter 25 for information about including security in a multiple-user environment.

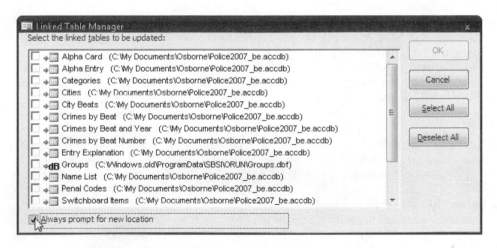

FIGURE 24-6   Setting to prompt for new table locations

You can also set up a security system that prevents Exclusive mode from opening by certain users and permits it for others. The database administrator must be able to open the database in Exclusive mode to perform duties, such as compacting and backing up the database.

NOTE *Access 2007 no longer supports database replication. If you have a database that was replicated in Access 2003 or earlier versions, you will not be able to save it in the new ACCDB format. You can, however, continue to use it in its MDB format or recreate it in the Access 2007 file format.*

Managing the Database in a Multiuser Environment

As soon as more than one user can open a database at the same time, someone should be assigned as the database administrator (DBA). The DBA is responsible for ensuring the integrity and security of the database. Among the issues that must be addressed by the DBA are the following:

- Controlling read/write access to the data
- Setting up user groups with the appropriate levels of access and security
- Adding new users to a group and removing users from a group
- Ensuring accurate, current record data and minimizing data-locking conflicts
- Editing database objects as necessary and ensuring that all users have current versions
- Backing up and compacting the database

Controlling Data Editing

If two users attempt to edit a record at the same time, the results can be unpredictable. Some form of data locking is necessary to ensure the integrity of the database. Allowing one user exclusive access to a record is called *record locking*. When a data page (a unit of data storage), recordset object (a table or query), or a database object is locked, it's read-only to all users, except the user who is currently entering or editing the data in it.

Access provides three levels of record locking, ranging from no locks at all to locking all the records in the recordset. You can set the default record-locking scheme in the Advanced group of options on the Advanced page of the Access Options dialog box (Figure 24-7).

Choose the level you want to use, and then check the Open Databases by Using Record-Level Locking check box. With record-level locking in effect, Access locks only a single record in the currently open database. This applies to accessing data in datasheets and forms. If you clear this check box, page-level locking becomes the default. This setting does not apply to action queries or SQL statements.

Set Default Record Locking

The Default record-locking setting applies only to datasheet views of tables and queries. If you want to set record locking for forms or reports, set the Record Locks property on the

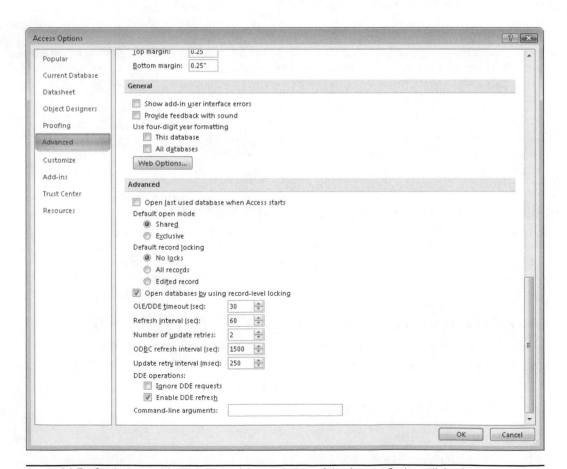

FIGURE 24-7 Setting record locking in the Advanced page of the Access Options dialog box

Data tab of the object's Property Sheet, as shown next. The choices are the same. Setting record locks for a report prevents changes in records in the underlying table or query while the report is previewed or printed. You can also set the Record Locks property for a query and override the default setting.

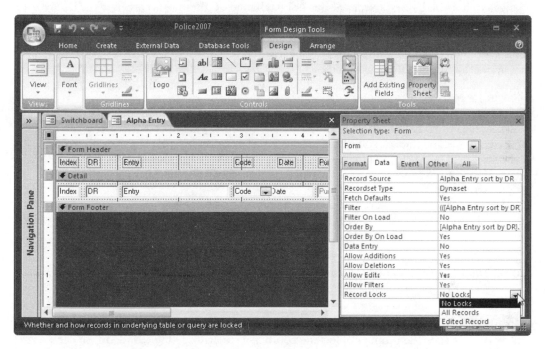

No Locks, the default setting when you start a new database, is called *optimistic record locking* because it's used where few record write conflicts are expected. Access doesn't lock the record during editing. The edited record is locked only at the exact moment it's being saved. The assumption here is that one user will probably have completed saving the record before another user tries to edit it. Using No Locks ensures that all records can be edited at any time, but it can also cause editing conflicts among the users.

When you try to save changes to a record another user has changed since you began editing it, a Write Conflict dialog box appears with the following options:

- **Save Record**   Saves the record with your changes, overwriting the other user's changes.

- **Copy to Clipboard**   Copies your version of the record to the clipboard for further analysis.

- **Drop Changes**   Discards your changes in favor of the previous changes.

The *All Records* record-locking strategy locks all records in the form or datasheet, as well as the underlying tables, for the entire time that the form or datasheet is open. No one else can edit the records. One case in which this strategy would be useful is when you're running an update query that applies to several different records and you want to make sure that all the affected records are locked until the query is completed.

The *Edited Record* record-locking strategy is called *pessimistic locking* because it's assumed that much competition will occur for access to records for editing. If it's important for all editing of a record to be completed before another user has access to it, the Edited Record strategy is required. As soon as one user begins to edit a record, no other user can make any changes to it until the first user saves his or her changes. Other users can view the record, but they cannot change it.

The only difference in the display of the record is that the universal symbol for No—the circle with a diagonal line through it—appears in the record selector instead of the pencil that appears with the No Locks method.

Choosing a Locking Strategy

The strategy you choose depends on your data, how many users share the application, and how they use the data. For most multiuser environments, the No Locks strategy can be the most effective, even though some brief write conflict errors can occur. The overall performance of the system is more efficient than with the other record-locking strategies.

If more imperative reasons exist for locking records during editing, use one of the other locking strategies.

If the data in a form, report, or query is acquired from an Open Database Connectivity (ODBC) database, Access treats it as though the No Locks setting were selected and disregards the Record Locks property setting.

NOTE   *The setting does not take effect if you open the database by selecting the filename from the list of Recent Documents that appears when you click the Microsoft Office button.*

Minimizing Conflicts

One way to reduce the number of locking conflicts is to arrange the workload, so each user attends to different parts of the database. For example, one user updates records for sales in the Western states, another does the same for the Southern area, and so on.

When two users try to update the same record and cause a conflict, Access tries several times to save the record, hoping that it will be freed from the lock, before displaying the Write Conflict message. The period of time that elapses between tries is specified in the Update Retry Interval setting in the Advanced page of the Access Options dialog box. The Number of Update Retries setting determines how many times Access should try to save the record before giving up.

You can try different combinations of these two settings. For example, set the Number of Update Retries to 0 to have Access display the Write Conflict message at once. Set both to higher values to reduce the number of write conflicts by letting Access try to save the record more times, with a longer interval between attempts. However, with this arrangement, users might complain that the system is running too slow. Experiment with these settings to settle on the right combination for your application.

Table 26-1 describes these and other settings that help avoid data-locking conflicts. The settings are found on the Advanced page of the Options dialog box.

Updating Records with Refresh and Requery

If the data in your shared database changes frequently and it's important for the user to have up-to-date data, you can use two methods to keep the data current:

Option	Settings	Description
OLE/DDE Timeout (sec)	0 through 300 seconds; default is 30 seconds	Controls the time to wait before retrying a failed OLE or DDE attempt.
Refresh Interval	0 through 32,766 seconds; default is 60 seconds	Sets the number of seconds between automatic updating of records in Datasheet or Form view. Setting to 0 results in no automatic updating.
Number of Update Retries	0 through 10; default is two tries	Sets the number of times Access tries to save a record locked by another user before displaying a Write Conflict message.
ODBC Refresh Interval	0 through 32,766 seconds; default is 1,500 seconds	Sets the number of seconds between automatic refreshing of records accessed using ODBC. Setting to 0 results in no automatic updating.
Update Retry Interval	0 through 1,000 milliseconds; default is 250 milliseconds	Sets the number of milliseconds between automatic attempts to save a record locked by another user.

TABLE 24-1   Advanced Options for the Multiuser Environment

- **Refresh**   Offers a periodic quick update of the data currently on the screen.
- **Requery**   Completely rebuilds the underlying recordset by running the query or applying the filter again.

Refresh updates only those records already appearing in Datasheet or Form view. When you refresh the datasheet or form, records are not reordered or deleted, and those that no longer meet the filter criteria also are not removed. To update the recordset to reflect these actions, you must requery the records.

The default interval for refreshing records is 60 seconds, which might be too long in critical situations. You can reset the interval to 10 or 15 seconds. If you set the interval too low, Access creates a lot of network traffic. To refresh a table, query, or form manually, open the table or query in Datasheet view or the form in Form or Layout view, and then on the Home tab's Records group, click the Refresh All down arrow and choose Refresh All or Refresh in the context menu. You can also press F9 to refresh the records.

Requerying completely rebuilds the underlying recordset. The easiest way to requery is to press SHIFT-F9.

TIP   *Requerying is somewhat of a nuisance to the user because the form or datasheet returns to the first record in the recordset. If you were working with a record deep in the recordset, you must manually return to it after requerying. Remembering the record number doesn't help much because the record order might have changed with the requery.*

Editing Shared Database Objects

Even though you do your best to have all the database object designs completed before setting up the database for shared access, changes are bound to be necessary later. Any local objects can be modified at any time, but the shared objects require special consideration.

Before you begin to make significant design changes to a shared database, be sure that you open it in Exclusive mode: click the Microsoft Office button and choose Open in the drop-down menu. Then in the Open Database dialog box, click the down arrow next to the Open button and choose Open Exclusive. Pick a time to do this when other users don't require access to the database, such as during nonworking hours.

If the required design changes are less invasive, you can safely modify the objects while the database is open in Shared mode. To make changes to a table design, the table must not be in use by another user. If the table or any query, form, or report based on the table is open, the table design cannot be changed. In this case, you can still view the table design, but Access informs you that the table is read-only.

The converse is also true—if you're modifying a table design, the table and any query, form, or report that is based on it is unavailable to another user. A good idea is to have the changes well-thought-out and specific before opening the table design. Then keep the table design open as briefly as possible.

NOTE *The Name AutoCorrect feature available in the list of Current Database options keeps track of object and field name changes, and tracks down locations where they're referenced. The changes affect all the references.*

Here are some helpful tips to keep in mind when you need to edit shared database objects:

- When you edit a query, form, or report design already in use by another user, that user won't see the new version until the object is closed and reopened.

- If the objects that you want to change are dependent on each other, be sure to edit them all at the same time, so that they'll be consistent.

- Make sure no one else is using the macro that you want to edit by opening the database in Exclusive mode. If you change a macro that someone's using, you can cause problems.

Summary

When multiple users need access to the same database, it's essential to ensure that all users have the same data. This chapter discussed a few of the ways this can be accomplished. Sharing a single file stored on a server with multiple users is one way. Another way is to split the database into a front-end database that contains the database objects and links to the data tables on the back-end database.

As multiple users make changes to the data at the same time on a LAN, provisions must be made to prevent conflicts from occurring. Various record-locking schemes are available in Access, some of which are quite lenient, while others are stricter.

In the next chapter, you will learn ways to keep your database secure and safe.

Secure a Database

The main purpose of database security is to prevent unauthorized access to the information, either for viewing or editing. Security can also prevent design modifications by unqualified individuals. Even the slightest change in a form design or a data validation rule can cause problems that can be difficult to locate and correct. Security also blocks hackers from getting into and damaging the database and spreading viruses in the system.

Access 2007 has added many new security measures that make it easier to apply security and to use a secured database. The new Trust Center was created to provide a central location to maintain security within folders that are designated as trusted locations.

New Security Measures

The following are a few of the new security features that make it safer to manage information in a database:

- You can browse in the database without having to enable the Visual Basic for Applications (VBA) code and macros that may contain damaging actions.

- You can set up a trusted location and place database files in it. Then you don't have to enable the database each time you want to use it.

- With the new Trust Center page in the Access Options dialog box, you can set and change all of the security settings in one place.

- You can encrypt a database with a password to keep others from accessing the data and objects.

In Access 2007, when you open a database that is stored in a trusted location, you won't see the Security Warning message box and the macros are enabled. If an earlier version of the database contains a valid digital signature from a trusted publisher, you can trust the contents. If you use a database from an untrusted location, it is disabled by default, and you must enable it each time that you open it.

NOTE *A publisher is a developer or company that creates databases. Reputable publishers are considered to be trustworthy.*

Enabling/Disabling Database Content

As you saw in earlier chapters, when you open a database, you often see the Security Warning message bar that tells you that certain contents within the database have been disabled. You can click the Options button to view your alternatives in the Microsoft Office Security Options dialog box (Figure 25-1).

You can leave the database content (VBA macro in Figure 25-1) disabled and continue to work with the database. If you trust the source of the database, you can choose to enable all the potentially harmful contents. When you close the database, all the contents are disabled again, and the next time you open the database, you'll have to enable them.

NOTE *You can close the Security Warning message bar without making a choice by clicking the Close button (X).*

Encrypting the Database

The encryption security tool combines encoding the database with requiring a password to open it. Encryption actually scrambles and compacts the database so that it is completely unreadable by a word processor or any utility program. Encrypting a database does not

FIGURE 25-1 Security Alert warnings

restrict access to database objects, but to open the database, the user must first enter a password. Decrypting the database reverses the process and restores it to its original form.

Encrypting with a Password

To encrypt the database, you must first open it in exclusive mode from the Open dialog box by doing the following:

1. Click the Microsoft Office button and click Open.

2. Locate and select the database in the Open dialog box. Then click the Open down arrow and choose Open Exclusive from the drop-down list.

3. With the database open, on the Database Tools tab's Database Tools group, click the Encrypt with Password command.

4. In the Set Database Password dialog box, enter the password and press TAB. Enter the password again to verify it.

5. Click OK.

   To open an encrypted database, you will be required to enter the database password and click OK.

About Security Problems with Linked Tables

Security problems might occur if one of the tables in a password-protected database is linked to a second database that does not require a password. The password for the first database is stored with the linking information in the second database. Any user who can open the second database can also open the linked table in the protected database. The password is also stored in an unencrypted form in the unprotected database, making it readable to any user.

NOTE   Encryption applies only to ACCDB database file formats. Earlier versions were encoded with a less stringent scrambling algorithm.

To remove the requirement for a password and restore the database to its original format, open the database in exclusive mode and on the Database Tools tab's Database Tools group, click the Decrypt Database command.

Using the Trust Center

The new Trust Center security system imposes strict criteria upon database components and determines whether it is safe to open the database or if the database should be disabled. The Trust Center enforces the criteria on macros, add-ins, and ActiveX controls, as you will see in the following sections. You can use the Trust Center to set specific security options and to create or change trusted locations.

NOTE   All changes in Trust Center settings do not take effect until after you close and reopen the Access database.

Creating a Trusted Environment

An Access database is made up of many components, rather than a single file, as with a Word document. The intricate relationships among the tables and other objects can create complex security issues. One solution is to place all the database components, once they are determined to be safe, in a trusted folder. When you open a database in a trusted location, you don't have to enable its contents. Another way to eliminate the need to enable a database upon opening is to identify the developer as trusted and place the name in the Trusted Publisher list.

Building a Trusted Location

You can place all macros, VBA code, and safe expressions in a trusted location so that you don't have to enable them every time that you open the database. You can use the Trust Center to create a trusted location and put the database or a copy in the trusted location, as follows:

1. Click the Microsoft Office button and choose Access Options.

2. In the Access Options dialog box, click Trust Center, and then click Trust Center Settings.

3. In the Trust Center Trusted Locations window, click Trusted Locations in the left pane.

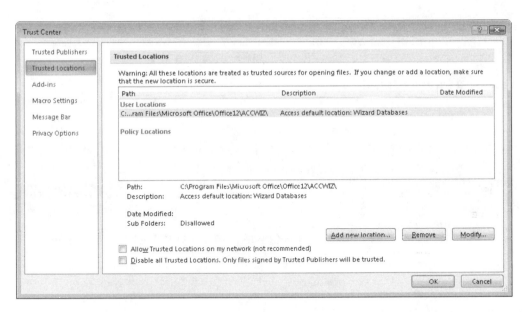

4. Click Add New Location and enter the name of the folder in the Path box of the Microsoft Office Trusted Location dialog box, or click Browse to find the folder you want.

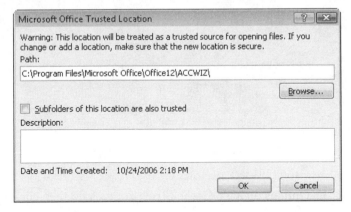

5. Check the option Subfolders of This Location Are Also Trusted if you want all subfolders to be considered trustworthy.

6. Type a description explaining the use for the location, if desired, and then click OK.

To remove the trusted location, return to the Trust Center Trusted Locations window, select the folder path, and click Remove. Then click OK. You can also use the Trusted Locations window to move the location to a different path by clicking Modify.

Creating a Trusted Publisher List

Anyone or any company who has created a macro, an add-in, an ActiveX control, or some other application extension is called a *publisher*. A trusted publisher is a developer who has a current and valid digital signature that is certified by a reputable certificate authority. If the developer is not involved with commercial projects, he or she can sign his/her own certificate rather that having to go through a certificate authority. (See the section "Creating a Certificate" later in this chapter.)

If the publisher's signature is valid, you will see the option Trust All Documents from This Publisher in the Microsoft Office Security Options dialog box (Figure 25-2). Choose that option and the publisher is added to the list.

To remove a publisher from the list, return to the Trusted Publishers list and do the following:

1. In the Access Options dialog box, click Trust Center, and then click Trust Center Settings.

FIGURE 25-2   Adding a publisher to the trusted list

2. Click Trusted Publishers.

3. In the Trust Center Trusted Publishers window, select the name in the list and click Remove.

Trusting Macros

Macros and VBA code are written by developers to carry out many types of frequently used commands. Hackers can create a macro that can invade your computer and spread a virus, so it makes sense to be cautious and protect your computer and its contents. The Trust Center monitors for macros and checks to see if they are safe using the following criteria:

- Is the macro signed with the developer's digital signature, and is the signature valid and current?

- Was the signature's certificate issued by a Certificate Authority (CA)?

- Is the developer who signed the macro trusted?

The macro is disabled if any of these criteria are not met, and the Security Warning message bar is displayed.

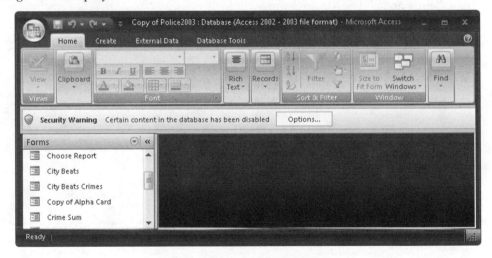

Click Options to open the Security Alert dialog box (Figure 25-2), where you can choose whether to enable the macros or not. Here are the choices:

- Help Protect Me from Unknown Content (Recommended)

- Enable This Content

- Trust All Documents from This Publisher

Specific information about the disabled content is displayed in the dialog box. For example, the VBA macro under question in Figure 25-2 was signed by "heather," whose certificate was self-signed. The certificate will not expire until January 1, 2012. You can click Show Signature Details if you need more information.

   The note in the dialog box indicates that the signature is valid, but the publisher is not currently included in your Trusted Publisher list. To add her to the list, as mentioned earlier, check the third option, Trust All Documents from This Publisher.

Dealing with Macro Problems

If the macro is not signed, you should make sure that you can trust the source before enabling the macro. Note that you can continue working with the database without enabling the macro.

   You may see a message indicating that the signature is not trusted if you have not added the macro source to your Trusted Publisher list. You should not enable any macros with invalid or expired signatures. Both of these problems can result from someone tampering with the macro. If the signature has expired but you have safely used the macro in the past, it is probably safe to enable it.

Changing Macro Security Settings

To change the trust level for macros that are not considered to be in a trusted location, go to the Trust Center and choose Macro Settings.

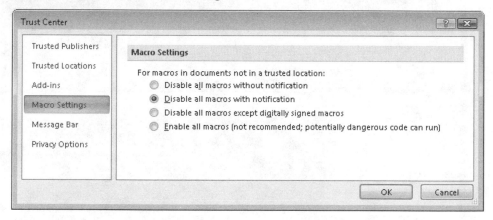

Choose from the four options:

- **Disable All Macros without Notification**   Blocks all macros and does not display a security warning. However, if you do trust some documents even though they have unsigned macros, put those documents in a trusted location.

- **Disable All Macros with Notification**   (Default setting) Notifies you with security alerts that some macros are unsigned. You can choose which ones to trust.

- **Disable All Macros Except Digitally Signed Macros**   Macros from trusted publishers can be run, but you are alerted if you have not added the publisher to your trusted list.

- **Enable All Macros (Not Recommended; Potentially Dangerous Code Can Run)** Allows all macros to run and can pose a problem with macros from hackers or other intruders.

NOTE *A fifth option may be offered:* Trust Access to VBA Project Object Model. *This option is for developers only. Developers create macros, VBA code, ActiveX controls, add-ins, and other application extensions for use by others.*

After making your choice, click OK twice to return to the database.

Trusting Add-Ins

Add-ins, also called *application extensions*, are functions that add special features to the Access program. For example, database templates, XML schemas, and Smart Tags are add-ons that extend the usability of Access. You can use the Trust Center to see which add-ins are currently installed on your computer.

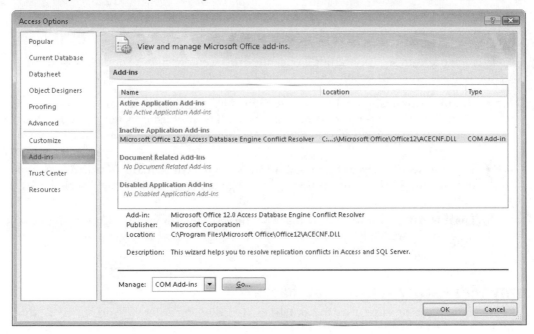

Add-ins are grouped in four categories:

- Active add-ins are registered and currently running in your database.
- Inactive add-ins are in your computer but not currently loaded.
- Document-related add-ins are template files that are used by currently open documents.
- Disabled application add-ins were automatically disabled because of the problems they caused, such as crashing the program.

The Trust Center enforces the same criteria as for macros with respect to validity, current digital signatures, certificates, and trusted publishers.

Declare "No Phishing"

"Phishing" is a technique used online by crooks in an attempt to get you to come up with personal information. They use all sorts of tactics such as pretending to be a well-known company, a bank, or even the Internal Revenue Service (IRS). They are looking for your name, address, and phone number, any password or Pin Identification (PID), a bank account or credit card number, or even your Social Security Number. With that information, the criminal can assume your identity and empty your bank account, take out new credit cards in your name, and perpetrate a lot of other scams.

Office 2007 has some new security alerts that display when it suspects phishing. See the Help topic "How Office helps protect you from phishing schemes" for more information.

To change add-in security settings, open the Trust Center window and click Add-ins. You will see three options:

- **Require Application Add-ins to Be Signed by Trusted Publisher**   Checks the file containing the add-in for a digital signature. If the publisher is not in the Trusted Publisher list, the add-in is not loaded and you will see a message that it has been disabled.

- **Disable Notification of Unsigned Add-ins (Code Will Remain Disabled)**   Available only if you have checked the first option. Then unsigned add-ins are disabled with no notification.

- **Disable All Application Add-ins (May Impair Functionality)**   Choose this option if you don't trust any add-ins. You will see no notice that they were disabled.

Security with Earlier Version Databases

If you applied user-level security to a database created in an earlier version of Access, that still works when you open the database in Access 2007. If the database has no security applied, it will open in disabled mode. In disabled mode, many components are inaccessible:

- VBA code and any references to code or unsafe expressions.
- Unsafe macro actions, such as those that allow the user to modify the database or access outside resources.
- Action queries that add, update, or delete data.
- Data Definition Language (DDL) queries that create or alter database objects.

- SQL pass-through queries that work with tables on the server without using the database itself.

- ActiveX controls.

You can choose to enable the content each time you open the database or you can apply a digital signature. A digital signature is an encrypted electronic stamp that authenticates database components. Another option is to place the database in a trusted location.

NOTE *If you convert the database to Access 2007, all the security settings are removed and the rules for ACCDB and ACCDE files apply instead.*

Creating a Certificate

Before you can apply your signature to the database, you need a digital certificate that authenticates the signature. If the database is for your own or your organization's use, you can use the SelfCert program to create the signature. If the database is for commercial use, you need to get the certificate from a commercial CA.

To create your self-signed certificate, do the following:

1. Click the Windows Start button and point to All Programs.

2. Click the Microsoft Office button, click Microsoft Office Tools, and click Digital Certificate for VBA Projects. You'll see the Create Digital Certificate dialog box.

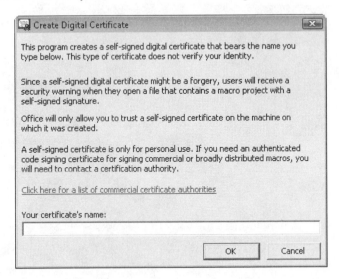

3. In the dialog box, enter a name for the new certificate in the Your Certificate's Name box.

4. Click OK twice. A message will inform you that the new certificate was created.

Code-Signing the Database

Applying a digital signature to a component is called *code-signing*. You can apply your signature to your database so that other certified users will know it is safe to use. When you code-sign your database, the security applies to all objects, not just macros and VBA code modules.

Open the database that you want to sign, and do the following:

1. On the Database Tools tab's Macros group, click the Visual Basic command.

2. In the Microsoft Visual Basic window, select the database. Choose Tools | Digital Signature.

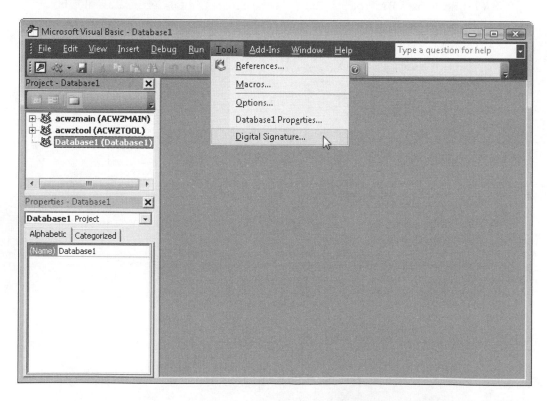

3. In the Digital Signature dialog box, click Choose.

4. In the Select Certificate dialog box, select your test certificate and click OK twice.

Access may not be able save your digital signature. If a problem occurs, you will see an error message with possible reasons such as these:

- The database is under Source Code Control.
- The database is opened as read-only.
- The database may be ACCDB or ACCDE file format and you need to use the Publish method to sign it.

NOTE *For more information about securing databases created in earlier versions of Access, see the Help topic "How security works with databases from earlier versions of Access opened in Office Access 2007."*

Summary

This chapter briefly scratched the surface of the many new security features provided in Access 2007. Look at the many Help topics for more information about securing your database worldwide.

Converting to Access 2007

When Access 2007 arrives, you'll probably want to convert your databases to the new version immediately. You can convert from any earlier version of Access with the information presented in this appendix. You might, instead, want to keep the database in the earlier version and run it with Access 2007. This is important if your database is accessed by more than one user and if all the users haven't upgraded to Access 2007 yet. You can convert an Access database created in Access 95 or later to the Access 2007 file format.

You can also convert an Access 2007 database file back to an earlier version as long as the ACCDB file does not contain any of the new features such as multivalued fields or attachments.

Deciding on a Conversion Strategy

Before setting out to convert the database, you will need to examine the way the database is used currently. Most likely, you'll want to convert it to take advantage of the new design features of Access 2007. If necessary, you can open the database and work with it in Access 2007 without conversion. If the database is one of the later file formats (2000 or 2002–2003) you will be able to view and edit data as well as make changes to object designs. If the database is from Access 95 or 97, you can work with the data, but you won't be able to save changes in the design of any of the objects. If you want to modify an object, you must open the database in the original version or convert it to Access 2007. See the section "Opening an Earlier Database" later in this appendix for more information.

There are significant differences between the Access 2007 ACCDB file format and the earlier MDB file format. You may want to look into the differences before converting a well-established database to Access 2007. See the Help topic "Differences between the ACCDB and MDB File Formats" for details.

For example, Access 2007 does not support replication or user-level security. If your database relies on these, keep the MDB format. If your database is shared among several users, not all of whom can convert to the Access 2007 ACCDB format, you can split the database and convert part of it to Access 2007 and keep other parts unchanged. This way, the database can be shared by users on different versions of Access.

Once you convert an MDB file database to ACCDB file, you're no longer able to open it with the original version of Access, but you can convert it back. You can convert an Access 2007 database back to Access 2000 or 2002–2003.

When the database is converted, the original database is preserved in its native file format and a copy is created in the format that you specify.

Converting a Database to Access 2007

Before you start to convert the database, make a backup copy. Keep this copy until you're satisfied that the database has converted correctly and that you've mastered Access 2007. You can convert the database to a different name in the same folder or use the same name in a different folder.

To convert the database to Access 2007 file format, do the following:

1. Click the Microsoft Office button and click Open. Browse for the file that you want to convert in the Open dialog box and then click Open. If you're operating in a multiple-user environment, make sure all other users have closed the database.

NOTE *If the database you are opening is earlier than Access 2000, the Database Enhancement dialog box opens, asking if you want to upgrade the database. See the section, "Opening an Earlier Database" for information about handling Access files from versions before Access 2000.*

2. Click the Microsoft Office button again and choose Convert.

NOTE   The Convert command is available only if the currently open database is an earlier version.

3. In the Save the Database in Another Format list, choose Access 2007 Database.

4. Then, in the Save As dialog box, enter a new name for the converted database and browse for a new location, if necessary. Then click Save.

NOTE   If you are using Windows XP, the Save As dialog box looks different but it works just the same.

You will see a warning message that the file has been upgraded and can no longer be shared with users of earlier versions.

Access converts the database to the file format that you chose. You might see messages about compile errors during the conversion, because some of the Visual Basic commands might no longer be valid. You can correct the code after conversion.

If the database that you're converting has linked tables, make sure that the tables remain in the original folder, so the converted database can find them. If Access can't find them, the converted database won't work properly. After you convert the database, you can move the linked tables to another location and use the Linked Table Manager to restore the links. The linked tables are not converted, so you must convert them separately.

You can link a table from earlier versions to a later version but not the other way around. For example, you can't link an Access 2007 table to an Access 2003 database.

NOTE   The form and report Layout views are new to Access 2007. To be able to use the Layout views, you must change the form or report Allow Layout View property on the Format tab on the Property Sheet to Yes.

Converting a Workgroup Information File (.mdw)

The Workgroup Information Files (WIFs) store permission information for secured databases. The files containing this information are .mdw files. No changes were made to the structure of .mdw files in Access 2007. So when you convert to the later version, the Workgroup Manager creates .mdw files identical to those in earlier versions. All such files created in Access 2000 through Access 2003 can be used in Access 2007.

Converting a Secured Database

If you applied user-level security to the database, it still works when you convert to Access 2007.

Converting a Replicated Database

Access 2007 no longer supports replicating databases. If a database was replicated in Access 2003, you will not be able to save it in the new ACCDB file format. You can, however, still open it in its MDB file format, where it is still supported by Access 2007.

To update a replicated database to the ACCDB format, you will need to create a new database and add all the objects from the replicated database. Before you start building the new database, open the replicated database in its original version of Access and make sure that all the hidden and system objects are showing by doing the following:

1. On the Tools menu, click Options to open the Options Dialog box.

2. On the View tab's Show Section, select Hidden Objects and System Objects. Then click OK.

3. Close the replicated database.

Now the replicated database is ready to be converted. Create a new blank database and open it in Access 2007. Then do the following:

1. On the External Data tab's Import group, click the Access command.

2. In the Get External Data–Access Database dialog box, locate the replicated database and click Open.

3. Click Import Tables, Queries, Forms, Reports, Macros, and Modules Into the Current Database, and then click OK.

4. In the next dialog box, click Select All on each tab or select just the objects you want. Do not select any tables at this time. Then click OK.

5. Save the import steps or just click Save Import.

6. Open the former version replicated database in Access 2007 and create a Make Table query for each table in the database. This builds a table in the new database with all the data from the tables in the replicated database.

NOTE *The Globally Unique Identifier (GUID) is a system field added to each replicated table in the replicated database. If the s_GUID field is the primary key, you will need to include it in the new table. If it is not, don't include it in the Make Table query.*

As the final step, create the same indexes and primary keys used in the replica's tables. Then establish all the relationships among the new tables to match those from the replicated database.

Converting to an Earlier Version

If you want to convert an open Access 2007 database to a different version, do the following:

1. Click the Microsoft Office button.
2. Point to Save As, and choose from the list of formats in the Save the Database in Another Format group.

Opening an Earlier Database

If you are not converting the database, you can still use the database created in an earlier version with your version 2007. You can open an Access 2000 or 2002–2003 format database in Access 2007 and use it as you normally would, but the new features of 2007 will not be available.

If you open an Access 95 or 97 database, Access 2007 offers to upgrade it for you. If you don't upgrade, you will not be allowed to make design changes. You can view objects and change data but not any object designs. You are warned that the database is opened as read-only. You must open the database using the version with which it was created to be able to modify object designs or add new objects.

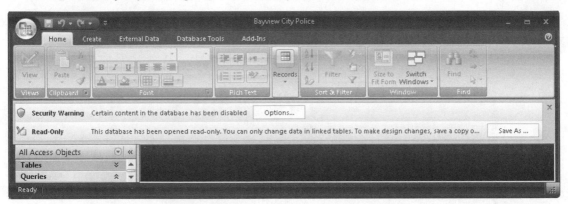

You can't link or import an Access 2007 table into an earlier version database running in Access 2007, but you can go the other way around and open the version 2007 database and export tables to the previous version database. You can also cut, copy, and paste data from version 2007 tables to previous-version tables.

Sharing a Database across Several Access Versions

To use a database with several versions of Access, you can create a front-end/back-end database. Leave the data in the oldest version as the back-end and convert the other objects to the later version front-end.

To build the shared-file Access database, do the following:

1. Convert the entire database to Access 2007.

2. Open the converted database, and on the Database Tools tab's Move Data group, click the Access Database command.

3. Split the database into a front-end and back-end, and then delete the back-end database created by the Database Splitter Wizard.

4. On the Database Tools tab's Database Tools group, click the Linked Table Manager command to link the new Access 2007 front-end to the tables in the previous-version database.

Now you have the best of both worlds: users of previous versions of Access can continue to use the previous version, while users who have upgraded to Access 2007 can add new features to the database objects in their front-end databases.

TIP *If the database is already a front-end/back-end application, you need only to convert the front-end and leave the back-end alone. Then run the Linked Table Manager to link the converted front-end to the original back-end database.*

NOTE *For more information about converting Access files, see the Help topic "Convert a Database to the Access 2007 File Format."*

What's on the CD

On the CD that accompanies this book is a reference resource that you can use to look up specific details of properties, specifications, formats, and other items that apply to designing and creating Access databases. It also contains all the material that you will need to reproduce the Access database objects described in the text. You have a choice of developing the database designs from scratch using the table data or viewing and working with the completed databases.

Using the Access Quick Reference

To use the Quick Reference, you must have Adobe Acrobat installed on your computer or you can download the latest version of the free Adobe Reader at http://www.adobe.com/products/reader/. To view the Quick Reference material, double-click the PDF file. When it opens, you'll see a listing of contents in the left pane and the space where the pages will be displayed on the right pane. If you select any topic on the left pane, the pages associated with the topic will automatically display on the right. You can use the magnification tools on the View menu to make the text more readable and to enlarge any detail on a given page.

The following shows an outline of the information in the Quick Reference, which you can readily reach on the CD.

Storing Information
Database Specifications
Database Templates
Database Objects
Database Properties
Relationships and Joins
Table Specifications
Table and Index Properties
Table Fields
Data Types
Field Properties
Display Formats
Custom Formatting Symbols
Custom Format Strings

Input Masks

User Interaction and Object Design
Ribbons and Tabs
Form and Report Design
Form and Report Specifications
Form and Report Format Properties
Form and Report Data Properties
Form and Report Event Properties
Form and Report Other Properties
Form and Report Section Properties
Dialog Box and Pop-Up Form Property Settings
Controls and Control Properties

Retrieving and Distributing Information
Filtering Records
Entering Filter Criteria
Creating Expressions
Arithmetic Operators
Comparison Operators
Logical Operators
Queries
Query Specifications
Query Properties
Aggregate Functions
Producing Reports
Page Setup and Options
Controlling the Print Process

Information Exchange
Text and Graphics Converters and Filters
Compatible File Formats
Import and Export Options and Specifications

Changing the Access Environment
Access Wizards and Builders
Setting Access Options
Customizing the Quick Access Toolbar

Programming with Macros and SQL
Macro Specifications
Macro Actions
SQL Syntax

Using the Access Database Files

All the files are contained in the Access Database Files folder on the CD. To reach the database files, do the following:

1. Insert the CD-ROM in your CD drive. If you set AutoPlay, the CD will open and you can skip to step 4.

2. Otherwise, click Start on the Windows desktop and choose Run.

3. Type your CD drive letter followed by a colon (:) in the Run dialog box and click OK.

4. Double-click the eula.pdf file to review the End User License Agreement that governs your use of the sample Access database files.

5. Double-click the Access Database Files folder icon to display a dialog box containing icons for all the files in the folder. You can tell the type of file by the accompanying icon.

You can now copy or import any of the files to your hard drive.

To use a complete sample database, you must import, rather than copy, the files to your system. To import the files, do the following:

1. Create a new empty Access 2007 database in a folder on your hard drive.

2. On the External Data tab's Import group, click the Access command.

3. In the Get External Data dialog box, choose the location of the CD and the filename. Then select Import.

4. Choose the first option to import any kind of objects and click OK.

5. In the Import Objects dialog box, click each object tab and choose Select All to import all the objects from the database.

6. The image files are embedded in the Home Tech Repair database, so you do not need to copy them unless you want to work with them separately.

To use only the tables, you can copy the HTR Tables and Police Tables databases directly to your hard disk.

PART IV

The Access Database Files folder on the CD-ROM contains the following files:

File Name	File Type	Contents
HTR2007.accdb	Access database	Complete Home Tech Repair database
HTR Tables.accdb	Access database	Home Tech Repair tables only
Police2007.accdb	Access database	Complete Bayview City Police database
Police Tables.accdb	Access database	Police tables only
Barb.gif	GIF image	Home Tech Repair Employee picture
Charlie.gif	GIF image	Home Tech Repair Employee picture
CopdRick.gif	GIF image	Home Tech Repair Employee picture
DickS.gif	GIF image	Home Tech Repair Employee picture
Doug.gif	GIF image	Home Tech Repair Employee picture
John.gif	GIF image	Home Tech Repair Employee picture
Rick.gif	GIF image	Home Tech Repair Employee picture
Tony.gif	GIF image	Home Tech Repair Employee picture
Bay2.gif	GIF image	Scanned drawing for Home Tech Repair Workorders table
Bay window.gif	GIF image	Scanned drawing for Home Tech Repair Workorders table
Fireplace.gif	GIF image	Scanned drawing for Home Tech Repair Workorders table

The HTR Tables and Police Tables databases contain only the data from the tables in the complete databases. Each table has a primary key field identified, but no relationships have been established between tables.

The HTR2007 sample database forms include hyperlinks to other locations. You need to edit the hyperlink addresses to match their location in your system. See Chapter 6 for information about editing hyperlinks.

The Badge Picture images are embedded in the Employees table in the HTR2007 database. If they don't appear, you can insert the images individually, using the techniques discussed in Chapter 6.

Index

Special Characters

- (hyphen), 155
– (minus sign), 141, 408
! (exclamation mark), 155, 227, 621
!>L0L 0L0 input mask, 130
(number) sign, 215
symbol, 130
& (ampersand) character, 130, 642
* (asterisk), 150, 179, 202–203, 230, 263, 646
* operator, 212
* symbol, 71
. (period), 576
: (colon), 266
? (Help button), 505
? (question mark) button, dialog box title bar, 24
@@ format setting, 71
@ character, 583
[ ] (brackets), 215, 242, 262, 484
\symbol, Input Mask Wizard, 130
^ (carat symbol), 594
{ } (curly brackets), 262, 594
| (vertical bars), 262
~ (tilde), 155
+ (expand indicator), 141, 164, 280
+ (plus sign), 408, 594
+ operator, 212
<= operator, 213
<>0 rule, 86
<> operator, 213
<01/01/08 rule, 86
< operator, 213
< symbol, 130
= (equal sign), 215, 576
= operator, 213
>=01/01/07 rule, 86
>= operator, 213
> format setting, 71
>L<?????????? input mask, 130
>LL0000-000 input mask, 130
> operator, 213
> symbol, Input Mask Wizard, 130
... (ellipses), 69, 579, 640
' (back quote character), 548
" " (double quotation marks), 215
" " (quotation marks), 225, 583
; (semicolon), 260

Numbers

00000-9999 input mask, 130
3-D chart, 473
11-point Calibir, 146
100 Or 200 rule, 86
(999) AAA-AAAA input mask, 130

A

absolute path, 120
ACCDB files, 736
ACCDE files, 546
Access 2007
    See also databases
    ACCDB files, 658, 733
    conversion to, 733–738
    copying or moving records from, 686–687
    modifying charts and graphs with,
        477–484
        editing chart legend, 479–484
        editing row source property, 478–479
        overview, 477–478
    saving output as external files, 687–689

═ D ═

F

G

S